10 0526737 1

THE NEW ECONOMIC CRITICISM

This collection explores the myriad ways in which economics and literature are mutually illuminating. Several essays employ economic principles and paradigms to offer striking new readings of literary and theoretical texts. These both extend current trends in literary scholarship towards historically informed methods, and interrogate those methods by exposing the material conditions under which texts are produced. Other essays present new work by economists schooled in feminist, literary and cultural theory, who suggest alternatives to the constraining models that dominate neoclassicalism. The volume thus demonstrates how economic criticism can both fruitfully examine texts for their economic form, content, and contexts, and also furnish new perspectives on cultural and economic history.

Covering a wide range of topics, the volume features essays by influential literary and cultural historians such as Marc Shell, Jean-Joseph Goux, and Regenia Gagnier, along with contributions by representatives of the vanguard of postmodern economics such as M. Neil Browne, Susan F. Feiner, Jack Amariglio and David Ruccio. It closes with a set of critical exchanges that outline further challenges for economic criticism.

Martha Woodmansee is Professor of English and Comparative Literature at Case Western Reserve University and Director of the Society for Critical Exchange. **Mark Osteen** is Associate Professor of English at Loyola College.

ECONOMICS AS SOCIAL THEORY
Series edited by Tony Lawson
University of Cambridge

Social theory is experiencing something of a revival within economics. Critical analyses of the particular nature of the subject matter of social studies and of the types of method, categories, and modes of explanation that can legitimately be endorsed for the scientific study of social objects, are re-emerging. Economists are again addressing such issues as the relationship between agency and structure, between the economy and the rest of society, and between enquirer and the object of enquiry. There is renewed interest in elaborating basic categories such as causation, competition, culture, discrimination, evolution, money, need, order, organization, power, probability, process, rationality, technology, time, truth, uncertainty, and value, etc.

The objective for this series is to facilitate this revival further. In contemporary economics the label "theory" has been appropriated by a group that confines itself to largely a-social, a-historical, mathematical 'modeling.' *Economics as Social Theory* thus reclaims the "theory" label, offering a platform for alternative, rigorous, but broader and more critical conceptions of theorizing.

Other titles in this series include:

ECONOMICS AND LANGUAGE
Edited by Willie Henderson

RATIONALITY, INSTITUTIONS AND ECONOMIC METHODOLOGY
Edited by Uskali Mäki, Bo Gustafsson and Christian Knudson

NEW DIRECTIONS IN ECONOMIC METHODOLOGY
Edited by Roger Backhouse

WHO PAYS FOR THE KIDS?
Nancy Folbre

RULES AND CHOICE IN ECONOMICS
Viktor Vanberg

BEYOND RHETORIC AND REALISM IN ECONOMICS
Thomas A. Boyland and Paschal F. O'Gorman

FEMINISM, OBJECTIVITY AND ECONOMICS
Julie A. Nelson

ECONOMIC EVOLUTION
Jack J. Vromen

ECONOMICS AND REALITY
Tony Lawson

THE MARKET
John O'Neill

ECONOMICS AND UTOPIA
Geoffrey Hodgson

CRITICAL REALISM IN ECONOMICS
Edited by Steve Fleetwood

THE NEW ECONOMIC CRITICISM

Studies at the intersection of literature and economics

Edited by
Martha Woodmansee and Mark Osteen

University of Nottingham
Hallward Library

London and New York

First published 1999 by Routledge
11 New Fetter Lane, London EC4P 4EE

Simultaneously published in the USA and Canada
by Routledge
29 West 35th Street, New York, NY 10001

Editorial matter and selection © 1999 Edited by Martha Woodmansee
and Mark Osteen; individual chapters © the contributors

Typeset in Garamond by Keystroke, Jacaranda Lodge, Wolverhampton
Printed and bound in Great Britain by Clays Ltd, Bungay, Suffolk

All rights reserved. No part of this book may be reprinted or
reproduced or utilized in any form or by any electronic,
mechanical, or other means, now known or hereafter
invented, including photocopying and recording, or in any
information storage or retrieval system, without permission in
writing from the publishers.

British Library Cataloguing in Publication Data
A catalogue record for this book is available from the British Library

Library of Congress Cataloging in Publication Data
The new economic criticism / edited by Martha Woodmansee and Mark Osteen.
p. cm.
Includes bibliographical references and index.
1. Criticism. 2. Economics. I. Osteen, Mark. II. Woodmansee, Martha.
PN51.N48 1999
809′.93355—dc21 98–20146
CIP

10052673 71

ISBN 0–415–14944–4 (hbk)
ISBN 0–415–14945–2 (pbk)

CONTENTS

FIGURES

PLATES

NOTES ON THE CONTRIBUTORS

Jack Amariglio, Professor of Economics at Merrimack College, is coauthor (with David Ruccio) of a book on postmodernism and economics (forthcoming from Princeton University Press). He is also the editor of *Rethinking Marxism: A Journal of Economics, Culture, and Society*, and (with David Ruccio and Stephen Cullenberg) a collection of essays entitled *Postmodernism, Knowledge, and Economics* (forthcoming from Routledge).

Linda Austin is Associate Professor of English at Oklahoma State University, where she teaches Victorian literature. She is the author of *The Practical Ruskin: Economics and Audience in the Late Work* (Johns Hopkins University Press, 1991) and several articles on James Thomson and economic discourse, including "James Thomson and the Continuum of Labor" (*Victorian Literature and Culture*, 1993). She is currently working on nostalgia and economics in nineteenth-century literature.

John R. Barberet is Assistant Professor of French at Case Western Reserve University. His essay "Baudelaire: Homoerotismes" will appear in a forthcoming collection, *Articulations of Difference* (Stanford University Press). Another essay, "Linking Producers to Consumers: Balzac's 'Grande Affaire' and the *Dynamics of Literary Diffusion*," will appear in *Making the News: Modernity and the Mass Press in Nineteenth-Century France*, forthcoming from University of Massachusetts Press. He is completing a book, *Scenarios of Diffusion and Reception from Balzac to Baudelaire.*

M. Neil Browne is Distinguished Teaching Professor of Economics at Bowling Green State University. His recent books include *The Legal Environment of Business: A Critical Thinking Approach*, 2nd edn. (Prentice-Hall, 1998) and *Striving for Excellence in College: Tips for Active Learning* (Prentice-Hall, 1997). His current research is concerned with the rhetorical role of the expert witness in legal proceedings, the impact of individualism on pay equity in Canada, Hong Kong, and Singapore, and the role of friendship in distinguishing between market and non-market processes.

Brian P. Cooper is a Diamond Postdoctoral Fellow at the New School for Social Research and author of *Family Fictions and Family Facts: Harriet Martineau, Adolphe Quetelet and the Population Question in England, 1798–1859* (forthcoming from Routledge).

Christina Crosby is Professor of English and Women's Studies at Wesleyan University. She is the author of *The Ends of History: Victorians and "The Woman Question"* (Routledge, 1991). Her current book project, from which the essay in this volume is drawn, is titled *Money Changes Everything: Literary Economies in Victorian Britain*.

Paul Delany is Professor of English at Simon Fraser University, Vancouver. His books include *D.H. Lawrence's Nightmare* (Basic Books, 1978) and *The Neo-Pagans* (The Free Press, 1987). He originally trained as an economist, and is completing a book on English literature and money since 1870. His work in progress also includes biographies of George Gissing and of the photographer Bill Brandt.

John Dupré is Professor of Philosophy at Birkbeck College, University of London, and Senior Research Fellow in the School of English and American Studies, University of Exeter. He is the editor of *The Latest on the Best: Essays on Evolution and Optimality* (MIT Press, 1987) and author of *The Disorder of Things: Metaphysical Foundations of the Disunity of Science* (Harvard University Press, 1993). He is currently working on a book criticizing reductive approaches to human behavior, with a focus on economics.

Nancy P. Epstein, a doctoral student of French culture at Ohio State University, is currently completing a dissertation on "The Random in Modern French Literature: A Theoretical Ecocritical Perspective."

Susan F. Feiner is an Associate Professor of Economics and Women's Studies at the University of Southern Maine, Portland. She is the editor of *Race and Gender in the American Economy: Views from Across the Spectrum* (Prentice-Hall, 1994), a collection of essays written from diverse economic perspectives on the causes and consequences of racial/sexual inequality. Her articles on feminist economics have appeared in numerous journals, including *Feminist Economics* and *The American Economic Review*.

Elaine Freedgood, an Assistant Professor of English at the University of Pennsylvania, has published essays in *Gender*, *Victorian Studies*, and *Nineteenth-Century Contexts*. She is currently working on a book titled *Locating Risk: Victorian Constructions of a Safe England in a Dangerous World*.

Regenia Gagnier is Professor of English at the University of Exeter in England. Her books include *Subjectivities: A History of Self-Representation in Britain, 1832–1920* (Oxford University Press, 1991), *Idylls of the Marketplace: Oscar Wilde and the Victorian Public* (Stanford University Press,

1986), and a forthcoming comparative study of the histories of economics and aesthetics. She has published on culture, neoliberalism, and the history of economics in many venues, most recently in *Feminist Economics*, *Journal of Economic Issues*, and *Political Theory*.

Jean-Joseph Goux, a philosopher by training, is the Lawrence Favrot Professor of French Studies at Rice University. His books include *Symbolic Economies* (Cornell University Press, 1990), *Oedipus Philosopher* (Stanford University Press, 1993), and *The Coiners of Language* (University of Oklahoma Press, 1994). He is presently working on a book on value, desire, and speculation.

Richard T. Gray is Professor of German at the University of Washington. He is the author of *Constructive Destruction: Kafka's Aphorisms* (Niemeyer, 1987) and *Stations of the Divided Subject: Contestation and Ideological Legitimation in German Bourgeois Literature, 1770–1914* (Stanford University Press, 1995). Currently he is working on a critical genealogy of German physiognomic theory which bears the working title *About Face: A History of German Physiognomic Thought from Lavater to Auschwitz*.

Howard Horwitz teaches in the English Department at the University of Utah. He has published *By the Law of Nature: Form and Value in Nineteenth-Century America* (Oxford University Press, 1991) and essays on American literature and critical theory. He is presently working on a book, *Administrative Aesthetics*, about the relation between literary practice and the emerging social sciences in America at the turn of this century.

Davis W. Houck is an Assistant Professor in the Department of Communication at Florida Atlantic University. With Amos Kiewe he is co-author of *A Shining City on a Hill: Ronald Reagan's Economic Rhetoric* (Praeger, 1991), which explores the intersection between presidential rhetoric and fiscal policy. He has recently completed a book manuscript entitled *Rhetoric as Currency: Hoover, Roosevelt, and the Great Depression*.

Gerhard Joseph, a Professor of English at Lehman College and the Graduate Center, City University of New York, has written on various nineteenth-century subjects, including two books on Tennyson: *Tennysonian Love: The Strange Diagonal* (University of Minnesota Press, 1969) and *Tennyson and the Text: The Weaver's Shuttle* (Cambridge University Press, 1992). He is currently at work on *The Guilty Art of the Copy*, a study of legitimate and illegitimate "copying" in nineteenth-century British and American literature.

Samira Kawash is an Assistant Professor of English at Rutgers University. She is the author of *Dislocating the Color Line: Identity, Hybridity, and Singularity in African-American Narrative* (Stanford University Press, 1997).

Amy Koritz is Associate Professor of English at Tulane University. She is author of *Gendering Bodies/Performing Art: Dance and Literature in Early Twentieth-Century British Culture* (University of Michigan Press, 1995). Her current research focuses on rhythm, work, and identity in American performance art in the 1920s.

Douglas Koritz is an Associate Professor of Economics at Buffalo State College and Visiting Professor of Political Economy at Vesalius College of the Vrije Universiteit in Brussels. He is a member of the Resurgent City Research Group and serves on the editorial board of the *Review of Radical Political Economics*. His primary areas of inquiry are the political economy of communities and urban "restructuring," as well as the culture and rhetoric of economics.

David Martyn teaches in the German department at the University of Bonn. He has published articles on literary theory and on eighteenth- and nineteenth-century French and German literature and philosophy. The essay that appears here is part of a forthcoming book entitled *Writing Ethics: Sublime Failures of Totalization in Kant and Sade*.

Margueritte S. Murphy is an Associate Professor of English at Bentley College and author of *A Tradition of Subversion: The Prose Poem in English from Wilde to Ashbery* (University of Massachusetts Press, 1992).

Mark Osteen, an Associate Professor of English at Loyola College in Maryland, is the author of *The Economy of* Ulysses: *Making Both Ends Meet* (Syracuse University Press, 1995), as well as numerous articles on twentieth-century literature and culture in such journals as *Modern Fiction Studies* and *Contemporary Literature*. He is currently completing a book on Don DeLillo's fiction, and editing the Viking critical edition of *White Noise*.

J. Kevin Quinn is Associate Professor of Economics at Bowling Green State University. His interests lie in methodology and the intersection of economics and ethics. He is the author of, most recently, "A Rhetorical Conception of Practical Rationality" (*Journal of Economic Issues*, 1996) and (with Neil Browne and Nancy Kubasek) "Resisting the Individualistic Flavor of Opposition to Model Rule 3.3" (*Georgetown Journal of Legal Ethics*, 1995). He is currently working on the implications of Gadamerian hermeneutics for economics.

David F. Ruccio is Associate Professor of Economics at the University of Notre Dame and an editor of the journal *Rethinking Marxism*. His essays on postmodernism and economics have appeared in numerous venues, including the *Journal of Post-Keynesian Economics* and *Marxism in the Postmodern Age* (Guilford, 1995). He has edited (with Antonio Callari) *Postmodern Materialism and the Future of Marxist Theory* (Wesleyan

University Press, 1996) and (with Jack Amariglio and Stephen Cullenberg) *Postmodernism, Knowledge, and Economics* (forthcoming from Routledge). At present he is working with Jack Amariglio on a book, to be published by Princeton University Press, on post-modern moments in economics.

Marc Shell is Professor of Comparative Literature and of English and American Language and Literature at Harvard University, where he is also the Director of the Center for the Study of Money and Culture. He is a recipient of a John D. and Catherine T. MacArthur Prize for 1990–95. His books include *The Economy of Literature* (Johns Hopkins University Press, 1978), *Money, Language and Thought* (University of California Press, 1982), and *Art and Money* (University of Chicago Press, 1995).

Janet Sorensen is an Assistant Professor of English at Indiana University, Bloomington. She is currently completing a book entitled *The Grammar of Empire: Language and Cultural Identity in Eighteenth-Century Britain.*

Michael Tratner, an Associate Professor of English at Bryn Mawr College, is the author of *Modernism and Mass Politics: Joyce, Woolf, Eliot, Yeats* (Stanford University Press, 1995). The essay included here is from a new book, *Deficits and Desires: Economics and Sexuality in Twentieth-Century Literature*, which will also be published by Stanford University Press.

Martha Woodmansee is Professor of English at Case Western Reserve University and Director of the Society for Critical Exchange. She has published widely at the interface of aesthetics, economics, and the law in such venues as *Cultural Critique*, *South Atlantic Quarterly*, and *Eighteenth-Century Studies*. Her books include *The Author, Art, and the Market* (Columbia University Press, 1994) and (with Peter Jaszi) *The Construction of Authorship: Textual Appropriation in Law and Literature* (Duke University Press, 1994).

ACKNOWLEDGMENTS

The papers collected in this volume grew out of a meeting sponsored by the Society for Critical Exchange with the generous support of the Center for the Study of Money and Culture at Harvard University and the Project on Rhetoric of Inquiry at the University of Iowa. The volume editors wish to thank Deirdre McCloskey for assisting in organizing the meeting, and Case Western Reserve University, the Society headquarters, for hosting it so generously. John Kuijper, a PhD student in the English Department at CWRU, aided us throughout the project – in preparing the papers for publication as well as in arranging the meeting – with rare resourcefulness, grace, and good humor.

Since the meeting, in autumn 1994, eight of the papers have been published elsewhere, and permission to reprint we herewith gratefully acknowledge: Linda Austin, "Smoking, the Hack, and the General Equivalent," reprinted from *Prose Studies* 18 (Aug. 1995): 159–70; Elaine Freedgood, "Banishing Panic: Harriet Martineau and the Popularization of Political Economy," reprinted from *Victorian Studies* 39.1 (Autumn 1995): 33–53, by Permission of the Trustees of Indiana University; Jean-Joseph Goux, "Cash, Check, or Charge?," *Communications* 50 (1989): 7–22; permission granted by Editions du Seuil; Richard T. Gray, "Buying into Signs: Money and Semiosis in Eighteenth-Century Language Theory," *German Quarterly* 69.1 (Winter 1996): 1–14; Gerhard Joseph, "Commodifying Tennyson: the Historical Transformation of 'Brand Loyalty,'" *Victorian Poetry* 35.2 (Summer 1996): 133– 47; Samira Kawash, "Fugitive Properties," from *Dislocating the Color Line: Identity, Hybridity, and Singularity in African American Narrative* by Samira Kawash (Stanford University Press, 1997); reprinted by permission of Stanford University Press; David Martyn, "Sade's Ethical Economies," reprinted with permission from *The Romanic Review* 86.1 (Jan. 1995): 45–63; Copyright by the Trustees of Columbia University in the City of New York; Marc Shell, "The Issue of Representation," from *Art and Money* by Marc Shell (University of Chicago Press, 1995): 72–86; permission granted by the University of Chicago Press.

INTRODUCTION

1

TAKING ACCOUNT OF THE NEW ECONOMIC CRITICISM

An historical introduction

Mark Osteen and Martha Woodmansee

When we organized a panel called "The New Economic Criticism" for the 1991 Midwest Modern Language Association (MMLA) convention, we were naming a phenomenon that we weren't entirely sure existed. Certainly there was no movement that called itself "New Economic Criticism"; in giving it a name, we were responding to our perception of an emerging body of literary and cultural criticism founded upon economic paradigms, models and tropes. Fortunately for us, this nascent movement took a firm hold in the 1990s, yielding exciting new work by both new and veteran critics, and establishing itself as one of the most promising areas of research in literary and cultural studies.

This critical corpus, we soon discovered, paralleled a movement in economics that attempts to use literary and rhetorical methods to unveil the discipline's buried metaphors and fictions. During our work for the MMLA panel, we learned that each side was largely unaware of the movement in the other discipline. Indeed, even literary economic critics seemed unaware of each other's work, mining the same veins without acknowledging other prospectors. The potential for critical exchange, for extension and expansion, seemed relatively untapped. These conditions inspired us to organize a conference in 1994 that brought together scholars from both fields to engage in critical dialogue. This volume grows out of that conference.

Our belief six years ago that economic criticism was a burgeoning and fruitful set of methods and discourses has been reinforced by recent developments: the first wave of economic criticism, which appeared during the late 1970s and early 1980s, has given way to a second, seemingly tidal wave of scholarship investigating the relations among literature, culture and economics. Why this explosion of new work? The reasons are multiple. Within literary studies, the critical pendulum has decidedly swung back toward historicist methods and away from deconstruction, semiotics, and the other formalist approaches that prevailed in the 1970s and early 1980s. Historicist and culturally aware literary critics have therefore sought new approaches derived from the methods and texts of other fields, one of which is economics. Second – both a cause and consequence of that theoretical shift – the economics of academic publishing has forced literary critics to seek untrammeled pathways. Third, the re-emergence of cultural studies lends itself readily (as Koritz and Koritz note in their contribution to this volume, perhaps too readily) to economic explanations. This change, in turn, has inspired a converse cross-fertilization in the work of economists such as Donald (now Deirdre) McCloskey and others, several of whom are featured in this volume. Fourth, the political economy of the 1980s thrust economics and its discussions of interest rates, stock market speculation, takeovers, leveraged buyouts, and so on, into the public attention as never before since the 1930s. Finally, and perhaps most importantly, just as physicists speak of "sweet" or "elegant" theorems and models, so literary and cultural critics sometimes happen upon particularly fertile fields for cultivation. As we hope this collection demonstrates, we believe that economics offers one of the richest available. Conversely, economists willing to entertain alternatives to the dominant paradigms of neoclassicalism have found literary studies to offer a wealth of new ideas and possibilities.

But the two "waves" of economic criticism are quite different: recent economic criticism may be characterized as a branch of New Historicism, itself a tributary of that wide stream called Cultural Studies. It is likely, however, that in developing new models and methods, economic criticism has abandoned other promising pathways. In this introduction, then, we wish to offer answers to the following questions: What is (and was) economic criticism? What can literary and cultural critics learn from economists? What can economists glean from literary and cultural studies? How will such critical exchanges enrich both disciplines? In offering our answers to these questions, we will present a history of economic criticism; an outline of its assumptions and principles; a survey of important recent work in both literary studies and economics; a provisional description of the forms of economic criticism; and a call for future work in relatively neglected discursive domains.

Origins and definitions

The first wave of economic criticism defined itself rather clearly. For example, in his book *The Economics of the Imagination* Kurt Heinzelman (1980) proposes a distinction between "imaginative economics," which addresses "the way in which economic systems are structured, by means of the imagination, upon what are essentially fictive concepts"; and "poetic economics," which scrutinizes "the way in which literary writers use this fictive economic discourse . . . as an ordering principle in their work" (11–12). Imaginative economics reads economics literarily; poetic economics reads literature economically. A second definition is proposed by Marc Shell (1978) in his highly influential study *The Economy of Literature*, where he writes that "literary works are composed of small tropic exchanges or metaphors, some of which can be analyzed in terms of signified economic content and all of which can be analyzed in terms of economic form"; hence, economic literary criticism seeks "to understand the relation between such literary exchanges and the exchanges that constitute the political economy" (7). All such criticism investigates "rationality defined according to the logic of exchange" (Purdy, 1993: 5).

Useful as these definitions are, they presuppose the very rift between discourses and disciplines that economic criticism – and this collection – attempts to bridge. The two fields were not always separate. When did the divorce occur? Heinzelman cites 1871, the publication date of Jevons's *The Theory of Political Economy*, which heralded the marginalist revolution in economics that eventually yielded neoclassical economics, the predominant mode today. But we, like a few other recent critics, would suggest an earlier date – one at least a century earlier, when the science of political economy emerged concurrently with the rise of that quintessentially bourgeois literary form, the novel. Several recent literary studies have explored the historical and cultural conditions surrounding the birth of these twin discourses. David Kaufmann (1995: 1), for example, asks why "economic theory and narrative fiction . . . both became objects of and media for" intellectual debate at the same period. He answers that "the rapid growth and institutional consolidation of commercial capitalism in the eighteenth century created a demand for new descriptions of and apologias for the economy, the state, morality and citizenship, a demand that was taken up by . . . both the field of political economics and the novel" (169).[1] Kaufmann follows Nancy Armstrong's influential argument that the novel emerged as a way of codifying the dichotomy between male and female spheres: the divorce of the economic from the literary is thus closely related to the gendering of culture and the consequent separation of the political and domestic domains in the late eighteenth century.[2] Thus, as James Thompson (1996: 27) observes, if the novel is "that discourse that describes or imagines and so constructs privacy and domesticity, political economy is the discourse that imagines or describes civil society and publicity."

And yet, recent work in economic literary criticism has also demonstrated how the two spheres profoundly conditioned each other. Thompson argues that the eighteenth century is the historical moment when the "concept of value underwent profound transformation and was rearranged into the various humanistic, financial, and aesthetic discourses that we know today" (1). What prompted these changes, he claims, is the "reconceptualization of money from treasure to capital and the consequent refiguration of money from specie to paper" (2). But this reconceptualization dramatically affected cultural

definitions of fictionality. Sandra Sherman (1996) argues that "the market in ideas, in literature – and the market constituted by commercial paper (both developing [in the early eighteenth century]) generated a mutually inflecting discursive field around the notion of 'fiction,'" such that the rise of "long-term credit implicated the culture in a new kind of narrativity" (2, 5).[3] Literary texts, and particularly novels, thus both produce and respond to reformulations of the nature of representation and credit embodied in money and in the economic system in general.

The history of this divorce between discursive domains in the eighteenth century helps to explain why so much recent economic literary criticism has focused on the English literature of the eighteenth and nineteenth centuries.[4] One might argue, however, as Martha Woodmansee does, that the dissociation of economics from the humanities is most integrally connected to the emergence of Romantic ideology, which defined literature (and indeed the arts generally) in opposition to commerce, and to the belief in the separation of aesthetic value from monetary value that endures to this day.[5] A significant impetus for this development was provided by authors seeking to earn their living by the pen in a period of rapidly accelerating competition.

Economies of authorship

In an essay on "The Condition of Authors in England, Germany, and France" that appeared in *Fraser's Magazine* in 1847 G.H. Lewes declared that:

> Literature should be a profession, not a trade. It should be a profession, just lucrative enough to furnish a decent subsistence to its members, but in no way lucrative enough to tempt speculators. As soon as its rewards are high enough and secure enough to tempt men to enter the lists for the sake of the reward, and parents think of it as an opening for their sons, from that moment it becomes vitiated. Then will the ranks, already so numerous, be swelled by an innumerable host of hungry pretenders[:] . . . barristers with scarce briefs, physicians with few patients, clergymen on small livings, idle women, rich men, and a large crop of aspiring noodles. . . .
>
> (Lewes 1847: 285)

That it should now be possible at all to earn one's living – the "income of a gentleman" – by the pen, if one has "health, courage, and ability," we owe to Samuel Johnson, according to Lewes:

> [A]ll honour to him! He was the first professional author – the first who, by dint of courage and ability, kept himself free from the slavery of a bookseller's hack, and free from the still worse slavery

> of attendance on the great. He sought his subsistence in public patronage, not in dedications to men of rank.
>
> (Ibid.: 286)

Lewes's sketch of the "conditions of authors" provides a convenient starting point for a typology of writing economies because it captures, economically, the whole spectrum – from patronage (including various types of "self-patronage"), to writing for hire, to the economy that Lewes finally celebrates the origins of in the career of Samuel Johnson: the free-lance status that, for Lewes, is distinguished by self-determination. As an "author by profession," a writer himself determines what he will write, and this expression of his individual genius finds acceptance first with publishers and then with an avid readership in a free market for books.

Lewes contrasts this ideal – and, indeed, idealized – "professional" economy of authorship with the "enslavement" of patronage on the one hand, and of hack writing on the other – as well as with writing on the side (that is, while deriving financial support from some other source). These four economies would seem to exhaust the possibilities, and we will attempt to flesh them out here in order to suggest where further research is needed, for we have not seen any kind of comprehensive typology of this kind.

Literary history has long situated the origin of professional writing in the career of Johnson – even identifying the originary moment in Johnson's refusal in 1755 of the Earl of Chesterfield's patronage. Only recently Alvin Kernan (1987: 105) described this incident, very much in the spirit of James Boswell's biography of 1791, as "the Magna Carta" of authorship. In 1755 Johnson was completing his *Dictionary* – a project that like much of his writing was commissioned by booksellers (181ff). Why, then, does this not make Johnson "a bookseller's hack" in Lewes's estimation? It would seem that while the ideal type of the professional author would write only "on spec" – either anticipating, or in the best scenario, "*creating* the taste by which he is to be enjoyed," to quote Wordsworth (1966: 182) – it is occasionally possible to accept a commission. However, an author who writes strictly, or even characteristically, on commission would presumably fall into the category of a hack – together with writers on salary who thus may be said to "work for hire," to use the legal term. This is in fact the economy in which most of the world's writing goes on – although we should never know this from our literary histories, which until recently have rendered such hackney writing invisible. We will return this economy below.

First let us look briefly at the other "evil other" of authors by profession: authors enslaved by "attendance on the great," working in a patronage economy. A profession of authorship evolved in tandem with the commodification of information that was speeded by the printing press. The spread of printing and the expansion of reading and the book market in the seventeenth, but especially the eighteenth century increased exponentially the opportunities for would-be writers. Writers had previously worked in church, court, and state bureaucracies, and in many cases their official duties, which might or might not involve writing, were light enough to leave them time to pursue their own projects. Such sinecures, as we now term them, are one of many forms of patronage, the dominant economy of authorship prior to the emergence of a book market (Korshin 1974). Early modern writers also found patronage among wealthy nobles, in whose households they worked as tutors, secretaries, personal librarians, and the like. Such private patronage could take the form of a simple grant or gift as well, and this form of patronage could in turn be "democratized" through subscription, a means of spreading the burden of supporting a worthy publication among a number of would-be patrons. Subscription increased in popularity in the eighteenth century, and even more traditional forms of patronage, far from disappearing, as is often assumed, persisted alongside the literary market, contributing to the support of writers even into the twentieth century. Dustin Griffin (1996) has recently taken up Paul Korshin's call for more study of this authorial economy, but further investigation is needed of its evolving forms.

We also need more study of how writing was viewed in patronage economies. Woodmansee has argued that in the age of patronage through the seventeenth century, writing was viewed as a *craft* on a par, from a printer-publisher's point of view, with the other crafts involved in book manufacture – papermaking, bookbinding, type-founding, or typesetting. The early modern writer, Woodmansee shows, was first and foremost the master of a body of rules, or techniques, preserved and handed down in rhetoric and poetics, for manipulating traditional materials to achieve meanings and effects prescribed by the individual or institution to whose patronage he owed his livelihood. He did not view himself, nor was he treated, as a privileged instance in the production process; indeed, in the early years of book manufacture the writer was the person of least account in this process (Woodmansee 1984a and 1994: 35–55; Plant 1974: 68). Authors could be had cheaply, compared with paper, type, good type-founders and -setters – or, indeed, for nothing if they were being subsidized by a patron.

With the spread of reading and growth in the market for a "lite" literature of entertainment and advice on secular subjects, which patrons were loathe to subsidize, publishers began paying authors for the right to publish their books. By the end of the sixteenth century writers were able to earn some income in this way, but not enough to support themselves by writing, except perhaps from writing for the stage (Feather 1988: 27). Publishers were not inclined to pay them substantial amounts for manuscripts as long as they could get these free – whether from writers who were able to count on patronage for their support; from the "backlog" of works (going all the way back to Greek and Roman times) that had yet to appear in print; by helping themselves to the manuscripts of contemporary writers without these writers' permission, or even knowledge; or simply by reprinting popular items that had been brought to market by their competitors. In Britain some order was brought to the trade in 1710 by the passage – at the instigation of publishers – of the first copyright statute, the Act of Anne.[6] Quite incidentally, it improved writers' situations too, chiefly by protecting publishers from piracy, thereby enabling them to pay writers more for the right to publish their manuscripts.

Gradually, more stable, or at least more predictable, market conditions ushered in the economy of writing that has received most of our attention – although it has never been the dominant economy: a free-lance economy in which writers might hope to earn a livelihood by the sale of their writing on the book market. Woodmansee and Jaszi (1994: 1–56) have investigated the reconceptualization of the activity of writing that this new economy fostered: a reconceptualization that downplays the social aspect of writing to foreground its individual aspects – figures it as essentially solitary and originary rather than collaborative; presents it as the product of inspired genius rather than the application of age-old techniques to inherited materials; and describes its results as new and original works expressive of the unique genius of their maker. This Romantic construction of creative production (one to which literary and composition studies in large measure still adhere) was fostered by the competition of the literary marketplace – as was also elite authors' reaction against a market-economic way of determining the value of their work, a reaction that resulted in the postulation of a specifically *literary* form of value distinct from the price a work will bring or from its popularity with readers, one that went so far as to make a work's ineffectuality – contemporary readers' indifference to it – a measure of the work's value. This reverse marketing strategy may be seen operating in Wordsworth's argument, in "Essay, Supplementary to the Preface" to *Lyrical Ballads* ([1815] 1966: 182), that "every Author, as far as he is great and at the same time original, has had the task of creating the taste by which he is to be enjoyed."[7]

Although celebrations of the market's liberation of writers from the slavery of patronage have persisted – from Boswell to Carlyle (1832: 396–98) and Macaulay down to Kernan – by the beginning of the nineteenth century, hostility toward the literary market economy on the part of writers unable to market their writings successfully had begun to produce nostalgic yearning for, and in some cases a return to, patronage. In the twentieth century the dominant literary tradition defined itself in opposition to the market economy. Literary Modernism, in addition to upping the Romantic ante by fashioning an entire aesthetics around opposition to the market, was – as Paul Delany shows in his contribution to this volume – financially sustained to a significant degree by patronage.

In a variation thereon, many authors have practiced "self-patronage." At one end of the spectrum we think of those who supported themselves on parental allowances or inherited money – authors like Milton, Pope, Byron, Keats, Shelley, Browning, Tennyson. Self-patronage did not, of course, prevent their writing from being treated as commodities. In the case Gerhard Joseph examines in this volume, Tennyson's popularity enabled his publisher to market his name as a known "brand" on the literary shelf. Through a curious etymological conjunction in the word "brand," Joseph argues, Tennyson seems in *Idylls of the King* to anticipate his own condition as a marketable commodity. However, Tennyson's work, lying within a burgeoning capitalist economy but invoking a time when possessions were inalienable and thus closer to gifts, also indicates the limits of the commercial market for books.

At the other end of the spectrum, "self-patronage" encompasses those who held day-jobs and sometimes even pursued successful careers that supported their writing – authors like Wallace Stevens or Anthony Trollope, whose habit of rising every morning at 5:30 a.m. to spend three hours writing before leaving for work is legendary. Christina Crosby shows in her essay in this volume that Trollope viewed his writing as a trade – an occupation demanding less inspiration than industry and perseverance, one whose value, far from being "inestimable," could be calculated precisely in terms of the number of pages and pounds sterling produced. Reviewing his career in his *Autobiography*, Trollope writes that he became convinced early on that

> in such work as mine the great secret consisted in acknowledging myself to be bound to rules of labour similar to those which an artisan or a mechanic is forced to obey. . . . A shoemaker when he has finished one pair of shoes does not sit down and contemplate his work in idle satisfaction. . . . The shoemaker who so indulged himself would be without wages half his time. It is the same with a professional writer of books. . . . I had now quite accustomed myself to begin a second pair as soon as the first was out of my hands.
> (Quoted in Crosby, 299 in this volume)

Presenting the writer as a humble book-cobbler, Trollope challenges the Romantic model of authorship that was widespread in the aestheticized 1880s when his autobiography appeared posthumously.

Trollope's construction of writing as a trade brings us, finally, to the fourth writing economy – that of writing for hire. This is without doubt the dominant economy in terms of the sheer number of words written – even if we ignore writing done on commission and include only writing on salary – for all those who write office memos and health care forms, computer manuals and advertisements, not to speak of screenplays and the like, write in the employ of some individual or institution. What distinguishes this host from the professional author in Lewes's schema is that in addition to receiving a salary, the "hack" also receives his instructions from – his or her task is defined by – another individual or institution into whose ownership the work passes on completion. Those who write in the employ of another individual or institution do not themselves determine what they will write; the purpose of a given piece of work and often even the means of accomplishing it are explicitly defined by the employer or the individual who commissions the work. And yet, this apparent "enslavement" to the marketplace has not been, nor is today, invariably experienced as confining. In her essay in the present volume, Linda Austin examines the creative liberation felt by "hack" writer James Thomson as a result of the very constraints imposed upon him by the tobacco trade journal for which he wrote. Thomson's experience demonstrates that "idealist aesthetics and capitalist production and exchange" are not necessarily incompatible.

In twentieth-century fiction one of the most colorful examples of such writing for hire is the Stratemeyer Syndicate, "author" of the Nancy Drew mysteries, the Rover Boys, Hardy Boys, and Bobbsey Twins – a veritable assembly line of contract and salaried writers which turned out over 1300 books under various pen names, with sales estimated at over two hundred million copies before it was sold to Simon & Schuster in 1984.[8] The Syndicate founder, Edward Stratemeyer, kept tight rein on his writers, as did his daughters, who took over the firm after his death in 1930. Writers typically worked from detailed outlines and according to guidelines which they provided (Johnson 1993: 6–17).

The economic situation of such large-scale "commodity-text publishers," to borrow Norman Feltes's term, was significantly enhanced by the copyright reform of 1909 (Feltes 1986: 1–17). Although in practice employed authors rarely exercised their rights, before 1909 they did in principle retain copyright in the writing they did on the job unless they had expressly relinquished it in a contractual arrangement with their employers. The Copyright Act of 1909 codified this advantage for employers by redefining the term "author" to include "an employer in the case of a work made for hire." Just what counted as a "work made for hire" was not explained in the statute, but the meaning of this term soon began to be decided in the courts. The courts continued to regard commissioned writing as a matter to be determined by contract between the two parties to the commission, but in the case of salaried writing, they applied the new "work for hire" doctrine with full force. And they rationalized this by appealing to the rhetoric of Romantic authorship – more precisely, by appealing to what Peter Jaszi (1991) has termed the "deep logic" of this model of authorship, according to which it is in the inspiration rather than in the execution that the crucial moment in creative production lies.[9] Insofar as an employer planned a given work and supervised employees' execution of it, the employer constitutes the genuinely creative party in production and, accordingly, the legal "author" of the work in question. In the wake of such decisions as *National Cloak and Suit Co.* v *Kaufman* (1911) there has emerged a whole new class of professional authors – corporations like Time-Warner, the Disney Corporation, and Microsoft – that are far more autonomous and self-determining than any of the professional authors celebrated by G.H. Lewes.

Despite the long and multifarious historical relationship between authorship and commerce, the separation of literary and cultural studies from economics has, until very recently, been maintained by both literary scholars and economists, each group suspicious of the other. Given this enduring bifurcation of disciplines, the challenge is to rediscover the contact points among literature, culture, and economics, to determine whether these cross-disciplinary exchanges are valuable, and to use each discourse as a monitor or counterpractice that will expose the weakness, blind spots, and biases of the other. One such blind spot has recently been pointed out by McCloskey, who claims that most literary critics' knowledge of economics begins and ends with Karl Marx. McCloskey further recommends that those engaging in economic literary criticism consider first the economy at the time of a work's production, and second the local economy of the producer/author, including her or his place in local divisions of labor, class, etc. (quoted in Gagnier and Dupré 1995: 1). As the following historical survey will demonstrate, most current economic literary criticism – influenced as it is by Foucault and cultural theory – is doing at least what McCloskey advises and sometimes more, examining how social forces and conditions both shape and are shaped by economic discourses and practices. The historical survey below outlines some of the myriad ways in which these interrelations are made manifest.

A second challenge comes by way of Jack Amariglio's and David Ruccio's essay in the present collection: the charge that literary critics use economic terms, metaphors, and paradigms with little or no awareness of how they are employed by economists. In so doing, the argument continues, literary critics replicate the abuses and myopias of neoclassicalism or Marxism and, perhaps worse, generate overgeneral or misleading "insights" based upon faulty premises. The criticism is valid. Nonetheless, although we believe that literary and cultural critics should familiarize themselves with what economists mean by terms such as "choice," "value," and "credit," we do not believe that literary critics should be limited by them. Indeed, many literary and cultural critics would point directly to this narrowness of definition and disciplinary practice as a major deficiency in contemporary economics. Even some economists agree that economics has long been dominated by a narrow scientism that, by ruling out of bounds any unconventional method or explanation, merely certifies the political status quo.[10] Economists, then, warn literary critics of opposed dangers: on the one hand, that of emulating the narrowness of conventional economic theory; on the other, that of expanding economic models and terms beyond their viability. With these challenges and hazards in mind, we present in this volume a number of critical interventions and exchanges that will help to refine and redefine economic criticism as both a literary-critical practice and as a constructive critique of economics – as both imaginative and poetic economics.

Language and money

In its movement from formalism to post-structuralism to historicism, economic criticism exemplifies the broader history of literary criticism in the last three decades. Of course, economic criticism existed even before 1960 in, for example, the brand of Marxism practiced by Lukács, the Frankfurt school, and Left critics of the 1930s. In the 1950s and 1960s, however, such approaches fell out of fashion, as the profession was dominated by the allegedly apolitical procedures of New Criticism. Thus in this period even economic criticism, which would seem to demand broader-based methods, focused almost exclusively on the manifest content of texts – characters' behaviors, monetary terms and tropes, etc. – often without detailed documentation even of the author's own financial habits or beliefs, and certainly without considering national or local economies or contemporary economic practices or theories. Two examples – similar, though separated by more than twenty years – are Donald Mull's (1973) and Peggy McCormack's (1990) studies of Henry James. While Mull's book – a formalist treatment of "cash and its conversion into the stuff of consciousness" (Mull 1973: 12) through close analyses of trope, character and event – remains a product of its time (the early 1970s) despite its brief discussion of James's attitudes about money, McCormack's study recalls New Criticism in its use of terms such as "capitalism," "consumption," or "commodities" with virtually no consideration of their complex and ideologically vexed meanings in other contexts. Although such work can offer useful insights into the "economies" of tropes and scenes, their presumption that texts are closed systems limits their value.

But formalist analysis, particularly if it approaches a text as a locus of exchanges and transactions, may still bear fruit. Ian Reid's recent narratological approach to narrative "dispossessions" and "exchanges," for example, introduces several useful "economic" models for framing the play of forces within texts and between texts and their authors. Unfortunately, Reid rarely connects the internal economies of texts either to their economic content or to the contexts within which the texts reside. Nonetheless, Reid's work both implicitly exposes a failing of almost all recent economic criticism – its disregard for what Marc Shell (1978: 7) calls the "tropic exchanges" within texts – and also demonstrates the necessity for historical awareness: without an explanatory context, economic terms seem to have been randomly chosen rather than dictated by intratextual, intertextual and extratextual dynamics. Unless one considers literary discourses as one of many social discourses in a time and place, there seems to be no compelling reason to use economic terms instead of, say, psychoanalytic ones to describe narrative dynamics.

A second form of economic criticism – generally but not exclusively instanced by pre-1990s work – addresses the economic habits of individual authors or schools to determine how these habits are (or are not) transferred into the writings. While generally adhering to Left or Marxist ideology, most of these studies are content to borrow the terms of a previous generation of social theorists without contesting them. In addition, many such studies aim mostly to "apply" various economic theories, terms or philosophies without considering how credit, value or money, for example, were understood in the culture at the time of a work's production and reception. These investigations, in short, still attend almost entirely to the manifest content of texts, and ignore both theoretical work in economic criticism and the history of economics itself.[11] The most sophisticated early criticism, however, does develop parallels between economic fictions or tropes in the texts and the tropes of the discipline of economics. Among the best early work of this kind is that of Heinzelman (1980), who analyzes "the language and logic which poetic and economic 'systems' share" (xi) through sound and enlightening economic readings of Spenser, Thoreau, and William Carlos Williams, and equally illuminating literary readings of the economic poetics of Mill, Marx, and Ruskin.

Like Heinzelman, the other founders of economic criticism have simply assumed what McCloskey and the rhetoric of economics movement has so laboriously tried to prove: that economics provides a ready-made system of tropes and fictions about value, debt, money, and exchange that underpins not only its own practices and texts, but also literary discourses that are less obviously economic. Economic criticism, in short, is predicated on the existence and disclosure of parallels and analogies between linguistic and economic systems. Thus any adequate theoretics of literary economics must begin with the axioms of Saussurian linguistics and post-structuralist theory – that all signs are arbitrary and related syntagmatically – and then address the similarly fictive or constructed nature of money and finance. Writers like Shell, Jean-Joseph Goux and Walter Benn Michaels have thus exposed and analyzed the historical and philosophical parallels – usually termed homologies – between economic and linguistic systems. Their work has laid the foundation for virtually all of the literary economic criticism that has followed.

Perhaps the earliest extended attempt to analyze the deep homologies between money and language, however, is F. Rossi-Landi's neglected book *Linguistics and Economics* (1975). Rossi-Landi's dense and difficult work retains value for its treatment of language as historical and social "capital" and for its detailed delineation of possible avenues for practical and theoretical investigations of the morphology of language and money. But Rossi-Landi's work is flawed by adherence to an old-fashioned Marxism that emphasizes production at the expense of consumption; thus, although he acknowledges the significance of "modalities of decodification and interpretation" (191), his view of language is ultimately instrumental, and ignores the fact that human beings are not simply "workers" who use language as a tool, but are themselves constructed by it. Moreover, Rossi-Landi's deterministic model, which describes the social origins and relations of linguistic exchange as "programs," leaves too little room for linguistic change. He gets into deeper trouble in trying to adapt the Marxian economic terms "use-value" and "exchange-value" for linguistic systems. Economics, he argues, is the study of "commodity-messages" (134); conversely, linguistic use-value is equal to the "message-content" of words or phrases, so that having a value is the same as having a meaning (139). But to recognize an utterance as a message means that a message (i.e., that an utterance is a message) has already been conveyed. Hence "use-value" – as a function of message-content – can be determined only if an exchange has already taken place. In short, Rossi-Landi defines linguistic use-value as exchange-value. His discussion, moreover, implicitly reveals a more profound problem: that the structures of linguistic and economic systems are not identical, and so distinctions or definitions that hold for one "economy" do not hold for another.

Nevertheless, Rossi-Landi helpfully defines the assumption or procedure underlying virtually all economic literary criticism: the existence of homologies between language and money. As he notes, homologies are not the same as analogies: dissecting an analogy is an *a posteriori* operation that assumes two objects have already been produced; the homological method, in contrast, studies comparable artifacts or entities both historically and ontologically in the hope of discovering a common anthropogenic root. Analogy posits a primary term or source from which others are derived, a "superimposition of the one upon the two; homology is the recognition of the original unity" (74, 75). This distinction implies that the discovery of a true homology prevents the establishment of hierarchies, and that when one does discover such hierarchies, one is really working with an extreme case of analogy, or what Rossi-Landi calls "isomorphism" (75). Ironically, his failed attempt to apply Marxian terminology to language implicitly demonstrates the difficulty of discovering true homologies. Perhaps, then, Rossi-Landi's most lasting contribution is to identify and exemplify the limitations of his own enterprise. Indeed, the homological method contains, as we will show, other potential dangers upon which critics founder. Nonetheless, the method retains the singular advantage of enabling one to study social forms "from the inside," and thereby to discover how certain essentials in human social behavior transcend historical and cultural differences (76).

Much more neutral ideologically than Rossi-Landi's work is that of Marc Shell, whose enormous impact on economic criticism can scarcely be overemphasized. In fact, Shell's (1982: 3) core insight that "money, which refers to a system of tropes, is also an 'internal' participant in the logical or semiological organization of language, which itself refers to a system of tropes," succinctly describes the major assumption upon which economic criticism has been built. Although Shell is concerned more with the logical, semiological, ontological, historical and aesthetic meanings of money itself than with economics per se, his early books remain extremely valuable not only for their analyses of historical homologies among monetary and other systems of representation, but for their recognition that texts themselves function as "economies" (a recognition, as we have noted, that is notably absent from much recent economic criticism). The unmatched erudition and breadth of Shell's work has also opened seemingly infinite avenues for future work: the study of money as art, symbol and medium; the concurrent origins of money and certain political and linguistic systems; the intertwined history of coinage and logic; the nature and cultural significance of credit, debt and usury, and the latter's relationship to national and ethnic identities; the political economy of art. For example, Shell's assertion that faith and credit involve "the ground of aesthetic experience," inasmuch as "the same medium that confers belief in fiduciary money (bank notes) and in scriptural money . . . also seems to confer it in [literature and] art" (1995: 73; 1982: 7) underlies both earlier (Vernon 1984 and Michaels 1987) and several more recent studies, including those of Sherman (1996), Brantlinger (1996), and Thompson (1996).[12] Shell's most recent book, *Art and Money* (1995), wittily surveys "modern iconological vacillations between art as money and money as art" (58) through explorations of Christian art and iconography and of the history of monetary and aesthetic representation in the United States. Although this new book sometimes (as Shell admits) resembles less an argument than a "repository of trivial anecdotes and facts" (119), his conclusion that the interrelations of art and commerce reveal both aesthetic and economic anxieties is so concretely and voluminously documented that even skeptical readers could not doubt that "the iconology of money and the economics of visual art converge" in innumerable and highly significant ways (134).

Jean-Joseph Goux's landmark work, which posits striking homologies between various "symbolic economies," represents a theoretical companion to Shell's scholarly montages. Synthesizing Marxism and post-structuralism, Goux's work (published in the 1970s but only recently translated into English) has begun to make a strong impact on Anglo-American criticism. His astonishingly ambitious project is nothing less than a genealogy of symbolic forms in all "domains of social reality where there are exchanges" (Goux 1990: 63). It proceeds by extending the notion of the "general equivalent" – in economics, the condition of money as a privileged commodity that thereby makes unlike things commensurable – to psychoanalysis, language and philosophy. For Goux, the Father is the general equivalent of subjects; language that of signs; the phallus that of objects, and so on (3–4). The generalized concept of exchange makes possible, for Goux, a definition of "major social formations as a *mode of symbolizing* that is both economic and significant" (4; his emphasis). Whether or not one accepts Goux's somewhat mechanical and at times ethnocentric historical model, his project offers a number of provocative definitions and distinctions. One of his most illuminating formulations builds upon Marx's history of money in Part I,

Chapter 3 of *Capital*, where he argues that money passes through three stages of development, from measure of labor, to medium of exchange, to means of wealth (Marx 1976: 188–244; cf. Thompson 1996: 32–4). Similarly, Goux delineates three functions of gold as money: its *real* function as a store of wealth; its *symbolic* function as a circulating medium (here gold can be replaced by symbols of itself); and its *imaginary* function as a measure of values (Goux 1990: 47–48; cf. Goux 1988: 15). This blend of psychoanalysis and economics clarifies both the social and psychological ramifications of the money form, and thereby furnishes an enormously helpful means of understanding both the history of symbolic forms and the behavior of individuals, whether real or fictional.[13]

Yet Goux's work exemplifies one of the hazards of the homological method, as pointed out by Fredric Jameson (1991: 198): the tendency for one form or another to assume a "privileged explanatory value." Although Goux protests that he does not "maintain [that] any direct, mechanical effect" of new forms of exchange "can account for the emergence of the thought or concept of universal measure" (1990: 93), the economic register seems for him both logically and ontologically prior. Indeed, although Goux seems to be tracing homologies, he may really be working with analogies or isomorphisms. In one place, for example, Goux writes that "the genesis of every major symbol . . . is *isomorphic* to the discrete genetic phases of the monetary form" (20–21; emphasis added). If so, then the linguistic or psychoanalytic registers are mere isomorphs of the protomorph, money: other semiotic forms are just vehicles of a pre-existent tenor. Elsewhere he writes that "*a mode of writing is representative of a mode of signifying exchange*" (72; emphasis in original): that is, writing represents something that precedes it – the economic. Goux's language is slippery (partly, no doubt, as a result of the translation), and sometimes he claims that he privileges the monetary only because monetary forms are more discussable than the others (13, 41). Nonetheless, the impetus of his argument presupposes the primacy of the economic – if not in content, then certainly in structure.

That is, Goux's analysis is based, like all economic literary theory, upon the presumption of the possibility of exchanges – metaphorical transfers – between different cultural registers, and specifically between linguistic and economic systems. Thus, both the method he employs – negotiating among various registers by discovering resemblances and then executing semiotic exchanges – and the content of his theory – which traces the effects of economic systems upon cultural formations – are grounded upon the same assumption: that exchanges (be they homological or economic) determine both social life and the discourse about social life. Indeed, all of Goux's various symbologies depend upon a paternal metaphor or "locus of the *standard*" (21; emphasis in original) – a rhetorical gold standard in which the money form acts as universal equivalent both within its own system and between itself and other cultural systems. Thus money not only underlies Goux's theoretical position; it also functions as a universal logical equivalent, or what Heinzelman (1980: 178) calls a "superior fiction." The belief in universal equivalents becomes an untranscendable horizon. In short, Goux's work courts, and perhaps succumbs to, an economism of form and content.

But this belief in homologies and in the usefulness of exchanges between different domains is not invalidated by its economistic presuppositions. In fact, even to argue against homologies one is forced to execute the same logical move that we have just employed in our use of "exchange": to develop a homology or analogy between economic exchange and verbal exchange, and thereby to carry out a metaphorical transfer between the two. Moreover, as McCloskey (1990: 24–25) points out, economists do the same thing, constantly arguing that "action X is just like action Y," seeking isomorphisms or homologies that enable them to discover a logical or rhetorical universal equivalent "underneath it all." In that sense, then, economic criticism and economics – whether self-critical or blithely uncritical – share a common set of principles and methods. Indeed, the same belief in the possibility and value of informed exchanges between literary and economic analysis underwrites the present collection. The question, then, is not whether homologies or metaphorical exchanges can be made; rather, it is what is lost or gained in such exchanges – an economic question, after all. It is therefore crucial for economic critics and economists to remain aware of the rhetorical structures of their own arguments, and to determine which exchanges are valuable and which are specious or worthless.

Such tough-minded self-criticism is necessary to avoid two principal hazards of the homological method: that it may become an "excuse for the vaguest kind of general formulations and the most unenlightening assertions of 'identity' between entities of utterly distinct magnitude and properties" (Jameson 1991: 187); and that it may assume identities rather than proving them. Finally, even when vigilantly guarding against such abuses, practitioners of this method face another danger succinctly described by Amy Koritz and Douglas Koritz in the present volume: that economic terms such as "capital," or "value," or "market," even when used only "metaphorically," come with the definitions and assumptions of conventional economics attached. In turn, such appropriations of economic terms may foster an "economism" that limits what can be conceived by restricting discursive fields and offering univocally economic explanations for overdetermined cultural phenomena.

The section in the present volume called "Language and Money" shows how the earlier work of Shell, Goux and others may still yield rich insights. Marc Shell's contribution, excerpted from *Art and Money*, traces how the nineteenth-century American debate about aesthetics and economics "connected the study of the essence of money with the philosophy and iconology of art." For Shell, it is language – or more precisely, inscription – that lends value to modern money. Janet Sorenson's essay analyzes homologies between the economic and linguistic theories of Daniel Defoe, a writer who both embodies and dramatizes the complex interrelations of fiction, finance, and gender in his life and work. She discovers in Defoe's character Roxana a symbol of his "radical ambivalence" about the exchange economy on which he bases his theories of nationalism, equivalence, and identity. Richard Gray incisively charts the historical development of homological thinking in eighteenth-century German thought. He demonstrates how Leibniz, Lavater, Herder, and Hamann's gradual recognition of the abstract, artificial nature of money led to a new "vision of language as an artificial construct," a "money of the mind." Finally, Goux's witty essay shows how a salesclerk's trite question – "cash, check, or charge" – repeats faithfully "the historical order of different forms of monetary usage." His contribution thus both concisely summarizes his major insights about the dematerialization of money and offers a preview of its rather frightening future in an "indefinite play of referrals which forever postpones the possibility of an actual value" denoted by anything but writing. The debates about representation depicted by Shell, Sorenson, and Gray eventually give way to the contemporary (and future) world of dematerialized money and electronic credits described by Goux, where the homology between language and money may soon become an identity.[14]

More recent economic criticism has focused on precisely this issue of representation. Perhaps chastened by suspicions of economism and slightly more skeptical about the validity of homologies, this recent work usually makes less totalizing or definitive claims. These studies tend to be more specifically historicist and more attentive to contextual discursive formations – law, banking, art history, etc. – as they impinge upon literary texts. One recurrent issue has been the relations between nineteenth-century literary realism and concurrent changes in the economic system. This issue is addressed in the early work of John Vernon, who investigates how the ambiguous meaning of money as both sign of material reality and a signifier of romantic aspiration reflects and is reflected by the anxiety about failures of perfect mimesis in the realistic novel (Vernon 1984: 19).[15] More recently, Walter Benn Michaels's brilliant *The Gold Standard and the Logic of Naturalism* (1987) treats with dazzling agility homologies between nineteenth-century realism and contemporary financial practices that enable him to consider how capitalist practices of representation construct various, and often conflicting, versions of subjectivity. Michaels explores the paradoxical logic of the gold standard, in which representation presupposes a "desire to make yourself equal to your face value" (22) and thus to eliminate representation altogether. If Michaels still pursues homologies, in method and spirit his book is quite different from the studies that precede it. Indeed, Michaels's study may be considered the inaugural foray into the predominant form of economic criticism practiced today – a limb of that spreading tree called New Historicism.

To illustrate the differences between Old and New Historicism, we may compare two studies of the relations between English literature and the world of finance: Norman Russell's *The Novelist and Mammon* (1986), and Colin Nicholson's *Writing and the Rise of Finance* (1994). Russell provides much useful information about the prevalence of "manias" in nineteenth-century English financial markets (a phenomenon also considered in the present volume by Elaine Freedgood and by Brian Cooper and Margueritte Murphy), and about the earnings and marketplace maneuvers of novelists like Dickens and Trollope. But he remains wedded to a view of the literary world as irretrievably different from financial culture, arguing that "the novelist was not primarily an academic, engaged in disputes with Scottish dons [such as James Mill], but an inventive craftsman [*sic*], whose particular genius would utilize the preoccupations and institutions of his time for his own inner purposes" (16): the novelist – a male, even though Russell discusses the work of Catherine Gore – has "inner purposes" that place him in commerce mostly with himself. Russell aims to show how novelists "used" or "responded to" financial crises and conditions in their fiction, but inadequately explores how the cultural nexus that includes finance also creates and ascribes value to novels and novelists, or how those fictional representations of the economy helped to produce the conditions they described.

Nicholson's work, appearing only eight years later, bears traces of the altered methods and revised vocabulary of post-Foucaultian criticism. Consider this sentence from his introduction: "What we encounter in Opposition and other writing is a complicated inscription of developing subjectivities constituting as they are being constituted by a developing political economy" (7). In addition to adopting a more fashionable lexicon ("subjectivities," "inscription"), the sentence is careful to recognize the reciprocity between social systems and individuals, and indeed to show how both derive from larger discursive forms. Thus, Nicholson is able to discuss the mutual effects of literary and economic tropes. For example, in reading *Gulliver's Travels*, he suggests that its diverse narrative strategies "acknowledge that in a new world of speculative fantasy any construction of its narrating subject in a position of dominance is itself a delusory fiction given that promissory notes of paper-credit are increasingly the alienating agency which positions and enables economic individualism" (10). As Thompson notes, this new brand of economic criticism encompasses "the way a whole discourse manages various kinds of knowledge," and realizes that changes in economics cannot be separated from "a discourse or language or discipline developed to represent just such changes" (Thompson 1996: 5, 8).[16]

Written in Michaels's wake, Howard Horwitz's erudite, detailed *By the Law of Nature* (1991) studies the concepts of nature, selfhood and property in nineteenth- and early twentieth-century America. His attention to debates about natural law allows him to consider a diverse set of economic issues; but again the most pressing problem is that of representation, and particularly the formation and sources of cultural value. Horwitz's book is among the first of the new breed; like much New Historicist writing, it bears a strong debt to philosophical pragmatism. In this regard, as will become more apparent below, new economic literary criticism shares at least one significant feature of the "critical economics" movement – antifoundationalism. Thus, although Horwitz retains the homological method, he is self-conscious about its pitfalls, and identifies his controlling trope not as homology but as "isomorphism," claiming not that events or structures in different registers are identical, but only that they have related morphologies and arise in kindred networks (19). If Horwitz's nuanced methodology largely avoids the traps of homology hunting, it nonetheless risks erecting its own universal equivalent – Nature.

In fact, New Economic Criticism almost inevitably confronts this problem of universal critical equivalents. As Jameson argues, studies like Michaels's sometimes seem to devolve into a "montage of historical attractions" that paradoxically elevate their disdain for theory into a quasi-theoretical principle (Jameson 1991: 190). Thus, for Jameson, Michaels and his ilk merely practice structuralism without structure (ibid.: 188). In other words, their anti-essentialism is magically transformed into a universal equivalent – an essentialism – in which the term "market" mystifies rather than illuminates economic conditions. Thus, claims Jameson, the anti-theoretical position is endowed, "against its own will and vocation, with a foundation that grounds it" (ibid.: 199). In similar terms, Goux (1990: 114) describes a gold standard as an anchor in a homological system that prevents signifiers from "drifting or floating in relation to the valences they are meant to signify." In Goux's terms, then, it appears that Michaels's negotiations themselves adhere to a logical gold standard of the very kind that he critiques: a faith in the commensurability of monetary and linguistic systems – in mimesis – that he himself shows to be faulty.

At bottom, perhaps all economic criticism is founded upon a faith in universal equivalents: our "gold standard" is a belief in the comparability of different cultural systems. In that sense, even New Historicist economic criticism reflects the infiltration of money into the very forms of logic that critics hope to analyze. Strangely enough, however, as Viviana Zelizer (1994) has observed, the modern discipline of economics shows little interest in the symbolic or imaginary aspects of money itself. It is simply assumed that all money is fungible, neutral, colorless, and thereby mirrors the depiction of economists themselves as neutral, rational observers dealing only with quantifiable entities (11–12). But as Goux, Shell, Michaels and the others prove, money is a language that speaks both the self and the society that uses it. Implicit in all of these studies is a perceived need to historicize money and to reattach it to the broader social world, an impulse that not only challenges the practices and assumptions of neoclassical economics, but that also implies the existence of alternative models.

Critical economics

One of the most significant insights shared by Heinzelman and Shell – one all but ignored in recent historicist literary criticism – is that all metaphors are in a sense economic, since the etymology of "metaphor" contains within it the concept of transfer or exchange (Heinzelman 1980: 10). For this reason, Shell demonstrates, money is an "internal participant" in the semiological organization of language: if language consists of economies, so also economics is a language. This latter assertion underlies what we shall call the "critical economics" movement, which aims to inject self-consciousness into the practices and paradigms of economics by exposing its metaphorical or fictive bases. The most important figure in this movement has been Donald (Deirdre) McCloskey, whose 1985 book *The Rhetoric of Economics* awakened economists to the radical idea (already a truism in the humanities) that their discourse was just that: a language comprised of tropes, tales and other rhetorical devices that are literary and rhetorical rather than scientific or natural. But McCloskey has not been fomenting revolution; her aims are the more modest ones of improving economics by forcing economists to question and refine their models (see McCloskey 1988: 285). Even so, McCloskey's work has been met with much resistance among economists, most of whom still adhere to the paradigms of neoclassicalism – mathematization, objectivity, free rational choice, exogenous tastes, etc. Others have attempted to extend McCloskey's insights (not always with her approval), particularly a growing cadre of feminist and neo-Marxists, some of whom (Amariglio, Ruccio, Feiner) are represented in the present volume.

McCloskey has been criticized both for going too far and for not going far enough. Marxists, for example, have asserted that McCloskey's anti-foundationalism is ambivalent and half-hearted, charging that after she demonstrates the invalidity of Cartesian first principles, she turns around and reinstates them. (This is a part of the argument presented by M. Neil Browne and J. Kevin Quinn in their contribution to this volume.) Those on the other side – Robert Solow, for example – worry that the rhetoric of economics movement "softens" the discipline. As Solow also notes, many of the early forays into economic rhetoric go around proclaiming, "look ma, a metaphor," but have no idea what to do with metaphors once they have found them (Solow 1988: 34). For literary critics, the problem is not that economists find metaphors, but that they seem not to know what a metaphor is: some economists use "metaphor" promiscuously to refer to any definition, short-hand phrase, or word, whether it has any metaphoric content or not. In short, just as economists claim that literary critics use economic terms ignorantly, so literary critics assert that economists know too little about literary terms.[17] Even McCloskey has sometimes failed to analyze her own tropes, and has thus been challenged for celebrating the "marketplace of ideas" without recognizing it as a metaphor. Critics claim that the "marketplace" notion simply translates *laissez-faire* economics into the intellectual sphere, which appears as a giant agora where good or bad metaphors fight it out and the best trope wins.[18]

As a step towards enhancing metaphorical self-awareness, Arjo Klamer and Thomas Leonard have provided a helpful introduction to tropes for the literarily impaired, along with a pathbreaking analysis of the three kinds of metaphors – constitutive, pedagogical, heuristic – used in economics. What economists fail to grasp, Klamer and Leonard (1994: 30) argue, is that metaphors underpin thought itself: they are not just instruments for our use, but actually shape subjectivity and reason. For Klamer and Leonard, the discovery that "a handful of metaphors constitutes discursive practices in economics" is itself a metaphor that may lead to a richer understanding of economics. How? By reminding economists of the fictive nature of their models and by revealing how practice differs from theory (44).[19] In contrast (and with his usual outrageousness), Stanley Fish asserts that recognizing the situatedness of economics will have no consequences whatsoever; indeed, he dubs the belief that knowledge of one's embeddedness in a situation helps us to escape the implications of those beliefs "antifoundationalist theory hope" (Fish 1994: 27). All we have in McCloskey's work, he claims, is a "new account of our epistemology," a "new belief about where our beliefs come from" (28). Antifoundationalists like McCloskey or the non-essentialist Marxists, claims Fish, cannot turn their hope into a lever to pry us away from the world given to us by beliefs. In a similar but more nuanced and detailed essay in this volume, Howard Horwitz argues that McCloskey's work is based upon a number of logical flaws: a confusion between constructing and construing reality; a self-contradictory conception of belief; a lack of clarity about the consequences of antifoundationalism.

In a response that has failed to satisfy either side, McCloskey also claims that becoming aware of the constitutive or pedagogical metaphors of economics will have little effect on the practice or outcomes of economics, other than cleaning it up and making it more honest. Indeed, these reassurances suggest that McCloskey is caught between antifoundationalist impulses and a deep loyalty to University of Chicago-style economic orthodoxy. Is the issue that economists use metaphors, or that they use faulty ones? If the first, it seems difficult to see why this condition is a problem, and impossible to conceive how to fix it, short of abolishing the discipline altogether. If the second is the issue, then the problem cannot be solved by a general theory, but only by scrutinizing and adjudicating each metaphor or story for its aptness, usefulness, and political ramifications.

Nonetheless, McCloskey's pathbreaking work has launched a wider, bolder challenge to the assumptions and practices of neoclassical economics. Some of these critical economists have targeted neoclassicalism chiefly for the shallowness of its model of human subjectivity. In their essay in this volume, for example, Browne and Quinn scrutinize three dominant metaphors in economics and outline their implications for ideas about human consciousness. They begin by critiquing the figure of rational economic man, who embodies the neoclassicalists' world of isolated, freely choosing individuals acting in their own self-interest. Elsewhere, sociologist Paula England (1993: 37) has criticized as narrow and androcentric this neoclassical paradigm of the "separative self." The exclusion of empathy and cooperative impulses handicaps economics, England charges, by preventing economists from adequately grappling with grave disparities in income and power: the allegedly neutral principles of neoclassical economics are thereby exposed as ideological (43). In their important article in the Kuiper and Sap collection, Diana Strassmann and Livia Polanyi (1995) isolate an irony in economists' belief in such isolated, self-interested, rational agents: it is rarely applied to economists themselves. That is, according to economists' own rationale, the positing of dispassionate, self-interested economic agents must be in economists' self-interest (132). But if economists' work is by definition self-interested, how can it also be disinterested?

To us as outsiders to the discipline of economics, the neoclassicalists' notion of subjectivity – which Jameson (1991: 270) describes as "little more than a point of consciousness directed onto the stockpile of materials available in the outside world" – seems severely attenuated. Moreover, the use of self-interest as a guiding principle seems to lead either to self-refutation or to tortuous or circular reasoning: one can easily redefine self-interest in such a way that even the most perverse, bizarre or self-destructive actions – such as heroin addiction – or sacrosanct institutions – such as marriage – are nothing more than instances of maximizing utility. Although economists do grant that many aspects of human behavior cannot be measured, and hence lie beyond the pale of inquiry, nonetheless many neoclassical economists seem compelled to expand the boundaries and thereby overreach themselves. Perhaps these economists would benefit from examining a literary work: Fyodor Dostoevsky's *Notes from Underground* ([1864] 1991), whose protagonist analyzes and embodies the paradoxes of self-interest. Written as a parody of Chernyshevsky's *What Is To Be Done?* (an apology for the portrayal of humans as enlightened and reasonable), *Notes from Underground* depicts humans, in contrast, as motivated by capricious, irrational impulses, including a perverse desire for self-abasement or humiliation. The Underground Man wonders "what if it so happens that a man's advantage *sometimes* not only may, but even must, consist exactly in his desiring under certain conditions what is harmful to himself and not what is advantageous," and goes on to show that "if there can be such a condition [and the Underground Man himself proves there can be] then the whole principle becomes worthless" (Dostoevsky [1864] 1991: 19). Indeed, the narrator demonstrates how humans will act *against* their own interest if only to prove that they are not bound by the obligation to act in their interest (26). One could, of course, argue in rebuttal that such actions are still a form of self-interest; but once self-destruction is reinterpreted as self-interest, and once the paradigm of self-interest is expanded beyond the very constricted realm of measurable economic phenomena, it loses its explanatory value. If human beings act willfully in opposition to what reason would term their self-interest, then one might wish to claim that other, irrational impulses and forces also motivate economic behavior.

The exposure of the deficiencies in the presumption of rational self-interest actuates the essays in the section in the present volume called "Economics of Irrationality." Susan Feiner's contribution (a companion to her piece in Kuiper and Sap) analyzes economists' favorite fictional character, *Homo economicus*, that straw man inevitably motivated by the goal of maximizing utility. For Feiner, *Homo economicus* remains profoundly infantile and eternally unsatisfied by markets, which assume the role of the withholding mother. Endlessly pursuing gratification, *Homo economicus* is compelled to consume incessantly, but never satisfies his desires. Moving from fictional Economic Man to Harriet Martineau, a real-life female literary economist, we learn from Elaine Freedgood how Martineau sought in *Illustrations of Political Economy* to reassure readers of the benefits of industrial capitalism, but was unable to allay even her own anxiety about its depredations. On an even wider scale, Margueritte Murphy and Brian Cooper suggest how Jean-François Lyotard's notion of "libidinal economy" exposes the failure of conventional economics to explain the recurrent manias or panics that plague economic systems, and thus lays bare an enormous blind spot in one of neoclassicalism's privileged beliefs.

Perhaps the most sustained and forceful challenges to neoclassicalism have come from a growing group of feminist economists, who have spotlighted the gendered nature not only of "economic man" but also of economics itself. Marianne A. Ferber and Julie A. Nelson's introduction to their valuable collection (1993) helpfully summarizes the challenges faced by feminist economics. One of these challenges is to end the demographic homogeneity that has reinforced the hegemonic conditions of a discipline dominated by white males who have come to regard their own biases and choices as universal. In the same volume, Diana Strassmann (1993) points out how these institutional practices restrict the "pattern of acceptable disagreement in a way that silences serious challenges to the primacy of self-interested individualism and contractual exchange" (55).[20] In their important essay, Nancy Folbre and Heidi Hartmann (1988) demonstrate how the conventional notion of separate economic spheres – the domestic realm for women and the market for men – produces the very conditions it analyzes. For example, women's alleged lack of egoistic self-interest – their "altruism" and lack of competitive spirit – has been used to claim (circularly) that women know they cannot participate in the marketplace and therefore choose the home as best suited to their "innate" qualities. Here the rhetoric of self-interest merely acts to protect "men's privileges from economic scrutiny" (192).

Much of the work by feminist economists has explored the origins of this bifurcation of spheres and examined its repercussions for the evolution of literary forms and economic science. Ferber and Nelson (1993: 12), for example, argue that the ideology of separate spheres is both a cause and symptom of the increasing detachment of economics from the other social sciences, the humanities, and the community in general.[21] The critique of gendered polarities – male vs. female, public vs. private, self-interest vs. altruism – thus furnishes a common arena where economic literary criticism and critical economics might meet to encourage both disciplines to contest these polarities and to seek new, less hierarchical and polarized models. One such model has been proposed by Folbre and Hartmann (1988: 198), who suggest that a better theory of interests would include some recognition of "solidarity" or "conditional altruism" in all spheres. The feminist critique, one hopes, will point toward a more fully social conception of economics that will contest the notion that all economic actions are performed by the isolated, rational, competitive monads depicted in neoclassicalism.

Two other sets of critiques have also shed light on the deficiencies of neoclassical economics. The first is a brand of "nonessentialist Marxism," so dubbed by practitioners such as Stephen Resnick, Richard Wolff, Jack Amariglio, and David Ruccio. Resnick and Wolff revive the Althusserian notion of "overdetermination" as a means of freeing the discipline from its positivism. For them, "overdetermination" implies that "every aspect of society is understood as totally constituted by all the influences emanating from every other aspect" (Resnick and Wolff 1988: 52). Such a concept is clearly at odds with conventional cause–effect logic: since all truths are plural and lack a definite essence, a full explanation for any circumstance, event or theory is impossible. These critics assert that resurrecting "overdetermination" will change the way economics is practiced, and consequently alter society as well. But it also seems possible that instead of the current situation, which they describe as "vain trumpeting at cross purposes of theories that each claims to hold a privileged communion with the truth" (60), we may instead find an endless series of articles proving that such and such a construction is "overdetermined." One is here reminded of a charge against deconstruction, which, as it began to dominate literary criticism, seemed to produce the same outcome over and over: a predictable (and sometimes self-congratulatory) discovery in every text of an "aporia" or deconstructive paradox. Thus, while overdetermination may change the terms of the debate, it may also simply replace one totalizing explanation (or non-explanation) with another.

One member of this school, Jack Amariglio, has provocatively argued that neoclassical economics is a modernist discourse that nonetheless contains "postmodern moments," which he defines as a recognition that all truths are "discourse-specific" – socially constructed and bounded in time and place (Amariglio 1990: 15, 24). The problem with McCloskey's subversion of neoclassicalism, writes Amariglio, is that it stresses only the form of argumentation while leaving the content untouched (25), and thus remains founded upon a modernist epistemology. Other modernist economists – Frank Knight, J.M. Keynes, G.L.S. Shackle – similarly permit postmodern moments to seep into their arguments by sometimes reluctantly recognizing the presence of uncertainty. Amariglio's argument holds a good deal of promise as a critique of the "Big Science envy" that characterizes neo-classicalism; the awareness that economic truths are situational and social may open new avenues for a reconsideration of paradigms such as "rational expectations."

However, the value of Amariglio's argument is undercut somewhat by an oversimplification – even demonization – of modernism that also infects some of McCloskey's work (see, for example, McCloskey 1990: ch. 1). Indeed, if Amariglio is right that Modernism generally emphasizes form over content and seeks to discover univeral truths, then his claim that Modernism upholds "the universality and eternality of Reason and Truth" (19) is itself a Modernist statement. Perhaps more importantly, there is a conflict at work between literary and social-scientific definitions of Modernism: whereas Amariglio's Modernists seem to be primarily eighteenth- and nineteenth-century scientists, literary Modernism usually refers to twentieth-century innovators such as André Gide, T.S. Eliot, James Joyce, and Virginia Woolf. These authors' picture of human culture as chaotic, fragmented, irrational, and situational closely resembles Amariglio's description of postmodernism; they also share his "postmodernists'" deep suspicion of general truth-claims. Many Modernist artists, moreover, recognized the repercussions of new scientific discoveries such as Gödel's theorems, which showed in 1930 and 1933 that no formal system complicated enough to include arithmetic can be both consistent and complete, and that no axiomatic system can establish definitively even its own consistency. Such conflicts in terminology will need to be clarified in order for literary and econonomic theorists to reach any mutual understanding. Nevertheless, Amariglio's essay retains value for its analysis of the incommensurability between economic theory – based upon a mechanistic, mathematized determinism – and its practice, which often must confront, only to explain away, its own uncertainties and situatedness.

All of these reconfigurations of conventional practices depend upon and invite a new understanding of the history and future of economics. In this regard, Mirowski (1994: 9) points out how the Anglo-American economic tradition has divorced itself almost entirely from a Germanic "historicist heritage that had argued for the desirability and even necessity of a separate and distinct mode for the study of society." Implicit in his argument is a perceived need to reattach economics to a broader notion of the social, one that Julie Nelson echoes in calling for a redefinition of economics that considers "humans *in relation* to the world" (Nelson 1993: 32; emphasis in original). This desire to resocialize and rehistoricize economic thought constitutes another potentially fruitful meeting ground for economists and literary/cultural critics. One example of the benefits of such a collaboration is provided in Regenia Gagnier and John Dupré's first contribution to the present volume, in which they demonstrate how the scientism of contemporary economics has occluded its biases and prevented proper consideration of values or goals outside of its allegedly neutral models. They conclude by calling for a new political economy that sees people as both producers and consumers, formed within the pains of labor and the pleasures of consumption.

Fundamental to these challenges to contemporary economics is also a rejection of essentialism in favor of models that present behavior and subjectivity as culturally constructed. This antifoundationalism is shared by both New Historicist literary criticism and much contemporary feminism. Unfortunately, however, one consequence of the antifoundationalism of post-modern economics has been a dispersal of its effects, so that, as in early economic literary criticism, the separate points of the various critiques have not cohered into a unified theory or set of theories (Ferber and Nelson 1993: 12). The critical economics movement, in short, still awaits its major statement. Moreover, while "poetic economics" is blooming in literary studies, "imaginative economics" – or what Willie Henderson calls "literary economics" ("a self-conscious awareness of the fictive element of economics discourse" and the value of metaphor or narrative in economic arguments [Henderson 1995: 14]) – is merely budding. Thus what A.W. Coats wrote in 1988 remains true: economics continues to lag behind other disciplines in questioning its own assumptions and in unbinding itself from mechanistic paradigms (Coats 1988: 64). One aim of the present collection, then, is to promote further self-questioning by showing what the methods and principles of economic literary criticism ("poetic economics") may offer to economics, and by suggesting how the two movements may collaborate to provide new theories and ask new questions that will improve both disciplines.

Giving and consuming

We believe that such collaboration will yield especially valuable dividends in two discursive arenas that have thus far remained outside the mainstream of both economics and literary economic criticism. The first encompasses a broad range of anti-bourgeois and anti-capitalist writing derived largely from French structuralism that blends anthropology, sociology, economics, and psychoanalysis: the theoretics of gift exchange. The second originated perhaps with the Frankfurt school, but has until recently been neglected by both the Left and Right: the economic and discursive analysis of consumption and consumerism. Both are spaces wherein economists and literary/cultural critics may fruitfully combine forces by wedding feminism, oppositional cultural criticism, economics, and psychoanalysis to literary theory and criticism. Taken together, these two sets of discourses – about giving and consuming

– may plant the seeds of a new set of principles for economics and economic criticism.

The primal text in gift theory is undoubtedly Marcel Mauss's 1925 anthropological romance, *Essai sur le don* (*The Gift*). Mauss's work has been appropriated by numerous thinkers, each of whom emphasizes a different aspect of his writing. Lewis Hyde (1983), for example, extends Mauss's ideas to posit a radical disjunction between market and gift economies that also, he claims, explains the social function and origin of artistic creativity. Novelist and eroticist Georges Bataille (1988) expounds an ambitious theory of "general economy" based upon the notion that expenditure rather than profit underlies many social forms. Jacques Derrida, the founder of deconstruction, has maintained a long dialogue with Mauss and Bataille going back at least to his essay "From Restricted to General Economy" in *Writing and Difference* (1978), and continuing with his recent books *Given Time I: Counterfeit Money* (1992) – which argues that Mauss's notion of the gift as entirely free from calculation is impossible – and *The Gift of Death* (1995). Jean-François Lyotard critiques Mauss's Utopian romanticization of "primitive" cultures only to replicate it in a different form in *Libidinal Economy* (1993) (both Derrida and Lyotard are insightfully treated in Amariglio and Ruccio's contribution to the present volume).

If the most troubling problem for "language and money" theorists concerns the viability of homologies between disparate cultural forms and types of representation, the problem for gift theorists lies in the relationship between gift exchanges and self-interest or profit. Is the gift economy (assuming there is such a thing) inherently different from the market economy, and if so does it embody or encourage a different set of behaviors and paradigms? Is gift-giving motivated entirely or mostly by altruism, or does it merely camouflage self-interest? Most investigations of gift exchanges have fallen into one of two camps. On one side are Bataille and Hyde. Hyde's stunning anthropology of gift exchanges as an alternative, or "erotic commerce" (1983: 163) has done much to reintroduce the subject to English-speaking audiences. For Bataille, the single most important phenomenon in human culture is not scarcity but the excess that cannot be used productively and hence must be spent or lost without profit (1988: 21, 23). As for Mauss so for Bataille the exemplary gift-giving ritual is the potlatch ceremony of Pacific Northwest Native Americans, in which giving extravagant gifts enables leaders to squander wealth intentionally and accrue prestige through loss (69). In Bataille's "general economy," human beings subsist not to save, but to "accede to the insubordinate function of free expenditure [dépense]" (1985: 129). Thus for Bataille, all meaningful social rituals – including and especially art and poetry – involve loss and sacrifice (ibid.: 120).

Both writers have been criticized in similar terms. Hyde's work is, like Mauss's, marked by a naïve Utopianism. In dividing economic actions into the supposedly incommensurable realms of market and gift, Hyde demonizes markets and sentimentalizes gifts, while ignoring the antagonistic or competitive aspects of ritual gift exchanges that even Mauss acknowledges.[22] Like David Cheal, who observes in his study of gifts how the "moral economy" of gift exchanges has long been associated in Western culture with female labor and female social roles, Hyde describes gifts as "female property" and gift exchanges as "female commerce" (Cheal 1988: 181; Hyde 1983: 93–108; cf. Zelizer 1994: 86–7). But while he recognizes the separation of economic spheres noted above, Hyde's notion of "female property" may reproduce the very bifurcation that he analyzes. Missing is a historical or anthropological recognition of *how* or *why* gift exchanges have been identified with femininity, and the relationship between "female property" and the historical condition of women themselves as "female property."[23] Hyde's thesis must be supplemented by work such as Gayle Rubin's influential 1975 essay "The Traffic in Women," which offers a counterargument to Lévi-Strauss's famous claim in his *Elementary Structures of Kinship* (1969) that the exchange of women provided the very foundations of culture. Hyde's study thus reveals the need to rethink the relationships between gifts and gender: this is another arena where literary criticism, cultural studies, and economics might meet for mutual enlightenment.

As for Bataille, critics charge that his "dépense" is merely another name for financial or social capital accrued through apparent, but not real, losses. According to these critics, Bataille readmits self-interest and profit through the back door by renaming conspicuous loss as social prestige. Barbara Herrnstein Smith, for example, charges that Bataille's "loss" retains most of the qualities of the bourgeois economics it aims to replace. In erecting expenditure as a central principle, Smith argues, Bataille simply recoups rationality with reversed valence and thereby replaces one universal equivalent with another: when "absolute loss" becomes a good, it ceases to be absolute (Smith 1988: 135–49).[24] It is certainly clear from the ethnographic evidence – including some presented by Mauss – that rituals such as the potlatch carry with them powerful obligations to reciprocate. Bataille does seem unsure whether "expenditure" really underwrites sociality itself, or is merely the motive for certain orgiastic moments of carnival; sometimes, too, expenditure seems to be merely another name for conspicuous consumption. Still, the recuperation of loss as prestige does not obviate the difference in intention between saving or profiting and squandering. Thus Bataille's work retains value as a critique of bourgeois economics, as a salutary reminder of the "irrational," even erotic motives underlying many economic behaviors – aspects that conventional economics fails to treat adequately.

The need to recontain or tame the gift economy may in fact tell us more about conventional economic assumptions than about gift exchanges. Indeed, Cheal lists this "economic rationalization" of gift exchanges as one of three means by which political economy trivializes and tries to dismiss gift-giving and -receiving (Cheal 1988: 7–8).[25] He argues that gift economies are not separate from capitalist economies, but rather coexist within and beside them. Cheal describes gifts as uniquely "redundant transactions": they transcend mere dutiful reciprocity; they bring no advantage or net benefit to recipients; they are often objects the recipient could have provided by him- or herself; they tend to be more than "merely sufficient" (12–13). Hence, gift transactions typify not political economy but "moral economy," a set of "normative obligations" that function mostly in smaller groups within the larger economic system (16ff). With this formulation, Cheal attempts to reconcile the separate spheres – gift and market, female and male, domestic and public – noted by Hyde and many other writers. However, his notion of a "moral economy" may inadvertently have the opposite effect of trivializing gift exchanges by limiting their range. A more useful model may be that of Pierre Bourdieu, who argues that the contradictory nature of gift exchanges – they are ritualized acts unlike others and at the same time necessarily implicated in a succession of reciprocal transactions – makes them unique. For Bourdieu (1977: 3–9), the defining characteristic of gift exchanges is the temporal separation of gift and counter-gift in an indefinite reciprocal cycle. Gifts are not the same as debts because the obligations they produce are cyclic and theoretically infinitely deferrable.

Even with its flaws and conceptual difficulties, gift theory, which foregrounds the many possible forms of social obligations, poses challenges to both economics and ethics. That is, gift exchanges reveal and complicate perhaps the fundamental norm of all economic behavior: reciprocity. Moreover, gift theory invites us to ask significant questions about other economic activities: are gifts entirely different from debts? If so, then what sorts of obligations do gifts involve? When is a gift also a debt? Investigations of the gift thus implicitly or explicitly address the nature of ownership and property: who owns a gift? How are persons – who are, according to Mauss, Hyde and Lévi-Strauss, inevitably symbolized in gifts given or received – constituted by property when property is not held by an individual? These questions are addressed in the section of the present collection entitled "Debts and Bondage." Nancy Epstein's essay focuses on Montaigne's notion of debt as bondage and his desire to preserve the self by shielding it from commerce with the marketplace. For Montaigne, friendship, presumably the realm of altruism, creates obligations that threaten the "capital of self." Epstein's Montaigne thus exemplifies the problems and paradoxes at the heart of bourgeois selfhood. David Martyn's contribution analyzes the ethics of reciprocity in Sade's *Justine* to show how Sade exposes gratitude as inherently self-interested. According to Martyn, what eludes the system of reciprocity for Sade is not gift but theft, which deactivates both gratitude and benevolence. Justine's narration, Martyn suggests, allows her to withhold the body her listeners wish to possess; thus her narrative economy, which remains indeterminate in its intentions and effects, lies outside of the ethical economy of reciprocity. Samira Kawash's fascinating historical foray demonstrates how the narratives of runaway slaves expose the boundaries of property and personhood by generating a third figure – the fugitive – residing outside of this polarity. Slaves who "steal themselves" at once violate the law of property and depend upon its sanction: to break the law, the slave (not legally a person) must be recognized as a person. Like Epstein and Martyn, Kawash teases out the limitations of bourgeois conceptions of selfhood by scrutinizing the complex relationships among bondage, narrativity, ownership, and obligation.

Theories of gift exchange and attendant questions about reciprocity, obligation, and altruism thus hold enormous potential for both economists and literary and cultural critics. Among the major issues might include: whether gift exchanges lie outside of economics and if so how; whether their female gendering is an unwanted result of exclusionary historical practices or a source of power; to what degree gift practices exist within conventionally "male" domains, and if so how they are to be described; whether an analysis of motives behind gift exchange provides an exemplary instance of overdetermination that can be described neither as altruism nor as self-interest; whether gift exchanges rely upon or produce a different understanding of selfhood than market exchanges; how eroticizing the economy (in the manner of Lyotard and Bataille) might alter economists' paradigms. Indeed, the viability of Mauss's work and of gift economics is indicated by the recent formation in France of MAUSS (the Mouvement Anti-Utilitariste dan les Sciences Sociales), which publishes a journal aimed at exploring "other, more generous ways of looking at human exchange than . . . the categories of 'interest' and 'utility'" (Purdy 1993: 13). The analysis of gift economies thus opens the possibility of a novel theoretics of the marketplace free from both Utopianism – whether of Mauss or Marx – and rigidly polarized thinking about gender and value.[26]

Polarization has likewise typified most work on consumerism and consumption, which has suffered from rigid theoretical and political divisions into Left vs. Right; high vs. popular culture; economics vs. literature, or the aesthetic vs. the commercial; the domestic realm vs. the public realm, etc. In economics, Left critiques of consumerism reside within a larger attack on capitalism; in contrast, the neoclassical viewpoint emerges from Marginalism's focus on individual consumer choices and tastes, and thus regards the consumer as *Homo economicus*, who goes about ahistorically and asocially maximizing utility by selecting from the panoply of goods and services whatever will satisfy his (rarely her) desires. In literary and cultural studies, the debate has been similarly polarized. In her book *Shopping With Freud*, Rachel Bowlby (1993) concisely characterizes the two schools of thought: in one model, the consumer is "a poor dupe, deluded by the onslaught of an irresistible and insidious advertising industry"; in the other, the consumer is the beneficiary of the ever-increasing choices offered by the dazzling wonders of consumer society (2–3). The former view is common in Left discourse which, conditioned by the writings of the Frankfurt school, seems unable to hide a distaste for mass culture that may derive as much from an elitist disdain for the popular as from any Marxian notion of alienation or capitalist abuses. The latter view is exemplified by the work of Lawrence Birken (1988), who argues that consumerism produces a democratization and enhancement of individual choice. Birken employs the homological method to draw persuasive parallels between the rise of consumer credit and deficit spending, and the emergence of a modern sexology that promoted erotic "spending."[27]

Few critics have found their way out of these tired dualities. But a small number of recent books – Bowlby's two studies (1985, 1993) of consumerism and literature, Thomas Richards's (1990) splendid historical analysis of the emergence of commodity culture in Victorian England, and Jennifer Wicke's (1988) deft and subtle treatment of the contemporaneous rise of advertising and literary modernism – have offered more nuanced models with which to treat the discourses of consumption and commodity culture. Richards (1990: 1), for example, demonstrates how "the fundamental imperatives of the capitalist system became tangled up with certain kinds of cultural forms, which after a time became indistinguishable from economic forms." He then traces – through rich and illustrative interpretations of both popular artifacts (such as ads for patent medicines) and high cultural icons such as Joyce's *Ulysses* – the ways that nineteenth-century capitalism developed its own characteristic discourses. For Wicke (1988: 1), the "dialectic between advertising and the novel reveals both how advertising was able to take on the status of a mass literature, enforcing its own codes of social reading, and how the novel relies on the conditions of advertising to permit it to become the major literary form." By examining Dickens, Henry James and Joyce, Wicke successfully resituates advertising without treating it as a mere "messenger-boy of ideology" (16) and without pandering to anti-Left backlash.[28] It is especially essential nowadays to reconceive the critical discourse about consumerism since, as Bowlby (1993: 2–3) notes, consumerist notions of "choice" have infiltrated virtually all aspects of social life, including voting, school selection, enrolling in college courses, and selecting a church; indeed, as Horwitz notes in the present collection, morality itself is often framed in terms of quasi-consumerist "choices."

Rita Barnard's (1995) book points to a positive direction for future critical discourse on commodity culture. Like Birken, Barnard adopts Warren Susman's term "culture of abundance" as a relatively neutral description of the rise of consumer-oriented mass culture in the early twentieth century (Birken 1988: 13–14; Susman 1984: xx). In demonstrating how the division between high and popular culture was gradually erased in the US during the 1920s and '30s, Barnard positions herself between consumerist apologists and the totalizing pessimism of Baudrillard and the Frankfurt school (Barnard 1995: 6, 13, 19). Against the Baudrillardian "conspiracy" theory of consumer society, she propounds a more measured formulation that treats the discourses of commodity culture not as a swindle but as a "bribe – a transaction that offers concrete benefits, including . . . a degree of comfort unparalleled in history" (19).[29] At the same time, however, she rejects what Roland Marchand calls "the parable of the democracy of goods" – that story in which consumption is celebrated as a pure expression of American ideals (Barnard 1995: 31; Marchand 1985: 217–22).

Although proceeding from a Left political stance, these studies have initiated a more sophisticated understanding of the power – and limits – of capitalist discourses. Their example, however, has been followed too rarely.[30] Thus the study of consumerism – in both its historical dimensions and its current manifestations – retains vast untapped reserves of discursive wealth. Achieving a workable set of models with which to approach consumerism is particularly important for an adequate understanding of twentieth-century economics and culture, a period that has, surprisingly, garnered much less attention from economic critics than have earlier eras. In literary studies, the treatment of relationships between aesthetic Modernism and Modernist economics has been handicapped by a vestigial formalism and a squeamishness about the distasteful politics of some of the period's luminaries.[31] Furthermore, studies of postmodernism rarely engage the actual workings of capitalist consumption or markets, simply repeating shibboleths like "late capitalism" or "global economy" instead of investigating specific instances that might produce surprising or overdetermined results.[32]

Three contributions to the present collection, all excerpted from important forthcoming books, indicate avenues for future research into the relationships between twentieth-century culture and economics. Paul Delany's "Who Paid for Modernism?" persuasively demonstrates the dependence of literary modernism on the patronage of a mostly female *rentier* culture of inherited wealth. Modernists who proclaimed their disdain for the commercial were protected from direct engagement with it by patrons who allowed them to mystify their own indebtedness. Ironically, it is precisely the "resistant" nature of High Modernist texts that eventually resituated them as "super-commodities" in the literary and cultural marketplace: difficult literary works eventually became a form of venture capital that could be invested and traded, but that was valuable only insofar as its means of production seemed to be anti-capitalist. Davis Houck turns his attention to John Maynard Keynes, a member of the Bloomsbury group – a coterie that contributed much to Modernist literature and aesthetics – to demonstrate how Keynes's rhetorical art, exemplified in two letters to President Franklin Roosevelt, helped to produce the very economic improvements that Keynes predicted. Through his rhetorical skill, Keynes was able to generate the image of economists as prophets that remains so powerful today. Michael Tratner's ingenious reading of Fitzgerald's *The Great Gatsby* addresses the relationship between American literature and economic policies like Keynes's by connecting the occupations of Fitzgerald's narrator and nominal protagonist – bond salesmen – to a broad change in attitudes about credit in the 1920s. Applying Birken's perceived parallels between sexology and deficit spending, Tratner illustrates how Gatsby's movement from gangster to *nouveau riche* – from illicit to licit bonds – symbolizes the results of the new valorization of domestic deficit spending. All three pieces thus explore the relationships between modernist writing and new concepts of the marketplace and all, in one way or another, suggest new ways of understanding how the rise of consumerism affected both economic policy and artistic production.

Redefinitions

We are now ready to offer some answers to the question, "What is economic criticism?" The historical survey we have provided suggests four separate, though related, approaches to the economics of literary texts.

1. Production

The most prevalent form of economic criticism investigates the social, cultural, and economic contexts in which individual or related works have been produced: here economic criticism comprises a branch of cultural studies or New Historicism. Such scholarship may consider, first, an individual author's views about money, his/her financial practices, profits from artistic labor, positioning within the marketplace, etc. Second, it may analyze the wider economy in which the author and his or her work reside, which includes the reception and evaluation of art or literary texts within the larger marketplace; it may examine the other cultural discourses (e.g., advertisements, popular cultural artifacts and practices) that impinge upon, influence, or parallel the text(s) under consideration; it may address the economic and social effects of gender, ethnicity, and sexual orientation on textual production. Finally, it should take account of the national, regional, or transnational economies during the time of a work's composition. For example, to make adequate sense of Charles Dickens's depictions of money, class, and bourgeois subjectivity, one might investigate: how his father's imprisonment for debt affected his attitude towards money and work; his manipulation of the market for his own works: how he responded to and incorporated public relations and advertising to become a kind of recognized brand name; the relationship between mass marketing and his seemingly obsessive industriousness; his labors to revise copyright statutes. One would also need to place Dickens and his work within the rapidly expanding industrial and imperialist economy and shifting class structures of Victorian England. Examples of this productionist or contextualist approach abound in recent economic criticism, and are amply represented in the present collection (see Sorenson, Crosby, Austin, Joseph, Delany, Wicke, Freedgood, and Tratner). Generally speaking, Productionist criticism is predominantly *extratextual*: it combines biographical, historical, and cultural methods as a means of framing texts and authors within small and large extratextual economies, but rarely examines the internal economies of the texts themselves.

2. *Internal circulation*

The second form of economic criticism supplements Productionist approaches by exploiting Shell's (1982: 3) insight that money is a "system of tropes" and an " 'internal' participant in the logical or semiological organization of language." Such criticism uses formalist methods to analyze the internal or intratextual "economies" of a text or texts. Fundamental to this approach is an understanding of texts as systems of exchange involving dynamic patterns of interlocking metaphoric transfer. Not surprisingly, the favored vehicles for such transfers are tropes that are also monetary in denotation. When applied to narrative works, such criticism usually begins by analyzing the actions and interactions of the characters – their exchanges, debts, purchases, losses, gifts, etc. – to show how they embody this internal tropic economy. For poetic texts, such criticism may examine the economic tropes in individual works (such as Wordsworth's use of a metaphorics of interest to represent memory in "Tintern Abbey"), within literary movements, or in an author's *oeuvre*, in order to chart repeated figural patterns and thereby also determine the author's evaluation of his or her own creative labor (as Heinzelman does). In short, the procedures of such formalist economic criticism are largely *intratextual.*

But if New Historicism sometimes neglects the intratextual in favor of extratextual economies, formalist economic criticism has been marred by its universalist, even ahistorical assumptions about the relationships between authors and social milieux. Thus the most successful economic criticism must combine several angles of attack, eschewing both narrow formalism and the indiscriminate connections and generalities of New Historicism. By combining these methods, a critic can mint unprecedented riches from texts, and at the same time show how microcosm mirrors macrocosm by concretely demonstrating the dense imbrication of cultural artifacts within a society. For example, a critic approaching a work like James Joyce's *Ulysses* would try to elucidate not only how that massive novel depicts in staggering documentary detail the economy of turn-of-the-century Ireland, but also how its textual economy mirrors Irish economic conditions. This critic might argue (as Osteen does) that the text betrays a constant fluctuation between control and extravagance, or saving and spending, that mimics the economic ambivalences of its author and of the real-life Irish living in 1904 under a fractured colonial economy. These socioeconomic conditions encouraged citizens to view certain prudent economic behaviors – such as maximizing utility – as English, and thus propelled many of them to continue the very behaviors that fostered British prejudice in the first place. But the formalist would also recognize that Joyce's oscillation between verbal meanness – in which words and characters are subjected to a stringent economic ethics of scarcity – and a comic extravagance of language – in which words are "spent" freely with apparently little thought for salvaging the semiotic economy of denotation typical of realism – enables him to transform his aesthetic labor with the English language into Irish cultural capital. In short, sensitive close reading of a text's intratextual economies of meaning can supply the microscopic lenses needed to supplement the telescopic vision of historicist criticism, which too often ignores economies of textuality for a single-minded pursuit of content, context and political consequence.

3. External circulation and consumption

This form of economic criticism focuses on such issues as the market forces at work in canonization; the selling or publicizing of art or literature; the changing dynamics of aesthetic value; the condition of authors or artists as commodities and celebrities, and so on. Here a critic might also address economies of reading – the interchanges between authors and readers, or texts and readers (whether theorized as contract, gift, debt, or dialogue) – and of reception, particularly the intertextual forces in literary history that impinge upon a text or texts. In this latter approach, a text may be presented as a kind of check or payment on which is inscribed the rewritten names of precursor authors or texts; using this approach, texts become records of accounts within an "intertextual economy" (Osteen 1995: 203).

Several recent critics (e.g., Guillory 1993; Woodmansee 1994; Erickson 1996) have explored the economics of canonicity and the role of authorship in debates about aesthetic value. But the economics of literary history, in which texts are presented as systems of historical exchange, is relatively unexplored territory. Underlying this method is an assumed homology between financial and literary debt – and the concomitant "interest" accrued over time – in which authors are perceived to appropriate and reuse textual materials as financiers or banks create wealth through debt: both generate value through temporal deferral. At issue here are the competing treatments of intertextuality propounded on the one hand by Derrida and Barthes – for whom every text is a tissue of unrecoverable citations – and on the other hand by writers such as Michael Riffaterre, for whom intertextuality generates a calculus of literary debt in which texts are viewed as escrow accounts and readers as auditors who must find specific precursors in order to take full account of textual meaning and thereby profit from the transaction.[33] Investigations of the intertextual economy might also consider problems of intellectual property, such as the nature and changing definitions of copyright, problems involving pastiche, plagiarism, forgery and artistic counterfeiting, and so on. Not surprisingly, in these matters one often discovers a synergy whereby the intertextual economy is made manifest through both an implicit and explicit metaphorics of money and debt. Thus, for example, Shell (1982: 47–83) shows how Shakespeare's appropriation in *The Merchant of Venice* of the Aristotelian understanding of *tokos* – meaning both interest and offspring – draws upon ancient notions of debt and derives from the history of usury and its relationship to anti-Semitism.

Intertextual economics should, however, be extended to encompass the discipline of economics itself, perhaps by investigating the reception and appropriation of classic economics texts such as *The Wealth of Nations* or *Capital*. For example, in his study of nineteenth-century literature and mass culture, Kevin McLaughlin (1995) explains how Marx deploys citation and imitation – which McLaughlin calls "quoting in reverse" (18) – to engender a subversive rhetorical technique aimed at destroying capitalism "from the inside" by using its own doctrines against itself. Similarly, Henderson offers a "literary approach" to economics "literature" that stresses the significance of intertextual relations between, for example, Harriet Martineau and *Robinson Crusoe*, or between Ricardo's work and Thomas De Quincey's "Dialogues of Three Templars on Political Economy" (see Henderson 1995: 16, 80–81, 91–111). Economists and theorists of contemporary culture might also join forces to reconsider the relationships between postmodern economic theories and practices and the prevalence of parody, pastiche and appropriation in contemporary literature and art.

4. *Metatheoretical*

The proliferation of economic approaches to literature and culture has brought a new set of problems. As we noted above (and as Amariglio and Ruccio suggest in their essay in the present volume), one of these problems has been an imprecision or promiscuity in the use of terms such as "economy," so that it comes to refer to any system of differences, whether or not that system involves value, money, scarcity, or labor (indeed, the present essay may strike some economists as guilty of this very promiscuity). A related danger is that overuse will empty such terms of their economic meanings and hence of their instrumental value. It is thus essential for economic criticism to continue to refine and justify its use of economic terms – to ask why, for example, one uses "economy" instead of some other term. The last form of economic criticism performs such metacritical operations, analyzing the practices, presumptions and protocols of economic criticism itself: its use of economic paradigms and terms (e.g., "value," "capital, " "economy"); its exploitation of the homological method; the degree to which this discourse is aware of its own biases. Of course, the present essay falls into this category, as do all similar attempts to discover the rifts and bridges between economic and literary/cultural studies and to generate useful critical exchanges between the disciplines. Indeed, at this stage in the development of this cross-disciplinary dialogue it is essential for all economic criticism – whether launched from the literary or from the economic side – to monitor and refine its assumptions and terms to avoid excessive generalization, the cavalier misuse or extension of terminology, and a simple-minded "economism" that ascribes complex cultural phenomena to one-dimensional causes.[34]

It is for this reason that we end this collection with a set of critical exchanges concerning the role and value of economic criticism and critical economics. In this final section, Jack Amariglio and David Ruccio provide a measured and well-informed discussion of economists' resistance to the infiltration of literary methods into their discipline, along with an even-handed and succinct critique of the excesses and errors of "anti-economics" theorists such as Bataille and Lyotard. Specifically, they suggest how theories such as Bataille's "general economy" erect an overarching principle or transcendental signifier that simply (as noted above) replaces one universal equivalent with another. Hence, many of these theories remain caught between "the desire to uncover the realm in which markets, capital, and self-interested rationality have not penetrated and the fear that such a space is no longer discursively possible." Nevertheless, write Amariglio and Ruccio, such anti-economic economics may correct the essentialisms of both Marxism and neoclassicalism, and therefore may indeed produce genuinely "economic" knowledge. In their response, Regenia Gagnier and John Dupré outline the historical shift from political economy to neoclassicalism, briefly chart the limitations of the latter, and reassert the central role that literary and cultural economic criticism may play in providing alternative understandings of the distribution of goods and services, the construction of tastes or preferences, and the social nature of human beings. Finally, in their concluding essay, Amy Koritz and Douglas Koritz alert us to the dangers of a strictly economic metaphorics, focusing particularly on the work of Bourdieu (in cultural theory) and Gary Becker (in economics). Although Bourdieu explicitly rejects economistic reductionism, Koritz and Koritz argue that his use of economic homologies often collapses similarities into identities and thus offers too little resistance to appropriation by neoclassical economics. On the other side, the axiomatic exchange theory postulated by Becker cannot represent any condition outside of its assumption of rational, self-interested maximizers of utility. Neither theorist can answer crucial ethical questions such as how one *should* act. As a corrective, Koritz and Koritz submit Lyotard's term "differend," which refers to the incapacity of any one discipline's rules or axioms to be simply applied to another. This final essay, then, reminds us of the need for refinement and self-consciousness about the limits of cross-disciplinary approaches such as the ones offered in the present collection.

Futures

All four of these methods "explore with increasing subtlety the complex ways in which *economic* dynamics, at every level of analysis, condition the production and reception of artworks and, more generally, condition the value of all cultural objects and practices" (Smith 1988: 129). For us, the greatest value of these critical interrogations and exchanges is to make us self-conscious about social behavior and compel us to reconsider long-standing ethical, philosophical, and economic questions: What drives people to make certain economic decisions instead of others? What is the economic condition of art works: that is, how do literary works both reflect and shape individual economic behaviors and the wider economic practices of an historical period? How do literary and cultural markets work, and how do they resemble other markets? How do financial markets work and what determines their dynamics? To what degree are linguistic and economic systems comparable? How does the increasing dematerialization of money mirror or mold other cultural practices and beliefs? What is the relationship between economic practices, laws or theories – property, credit/debt, money – and subjectivity? This volume, along with the critical studies that we have cited, present a myriad of new ways to frame these questions and to consider possible answers.

How can economic criticism and critical economics continue to enhance our understanding of culture? We have already sketched out two discursive domains – gift theory and consumption – that promise much for future work. But we also need more innovative examinations of neglected realms of economic storytelling – for example, accounting ledgers, counterfactual hypotheses – and their relations to other forms of narrative accounting. In addition, we need more and better treatments of the role of gender and ethnicity in both economics and literary economics: how, for example, does gender impinge upon economic stories and stories of economics? While we need to bring the "non-economic" or "anti-economic" theories of writers like Bataille, Mauss, and Lyotard to bear upon Marxist and neoclassicalist assumptions (as for example in this volume's contributions by Cooper and Murphy and by Koritz and Koritz), at the same time we need more hard-eyed analyses that will ferret out the errors and excesses of such theories. We also need further treatments of how social phenomena that are usually framed as "economic" may be deepened by considering their wider cultural meanings or ramifications. We need further discussions of how our understanding of books or other cultural artifacts must be modified in the age of "mechanical reproduction" or "late capitalism," where everything is commodified and everything is an image. And we need futher consideration of the economic and psychological effects of electronic money such as credit cards, debit cards, and "smart cards."

Finally, just as we literary critics need to be more self-conscious about our use of economic terms and paradigms, so economists need to be better informed and more subtle in their deployment of literary terms such as "metaphor" or "story." In general, we need more measured, well-informed, disciplined scholarship and research from both fields in order to make economic literary criticism more economic (but without replicating its narrowness of definition and disciplinary rigidity) and critical economics more social and more critical. With these goals in mind, we invite you to read the essays that follow as points of intersection between the disciplines, and as critical exchanges aimed at enriching both literature and economics.

Notes

1 One such apologia in the early nineteenth century was written by Harriet Martineau, whose *Illustrations of Political Economy* is discussed by Henderson (1995: 63–90) and compellingly analyzed in the present volume by Elaine Freedgood.

2 Other recent literary studies exploring this separation of spheres in the eighteenth and nineteenth centuries include Copeland (1995), Nunokawa (1994), Gallagher (1994), Scheuermann (1993). Many of them conclude, with Kaufmann (1995: 28), that the "domestic novel and the masculine world of commerce are not so different after all." As we suggest later in this introduction, this divorce between the political and domestic has also provided much useful fuel for feminist economists.

3 The books by Sherman (1996), Thompson (1996), and Nicholson (1994) have much in common, particularly in regard to their treatment of the homologies between the evolution of financial credit and new attitudes about fictional literature. All three are also heavily indebted to the work of economic historians, particularly J.G.A. Pocock's *Virtue, Commerce, and History* (1985), and *The Machiavellian Moment* (1975). See also Patrick Brantlinger's (1996) study of the relations between credit and the literature of empire.

4 In addition to the studies cited above, those of Vernon (1984), McLaughlin (1995) and Heinzelman (1980) also scrutinize the relationships between nineteenth-century literature and economics. Among eighteenth-century writers, Defoe has garnered the most attention by economic critics. The reasons are many, but the most salient may be his unequaled prolixity and versatility as the author of both economics tracts and of fictional narratives that dramatize his economic theories and depict the conceptualization of money and credit. In addition to Sherman's (1996), earlier studies by Novak (1962), Dijkstra (1987), and Meier (1987) deal primarily with Defoe; he also plays a major role in Thompson (1996), Nicholson (1994), and Brantlinger (1996). The nineteenth-century English author whose works have most frequently been subjected to economic readings is undoubtedly Charles Dickens, again because of the complicated and fascinating relations between his fictional texts – which invariably revolve around economic issues – and his important position in the nineteenth-century literary marketplace. For exemplary discussions of Dickens and economics, see Nunokawa (1994: 19–76), Russell (1986: 96–103, 132–48, 191–201), Miller (1995: 119–58), Houston (1994), Walsh (1993), Klaver (1993), and Carlisle (1996); for illuminating treatments of Dickens's relationship to the marketplace, see McLaughlin (1995: 83–121) and Wicke (1988: 19–53).

5 Woodmansee (1984, 1994). In this regard, see also Bourdieu (1985) and Smith (1988: esp. 125–49).

6 On British copyright, see Feather (1994) and Rose (1993); on the emergence of authors' rights in Germany and France, see Woodmansee (1984a) and Hesse

(1990), respectively. The situation in the United States is treated in Jaszi (1991) and Rice (1997: 74–96).

7 See Woodmansee (1994: 111–47); see also Erickson (1996: 49–69), and Schoenfield (1996).

8 The figures are taken from Deidre Johnson's 1982 study (quoted in Billman 1986: 2). See also Johnson (1993: ix).

9 We thank Peter Jaszi for his indispensable help in clarifying for us the history of authorial economies. Any remaining errors are our own.

10 The essays in the present volume by Susan Feiner, Neil Browne and Kevin Quinn, Regenia Gagnier and John Dupré, Brian Cooper and Margueritte Murphy, Jack Amariglio and David Ruccio, as well as the works cited below by Feiner, Amariglio, Klamer and his collaborators, Strassmann, Folbre and Hartmann, and Ferber and Nelson all criticize contemporary economics on these or related grounds.

11 Other examples of content-based criticism include Male (1980), Watts (1990), Scheuermann (1993) and Copeland (1995). The latter two studies do, however, successfully address contemporary financial values and the gendering of economic spheres.

12 Both of the key insights cited here owe much to Georg Simmel's magisterial study of 1900, *The Philosophy of Money*; see esp. 179 and 441.

13 Goux's later book, *Les Monnayeurs du Langage* (translated in 1994 as *The Coiners of Language*) forms the praxis for the earlier book's theory, as Goux tests his theses through readings of Modernist French and German literature.

14 For a similar, if rather hyperbolic, treatment of the future of money, see Gleick (1996).

15 As DiPiero (1988: 5) notes, Vernon's work is weakened by an insufficiently rigorous conceptualization of the historical conditions behind mimesis (that is, how realism suppresses its history) and by a slippage in his presentation of the functions of money, which is sometimes described as an object of desire, but at other times a force that resists desire.

16 Thompson lists Nicholson (mistakenly, perhaps) among those in the "Old" historicist group. Thompson's study is one of the most theoretically sophisticated and best informed of the recent work in economic criticism.

17 To wax pedantic for a moment, we might point out that Solow himself seems unclear about the definition of metaphor. In his "Comments" in Klamer, McCloskey and Solow's (1988) collection, he refers to Robert Burns's "love is like a red, red rose" as a metaphor (34), when in fact – as any good first-year literature student could tell you – it is a simile. A similarly indiscriminate use of "metaphor" appears in Strassmann and Polanyi (1995: 131): they describe the argument that all knowledge is situated as a "metaphor," which it is not.

18 Strassmann (1993: 56–57), for example, shows how the metaphor (she calls it a "story") of the free economy of the intellect actually solidifies the disciplinary status quo by eliding racial, gender and other exclusionary biases that bar access to those outside the mainstream.

19 Similarly, Philip Mirowski helpfully outlines four "metaphorical narratives" underwriting economics in order to demonstrate how antifoundationalism offers an entirely new notion of what economics is and does. According to Mirowski, remembering that the Natural and the Social are both culturally constructed

yields a novel sense of history as an oscillating process rather than a linear narrative (see Mirowski 1994: 10–15).

20 See also Strassmann and Polanyi (1995), who illustrate how certain economic stories in textbooks presuppose and thereby perpetuate purblind assumptions about race, class, and gender.

21 In a similar vein, David Moore (1994) suggests some of the ramifications that feminist literary criticism might have for accounting practices.

22 For critiques of Hyde, see Leland (1988) and Rzepka (1995: 52–58). Rzepka argues that Hyde's positioning of literary production in the realm of gift exchange mystifies the labor involved in such production, but Rzepka's own understanding of texts as gifts may also involve mystification, in that it reconstitutes the author as Romantic creator rather than as an effect of the interaction between text and reader.

23 For a more detailed analysis of Hyde and the gendering of gifts in relation to James Joyce's *Ulysses*, see Osteen (1995: 30–33, 430–44). For a more general treatment of the gendering of gift exhanges, see Komter's contribution to her essay collection (1996).

24 Smith also criticizes Jean Baudrillard's related attempt, in *For a Critique of the Political Economy of the Sign*, to create a value beyond economic exchange and proft (Smith 1988: 215). For an illuminating analysis of the range of obligations in gift exchanges, see Sahlins (1972: esp. 193–95); for a more sympathetic treatment of Bataille, see Richman (1982).

25 The other methods are what he calls "capitalist transformation" (in which gifts are said to be important only in "primitive" economies), and "emotional sequestration" (in which the gift economy obtains only within family circles): see Cheal (1988: 4–7).

26 Excerpts from Cheal's and Bourdieu's work are provided in Komter's (1996) helpful collection, which also includes important essays by Malinowski, Lévi-Strauss, Simmel, Alvin Gouldner, Amartya K. Sen, and others. Two new studies, both of which became available just as this volume was going to press, offer important new perspectives on gift theory. John Frow's *Time and Commodity Culture* (1997) includes a valuable synoptic essay on the relationship between gifts and commodities. Vincent Pecora's (1997) study analyzes Mauss and Bataille in detail and offers a brief critique of Hyde (303–4 n29), as part of a compelling argument that the opposition of the gift and market economies is largely a restatement of Aristotle's distinction between *oikos* and *agora*.

27 As Gagnier and Dupré suggest in their second contribution to the present volume, Birken's notion of consumption fails to account for differences in gender, class, or wealth, and too readily reproduces the panglossian assumptions of neoclassicalism.

28 Wicke's introduction (1988: 7–17) also provides a helpful historical outline of the cultural debates about advertising discourse.

29 Barnard's formulation owes a good deal to Michel de Certeau's argument that consumers resist the terms offered by advertising and maintain opposition by "poaching" or "stealing" from the powers that be (Barnard 1995: 20; Certeau 1984: 18, 30–32).

30 Baudrillard took steps in this direction in his 1970 work, *La Societé de consommation*, where he criticizes both neoclassicalist presumptions of free choice

and the Galbraithian argument that consumers are coerced into accepting created needs. But Baudrillard's argument is marred by a totalized view of consumption as a "complete system of values" (1988: 49). Still, Baudrillard's description of consumption as a system of signs involving "social labor" (53) has provided a starting point for critics such as Wicke, Richards, and Osteen.

31 Although the studies by Wicke (1988), Goux (1994), Barnard (1995), Godden (1990), and Osteen (1995), along with Jameson's *Postmodernism* (1991), are virtually the only extensive studies of twentieth-century literature and economics, new work by Wexler (1997), Dettmar and Watt (1996), Willison *et al.* (1996) and forthcoming work by Delany and Tratner promise to provide new directions and establish new insights into the relationships among art, money, and the marketplace in our century. Delany's essay in the present collection, although it shares a title with Wexler's study, was originally given as a conference paper in 1994, and thus antedates her book's publication.

32 An exception is Godden's *Fictions of Capital* (1990). Although Godden is heavily influenced by Ernst Mandel's *Late Capitalism*, he takes pains to show how the processes by which wealth is created and stolen are based upon the decisions of "historical subjects," and conditioned by the "class history that produces those subjects." For Godden, economic relations are always social relations (Godden 1990: 3, 4, 9).

33 See especially Riffaterre's *Semiotics of Poetry* (1978: 85–86). Derrida's "infinite citationality" thesis may be found in numerous places, but especially in "White Mythology" in *Margins of Philosophy* (1982: 302). For a more detailed discussion of these two competing versions of the intertextual economy, see Osteen (1995: 228–33).

34 For a useful outline of some objections to and potential value of economic criticism, see Smith (1988: 114–16).

References

Amariglio, Jack (1990). "Economics as a Postmodern Discourse." In *Economics as Discourse: An Analysis of the Language of Economists*. Ed. Warren J. Samuels. Boston: Kluwer, 15–46.

Armstrong, Nancy (1987). *Desire and Domestic Fiction: A Political History of the Novel*. New York: Oxford University Press.

Barnard, Rita (1995). *The Great Depression and the Culture of Abundance*. Cambridge: Cambridge University Press.

Bataille, Georges (1985). "The Notion of Expenditure." In *Visions of Excess: Selected Writings 1927–1939*. Ed. Allan Stoekl. Trans. Allan Stoekl, Carl R. Lovitt, and Donald M. Leslie, Jr. Minneapolis: University of Minnesota Press.

—— (1988). *The Accursed Share*. Trans. Robert Hurley. New York: Zone.

Baudrillard, Jean (1970). *La Société de consommation*. Paris: Gallimard.

—— ([1972] 1980). *For a Critique of the Political Economy of the Sign*. St. Louis: Telos.

—— (1988). *Selected Writings*. Ed. Mark Poster. Stanford: Stanford University Press.

Billman, Carol (1986). *The Secret of the Stratemeyer Syndicate: Nancy Drew, the Hardy Boys, and the Million Dollar Fiction Factory*. New York: Ungar.

Birken, Lawrence (1988). *Consuming Desire: Sexual Science and the Emergence of a Culture of Abundance, 1871–1914*. Ithaca: Cornell University Press.

Bourdieu, Pierre (1977). *Outline of a Theory of Practice*. Trans. Richard Nice. Cambridge: Cambridge University Press

—— (1984). *Distinction: A Social Critique of the Judgment of Taste*. Trans. Richard Nice. Cambridge, MA: Harvard University Press.

—— (1985). "The Market of Symbolic Goods." *Poetics* 14: 13–44.

Bowlby, Rachel (1985). *Just Looking: Consumer Culture in Dreiser, Gissing and Zola*. New York & London: Methuen.

—— (1993). *Shopping with Freud*. London & New York: Routledge.

Brantlinger, Patrick (1996). *Fictions of State: Culture and Credit in Britain, 1694–1994*. Ithaca: Cornell University Press.

Carlisle, Janice (1996). "Introduction: Biographical and Historical Contexts." In *Great Expectations*. By Charles Dickens. Ed. Janice Carlisle. Boston & New York: Bedford/St. Martin's Press.

Carlyle, Thomas (1832). "Boswell's Life of Johnson." *Fraser's Magazine* 5: 379–413.

Certeau, Michel de (1984). *The Practice of Everyday Life*. Trans. Steven F. Rendell. Berkeley: University of California Press.

Cheal, David (1988). *The Gift Economy*. London & New York: Routledge.

Coats, A.W. (1988). "Economic Rhetoric: The Social and Historical Context." In *The Consequences of Economic Rhetoric*. Ed. A. Klamer, D.N. McCloskey and R.M. Solow. Cambridge: Cambridge University Press, 64–84.

Copeland, Edward (1995). *Women Writing About Money: Women's Fiction in England, 1790–1820*. Cambridge: Cambridge University Press.

Derrida, Jacques (1978). "From Restricted to General Economy: A Hegelianism without Reserve." In *Writing and Difference*. Trans. Alan Bass. Chicago: University of Chicago Press.

—— (1982). "White Mythology." In *Margins of Philosophy*. Trans. Alan Bass. Chicago: University of Chicago Press.

—— (1992). *Given Time: I. Counterfeit Money*. Trans. Peggy Kamuf. Chicago: University of Chicago Press.

—— (1995). *The Gift of Death*. Trans. David Wills. Chicago: University of Chicago Press.

Dettmar, Kevin J.H., and Stephen Watt, eds. (1996). *Marketing Modernisms: Self-promotion, Canonization, and Rereading*. Ann Arbor: University of Michigan Press.

Dijkstra, Bram (1987). *Defoe and Economics: The Fortunes of* Roxana *in the History of Interpretation*. New York: St. Martin's.

DiPiero, Thomas (1988). "Buying into Fiction." *Diacritics* 18.2: 2–14.

Dostoevsky, Fyodor ([1864] 1991). *Notes from Underground & The Grand Inquisitor*. Trans. Ralph E. Matlaw. New York: Meridian.

England, Paula (1993). "The Separative Self: Androcentric Bias in Neoclassical Assumptions." In *Beyond Economic Man: Feminist Theory and Economics*. Ed. M.A. Ferber and J.A. Nelson. Chicago: University of Chicago Press, 37–53.

Erickson, Lee (1996). *The Economy of Literary Form: English Literature and the Industrialization of Publishing, 1800–1850*. Baltimore: The Johns Hopkins University Press.

Feather, John (1988). *A History of British Publishing*. London: Routledge.

—— (1994). *Publishing, Piracy and Politics: An Historical Study of Copyright in Britain*. London: Mansell.

Feiner, Susan F. (1995). "Reading Neoclassical Economics: Toward an Erotic Economy of Sharing." In *Out of the Margin: Feminist Perspectives on Economics*. Ed. E. Kuiper and J. Sap *et al*. New York and London: Routledge, 151–66.

Feltes, N.N. (1986). *Modes of Production of Victorian Novels*. Chicago: University of Chicago Press.

—— (1993). *Literary Capital and the Late Victorian Novel*. Madison: University of Wisconsin Press.

Ferber, Marianne A., and Julie A. Nelson, eds. (1993). *Beyond Economic Man: Feminist Theory and Economics*. Chicago: University of Chicago Press.

Fish, Stanley (1988). "Comments from Outside Economics." In *The Consequences of Economic Rhetoric*. Ed. A. Klamer, D.N. McCloskey and R.M. Solow. Cambridge: Cambridge University Press, 21–30.

Folbre, Nancy, and Heidi Hartmann (1988). "The Rhetoric of Self-interest: Ideology and Gender in Economic Theory." In *The Consequences of Economic Rhetoric*. Ed. A. Klamer, D.N. McCloskey and R.M. Solow. Cambridge: Cambridge University Press, 184–203.

Frow, John (1997). *Time and Commodity Culture*. Oxford: Clarendon Press.

Gagnier, Regina, and John Dupré (1995). "Economists, Marxists, Critics: Whose Economics?" Paper presented at the Modern Language Association Meeting, Chicago, December.

Gallagher, Catherine (1994). *Nobody's Story: The Vanishing Acts of Women Writers in the Marketplace, 1670–1820*. Berkeley: University of California Press.

Gleick, James (1996). "Dead as a Dollar." *New York Times Magazine*, 16 June. 6.26–30, 35, 42, 50, 54.

Godden, Richard (1990). *Fictions of Capital: The American Novel from James to Mailer*. Cambridge: Cambridge University Press.

Goux, Jean-Joseph (1988). "Banking on Signs." Trans. Thomas DiPiero. *Diacritics* 18.2: 15–25.

—— (1990). *Symbolic Economies: After Marx and Freud*. Trans. Jennifer Curtiss Gage. Ithaca: Cornell University Press.

—— (1994). *The Coiners of Language*. Trans. Jennifer Curtiss Gage. Norman: University of Oklahoma Press.

Griffin, Dustin (1996). *Literary Patronage in England, 1650–1800*. Cambridge: Cambridge University Press.

Guillory, John (1993). *Cultural Capital: The Problem of Literary Canon Formation*. Chicago: University of Chicago Press.

Heinzelman, Kurt (1980). *The Economics of the Imagination*. Amherst: University of Massachusetts Press.

Henderson, Willie (1995). *Economics as Literature*. London & New York: Routledge.

Hesse, Carla (1990). "Enlightenment Epistemology and the Laws of Authorship in Revolutionary France, 1777–1793." *Representations* 30: 109–37.

Horwitz, Howard (1991). *By the Law of Nature: Form and Value in Nineteenth-Century America*. New York & Oxford: Oxford University Press.

Houston, Gail Turley (1994). *Consuming Fictions: Gender, Class, and Hunger in Dickens's Novels*. Carbondale: Southern Illinois University Press.

Hyde, Lewis (1983). *The Gift: Imagination and the Erotic Life of Property*. New York: Random.

Jameson, Fredric (1991). *Postmodernism: or, The Cultural Logic of Late Capitalism*. Durham: Duke University Press.

Jaszi, Peter (1991). "Toward a Theory of Copyright: The Metamorphoses of 'Authorship.'" *Duke Law Journal*: 455–502.

Johnson, Deidre (1993). *Edward Stratemeyer and the Stratemeyer Syndicate*. New York: Twayne.

Kaufmann, David (1995). *The Business of Common Life: Novels and Classical Economics between Revolution and Reform*. Baltimore: The Johns Hopkins University Press.

Kernan, Alvin (1987). *Printing Technology, Letters, and Samuel Johnson*. Princeton: Princeton University Press.

Klamer, Arjo, and Thomas C. Leonard (1994). "So What's an Economic Metaphor?" In *Natural Images in Economic Thought: "Markets Read in Tooth and Claw."* Ed. P. Mirowski. Cambridge: Cambridge University Press, 20–51.

Klamer, Arjo, Donald N. McCloskey, and Robert M. Solow, eds (1988). *The Consequences of Economic Rhetoric*. Cambridge: Cambridge University Press.

Klaver, Claudia (1993). "Revaluing Money: *Dombey and Son*'s Moral Critique." In *Literature and Money*. Ed. A. Purdy. Amsterdam and Atlanta: Rodopi, 105–36.

Komter, Aafke E., ed. (1996). *The Gift: An Interdisciplinary Perspective*. Amsterdam: Amsterdam University Press.

Korshin, Paul. J. (1974). "Types of Eighteenth-Century Literary Patronage." *Eighteenth-Century Studies* 7: 453–73.

Kuiper, Edith and Jolande Sap, *et al*. (1995). *Out of the Margin: Feminist Perspectives on Economics*. New York & London: Routledge.

Leland, Blake (1988). "Voodoo Economics: Sticking Pins in Eros." *Diacritics* 18.2: 38–46.

Lévi-Strauss, Claude (1969). *The Elementary Structures of Kinship*. Rev. edn. Trans. James Harle Bell, John Richard von Sturmer, and Rodney Needham. New York: Beacon.

Lewes, George Henry (1847). "The Condition of Authors in England, Germany, and France." *Fraser's Magazine* 35: 285–95.

Lyotard, Jean-Francois ([1974] 1993). *Libidinal Economy*. Trans. Iain Hamilton Grant. Bloomington: Indiana University Press.

Macaulay, Thomas B. (1831). "Review of Croker's Boswell." *Edinburgh Review* (Sept.): 1–38.

Male, Roy R., ed. (1980). *Money Talks: Language and Lucre in American Fiction*. Norman: University of Oklahoma Press.

Mandel, Ernest (1978). *Late Capitalism*. London: Verso.

Marchand, Roland (1985). *Advertising the American Dream: Making Way for Modernity, 1920–1940*. Berkeley: University of California Press.

Marx, Karl (1976). *Capital*. Vol. 1. Ed. Ernest Mandel. Trans. Ben Fowkes. Harmondsworth: Penguin.

Mauss, Marcel ([1925] 1967). *The Gift: Forms and Functions of Exchange in Archaic Societies*. Trans. Ian Cunnison. New York: W.W. Norton.

McCloskey, Donald N. (1985). *The Rhetoric of Economics*. Madison: University of Wisconsin Press.

—— (1988). "The Consequences of Rhetoric." In *The Consequences of Economic Rhetoric*.

Ed. A. Klamer, D.N. McCloskey and R.M. Solow. Cambridge: Cambridge University Press, 280–93.

—— (1990). *If You're So Smart: The Narrative of Economic Expertise*. Chicago: University of Chicago Press.

—— (1994). *Knowledge and Persuasion in Economics*. Cambridge: Cambridge University Press.

McCormack, Peggy (1990). *The Rule of Money: Gender, Class and Exchange Economics in the Fiction of Henry James*. Ann Arbor: UMI Research Press.

McLaughlin, Kevin (1995). *Writing in Parts: Imitation and Exchange in Nineteenth-Century Literature*. Stanford, CA: Stanford University Press.

Meier, Thomas K. (1987). *Defoe and the Defense of Commerce*. Victoria, BC: University of Victoria.

Michaels, Walter Benn (1987). *The Gold Standard and the Logic of Naturalism: American Literature at the Turn of the Century*. Berkeley: University of California Press.

Miller, Andrew H. (1995). *Novels Behind Glass: Commodity Culture and Victorian Narrative*. Cambridge: Cambridge University Press.

Mirowski, Philip, ed. (1994). *Natural Images in Economic Thought: "Markets Read in Tooth and Claw."* Cambridge: Cambridge University Press.

—— (1994) "Doing What Comes Naturally: Four Metanarratives On What Metaphors Are For." *Natural Images in Economic Thought: "Markets Read in Tooth and Claw."* Ed. P. Mirowski. Cambridge: Cambridge University Press, 3–19.

Moore, David Chioni (1994). "Feminist Accounting Theory as a Critique of What's 'Natural' in Economics." In *Natural Images in Economic Thought: "Markets Read in Tooth and Claw."* Ed. P. Mirowski. Cambridge: Cambridge University Press, 583–610.

Mull, Donald L. (1973). *Henry James's "Sublime Economy": Money as Symbolic Center in the Fiction*. Middletown, CT: Wesleyan University Press.

Nelson, Julie A. (1993). "The Study of Choice or the Study of Provisioning? Gender and the Definition of Economics." In *Beyond Economic Man: Feminist Theory and Economics*. Ed. M.A. Ferber and J.A. Nelson. Chicago: University of Chicago Press, 23–36.

Nicholson, Colin (1994). *Writing and the Rise of Finance: Capital Satires of the Early Eighteenth Century*. Cambridge: Cambridge University Press.

Novak, Maximilian E. (1962). *Economics and the Fiction of Daniel Defoe*. Berkeley: University of California Press.

Nunokawa, Jeff (1994). *The Afterlife of Property: Domestic Security and the Victorian Novel*. Princeton: Princeton University Press.

Osteen, Mark (1995). *The Economy of* Ulysses*: Making Both Ends Meet*. Syracuse: Syracuse University Press.

Pecora, Vincent P. (1997). *Households of the Soul*. Baltimore: The Johns Hopkins University Press.

Plant, Marjorie ([1939] 1974). *The English Book Trade: An Economic History of the Making and Sale of Books*. 3rd edn. London: Allen & Unwin.

Pocock, J.G.A. (1975). *The Machiavellian Moment: Florentine Political Thought and the Atlantic Republican Tradition*. Princeton: Princeton University Press.

—— (1985). *Virtue, Commerce, and History: Essays on Political Thought and History, Chiefly in the Eighteenth Century*. Cambridge: Cambridge University Press.

Purdy, Anthony, ed. (1993). *Literature and Money*. Amsterdam and Atlanta: Rodopi.
Reid, Ian (1992). *Narrative Exchanges*. New York & London: Routledge.
Resnick, Stephen, and Richard Wolff (1988). "Marxian Theory and the Rhetorics of Economics." In *The Consequences of Economic Rhetoric*. Ed. A. Klamer, D.N. McCloskey and R.M. Solow. Cambridge: Cambridge University Press, 47–63.
Rice, Grantland S. (1997). *The Transformation of Authorship in America*. Chicago: University of Chicago Press.
Richards, Thomas (1990). *The Commodity Culture of Victorian England*. Stanford: Stanford University Press.
Richman, Michèle (1982). *Reading Georges Bataille: Beyond the Gift*. Baltimore: The Johns Hopkins University Press.
Riffaterre, Michael (1978). *Semiotics of Poetry*. Bloomington: Indiana University Press.
Rose, Mark (1993). *Authors and Owners: The Invention of Copyright*. Cambridge, MA: Harvard University Press.
Rossi-Landi, Ferruccio (1975). *Linguistics and Economics*. The Hague: Mouton.
Ruben, Gayle (1975). "The Traffic in Women: Notes on the 'Political Economy' of Sex." In *Toward an Anthropology of Women*. Ed. Rayna R. Reiter. New York & London: Monthly Review, 157–210.
Russell, Norman (1986). *The Novelist and Mammon: Literary Responses to the World of Commerce in the Nineteenth Century*. Oxford: Clarendon Press.
Rzepka, Charles J. (1995). *Sacramental Commodities: Gift, Text, and the Sublime in De Quincey*. Amherst: University of Massachusetts Press.
Sahlins, Marshall (1972). *Stone Age Economics*. Chicago: Aldine.
Scheuermann, Mona (1993). *Her Bread to Earn: Women, Money, and Society from Defoe to Austen*. Lexington: University Press of Kentucky.
Schoenfield, Mark (1996). *The Professional Wordsworth: Law, Labor and the Poet's Contract*. Athens, GA: University of Georgia Press.
Shell, Marc (1978). *The Economy of Literature*. Baltimore: The Johns Hopkins University Press.
—— (1982). *Money, Language and Thought: Literary and Philosophical Economies from the Medieval to the Modern Era*. Berkeley: University of California Press.
—— (1995). *Art and Money*. Chicago: University of Chicago Press.
Sherman, Sandra (1996). *Finance and Fictionality in the Early Eighteenth Century: Accounting for Defoe*. Cambridge: Cambridge University Press.
Simmel, Georg ([1900] 1978). *The Philosophy of Money*. Trans. Tom Bottomore and David Frisby. London: Routledge.
Smith, Barbara Herrnstein (1988). *Contingencies of Value: Alternative Perspectives for Critical Theory*. Cambridge: Harvard University Press.
Solow, Robert M. (1988). "Comments from Inside Economics." In *The Consequences of Economic Rhetoric*. Ed. A. Klamer, D.N. McCloskey and R.M. Solow. Cambridge: Cambridge University Press, 31–37.
Strassmann, Diana (1993). "Not a Free Market: the Rhetoric of Disciplinary Authority in Economics." In *Beyond Economic Man: Feminist Theory and Economics*. Ed. M.A. Ferber and J.A. Nelson. Chicago: University of Chicago Press, 54–68.
——, and Livia Polanyi (1995). "The Economist as Storyteller: What the Texts Reveal." In *Out of the Margin: Feminist Perspectives on Economics*. Ed. E. Kuiper and J. Sap. *et al*. New York & London: Routledge, 129–45.

Susman, Warren (1984). *Culture as History: The Transformation of American Society in the Twentieth Century*. New York: Pantheon.

Thompson, James (1996). *Models of Value: Eighteenth-Century Political Economy and the Novel*. Durham, NC: Duke University Press.

Vernon, John (1984). *Money and Fiction: Literary Realism in the Nineteenth and Early Twentieth Centuries*. Ithaca: Cornell University Press.

Walsh, Susan (1993). "Bodies of Capital: *Great Expectations* and the Climacteric Economy." *Victorian Studies* 37.3: 73–98.

Watts, Cedric (1990). *Literature and Money: Financial Myth and Literary Truth*. New York & London: Harvester Wheatsheaf.

Wexler, Joyce Piell (1997). *Who Paid for Modernism? Art, Money, and the Fiction of Conrad, Joyce, and Lawrence*. Fayetteville: University of Arkansas Press.

Wicke, Jennifer A. (1988). *Advertising Fictions: Literature, Advertisement, and Social Reading*. New York: Columbia University Press.

Willison, Ian, Warwick Gould, and Warren Chernaik, eds. (1996). *Modernist Writers and the Marketplace*. London: Macmillan; New York: St. Martin's Press.

Woodmansee, Martha (1984a). "The Genius and the Copyright: Economic and Legal Conditions of the Emergence of the 'Author.'" *Eighteenth-Century Studies* 17: 425–48.

—— (1984b). "The Interests in Disinterestedness: Karl Philipp Moritz and the Emergence of the Theory of Aesthetic Autonomy in Eighteenth-Century Germany." *Modern Language Quarterly* 45: 22–47.

—— (1994). *The Author, Art, and the Market: Rereading the History of Aesthetics*. New York: Columbia University Press.

——, and Peter Jaszi, eds. (1994). *The Construction of Authorship: Textual Appropriation in Law and Literature*. Durham, NC: Duke University Press.

Wordsworth, William ([1815] 1966). "Essay, Supplementary to the Preface." *Literary Criticism of William Wordsworth*. Ed. Paul M. Zall. Lincoln: University of Nebraska Press.

Zelizer, Viviana A. (1994). *The Social Meaning of Money*. New York: Basic Books.

Part I

LANGUAGE AND MONEY

2

THE ISSUE OF REPRESENTATION

Marc Shell

> A descriptive analysis of bank notes is needed. The unlimited satirical force of such a book would be equaled only by its objectivity. For nowhere more naively than in these documents does capitalism display itself in solemn earnest.
>
> (Benjamin 1979b: 96)

The United States, the first place in the Western world where paper money was widely used,[1] is an interesting locale for the study of representation and exchange in art. This is not only because the United States sometimes presents itself as a "secular" – hence supposedly non-Christian – state. It is also because in nineteenth-century America there raged an extensive debate about paper money that, like the discussion of coinage in "religious" Byzantium, had aesthetic as well as political implications.

In the American debate, which blended the self-interested struggle between "hard money" creditors and "soft money" debtors with various disputes about the issue of representation, "paper money men" (as advocates of paper money were called) were set against "gold bugs" (advocates of gold).[2] It was shadowy art against golden substance. The zealous backers of solid specie associated gold with the substance of value and disparaged all paper as the "insubstantial" sign. A piece of paper counted for relatively little as a commodity and thus, they said, was "insensitive" in the system of economic exchange. Over the first half of the century, paper issued by banks (and supposedly backed by gold) was their primary focus. During the Civil War, controversy swirled over the government-issued "greenbacks" – monetary paper backed by no metal at all. Monometallists, at the end of the century, grew alarmed when some politicians wanted the government to declare silver to be money and to issue banks notes on this augmented monetary "base."

Credit, or belief, involves the ground of aesthetic experience, and the same medium that confers belief in fiduciary money (bank notes) and in scriptural money (accounting records and money of account, created by the process of bookkeeping) also seems to confer it in art. So the "interplay of money and mere [drawing or writing] to a point where," as Braudel says, "the two be[come] confused" involved the tendency of paper money to play upon the everyday understanding of the relation between symbols and things.[3] The sign of the monetary *diabolus*, which Americans said was like the sign impressed in Cain's forehead,[4] became the principal icon of America.

The American debates, viewed historically, were a plank in a cultural bridge to the contemporary world of electronic credits and transfers and government money unbacked by metal or other material substance. The shift from substance to inscription in the monetary sphere began early, with the first appearance of coins. Coins as such were fiduciary ingots that passed for the values inscribed – values to which the metallic purity and weight of the coins themselves might be inadequate – thanks to a general forbearance and acceptance of the issuing authority on the part of buyers and sellers. Whether or not this workaday tolerance of political authority came on the heels of traders customarily overlooking the clips and wear and tear in old-fashioned ingots, the first appearance of coins precipitated a quandary over the relation between face value and substantial value – between, as it were, intellectual currency and material currency. As early as Heraclitus and Plato, idealist thinkers had wondered about the link of monetary hypothesizing with logical hypothesizing, or monetary change making with dialectical division. But awareness of the specific difference between inscription and thing exploded with the introduction of paper money.

For Americans the value of paper – the material substance on which monetary engravings were now printed – clearly had next to nothing to do with paper notes' value as money. Bank notes were backed by land; or by gold in a vault somewhere; or by silver; or by loans; or perhaps by actual or potential government power. (*Exitus in dubio est*, "the issue is in doubt," read the "continental" notes of the American Revolution.) But the precise connection between gold and paper seemed the stuff of mystery. Paper money thus regenerated a cultural disturbance that extended beyond money *per se* to include the artistic experience.

In Poe's famous story "The Gold-Bug," the treasure-hunting protagonist cashes in a devilishly "ideal" cryptographic drawing for "real" gold. The link between the economic and aesthetic realms that drives Poe's protagonist, with his golden bug and his bug for gold, is expressed inadvertently in *Gold Humbug*, H.R. Robinson's "joke" note depicting a devilish treasure hunt for the gold that "real" notes ("gold humbug") are supposed to represent (Plate 2.1). He and Napolean Sarony represented themselves as sellers of artful joke notes in much the same way that they represented bankers and legislators as sellers of genuine or counterfeit notes.[5] (Likewise, Johnson, in his joke note *Great Locofoco Juggernaut*, made the usual association of gold deposits, which back up paper money, with fecal deposits, which issue from the backside.)[6]

Plate 2.1 H.R. Robinson, *Gold Humbug*, caricature of a shinplaster, United States, 1837. At the right, Andrew Jackson chases the "gold humbug." Courtesy, American Antiquarian Society, Worcester, Massachusetts.

LAW, als een tweede Don-Quichot, op Sanches Graauwtje zit ten spot.
Dulcinia en 't Actie Roth,
Verzoekt den Lawen Don-Quichot,
Op Sanches Eseltje gezeeten,
(Wyl Rosinant wat hooy gaat vreeten)
In 't groot betoovert Actie-huis.
En Sanche, tot zyn droevig kruis
Moet voor Bombario hier speelen;
Het kan den bloed zo zeer verveelen;
Hy kruipt zyn baas na als een pad:
En Hointjemaat to drommols plat
Weet vast een ider te bespotten,
Daar een Zot maakt veel duizent Zotten

These American cartoonists worked within a tradition that includes France in the 1790s and Germany in the 1920s. "Bombario" of eighteenth-century Europe, who is named on the idealist Don Quixote's saddles in cartoons from the John Law paper money fiasco (Plate 2.2), became the gold humbug of nineteenth-century America.

Thomas Nast's cartoon *A Shadow is Not a Substance* (Plate 2.3), which appears in Wells's *Robinson Crusoe's Money* (1876), depicts the relation between reality and idealist appearance as both monetary and aesthetic; and it helps to explain many American artists' and economists' association of paper money with spiritualness, or ghostliness,[7] and their understanding of how an artistic appearance is taken for the real thing by a devilish suspension of disbelief. Congress, it was said, could turn paper into gold by an "act of Congress," like the devilish *Tat* (deed) at issue in the paper money scene orchestrated by Mephistopheles in Goethe's *Faust*. Why could not a Faustian artist turn paper with a design or story on it into gold? Thus Nast's cartoon *Milk Tickets for Babies, in Place of Milk* (Plate 2.4), also from Wells's book, shows one paper bearing the design of a milk cow and the inscription "This is a cow by the act of the artist," and another paper that reads "This is money by the act of Congress"; his *Ideal Money* has similar inscriptions reading "Soft-Soap / by an / Act of Congress / This is Money" and "By an Act of Congress this Dipper Full is $10,000" (Plate 2.5). (Some *Notgeld*, or "emergency money," from Germany of the inflationary 1920s quotes *Faust* and includes the inscription: "One liter of milk for 550 billion German marks" (Plate 2.6). Other German emergency bank notes ironically quote passages from *Faust* like "Such currency . . . bears its value on its face" (Plate 2.7).)

The American debate about paper money was concerned with symbolization in general, hence with both money and aesthetics. Symbolization in this context concerns the relation between the substantial thing and its sign. Solid gold was conventionally associated with the substance of value. Whether or not one regarded paper as an inappropriate and downright misleading "sign," that sign was "insubstantial" insofar as the paper counted for nothing as a commodity and was thus "insensible" in the economic system of

---

Plate 2.2 opposite: Cartoon, *John Law as Don Quixote*, Netherlands, 1720. "*Law, als een tweede Don-Quichot, op Sanches Graauwtje zit ten Spot*" [Law, like another Don Quixote, sits on Sancho's ass, being everyone's fool]. The engraving shows John Law riding an ass. On the flag is "*Ik koom. Ik koom Dulcinea*" [I come, I come Dulcinea]. A coffer filled with bags of money is inscribed "Bombarioos Geld kist 1720" [Bombario's (humbug's) money box, 1720]. Behind Law is a devil, the "Henry" of the text; he holds up the tail of the ass. The ass voids papers inscribed 1000, 0, 00, and so on. From *Het groote tafereel der dwaasheid* (Amsterdam, 1720) Buffalo and Erie County Library, Buffalo, New York.

Plate 2.3 Thomas Nast, *A Shadow Is Not a Substance*, 1876. From Wells, *Robinson Crusoe's Money*. Harvard College Library.

exchange. (The French symbolist poet Stéphane Mallarmé, who was much interested in the international Panama financial scandal – during the decade of the 1890s when Americans were focusing on the Cross of Gold presidential campaigns – wrote in this context that "everything is taken up in Aesthetics and in Political Economy."[8])

The American debate about aesthetics and economics connected the study of the essence of money with the philosophy and iconology of art. Joseph G. Baldwin thus explored how paper money asserts the spiritual over the material;[9] and Albert Brisbane, in his midcentury *Philosophy of Money*, provided an "ontology," as he called it, for the study of monetary signs. Clinton Roosevelt, a prominent member of the Locofocos (a political party of the period), argued in his *Paradox of Political Economy* in 1859, when the "gold bug" Van Buren had lost the presidency, that the American Association

MILK-TICKETS FOR BABIES, IN PLACE OF MILK.

Plate 2.4 Thomas Nast, *Milk-Tickets for Babies, in Place of Milk*, 1876. From Wells, *Robinson Crusoe's Money*. Harvard College Library.

for the Advancement of Science should establish an "ontological department for the discussion and establishment of general principles of political economy."[10]

Such a discussion already existed in Germany in the shape of a far-ranging debate between the proponents of idealism and the proponents of realism. It was this debate that Thomas Nast brought to American newspaper and book readers in the second half of the century in such Germanic cartoons as his devilish *Ideal Money* (Plate 2.5). For Nast and his collaborator Wells – as for many Americans living during the heyday of paper money controversies and *trompe l'oeil* art – paper could no more be money than "a shadow could be the substance, or the picture of a horse a horse."[11]

Plate 2.5 Thomas Nast, *Ideal Money*, From *Harper's Weekly* 48 (19 January 1878). Beneath the title, *Ideal Money*, in small script: "'Universal Suffrage can, if it likes, repudiate the whole debt; it can, if it likes, decree soft-soap to be currency.' – *The Louisville Courier-Journal*". Courtesy of Library of Congress, Washington, D.C.

Plate 2.6 Emergency money (*Notgeld*), bank note, *Eine Billion Mk.* (American, one trillion German marks; British, one billion German marks), Stadt Vohwinkel, November 1923. Quoting Goethe's *Faust*, 2802–4: "For gold contend, / On gold depend / All things and men . . . Poor us!" In right border, beginning at top: "550 Milliarden, ein Liter Milch" (American, one liter of milk for 550 billion German marks) Money Museum of the Deutsche Bundesbank, Frankfurt.

The problem, from the viewpoint of aesthetics, involves representation as *exchange*. A painting of grapes, a painting of a pipe, or a monetary inscription generally stands for something else – it makes the implicit claim: "I am edible grapes," "I am a pipe," or "I am ten coins." Sometimes observers are trumped into taking the imitation for the real. For example, birds are said to have pecked themselves to death on the grapes painted by the ancient Greek artist Zeuxis. (He was the first artist known to become very rich.)[12] People who read the inscription under Magritte's *trompe l'oeil* (trumping, or fooling the eye) pipe may never roll up the canvas and smoke it like a cigar (Plate 2.8),[13] but Magritte here plays with our "commonsense" suspension of disbelief when we approach an artistic representation. We take the painting for a pipe on some level. But pipes and grapes, however much they are representable artworks, are also more or less "original" objects.[14] Money, on the other hand, is not. A piece of paper money is almost always a representation, a symbol that claims to stand for something else or to be something else. It is not that paper depicts and represents coins, but that paper, coins, and money, generally, all stand in the place of something else.

Plate 2.7 Emergency money (*Notgeld*), bank note, Schleswig-Holstein, 1920s. Quoting the paper money scene from Goethe's *Faust*, 6119–20: "Such currency, in gold and jewels' place, / Is neat, it bears its value on its face" (trans. Arndt). Money Museum of the Deutsche Bundesbank, Frankfurt.

(Just as bank notes sometimes visually suggest that they represent or are coins, as do the American bank notes in Plate 2.9 [Hessler 1974: 17] and various Chinese bills that depict rolls of coins,[15] so postage stamps often depict monetary tokens, as do those in Plate 2.10, and issuing postal authorities frequently claim the banker's prerogative to issue regular currency.[16] Similarly, some playing cards suggest visually that they represent or are coins, much as the coins they represent suggest specie: examples would include the round coinlike cards from the "suit of coins" in Plate 2.11 and the tarot knight holding a coin in Plate 2.12.[17] Playing cards as such are linked with the historical beginnings of paper money, and even in the modern era playing-card money has been issued during periods of financial crisis.[18] In gambling card games, moreover, the relation between what is played with and what is played for – the playing card as numeric marker and as money – is like that in such coin games as "heads or tails" (*croix et piles*). Blaise Pascal used this game to help explain why it is best to bet on the existence of God and the true *croix*, or cross; and probability theorists and econometricians generally have used this game to explain the link between likelihood and likeness – the likelihood that a perfectly weighted coin will land on heads or tails, say, and the likeness, bordering on infinitesimally close identity, between coins of the same denomination.[19])

Plate 2.8 René Magritte, *This Is Not a Pipe*, 1926. Photothèque René Magritte-Giraudon. © 1994 C. Herscovici, Brussels/Artists Rights Society (ARS), New York

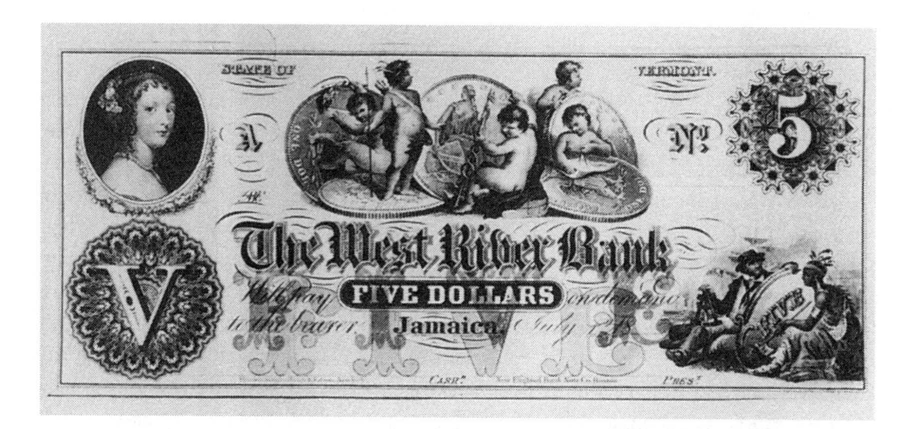

Plate 2.9 Bank note, the West River Bank of Jamaica, Vermont; issued jointly by Rawdon, Wright, and Edson and the New England Bank Note Company, nineteenth century. American Numismatic Society, New York.

Plate 2.10 Stamps showing coins or paper money: Hungary, 1974, 1975, and Grenadines of St Vincent, West Indies, 1976.

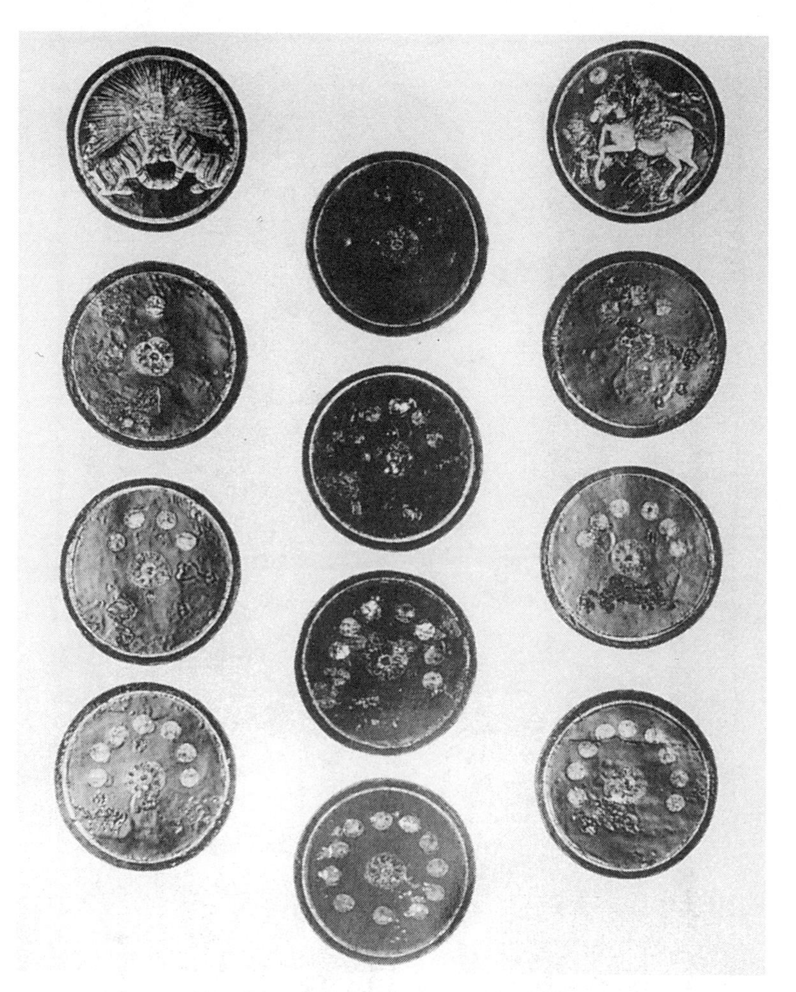

Plate 2.11 Playing card set, Mamluk/Indian, *ca.* 1775. Suit of money (*darahim*), king, vizir, and numbers 1–10. L.A. Mayer Memorial Institute for Islamic Art, Jerusalem.

Nast's cartoon *Milk Tickets for Babies, in Place of Milk* (Plate 2.4) displays most clearly the gold bug's characteristic thinking about representation as exchange. It illustrates quite literally the tendency to confound artistic confidence with political or economic credit to the point where money becomes art and art becomes money. One of the cartoon's bank notes reads, "This is a cow by the act of the artist," where the word "cow" appears inside the picture of a milk cow. Another paper, "This is milk by the act of con," suggests the *con*gressional *con*fidence game by which Americans are *con*ned and recalls for us Calvin's remark about lactary relics that "had Mary been a cow

Plate 2.12 *Knight of Coins*, from uncut sheet of *taroochi* (tarot cards), fifteenth or sixteenth century. Coins is a feminine suit. Metropolitan Museum of Art, Bequest of James C. McGuire, 1931. (31.54.159).

all her life she could not have produced such a quantity." "This is money by the act of cannibals" recalls similarly the association of coins with communion tokens and the Eucharist. Still another bank note reads, "This is not a rag baby but a REAL BABY by act of Congress."[20] Carlyle wrote about such "rags" in his *French Revolution*: "Bank paper, wherewith you can still buy when there is no gold left; Book-paper, splendent with Theories, Philosophies, Sensibilities, – beautiful art, not only of revealing Thought, but also of so beautifully hiding from us the want of Thought! Paper is made from the *rags* of things that did once exist; there are endless excellencies in Paper" (Carlyle [1837] 1902: 37; my emphasis). More important, the paper money inscription "This is money by the act of Congress," appearing as the work of an artist, suggests an identity, indeed rivalry, between the authority of the artist and that of the banker or statesman. Both artist and politician seem able to take an apparently valueless piece of paper and, by virtue of words or drawings, make it as valuable as exchange note or the valuable "original" for which the note is purportedly exchangeable.

The tension is that between political nation and individual imagination, as suggested in Paul Cotton's joke note drawn on "the Bank of the Imagi-Nation" (Plate 2.13). Latin American artists of the modern period, working in post-colonial contexts rife with political tyranny and monetary inflation, similarly consider money as fiction and fiction as money: in Jac Leirner's *Os cem* (1986–7), for example, "the bank note is," as Leirner herself says, "almost an absence." (The pun on *cem* and *sem* – "hundred" and "sign" – is crucial to her title.)[21]

Can the artist, in a regime of paper money, manufacture money as if he or she were a bank? Some artists would have it that way. Many artists in the twentieth century thus draw, or draw on, checks as a conceptual jest. Marcel Duchamp, for example, paid his dentist Daniel Tzanck with a hand-drawn check that presumably enabled the bearer to draw on funds at "The Teeth's Trust Company"; the artist later repurchased the check for more than he had drawn it for (Plate 2.14).[22] Duchamp hints at the same exchangeability of paper for money in his reworking of a label for photographic paper; he cut the label so that it reads "papier au . . . d'argent," or "silver paper."[23]

Instances where monetary value is similarly linked to originary signature include the artist Daniel Spoerri's opening his checkbook one day, writing out a series of checks payable to cash at ten deutsche marks each, and selling them as art for twenty deutsche marks apiece. "In exchanging art for money," Spoerri explained, "we exchange one abstraction for another" (Weschler 1988: 44). Don Judd likewise paid a bill to the fortuitously named art collector Henry Geldzähler with a photocopied five dollar bill.

In such gestures the combination of representation and value derives from the imprimatur or signature of the artist, not the state. It is the artist who certifies, who sug*gests* – from *sur-gere*, "to carry over," as in a metaphorical conveyance. Hence the signature is fetishized – as hinted in Carl Reutersward's

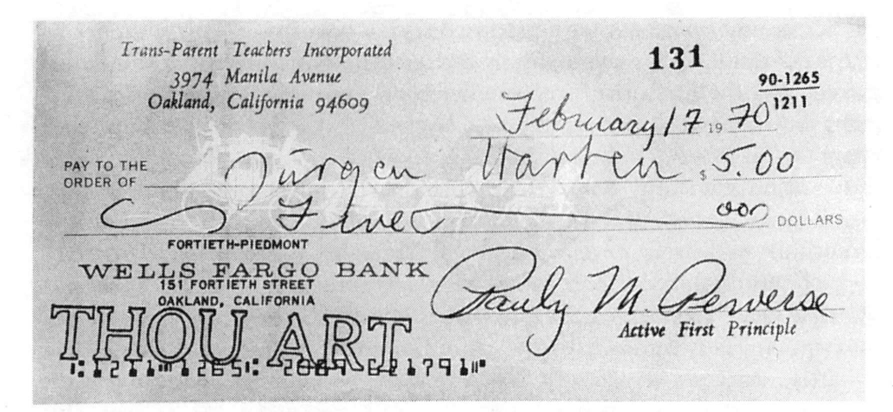

Plate 2.13 Paul Cotton, *Check Drawn on the Bank of the Imagi-Nation*, Wells Fargo Bank, 1970. "This check is a detail in a collaborative drawing by the Trans-Parent Teachers Incorporated. Uncashed, its value is twelve times the written amount to be paid by the collector". Courtesy of Jürgen Harten, Städische Kunsthalle, Düsseldorf

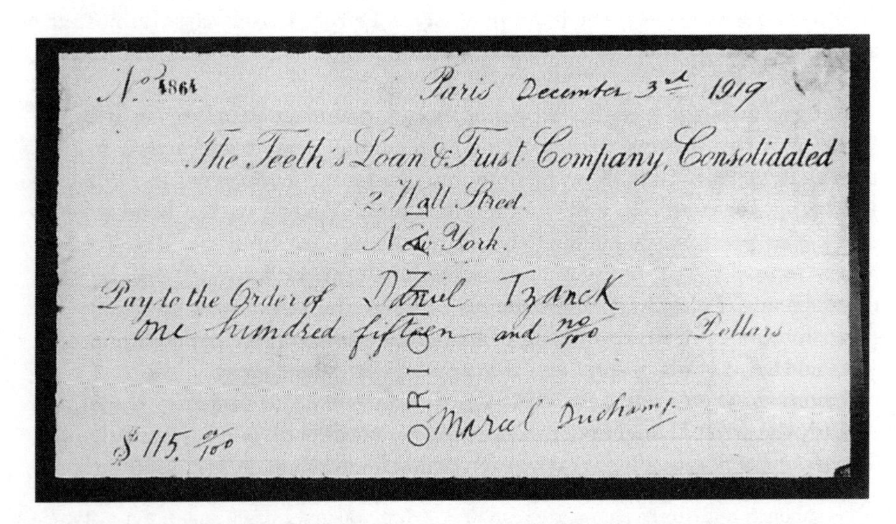

Plate 2.14 Marcel Duchamp, *Tzanck Check*, Paris, 3 December 1919. Enlarged manuscript version of a cheque, 8 × 15 in. Handwritten in black. Vertically, in red: ORIGINAL; printed with rubber stamp in red, as background: "The Teeth's Loan & Trust Company, Consolidated." From *Boite en valise*, Galleria Schwarz (Milan, 1963 edn), Coll. S.C., Montreal. © 1997 Artists Rights Society (ARS), New York/ADAGP, Paris/Estate of Marcel Duchamp.

The Great Fetish, which reproduces Picasso's signature as a cult object.[24] A signature is like a thumbprint guaranteeing the aura of the authentic, as Galton says in his nineteenth-century American work on detection and fingerprinting. Edward Kienholz's watercolors, described in *Life Magazine*'s "Paper Money Made into Art You Can Bank On," are each signed with his thumbprint. The watercolors sold for the amount of money stamped on the face – ranging from one dollar to ten thousand dollars. Kienholz wrote in an exhibition essay, "What I have done is, in effect, to issue a kind of currency which is not dependant [*sic*] on the normal monetary system."[25] "The fetish of the art market," says Walter Benjamin in his 1937 study of Eduard Fuchs and the mass cult of the leader, is "the old master's name" (Benjamin 1979a: 384, 386).

Notes

1 Paper money had circulated in Europe at earlier times, as discussed by Adam Smith in *Wealth of Nations*. But historians generally distinguish the popular, long-term use of paper money in America from its restricted use by merchants and bankers in eleventh-century Italy, for example, or from its short-term use by the French during the paper money experiments of the 1720s. Historians also distinguish the common use of scriptural money from fiduciary money, which began its widespread, long-lived use in America (see Wagenführ 1959: 73–76; Braudel 1975: 357–72; and Newman 1967). Benjamin Franklin, that all-American, was already printing paper money for colonial governments in 1728. The next year he published the *Necessity of a Paper-Currency*, in which he discussed the money backed only by government commitment. In the Revolution, the Continental Congress issued "Continentals." After independence, commercial banks in the major seaports and the federal bank of the United States began issuing bank notes. With the nineteenth century came the "outburst" of private banks in all parts of the nation.

2 Thomas Love Peacock, in *Paper Money Lyrics* (1837), uses the term "paper money men." St. Armand (1971: 7n) writes that at "the end of the nineteenth century the term 'gold bug' was [also] applied in America to scheming capitalists like Jay Gould ['gold'], who tried to corner the gold market, or to fanatical advocates of a gold standard over a silver standard."

3 Braudel (1975: 357–58). On credit and belief, see Shell (forthcoming).

4 "You sent them these notes out into the world stamped with irredeemability. You put on them the mark of Cain, and, like Cain, they will go forth to be vagabonds and fugitives on the earth." Congressman George Pendleton (Ohio) thus opposed the issuance of legal tender on 29 January 1862 (*Congressional Globe*, 37th Cong., 2nd sess., lines 549ff..

5 Robinson also made maps of the "gold regions" of the United States "embracing all the new towns and the dry and wet diggins" (Robinson 1848; see the collection of Robinson's caricatures at the Bancroft Library, University of California, Berkeley). On the relationship of Robinson's "Gold Humbug" to Poe's story, see Shell (1982: 13). "To the various meanings of 'goldbug' I consider there

should be added the *gul-baug* – 'the money-like gold ring' – of Scandinavian sagas" (Du Chaillu 1889: 2. 16, 476–77; Del Mar 1983: 256–57).

For other cartoons about paper money in the Unites States, see Homer Davenport's *The Dollar or the Man?* (1900) and such cartoons as Walter McDougall's *The Royal Feast of Belshazzar and the Money Kings* (in *New York World* 1884), Davenport's *Caricature of Mark Hannah* (with a suit covered with dollar signs; 1883), and John Tirney McCutcheon's *A Wise Economist Asks a Question* (1932; cited in Pogel and Somers 1980: 109–10). See also Carmon (1926–28); Wynn Jones (1975); Murrel (1933–38); and White (1862). Cf. American joke coins (e.g., Hefferton's "Lincoln Memorial" and O'Dowd's "Silver Certificate," cited in Lipman 1970: 80), various nineteenth-century German pseudo-bank notes (Harten 1978: 1. 46, 2. 142), and French joke bank notes (Grand-Carteret 1894: 375–83).

6 Johnson's caricature of a shinplaster (1837) thus expresses visually the same link between the bug for gold and money grubbing that motivates Poe's story and that later in the century informed much psychologizing about money and feces. Many money devil cartoons, indeed, show the money devil defecating ducats – a psychoanalytic interpreter's delight. A few focus on the devil's much-talked-about tail. See my discussion of Poe's *Dukatenscheisser* and of medieval illuminations of hybrid creatures defecating into bowls held by apelike money devils (Shell 1982: 11–12, 18), and my summary history of the "money complex" in psychoanalysis since the publication of Freud's essay "Character and Anal Erotism" (app. 3, 196–99). For an illustration of Johnson's work (and historical background), see Johnson (1971).

7 In Goethe's *Faust*, the bank note (*Geldschein*) as ghost is a major theme; and in Karl Marx's works, paper money is frequently associated with the "shadow" of Peter Schlemiel. On this meaning of "ghost" (cf. German *Geist*, meaning spirit), see Shell (1982: 21, 84–130); and for the American context, see William Charles's *The Ghost of a Dollar, or the Banker's Surprise* (*c*.1810, a cartoon in the collection of the American Antiquarian Society, in Murrel 1933–8: no. 74).

8 "Tout se résume dans l'Esthétique et l'Economie politique" (Mallarmé 1945: 656; see *National Observer* 25 February 1893). Cf. Derrida (1972: 292). French fiction writers – including Paul Claudel, Alphonse de Lamartine, Alphonse Daudet, Guy de Maupassant, and others – have long written for financial journals; much of this writing remains unstudied, but some is now being edited by Jean-Marie Thiveaud (1988). On the Panama scandal, see Bonin (1989: esp. 225–39 ("L'argent mythique") and 249–51).

9 Baldwin's *Flush Times of Alabama and Mississippi* (1853) concerns "that halcyon period, ranging from the year of Grace, 1835, to 1837 . . . that golden era, when shinplasters were the sole currency . . . and credit was a franchise" (1). Baldwin's narrator tells the story of a man who "bought goods . . . like other men; but he got them under a state of poetic illusion, and paid for them in an imaginary way" (4). "How well [he] asserted the *Spiritual* over the *Material*!" exclaims the storyteller (5). See Schmitz (1977: 473–77).

10 Roosevelt (1860); See Dorfman (1946: 2. 660–61).

11 Wells ([1876] 1931: 57); cited by Michaels (1987: 146).

12 The story of Zeuxis trimming his robe with gold is also relevant (Bann 1989). The business of exchanging images involves visual puns as well as linguistic ones.

Félix Labisse's exchange of image for thing is the typical punning *gesture* in the modern period. One of his works, which depicts a hand, has the inscription, "Mon amour, vous m'avez demandé ma main, je vous la donne" (My love, you have asked me for my hand, I give it to you; Harten 1978: 2. 67). On the tale of Zeuxis, see also Wagenführ (1959: 222).

13 Cf. Foucault's *This Is Not a Pipe* (1982).

14 Nevertheless, it is worth remarking again the old argument that, as Mitchell (1986: 17, cf. 90) puts it, "when a duck responds to a decoy, or when the birds peck at the grapes in the legendary paintings of Zeuxis, they are not seeing images; they are seeing other ducks, or real grapes – the things themselves, not images."

15 Samhaber (1964: 47). Likewise, much nineteenth-century Chinese playing card money depicts coins (Prunner 1969).

16 In France the Musée de la Poste held its exhibition titled *Les Couleurs de l'argent* in early 1992 just as the national postal service attempted, unsuccessfully as it turned out, to take over one of the traditional moneylending roles of regular banking institutions.

17 In many playing card systems there are suits signifying money. In the Indian and Persian systems, for example, there are the suits of *safed* (for silver coin) and *surkh* (for gold coin) (Leyden 1977: 8–9); in Mamluk cards there is the suit of *drachme* (Leyden, "Oriental Playing Cards" 16–17; cf. Mayer 6–8); and in Italy there is the suit of *denari*, from which the French suit *caro* developed (Leyden, letter to author, 14 November 1979). Note the likely etymological link between the ace in card games and the *as*, or *aas*, in the Roman monetary system (Del Mar [1896] 1983: 17–18).

18 Paper money made from playing cards was used in Canada in the seventeenth century (McLachlan 1911), in France during the Revolution, and in Germany and Austria during World War II (Beresiner 1979: 82ff.). The history of playing card paper money, which is loosely connected with that of gambling as a type of early capitalism, is not well known. Chinese money playing cards may have inspired playing cards in Central Asia and Mamluk Egypt – and from there in Italy and the rest of Europe. The round form of other Indian playing cards, with gold foil used as decoration, is linked with their being made in the shape of coins (Prunner 1969). On the tarot pack, see Moakley (1966).

19 See "Likeness and Likelihood," in Shell (1982: 194–95).

20 On the "bodiless and homeless Rag baby of fiat money," see Thomas Nast St. Hill's brief remarks in Nast (1976: 96).

21 In the same punning vein are such works as Cildo Meireles's *Zero Cruzeiro* (1970s) and Waltercio Caldas's *Dinheiro para Treinamento* (1977).

22 "J'ai racheté ce cheque, vingt ans après, beaucoup plus cher que ce qui était marqué dessus," said Duchamp to Pierre Cabanne (Duchamp 1971: 116). Concerning this check, see also Heinzelman (1980: chp. 1). Cf. Duchamp's "L'obligation pour la roulette de Monte Carlo," in *Il real assoluto* (Duchamp 1969: no. 368); his *Czeck Check* (ibid.: no. 374); and his *Cheque Bruno* (ibid.: no. 377).

23 Depicted by Clair (1977: 55). There is a pun on *au*. First, the French *eau* (meaning both "water" and "perfume") suggests that paper money is the perfume of silver. Second, *au* (as the English *owe*) suggests a relation to a credit economy dependent upon checks. Compare the association with silver nitrate. Cf. Lyotard (1990).

24 For an example of the thematic of the signature as fetish, see Reuterswärd's *The Great Fetish: Picasso's Signature, a Sleeping Partner* (no. 2/2, 1974–7, a steel and bronze sculpture, 172 × 482 × 90 cm). Reuterswärd's *L'Art pur l'or* depicts the sign of an investment firm in Liechtenstein that sells artists' signatures. His question is: "Wie wäre es, wenn wir uns auf den wichtigsten Teil des Kunstwerks konzentrieren, DIE SIGNATURE?" (An der Schlur / Oberbayen, 27 March 1975); in Harten and Kurnitzky (1978: 2. 177–79).

25 The quotation is from the artist's essay in the Finnish catalogue *Kienholz*. Kienholz's *Watercolors* were exhibited at the Eugenia Butler Gallery (Los Angeles) in 1969.

References

Baldwin, Joseph G. (1853). *The Flush Times of Alabama and Mississippi: A Series of Sketches*. New York: Appleton.

Bann, Stephan (1989). "Zeuxis and Parrhasius." In *The True Vine: On Visual Representation and the Western Tradition*. New York: Cambridge University Press.

Benjamin, Walter (1979a). "Eduard Fuchs, Collector and Historian." In *One-Way Street and Other Writings*. Trans. Edmund Jephcott and Kingsley Shorter. London: NLB, 349–86.

—— (1979b). "Tax Advice." In ibid.: 96.

Beresiner, Yasher (1979). "Legal Tender." *Journal of the Playing Card Society* 7 (May): 82–83.

Bonin, Hubert (1989). *L'Argent en France depuis 1880*. Paris: Masson.

Braudel, Fernand (1975). *Capitalism and Material Life, 1400–1800*. Trans. Miriam Kochan. New York: Harper & Row.

Carlyle, Thomas ([1837] 1902). "The Paper Age." In *The French Revolution: A History*. Ed. C.R.L. Fletcher. New York: G. Putnam's Sons.

Carmon, Walt, ed. (1926–28). *Red Cartoons from* The Daily Worker. 2 vols. New York: The Daily Worker.

Clair, Jen (1977). *Duchamp et la photographie: Essai d'analyse d'un primat technique sur le développement d'une oeuvre*. Paris: Chene.

Davenport, Homer (1898). "Caricature of Mark Hannah." In *Cartoons*. New York: DeWitt.

—— (1900). *The Dollar or the Man? The Issue of Today*. Boston, MA: Small, Maynard.

Del Mar, Alexander ([1896] 1983). *History of Monetary Systems*. Orono, ME: National Poetry Foundation, University of Maine at Orono.

Derrida, Jacques (1972). "La Double Séance." In *La Dissémination*. Paris: Éditions du Seuil.

Dorfman, Joseph (1946). *The Economic Mind in American Civilization, 1606–1865*. New York: Viking.

Du Chaillu, Paul B. (1889). *The Viking Age: The Early History, Manners, and Customs of the Ancestors of the English Speaking Nations*, 2 vols. New York: Scribner.

Duchamp, Marcel (1969). *The Complete Works of Marcel Duchamp*. Ed. Arturo Schwarz. New York: Abrams.

—— (1971). *Dialogues with Marcel Duchamp*. Ed. Pierre Cabanne. Trans. Ron Padgett. London: Thames & Hudson.

Foucault, Michel (1982). *This Is Not a Pipe*. Illus. and letters by René Magritte. Trans. and ed. James Harkness. Berkeley: University of California Press.

Grand-Carteret, John, ed. (1894). *Le Livre et l'image: Revue documentaire illustrée mensuelle*. Vol. 3. Paris: Rondeau.

Harten, Jürgen, and Horst Kurnitzky (1978). *Museum des Geldes: Über die seltsame Natur des Geldes in Kunst, Wissenchaft und Leben*, 2 vols. Städtische Kunsthalle Düsseldorf und Kunstverein für Rheinlande und Westfalen. Düsseldorf: Städtische Kunsthalle.

Heinzelman, Kurt (1980). *The Economics of the Imagination*. Amherst: University of Massachusetts Press.

Hessler, Gene (1974). *The Comprehensive Catalogue of U.S. Paper Money*. Chicago: Regnery.

Johnson, Malcolm (1971). *The Great Loco Foco Juggernaut*. Drawn by D.C. Johnston. Barre, MA: Imprint Society.

Krooss, Herman Edward (1969). *Documentary History of Banking and Currency in the United States*. New York: Chelsea.

Leyden, Rudolph von (1976). "Oriental Playing Cards: An Attempt at Exploration of Relationships." Trans. Fred G. Taylor. *Journal of the Playing Card Society* 4, Suppl. 2: 1–37.

—— (1977). *Indische Spielkarten: Inventarkatalog der indischen Sammlung des Deutschen Spielkarten-Museums*. Leinfelden-Echterdingen: Das Museum.

Lipman, Jean (1970). "Money for Money's Sake as Art." *Art in America* 58 (Jan.–Feb.): 76–83.

Lyotard, Jean-François (1990). *Duchamp's TRANS/formers: A Book*. Venice, CA: Lapis.

Mallarmé, Stéphane (1945). *Oeuvres complètes*. Ed. Henri Mondor. Paris: Gallimard.

Mayer, Leo Ary (1971). *Mamluk Playing Cards*. Ed. R. Ettinghausen and O. Kurz. Leiden: Brill.

McLachlan, R.W. (1911). *The Canadian Card Money: A Bibliography*. Montreal.

Michaels, Walter Benn (1987). *The Gold Standard and the Logic of Naturalism: American Literature at the Turn of the Century*. Berkeley: University of California Press.

Mitchell, W.J.T. (1986). *Icononology: Image, Text, Ideology*. Chicago: University of Chicago Press.

Moakley, Gertrude (1966). *The Tarot Cards Painted by Bonifacio Bembo for the Visconti-Sforza Family: An Iconographic and Historical Study*. New York: New York Public Library.

Murrel, William (1933–38). *History of American Graphic Humor*. New York: Whitney Museum of American Art.

Nast, Thomas (1976). *Cartoons and Illustrations by Thomas Nast*. Text by Thomas Nast St. Hill. New York: Dover.

Newman, Eric P. (1967). *The Early Paper Money of America*. Racine, WI: Whitman.

Pogel, Nancy, and Paul Somers, Jr (1980). "Editorial Cartoons." In *Handbook of the American Popular Culture*. Ed. M. Thomas Inge. Westport, CT: Greenwood.

Prunner, Gernot (1969). *Ostasiatische Spielkarten*. Bielfeld: Deutsches Spielkarten Museum.

Robinson, H.R. (1848). *A Correct Map of Alta California and the Gold Region: From Actual Survey Embracing All the New Towns and the Dry and Wet Diggins*. New York: H.R. Robinson.

Roosevelt, Clinton (1860). "On the Paradox of Political Economy in the Coexistence of Excessive Population." *Proceedings of the American Association for the Advancement of Science*. Aug. 1859. Philadelphia: John C. Clark, 344–52.

Samhaber, Ernst (1964). *Das Geld: Eine Kulturgeschichte*. Munich: Keyserche.

Schmitz, Neil (1977). "Tall Tale, Tall Talk: Pursuing the Lie in Jacksonian Literature." *American Literature* 48: 473–77.

Shell, Marc (1982). *Money, Language, and Thought: Literary and Philosophic Economies from the Medieval to the Modern Era*. Berkeley: University of California Press.

—— (forthcoming). "Les Lis des champs: *Assurance, insurance, et ensurance*." *Revue d'economie financière*.

St. Armand, Barton Levi (1971). "Poe's 'Sober Mystification': The Uses of Alchemy in 'The Gold-Bug.'" *Poe Studies* 4: 1–7.

Thiveaud, Jean-Marie (1988). "L'Ambassadeur-poète, Paul Claudel devant la crise de 1929." *Revue d'economie financière* 5/6 (Sept.): 283–92.

Wagenführ, Horst (1959). *Der goldene Kompass: Vom Werden und Wandel des Geldes, mit einem Lexikon der europäischen Wahrungen*. Stuttgart: Schüler.

Wells, David A. ([1876] 1931). *Robinson Crusoe's Money; or, The Remarkable Financial Fortunes and Misfortunes of a Remote Island Community*. Illus. Thomas Nast. New York: P. Smith.

Weschler, Lawrence (1988). "Onward and Upward with the Arts: Value." *New Yorker* 18 Jan.: 33–56; 25 Jan.: 88–98.

White, Richard Grant (1862). "Caricature and Caricaturists." *Harper's Monthly Magazine* April: 586–607.

Wynn Jones, Michael (1975). *The Cartoon History of the American Revolution*. New York: Putnam.

3

"I TALK TO EVERYBODY IN THEIR OWN WAY"

Defoe's economies of identity

Janet Sorensen

While living in Edinburgh in 1707, promoting union between England and Scotland and acting as a spy for Robert Harley, Daniel Defoe, like many of his wealthy Lowland cohorts, attended meetings of the burgeoning Society in Scotland for Propagating Christian Knowledge (SSPCK). Identifying linguistic conversion of Gaelic-speaking Highlanders to English as the fulcrum upon which the SSPCK could rest their hopes for a larger cultural and political Highland conversion, the Society argued, "Nothing can be more effectual for reducing these countries to order, and making them usefull [*sic*] to the Commonwealth than teaching them their duty to God, their King and country and rooting out their Irish language" (SSPCK 1716). While a separate linguistic community existing within the newly consolidated British nation might problematize the political and cultural identity necessary for successful union, the exchange of Gaelic for English, they hoped, would eradicate such troubling difference. Aiming to sublimate linguistic and cultural difference through seamless translation, the Society deployed a universal grammar, exchanging words as neutral counters for ideas. Further, their vision of linguistic exchange – in which difference initiates a translation or substitution, whereby it is made the same – parallels the rising form of commodity exchange. Both commodity exchange and linguistic exchange in this imperial context share a dehistoricizing and universalizing movement. The English language, in turn, functions, like money, as a universal equivalent, constructing and abstracting difference in its circulation.

This way of thinking about language and its structures of exchange was not limited to England's Celtic periphery in Scotland but inflected eighteenth-century English identity itself, influencing texts we now consider part of the canon of English literature. In this essay I hope to show that this model of exchange, its bearing on identity, and the contradictions it produces are evident in the writings of even that most English of authors, Daniel Defoe.[1]

His *The Fortunate Mistress . . . Roxana* (1724) features a heroine who masters the exchange economy of late seventeenth-century England and does so, in part, by her ability to translate and subsume linguistic and cultural difference.

The attempt to analyze Defoe's relationship to the expanding British empire around him is a notoriously tortuous endeavor; his writings exhibit multiple, contradictory positions. I set out, then, not to locate Defoe squarely in one camp or the other, but instead to read the semiotic economy of several of his texts, particularly *Roxana*, as representing an emerging system of exchange – both linguistic and economic – influenced by that rising empire. I discuss *Roxana* because, of all Defoe's novels, it is the most complex meditation on exchange. In tracking Roxana's inordinate success at accumulation, the text celebrates an atemporal exchange identity.[2] Yet in depicting the return of her daughter, abandoned in Roxana's adherence to the logic of the market, the text grapples with and feminizes the suppressed temporal dimension of the rising commodities exchange process. I want to link the symbolic economy of this popular novel to a particular exchange logic and its contradictions. For *Roxana* stages a similar exchange logic: reducing difference to equivalence, translating value across cultures by means of a universal equivalent. At the same time it also reveals the doubled, concealed, even contradictory, quality of that exchange.

Defoe, in his wide range of cultural practices, from propagandist and hack writer to economist and tourist, images the nation on a model that owes more to international exchange than to an integral, autonomous cultural body. It is true that Defoe's language and narrative structures announce and maintain a conscious distance from foreign influence; we can note that Defoe's vocabulary "contains a higher proportion of words of Anglo-Saxon origin than that of any other well-known writer" (Watt 1967: 101) and that *Roxana* departs from the French model of the *chronique scandaleuse* in its first-person narration.[3] Yet Defoe's very forms of constructing the ideological space of the nation were influenced by a semiology predicated on empire – a semiotic economy that produces and then subsumes signs of difference within a unified cultural identity. This universalizing vision of language would give rise to an ambivalence about English claims of imperial superiority over and equivalence to the colonial culture and its language.[4]

This ambivalence is in evidence in the relationship between England and the Highlands in its "internal colonization" of that region.[5] As Paula Backscheider (1989: 209) has put it, Defoe, though sympathetic to the Scots, "did believe wholeheartedly in the Union, envisioning a 'manifest destiny' for his island." Like many of his English and Lowland Scots contemporaries, Defoe identified Gaelic with Jacobitism and Catholicism, marking it as threateningly different.[6] Yet in insisting on the need to convert Gaelic speakers into English speakers, as he and the other supporters of the SSPCK had done, Defoe assumed that these languages and their world views had enough in common to make such conversion possible. Further, underpinning the SSPCK's proposed projects for English translations and English usage in schools and professional life was the promise that English, functioning as a standard, could eradicate difference across time and space.

We can detect a parallel movement in Defoe's *A Tour through the Whole Island of Great Britain* (1724–6), which carries a subtext of Scottish incorporation. Although much of Defoe's description of Scotland in Letters 11–13 of *A Tour* catalogs Scotland's distinctness – its unimproved commerce, its unique system of measurement, etc. – that distinctiveness, like the distinctiveness of England's regions, is incorporated into the social and cultural entity of Britain and its progress. Ultimately, the description of Scotland follows the same pattern that Defoe's descriptions of all of England's diverse regions follow: differences – in commodities, customs, language – all feed into the national unity of Britain through exchange with the nation's center, London.

"I am all to every one that I may gain some": translating difference into identity and accumulation

In his own interventions as a spy, propagandist, and demographer, and in his cultural imaginings of the British nation, Defoe participated in a symbolic economy akin to this imperial linguistic model. Consider the way in which he articulated his own multiple identities as a spy in Edinburgh. In a letter to Harley, Defoe writes:

> I converse with Presbyterian, Episcopall-Dissenter, papist, and Non Juror. . . . I Talk to Everybody in Their Own Way. To the Merchants I am about to settle here in trade . . . With the Lawyer I want to purchase a House and Land to bring my Family & Live Upon it . . . With the Glasgow Mutineers I am to be a fish Merchant, with the Aberdeen men a woolen and with the Perth and Western men a Linen Manufacturer, and at the end of all Discourse the Union is the Essentiall and I am all to Every one that I may Gain some.
>
> (Quoted in Novak 1962: 2)

Here Defoe exploits diversity. He assumes protean shapes, but the purpose of assuming these varied personae is "Union," the conversion of these separate entities – and ultimately the two entities of England and Scotland – into one. Defoe exchanges his own identity for a series of alternative identities, and his different disguises all have a homogenizing end in mind.[7] Defoe's most effective means of adopting these varied identities is language, hence his claim that "I Talk to Everybody in Their Own Way." He describes himself as translating himself into the position of others through language. Language and translation also function in this passage as a figure for difference and a dissembling, or, more accurately, a deceptively assimilating, identity. This ability to exchange one persona or language for another is also demonstrated by Defoe's fictional character Roxana. She too displays how fluidity and movement shape an unstable identity. In *Roxana*, his final novel, Defoe tracks the title character's accumulation of capital as she assumes and exchanges a variety of disguises while engaging in a series of exchanges (of self and sex for money). While this narrative movement is characteristic of a number of his fictions, in *Roxana* Defoe goes beyond a mere staging of the propulsive movement of exchange and the accumulation it seems to generate, to explore the ambiguities concealed in the equations between money and commodities. Roxana's accumulation through exchange appears rather straightforward; difference is constructed and exchanged for the universal equivalent, money. The text, however, unpacks the layers embedded in those exchange operations, revealing a complex, contradictory set of identities and temporalities.

Roxana's exchange economy is analogous to the symbolic economy of what I will call "imperial grammar," where the difference – and constructed "otherness" – of the Gaelic language is reduced to the "universal equivalent" of English. In a process that wavers between description and construction, Roxana continually invokes national and cultural difference. The novel juxtaposes France, from which "Protestants were Banish'd . . . by the Cruelty of their Persecutors" to London, "a large and gay City" (Defoe [1724] 1986: 5), and contrasts the legal system of England, where "they must prove the Fact or give just reason for their suspicions" to that of France, where law is mysterious and "How such things were carried on I knew not" (117). The French, we are told, are distinctly nosy: "the People of Paris, especially the Women, are the most busie and impertinent Enquirers . . . in the world" (67). The Romans "have an Air of sharping and couzening, quarreling and scolding" (103); the women of Naples lead a "loose life" (102); Persian women are "wild and *Bizarre*" (179). In addition, Roxana continually refers to linguistic differences between cultures. For instance, she tells us that a "mistress" in France is "in English, a Whore" (115).

Roxana, however, does not derive her identity in opposition to these other cultures. Alone in a strange country after the murder of her lover, Roxana is able to universalize her experiences in foreign places, to translate difference by assimilating it. Often this means a literal translation of different languages. Her abilities as a polyglot provide her with a linguistic skeleton key which she uses to enter and assume and/or construct a variety of identities. She is able to translate infinitely, learning to speak English, French, Dutch, Italian, and Turkish. She writes,

> I learnt the *Turkish* Language . . . and some Turkish, or rather Moorish Songs, of which I made Use, to my Advantage . . . I need not say I learnt *Italian* too, for I got pretty well Mistress of that,

> before I had been there a Year; and as I had Leisure enough, and lov'd the Language, I read all the Italian Books I cou'd come at.
>
> (Defoe [1724] 1986: 102)

Roxana masters these languages, these moments of difference. She even consumes them in reading. Her linguistic proficiency allows her to circulate with ease; she rarely succumbs to that loss of power – and of self – immanent in the inability to understand the language of a foreign place. All languages are finally translatable and translated into English, which functions as a universal equivalent in the novel. English readers have these differences translated for them into English, whereby they too can consume them. This consolidates a national subject who confronts a variegated panorama of cultural difference in a safe, consumable form, leveled by the translation, or exchange, into English.

Roxana's universalizing linguistic exchanges represent the theory and practice of what I am calling "imperial grammar." These translation practices are informed by and reinforce an understanding of language as a transparent representational system directly mappable onto an objective reality, or at least onto the idea or sensory impression of an objective reality, an understanding of language that enables the word/coin analogy that Richard Gray has mapped out in his essay in this volume. The linguistic economy between English and Gaelic, for instance, saw language as reducible to a one-to-one exchange relationship between words of different languages. In addition, however, the exchange of Gaelic for English asserts the superiority of English, the "universal equivalent." That is to say that word "coins" for the same object in different languages do not have the same value, and that difference introduces the ambivalence between equivalence and superiority mentioned in this essay's opening. At the same time, that superiority must be seen to exist outside of historical relationships and contexts, inhabiting a spatial rather than a temporal system of meaning and exchange. If English or Gaelic were situated within a larger network of history, or each within its own distinct syntax, the view of language as universal and transparent – and therefore seamlessly exchangeable – would collapse under its own contradictions.

This view of language, which suppresses its relational, contingent, historically specific relations of meaning production, instead trades in linguistic difference across space. To facilitate such exchange, language should be as plain and simple as possible. And indeed, Defoe, in his *Essay Upon Projects* (1697) and various *Review* articles, repeatedly emphasizes the importance of a plain, clear prose style. He writes: "easy, plain, and familiar language is the beauty of speech in general" and maintains, in the same *Review* article, that "perfect stile" would be "that in which a man speaking to five hundred people, of all common and various capacities, should be understood by them all in the same manner with one another," believing that plain language enabled exchange of meaning between disparate groups. Defoe's predilection for "plain" prose has a variety of sources, including Thomas Sprat's writings and the dissenting tradition in which Defoe had been educated. I want to argue for an additional influence: the exchange of language between a growing number of diverse peoples, both in imperial and national contexts.

Defoe's interest in language was very much motivated by its importance to the improvement of the nation. For Defoe, the nation, like the empire, is an extremely heterogeneous community pulled together through exchange – including linguistic exchange – through which a national identity becomes possible. Defoe's definition of "perfect stile" allows exchange between vastly different groups – between laborers and city merchants, say – within a single linguistic community.[8] In his *Essay Upon Projects*, which contains a variety of proposals for improving the nation, Defoe urges the formation of a language academy, the role of which would be to facilitate and monitor linguistic exchange. Such calls for language academies were common in early eighteenth-century Britain, reflecting the anxiety around linguistic value which Richard Gray has described in his essay in this volume. In his effort to discourage swearing, for instance, Defoe does not appeal to its being "sinful and unlawful" (Defoe [1697] 1969: 238). Instead he recommends that "gentlemen" write out these "Common-Places [swear words] . . . then let them turn them into Latin, or translate them into any other Language, and but see what a Jargon and Confusion of Speech they make together" (239). It is the untranslatability, the inexchangeable quality of swear words, which would make them a primary target of Defoe's proposed language academy. Particular to one linguistic group, swear words are not universally translatable and so lack meaning or value in exchange. Similarly, the academy would ensure that "'twou'd be as Criminal then to *Coin Words*, as *Money*" (237). Here Defoe overtly compares words to a monetary exchange medium; coining words would be, like coining counterfeit money, an attempt to create value from nothing, in a sense to devalue all words. The regulatory agency of the academy would remove any "false coins" which might disrupt fair exchange.

This eye toward international exchange across the British empire influenced Defoe's proposal to make the national language uniform with the help of an academy. The standardized English constructed throughout the eighteenth century – without the help of an academy – became the standard across parts of the globe; its enforced ascendancy in Scotland is an early case in point. Here, as in other cases, Defoe was influenced by Locke, who was, according to John Caffentzis (1989), "the first self-conscious theorist of the Great Transformation of the English language that started during this period, which would turn the peculiar pidgin of the European World into *the* computable language." The international market and the understanding of language as stable depended on each other. As Caffentzis has put it: "the existence of the world market depended upon determinacy of translation across many languages, societies and fashions; and surely Locke, operating near the center of the world power that claimed to steer that very market, was conscious of the implications of his 'semantic' analyses" (ibid.: 84). Alternatively, the understanding of language that makes that "determinacy of translation" possible is derived from the experience of empire, as its technologies of codification permit the ability to think and construct a standard at all.

Defoe repeatedly engages this technology in his construction of the nation, as difference – in language, in goods – becomes the site of a homogenizing exchange. His *Tour* provides one instance where the nation functions in the same spatial economy that empire does. *A Tour* describes a variety of regions, emphasizing their diverse natural resources and products (as well as their particular "Customs, Manners, speech"; Defoe [1724–6] 1971: 41). It then universalizes these commodities, as all participate in a uniform movement to the nation's center, London. He writes: "this whole kingdom, as well as the people, as the land, and even the sea, in every part of it, are employed to furnish something, and I may add, the best of every thing, to supply . . . London with provisions . . . corn, flesh, fish, butter, timber, clothes" (41). While much of Defoe's *Tour* marks regions of Britain as separate and distinct because of their unique resources, the list reduces all of these resources and their particularity to a moment of sameness as commodities. The list defines them as identical, in that they are all goods for exchange and consumption in London. Defoe repeats this gesture in each circuit: each trip to and from a particular region records, or we might say helps to construct, that region as distinct. That difference is then abnegated, as the products of the diversity feed into the nation's syncretic but unified center. This semiotics of metonymy or synecdoche, of diverse parts representing a whole, is shared by an imperial and national model as defined by Defoe.[9] Defoe is working early enough in the development of ideas about the nation that he does not directly wrestle with the resulting contradictions of a shared model of identity for nation and empire. However, his texts' ambivalences, as we shall examine in *Roxana*, reflect those contradictions.

Roxana's subsumption of diversity, her ability to assimilate and to find identity precisely in that process of exchange, is analogous to Defoe's model of the nation. Her ability to universalize is evident when she translates for her English audience. Moments of difference, such as the mistress/whore distinction cited above, are translated into universals. Her assumption seems to be that "call it what you will, a whore is still a whore." Although one might try to disguise the true nature of a whore by calling her the French "mistress," it is the *English* word and meaning that operates in all times and places. These transparent translations invoke a theory of language that emphasizes the stable determinacy of the signified. Roxana conflates a universally valid morality with English morality. "Several countries abroad" might deviate from true moral behavior, or call it by another name, but this does not alter true English morality. This suggests that there is a universal, English morality, which other cultures obscure through a perversion of language. The desire for pure determinacy, possible only through abstraction, and the reality of indeterminacy, produced in the contingencies of life, poses one of the key contradictions troubling the symbolic economy of Defoe's texts.

Like the English language in the linguistic realm, English morality represents the universal equivalent of all moralities. The concept of a universal equivalent figures on many levels in *Roxana*, most directly in the form of money. The text is replete with images of conversion of commodities into money, and the ease of circulation and profit such conversion brings. Roxana, who, like Moll Flanders, acts as a human calculator throughout the text, continually translates goods into their monetary value. One instance of many is her description of the "suit of Lace, upon my Head, which would have been worth in England, 200£ Sterling" (Defoe [1724] 1986: 71). If all linguistic – and cultural or material – difference is laundered in the moment of translation into Roxana's language of mastery, similarly the moment of the exchange of a material commodity into money universalizes and abstracts qualitative, physical difference, and specific history. Money means power and control, especially because, as Locke had recently pointed out, it circumvents time. While goods such as food and clothes spoil and wear out in time, money endures, extending one's property beyond what is useful in the here and now to the indefinite future, and functioning as a standard outside of time, as standards often claim to be.

Alternatively, the ability to translate or convert goods into money allows the same invisibility and control that Roxana's ability to translate language allows, and the same movement in space, enabling her to cross the Channel, for instance. Here Defoe highlights the functionalist understanding of language that Richard Gray in this volume has identified as emerging in this period. Defoe's response to this functionalism is ambivalent, as we shall see. Enabling movement in space, money also eradicates cultural difference. Roxana buries her Protestant husband in a French Catholic cemetery "with all the Ceremonies of the Roman church . . . by the help of Money to a certain Person" (54). The Dutch merchant purchases his "Naturalization" as an Englishman. He also informs Roxana that "money purchas'd Titles of Honour in almost all Parts of the World" (240); in other words, money instantly replaces the time of genealogy and tradition. Under the logic of the universal equivalent, anything, including titles and nationalities – those most "naturalized" distinctions – are salable, denaturalized, reducible to a universal market value.

Roxana and her servant Amy both explicitly invoke a figure of an atemporal imperial commerce to describe their profitable manipulation of difference. They use a narrative of wealth derived by movement through space to conceal their histories. Amy tells a curious guardian of one of Roxana's many children that "she had been out of *England*, and was but newly return'd from the *East-*

Indies . . . for it was not a strange thing for young Women to go away poor to the *East-Indies*, and come home vastly Rich" (193). Roxana also later reflects "that I was like a Passenger coming back from the *Indies*, who having, after many Years Fatigues and Hurry in Business, gotten a good Estate, with innumerable difficulties and hazards, is arriv'd safe at *London* with all his Effects" (243). Like the fortunes made in the outposts of the colonial empire, her wealth is procured invisibly, almost mysteriously. In the imperial context, movement across space and the exchange of goods, rather than visible labor over time, generates wealth. The East Indies is a space of radical difference, and the figure of a successful manipulation of that space is offered as the model for the accumulation in which Amy and Roxana have been engaged. That difference can be translated into money, which in turn has meaning in the home space of England.

Translating the translator: Roxana and the layered identity of the commodity

If at one point she compares herself to a profiteer of empire, at another point Roxana compares herself to a colonial subject. Her money has translated into status and title, and yet she revealingly writes:

> 'twas so Big, and so Great, to hear myself call'd *ladyship*, and *Your Ladyship*, and the like; that I was like the *Indian* King at *Virginia*, who having a House built for him by the *English*, and a Lock put upon the Door, wou'd sit whole Days together, with the Key in his Hand, locking, unlocking, and double-locking the door, with an unaccountable Pleasure at the Novelty.
>
> (Defoe [1724] 1986: 246)

In this complicated passage, Roxana expresses a shrewd if fleeting analysis of her situation. Hers is not a position of power, as the titles she acquires might indicate. Instead, she is a slave to the title. While the Indian King is delighted with the acquisition, the reader is aware of his folly, of the uselessness of the house and key, suggested by his misrecognition of the lock's function. The image of the king sitting in his locked house suggests an unknowing entrapment, a captivity in which he has unwittingly participated. He has, the reader recognizes, made a bad deal, much like a child who is unaware of the "real" value of goods. This image would be familiar to contemporary readers aware of popular travel accounts and their stories of similarly infantilized foreign populations, with similarly "naïve" relationships to goods. And yet Roxana compares herself to this child-like Indian king. Consequently, we may assume that she too has made a bad deal, that the title was not "worth" what we know she has paid for it, and this suggests a critique of the atemporal exchange economy and spatial understanding of value with which Roxana operates.

For all the seeming control her mastery of disguises affords her, Roxana is not simply the translator, the narrator, the trader of commodities. She is also the translated, the narrated, the commodity. Her landlord "translates" her into monetary value when "he pull'd out a silk Purse, which had three-score Guineas in it, and threw them into my Lap" (42). The physical connection of the purse to the body and the cavalier act of the toss suggest that Roxana's position is not one of total control. In referring to herself as, simultaneously, a pretty surface and a "carcass," Roxana suggests this doubled sense of self as a piece of meat to be sold. Thus while she fetishizes titles and goods throughout the text, she is herself fetishized. "I was really his Idol" (70), she declares, referring to the defining gaze of the Prince. Like an idol, she is worshipped, but only as an object.

Like a commodity, Roxana establishes an equivalence between herself and commodities, drawing a direct parallel between herself and her house, for instance. Her neighbors "saw me in Rags . . . thin and looking almost like one Starv'd, who was before fat and beautiful: The House, that was before handsomely furnish'd with Pictures and Ornaments . . . was now stripp'd, and naked" (17). When circumstances force Roxana to prostitute herself, we are invited to see her as equivalent to "a large very good leg of Veal [and] a Piece of the Fore-Ribs of Roasting Beef" (25). Superior commodities soon outstrip these humble goods. When thieves murder her landlord, Roxana receives (or takes), in exchange for the intimate relationship they have shared, "his Ring . . . 700 Pistoles . . . Plate, and the Household-Stuff" (56). The lists of commodities which she recites, like the list from *A Tour* quoted above, flatten out any distinction between the items (and between herself and the items) in the empty time of repetition.

It is from this crucial perspective – the story of a commodity and its hidden history – that Defoe's novel unwittingly interrogates the spatial semiotic economy of imperial exchange and accumulation. The commodity's-eye view provided by this perspective reveals the layered, relational qualities of identity and exchange. This perspective will be especially helpful in analyzing the suppression and then re-emergence of a submerged social history in what is presented as a timeless moment of exchange. In Defoe, this temporal perspective is feminized: the subject/object split evident in Roxana's status can be directly linked to the commodification of her sexualized body, as she occupies the position of a prostitute. When Roxana refers to herself as a "*Man-Woman*," she does so to defend her assertion that "as I was born free, I wou'd die so" (171) and to signify her power to accumulate – like a man. The term "man-woman," however, also connotes a doubleness, even a dialectic between the control of property, which she identifies with men, and the lack of that control – and the status as property – which she identifies with women. Despite Roxana's dizzying ascent to the pinnacle of financial success, her status as a woman means that success is purchased through an objectification of self. For this reason, we may begin to understand Defoe's representation of the suppressed social history and temporality behind exchange as feminized. His female narrator's status as a commodity reveals multiple levels of the exchange equation.

As a commodity, Roxana adopts novel foreign personae which are, on one level, defining characteristics of the commodity form: the commodity presents itself as something new and different in order to tempt an exchange. For instance, Roxana playfully assumes a Turkish identity in costume and dance, with which she thinks she lures the king himself. Yet the commodity is also doubled because it must be viewed as not only different from but also the same as other commodities. In order to be exchanged, commodities must seem to share a common denominator. The commodity, like the word in the context of imperial grammar, announces itself as having no history, as inhabiting, rather, a spatial economy that erases historical difference to appear the same for exchange. Like a commodity, she maintains a social anonymity, attempting to position herself outside of social historical contexts. Seeming to circulate outside of time, her years of sexual liaisons and childbirth tell little on her surface; she seems ageless. Similarly, Amy, though "between forty and fifty" near the novel's end, is still "a wild, gay, loose Wretch, and not much the graver for her Age" (265). The commodity's identity derived through its hidden history is superseded by an identity derived from its relation to other commodities in space, not from its relation to itself through time.

The commodity, marked by a series of slippages and displacements, is ultimately discernible only relationally, particularly in the moment of exchange. Roxana, like the commodity, reveals her value only when equated with another commodity. In that exchange equation, a transformation takes place: one of the commodities becomes a symbol of the other's value. Thus the identity of the two commodities changes in the equation relationship. Visible and invisible, made material only through an exchange relationship, value seems to flicker mystically within, above, around the commodity. A distinctly atemporal entity, the value and identity of the commodity are instantaneous, apparent briefly in an exchange relationship of self and other via a numerical grammar. As value glimmers elusively in moments of exchange, these relational terms of value identity in *Roxana*'s economy cast value as fiction. There is no direct referent, no essential object of value. This characterization of value's shaky, indeterminate status is hard to square with the referentiality of universal exchange Defoe so clearly seeks. This discrepancy might explain Defoe's feminization of the hidden temporality of commodity exchange as represented in Roxana. He attempts to distance her from a masculine honest trade represented by the novel's Dutch merchant, who is devoid of that troubling temporality and indeterminacy. The novel reads Roxana's timeless, ageless quality as a sign of her duplicity and emphasizes that duplicity in her status as a prostitute, a status defined by invisibility or, at least, disguise.

Throughout the eighteenth century, commerce's capriciousness and volatility, and its inscrutability, were feminized. Part of the text's cultural work is its attempt to suppress the fanciful, temporally marked elements of commodity exchange – which Defoe castigates and genders female – and to assert by contrast a trustworthy, respectable, atemporal trade. The reader might not allow him- or herself to be seduced by the sweeping forward motion of Roxana's accumulation or even by the detailed description of her fine fabrics, plate, and jewelry. Yet we cannot deny the novel's unambiguous moral center in the Dutch merchant. Beyond reproach, the Dutch merchant is who he says he is and does what he says he will do. He honors Roxana's bills, for instance, when he has every opportunity to cheat her. There is a transparency between the name and the man; he "acted as honest Men always do; with an upright and disinterested Principle; and with a Sincerity not often to be found" (122). There is no double identity here, no destabilizing gap between signifier and signified. Further, there is little possibility for the resurfacing of the social traces that taint Roxana's gains. As a man, he will have neither the adornments (such as Roxana's Turkish costume) nor the relationship to children that makes them irrefutable legacies of Roxana's multiple identities, and that indelibly maps a temporal frame on to her identity. Although he too has a child he reclaims, this fact does not bestow the same bitter legacy. The suggestion seems to be that ultimately the powers of trade and translation are and should be resolutely masculine.

In contrast, the text genders Roxana's deceptive method of exchange and of signifying value as feminine. To convince the prince that she is ingenuous, she makes him "wipe my face so hard, that he was unwilling to do it, for fear of hurting me" (72) and gives him an "undeniable Demonstration" (73) of the fact that she does not paint. Here, however, a fundamental duplicity cleaves signifier and signified. Roxana's honest visage signifies something very different from the dishonest woman the reader knows her to be. Duplicity forges her very identity, as it forges the identity of the commodity. In instances of her self-bifurcation she describes herself as a "sham lady" (307) and a counterfeit (213). She has a "history," a past of sexual liaisons which for women, in part because they are commodities, is impossible to escape. The split between who Roxana is and who she says she is disrupts the seamless homogenization of exchange. In that split a temporal dimension intrudes, introducing a radical difference that makes one-to-one exchange impossible. In doling out punishment to Roxana, as her suppressed history resurfaces, the text warns of the dangers of a feminized commerce of duplicity over time – a move, however, which implicates all exchange.

Telling time: the multiple temporalities of exchange and inexchangeable temporalities

In bracketing her personal history in order to accumulate, Roxana's personal temporality is replaced with an alternative sense of time – the empty time of interest accumulation. The submerged time of personal history, however, re-emerges briefly in several close calls – as when the jeweler recognizes the jewels Roxana tries to sell as the ones that were assumed stolen from her murdered lover – and then in the full-blown assertion of the claims of the past in the form of her long-lost daughter. Roxana and the commodities that serve as the basis of her identity become readable as social hieroglyphics, and the appearance of these once-hidden, inscribed objects halts the narrative progress of linear accumulation through timeless exchange in the novel.

This would suggest that there are aspects of the past, elements of Roxana's relational (repressed) identity, that are non-convertible, and their telling would make Roxana inexchangeable. Roxana finally cannot abstract or repress these relationships by translating them seamlessly into her own identity. Roxana cannot totally suppress her earlier identity as a mother, for instance, which again feminizes the social/historical context that will act as a drag on her ability to circulate. Her daughter Susan, the boldest and most protracted assertion of the past, detects Roxana's assimilations and attempts to pin her down to one inexchangeable identity – that of her "natural" mother. The text, then, sets up a tension between two mutually exclusive Roxana identities: one known through atemporal relationships to things and objectified people, the other known through temporal (past) relationships.

The novel depicts the vertiginous, catastrophic return of that suppressed past when her daughter Susan begins to "haunt" her. Like a ghost, Susan is representative of "a past that will not stay past."[10] Susan, as Roxana's child and servant, bears witness to Roxana's past, presenting the strongest case of both identity and radical alterity to Roxana – they even share the same name. In response to the threat posed by this past-revealing Other, Roxana attempts to level Susan's particularity, referring to her, not as Susan, or even "my daughter," but as "the Girl" or "she": impersonal, generic categories.

The narrative break – where Roxana ends her story, only to narrate it again – indicates a schism between one superficial reality and a historical, problematic underside, even introducing a recursive temporality. We do not, then, get a mere atemporal inventory of the commodities she accumulates – an instantaneous, ahistorical identity. To know Roxana through the second narrative is to know the history excluded from her commodity identity: the number of men she has been with, the children she has left behind – the residue of her exchanges. This is not the constant present elicited in the pattern of commodity exchange.

Again, this temporal quality is feminized. Roxana has narrated the story of her two sons, "one at Messina, and the other in the Indies" (265). They, like Roxana, have learned to trade in commodities, living out the literal life of merchants of exotic goods of empire that Roxana uses as a figure to describe her own business. Presumably, they inhabit a symbolic economy of atemporal exchange similar to Roxana's. There is no haunted past either for them or for Roxana in relation to them; they partake in the linear process and homogeneous empty time of accumulation. Roxana has not, however, discussed her daughters, who have not been traders in commodities, but instead have been servants, with only their labor to sell. Susan, whose story is presented as an afterthought, haunts the spatial symbolic economy of Roxana like a specter.[11] Her appearance seems entirely external to the accumulation-for-accumulation's-sake logic which dominates the novel. As a social trace, Susan exists in a temporality clearly different from her mother's. When the Quaker tells Susan she will warn Roxana of her arrival, Susan appeals to a recursive temporality, threatening that "a Curse wou'd follow her, and her Children after her" (322). This is a sense of the past as exerting influence for years, a temporality not instantaneous and unmarked but enduring, leaving its trace on generations. Echoing Susan's recursive temporality, Roxana remarks: "the blot can never be wip'd out by the most glorious Actions; nay if [the illegitimate child] lives to raise a Family . . . the Infamy must descend even to its innocent Posterity" (81). These beliefs imply that, despite the seeming illegibility of time's movement, the past can play a role in the future, usually a malevolent one, and certainly not the salutary invisible repetition of interest accumulation. This temporality is gendered female, accruing to Roxana and her daughters.

This points to the crux of the problem, the central contradiction of the symbolic economy of the novel and, implicitly, of Defoe's other narratives of exchange. Items exchanged – both persons and things – inevitably conceal a history, which it is narrative's job to tell. Yet reintroducing the suppressed contextual, diachronic aspects of the commodity's identity disrupts the symbolic economy in which it circulates. Jean-Joseph Goux, in his analysis of this symbolic economy, insists on the centrality of time to a complete understanding of the mechanism of value: "only a genesis of values, a genesis of the value form, can deconstruct the artifice of their hypostasis" (Goux 1990: 11).[12] Thus we must reintegrate the production history of the commodity, the historical rise of a general equivalent, the social history of Roxana, and the historical, social context of languages into the analysis of trade and imperial grammar in Defoe's texts.

These histories are, of course, noticeably absent in Defoe's *Tour*. Defoe's model of the nation is, in part, spatial and atemporal because it is a *trading* nation. He proudly describes near-perfect trade at the cloth market at Leeds: "thus, you see, ten or twenty thousand pounds value in cloth . . . bought and sold in little more than an hour. . . . By nine a clock the boards are taken down, the trestles are removed, and the street cleared, so that you see no market or goods any more than if there had been nothing to do" (Defoe [1724–6] 1971: 502). Defoe's description makes trade sound like nothing so much as an extensive legerdemain. And, like well-executed legerdemain, it should leave no trace. There is neither a visible history that goods have been bought and sold there, nor a record of where they have gone. The extension of these goods throughout England consolidates the movement of trade. That consolidation, however, is seamless, appearing to occur almost outside of time.

There is a strange parallel here between the image of Roxana as a person without a past and Manuel Schonhorn's description of Defoe's own negation of a social past in his non-fiction. Schonhorn (1982: 78) writes: "Unlike his contemporaries, Defoe rejected all models of the past, antiquity, and custom." In *A Tour* Defoe repeatedly asserts that he is not interested in history. Near the opening of that text he writes: "the looking back into remote things is studiously avoided" (Defoe [1724–6] 1971: 43). At another point he argues of a certain manufacturing process: "we cannot trace it by history" (546). Despite Defoe's efforts, however, history does often assert itself in *A Tour* as well as in *Roxana*. He resignedly writes in *A Tour*: "though I am backward to dip into antiquity, yet no English man, that has any honour for the glorious memory of the greatest and truest hero of all our kings of the English or Saxon race, can go to Carlisle, and not step aside to see the monument of King Edward I" (556). History thus appears, in a non-linear fashion, throughout the text. Defoe mentions random bits of history as he describes the spaces of his circuits, creating a fragmented palimpsest, where each space signifies a randomly layered set of historical references. Schonhorn (1982: 82) asks: "What does this scorn of tradition, treatment of past actions as discrete, discontinuous, and detached from a comprehensible present, mean for the fiction?" It means, in part, that we must read Defoe's work – fiction and non-fiction – as inflected by the logic of the commodity, a logic that parallels the relationship Schonhorn describes Defoe as having to history, a logic that I have been tracking in *Roxana*.

This logic is analogous to the spatial economy of imperial grammar. Defoe's theory of language also suppresses the temporal element of language as it asserts the most proper authority for correct usage. In *An Essay Upon Projects* he writes,

> The Voice of this Society should be sufficient Authority for the Usage of Words, and sufficient also to expose the innovation of other men's Fancies; they shou'd preside with a Sort of Judicature over the Learning of the Age, and have liberty to Correct and Censure the Exorbitance of Writers . . . no Author wou'd Coin without their Authority.
>
> (Defoe [1697] 1969: 236)

Most important to our argument here is the static temporality the academy would impose. Leaving no room for change, it would remove innovations, eliding the temporality of both future usage and alteration of the past, as it seeks to weed out "Erroneous Customs," the common practice of the people through time. It would instead regulate language in the interest of exchange through principles and standards. Defoe hints at the goal of such an academy's efforts. The academy in Paris has achieved "the Language allow'd to be most universal" and it is "now spoken in all the Courts of Christendom" (228).

Similarly, Defoe's academy would set out to establish a universal language, usable across time and space, an imperial grammar participating in the same atemporal symbolic economy.

The call for honest trade and honest language usage speaks to a nervousness concomitant with the realization that exchanges of words, of commodities, of languages are open to deceit. Richard Gray, in this volume, underscores precisely this nervousness in eighteenth-century writings on language and money. Just as a certain type of trade is policed in *Roxana*, so Defoe, in his call for an academy, hopes to regulate word usage along atemporal, universal principles. Both texts hold up a standard designed to propagate the dream of a traceless, homogeneous, universal and universalizing exchange. As Roxana's experience reveals, however, identity predicated on the ability to master and efface difference through exchange will always be haunted by the threat of the return of that difference. Like the commodity's oscillating movement between sameness and difference, her suspension of a distinct and troubling history can only ever be temporary.

What distinguishes *Roxana* from Defoe's other novels and also from some of his non-fiction writing is its acknowledgment, if confused and ambiguous, of an historical temporal dimension. By this I mean, not linear progress, but a sense of a heterogeneous past's ineluctable influence on the present. We have seen the disorder that that particular temporal dimension wreaks on Roxana's economy. Roxana's seemingly instantaneous relational identity derived through commodity exchange contains a residual past, a competing temporality. The reading of a social past into various commodities redirects, even halts, the narrative. The Turkish costume, for instance, once the foundation of her highest exchange value, comes to inhibit her ability to circulate when it nearly exposes her "true" identity.

This temporal dislocation is related to the displacement of human relations onto objects in commodity fetishism. As human becomes object in the form of Roxana, so object becomes human in the form of the dress. What Roxana had adopted gingerly to conceal her own identity and efface her past becomes the clue to establishing her identity years later. Ridden with Roxana's repressed social history (and that of the Turkish slave from whom she takes it), it virtually speaks for itself, telling, through Susan, the secret adventures of Roxana. Conversely, the Georgian women who come to dance with the "Turkish" Roxana cannot speak. Voiceless, they represent a past which interrupts, even precludes, the narrative. This temporality is feminized in the figure of these silent yet resonant women.

The limits of translation: the nation in time

Defoe does not consciously recognize and represent the contradictions of commodity exchange. Instead, in this relatively early era of capital, competing accounts of value, shifting semiological systems, and evolving social relations produce and are produced by cultural productions such as *Roxana*. Finally, Defoe's texts register suspicion of the myth of a purely spatial, atemporal trade. In fact, Defoe admits that exchanging words effectively necessitates a usage that is less than plain, arguing: "Things seem to appear more lively to the Understanding" if "insinuated under the cover of some Symbol or Allegory."[13] This becomes increasingly true if the thing meant to be made "more lively to the understanding" is the idea of a national identity. The imperial grammar model is ultimately inadequate to the task of consolidating a national identity. The syncretic identity produced out of exchange across space forecloses the possibility of a (fictional) distinctly national identity developed through time. "Talking to each in their own way" is an all-encompassing gesture, hollow at its core and incapable of creating or maintaining borders. Identity through universalizing exchange in space erases the particularity and history, the identity across time, of the nation. Later eighteenth-century writers will reject this heterogeneous figure for the nation, blaming commerce for its rise, and calling the process corruption. As a result, the myth of timeless spatial exchange will be rejected. Replacing a spatially imagined nation will be a myth of a people unified across time by custom and by a feminized temporality, precisely the kind so frightening to Defoe in *Roxana*.

Defoe begins, perhaps unwittingly, to represent the tensions and contradictions of the symbolic economy he defends at other times. He complicates, on a number of levels, his own ideas of transparent exchange and the identity produced there. His character Roxana represents both a temporality in which the instant of exchange evacuates time itself and a temporality in which a hidden social past weighs heavily upon the future. Her tentative individuality reflects a commodity logic which incorporates both universality and a hidden particularity. In a dialectical process of the assertion and abnegation of difference, she speaks in many languages. Yet she speaks in these languages in order to convert them into a universal language, a standard and universal equivalent. Against the grain of that universalizing movement, however, is written the story of its own impossibility. Hers is an identity informed by movement across space, translation across cultures, and homogenizing exchange of difference. In narrating her story as one of simultaneous accumulation and disintegration, Defoe registers a radical ambivalence about the exchange economy which formed the basis of his image of national identity.

Notes

1 Much as writers such as Madeleine Kahn (1991) have shown that Defoe's novels are intersected by the suppressed history of women writers, I argue that imperial commodity relations, and their semiotic economy, also traverse the writings of "the father of the English novel."

2 I depart from Veronica Kelly (1993), who embraces *Roxana*'s "postmodern" pleasure of counting outside of history and critiques the novel's representation of linear history as a sign of its bourgeois modernity. Instead I see the atemporal counting as the flip-side of the linear temporality of accumulation. Capital accumulation and commodity exchange efface the multiplicity of histories by posing both an empty linear time and a series of atemporal exchange moments instead.

3 Bill Warner has pointed out to me the distinction between Defoe's novels and their French contemporaries.

4 Cheyfitz (1991) develops this analysis. Such ambivalences were common in the relationship between Scotland and England, as the ideology of incorporation sat uncomfortably alongside imperial practices of cultural domination. Partha Chatterjee (1993) also describes the dialectical relationship between colonial imitation and national distinction – a dialectic also applicable in the Scottish context.

5 I take the phrase "internal colonialism" from Michael Hechter (1982). Hechter's characterization of the relationship between England and the "Celtic fringe" (Ireland, Scotland, Wales) as one of internal colonialism is problematic, as it fails to account for the role Lowlanders played in assimilating Scotland to England, for instance. Yet in its connotation of the economic, political, and cultural domination of the Highlands, it is entirely appropriate.

6 On Lowland and English political characterizations of Gaelic, see Durkacz (1983).

7 Defoe's other notable impetus to assuming multiple identities was as an author playing the market.

8 Defoe's dream of a national community constructed through a homogenous, uncontested language resembles the "linguistics of community" criticized by Mary Louise Pratt (1987: 56). Pratt offers an alternative model, a "linguistics of contact," whose "center is the operation of language across lines of social difference, a linguistics that focused on modes and zones of contact between dominant and dominated groups . . . that focused on how such speakers constitute each other relationally."

9 James Bunn (1980) has described the semiotics of metonymy of the eighteenth-century British empire.

10 I take this phrase from Deidre Lynch, who in discussion used it to describe, in part, the driving force of the gothic.

11 The reference to a "haunting specter" is not a facetious allusion to Marx and Engels's *Manifesto*. The argument is not that Susan represents a nascent proletariat – although as Roxana's servant she does perform labor, an activity surprisingly unrepresented in a text that tracks the accumulation of capital. I merely mean to suggest that history, suppressed in the movement and exchange of capital, continues to exist and, if remembered and used, poses a threat to that accumulation and movement. Consider the *Manifesto*'s well-known analysis of the atemporality of the social system organized around capital: "Constant revolutionizing of production, uninterrupted disturbances of all social conditions, everlasting uncertainty and agitation distinguish the bourgeois epoch from all earlier ones. All fixed, fast-frozen relations, with their train of ancient and venerable prejudices and opinions, are swept away, all new-formed ones become antiquated before they can ossify" (Marx and Engels 1975: 37).

12 Marx argues, and Goux along with him, that at the universal equivalent's origin is the basic equation in which one commodity is valued in terms of another commodity, and that this commodity comes over time to be regarded as money, the universal equivalent, through social custom and habit. Though the source of the universal equivalent's value is customary practice through time, its identity as a standard deceptively announces a timeless, placeless value. *Roxana* registers these dual temporalities, both in the power that comes from Roxana's ability to circulate seemingly outside of time (in this sense she herself might be representative of a universal equivalent) and in the irrefragable fact of social history informing that power.

13 From a letter in *Mist's Weekly Journal*, cited in Aikins's useful discussion (1985: 535).

References

Aikins, Janet E. (1985). "Roxana: the Unfortunate Mistress of Conversation." *Studies in English Literature* 25: 529–56.

Backscheider, Paula (1989). *Daniel Defoe*. Baltimore, MD: Johns Hopkins University Press.

Bunn, James (1980). "The Aesthetics of British Mercantilism." *New Literary History*: 303–21.

Caffentzis, John (1989). *Clipped Coins, Abused Words, and Civil Government: John Locke's Philosophy of Money*. Brooklyn: Autonomedia.

Cheyfitz, Eric (1991). *The Poetics of Imperialism*. Oxford: Oxford University Press.

Chatterjee, Partha (1993). *Nationalist Thought and the Colonial World*. Minneapolis: University of Minnesota Press.

Defoe, Daniel ([1697] 1969). *An Essay Upon Projects*. Menston, W. Yorks.: Scolar.

—— ([1724] 1986). *Roxana, the Fortunate Mistress*. Oxford: Oxford University Press.

—— ([1724–6] 1971). *A Tour Through the Whole Island of Great Britain*. Ed. Pat Rogers. Harmondsworth: Penguin.

Durkacz, Victor E. (1983). *The Decline of the Celtic Languages*. Edinburgh: John Donald.

Goux, Jean-Joseph (1990). *Symbolic Economies: After Marx and Freud*. Trans. Jennifer Curtiss Gage. Ithaca: Cornell University Press.

Hechter, Michael (1982). *Internal Colonialism: The Celtic Fringe in British National Development, 1536–1966*. Berkeley: University of California Press.

Jacobsen, Susan L. (1992). "A Dialogue of Commerce: Defoe's Roxana as Mistress and Entrepreneur." In *Compendious Conversations*. Ed. Kevin L. Cope. Frankfurt am Main: Lang, 218–33.

Kahn, Madeleine (1991). *Narrative Transvestism*. Ithaca: Cornell University Press.

Kelly, Veronica (1993). "The Paranormal Roxana." *Postmodernism Across the Ages*. Ed. Bill Readings. Syracuse: Syracuse University Press, 138–49.

Marx, Karl, and Friedrich Engels (1975). *Manifesto of the Communist Party*. Peking: Foreign Language Press.

Novak, Maximillian E. (1962). *Economics and the Fiction of Daniel Defoe*. Berkeley: University of California Press.

Pratt, Mary Louise (1987). "Linguistic Utopias." In *The Linguistics of Writing*. Ed. Nigel Fabb. New York: Methuen, 48–66.

Schonhorn, Manuel (1982). "Defoe, the Language of Politics, and the Past." *Studies in the Literary Imagination* 15: 75–82.
Society in Scotland for Propagating Christian Knowledge (SSPCK) (1716). *State of the Society in Scotland for the Propagation of Christian Knowledge*. Edinburgh.
Watt, Ian (1967). *The Rise of the Novel*. Berkeley: University of California Press.

4

BUYING INTO SIGNS

Money and semiosis in eighteenth-century German language theory

Richard T. Gray

Monetary culture means that life is caught up . . . in its means.
(Georg Simmel [1907] 1984: 336–37[1])

The metaphorical field circumscribing analogies between language and money is undoubtedly one of the most productive in all of Western culture. Quintilian's admonition that one expend words as carefully as one spends money (1921–2: I. 6, 1), Ovid's remark that words, like coins, are minted by public authority (1979: III. 479f), Nietzsche's famous comparison of current words to coins that have lost their impression due to overcirculation (1988: 881), and Saussure's identification of linguistic significance with monetary value (1966: 115): what all these metaphors have in common is that they draw on issues of monetary practice to elucidate the operation and use of language. The historical extension of this metaphorical field is matched by its broad cultural dispersion throughout the European languages: comparisons between money and language are just as likely to be found among English or French writers as they are among German ones.[2] The unusual vitality of this analogy between money and language is further reflected in the expansive semantic territory it encompasses. Aside from the common identification of words with coins, many other elements drawn from the sphere of finance, such as the notions of circulation, exchange, credit, banking, counterfeiting, investment, etc., are frequently applied as metaphorical vehicles for the illumination of linguistic practices. The vitality and diversity of this metaphorical field gives the best indication that the analogy between money and language in particular, and between the realms of economics and linguistics in general, is underwritten by a wealth of substantive capital. Indeed, as Jean-Joseph Goux (1990: 110) has argued, the coherence and organic nature of this relation indicates that what is at work here is not a mere analogy, but rather a deep-seated isomorphism between the domains of money and language.

In the revolutionary year 1789, Friedrich Gedike, the editor of the *Berlinische Monatsschrift*, one of the leading organs of Enlightenment culture in Germany, published an article entitled "*Verba valent sicut numi*: or, On Verbal Coins." Gedike's primary purpose in writing this essay was the rehabilitation of the word "Enlightenment," which, according to his assessment, had taken on negative connotations over the course of its use and abuse (Gedike 1789: 260–61). But what makes Gedike's essay a revealing historical document is not so much his perceived need to salvage the concept of Enlightenment by delimiting its signification as the fact that to accomplish this he persistently relied on comparisons between monetary and linguistic economies. Indeed, Gedike's essay can be viewed as a kind of metaphorical treasury in which is stored a more or less complete inventory of the analogical connections between money and language that were current in German language theory during the final decades of the eighteenth century: as coins serve to ease material commerce, so do words facilitate intellectual commerce; as money condenses wealth into a more portable and useful form, so do words make knowledge more flexible and manageable; words have values, as do coins, but like the latter their face values are often inconsistent with their actual material worth; the meanings of words can shift with each usage, just as the value of coins can vary at different times of their circulation; much like the "clippers and pickers" (*Kipper und Wipper*) profit from conscious manipulations of the value of coins, linguistic counterfeiters lend the stamp of credibility to words of meager intrinsic worth in order to deceive their interlocutors; moreover, just as the seigniorage, the cost of minting, is deducted from the metal content of a coin, so that the metallic value even of legitimate currency never completely measures up to its face value, the meaning of words that have just been freshly coined can also never be established with total accuracy and precision; finally, just as there are wardens of the mint whose charge it is to guarantee the weight of the coinage and to draw light coins out of circulation, so there must be wardens of language who oversee the coining of phrases and police their usage (253–56). Clearly, Gedike sees himself as just such a warden over the mint of language, and he hopes that his essay will help his contemporaries distinguish between "true and false enlightenment" as between "true and false ducats" (270).

Gedike's essay bears testimony to the obsession of the late eighteenth century with exploring the isomorphism between the function and value of monetary currencies in the proto-capitalist economy and the function and value of words in the economy of linguistic truth. Gedike's inflated use of the money–language conceit is grounded in an awareness of its prevalence in the language theory of the eighteenth century. Indeed, this image is veritably omnipresent in theoretical discourses on language in this period. What is more, Gedike's essay is representative of the way in which eighteenth-century authors explored the richness of this metaphorical field, mining not only the mother lode, but also its many associative veins. Yet the depth to which this homology penetrated the thought of bourgeois intellectuals in this period is probably best demonstrated by the fact that the metaphorical exchange between the realms of economics and linguistics ran in both directions, so that just as monetary images were employed to describe the functioning of language, examples from the realm of language were used in economic treatises to elucidate the operation and essence of money. The French physiocrat A.R.J. Turgot remarked already in 1769 on the underlying systematic, formal affinities between money and language. "Money has in common with measures in general," he argued in the essay "Value and Money," "that it is a type of language, differing among different peoples and in everything that is arbitrary and conventional, but of which the forms are brought closer and made identical, in some respects, by their relation to a common term or standard" (Turgot [1769] 1969: 133). Language, like money, Turgot had already recognized, is governed by the logic of the general equivalent.[3] Similarly, the eighteenth-century German economist Johann Georg Büsch identified the semiotic nature of money and language as the basis of their inherent relationship. In his *Abhandlung von dem Geldumlauf* (*Treatise on the Circulation of Money*) of 1780 he noted: "We have languages as signs of concepts. We have money as signs of the value of things" (Büsch 1780: 1. 151). Thus, already for Büsch the monetary and linguistic economies appeared as systems whose operation depended on the circulation of signs. Indeed, as we will see, this semiotic affinity forms the principal *tertium comparationis* that underwrites the analogy between money and language for eighteenth-century thinkers.

Succumbing at this juncture to an urge for historical speculation, let me sketch briefly some of the sociological and intellectual-historical factors that help to account for this rampant appropriation and exploitation of the money–language conceit in eighteenth-century letters. It can scarcely go unnoticed, first of all, that this century was one of far-reaching economic and monetary change. As a counter to the increasing implementation of mercantilistic economic and monetary policies, the physiocratic doctrine emerged and became one of the most hotly debated issues of the day. Of primary importance in drawing general attention to the operation of monetary systems was certainly the infamous instability of the major European currencies during this period, due largely to the corrupt intervention of political authorities into the practices of coinage and currency (see Smith [1776] 1970: 131). No doubt the introduction of paper currencies in the form of bank notes was an event for many no less earth-shattering than the Lisbon earthquake of 1755, since it called into question the traditional definition of money as a commodity with intrinsic value. The effects of John Law's monetary reform in France between 1716 and 1720, which included the introduction of paper money, are well known and scarcely need mention.[4] Less well known are the manipulations of the value of the Prussian Thaler undertaken by Frederick the Great during the Seven Years' War in order to finance his war debt.[5] The result of these manipulations of the Prussian monetary system was a steep decline in the value of the Thaler, not only leading to widespread mistrust of this coin and of the state whose stamp guaranteed its value, but opening the door to general misgivings about the institution of money itself. Finally, due to the discovery of large quantities of silver and gold in the New World and their influx into Europe, the value of these metals underwent substantial fluctuations, and this, in turn, led to a radical destabilization of the value of gold and silver coins.[6] The upshot of these diverse events for the populace was an intense psychological uncertainty concerning matters of money and value, predicated on the unsettling recognition of the fundamentally abstract nature of money, a substance whose materiality had hitherto scarcely been called into question. What was beginning to make itself felt, in short, was the paradigm shift from a substantialist to a functionalist conception of money. Consistent with this transformation was the mercantilistic theory of monetary circulation, which played down money's significance as a commodity and began to see it as a mere expedient of commerce and exchange, an "oil which renders the motion of the wheels [of trade] more smooth and easy," in the words of David Hume (1854: 309).

Taking the other side of the coin, the eighteenth century was a time of intense deliberation on the origin, nature, and function of language. Central here is the emergence of the discipline of semiotics as fundamental to the science of knowledge, a proposition first advanced by Locke in his *Essay Concerning Human Understanding* (1689) and subsequently carried over into German philosophy by Johann Heinrich Lambert in his *Neues Organon* (1764), one of whose four parts dealt explicitly with the nature of signs and their role in the discovery of truth. As Ulrich Ricken (1985: 10–17) has argued, language theory of the eighteenth century was marked by a transition from the rationalist Cartesian paradigm to the sensualist, sign-oriented model advanced by Locke and Condillac. This shift was significant because it led to a reconceptualization of language, previously viewed as a mere communicative vehicle, which recognized in it a cognitive, creative, knowledge-producing medium. But the insight into the semiotic nature of language was both a boon and a bane for eighteenth-century philosophy: a boon because it made possible this knowledge-productive conception of an *ars characteristica* or an *ars combinatoria*, a calculative sign-language on the basis of whose manipulation previously unknown truths could be discovered;[7] a bane because, to quote John Locke, words "interpose themselves so much between our understandings, and the truth which it [*sic*] would contemplate and apprehend, that, like the medium through which visible objects pass, the obscurity and disorder do not seldom cast a mist before our eyes, and impose upon our understandings" ([1690] 1965: 274). The same was true for the eighteenth-century conception of money. In fact, one of the major economic debates of the eighteenth century turned on the semiotic character of money: whereas progressive economists such as Adam Smith had recognized that as pure sign, that is, in the form of paper currencies, money could function as a stimulator of trade and a catalyst to the increase of wealth (Smith [1776] 1970: 388–97, 420–24), more conservative economists like Turgot asserted that this "sign-money," as it was already called, was but a mere deceptive sleight of hand, an economic edifice built without a foundation (Turgot [1769] 1969: 4–5). This, then, is the most significant point of convergence between the eighteenth century's philosophy of language and its theory of money: both were conceived principally as semiotic intermediaries whose interposition in their respective domains of exchange had the potential to be either immensely productive or immeasurably destructive. Indeed, the recognition of the semiotic nature of words and money extended deep into the theories of each discipline. For just as the philosophers of the eighteenth century came to realize that words are signs twice removed – signs of concepts that in turn are signs of things – economists came to understand "sign-money," defined as any currency in which the symbolic value stamped upon it does not coincide absolutely with its real value as precious material,[8] explicitly as a sign of a sign, specie being understood as an immediate sign of value. In an essay published in Gedike's *Berlinische Monatsschrift* in 1796, the economist Moses Wessely can thus propose the following definition: "*Symbolic money*, the symbolic sign of a bill of exchange drawn on society (*paper money*), is only the representative of a representative" (1796: 308). This understanding of verbal expression and emergent "symbolic money" as second-order systems of signification is perhaps the fundamental homology that underpins the comparison of money and language in the eighteenth century.

Well before the French Revolution, German intellectuals were aware that they were living in a time of profound intellectual transformation. The economic and monetary revolutions of the eighteenth century, marked by the shift from a substantialist to a functionalist paradigm, were perhaps the most concrete, tangible forms in which these changes were experienced. In monetary theory this transformation expressed itself in the recognition that with the introduction of paper currency, two of the functions traditionally served by money as specie, to be a store of value as well as a medium of exchange, had been disassociated. Wessely (1796: 311) articulated this split by asserting that paper money only has value when used in exchange for something, that is, when being spent, whereas specie has value independent of its role in the circulation of goods. Wessely's attitude toward "symbolic money" was characteristically ambivalent: although he recognized its beneficial effects as a stimulant to circulation, useful especially during economic declines, he also attacked the "spirit of speculation" it introduced and warned that the use of paper money amounted to nothing other than the mortgaging of the energies of future generations in order to satisfy the needs of the present (308, 310).

It was a friend of Moses Wessely's, the dramatist, essayist, and aesthetician Gotthold Ephraim Lessing, who articulated this paradigm shift most poignantly, while simultaneously associating this transformation in the monetary realm with parallel changes in the spheres of thought and linguistic expression. In his late drama *Nathan der Weise* (*Nathan the Wise*, 1779), Lessing portrayed his protagonist facing the recognition that in the modern world two systems of understanding and expression, each of which articulates its own "truth," contest one another. In his audience with Sultan Saladin, the Jew Nathan is taken unawares when, expecting to be petitioned for a loan of money, he is asked instead to make a statement of absolute truth. Before responding with the famous parable of the three rings, Nathan deliberates on this request in a trenchant monologue:

> . . . I thought of money;
> And he wants – truth. Yes, truth! And wants it so –
> So bare and blank – as if the truth were coin! –
> And were it coin, which anciently was weighed! –
> That might be done! But coin from modern mints,
> Which but the stamp creates, which you but count
> Upon the counter – truth is not like that!
> As one puts money in his purse, just so
> One puts truth in his head? Who is the Jew here?
>
> (Lessing 1954–8: 2.402)

Challenged to a statement of truth in a situation with potentially menacing personal and political ramifications, Nathan recognizes that he must choose between two distinct forms of truth, the "ancient" and the "modern." The Sultan, who functions as the representative of the modernist paradigm, treats truth as though it were mere symbolic money, a token that could stand in to assist in counting up a debt. Thus the Jew Nathan, the usurer in economic matters, accuses Saladin of being a usurer in matters of truth and language, and he hence justifiably asks who the real "Jew" is. For Lessing's Nathan the conflict of truths can be reduced to an essential antithesis between contrary systems of value. In ancient times the currency used to measure value had its own inherent worth, established intrinsically by the preciousness of the material that represented it. In the modern age, by contrast, value becomes extrinsic and systematic; it no longer resides in the material through which it is expressed, but has become instead purely symbolic, lent currency by the arbitrary stamp imposed by political authority. Specie, as a manifestation of eternal, intrinsic value, stands in for ancient "truth" as the reconfirmation of the known. Michel Foucault (1970: 30) has described this mode of thought, which he associates with what he calls the Renaissance episteme, as a form of knowledge that "condemned itself to never knowing anything but the same thing." Over against this epistemic pattern, in Foucault's model, stands the Classical mode of thought. Its purpose is not, as in the Renaissance episteme, "to attempt to rediscover beneath [signs] the primitive text of a discourse sustained, and retained, forever," but rather "to discover the arbitrary language that will authorize the deployment of nature within its space, . . . to fabricate a language, and to fabricate it well – so that, as an instrument of analysis and combination, it will really be the language of calculation" (62–63). One of the intellectual constants in eighteenth-century language theory, as the passage from Lessing's *Nathan* makes clear, is the assumption of a homology, on the one hand, between specie as a manifestation of intrinsic value and "ancient" truth as the reiteration of the already known or believed, and, on the other hand, between symbolic money as a mere placeholder of absent value in the calculus of economic circulation and "modern" truth as a speculative form of knowledge that employs arbitrary signs to generate new "truths."

The disquiet about the incipient paradigm shifts in the economies of money, knowledge, and truth that were transpiring during the eighteenth century manifests itself in exemplary fashion, as the passage from Lessing's *Nathan* demonstrates, in analogies between money and language. This is especially true of eighteenth-century German language theory. In what follows I will concentrate on the use of money metaphors in reflections on language by four German thinkers: Gottfried Wilhelm Leibniz, Johann Kaspar Lavater, Johann Gottfried Herder, and Johann Georg Hamann. These textual examples serve not only to document the persistence of this homology between money and language in the language theory of the time, but also to help us assess how the historical shakedown occurring in the realm of monetary policy unconsciously influenced the way people thought about language. My hypothesis is that the move from a substantivist to a functionalist (or from what Ricken terms a Cartesian to a sensualist) conception of language cannot simply be understood as an intra-philosophical development, as historians of language and philosophers have generally tended to treat it, but that it was profoundly affected by a cross-fertilization with ideas that emerged in economics, particularly with regard to advances in monetary policy.

In paragraph five of his *Unvorgreifliche Gedanken, betreffend die Ausübung und Verbesserung der teutschen Sprache* (*Unpresuming Thoughts Concerning the Use and Improvement of the German Language*), first published in 1719, Leibniz attempts to elucidate the character of words as signs by enlisting an analogy to money. The specific metaphorical vehicle he selects, token money, gives evidence that the historical shift from a substantivist to a functionalist monetary system had begun to remap the metaphorical relationship between money and language already quite early in the eighteenth century:

> However, where the use of language is concerned, it is the case . . . that words are not only the signs of concepts, but also of things, and that we need signs not only to express our opinion to others, but even to assist our thoughts themselves. For just as in large trading centers,

> as in games and in other places, one does not always pay with money, but in its place makes use of notes or tokens until the final settlement of accounts or payment is made, so, too, reason makes use of the representations of things, especially when a great deal of thinking must be done, namely by replacing them with signs, so that it is not necessary repeatedly to call to mind the thing every time it occurs.
>
> (Leibniz [1719] 1966: 520)

Leibniz gives the money–language metaphor a peculiarly modern twist insofar as the traditional analogy between words and specie is replaced by the comparison between words and symbolic money. While the issuance of such paper notes, or bank notes, had its inception as early as 1407 at the bank of Genoa, these paper currencies were a relatively uncommon phenomenon in Germany at the time Leibniz published this treatise, and this fact underscores the radicality of Leibniz's modification of the traditional metaphor. But as the quotation makes apparent, this transmogrification is by no means wanton; indeed, it serves to elucidate some of the fundamental aspects of words when conceived explicitly as signs. It is important to note, first of all, that at about the same time as Locke, Leibniz too arrived at the conclusion that words are second-order signs insofar as they do not immediately signify things themselves, but rather represent our mental conceptions of these things. The comparison with bank notes as second-order signs of first-order monetary signs is eminently adequate to the illumination of this semiotic reduplication. Second, Leibniz stresses the centrality of verbal signs not only as mediators in the act of communicative exchange, but also in the very process of thought itself. Here, too, symbolic money supplies an appropriate analogy for the elucidation of this inter- and intra-active function, for this sign-money not only passes as currency in commercial exchange, but also serves as a token, a counter, by which people can take stock of their bank assets. Finally, Leibniz refers to the fundamental role signs play in the economy of thought and expression, a doctrine that was central to Enlightenment semiotics (Wellbery 1984: 229–30): signs perform an abbreviating function for reason, since they can be manipulated more easily and efficiently than either the things themselves or their concepts. It was precisely this argument of efficiency and increased productivity, of course, that was touted as one of the primary virtues of bank notes by their eighteenth-century advocates. The economist Johann Büsch, for example, refers to the ability of symbolic money to produce wealth and drive economic growth as the "magical power of money" (Büsch 1780: 1. 78). It is no coincidence that in his treatise on language, Leibniz uses a strikingly similar metaphor to elucidate the productivity of language when understood as a system of signs, calling it a "cabbala" (Leibniz [1719] 1966: 521).

Leibniz's exploitation of the conception of ersatz money as a means for concretizing the operation of signs in the economies of thought and language does not end here. In paragraph seven of this same treatise he turns to the images of the "counter" and the "promissory note" in order to explain how thought is made more efficient and productive by the implementation of signs:

> For this reason one often uses words as ciphers or as counters, in the place of representations and things, until one moves step by step to the final sum, and with the reasoned conclusion arrives at the thing itself. From this it becomes evident how important it is that words, as models and, as it were, the promissory notes of reason, be properly conceived, properly distinguished, adequate, abundant, free-flowing, and appropriate.
>
> (Ibid.: 521)[9]

This "art of signs," which Leibniz compares with algebra, forms the basis for the theory of productive – rather than merely re-productive – knowledge that represents one of the central accomplishments of Enlightenment epistemology. "[By means of this art of signs] we are able today," Leibniz maintains, "to discover things at which the ancients were not able to arrive; and yet the entire art consists in nothing but the use of properly employed signs" (ibid.). Leibniz's exploitation of metaphors from the realm of nascent capitalist economics thus helps him formulate and explain the theory of productive knowledge that is characteristic of the functionalist conception of language. Symbolic money, Leibniz realizes, as a sign of value that, stripped completely of its materiality, stimulates the circulation of commodities, is intimately related to an instrumental knowledge that deploys arbitrary signs for the purpose of calculation and discovery.

Leibniz goes to great pains to stress that this epistemological calculus depends on the adequacy of signs: they must be "properly conceived," "properly employed," "adequate," and "appropriate" if this mental magic is to arrive at truth. However, he is generally at a loss when it comes to defining precisely what makes any particular sign "proper," "adequate," or "appropriate." Clearly, the entire palette of metaphors he has exploited to explain these signs has emphasized nothing if not their ultimate arbitrarity, their role as conventionalized tokens that by definition have no intrinsic connection with the concepts or things they represent. Adequacy can no longer be defined in terms of the referentiality between signs and concepts, but can be gauged only by the efficient functioning of the epistemological equation: productivity becomes the sole measure of proper signs.

Leibniz himself could not accept this conclusion. Despite his consistent application of metaphors that would seem to indicate that he was a convinced nominalist, he turns out, in fact, to be a closet metallist, at least where his theory of language is concerned. For later in this same treatise, when he attempts to explain the referential connection between verbal signs and the concepts or things they signify, he explicitly asserts that "words do not evolve as arbitrarily or accidentally as many people believe" (536). He goes on to theorize that words originally evolved out of the imitation in sound of the concepts they signified. The German word *Welt* (world), Leibniz proposes, is etymologically related to the German words *Wirren*, *Wirbel*, and *Wogen* (whirl, whirlpool, wave), as well as to the English word "wheel", and he identifies the common phoneme "w" in these words with the gyrating motion each of them describes. In pronouncing this phoneme, he suggests, the articulatory organs imitate this circular movement (535–36). This hypothesis, which Hans Aarsleff (1982: 65) has dubbed the "affective theory of the sound–thing connection," obviously stands in egregious contradiction with the metaphors of the "note," the "counter," and the "promissory note" that Leibniz employs to explain the thought-economy and calculative productivity made possible by explicitly arbitrary linguistic signs.

For the moment I want simply to make a note of this contradiction in the critical balance-sheet, without yet calculating the bottom line. Before doing that it is necessary to determine whether this equivocation is unique to Leibniz, or if it is present in the works of other German writers, as well. Only once we have seen that it also occurs in modified form in Lavater's, Herder's, and Hamann's writings on language will we have accumulated enough evidentiary capital to risk a speculative historical conclusion.

It is perhaps not insignificant that Lavater, Herder, and Hamann have in common a coherent intellectual and spiritual background: all three of them were trained as Protestant preachers, inspired in part by the Pietist teachings so prevalent in the Protestant areas of the German-speaking world in the late eighteenth century. Given this background we would spontaneously expect them to argue for a substantivist theory of language as the non-mediated word of God, and, indeed, this is generally the case. But even when they make substantivist arguments about the nature of language as semiotic system, their rhetoric often betrays elements that run counter to this position. This is nowhere so true as when they turn to metaphors drawn from the realm of monetary practice to elucidate the operations of language.

In the 1770s Lavater achieved European fame – some might say, with some justification, European infamy – for his theory of physiognomics. The motivating impulse behind Lavater's physiognomical theories was a crusade against arbitrarity in all its forms, in particular against semiotic arbitrarity (see Gray 1991: 138–41). Physiognomics for Lavater was the worldly incarnation – literally – of a natural semiosis that closely approximated the cognitive immediacy he held to be the principal characteristic of divine consciousness. In his *Aussichten in die Ewigkeit* (Views on Eternity), a set of essays published between 1768 and 1778 in the form of a collection of letters, Lavater recorded the principles that informed his religious philosophy, and it was here that he first set down his belief in the language of physiognomy as an approximation of divine language. But what is especially curious about

Lavater's views is the manner in which they integrate central recognitions of Enlightenment epistemology with the transcendentalism of the religious fanatic. In the thirteenth letter of this collection, for example, Lavater gives a capsule summary of Enlightenment cognitive theory when he distinguishes "intuitive cognition" from "symbolic cognition" on the basis of the types of signs they employ:

> If an object has an immediate effect on our senses, the impression we are conscious of as a result of this effect is called *sensual*, *intuitive* cognition, *perception*, experience. If an object does not have an immediate effect but instead is represented to us by means of *arbitrary* signs, then our cognition is *nonsensual*, *logical*, *symbolic*.
>
> (Lavater 1768–78: 3. 2–3)

The crucial distinguishing feature between these two types of knowledge, according to Lavater, is their degree of mediacy or immediacy. Intuitive cognition requires either no mediation at all, or mediation by means of natural signs that are intrinsically related to the objects they signify. Symbolic cognition, by contrast, depends on the intervention of arbitrary signs. For Lavater, as for Enlightenment epistemology in general, the relationship between these types of cognition is conditioned by a specific telos: the aim of human cultural development is the progressive elimination of arbitrary signs, their elevation to the status of natural signs, so that ultimately symbolic, mediated knowledge would be completely replaced by intuitive, immediate knowledge (Wellbery 1984: 7). For Lavater this telos takes the form of a projection into the afterlife, where human cognition merges with the perfect cognition of the Christian divinity (Lavater 1768–78: 3. 21–22).

When in the sixteenth letter from this collection Lavater sets about distinguishing this heavenly language from worldly language, he draws on an analogy from the realm of economic exchange:

> We would have just as little need of money if we possessed everything we wish to possess; or if we could exchange thoughts for thoughts, sensations for sensations with just the same ease with which we exchange compendious money for voluminous things. Money is not wealth, it is only a sign of wealth; the sign loses all its value when the signified thing is available in large enough quantities. All words, signs of thoughts, seem to lose their value, and will presumably disappear, when we will become capable of communicating our thoughts *immediately* to one another.
>
> (Ibid.: 3. 104–5)

What interests me here is not Lavater's transcendentalist perspective, but the principles underlying his conception of money that allow it to serve as a metaphor for human language, understood as a counter-position to the pure, immediate language of heaven. Clearly, Lavater is working with a peculiarly modern conception of money as a purely symbolic mediator: money has no intrinsic value, is not specie, but has been reduced completely to a sign of value, to symbolic money. But what is especially curious – and especially telling – about Lavater's argument is his absolutization of symbolic money as money *per se*. He does not, as one might expect, juxtapose paper money and solid coin in order to distinguish between the artificial language of worldly existence and the genuine expression of the transcendental realm, but focuses instead on the notion of money in general as a medium of exchange. Money becomes the focal counter-example for an elucidation of divine language precisely because of its mediative nature, which Lavater obviously accepts as its primary function. The reduction of money to its role as mediator, of course, is one of the central principles of mercantilist economics, and Lavater's metaphor is capitalized by a rich investment from this economic philosophy. This metaphor, in fact, forms the locus of an ideological dialectic that invades Lavater's discourse. For in order to project the divine world as the transcendence of a worldly mediacy whose paradigmatic representatives are money and the arbitrary sign, Lavater must first acknowledge that these principles dominate economic and communicative exchange in the bourgeois world. In other words, Lavater already assumes an empirical reality whose economic and linguistic systems are so dependent on mediation, arbitrarity, and nominalism that the only world he can imagine free of these principles is the transcendent realm of divine immediacy.

If Lavater accepts the nominalism of the quotidian world only to overcome it ideologically in a substantialist vision of the transcendental, Herder's theory of language develops as an attempt baldly to deny that human language originates as a nominalist structure. In his *Abhandlung über den Ursprung der Sprache* (*Treatise on the Origin of Language*, 1772), Herder rejects the very conception of arbitrary signs, and he argues that all languages have as their source the same set of natural signs (500). He is especially emphatic in his repudiation of the idea that human language evolves by means of "arbitrary societal convention"; "primitive man, the recluse in the woods, would have had to invent language for himself. . . . It was the understanding of his soul with itself, an understanding that was just as necessary as it was necessary that the human being was a human being" (428). Language emerges, according to this theory, in a process of Adamic naming in which human beings stamp the "signature of the soul on a thing." Herder attempts to support this argument by appealing to an analogy with money: "And wouldn't for the first human being such a signature of the soul on a thing, by recognition, by characteristic feature, by language, not be just as much the mark of ownership as a stamp on a coin?" (486). Unfortunately, the metaphor Herder chooses is inconsistent with the substantialist theory he seeks to defend. What he apparently wants to say is that just as the stamp on a coin signifies the authenticity of its minting, the word, as a signature of the soul on a thing, is a brand that signifies ownership. But the stamp on a coin is not a sign of possession for those who use it, but only for the political authority that issues it, and it seems unlikely that Herder wanted to suggest such an authoritarian origin for language. Moreover, the stamp, as the mark of that political authority who stands behind the coin, serves merely to guarantee the weight and purity of the metal of which it is made. Thus, according to Adam Smith, the practice of affixing "a public stamp upon certain quantities of . . . metals" arose in order "to prevent . . . abuses, to facilitate exchanges, and thereby to encourage all sorts of industry and commerce" (Smith [1776] 1970: 129). Viewed from this perspective, the stamp on the coin is nothing if not the embodiment of convention: it is, quite literally, the coin's nominalist aspect. We recall that for Lessing's Nathan it is precisely coin "which but the stamp creates" that marks the paradigm shift from ancient, intrinsic money to the valueless symbolic currency of the modern world. What is noteworthy about Herder's metaphor, then, is that it actually undercuts the position he wants to defend. The fact that he turns to a money metaphor at all to buttress his conception of language's origin testifies to the fact that during this period the appeal to this metaphorical field was nothing if not obligatory for theoreticians of language. What Herder's metaphor betrays is that, even when he was still consciously attempting to support a substantivist view of language, he – like Leibniz and Lavater – had unconsciously come to accept the abstract, symbolic nature of a nominalist money "which but the stamp creates."

Herder explicitly acknowledges the conventionality of minted coins in the first collection of his fragments *Über die neuere deutsche Literatur* (*On Recent German Literature*, 1767). Here he also employs the comparison of words to coins, but this time instead of applying it positively to underwrite the inherent significance of words he uses it negatively to emphasize their abstract, arbitrary character: "Allow me to compare words that refer to abstract ideas [with coins]. Both are arbitrarily coined and become current by means of an arbitrarily established value; the most solid ones among both are hoarded as treasures, while the smaller ones are used to make change" (42). In this comparison, modern, abstract languages are likened to monetary economies in which value and significance are arbitrarily ordained and attain currency based solely on conventionalized usage. Some of these abstract words are "solid" coins whose nominal value closely approximates their inherent worth; others are inferior coins, token money, in which denomination and substance are greatly divergent. The concession that even abstract words can represent treasures worthy of hoarding stands apart from the otherwise austere critique of abstraction in language that Herder expresses both throughout this series of essays and in his *Abhandlung über den Ursprung der Sprache*. But what is especially significant is Herder's ability to exploit the comparison between money and language to defend both a traditional substantialist and a modern nominalist theory of language. That the nominalist interpretation of money and of language has already noticeably infiltrated Herder's thought is indicated by the fact that even when used to support a substantialist interpretation of language, the image of money he invokes is ineluctably, if subliminally, nominalist in character. Thus, while Herder is vociferous in his attack on the "spirit of commerce" whose increasing dominance in the bourgeois world he laments, and warns his contemporaries that this commercial spirit threatens to supplant the spirit of wisdom ([1769] 1967: 383, 410), his own theory of language is unwittingly informed and infected by this very spirit of commerce.

Although German bourgeois intellectuals of the eighteenth century apparently could not escape the contagion of capitalist commercialism, few confronted the realities of the emerging international market and its nominalist monetary economy as directly as did Johann Georg Hamann. To be sure, like Leibniz, Lavater, and Herder, Hamann also hypostatized an ideal mode of thought believed to exist beyond the abstraction of money and arbitrary signs. However, Hamann identified this realm of immediacy not as an originary, affective natural language, as did Leibniz and Herder, nor as divine cognition, as did Lavater, but rather as the domain of religious belief. In a letter to Friedrich Jacobi dated April 30, 1787, Hamann states apodictically: "Belief is not for everyone, and also not communicable like a commodity" (1955–79: 7. 176). In a bourgeois world increasingly dominated by the principle of exchange, belief becomes for Hamann the only mode of human thought that escapes the logic of commodification. To be free of this logic, however, is to be non-communicable in a double sense: neither transferable as a commodity, nor communicable through language, so that belief takes on – coherent with Pietistic views – a wholly personal and monadic character. Striking also is Hamann's anti-egalitarian posture: if the free market is the great democratizer that makes – in theory, at least – all things available to all people, then religious belief is the only value not subject to this marketability.

If Hamann can rescue belief from the abstraction of exchange only by denying that it is a language, then this bespeaks an acceptance of language as a fundamentally arbitrary system. And indeed, Hamann is one of the first German intellectuals to come to terms in a significant way with the arbitrarity of the linguistic sign. In his "Metakritik über den Purismus der Vernunft" ("Metacritique of the Purism of Reason," 1784), he admits that the meaning of words derives from the "connection of an *a priori* arbitrary and indifferent . . . verbal sign with the intuition of the object itself" (Hamann [1784] 1967: 226). At the same time, he cannot give himself over absolutely to this doctrine, so he restricts it with the qualification that the connection between verbal sign and object, although *a priori* arbitrary, is *a posteriori* necessary. Arbitrarity is thereby sublated into the pragmatic principle of the consistent and accurate use of any particular verbal sign. It is consistent with

Hamann's qualified acceptance of the arbitrary nature of the linguistic sign that the application of monetary metaphors in his discussions of language underscores language's functional, systematic aspects. In a passage from his *Sokratische Denkwürdigkeiten* (*Socratic Memoirs*, 1759), for example, Hamann stresses precisely the relativity and context-boundness of meaning: "Words have their value, like numbers, based on the place in which they stand, and the determination and relations of their concepts are, like coins, variable according to time and place" (Hamann [1759] 1972: 75). Of significance here is not only Hamann's historicizing thesis, which opens up linguistic signs to variable interpretation over time, but also his assertion that the meanings of words cannot be separated from the relationships they enter when used in certain contexts. Hamann obviously assumes that coins do not possess any absolute, intrinsic value, and he uses this understanding of money to deny that words have any specific *a priori* meanings. What makes Hamann's appropriation of the coin–word analogy so radical is the way it breaks with the traditional use of this analogy. For if the comparison of words and coins is generally employed to elucidate the referential function of language, Hamann's emphasis on the context-boundness of coins and words evokes its systematic, syntagmatic function. He thus reveals himself to be a proto-structuralist who anticipates the Saussurian insight that the value of verbal signs is determined by their relational structure with other signs.

The metaphor with which Hamann opens his essay "Vermischte Anmerkungen über die Wortstellung in der französischen Sprache" ("Mixed Remarks on Word Order in the French Language," 1761) likewise relies on an analogy between money and language that highlights their structural and systematic isomorphism:

> Money and language are two objects whose examination is as profound and abstract as their use is universal. Both stand in a closer relationship than one would otherwise suppose. The theory of one explains the theory of the other; for this reason, they appear to derive from common grounds. The richness of all human knowledge is based on the exchange of words. . . . All the goods . . . of commercial and social life relate to money as their general measure.
>
> (Hamann [1761] 1967: 97)

Hamann appears in this passage as a precursor of Karl Marx insofar as he not only acknowledges money as the general equivalent in bourgeois commerce, but also recognizes that in the capitalist market society all human interactions are mediated by money as the absolute measure of all things (see Marx 1977: 562–67). The same insight that underwrites Marx's critique of money as the embodiment of human alienation informs Hamann's variation on the comparison of words and coins: this is the awareness that money concretizes a basic form of representation and symbolization that extends into myriad realms of human intersubjective conduct. Hamann's metaphors indicate that he perceives the intimate interrelationship between the linguistic and financial domains as structured systems. The common element that determines their isomorphism is their character as processes of exchange based on the circulation of arbitrary signs. With this we return to the proto-capitalist theory of symbolic money's productive power that also informed Leibniz's use of the money–language metaphor.

We are justified, I believe, in taking Hamann's statement about the close relationship between money and language at face value: to eighteenth-century philosophers of language economic theory appeared to be intimately related to the theory of language. But what the examples from Leibniz, Lavater, Herder, and Hamann demonstrate is an incipient equivocation and transformation in the conception of the money–language analogy. If this metaphor traditionally endorsed a substantivist theory of referential meaning by comparing truthful words with full-weight coins whose constant value is guaranteed by their intrinsic worth, in the eighteenth century this variation of the metaphor is increasingly supplanted by one that underscores the nominalist view that the truth of words, like the value of symbolic money, is established extrinsically and syntagmatically by their systematic function in the circulation of language. This has far-reaching implications especially where eighteenth-century semiotics is concerned; for if semiotic thought of this period is constantly rent by an ambivalence toward the arbitrarity of linguistic signs, which it views simultaneously as the instrument of productive thinking and the source of delusion and error (Wellbery 1984: 5), then this conflicted assessment reflects the eighteenth century's ambivalence toward token money as the arbitrary representation of economic value, as well. The fact that the four thinkers discussed here attempt to hold on to a substantialist view of linguistic truth while simultaneously employing monetary metaphors that tend rather to valorize the functionalist, nominalist conception of linguistic signs, betrays the degree to which they were ultimately attracted by the possibilities of a semiotic system that, like the token money of emergent capitalist theory, would be capable of producing and increasing knowledge based simply on the deployment of well-made signs. Leibniz, Lavater, and Herder, at least, were linguistic and epistemological "metallists" who nonetheless unconsciously transferred the virtues of paper currency to their theories of language and knowledge. They accepted the abstract, arbitrary nature of money before accepting the nominalist, conventional, and systematic interpretation of language. However, they unwittingly read the abstract character of money into their theories of language by way of their use of money metaphors. Hamann is the first openly to embrace this modern, structuralist conception of language and apply metaphors of money that are coherent with this view. What we witness in the intellectual trajectory from Leibniz to Hamann, then, is the gradual jettisoning of substantivist conceptions of language through the analogy with an increasingly functionalist monetary system. This is a process by which these bourgeois intellectuals literally buy into signs. Experiencing in the concrete economic realm of capitalistic monetary practice the productive potential of "properly employed signs," they begin to accept a vision of language as an artificial construct, a relational system of arbitrary tokens with the potential vastly to increase the stores of human knowledge. The vision they share, to a greater or lesser degree, is a conception of language as a money of the mind, and they imagine themselves becoming the *nouveaux-riches* of bourgeois thought.

Notes

1 All translations from the German are my own.
2 On the temporal extension and cultural breadth of the metaphorical field money–language, see Weinrich 1958: 511–14.
3 For Goux the homology between language and money is structured principally around the reference to a general equivalent (see the essay "Numismatics: an Essay in Theoretical Numismatics," in Goux 1990: 9–63).
4 For a detailed account of the Law reforms and their consequences, see Gaettens (1955: 100–26), and Minton (1975).
5 For an eighteenth-century reaction to the Prussian monetary crisis, see Barkhausen (1776: 537 and 551). Gaettens (1955: 147–72) gives an historical overview of the problems the Prussian mint faced at this time.
6 See Smith ([1776] 1970: 135), and also Streuensee (1789: 227).
7 On this knowledge-productive aspect of signs, see Leibniz, (1960: 90–92).
8 On the definition of sign-money in eighteenth-century economic theory, see, for example, Streuensee (1789: 244–47).
9 Significantly, this comparison of verbal signs to debt-counters is not unique to Leibniz. The same image is employed by Locke, who identifies the misuse of words with the "misplacing of counters in the casting up a debt" (Locke [1690] 1965: 278).

References

Aarsleff, Hans (1982). *From Locke to Saussure: Essays on the Study of Language and Intellectual History*. Minneapolis: University of Minnesota Press.
Barkhausen, Heinrich Ludwig (1776). "Über den 20. und 24. Geldfuß." *Deutsches Museum* 1: 535–52, 575–93.
Büsch, Johann Georg (1780). *Abhandlung von dem Geldumlauf in anhaltender Rücksicht auf die Staatswirtschaft und Handlung*, 2 vols. Hamburg & Kiel: Carl Ernst Bohn.
Foucault, Michel (1970). *The Order of Things: An Archaeology of the Human Sciences*. New York: Vintage-Random House.
Gaettens, Richard (1955). *Inflationen: Das Drama der Geldentwertungen vom Altertum bis zur Gegenwart*. Munich: Richard Pflaum.
Gedicke, Friedrich (1789). "Verba valent sicut numi; oder von der Wortmünze." *Berlinische Monatsschrift* 20: 253–75.
Goux, Jean-Joseph (1990). *Symbolic Economies: After Marx and Freud*. Trans. Jennifer Curtiss Gage. Ithaca, NY: Cornell University Press.

Gray, Richard T. (1991). "The Transcendence of the Body in the Transparency of its En-Signment: Johann Kaspar Lavater's Physiognomical 'Surface Hermeneutics' and the Ideological (Con-)Text of Bourgeois Modernism." *Lessing Yearbook* 23: 127–48.

Hamann, Johann Georg ([1759] 1972). *Sokratische Denkwürdigkeiten. Sturm und Drang: Kritische Schriften.* Ed. Erich Loewenthal, 3rd edn. Heidelberg: Lambert Schneider, 63–84.

—— ([1761] 1967). "Vermischte Anmerkungen über die Wortstellung in der französischen Sprache." In *Schriften zur Sprache.* Ed. Josef Simon. Frankfurt/Main: Suhrkamp, 95–104.

—— ([1784] 1967). "Metakritik über den Purismus der Vernunft." In *Schriften zur Sprache.* Ed. Josef Simon. Frankfurt: Suhrkamp, 219–27.

—— (1955–79). *Briefwechsel.* Ed. Walther Ziesemer and Arthur Henkel, 7 vols. Wiesbaden: Insel.

Herder, Johann Gottfried ([1767] 1985). *Über die neuere deutsche Literatur: Fragmente.* Ed. Regine Otto. Berlin: Aufbau.

—— ([1769] 1967). *Journal meiner Reise im Jahr 1769. Sämtliche Werke.* Ed. Bernhard Suphan, 1877–93. Vol. 4. Hildesheim: Olms, 343–461.

—— ([1772] 1972). *Abhandlung über den Ursprung der Sprache. Sturm und Drang: Kritische Schriften.* Ed. Erich Loewenthal. 3rd edn. Heidelberg: Lambert Schneider, 399–506.

Hume, David (1854). "Of Money." In *The Philosophical Works.* Vol. 3. Boston, MA: Little, Brown, 309–23.

Lambert, Johann Heinrich ([1764] 1965). *Neues Organon oder Gedanken über die Erforschung und Beziehung des Wahren und dessen Unterscheidung vom Irrthum und Schein*, 4 vols. Hildesheim: Olms.

Lavater, Johann Kaspar (1768–78). *Aussichten in die Ewigkeit*, 4 vols. Zurich: Orell, Geßner.

Leibniz, Gottfried Wilhelm (1960). *Fragmente zur Logik.* Ed. and trans. Franz Schmidt. Berlin: Akademie Verlag.

—— ([1719] 1966). *Unvorgreifliche Gedanken, betreffend die Ausübung und Verbesserung der teutschen Sprache. Hauptschriften zur Grundlegung der Philosophie.* Ed. Ernst Cassirer. Vol. 2. Hamburg: Meiner, 519–55.

Lessing, Gotthold Ephraim (1954–8). *Nathan der Weise.* In *Gesammelte Werke.* Ed. Paul Rilla, 10 vols. Berlin: Aufbau, Vol. 2: 319–481.

Locke, John ([1690] 1965). *An Essay Concerning Human Understanding.* Ed. Maurice Cranston. London: Collier.

Marx, Karl (1977). "Ökonomisch-philosophische Manuskripte aus dem Jahr 1844." In *Marx–Engels Werkausgabe.* Ergänzungsband, Teil 1. Berlin: Dietz, 465–588.

Minton, Robert (1975). *John Law: The Father of Paper Money.* New York: Association Press.

Nietzsche, Friedrich (1988). "Über Wahrheit und Lüge im außermoralischen Sinn." In *Sämtliche Werke: Kritische Studienausgabe*, 15 vols. Ed. Giorgio Colli and Mazzino Montinari. Munich: Deutscher Taschenbuch Verlag, Vol. 1: 871–90.

Ovid (1979). *Ars Amatoria.* Ed. and trans. John Henry Mozley. 2nd edn. Cambridge, MA: Harvard University Press.

Quintilian (1921–2). *Institutio Oratoria.* Ed. and trans. Harold Edgeworth, 4 vols. New York: Putnam.

Ricken, Ulrich (1985). *Probleme des Zeichens und der Kommunikation in der Wissenschafts-und Ideologiegeschichte der Aufklärung*. Berlin: Akademie-Verlag.

Saussure, Ferdinand de (1966). *Course in General Linguistics*. Ed. Charles Bally and Albert Sechehaye. Trans. Wade Baskin. New York: McGraw-Hill.

Simmel, Georg ([1907] 1984). *Philosophie des Geldes*. 2nd edn. Ed. David P. Frisby and Klaus Christian Köhnke. Frankfurt: Suhrkamp.

Smith, Adam ([1776] 1970). *The Wealth of Nations*. Ed. Andrew Skinner. Harmondsworth: Penguin.

[Streuensee, Karl August von] (1789). "Ueber Rechnungsmünze, Geld und wirkliche Münze." *Berlinische Monatsschrift* 20: 220–52

Turgot, A.R.J. ([1769] 1969). *The Economics of A.R.J. Turgot*. Ed. and trans. P.D. Groenewegen. The Hague: Nijhoff.

Weinrich, Harald (1958). "Münze und Wort: Untersuchungen an einem Bildfeld." In *Romanica: Festschrift für Gerhard Rohlfs*. Halle: VEB Max Niemeyer Verlag, 508–21.

Wellbery, David (1984). *Lessing's* Laokoön: *Semiotics and Aesthetics in the Age of Reason*. Cambridge: Cambridge University Press.

Wessely, Moses (1796). "Geld und Zirkulazion." *Berlinische Monatsschrift* 27: 301–12.

5

CASH, CHECK, OR CHARGE?

Jean-Joseph Goux

Trans. John R. Barberet[1]

When the consumer whose shopping cart is overflowing stops at the cashier in an American supermarket, an all but ritual question is posed in a tone at once vacant and threatening: "CASH, CHECK, OR CHARGE?" The cashier, of course, wants to know by which of these three methods of payment the customer wishes to pay for his purchases: in banknotes, with a check, or with a credit card? The significance of this daily commercial ritual lies in the fact that the customer is confronted with a stereotypical question that repeats faithfully, in the sequence of possible means of payment, the historical order of different forms of monetary usage, from oldest to newest.

Payment by cash (from the French *caisse*) remains faithful to the well-established practice of the bank note. Payment by check prolongs the English innovation that still stunned Jevons in the 1870s and only became generalized in retail commerce much later. Finally, payment by charge, the latest and still-evolving mode of payment, appeared in the 1950s and initiated the electronization of monetary transactions, inaugurating the monetic era.

Thus, several historically datable means of acquitting oneself of a debt persist in combination without, for the moment, excluding one another. Each buyer enters by his own choice into a system of operations which situates him in a different order of exchange. At one end of this historical sequence there still persists, perhaps, the recollection of – or at least the structural necessity for – the precious metal which that bank note, until recently convertible into gold, was supposed to represent in everyday circulation. At the other end, that of "settlement by writing" (ledger entries) and mechanographical operations, literal monetary signs are nowhere to be found, but only "transfer orders." Bits of information are recorded.

"Cash, check, or charge?": three modes of payment, three monetary systems, each of which situates the buyer in a different relation to "money," offering a daily choice between different symbologies of value. Exactly what these differences involve is undoubtedly beyond the scope of the person who responds, for various, often contingent reasons, to the mechanical question of the cashier. And yet, doesn't this trifling question reveal an entire social semiotic, an entire mode of symbolizing, implying not only a certain status of the sign and of value, but more implicitly a certain structural relationship to the law, to the state, to the private and the public, to representation, to reality, to materiality and ideality? Does it not imply and perform, in each of its practices, the coherent mode of a social institution, with its implicit philosophy and its pre-reflexive postulates?

The fact that our century has experienced what has come to be called the dematerialization of money, leading to a radically nominalist conception of the monetary instrument and culminating in inconvertibility and floating exchange rates, and that this same century is also marked by an unprecedented rupture in the mode of representation as well as by a deepening concern with the nature of the sign and the philosophical status of language, is certainly not a simple coincidence. In monetary practice, an unprecedented order of signs and values is taking form, tracing and accompanying in its own way the questioning of assumptions and the dislocations that contemporary thought has tried to conceptualize. The collapse of referents, the dissolution of exchange standards, the dissociation of the sign from what it signifies, the evacuation of all "presence" or of any "treasure" regulating the play of signifiers, the indefinite deferral of meaning in the pure operations of writing: it is to this extreme crisis of language in the broadest sense that the new monetary nominalism corresponds – by a contagion or a parallelism that we should not rush to simplify.

Accompanying the historical disappearance of gold-money, which reigned during the last century, is the unraveling of a moment of privileged conjunction, within the same body, of the three functions of the monetary object, which were not always unified and which, today, are no longer unified. At once the *ideal* measure of value, the *symbolic* instrument of exchange, and the *real* means of reserve, gold-money brought together the functions of *archetype*, of *token*, and of *treasure* into a single object.[2] Customarily money was considered the historical braiding of these three functions. Yet money in this sense no longer exists. The braid has come unwoven. There is no longer a body that is elevated into a standard for values while still circulating in the daily market and remaining capable of being hoarded as a guarantee of stable value. The three functions have come asunder. The inconvertible signifier that circulates today, that floats, that always postpones its "realization," guarantees the monetary function in the realm of pure symbolicity, but only by mourning the loss of the unlocatable (or floating) standard and the uncertain reserve value, secured by nothing.

And what if this mutation of the sign and this mourning of representation were only the prelude to a still unknown ascendancy: the total bankerization of existence, by the combined powers of finance and computers?

Let us consider for a moment the one-dollar "greenback." Clearly this bank note was conceived in such a way that an emblematic power emanates from it and transforms it into a potent political symbol. It is a civil monument that, though made of paper, is nonetheless ceremoniously laden with all the insignia of the state's officialdom. There is something solemn in this rigorous symmetry of the layout, in this concentrated arrangement of all the great symbols of the nation. On one side, in the center there is the portrait of a founding father, the first president, Washington, flanked on either side by the seals of the United States Treasurer and of the Secretary of the Treasury. On the other side, to the right and to the left of the central motto *In God We Trust*, there are two circles wherein the "Great Seal of the United States" is inscribed: a truncated pyramid with a triangular eye rising above it, accompanied by the Latin mottoes *Annuit coeptis* and *Novus ordo seclorum*; and on the right-hand side, the eagle carrying in its claws the symbols of peace and of war (the olive branch and the bundle of arrows), holding in its beak another Latin motto, *E pluribus unum*. We could go into further detail, but these elements already speak for themselves in their conjunction on the same rectangle of paper, where there appears in small capitals the annotation indicating the

Plate 5.1 US dollar bill

universality of this means of payment: "This note is legal tender for all debts, public and private."

On this bill, the simple functionalism of the bank sign has not yet abolished the richness of the civil symbols; or rather, this emblematic proliferation is still necessary to uphold the function of the sign. The State (and its Treasury), God (and our faith in Him), the Father (founder), the dead and sacralized Language (Latin): all these powerful, central[3] signifiers converge, combine, and intensify each other so as to provide the bank note with its force. It is the State in all of its foundational stability that guarantees the value of the bill, under the authority of the Treasury. By design, despite the fact that the convertibility of the dollar into gold has been *de facto* suspended for over a decade, the American bill, through the almost Roman austerity that characterizes its engraving, remains strongly marked by the emblems of civil religion: that is, by the imaginary realm of guaranteed value and fixed standards. The value of the bill still refers to a certain depth, a certain verticality. Somewhere, a treasure is present, a reserve, a fund, upon which this bill is staked. There exists an underlying, protected value, which the State holds, preserves, and guarantees by its institution, and which this bill represents (Plate 5.1).

But if the bank note solemnly offers itself as a political symbol marked by the regulating and founding role of statist mediation, within a civil space governed by the mechanism of representation, does not the practice of payment by check refer to a very different configuration, one that is superimposed on the previous one rather than following or abruptly displacing it? And can we not see, in the generalization of the check, the indicator (as well as the operator) of another means of signifying, a different conjoining of politics, representation, sign, and subject?

What is most striking about the check, by comparison with the bank note, is the movement from a purely public and political realm of personalization (the signature of the treasurers of the State) to a private realm of personalization, which engages identities in a wholly different way. Whereas the bank note mediates a relationship in which buyer and seller remain anonymous, as if all of the responsibility and the insurance of coverage were delegated to a third party, i.e., the State, a transaction by check is a tripartite operation, wherein each party is identified by a proper name: the banker, the bearer, the beneficiary. The invisible reserve that serves as funds for the transaction is no longer the public Treasury, but the assets belonging to a private individual holding an account in a private bank. Strictly speaking, a check is not money, which is exchanged anonymously and exhausts its function of contracting out a debt in the reciprocity of a *quid pro quo*; instead, it is a "transfer order" given by a clearly named bearer, to be processed by a particular bank, and payable to a particular person, no less clearly named. In the case of scriptural money, or rather settlement by writing, one enters therefore into another semiotic or praxiologic space, where the marks are not so much signs of value (as they are in a realm of representation where materialized values are still visible on the horizon as a referential guarantee) as they are signs of operations upon values, such that the signs in themselves are not endowed with a meaning or a value subject to direct appropriation, but are launched into an indefinite play of deferral, of referral (traces of operations upon traces), without involving any direct exchange, or even the designation, of a materialized value ("treasure").

Bank assets have become the inscription of a credit that, in turn, is referred back into an indefinite system of inscribed credits. Everything happens as if "scriptural money" involved a process of substitution that is no longer directly backed up by materialized value. The status of the sign in the *banking* realm could thus be opposed to its status in the *market* realm, wherein the material presence of a commodity (including commodity-money) guarantees the correlation between representation and equivalence.

The banker's reserves are a depository. But this depository is constituted of funds that are in turn credits. The "treasury" of a bank (according to an increasingly obsolete expression whose proper signification will soon be forgotten) is nothing more than signs of operations upon credits. The assets are scriptural. Everything happens as if the judicial personalization of the operation were intended to compensate for the dematerialization of money, within legal constraints.

It could rightly be asked if the profound rupture in semiotic (Peirce), linguistic (Saussure), or aesthetic (cubism, abstract art) conceptions at the end of the last century and the beginning of this one – all of which involve an attempt to found meaning on the reciprocal and differential relation between a signifier and another signifier, in an indefinite play of deferrals and referrals, instead of on the direct relationship between a sign and the thing it signifies or represents – is indeed perfectly congruent with this socio-symbolic transformation of the monetary status of the sign.

We all know how Saussure sought to rethink the nature of the linguistic sign by attempting to break with the "simplistic" conception of language-as-nomenclature in favor of a conception of language-as-system. Far from establishing a rigid and isolable relationship among a word, an idea, and a thing, language is a system of differential values, i.e., of pure values determined by nothing outside of the momentary arrest of its terms. The passage from language-as-nomenclature (where a word is worth the signified thing) to language-as-system (where it is the relation of words among themselves that determines value) certainly evokes the passage from a representative money to a scriptural money in a system where the speculative and banking axis of currency exchange and financial operations is more important than the axis of commercial exchange (where money stands in for the commodity, and vice versa). It is indeed remarkable that the Saussurian break in linguistics invokes in its favor a monetary conception that presupposes the privileged and almost monopolistic status of the axis of currency exchange (where money is exchanged for other money) over the axis of commercial exchange (where money is exchanged for a commodity). Saussure conceptualizes value in linguistics according to an economic model of value borrowed directly from monetary nominalism.

This paradigm shift in the conception of the sign is all the more remarkable in that it is contemporaneous with the new monetary conceptions of Knapp (who in 1905 extended to an unprecedented degree the concept of the "decided" and purely nominal value of the monetary sign issued by the State) and of Hilferding, who, in *Daz Finanz Kapital* (published in 1910, the same year Kandinsky produced the first abstract painting), advanced for the first time the theory of the domination of financial capital over industrial and commercial capital in the new stage of capitalism.

Wittgenstein's research also participated in the same paradigm shift. By moving the focus of philosophy toward language games, he problematized right from the outset the simplistic notion of the referent expressed in the Augustinian postulate that "the individual words in language name objects" (Wittgenstein 1958: 2).[4] And once again, as we might have expected, the monetary metaphor is not absent, in rigorous conformity to the economic axiology that permeates the subtext. When he wants to critique, and even mock, the belief in a meaning different from the word itself, Wittgenstein writes: "You say: the point isn't the word, but its meaning, and you think of the meaning as a thing of the same kind as the word, though also different from the word. *Here is the word, there the meaning. The money, and the cow that you can buy with it* (ibid.: 49; emphasis added). Thus, Wittgenstein is ridiculing a conception of language patterned on the commercial mode, according to which a word refers to the signified thing that is its equivalent, just as money refers to the commodity (in the village market, where the peasants buy or sell cows).

It seems, then, that the most powerful theories of the sign, which call into question the Aristotelian and Stoic triad (signifier, signified, referent) and which Derrida has been pursuing in his deconstructive grammatology – where these theories find their most acute philosophical radicalization – correspond to the overthrow of the status of the sign inaugurated by the practices of monetary nominalism, along with those of scriptural money and the inconvertible bank note. We should avoid interpreting the causality of this correspondence too hastily, since there is no simple way of accounting for it, and it poses considerable problems. Yet it is remarkable that the loss of any material referent (treasure) or of any ideal measure of value (standard) in today's monetary system is analogous to the attempt on the part of grammatology to re-conceptualize the status of the sign by opposing it to the metaphysics of the transcendental signified. A shared dynamic transforms all money into a form of writing (and no longer into a value-sign of the exchange, or even less into a "thing" possessing value) in the indefinite mobility of displacements and referrals where all we encounter are traces leading to other traces, such that the clearing of all accounts would never be possible or even thinkable. In both the monetary and grammatological realm, we no longer find a full-fledged (as in gold-money), certain guarantee of stable meaning (value) being circulated, but rather writings about writings with no assignable term or end: an indefinite play of referrals that forever postpones the possibility of an actual value that would not be anything but more writing.

Such a grammatology of banking – wherein money, in the classical sense, has disappeared to make room for the system of "settlement by writing" (along with the entire system of credit and the system of deferment to which credit is tied, and therefore with the disappearance of the "present" as central temporal reference) – can only disrupt our most tenacious philosophical categories. Money, that Greek invention, has been linked to the birth of philosophy: to wit, the ternary structure of Aristotle's and the Stoics' semiotics. The end of this type of money (and of this mode of signifying, which was rediscovered and carried to its apogee in the last century) can only correspond to a weakening of such a metaphysics.

If writing, in the narrow sense, has slowly detached itself from the original conditions in which words are exchanged by living speakers present to one another, scriptural money has become detached from the concrete conditions of commercial exchange, pursuing the internal logic of the autonomization of the signifier, a logic most visible in banking and brokerage systems. As an artificial procedure that separates the individual living speaker from her- or himself, writing actualizes from the beginning all of the ambiguities inherent in this technique: the management of scriptural money becomes the most critical point of conjunction between the economy and the techniques of the signifier. The history of writing and the history of money converge spectacularly in monetary technology.

Plastic money, or payment by *charge* (with a bank card or credit card) inaugurates an additional rupture. By freeing us from the personal labor of writing by hand, the card opens the way to all the ulterior possibilities of the automatization of operations. By borrowing from the arrangement of checking practices already in place (a bank, a bearer, a beneficiary), the card multiplies the power of the automatized communication of banking information. It permits direct access on automatic tellers without the intervention of a human agency. It is the owner of the card who, in dialogue with the machine, performs some of the transactions previously performed by bank personnel. The purely informational essence of money is becoming more and more apparent. This time, nothing is physically "exchanged": signals alone are emitted and recorded.

The so-called "smart card," which is replacing the first generation of plastic money, represents an important and rapid development in this process of automatization, where the operation upon transfer orders is further and further removed from human labor. In this case, the card not only contains the rather simple possibility of code-activating the processing operations of the automatic teller, but furthermore, thanks to the microchip embedded in the thickness of its plastic substance, performs all by itself some of the operations of memorization and processing once performed by the bank. Everything happens as if the "smart card" (in a manner unrelated to the old bank note) had *internalized* the practices of banking operations, synthesizing in its microchip memory the traces out of which scriptural money was made, and permitting the self-processing of these traces in dialogic interface with the banking system.

Because processing power and memory capacity have been internalized in the card itself, the opposition between the immobilized, stable sign and the operation performed upon the sign has been overcome, and the card-holding subject is now the individual bearer of a disseminated component of banking competence. The banking card is no longer scriptural money, but rather an operative power in banking communication: just as if a book, instead of being an immutable, printed entity that "must be read," had acquired the capacity to enter into relations with other books so as to write itself differently. One may wonder if it isn't the very notion of writing itself as a "lasting" and "dead" trace (traditionally opposed to living speech) that has in turn been subverted. Speech no longer reveals itself structurally as a form of writing, but writing itself has become, strangely, a form of "speech," if the very idea of speech involves the unforeseeable, active production of new constellations of meaning in the communicative nexus.

Although it is still hard to say which kind of subjectivity, which ontological status of the "sign," corresponds to the smart card, it is nevertheless already possible to grasp how what we have called the "operative subject" (to distinguish it from the "perspective subject")[5] becomes remarkably manifest in this type of transaction.

For that matter, the purely informational essence of money is revealed in this decisive step, such that the strategic interest in disengaging the close structural homology between money and language appears here in its most restrictive historical necessity: money *is* "language," information, writing. We are no longer dealing here with a homology but (in a word) with an identity. What previously lay concealed behind metallic monetary circulation, the archaic and almost incredible "commodity-money," becomes obvious in the generalization of scriptural money and, even more so, of micro-calculating money that self-remembers and self-performs.

Such is pure language, the autonomized signifier: on the condition that we add that these traces always refer back to a juridical identity, that of the proprietary agents, who are saddled with the juridical constraints (ultimately violent) of debt. The trace is regulated and drawn into the movement of the deferred by the increasingly complicated, deviated, and derived circulation of a debt never paid off. A juridical force is therefore joined to an ethical value: the inherent promise of credit as well as of debit. The banking system is the active recording, the permanent scriptural management of an immense intertwined movement of promises made between juridical subjects. It includes therefore, according to the very structure of the deferred, the time factor – and precisely the future – as its constitutive, obligatory orientation. A society dominated by banking activity, and thus by credit, makes use of time and expectation, makes use of the future (as if all of its activities were totalized and accounted for in a time ahead of its own) by furnishing itself with an advance on itself in a gesture of expectation and reckoning.

Whereas gold, dear to Balzac's bourgeois, and the bank note itself (which is at the beginning still a "sign of gold") can be considered the emblem of market society and of the central and sacred role of the State (which monopolizes the coining of money), scriptural and subsequently electronic money are the hallmarks of a very different society, marked by the increasingly generalized appropriation of monetary services by banking networks and by the increasing "bankerization" of life, itself an effect of the dizzying linkages between finance and computer technology.

We have come a long way from Old Man Grandet and his well-hidden stash of gold coins which, as his neighbors in Saumur believed, provided him every night with "ineffable pleasures." Accelerated bankerization has produced and continues to manufacture an entirely different imaginary. In order to seduce and convince, money appears therein tied to a nomadic and exotic sensibility that has nothing in common with quivering confinement and fanatical accumulation. Money is no longer about "economy" in the sense of thrift and saving.

Let us open, for the sake of entertainment, some weekly magazine. A full-page advertisement calls out to us:

> Whether you need rupees for a rug in Kashmir, or dollars for an emergency in Seattle, there are over 200,000 places worldwide where your Visa card means cash. The Visa symbol means you have instant access to dollars or drachmas, cruzados or pesos at over 190,000 banks in the U.S. and abroad. . . . [The Visa symbol] means easy access to cash in any language.
>
> (Plate 5.2)

The text of this advertisement is highly revelatory of the axis orienting the banking imaginary. It expresses a perfectly "Saussurian" conception of the monetary sign. The purchase price of the rug (money exchanged for the commodity) is less important than the very possibility of ubiquitous and perpetual currency conversion. If value in economics can be expressed along two axes: (1) the exchange of a thing (money) for a dissimilar thing (bread), and (2) the conversion of similar things into more similar things (money for money), then it is this second axis or this second value that is privileged (just as Saussure privileges homologically the linguistic sign) in banking activity. This activity bases the omnipotence of universal equivalence upon such a status of value. The universality of equivalence does not arise here out of

Plate 5.2 Visa advertisement. © 1987, VISA USA Inc. All rights reserved

commerce, but through banking protocols according to which a currency conversion (a transferral) is always and everywhere possible, and which holds entirely under its sway the possibility of the purchase or the second order of equivalence, in conformity with the money–commodity axis.

This imaginary, wherein cash would necessarily be mediated by a card capable of converting your money into foreign currency, perfectly expresses the domination of financial capital over commercial transactions, as well as the privileging (which goes to the foundations of structuralism) of the axis of convertibility over the axis of exchangeability in the determination of value. At the level of signs, this imaginary corresponds to the de-emphasis of the referent (the thing itself in its tangible presentness) in favor of pure value.

But let us beware: this monetary polyglotism that allows one to feel at home throughout the world, thanks to the possession of a universal instrument of conversion, is not granted to just anyone. It is a privilege: "You are assured of a privileged place in the greatest network in the world," says the ad for Premier Visa; "You are a member, not a number," says an American flyer for American Express. This privilege separates you from the rest. Your relationship to monetary signs, despite their abstraction and universality, is just as personalized, you are invited to believe, as the relationship between a composer and the music he creates. You are a conductor for whom music, that universal language, constantly requires a renewed personal interpretation. This paradoxical conjunction between an imaginary realm of personalization (which must convince you that the bank has chosen you) and an imaginary realm of the most abstract universality is realized and expressed in a full-page ad for MasterCard ® (which also shows, in its own way, that there exists a certain aesthetics that necessarily corresponds to this "abstraction").

A musician endowed with the refined features of a sensitive and thoughtful artist articulates, from behind a credit card, an emphatic endorsement:

> Substance makes music a universal language. Music is not as simple as printed notes on a page, it's the thought behind them. The composer's intention cannot be realized without a conductor and musicians to interpret, instruments to play and an audience to listen.
>
> The Gold MasterCard is not simply a card I carry in my wallet. It's an instrument of credit that speaks a universal language understood everywhere in the world. It gives me both the possibilities and the substantial credit line my busy life requires.
>
> Whether in Europe conducting or composing at home, the Gold MasterCard is an instrument of possibilities.
>
> (Plate 5.3)

Thanks to the credit card (wondrous incarnation of sensitivity, power, and abstraction), I can speak a language as universal as music, one that, like music, requires the creative personality of the one who composes and interprets it, as well as the existence of those who play it. There is more to money than mere numbers. Isn't the banking system that is at my disposal (that I can "perform") anywhere in the world much like the orchestra that travels the globe to interpret and execute the abstract "score" of "notations" by giving them substance? In my dealings with the bank, I compose and interpret, like a conductor; I am not shackled by rules. I am, as it says on the top of the ad, a "master of possibilities."

Plate 5.3 MasterCard advertisement

The credit card: a universality of value that grants purchasing power throughout the world, thanks to the global networks of my bank that transcend, by the power of their transnational connections, all local particularities including the unusual idioms of carpet merchants and cow vendors.

If the bank note, whose state issuance ensures that its validity is circumscribed within well-defined boundaries, clearly marked the national limits of monetary exchange (like a language spoken by a nation), the credit card also becomes one of the no less clear signs of the epoch of multinational or transnational capitalism (of which electromagnetics is the medium).[6]

Henceforth, every movement (touristic or financial) is an exalted adventure, yet at the same time guaranteed to be risk-free – because my bank is with me. It protects me. It is my personal assistant as I wander the globe. It frees me of all material problems. This is what the Premier Visa card promises: access to a realm beyond even Jules Verne's imagination:

> Before receiving your Premier card, you already belonged to this small circle of great travelers, whose business or curiosity leads them across five continents. From now on, with your Premier card, happier than Jules Verne's Phileas Fogg, you will no longer need to concern yourself with financial problems . . . or smaller ones: quick cash, assistance, insurance, reservations, your card is there, like a magic key, to simplify everything.
>
> The following pages will show you how the credit extended to you by your bank or financial institution will accompany you from now on throughout the world . . . without a carpetbag stuffed with bank notes.
>
> Your card, which we have created for you, is the ideal tool of the great traveler.
>
> (Visa 1987b)

The card is in charge of everything. No longer the manager of monetary deposits, the bank is a worldwide presence that helps and protects you. Everything happens as if the increasing abstraction of the monetary sign is compensated for by (all the while enabling) a total bankerization of life. Not only does the card allow you "to obtain money every day, at any hour, throughout the world" (even money you don't have in your account, thanks to "your worldwide credit"), it does even more: you are completely covered, in terms of assistance and insurance: "With the Premier card, there is no need to worry about insurance or assistance during your travels throughout the entire world: you are fully covered." Medical aid, hospitalization, repatriation, theft, death, disability ("including 'risks of war' – kidnappings, riots, hijackings"): there are hardly any risks that the bank does not anticipate and cover automatically, incorporating functions of risk-coverage that previously escaped its purview.

Such is the dynamic. The bank, having become telematized, rapidly exceeds its limited secular role in order to appropriate the at-home (tele-payment, tele-transfer) and the far-away (currency exchange anywhere), the present (cash) and the future (credit, insurance, retirement) in a providential bankerization affecting all aspects of life.

Notes

1 I wish to thank Georgeta Georgescu for her assistance with this translation.
2 On this distinction, see Goux (1990: 47–53, and 1994: 30–37).
3 Curiously, the emblems on the American bank note seem to confirm the analysis of the most central axiological signifiers performed in numismatics. See Goux, "Numismatics: An Essay in Theoretical Numismatics," (in 1990: 9–63).
4 Wittgenstein is summarizing Augustine's remarks in his *Confessions*, I.8 [JRB].
5 See Goux (1978). Portions of this work have been included in *Symbolic Economies*; for "operative subject," see 1990: 196.
6 This paragraph does not appear in the original French, and was added by Goux to this English translation [JRB].

References

Goux, Jean-Joseph (1978). *Les Iconoclastes*. Paris: Seuil.
—— (1990). *Symbolic Economies: After Marx and Freud*. Trans. Jennifer Curtiss Gage. Ithaca: Cornell University Press.
—— (1994). *The Coiners of Language*. Trans. Jennifer Curtiss Gage. Norman: University of Oklahoma Press.
Master Card (1986). Advertisement. *Harper's Magazine* Dec.: 16.
Visa (1987a). Advertisement. *Newsweek* 7 April: 72.
—— (1987b). "Your Premier Visa Card." Direct mail advertisement. March.
Wittgenstein, Ludwig (1958). *Philosophical Investigations*. Trans. G.E.M. Anscombe. 3rd edn. London: Basil Blackwell & Mott.

Part II

CRITICAL ECONOMICS

6

DOMINANT ECONOMIC METAPHORS AND THE POSTMODERN SUBVERSION OF THE SUBJECT

M. Neil Browne and J. Kevin Quinn[1]

The benign view of metaphors emphasizes their creativity and fecundity. Certain metaphors indeed have the potential to blast us to a new level of appreciation or understanding. They move us through imagery and past experiences to a more edifying awareness. After encountering them we are somewhere that previously seemed unapproachable. How limited we would be without the generative jolt provided by metaphors. But while the literature touting metaphors from this perspective has a liberating impact on thought, its fascination with creative lunges stimulated by self-conscious analysis of metaphorical structures can easily lapse into an undersocialized, decontextualized embrace of "productive" metaphors.

A more robust analysis of metaphors, while acknowledging both their indispensability and instrumentality, requires more than a glance at their ideological power as legitimizing devices (Shulman 1992: 433). That particularly dominant metaphors would play such a social role is implicit in the concept of the embodied subject that underlies the argument of this paper (Gadamer 1988; Merleau-Ponty 1962). The inspiration for this full-blooded look at metaphors is wonder – wonder at *why* certain metaphors are so compelling at particular times in particular places for specific communicators. Or: *why* does one trope convince while another, no less empirically grounded or vivid, falls flat (Toulmin 1990: 6–8)? Propelled by this wonder, our exploration directs us inescapably to the values and social relationships that permit a metaphor to enjoy contingent salience.[2]

Those of us excited about renewed interest in rhetoric in the human sciences are unusually appreciative of what one of our distant contextualist predecessors, Giambattista Vico, summarized as *entrar*: the values, the ideals, and the organizational modes of human communities (Berlin 1990). Applying this awareness to the use of metaphors in economic analysis requires us to focus on the seminal work of Deirdre (Donald) McCloskey. While Arjo Klamer and others, including Jack Amariglio, have greatly enhanced our awareness of the omnipresence and significance of rhetoric in the social sciences, it is McCloskey's eloquence and scholarly output that economists immediately recognize as exemplary of a rhetoric that is not "mere."[3] In this paper we take a critical stance toward certain aspects of McCloskey's treatment of rhetoric, but we are nonetheless heavily indebted to her work.

By replacing the objective observer and correspondence theory with agreement within the responsible community as the epistemological polestar, McCloskey and other analysts building on Rorty's work have sanctioned particular metaphors, the dominant ones. Skulking not too far below the surface of the logic for this approval is the enchanting appeal of a free marketplace of ideas. A melange of associated democratic images provides additional tacit appeal. What else is there, a supporter of this perspective might blurt out, that provides greater edification or truth-value than the considered expertise of the pertinent discourse community?

While dominant metaphors are revealing and reinforcing, they may preclude and stultify more than liberate thought. Our native belief perseverance (see Kahneman *et al.* 1982) both as individuals and communities creates a powerful bias against emergent metaphors that are disruptive or Utopian.[4] In economics this tendency is especially pronounced because economics is remarkably hegemonic when compared to the other social sciences.[5]

As prelude to speculating about potentially restrictive effects of this condition, the first section of this paper suggests the centrality of three metaphors that activate and legitimize market exchange as an allocative and distributional instrument. Then we go on to adumbrate an argument that the postmodern rejection of the subject is highly relevant to an enhanced understanding of the restrictive role of dominant economic metaphors.

The link between rhetoric and postmodernism is tight. Although the "rhetoric of economics" movement is probably the chief voice of postmodernist sentiment in our discipline, it is a source of affirmative postmodernism rather than of the skeptical neo-Nietzschean variety (Rosenau 1992: 15). Its practitioners, unlike Descartes, Galileo, Hobbes, Kant, and their modernist descendants, privilege the oral, the local, the timely, and the particular. But the belief in certitude and systematicity still reigns in economics, despite the claims of the heterodox that positivism died in the 1960s (Dillon 1991: 1–15).

While postmodernism takes an impressive array of forms (Toulmin 1990: 6–8), this paper follows the suggestion of David Ruccio that the strategies and perspectives of deconstruction and post-structuralism offer the most fruitful avenue for enriching economic discourse (Ruccio 1991: 495–97). Within this tradition, one dominant metaphor serves as an analytical *bête noire*: the solitary, unified subject (Rosenau 1992: 21).[6] In this paper we intend to challenge the belief in the disembodied subject to which the "rhetoric of economics" movement remains wedded. It is the lone voice in the postmodern conversation still giving credence to a figure long since buried by others.

The metaphors by which our clan is known

To claim that metaphors are fundamental to economic claims is trite for those relatively few economists who think of knowledge as discursive. However, for most of us licensed to speak about economic matters with authority the claim doesn't even rise to the level of controversy.[7] Despite the multitude of diverse voices urging us to focus on metaphor as productive "evidence" (Ricoeur 1977: 138–50 and Wheelwright 1967: 3–6 among them), economists, to the extent they consider the issue at all, would probably agree with Hobbes that to use words metaphorically is to encourage deception, because we are thereby using words in senses different from what they really mean.[8]

A perusal of principles of economics texts supports McCloskey's portrayal of a pervasive modernism in economics, and the consequent desire to view with distaste anything as squishy as a metaphor (McCloskey 1985: 36–38). Instead, our students are assured that economists are convinced by facts (always established by careful observation, referred to not accidentally in the passive voice) and logic (reliable, unemotional, and often intricate). Representative passages to substantiate this claim hardly seem necessary, but several can serve to remind us of the conventional methodological wisdom:

> Economic science . . . is an attempt to find a body of laws of nature. . . . Science tries to discover and catalog positive statements that are consistent with what we observe in the world. Science is silent on normative questions. . . . A difference of opinion on a positive matter can ultimately be settled by careful observation and measurement. . . . Economists observe, measure, and explain what they see. Understanding what makes things work requires the discovery of laws. This discovery is the main task of economists.
>
> (Parkin 1990: 22)

> Economists verify or reject theory by an appeal to facts. They may draw upon casual observation, insight, logic or intuition to frame hypotheses. . . . The systematic and repeated examination of relevant facts tests the validity of hypotheses. . . . Principles and theories are meaningful statements drawn from facts, but facts, in turn, serve as a constant check on the validity of principles.
>
> (McConnell and Brue 1993: 14–15)

This portrayal of economic method is so standard that it is a strain to find contrary voices. As an approach to knowledge, it resonates with the Platonic doctrine that truth should be achieved without the use of fancy garb to dress it. Presumably figures of speech threaten to tempt us away from the solid grounding provided by facts and logic.

Because prevalent economic opinion seems so rigid in this regard, and additionally because we cannot imagine arguments more eloquent or compelling than those already provided by McCloskey (1990), this paper simply assumes the power and prevalence of metaphorical structures in economic reasoning. To identify dominant metaphors shaping economic arguments is hardly a certain enterprise given mainstream attitudes about the worth of tropes. Metaphors may be omnipresent, but they will hardly ever be acknowledged or defended. Ferreting them out requires inference or guesswork. Our speculations about dominant metaphors are just that, but we think economists willing to consider our argument will not be shocked by our inclusions. If they are dominant, as we are claiming, there will be few surprises on our list. In each case the metaphor seems constitutive (Boyd 1979: 402) in that it is difficult to consider mainstream economics apart from that metaphor.

Robinson Crusoe

Robinson Crusoe, a literary invention of the eighteenth-century writer Daniel Defoe, continues to represent *Homo economicus* in the literature of economics. The image of the shipwrecked, isolated Crusoe has appealed to economists for over two centuries, providing a narrative basis for the theoretical formulations of Ricardo, Edgeworth, Koopmans, Barro and others, as well as continuing to remain a staple of textbook fare. McCloskey (1995: 203) discusses the literary origins of *Homo economicus* in Robinson Crusoe: "*Homo economicus* may or may not be bad company for us, but literary artists, not worldly philosophers, are responsible for getting us acquainted." A frequently stated basis of this appeal is the primitive yet charming simplicity of Crusoe's life on the island as sole producer and consumer of goods and services. Because it is not cluttered with social relations, family, government, and so on, the "Robinson Crusoe economy" is a metaphor that allows economists to focus on what is "essential" about consumer and producer choice under conditions of scarcity.[9]

However, some of the story's appeal may have to do with elements that are not explicitly acknowledged by economists who are drawn to it. One is the way that the story portrays the behavior of Crusoe as "natural." Crusoe, drawn by a desire to flee the comfort and stifling tradition of his middle-class home, goes adventuring. In the course of these adventures he becomes stranded on an island for thirty years. No analysis of the frames of meaning that created the perceiving Crusoe, not any of what Freire calls conscientization (Prilleltensky 1989: 800), weighs down Crusoe's engagement with his new home.

Nothing he has previously learned is of any use to him on the island, in the view of economists, who accordingly represent it as a "state of nature." That is, they represent his behavior on the island as a return to the natural life: he is simply obeying his own natural propensities by working, consuming, and resting in optimal proportions while meticulously recording these activities in his ledger. His rational, calculating behavior represents a rejection of tradition, family, and society for a more "natural" relationship to the material world. It reflects the historical and universal nature of man in action.[10]

The insightful feminist analysis of Robinson Crusoe stories by Ulla Grapard reminds us that something else gets pushed to the margin when economists use Crusoe as their "quintessential economic man" – questions of gender. There are no women on the island, allowing Crusoe to get on with the pleasures of ownership and control. However, nature and wilderness in this tale are often linked metaphorically to an unspoiled, passive female ("virgin") which Crusoe penetrates and controls. Recent feminist and post-colonial scholarship has argued that such constructions of nature as passive and "feminine" inaugurate the "Other" against which the Subject can be defined (see Bordo 1987; Harding 1986; Said 1979; Spivak 1988). In other words, far from being universal, the character of Crusoe is "masculine," in contrast to the feminine world of his island, and to the irrational, "soft," sweet, and child-like Friday (Grapard 1995: 45–46). Far from being the "representative agent," Crusoe is the masculine agent who has free rein to appropriate and control the resources of his passive and inferior Others (i.e., nature, the colonial subject Crusoe, the wife who keeps his house when he finally leaves the island, and the slaves on his Brazilian sugar plantation who make him rich).

Thus, as Grapard articulates so well, the universal subject that Crusoe is supposed to represent in economic theory is in fact a masculine subject who is historically and socially constructed in the discourse of Western science and philosophy. His behavior is not so much "natural" as it is unrelentingly British and middle-class. He acts in a world of racism and exploitation that is theoretically at odds with the ideals of the free market that economists often associate with Robinson Crusoe stories. And yet he remains for many economists the "quintessential economic man," the subject of economics. Other subjectivities based on gender, class, and race are relegated to the margins of the discipline in favor of this "representative" agent.

Machine

Even Robinson Crusoe requires some tools. For economists, human agents interact with a machine-like economic system as they barter and trade for goods and services. The machine metaphor is not only in common use among economists; it also provides a meta-metaphor for economic thought, capturing in its complex imagery the core modernist principles of foundationalism, objectivism, and control (Wendt 1990: 48–49).

The economy as machine suggests a process of exchange in which the only active agent shaping the outcomes is the human subject who works and consumes after having been handed a specific assemblage of productive forces. The machine has been mailed to us in a box with no return address. It is not our role to question the legitimacy, effectiveness, or beauty of the machine; we are just to use it for our ends. The detachment of the machine from the subjects who will make use of it elevates the economic agent to the level of the heroic (Nelson 1993b: 124–26). We control the machine's output.

Machines do not discriminate; they do their predetermined task without recognition of race or sex.[11] We are justifiably wary of potential abuse of power by human subjects, but the machine is benign; after all, it's just an object. Our choices will determine the quality of the life we eventually experience; the machine is our innocent helpmate. The machine metaphor for the economy is first cousin to the tool metaphor, a machine being among other things a sophisticated tool. The effect of thinking of economic arrangements with this metaphor is to make certain questions impertinent.

For example, consider the question of education vouchers for private education. An economist is trained to pose the question of private vs. public education as a question of finding the best means to an independently defined end – an implicit use of the tool metaphor. But such a formulation of the issue means that we have ruled out of bounds questions about whether we are indeed providing the same "good" when we provide education privately. We have excluded the possibility that the "publicness" of public education may be constitutive (Anderson 1993: 162) of the good provided. The means/end formulation, which makes different economic arrangements better or worse tools for the provision of an independently defined end, has already settled this question. Although the question can still be asked, as we have just done – by challenging the metaphor – the means/end/tool metaphor places the burden of proof on those who believe that economic institutions constitute both the goods they provide and the individual agents who "employ" them for their purposes. And where the burden of proof is placed matters greatly when we have rejected a Cartesian account of knowledge for a rhetorical one: no uninterpreted "facts" will settle issues like this (Taylor 1995: 35).

The consequences of the machine metaphor are boldly apparent in the research program of the New Institutionalists. (A critical survey can be found in Hodgson 1988.) Here the goal, quite explicitly, is to treat all institutions as instrumental solutions to problems faced by interacting rational atoms. Collective action is, from this perspective, problematic until we have given an individualistic explanation that makes it instrumentally rational for the self-seeking individuals who engage in it. Like the alchemist's quest for the philosopher's stone, this may be futile.[12]

Under the grip of the machine metaphor, however, the quest continues. The mutual implication of our master metaphors is apparent here, too: our self-sufficient Robinson Crusoes build the institutions they need to solve the problems they encounter in their attempts to maximize satisfaction. An agent less self-sufficient than Robinson might well find institutions to be essential to finding out who he is rather than just tools for getting what he wants. This expressive, rather than instrumental (Taylor 1989: 506) role of institutions can rarely get a hearing in economics departments as currently constituted because it cannot penetrate the closed circle of explanation shaped by our mutually reinforcing master metaphors.[13]

One last example of the playing-out of the master-metaphor of institutions as tools should be noted: the versatile notion of the "implicit contract." Explicit contracts, of course, confirm the instrumental nature of the contracted-for arrangements. Where there is no such contract, the picture of an implicit contract puts the arrangement under study back into the instrumental mold. Do hierarchical relationships within the firm or the family threaten to undermine our picture of the social world as the free creation of self-sufficient rationally choosing agents? These arrangements – like the state itself in the contractarian tradition in political philosophy – must then have been the product of implicit contracts.

Auction

Our choices are exercised, according to common economic lore, at an auction. This metaphor, like other dominant tropes in economics, names or acknowledges the passive institutional setting in which the subject determines his or her economic fate. The auction "is held," with emphasis on the passive voice. Discrepancies in knowledge, aggression, embedded human capital, trustworthiness, and wealth among participants are epiphenomenal.

The salient trait of auctions as they are discussed by economists is the presence of many, well-informed bidders (Thurow 1983: 21). The magnitude of the auction allegedly protects against cartels, exploitation, or moral perversity in eventual allocative and distributional results (Lindsay and Shanor 1982: 215). Similar dependence on the protective impact of huge numbers of bidders at the auction can be found in the compensating wage differential (see Filer 1985) and human capital theory (see Polachek 1984) literatures. The assumption of knowledgeable bidders then provides assurance that those who are bidding will make a direct, accurate link between their well-ordered utility functions and the bid they choose to make.

Exploration of the origins of the auction, the impact of the auction model on eventual outcomes (Lane 1991: 108), and heterogeneous capacities of the bidders are, not so strangely, absent from discussions of marketplace auctions. As with the other dominant metaphors, here the market process is portrayed as friendly. Support for resulting prices, incomes, and output levels is garnered by emphasizing the controlling role of the eventual chooser. Such treatment of the subject implicitly rejects the importance of Heideggerian disclosure or even of more socialized forms of individualism (Sampson 1988: 20–21).

The auction metaphor has of course been famously challenged in macroeconomics by Clower and Leijonhufvud (1975). Looking at Walras's use of the metaphor to describe the achievement of general equilibrium, they asked, in effect, "if this is an auction, then where's the auctioneer?" And they pointed out that Walras's use of the metaphor, in which prices were called out but no trades executed until a market-clearing vector had been found through "tattonnement," begs all the important questions about coordination among decentralized agents, for example, where trading takes place in real time at non-equilibrium prices, altering the equilibrium itself. In important ways, according to Leijonhufvud, it was the grip of this metaphor that made the depth of Keynes's challenge unappreciated. Keynesian economics, he writes, was best understood as economics without an auctioneer (Leijonhufvud 1979: 48). Treating the entire economy as a single huge auction, Leijonhufvud might have said, echoing Wittgenstein, is to let words go "on holiday."

This incident in the history of economic thought stands out for its singularity: it is rare for an economist to leave aside "facts and logic" and intervene in debate by criticizing the metaphors employed, metaphors whose nature it is, as frames for seeing anything at all, to be themselves unseen. The role of "therapist" *à la* Wittgenstein, showing us how we are in the grip of a certain picture that preforms our questions and possible answers, is not a role the typical economist is well suited to play. Confident in our possession of a sure-fire method for uncovering facts, we instead relegate quibbles about metaphorical adequacy to the history of economic thought – the refuge of the literary, non-scientific throwbacks in the discipline.

The fate of Leijonhufvud's intervention shouldn't be surprising in light of the power of the profession's master metaphors to celebrate self-sufficient agents wielding institutional tools to achieve predefined ends. If, for Leijonhufvud, macroeconomic policy threatens, because of its ability to substitute for the missing auctioneer and help to solve coordination problems, to be potentially creative and enabling rather than constraining, the New Classical Economics, following hard on the heels of this work, closed the doors on this possibility by making the state itself non-autonomous. The ubiquitous representative agent with "rational" expectations has already anticipated all possible moves by state policy makers and altered his or her behavior accordingly, rendering all policy ineffective.[14] The auctioneer, the absence of whom in Leijonhufvud's account threatened to blow up the auction metaphor, is no longer necessary – our worries about coordination have been allayed by adding "rational" expectations to the sovereign subject's powers. Keynesian appeals to institutions such as long-term contracts are said to be "undertheorized" because they haven't imposed optimizing logic on those institutions themselves.

While it might be possible to suggest economic metaphors that are inconsistent with the assumption of an isolated, autonomous subject, the dominant metaphors with which we are familiar all complement the popular

Robinson Crusoe trope. They tend to ignore the social patterns that permit and encourage recognition that the target concept or process (what we are seeking to understand) is linked in a particular fashion to the source (the relatively well-known entity that we are using in the metaphor to extend meaning or understanding).

Rhetoric, dominant metaphors, and postmodernism

Given the nature of the dominant metaphors in economics, it would seem that a meeting of economics with the deconstructivist and anti-humanist sensibilities of postmodernism would generate a lot of fireworks. However, the first sustained incursion of a form of postmodern thinking into the discipline by McCloskey (1985) seemed to carry very few implications for the substance of economics. McCloskey skilfully deployed the insights of anti-Cartesian thinkers such as Rorty to undermine the economist's self-image as a scientist in the heroic Cartesian sense. She made us much more aware of the inevitability of metaphor in the construction of knowledge. Objective "Truth" is replaced by the "truth" (small "t") of consensus within the speech community of economists. But this criterion doesn't threaten the dominant metaphors in economics, however newly conscious of their metaphorical status we are by virtue of McCloskey's work.

The paradox of McCloskey's stance, as Mirowski has pointed out, is that the Cartesian epistemology that she has in her sights is mixed up both in its genesis and its logic with the concept of *Homo economicus* and thus with the whole logic of the dominant metaphors: "ontogeny recapitulates epistemology" (Mirowski 1988: 120). McCloskey, though, does not seem to feel any tension here at all: her Chicago-style economics coexists in harmony with her fairly thoroughgoing critique of Cartesian epistemology. McCloskey seems quite comfortable hunting and fishing with *Homo economicus* during the day and then retiring to the drawing room to become a critic of the epistemology that produced her – and much else – during the evening.

Charles Taylor's distinction (1987: 465–66) between two modes of post-modern thought may help us to understand McCloskey's stance. On the one hand, there are those thinkers whose quarrel with Cartesian epistemology is confined solely to the latter's foundationalism – its attempt to ground our knowledge in some ultimate way, whether it be "clear and distinct ideas," the transcendental conditions of the possibility of experience, or observation statements capturing the data untainted by any interpretation. Taylor mentions Rorty and Quine as good representatives. Both have shredded any such foundational thinking. But curiously, says Taylor, for these thinkers there is no break with the Cartesian subject in several important respects: the thinker, albeit foundationless, remains isolated, asocial and punctual (i.e., instrumental). Taylor claims that really and truly to get beyond epistemology we need to jettison not only foundationalism, but also atomism, individualism, and instrumentalism as well.[15]

Evidently, a thoroughgoing end-of-epistemologist in Taylor's sense will have a lot more to do in economics as presently constituted than disabusing its practitioners of their outmoded positivist methodology. He or she would want to point out not only that what they do every day is to engage in metaphorical thinking but also that the dominant metaphors they use may be seriously suspect. Rorty's version of the end of epistemology, however, would not take this second step. Like poetry for Auden, anti-foundationalism "makes nothing happen." People are to go on doing what they have been doing while giving up the notion that they have or should want any grounds for so doing.[16] Postmodernism understood in this fashion as *mere* anti-foundationalism amounts to a sort of euthanasia of the critical faculty. Implicitly, the mere anti-foundationalist shares with the foundationalist the conviction that knowledge and criticism must be understood on the Cartesian model. For the latter, then, because we do engage in knowledge and criticism, the Cartesian model must be correct. For the former, accepting the same premise but (rightly) rejecting the Cartesian model, the nihilist conclusion that knowledge and criticism are impossible follows inescapably.[17]

McCloskey's "mere" anti-foundationalism explains the immunity of the dominant economic metaphors to her rhetorical approach. McCloskey (1994: 338) notes: "nothing is implied by analysis. In particular, realizing that a language game is being played, with certain elaborate rules, does not imply that one wants to stop the game or even change its direction"; and again: "it does not follow, contra Mirowski and others, that because I have noticed some of the rules of economic discourse that I must be committed to overthrowing them" (339). If the Cartesian God is dead, then everything is permitted. Only if one clings to the notion of truth as necessarily literal will the revelation that everything is a metaphor entail the conclusion that distinguishing good from bad metaphors can only be done by means of aesthetic criteria.[18]

The inevitable tension in the position of the "mere" anti-foundationalist, his or her clinging to the ghost of what he or she claims to have left behind, becomes acute in the case of the rhetoric of economics movement: the dominant economic metaphors that go unchallenged are intimately associated both logically and historically – as Mirowski has shown – with the knowing subject of Cartesian epistemology, ostensibly under attack by McCloskey. As Mirowski (1988: 120) notes:

> The neoclassical school of economics had only recently adopted all the trappings of the Cartesian world view – mathematical formalism, axiomatization, derogation of literary narrative, and mimesis of natural science terminology and attitudes – but had also endowed their mannequin of rational economic man with exclusively Cartesian powers and abilities: transparent individual self-knowledge, mechanical

algorithms of decision making, independence from all historical determination, and all social action ultimately explained by rational individual assent.

As part and parcel of her anti-Cartesianism, for instance, McCloskey recognizes the social embeddedness of the knowing subject, but this recognition does not seem to have any consequences for the asocial economic subjects (the Robinson Crusoes, the representative agents) enshrined in the dominant metaphors. By contrast, it is precisely the intersubjectivity of knowledge that led Habermas to the important notion of communicative rationality, a concept that, had McCloskey exploited it, could have had revolutionary consequences in a discipline which unabashedly reduces rationality to instrumental rationality.

Instead, in McCloskey, the dominant metaphors themselves influence her account of the intersubjectivity of knowledge: the speech community of economists becomes a "market" in ideas that finds its own optimal solutions. A genuinely non-Cartesian account of science and rationality might well have been a potent weapon for evaluating the dominant metaphors of our clan. Instead, in McCloskey the potential targets have disabled the weapon through the reductive account of intersubjectivity in science as a market.

McCloskey (1994: 336) argues that her neoclassicalism "takes the order of the economy to be the same as the order of speech" and that her work in fact reverses the marketplace-of-ideas metaphor, showing that "the market itself is a conversation, to be negotiated, driven by rules of talk." It is certainly true that *Homo economicus* speaks, and speaks essentially, in McCloskey's work. This theme is most developed in her "The Economy as a Conversation" (ibid.: 367–78). But the sort of speech *Homo economicus* engages in, in McCloskey, is predominantly instrumental. Donald Trump is served up as an exemplar of the economic agent as rhetor, for example (ibid.: 369–70). A distinction crucial to another anti-foundationalist, Habermas, who, like McCloskey, would substitute conversation and communication for the Cartesian model of science – the distinction between strategic and communicative action, and the corresponding distinction between instrumental and communicative rationality – is frustratingly elided in McCloskey's work. On one page (373) we find the establishment of trust analyzed, in good new-institutionalist fashion, by appeal to the instrumental logic of the iterated Prisoners' Dilemma; while on the next we find the "earning of profits" treated as a Wittgensteinian practice ("something we bourgeois Westerners do"), needing no instrumental justification.

As the rhetorician James Boyd White has pointed out, "persuasive speech" can be of two very distinct kinds. One, "honest persuasion" (*peithos*), persuades by "constituting a community" between speaker and listener (White 1985: 6). Another form of persuasive speech White calls *dolos* – "a sort of trick, or deceitful stratagem" (7). The latter is persuasion as "the art of manipulating others to adopt one's position" while the former is "the art of stating fully and sincerely the grounds upon which one thinks common action can and should rest" (17). White associates *dolos* with means–ends rationality and market economics (21). In McCloskey's work, these two crucially different forms of persuasive speech are never distinguished – the persuasive speech of an advertiser or of a Donald Trump is treated on a level with the "persuasive speech" of the economist-rhetor.

Symptomatically, one of the scarier aspects of a thoroughly instrumental society – the way in which *peithos* itself becomes the raw material of *dolos* (and thus loses its character as *peithos*) as capitalists learn to employ constitutive, community-creating rhetoric the better to motivate their employees – is offered up by McCloskey not as a *prima facie* problem with market economies, but as one more bit of evidence that the order of the economy mirrors the order of speech. "Motivating people by deals will work only if the deals convey to them the right story of their own lives," she comments, after excerpting a novelist's account of an entrepreneur persuading his employees to "reach by their own reasoning the solutions he had himself already determined upon" through an adroit use of what he mistakenly calls the "Socratic Method" (McCloskey 1994: 374).

When McCloskey argues that her critics misunderstand her by failing to see that she reads the "marketplace of ideas" both ways, therefore, we are not reassured. In fact, if the metaphorical marketplace of ideas in economics works like the speech-saturated marketplace he presents in "The Economy as a Conversation," then *caveat emptor*.

We should point out that other postmodern economists have taken a different turn that challenges this "free marketplace of ideas" metaphor. As Strassman (1993: 57) notes, the market is not free to begin with. There are barriers to entry that constrain the economic conversation. (Colander and Klamer's 1989 anthropological investigation of the graduate school experience shows this all too starkly.) However, many postmodern scholars inside and outside of economics (including Strassmann) do not want to replace McCloskey's metaphor with the alternative "imperfectly competitive marketplace of ideas" either. If women and minorities, radicals and feminists were finally let into the club, would it dramatically affect the nature of the dominant metaphors? Maybe not, if these metaphors are "always already" produced by the discursive practices of modernist economics, practices that are conditioned by the "meta-narratives" of modernism that structure meaning. McCloskey's quietism may be challenged by a recognition of, and an incredulity toward, the meta-narratives that allow certain metaphors to enjoy contingent salience.

We believe this challenge is evident in projects that range from Amariglio's (1990) archaeology of the postmodern moments in post-Keynesian thought, Resnick and Wolff's (1987) anti-essentialist "rethinking" of Marxian theory, and Mirowski's (1989) demonstration of the ill-fated marriage of nineteenth-century physics metaphors and economic theory in *More Heat Than Light*, to Rossetti's (1993) exploration of the connections between feminist economics and postmodernism, and Strassman's (1993) and Nelson's (1993a) work on the gendered construction of economic conversations. While the nature of these projects is quite varied,[19] they all recognize that the parallel between the autonomous, rational, objective theorist of economics and the knowing subject in economics – the rational agent – means that epistemological critiques of economics will have implications for its content as well. This postmodern stance reflects the "deeper" end-of-epistemology, which Taylor's work suggests in its radical rethinking of the atomism, individualism, and instrumentalism central to the modernist project.

The rejection of the unified Cartesian agent in economics need not be based on a search for a subject that is more "real" in an empirical sense. Instead, it can take the form of an immanent critique, pointing out what the dominant, essentialist discourse makes invisible. It may reveal the "others" against which the Cartesian subject is defined. For example, a deconstructive reading of some of the texts of economics might show how these "others" often threaten to disrupt modernist economic discourses, causing economists to pull back from the implications of their own analyses. Amariglio's deconstructive reading of Knight's and Shackle's work on uncertainty is a good example of this. He shows how both authors develop notions of uncertainty that tend to disrupt deeply held notions of the knowing subject, only to resuscitate the heroic subject with last-minute disclaimers: for example, Shackle's concept of "bounded uncertainty" that limits the scope of uncertainty in a way that maintains the subject's ability to choose rationally (see Amariglio 1990: 36)

Feminist economists have also provided immanent critiques of the representative agent in economics. Feminists have long pointed out that the purportedly "universal" subject is in fact a representation of male behavior in the masculine sphere of public space. Some have called for an economics that is more "inclusive," one that will take gender into account. But as Jane Rossetti asserts, the plea for a more inclusive concept of human agency should be changed to one that recognizes that gender is already "in" the one that is currently dominant (Rossetti 1993: 15).

A feminist postmodernism would want to show the way that the subject is constructed in a web of binary oppositions such as mind/body, culture/nature, public/private, subject/object, reason/emotion and masculine/feminine, in which the first term is assumed to be prior to and superior to the second (Bordo 1987: 93–94; Williams 1993: 144). The subject pole is separated from the concepts on the object pole, which are considered inferior and are pushed to the margins. This means, on the one hand, that the universal subject is in fact a particular subject, a masculine subject. It also means that the metaphors and narratives which rely on this subject have already "assigned" an implicit role to women, minorities, nature, etc., thereby creating a space for a critique of the values of dominant metaphors. As Rossetti (1993: 15) argues: "Bringing this aspect out into the light opens another avenue for criticism and reconstruction that should be used. Bringing consideration of the hitherto subordinate and overlooked into the discussion is shown to be necessary, not magnanimous on the part of those involved in the dominant discourse."

The postmodern turn that decenters and fragments the subject, exposing the discursive limits of modern economics' embrace of a centered and "separative" self, may provide a means to critique and perhaps displace the dominant metaphors in economics. An approach to the rhetoric of economics that has become more than "mere" may well be far less quietist than the version McCloskey has given us. It may well be that the Cartesian knowing subject will not get the burial he deserves in our discipline until he has been joined in the family mortuary by his first cousin, the economic acting subject, *Homo economicus*.

Notes

1 This paper would not have been possible without the insight, arguments, and critique provided by Suzanne Bergeron. She contributed to its development from inception to completion. We also want to acknowledge the creative role of Wesley Hiers, the research assistant of any academic's dreams.
2 A graphic illustration of this process is Herodotus's story of Darius's curiosity about the metaphorical content of eating the corpses of our parents. The sharply divergent reactions of Greeks and Indians at Darius's court had their foundation in the moral hierarchy and conventional narratives of their respective civilizations.
3 Perhaps the best single source of diverse perspectives on the rhetoric of economics is the conversational article in which Klamer and McCloskey (1989) highlighted their divergent reactions to the structure of the market for economic ideas.
4 This use of "Utopian" draws on Mannheim's distinction between utopian and ideological constructs (Mannheim 1951: 36).
5 It is with great pride rather than bemusement that mainstream economists refer to *the theory* as if its boundaries and contents were canonical.
6 Edmund Sullivan's (1990) work in psychology provides an outstanding model of this approach and the insights it produces.
7 This point was driven home to one of us recently when, upon finishing a presentation about the role of metaphor in economics at the Southern Economic Association, he was challenged by an agitated economist who blurted out, "I did not get my economics from some metaphor; I got it from Arrow and Debreu."
8 I.A. Richards colorfully labels such essentialism as it applies to language "the proper meaning superstition" (Richards 1936: 11).
9 As Hewitson (1994: 143) notes, neoclassicals have even managed to discuss exchange without social relations: "Hal Varian, for example, has eliminated Friday as a necessary component of an exchange model. Crusoe is able, in his role as a producer who is interested in hiring labor, to make contracts with

himself in the role of a worker. . . . 'Their' exchanges take place in 'intra-subject' markets."

10 Marx argues that the neglect of the social and historical nature of the production process represents a grave misuse of the Robinson Crusoe stories by Smith and Ricardo, for in their emphasis on Crusoe's behavior as a return to nature they neglect to consider that he himself was shaped by historical forces before he ever set foot on the island (Marx 1977: 346).

11 See Browne (1987) for a more extended discussion of "impersonality" as a convenient metaphorical attribute possessed by the market as machine.

12 See Hurley (1989: 136–56) for a persuasive argument that attempts to give individualistic explanations of collective action – such as voting – have been ultimately question-begging: assuming the very cooperation they are meant to explain.

13 For an extraordinary reading of Robinson himself as expressively rather than instrumentally involved with the world around him, see Elizabeth Bishop's (1979) poem, "Crusoe in England." Looking back on his time on the island, Bishop's Crusoe says: "Just when I couldn't stand it / another minute longer, Friday came. / (Accounts of that have everything all wrong)." Even his tools become more than tools: "The knife there on the shelf – / It reeked of meaning, like a crucifix. / It lived . . .". The last lines of the poem are an understated lament: "And Friday, my dear Friday, died of measles / seventeen years ago come March."

14 See Hoover (1988) for a comprehensive discussion of the philosophical underpinnings of New Classical Economics.

15 We cannot do justice to Taylor's subtle and important argument in a paragraph and footnote. For a full version, see Taylor (1989). He argues that the "epistemological construal" of knowledge – the picture of the knower as striving, through an orderly method, to obtain a "correct representation of an independent reality" (1987: 466) – is bound up as both cause and effect with a moral ideal of "self-responsibility" and freedom and

> that this notion of freedom has been interpreted as involving certain key theses about the human agent. . . . The first is the picture of the subject as ideally disengaged, that is, as free and rational to the extent that he [*sic*] has fully distinguished himself from his social and natural worlds, so that his identity is no longer to be defined in terms of what lies outside him in these worlds. The second, which flows from this, is a punctual view of the self, ideally ready *qua* free and rational to treat these worlds – and even some features of his own character – instrumentally, as subject to reordering in order better to secure the welfare of himself and other like subjects. The third is the social consequence of the first two: an atomistic construal of society as constituted by, or ultimately explicable in terms of, individual purposes.
>
> (471)

For Taylor a true overcoming of epistemology – such as has been attempted by Heidegger, Merleau-Ponty, and Wittgenstein – challenges this whole nexus of beliefs, a much wider and deeper task than the anti-foundationalism of a Rorty or a Quine, which leaves these anthropological beliefs intact.

16 Stanley Fish (1988) offers a similar version of this species of postmodernism: "What we now have as a result of the rhetorical, postmodern, deconstructive, poststructuralist, neopragmatist revolution is a new account of our epistemology, that is, a new account of where our beliefs come from. The mistake is to think that by adding this new belief, our other beliefs about things other than epistemology will be altered" (29); "while it is true that it matters what metaphor one uses, this truth will not help you do anything in the world. Nothing whatsoever" (23). Note the stark contrast with the remarks from Taylor cited above.

17 Nussbaum (1990: 229) makes this fairly common argument in her critique of Stanley Fish:

> Just as, in Nietzsche's account, the news of God's death reduces modern human beings to Nihilism, that is to the view that all preferring and valuing are groundless and anything goes, so for numerous contemporary theorists the collapse of the hope that we could walk out to the world and see it in all its unmediated presentness, as it truly is in itself, has left only the thought that no descriptions can be defended as superior to any others. . . . [O]ne suspects that the retreat to skepticism or subjectivism betrays a residual commitment to metaphysical realism as the only form of truth worth having: failing that, we do not seem to have anything worth preferring to anything else.

18 McCloskey has made this distinction herself many times in her programmatic statements. A tenable postmodernism, she has said, does not reject reason, but the Cartesian notion of the latter.

19 A caveat: We think, with McCloskey, that it is important to look at what this work does – not just at what it says it does. Especially in the case of self-consciously "postmodernist" or post-structuralist work, its programmatic statements often betray a modernist equation of incommensurability with unreason, implying that criteria for paradigm choice must be irrational. We believe that in the work itself we can find resources for rational criticism of the dominant metaphors, where "rationality" is understood rhetorically, and even where its programmatic statements seem to exclude this possibility as essentialist or a new "meta-narrative."

References

Amariglio, Jack (1988). "The Body, Economic Discourse, and Power: An Economist's Guide to Foucault." *History of Political Economy* 20: 538–613.

—— (1990). "Economics as Postmodern Discourse." In *Economics as Discourse: An Analysis of the Language of Economists*. Ed. Warren J. Samuels. Boston, MA: Kluwer, 15–46.

Anderson, Elizabeth (1993). *Value in Ethics and Economics*. Cambridge, MA: Harvard University Press.

Benhabib, Seyla (1986). *Critique, Norm and Utopia*. New York: Columbia University Press.

—— (1987). "The Generalized and the Concrete Other: The Hohlberg–Gilligan Controversy and Moral Theory." In *Women and Moral Theory*. Ed. Diana Meyers and Eva Feder Kittay. Totowa, NJ: Rowan & Littlefield, 154–77.

Berlin, Isaiah (1990). *The Crooked Timber of Humanity*. New York: Vintage, 8–14.

Bishop, Elizabeth (1979). "Crusoe in England." In *The Complete Poems*. New York: Farrar, Straus, & Giroux.

Bordo, Susan (1987). *The Flight To Objectivity*. Albany: State University of New York Press.

Boyd, Richard (1979). "Metaphor and Theory Change: What Is 'Metaphor' a Metaphor For?" In *Metaphor and Thought*. Ed. Andrew Ortony, Cambridge: Cambridge University Press, 356–408.

Browne, M. Neil (1987). "The Metaphorical Constraints to Pay Equity: Why So Many Economists Are Outraged by Comparable Worth." *Population Research and Policy Review* 48: 29–46.

Clower, Robert W., and Axel Leijonhufvud (1975). "The Coordination of Economic Activities: a Keynesian Perspective." *American Economic Review* 14 (May): 82–88.

Colander, David, and Arjo Klamer (1989). *The Making of an Economist*. Boulder, CO: Westview.

Defoe, Daniel (1965). *The Life and Adventures of Robinson Crusoe*. New York: Penguin.

Dillon, George L. (1991). *Contending Rhetorics*. Bloomington: Indiana University Press.

Filer, R. (1985). "Male–Female Wage Differences: The Importance of Compensating Differentials." *Industrial and Labor Relations Review* 426: 426–37.

Fish, Stanley (1988). "Comments from Outside Economics." In *The Consequences of Economic Rhetoric*. Ed. A. Klamer, D.N. McCloskey and R.M. Solow. Cambridge: Cambridge University Press, 21–30.

Gadamer, Hans-Georg (1988). *Truth and Method*. Rev. edn. New York: Seabury.

Grapard, Ulla (1995). "Robinson Crusoe: The Quintessential Economic Man?" *Feminist Economics* 3: 33–52.

Harding, Sandra (1986). *The Science Question in Feminism*. Ithaca: Cornell University Press.

Habermas, Jurgen (1992). *The Philosophical Discourse of Modernity*. Cambridge, MA: MIT Press.

Hewitson, Gillian (1994). "Deconstructing Robinson Crusoe: A Feminist Interrogation of 'Rational Economic Man.'" *Australian Feminist Studies* 20 (Summer): 130–48.

Hobbes, Thomas (1950). *Leviathan*. New York: Dutton.

Hodgson, Geoffrey M. (1988). *Economics and Institutions*. Philadelphia: University of Pennsylvania Press.

Hoover, Kevin (1988). *The New Classical Macroeconomics*. Oxford: Basil Blackwell.

Hurley, Susan (1989). *Natural Reasons*. Oxford: Oxford University Press.

Kahneman, Daniel, *et al.* (1982). *Judgment under Uncertainty: Heuristics and Biases*. Cambridge: Cambridge University Press.

Klamer, Arjo, and Donald McCloskey (1989). "The Rhetoric of Disagreement." *Rethinking Marxism* 140 (Fall): 140–61.

Klamer, Arjo, Donald N. McCloskey, and Robert M. Solow, eds (1988). *The Consequences of Economic Rhetoric*. Cambridge: Cambridge University Press.

Lane, Robert E. (1991). *The Market Process*. Cambridge: Cambridge University Press.

Leijonhufvud, Axel (1979). *On Keynesian Economics and the Economics of Keynes*. Oxford: Oxford University Press.

Lindsay, C., and C. Shanor (1982). "*County of Washington* v. *Gunther*: Legal and Economic Considerations for Resolving Sex-based Wage Discrimination Cases." *Supreme Court Review* 185: 185–233.

Mannheim, Karl (1951). *Ideology and Utopia: An Introduction to the Sociology of Knowledge*. New York: Harcourt Brace.

Marx, Karl (1977). *Selected Writings*. Ed. David McLellan. Oxford: Oxford University Press.

McCloskey, Donald N. (1985). *The Rhetoric of Economics*. Madison: University of Wisconsin Press.

—— (1990). *If You're So Smart: The Narrative of Economic Expertise*. Chicago: University of Chicago Press.

—— (1994). *Knowledge and Persuasion in Economics*. Cambridge: Cambridge University Press.

—— (1995). "Sophisters, Economists, and Calculators." In *Rhetoric and Pluralism*. Ed. Frederick Antczak. Columbus: Ohio State University Press, 187–210.

McConnell, Campbell R., and Stanley Brue (1993). *Microeconomics*. 12th edn. New York: McGraw Hill.

Merleau-Ponty, Maurice (1962). *The Phenomenology of Perception*. New York: Humanities.

Mirowski, Philip. (1988). "Shall I Compare Thee to a Minkowski–Ricardo–Leontief–Metzler Matrix of the Mosak–Hicks Type? Or, Rhetoric, Mathematics and the Nature of Neoclassical Economic Theory." In *The Consequences of Economic Rhetoric*. Ed. A. Klamer, D.N. McCloskey, and R.M. Solow. Cambridge: Cambridge University Press, 117–45.

—— (1989). *More Heat Than Light*. Cambridge: Cambridge University Press.

Nelson, Julie A. (1993a) "Gender and Economic Ideologies." *Review of Social Economy* 287 (Fall): 287–301.

—— (1993b). "Value-free or Valueless? Notes on the Pursuit of Detachment in Economics." *History of Political Economy* 121 (Winter): 121–45.

Nicholson, Linda, ed. (1990). *Feminism/Postmodernism*. New York: Routledge.

Nussbaum, Martha (1990). *Love's Knowledge*. Oxford: Oxford University Press.

Parkin, Michael (1990). *Economics*. Reading, Berks: Addison Wesley.

Polachek, Simon (1984). "Women in the Economy: Perspectives on Gender Inequality." In *Comparable Worth: Issue for the 80s*. A Consultation of the US Commission on Civil Rights, 6–7 June. Washington, D.C.: US Commission on Civil Rights.

Prilleltensky, Isaac (1989). "Psychology and the Status Quo." *American Psychologist* 795 (May): 795–802.

Resnick, Stephen, and Richard Wolff (1987). *Knowledge and Class*. Chicago: University of Chicago Press.

Richards, I.A. (1936). *The Philosophy of Rhetoric*. London: Oxford University Press.

Ricoeur, Paul (1977). *The Rule of Metaphor*. Toronto: University of Toronto Press.

Rosenau, Pauline M. (1992). *Postmodernism and the Social Sciences*. Princeton: Princeton University Press.

Rossetti, Jane (1993). "The Ambiguous Benefits of Postmodernism for Feminist Economists." Unpublished manuscript.

Ruccio, David F. (1991). "Postmodernism and Economics." *Journal of Post Keynesian Economics* 495 (Summer): 495–510.

Said, Edward (1979). *Orientalism*. New York: Vintage.
Sampson, Edward E. (1988). "The Debate on Individualism." *American Psychologist* 15 (January): 15–22.
Shulman, Steven (1992). "Metaphors of Discrimination: A Comparison of Gunnar Myrdal and Gary Becker." *Review of Social Economy* 50: 432–52.
Spivak, Gayatri Chakravorty (1988). *In Other Worlds*. New York: Routledge.
Strassman, Diana (1993). "Not a Free Market: The Rhetoric of Disciplinary Authority in Economics." In *Beyond Economic Man: Feminist Theory and Economics*. Ed. Marianne A. Ferber and Julie A. Nelson. Chicago: University of Chicago Press.
Sullivan, Edmond (1990). *Critical Psychology and Pedagogy*. New York: Bergin & Garvey.
Taylor, Charles (1987). "Overcoming Epistemology." In *After Philosophy: End or Transformation?* Ed. Kenneth Baynes, *et al*. Cambridge, MA: MIT Press, 464–88.
—— (1989). *Sources of the Self*. Cambridge, MA: Harvard University Press.
—— (1995). *Philosophical Arguments*. Cambridge, MA: Harvard University Press.
Thurow, Lester (1983). *Dangerous Currents: The State of Economics*. New York: Random.
Toulmin, Stephen (1990). *Cosmopolis: The Hidden Agenda*. New York: Free Press.
Tullock, Gordon (1986). "In Search of Exploited Workers: One Businessman's View of Comparable Worth." *Harvard Journal of Law and Public Policy* 95: 95–97.
Watt, Ian (1988). "Individualism and the Novel." In *Daniel Defoe's* Robinson Crusoe. Ed. Harold Bloom. New York: Chelsea.
Wendt, Paul (1990). "Comment on Amariglio." In *Economics as Discourse: An Analysis of the Language of Economists*. Ed. Warren J. Samuels. Boston, MA: Kluwer, 47–64.
Wheelwright, Philip (1967). *Metaphor and Reality*. Bloomington: Indiana University Press.
White, James Boyd (1985). *Herakles' Bow*. Madison: University of Wisconsin Press.
Williams, Rhonda (1993). "Race, Deconstruction and the Emergent Agenda of Feminist Theory." In *Beyond Economic Man: Feminist Theory and Economics*. Ed. Marianne A. Ferber and Julie A. Nelson. Chicago: University of Chicago Press, 144–53.

7

THE TOGGLING SENSIBILITY

Formalism, self-consciousness, and the improvement of economics

Howard Horwitz[1]

> Unearthing constitutive metaphors may not by itself accomplish change, but a statement that 'a handful of metaphors constitute discursive practices in economics' could be the heuristic metaphor that leads us to a richer understanding of economics. It compels us to develop a conceptual framework with which we can interpret and characterize alternative discursive practices in economics. The characterization will help us understand.
>
> (Klamer and Leonard 1994: 44)

The above passage, I think, conveys very nicely the aims and method of the now decade-old rhetoric of economics movement. The movement aims to be revisionary. By "exposing" the constitutive metaphors driving both economic discourse and our assent to its authority (Klamer and Leonard 1994: 41), rhetorical economics makes possible, even "compels," the conceptualization of "alternative discursive practices in economics." What is the mechanism of revisionary reconceptualization? Jack Amariglio, Stephen Resnick, and Richard Wolff (1990) elucidate the process. Exposing the rhetorical character of economic discourse and behavior shows these to be cultural and normative rather than natural and rationalist, based on some universal logical imperative. "Abandoning the search for the essence of economic theory," they write, "leads to a deconstruction and reconstitution of the economics discipline," and thus makes possible changes in the discipline that could precipitate changes in the policies economics bolsters and promotes. Amariglio, Resnick, and Wolff themselves espouse what they call a "nonessentialist Marxism" (137), but the revisionist aspirations of the rhetorical economists are fundamentally methodological rather than merely partisan. In the words of the movement's leading theorist, Deirdre (Donald) McCloskey – an unabashed neoclassical whose 1985 book has given the movement its name – supplanting the current formalism of economics with rhetorical analysis will "improve" the practice of economics and perhaps, too, economic practice.

In its activism, the rhetoric of economics movement typifies post-structuralist approaches that have over the last twenty years become influential in other social science and humanistic disciplines, including political science and the law. Generally, post-structural analysis employs what is called the linguistic or interpretive turn to examine a discipline's claims about the foundations of its procedures. Knowledge, the post-structuralist (rightly) argues, does not result from direct contact with phenomena but emerges within conventional and habitual structures. Knowledge, then, is not founded on a universal logic but on interpretations of phenomena, and it follows that disciplines are social achievements rather than what Philip Mirowski (1994a: 6) calls natural kinds.[2] The fundamental premises, methodology, and practices of a discipline (or any other community) are contextual and normative rather than necessary; they could be otherwise and they can change. Many commend the potential consequences of the post-structuralist critique: dissuading practitioners from foundationalism – from a conviction that they are merely realizing metaphysical principles – frees them to devise alternative practices.

Post-structuralists, then, tend to be methodological radicals.[3] They pursue practical reform by undermining premises about cognition that supposedly underlie a discipline's methodology; the philosophical challenge is the foundation for a political challenge. The rhetorical movement in economics, which we might generally name "critical economics," may be said to epitomize post-structuralism's practical aspirations. Economics can envision concrete effects in ways a discipline like English, my own, can scarcely imagine. Economics' sphere of study is undeniably material, whereas we in English must characterize our influence in unavoidably metaphorical terms. We must speak of the structure of consciousness, of ideology, of the linguistic constitution of knowledge; economists can address these matters, and tax and labor and trade policies too. Appropriately, then, and perhaps ironically, the rhetoric of economics movement assaults the very way its discipline claims to be concrete.

McCloskey and others object to the methodological formalism of orthodox economics. Its formalism consists of its claim to be a purely logical analysis of metaphysically given facts. Economic formalism purports to derive its practice, and hence its authority, from the nature of the object under scrutiny and the nature of the subject performing the analysis. Economics devises measures that correspond to the activity it studies; economic knowledge is therefore absolutely objective. This analysis, moreover, is purportedly conducted by (and measures the effects of) rational selves, able to comprehend fully the reasons for and consequences of economic activity. McCloskey objects that this model of economics has tended to fetishize fact and logic and to deny that economics relies on narrative and metaphorical strategies for its form and authority. Economists, like anybody else, make arguments rhetorically by using all four elements – fact, logic, metaphor, and narrative – of the rhetorical tetrad composing classical rhetoric and deeply informing humanistic and social discourses at the time of economics' eighteenth-century origins. Economics is an art, McCloskey contends, a rhetorical art in the classical sense, and the discipline's repression of this fact over the last thirty years has led both to misguided claims about its authority and, as McCloskey colloquially and pithily puts it, to bad economics.[4] Some orthodox economists have objected that McCloskey's rhetorical analysis softens up economics, jeopardizing its status as a science. Members of the movement counter that no science operates without rhetoric; all arguments are rhetorical. Moreover, they contend, the rhetorical critique of economic science is not merely critical but remedial.

How will rhetorical analysis improve economics? In the best philosophical sense, the critique itself provides the basis for reform. Rhetorical economics would restore economics as a human science by reintegrating its now exaggerated technical aspects with its humanistic basis. This integration is achieved through a "self-conscious reading" of the discipline. "Economics . . . can be improved by rhetorical self-consciousness," McCloskey writes (1994: xiii, 306). Klamer (1990a: 22) explains this claim: since all economic discourse is "metadiscourse," a reflection "on our lives as economic agents," studying economic rhetoric best teaches us about economic life. Klamer and Leonard (1994) add that conceiving of economics as a discursive practice rather than a purely formal, "mechanistic" enterprise would undermine our basic forms of self-identification; because "constitutive metaphors are us," "expos[ing]" these metaphors induces a "painful" self-transformation. No longer "blind to [our] practice," we can begin to "characterize alternative discursive practices in economics" (43, 41, 44). Resnick and Wolff (1988) contend that it is precisely in "being thoroughly self-conscious" about its status as a "particular knowledge construction" (rather than a "true" theory) that non-essentialist Marxism can present an alternative to conventional economic models (48–49, 57, 60–62).

There are no doubt differences in the way the neoclassical McCloskey and, say, avowed neomarxists like Amariglio, Resnick, and Wolff think self-consciousness about one's practice would improve economics. But self-consciousness, what McCloskey calls the "reflexive position" (1994: 213), is the collective, standard recommendation. In the absence of a universal logic to govern practice, the discipline must monitor and recast itself through self-consciousness. I find this methodological counsel, although typical of critical theory in all disciplines, at best circular. If the villain of the critical economists' scenario is formalism – the fantasy that one's practice derives from the form in which cognition proceeds – then does not the call to self-consciousness as remedial reproduce this very formalism? The rhetoric of economics movement must of necessity resort to formalism, however; otherwise, the rhetorical approach could not have any practical consequences because it would not exist.

McCloskey charges economists with selling snake-oil, specifically their ability to predict and run the economy without assistance from, or more importantly effort by, the citizens who honor their expertise. Economists' policies supposedly allow the economy to run automatically. Their product purports to be social engineering on the order of physical engineering, but it is snake-oil because economists do not "use all the resources of human reasoning" (McCloskey 1990: 5). Since World War II, economics has been afflicted by "modernism," a narrowing of intellectual focus and formalization of evaluative criteria. As McCloskey sketches the story, this modernist mode sprang up in various disciplines after World War I (although arguably this tendency reigned at least by 1880). Certain philosophers attempted to narrow their subject matter to an artificial language, architects reduced their subject to a cube, and painters reduced theirs to a surface. Modernist formalism, then, reduces the work of an art or discipline to a few formal operations supposedly based in and reflecting the form of the phenomenon or operation itself.

McCloskey reminds us that economics has traditionally been a broad discipline. Since the eighteenth century, when certain members of faculties of moral philosophy, like Smith and Malthus, were first designated economists, economics has traveled among and had transactions with many branches of knowledge and philosophy (hence Robert Heilbroner famously dubbed economists "the worldly philosophers"). Thus, the statistical (merely material) concerns of economics were never (certainly through Keynes's *General Theory*; cf. 1964: vii–viii) conceptually removed from its human concerns, its human effects. When economists belatedly adapted the modernist intellectual fashion, however, they reduced their field to questions of fact and logic, to equations and statistics, and they abandoned "the wider work of moral philosophy" (McCloskey 1994: xii). As a result, complex cultural matters including human intentions, motivation, and ethics were reduced to formulae measuring production, consumption, employment, trade balances, interest rates, exchange rates, etc. In McCloskey's view, this modernist idolatry of facts and formulae has been the ruin of economics, and has "led us to build high-rise slums and high interest rate economies" (1990: 5).

Others tell a similar tale. Amariglio criticizes the "cultural formalisms" underlying modernist disciplines and movements. Formalism was modernism's method for discovering the timelessness it presupposed as the ultimate principle of order. "Modernist discourse" pays "close attention . . . to form and most especially to those forms thought to express the essence of all things," because it posits that the meaning of phenomena inheres in their "formal conditions" rather than in the historical – i.e., contingent – conditions of their production (Amariglio 1990: 17–18). Modernist formalism was meant to manifest and secure a rationalist, unified self, but even in modernist discourse, Amariglio contends, this self is illusory. Robert Heilbroner concisely presents a parallel argument. His operative term is not rhetoric or, as it is for Amariglio, discourse, but ideology: "ideology permeates – indeed, constitutes – our social vision," and "there is no escape from it in seeking to explain that portion of social reality we denote as 'the economy'" (Heilbroner

1990: 111). Economics, like any other interpretive practice, is ideological rather than disinterested and objective.

Amariglio and Heilbroner discover economics continually trying to disguise, from itself and its audience, the presence of, for Heilbroner, ideology, and, for Amariglio, discourse, the fragmented self, and epistemological "uncertainty." Amariglio and Heilbroner seek a discipline whose fundamental assumptions recognize the historical constructedness rather than formal necessity of knowledge, and some form of Marxism seems to both more satisfactory. For her part, McCloskey charges the modernist experiment in economics with rhetorical "immoderation": aggrandizing the so-called scientific half of the rhetorical tetrad, fact and logic, and denying any dependence on the so-called humanistic half, narrative and metaphor. Of course economists, like anyone else, use story and metaphor, for facts and logic alone do not constitute discourse. Facts make sense only insofar as they are arranged in some narrative order; moreover, these narratives always are conveyed through metaphors.

Economists' denial of rhetoric – a familiar rhetorical ploy, of course – is the critical economists' central charge against the discipline's claim to authority. It is at best disingenuous for economics to deny its embeddedness in and dependence on the medium in which economics proceeds. McCloskey calls this medium rhetoric; others call it ideology, discourse, interpretation, the linguistic, or history. Economics' disavowal of its operative medium is supposed to stymie attempts to challenge the validity of economic analysis, to read economic analysis critically. As McCloskey puts the point, if economic facts and logic are in fact autonomous criteria, they are (as economists mean them to be) unassailable, enjoying unchecked (immoderate) analytical force. If the marshalled facts seem at all plausible, conclusions are unchallengeable, and citizens become likely to swallow wholesale the proclamations of economic experts – which, in McCloskey's view, is the primary objective of snake-oil economics. McCloskey and Klamer propose what they call a "literary solution" to economists' immoderation. Others propose comparable modes of inquiry: hermeneutics (Lavoie 1990; Wisman 1990), discourse analysis (Amariglio 1990), ideological analysis (Heilbroner 1990; Wisman 1990), sociological analysis (Rector 1990), deconstruction (Amariglio 1990; Rossetti 1990). All proposals emphasize the linguistic foundation of knowledge and social interaction and recommend some form of linguistic analysis and methodological reflection as the method for understanding the socially constructed quality of experience and social reality and for remedying modernism's vicious formalism.

For now, McCloskey's rhetorical method can stand as the exemplary case. The rhetorician combats formalism by using all four elements of the tetrad critically:

> use the stories and metaphors [at work in economic discourse] to criticize each other. Each part of the rhetorical tetrad, in other words,

> places limits on the excesses of the others. If you are fanatical about stories alone or about metaphors alone (or logic or facts alone . . .) you will start saying silly and dangerous things in the other realm.
> (McCloskey 1990: 4)

Rhetorical analysis lets the four elements of economic discourse serve as checks on each other in economic stories along with their attendant policy recommendations. One of McCloskey's wittiest examples for illustrating how her rhetorical method works concerns the debate over recent American fortunes in international competitiveness. Has America been suffering a decline of late? McCloskey addresses this question by revisiting the same debate about Britain's economic fortunes after 1870. The debate has taken place between the "pessimists" and the "optimists." Like those now anxious to recover America's once (albeit brief) unchallenged command over the global economy, McCloskey's pessimists speak of Britain's failure – its decline relative to other nations, including former colonies; the optimists (a group that includes McCloskey) tell a story of enduring economic strength.

The discrepancy between the competing accounts is dramatic, but McCloskey contends that the dispute is not about facts – these don't seem to be in question – but rather about rhetoric, about what narrative and metaphorical frameworks should convey the facts. "The way of telling stories," McCloskey writes, "shape[s] one's opinion about Victorian failure." If one "wants to tell" a story of international (imperial) supremacy that should have remained unchallenged, then the facts and figures can be used to demonstrate that Britain suffered a damnable decline after 1870. Conversely, "optimists like me [McCloskey] want the story to be one of 'normal' growth, in which 'maturity' is reached earlier by Britain. The failures were by international standards small, say the optimists" (McCloskey 1990: 45). In McCloskey's summary, the two camps employ conflicting metaphorical and narrative frameworks. The pessimists view international economic development jingoistically, as a sporting competition with only one winner, ideally the home-team. Second place, third place, or any other so-called place in relation to world-wide supremacy, is failure. The optimists prefer different metaphors and narrative structures, maturity and development.

It is important to note that for McCloskey the appearance of metaphor in no way undermines the validity of analysis. The crucial question concerns the appropriateness of metaphors to the story and the facts. Do fact, story, and metaphor *fit* each other? From this perspective, which she adapts from the rhetorical and pragmatist traditions, the pessimists' sporting jingoism strikes McCloskey as visibly partisan.[5] Their stories just don't fit the facts. McCloskey believes that this idea of fit – the fit among facts, stories, and metaphors – makes her analysis therapeutic as well as diagnostic. She repudiates modernist (positivist, objectivist, formalist) claims to speak the Truth, to speak without metaphor, as Thoreau characterized the language of nature. The validity of accounts is measured not by their "truth or accuracy" but by the "aptness or rightness" of the relation between metaphors and facts.

It is the aptness of narratives and metaphors that makes some narratives "better" than others. If economists (or any other interpreter of texts or social arrangements) would make their preferred narratives and metaphors explicit (rather than presenting them as positive, absolutely objective, indisputable facts, as the modernists tend to do), the rhetorical elements of an argument could "be tested for their aptness" (McCloskey 1990: 64–65, 90). Rhetorical economics will be more verifiable, more accessible, and less arrogant than formalist economics, because the complex of elements composing economic arguments will be more visible. Rhetorical economics will be "better" economics because: (a) it will be more aware of the way its various elements fit together and therefore better able to scrutinize itself; and (b) it will be more available to public review and hence public comprehension and refinement. Thus, reintegrating the elements of the rhetorical tetrad will shore up the ethics of economic analysis and debate.

Critiques like McCloskey's of the absolute objectivity of economic knowledge have produced the most resistance among positivist economists. The rhetorical economists tend to speak not of the truth of beliefs, but of the constitutive frameworks in which facts appear and make sense (see Klamer and Leonard 1994; Amariglio 1990; or Bicchieri 1988; Rossetti 1990). Some extend this critique. For Backhouse, Dudley-Evans, and Henderson (1993), the fact that different readers or observers bring "different perspectives" to a text or phenomenon means that we should not "seek to determine the 'meaning'" of such phenomena (17). There is no inherent meaning to interpret, and hence no correct interpretation can be arrived at. Likewise, Amariglio, Resnick, and Wolff (1990: 121) deny that their "anti-essentialist" Marxism is "the 'correct way' of understanding economic phenomena."

Following Stanley Fish, economists often refer to this way of speaking about knowledge as antifoundationalism, the denial that practice can be grounded "on a firmer footing than can be provided by mere belief" (Fish 1985 112).[6] Less discursively minded economists grow nervous about this view (see Solow 1988: 31–32; Lewis 1992). Uskali Maki (1993) argues that with only a coherence theory of knowledge – a sense of how specific beliefs fit with other beliefs – and without a correspondence theory of knowledge stipulating the relation of beliefs to phenomena exterior to them – McCloskey cannot make truth claims for her propositions, whether they concern economics in general, rhetoric in general, or British Victorian economics in particular. A subtler version of this argument appears in E. Roy Weintraub's (1990) response to Heilbroner: "Heilbroner's [antifoundationalist] claim itself is deconstructed by the situated nature of his own theoretical beliefs." Since Heilbroner denies the existence of a "neutral place" from which knowledge can be free of ideology, he cannot, as merely another "situated subject," make any positive or privileged (in this case Marxist) claims about the economy or recommendations about how to analyze and manage it.

In *Knowledge and Persuasion* (1994), McCloskey does an excellent job of forestalling such a criticism.[7] Here, following William James and Richard Rorty, McCloskey dismisses "metaphysical questions" as "unanswerable" (266). A formalist methodology aspiring to what Amariglio (1990: 19) calls a "universal formal principle," a universal logic, must have recourse to the metaphysical essence and foundation of being and truth. No such essence exists; existence, meaning, and knowledge are functions of specific situations and contexts. Classic philosophical formalism judges the validity of beliefs according to the form (foundation) of knowing; unless purified of historical contingency – beliefs, interests, and the like – unless based in some neutral encounter with the object of scrutiny, knowledge cannot be deemed valid. But the validity of knowledge is not a function of the form it takes. Knowledge is never unmediated, and belief, rather than needing to be grounded in the phenomenon itself, is "justified belief" (McCloskey 1994: 277), justified with respect to other beliefs that seem indefeasible, with reference, that is, to a large complex or network of beliefs that seem true. No "first instance of knowing," as Descartes (1980: 67) called it, is available or possible, but the fact that particular beliefs are (necessarily) premised on other beliefs does not in itself invalidate them or even challenge them in any way.

Although she discredits relativism, McCloskey does occasionally employ language that leaves her vulnerable to the charge. "The world is still there," she writes, "but we are still constructing it" (McCloskey 1994: 212). She is conflating here the semantically distinct terms construal and constructing, as do many post-structuralists like Fish, who throughout *Is There a Text in This Class?* (1980) writes that interpreters and interpretive communities "produce" the meaning of texts. If we produce the meaning of texts, however, we are not reading them but writing them and we might as well abandon any claim to knowledge distinct from sheer preference.[8] Likewise, the truth of a proposition or interpretation is not determined by one's interpretive community, whose authority Fish examines in *Is There a Text in This Class?* and whose authority McCloskey happily emphasizes. Specific communities make available the conventions for evaluating interpretations, but they do not necessarily supply the foundation for belief. Their authority, that is, concerns the reception rather than the validity of an interpretation, the terms of which may derive from far-flung arenas (although still identifiable as communities in the broadest and therefore trivial sense of the word). McCloskey (1994: 310) is wrong to claim that a speech community supplies "a tighter, not a looser, constraint" on arguments "than the formula of modernism."[9] Like formalism, an interpretive community supplies intrinsically no constraint on (or governance of) interpretation. Interpretation is structured by the networks of beliefs within which experience takes shape. These structures possess no metaphysical basis, nor are they necessarily coextensive with any particular community.

McCloskey herself intuits this fact, even if she sometimes misstates the case. She endorses the notion of "small-t truth" (ibid.: 309). This idea derives from James and Rorty, and it means that our beliefs feel true because they are justified by reference to networks of other justified beliefs, beliefs at that point unchallenged. Such unchallenged background beliefs do not derive from metaphysical conditions, nor are they authorized by a community; they are unchallenged, rather, because the structure of our beliefs – which may be entirely at odds with those of any particular community – renders us at that moment unable to doubt them.

McCloskey's espousal of small-t truth should incline her to avoid substituting "construction" for construal. Like many critics of positivism, including her fellow critical economists, McCloskey wishes to avoid the implication that "construal" must be based in some epistemologically pure condition. But insisting that the observer constructs phenomena jeopardizes the validity McCloskey clearly believes her accounts of economic history possess. "Construction" does not claim to involve phenomena different from our beliefs. "Construal" does make such claims (although they are of course fallible), and the validity of construal, its quality of feeling justified, is a function of habitual structures of belief. No more metaphysical grounding is necessary and indeed would be self-defeating.[10] In the acontextual interpretive environment someone like Descartes aspires to – in which we arrive at metaphysically grounded, true beliefs only once we have unburdened ourselves of our fallible, habitual, particular beliefs – interpretation would be impossible and superfluous precisely because the knower would lack a frame of reference in which perceptions would make sense.[11]

McCloskey refreshingly avoids this paradox by distinguishing between "empirical" study – study "devoted to studying the world" – and "empiricist" study – "devoted to a particular account of the relation between sense data and thought" (McCloskey 1994: 248). We have empirical experiences, encounters with phenomena, all the time. (Perhaps "evidentiary" is yet an even less loaded term.) Empiricist study, however, is impossible. In the empiricist, Cartesian ideal, knowledge would be caused by phenomena, directly intuited in the mind. But such a condition would not be knowledge; it would be identity between the phenomenon and the idea. As C.S. Peirce and James pointed out, knowledge, indeed all consciousness, requires the difference between the phenomenon and the cognitive faculty that makes knowledge knowledge *of* something. We always *have a relation* to objects of knowledge – we have an account of them – and therefore the fact of that relation is irrelevant to the validity of our beliefs.

I have tried to refine McCloskey's point about "small-t truth" in order to reemphasize and extend her own position in *Knowledge and Persuasion* about the status of beliefs. We cannot look to the status of our beliefs *per se* – to their ontological status or origin – to adjudicate among disputes or dispel doubts. No arena independent of the contexts in which we hold beliefs exists to provide a neutral ground on which to base and judge beliefs. Therefore the formalist methodology of economics – in which you adjudicate disputes by judging the status (ontological form) of competing beliefs – is untenable. The rhetorical or linguistic models of the critical economists are meant to some extent to supplant Being as a check on our beliefs and practices.

I doubt, however, that the rhetorical model can help us monitor our views. Any such prospect depends on distinctions as untenable as the classical formalist distinction between Being and practice. Recall that for McCloskey the analytical virtue of the rhetorical model is that it enables one to use the four elements of the rhetorical tetrad to "criticize each other" and "place . . . limits on the . . . the others" (McCloskey 1990: 4). But for the four elements of the tetrad to enable self-criticism, placing limits on the jurisdiction of the other elements, they must be more distinct than McCloskey herself thinks them to be. It is she after all who argues that facts make no sense (could they even be recognized as facts?) unless they are part of a story and expressed through narrative and metaphor. Fact, logic, story, metaphor are inseparable, different aspects of an elaborate and elaborable account of events or conditions. But if the four elements are differentiable aspects, none enjoys the independence that would qualify it to serve as a check on accounts of the other categories. Indeed, the four categories are versions of each other.

Consider the relation between facts and the other elements of the tetrad. A fact counts as a fact only in relation to other facts and stories, etc., that seem apt or valid according to criteria we currently find persuasive. That is, a fact exists and appears valid only in a context, and if we rehearse this context, as we sometimes are called upon to do or otherwise feel the need to do, it displays a narrative dimension; for the relation of part to part – of one fact to other facts in relation to which any fact counts as a fact – becomes palpable only temporally. To be comprehensible, a context – even if defined as purely logical – must have a dimension that feels temporal, a point consistent with the etymology of the word "fact" (past participle of the Latin *facere*, to do), wherein facts emerge as part of some action. Facts, then, to be facts, are accounts of objects or events or conditions which themselves belong to larger accounts, and thus are always part of narrative. To have a fact is already to have a story, and to dispute a fact is to dispute its contextualizing story, and to dispute a story is in effect to dispute the facts of that story. In short, to dispute one category of the tetrad – fact or story or metaphor – is *de facto* to dispute its attendant, contextualizing categories.

We would do well to say that disputes are always disputes about facts after all. McCloskey's tale about the pessimistic and optimistic historians of British Victorian economic development illustrates this claim. McCloskey emphasizes that the discrepancy between the competing accounts, while dramatic, is not about facts but rather about rhetoric. With the facts not in dispute, the key question is, in what narrative and metaphorical framework should facts appear? McCloskey is using the term "fact" here too narrowly. "Fact," here, must mean merely something like trade or employment statistics. McCloskey would ask, further, what do these facts mean? Was the British economy continuing to grow and was its growth diminished by the growth of other national markets and industry? But how is the answer to such questions not an account of a "fact"? Yes, it was growing, or no, it was not growing; or its rate of growth is acceptable or not acceptable, according to specifiable criteria. Klamer and Leonard (1994) are right to argue that constitutive metaphors – in this debate concerning the "maturity" or, in contrast, imperial domination of an economy – frame our questions, analysis, and conclusions. But these are all facts in a broad sense, by definition what any argument or account is about: it is a fact that the proper metaphorical framework in which to view British economic development is "maturity," or else "imperial domination," or else something else. In other words, facts (in this case, trade statistics and the like) in two competing stories are not really the same facts.

McCloskey's rhetorical analysis, then, in which facts check stories and vice versa or in which disclosing constitutive metaphors helps us assess the validity of those metaphors, is in principle circular rather than critical. In the rhetorical procedure, one account (of facts, story, metaphor) is enlisted in relation to another account (of facts, story, metaphor), in essence the same account under a different description, as Donald Davidson or Richard Rorty might say.[12] The procedure is as likely to confirm as to challenge belief, preference, or prejudice, and either result is a function of particular configurations of beliefs rather than of any formal rhetorical procedure. In itself, the exposure of fundamental premises in no way affects our investment in those premises. It therefore cannot help resolve a dispute between two observers who hold competing accounts of a situation. The first observer will look at the relation of story and metaphors to some facts and decide that the story and metaphors are apt; the second will decide the same about his or her story and metaphors. To believe a story (or a fact) means already to think that it is apt, that the elements fit; if you didn't, you wouldn't believe it. Circular as it is, then, the rhetorical model does no work; it is not an analytical method, or what Klamer (1990b: 151) calls "a mode of inquiry," or even a general approach. It is merely exhortation.[13]

For the rhetorical model to do any work, rhetorical analysis must itself be diagnostic and therapeutic, but any such claim recycles the very formalism that economic rhetoricians disdain in modernism. Note how closely the circular rhetorical method parallels that of a prototypical modern formalist, I.A. Richards, whom McCloskey cites as an emblematic rhetorician (McCloskey 1994: 36). In *Practical Criticism* (1929), Richards protests that his students at Cambridge are inept interpreters of poems. Richards views interpretation as in principle difficult because language is inherently ambiguous. To overcome ambiguity and the distortions of our preconceptions, Richards tries to devise a formal procedure that will furnish "a reasoned general technique for construing" and thus help us disambiguate poems (294). He breaks meaning into four contributory parts: sense, tone, intention, aim. The reader identifies one element and then uses it to determine the others. But Richards himself asserts numerous times that the four contributory elements of meaning are inseparable and very hard to distinguish. He speaks of the inevitable "combination" of functions, or even of how excessive focus on one contributory meaning will "interfere" with our comprehension of the others (176–77). And he is right about this commingling. Take the example of irony. An ironic remark means something other than the dictionary meaning of its individual words. Hence, identifying the apparent "sense" can only be misleading, since the meaning of the utterance may have nothing to do with the dictionary meaning of its words. Nor can identifying the tone help you understand the so-called "sense" of the utterance, for sense and tone here are identical. If you have an account of tone, you already have an account of sense and intention, indeed of the entire utterance. Any interpretation may well be wrong or appallingly incomplete, but Richards's four contributory meanings provide no help in understanding the others, because these categories, really, don't exist; instead you already have an account of the whole utterance.

If Richards's model is a high modernist formalism, so is McCloskey's, identical in structure to Richards's purported method. Both offer a circular theory of analysis (literary interpretation, for Richards, and for McCloskey rhetorical analysis of economics – although both are species of interpretation). Because it is circular, the rhetorical model cannot improve the discipline. I suspect that McCloskey recognizes the circularity of her method, because, as does Richards late in his book, she in effect abandons it in *Knowledge and Persuasion* (1994).[14] In this book she mainly exhorts us to possess "rhetorical self-consciousness," achieved through what she calls, following Richard Lanham, toggling. "Rhetorical self-consciousness [is] the ability to toggle between looking at and looking through a text," "to toggle between two knowings" of a text or experience. Virtue comes of toggling. "Good" people toggle; bad, intolerant people (monists) do not. Toggling is "necessary for wisdom" (293–94). Toggling is the mechanism through which rhetorical analysis supplies "procedural . . . justice" (295).

Rhetorical self-consciousness will make us good, but this summons is overtly formalist. In her anti-formalist bearing, McCloskey is careful to remind us that rhetorical analysis has no intrinsic results. Rhetoric "is not intrinsically anything" (339). Elsewhere, McCloskey has wondered "how economics would be different without [positivism]," and concluded, "Not much" (McCloskey 1989: 236). She pursues her historical work this way, making evidentiary arguments that challenge other evidentiary arguments. But McCloskey also displays a formalist demeanor, requiring a formal procedure to insure the aptness of our accounts (as if to compensate for the fact that, as she recognizes, our accounts are not grounded in Cartesian first instances of knowing). In her formalist temper, McCloskey can castigate positivism as "childishly rigid" and "absurd, the sort of positivist nonsense that so blights modern economics (ibid.: 237; 1991: 130). She is proud to say that she "pursu[es] a program of goodness" in *Knowledge and Persuasion* (1994: 95), and she casts toggling as the salutary formal method.

Toggling supposedly engenders wisdom and virtue by "allow[ing] one to see that one's view is a view." "Looking at and looking through" texts and beliefs exposes the partiality of knowledge, as when traveling abroad "throws light on life at home." "You can see two sides. You are tolerant, without by any means abandoning the responsibility to choose," presumably among diverse or even incommensurate cultural practices. McCloskey is emphasizing here that toggling "does not imply indifference between the views"; it is not relativism but an expansion of perspective (ibid.: 294). Presumably, when we look *at* a belief or argument or text, we behold it as real, as a matter of conviction with which we may or may not concur. When we look *through* a belief or account, in contrast, we discern it as a construct, as a view among other views with no special reality other than its structural coherence, and therefore with no special privilege. Toggling makes us more tolerant, then, because in seeing our beliefs for the constructs they are, we are less committed to them, freed from their limits because we now see their limits, i.e., the fact that they are limited, not necessary, not compelled by the phenomena of which they are accounts.

This vision of moral improvement is epistemologically incoherent. It imagines that, when toggling, we believe our beliefs and don't believe them too. McCloskey becomes Descartes here. Descartes, too, undertakes his methodological project to secure virtue. He advances his rationalist proof of being in order to convince the unfaithful of the existence of God. From God come not only properly grounded beliefs but virtue. For Descartes as for McCloskey, beliefs grounded in the proper method are by definition virtuous. (When beliefs result from toggling, they signal increased tolerance.) McCloskey is not advocating with Descartes "the general destruction of [one's] former opinions" since they derive from habitual structures (Descartes 1980: 57). Such an emptied self would lack the criteria – structures of beliefs – to make judgments. But McCloskey's virtuous self must be at least partially empty – that is, partially loosened from its investment in or commitment to its beliefs, to itself. Otherwise you could not look *through* a belief at the same time that you behold it (which really means to look by means of it). Only a self at least partially unsaturated by or freed from beliefs can disbelieve what it believes. More precisely, the possibility for self-criticism and for disciplinary and political reform seems to come from the part of us that is empty, which means from a part that possesses no criteria for judging nor, therefore, for self-revision.

McCloskey tries hard to deflect the charge of relativism. But toggling can occur only if the self is at least momentarily uncommitted to its beliefs and therefore unable to dispute others. McCloskey uses her example of the toggling traveller to imagine the activity of the toggling economist. The toggler "can evaluate the standard of living in America and India using either the point of view of American prices . . . or Indian prices." Knowing that two perspectives exist "is wisdom. . . . Pick one view, know what you're doing, and from time to time, for the hell of it, toggle." Note here the unmotivated nature of toggling. We toggle (revise our views?) not because we are dissatisfied with beliefs we currently hold, but for the hell of it. Toggling is "the ability to try out different perspectives" (McCloskey 1994: 295), but there seems to be no reason to try them out, and in trying something out, as in trying something *on*, we have no commitments to that perspective.

Toggling represents a consumerist model of belief, as if, presented with an array of beliefs, we get to choose beliefs we prefer rather than believing ones that feel true. In *If You're So Smart* (1990), McCloskey suggests that one must "choose" which story to tell about a series of facts (55). But if we must choose an interpretation of a situation or event, it is because we at that moment do not believe it, have no commitment to any particular account of that situation (otherwise we wouldn't need to *choose* an account). In such a situation the information in our purview doesn't really make sense to us, and we arbitrarily choose a story that suits our preferences or some agenda. Toggling "for the hell of it" is choosing our beliefs in this way. It means, however, that we have no commitment to the account we tell. If we have no commitment to the toggled perspective, then we have not really inhabited it and therefore there is no reason to think that it will have any effect on our beliefs or values. In analyzing a problem, we don't try perspectives on; we do not choose from which perspective, the American or the Indian, we will examine economic development. We operate within a particular frame of reference or perspective because it fits a situation, seems appropriate to the problem at hand, while others do not.

Of course we are not limited to the American or Indian perspectives. We may believe (or be persuaded) that there is a more salient international or global perspective that is most appropriate to considering economic developments in both America and India. We believe so, however, not because we have tried on this perspective but because it seems compelling and the others do not. Or perhaps the African perspective (or the Alaskan perspective, etc.) is compelling, and the others must be seen through this more constitutive framework. Toggling, then, the method of rhetorical self-consciousness, cannot result in more (or less) tolerance because it doesn't exist. We cannot suspend our beliefs to try on different perspectives.[15]

We believe what we believe. This ontological fact does not mean that we cannot be tolerant or cannot learn from new experiences, even to the point of being converted to a radically different perspective. But this transformative process does not involve a trying-on of perspectives, a partial or temporary suspension of the self in a moment in which we don't believe what we believe, or believe less than we believe; rather, it involves precisely transformation of our beliefs, of ourselves, a reconfiguration of our beliefs that feels fundamental and therefore can be characterized as a transformation of perspective. If new experiences make us more tolerant, it is because beliefs that we already hold have disposed us to regard as too narrow the range of opinions or behaviors we now find acceptable. In this transformation, however, the self is never suspended and another tried on. The self abides, even as it is changing, perhaps unrecognizably.

Toggling, then, is nothing other than a sensibility, an exhortation to respond to new experiences in one way rather than others. When experiencing new things, be tolerant; or more generally, when experiencing, be tolerant. Again, however, this advice reprises the very formalism that McCloskey decries. A particular moral response seems built into the condition of being. Without this formalism – which, let me repeat, is circular and therefore does not exist – the exhortation to rhetoric would have no force.[16] One might wonder, too, why it is that toleration is a superior response to situations. Why am I a better person if I tolerate the white supremacist, the neo-Nazi, the racial bigot, the wife beater, the child abuser, legislators who cut funding for public education, Republicans, Democrats, neoclassical economists, Marxists, people who like opera, people who hate opera, advocates of rhetorical self-consciousness, or debunkers of such advocacy? Why should I tolerate anyone whose conduct violates what I take to be some fundamental moral principle? Personally, I believe tolerance is in general an excellent social and political principle. But this rule of thumb does not follow from toggling, from trying on perspectives; it follows, if it follows at all, from beliefs I hold about the golden rule, about the proper way to organize a society, about tolerance itself, and about a host of other matters, some of which are specifiable and some of which are not.

I fail to see, therefore, how economics and more generally scholarly and moral life "can be improved by rhetorical self-consciousness" (McCloskey 1994: 306), precisely because rhetoric is indeed, as McCloskey notes but then forgets, intrinsically nothing. Self-consciousness in itself does not convince anyone of anything. We can discern an idealism about method and consciousness similar to McCloskey's in Klamer and Leonard's (1994) idea that rhetorical analysis of constitutive metaphors will help us account for differences and the lack of communication among neoclassical economists, Marxists, post-Keynesians, institutionalists and others, and may therefore improve communication and debate among economists. However appealing, this is a wishful sentiment. Will neoclassicals and Marxists be surprised to learn that they employ incompatible constitutive metaphors? They already know that they embrace very different, even hostile, fundamental premises: they view economic phenomena from very different frameworks, and this difference is what their different constitutive metaphors express. The clear light of rhetorical analysis will make their disputes no more readily adjudicable; perhaps less so, now that the debate concerns not just production statistics and profit margins but fundamental premises. Perhaps Klamer and Leonard mean that discussion among economists will become more civil; but if you previously found the neoclassical or the Marxist or the Austrian economist pernicious and worthy only of disdain, you are not likely to become more tolerant of your opponents because you are reminded that you and they merely hold incompatible views of society – that's why you find them odious in the first place.

One goal of the critical economists is to develop what William Waller and Linda Robertson (1990: 1040–41) have called a more "open discourse community." By making our premises and persuasive strategies more explicit we may include more people in the economic conversation and make it more comprehensible to non-specialists. This is surely another admirable sentiment, but it leaves fundamental disagreement intact. McCloskey (1994: 391) urges economists "to agree on some particular, human, rhetorical standard by which the quarrel can yield progress." This exhortation presumes too much. It assumes we *can* agree on a standard, and since the standard is a standard of conduct, it presumes that by agreeing to talk in a certain way, economics will do its job better. McCloskey presumes, here, a genteel model of disciplinary practice. In the chapter "Rhetoric as Morally Radical," she fashions a dialogue to illustrate how inquiry and a rhetorical community should work. The dialogue takes place between herself and Arjo Klamer, old friends and collaborators contemplating important ideas. This is a charming ideal, but McCloskey's control group is biased and cannot be representative. Moreover, again, it is formalist, thinking that the results of inquiry follow from the form it takes. Here, intellectual trust itself improves the discipline.

But can it? How does the trust and respect informing this dialogue yield superior results? As some others before me have observed, the rhetoricians or critical economists take for granted the relation between talk about economics and economic activity. As Weintraub (1990: 126; author's italics deleted) has argued, "doing economics is a different activity from talking about doing economics." Heilbroner (1988: 42–43) denies that a rhetorically oriented economics conversation would "make sense out of economic experience," since it concerns "style" rather than "substance." Fish (1988: 25–26) undercuts the rhetoricians' strongest claim that rhetoric helps us evaluate economic arguments: noting that all arguments are rhetorical does not help us determine which rhetorical performances are superior or acceptable or bankrupt. According to these criticisms, rhetorical analysis may possibly (although its circularity makes me doubt it) teach us about how economic discourse works, how it persuades; but such instruction alone does not help us manage the economy or establish priorities in examining the economic environment (see also Gerrard 1993). Part of the rhetoricians' point is that we must include talk about the economy (in the workplace, in the media) in our analyses of economic performance. If such talk affects, say, productivity or consumer confidence, then try to measure it. But the talk alone is not economics.

The rhetoricians would counter, with some legitimacy, that Weintraub, Heilbroner, and Fish miss the point: they retain too firm a distinction between the substance and mode of discourse. The critical economists contend that one cannot radically distinguish talking about doing economics from doing economics. There is no "just doing" economics. The substance of economic analysis is, on this view, scarcely distinguishable from the manner of the analysis. Therefore reading economic texts better will (or at least can) improve the discipline by improving our talk about the economy. Even on the rhetoricians' own terms, however – and bracketing for the moment the inability of the rhetorical approach to disclose anything – this claim is again circular. If economics talk and economics practice are the same, then the reasons for criticizing an economic text are substantive (economic) rather than rhetorical after all. The critic will find an economic text wanting not because its author has poorly integrated the tetrad, but because its economics are wrong; poor integration of the tetrad is only the sign of economic error. From this point of view, it isn't that the economic rhetoricians are not doing economics; they are not doing rhetoric.

McCloskey unwittingly concedes more than this point when she proudly declares that "a literary, humanistic, rhetorical approach to economics provides the economist . . . with a place where she can stand outside the field" (1994: 383). There's an emblematic logical contradiction here: if I stand outside a "field," then why am I qualified to criticize or practice it? McCloskey would counter that economics is too narrow and too narrow-minded; we need to study other fields to place checks on (i.e., broaden) economics. The rhetorical economist, however, is never outside the field. The field is never more "open" (in the ontological sense that this term must mean) than it ever was. If you use strategies or information or premises from another discipline to criticize economics texts, then these items are at that moment precisely tools of economic analysis, and their value as tools is weighed according to the criteria of economics, not of rhetoric or English (a good thing, too). If the discipline is so misguided that it is asking the wrong questions, then fashion better ones, or dissolve the discipline; but such determinations are not the result of extradisciplinary analysis but of convictions about how we should act in the momentous arenas treated by economics.

Neither should the critical economists be hopeful, nor their positivist readers feel too nervous, about the consequences of rhetorical analysis, phantoms that they are. It is not the rhetorical or discursive form of analysis that causes us to adjust or abandon current economic principles. It is the content of an analysis and of our response to it – the content rather than the form of our beliefs about a topic – that leads us to act in one way rather than another.[17] The contingency of revision (of beliefs and practice) implied by this fact, however, incites the critical economists to try to discover the very formalist foundation for belief and analysis that they readily debunk in others. Revision – of economics and of the self – may or may not occur. Our responses to experience depend on a variety of factors and variables. The rhetoricians reprise formalism precisely to guarantee revision and therefore the efficacy of their practice.

Even the most sophisticated examples of discursive analysis illustrate this tendency. Take, for example, Amariglio's (1990) deconstruction or "postmodern discourse analysis" (17) of the persistence of the idea of uncertainty in modernist economic writing. Amariglio would undermine modernist discourse by permitting the "postmodern moments of uncertainty . . . more freedom to operate within that discourse" (41). He contends that his method is more actively "subversive" than McCloskey's because more interior to economics, more "at the core of modernist economic discourse" (27). McCloskey, a rather passive observer in Amariglio's account (as in Heilbroner's), discloses rhetorical patterns but leaves the content of modernist economics "untouched" (25). McCloskey can only "call attention" to rhetorical patterns; Amariglio's deconstruction can undermine the authority of modernist economics more effectively because it "trace[s] the way certain concepts within modernist economic discourse 'deconstruct' the very modernism they are thought to reflect" (16).

For Amariglio, the persistence of "uncertainty" as a concern undermines the modernist commitment to the self as a unified, rational calculator and thereby gives us "more freedom" to entertain "alternative economic discourses" (41, 27). I need scarcely note the formalism of Amariglio's enterprise. He, like the modernists whose formalism he censures, thinks that the substance and force of his analysis is authorized by the form it takes (here, deconstruction with its non-unified self). As he, along with Resnick and Wolff, describe their anti-essentialist method, it is as if getting to the core of economic discourse permits a McCloskeyan toggling. Once we see from within the untenability of economics' account of the self, and once we see that economic discourse consists of incommensurate knowledge "constructions" of economic reality rather than empiricist and adjudicable theories, then we are freed from economics' dominant scientism to consider alternatives. In this logic, finding at the core of economics a logical gap and an incommensurateness among its models permits us to conclude that "no discipline of economics exists" (Amariglio *et al.* 1990: 109) and frees us from the hold of the discipline to imagine alternatives to it.

These authors have not, of course, formulated their non-essentialist Marxism because, loosened from conventional constraints, they are now free to imagine previously unthinkable alternatives. Non-essentialist Marxism was already included (if only as censured) in the discipline. Certainly the critique of the neoclassical subject circulates in Thorstein Veblen's famous passage on the absurdity of "the hedonistic conception of man" as a "self-contained globule of desire" (Veblen 1919: 73–74). Nor do their methodological alternatives actually disclaim positive existence. Amariglio, Resnick, and Wolff (1990) truly believe that the orthodox model is wrong and that non-essentialist Marxism is a more effective model of analysis, and they have set out to demonstrate both theses. These authors positively reject the neoclassical account of the economic subject. Amariglio is wrong to claim that the persistence of the idea of uncertainty itself undermines economic discourse.[18] This is what he is trying to do. He traces this motif in order to persuade others that his alternative, despite his express denials, is logically and, indeed, empirically superior to modernist models, since his premises better fit the constitution of the subject.

Finally, the discursive nature of knowledge and the incommensurateness among economic theories do not in themselves discredit modernist economics. Even if the modernists' conception of the self as rational calculator is wrong, their measurements are not necessarily wrong. Economists' measurements and analyses are inept or proficient because they are inept or proficient, not because their methodological justifications are right or wrong, consistent or inconsistent. Even if we mischaracterize our fundamental premises, our practices and results may still fit a situation. The appropriateness of an analysis to a situation is a function of how well it fits the situation. It is therefore, however, no more than an evidentiary claim. This fact makes Amariglio, Resnick, and Wolff, like McCloskey and Klamer and no less than the dreaded positivists, nervous, and they seek to secure their specific, evidentiary arguments in something firmer. They resort to formalism for precisely the reason that the positivists resort to it, to ground otherwise falsifiable claims in something firmer than evidence and belief.

Amariglio provides no hint of what political or policy consequences follow from his deconstructive analysis. How should the absence of a rational economic subject affect evaluation of trade policy or tax or labor policy or homelessness or exacerbated polarization in income distribution or national health insurance legislation? Positions on these matters derive not from any formal procedure but from the beliefs the procedure is claimed to monitor. Typically circular and inconsequential, Amariglio's forceful analysis exemplifies the abiding formalist mistake of the critical economists, without which, however, they would have nothing to talk about since the rhetorical/discursive turn is not a mode of analysis. Talking about how economists talk is at best another way of characterizing beliefs about economics and so cannot *per se* improve economics; at most it might alter the vocabulary of debates. Rhetorical self-consciousness neither frees us to entertain formerly unpersuasive ideas like uncertainty and the non-essential self, nor makes alternative practice more (or less) possible to conceive. If it is anything at all, rhetorical self-consciousness – or rather talk about such consciousness, since such self-consciousness does not exist – is moral talk signaling that fundamental premises are already under challenge. The reasons for the challenge are substantive and motivated rather than metacritical. Rhetorical or discursive analysis is not the challenge, only its formalist guise.

Notes

1 I appreciated the opportunity to present an earlier version of this essay at the Conference on the New Economic Criticism held at Case Western Reserve University in October, 1994, organized and hosted by Martha Woodmansee and Mark Osteen, with Deirdre McCloskey. This terrifically run conference was an excellent forum for intellectual exchange: the talk was stimulating and I received helpful responses to my paper.

2 For a discussion of the linguistic or interpretive or hermeneutical turn as it pertains to economics, see: Backhouse, Dudley-Evans, and Henderson (1993: 1–6); Lavoie (1990); Samuels (1990); Bicchieri (1988). For discussions of the linguistic turn in other disciplines, see Jay (1982), LaCapra (1983), Toews (1987), White (1978), Geertz (1973), and Rorty (1984, 1989, 1991). On this point and others, Geertz's work and Rorty's work are regularly cited in manifestos of the movement.

3 Lavoie observes that the contributors to his volume, *Economics and Hermeneutics*, tend to be "radicals, challenging the way economics is done today" (Lavoie 1990: 3).

4 McCloskey mounts this critique throughout *If You're So Smart* (1990) and in *Knowledge and Persuasion* (1994).

5 McCloskey emphasizes the rhetorical tradition as the source of this idea in *If You're So Smart* (1990), where references to the pragmatist tradition are surprisingly absent. She invokes the pragmatist tradition in *Knowledge and Persuasion* (1994: 210–15, 345–49).

6 One might say that the critical economists occupy the category that Fish calls in this essay and in his "Comments" at the 1986 conference on the Rhetoric of Economics "antifoundationalist theory hope" – the hope that antifoundationalism rather than familiar positivist theory can improve our practice – while their opponents represent Fish's category of "antifoundationalist theory fear" – fear that antifoundationalism will jeopardize the ability of a discipline to make claims for its expertise. Neither response, Fish argues, is warranted, and my argument partly borrows from Fish's take on such matters.

7 I developed an argument akin to Maki's and very similar to Weintraub's in the version of this essay called "Why Should We Believe You?," circulated at the Conference on the New Economic Criticism. While such an argument still seems to me partially relevant to rhetoric of economics arguments, McCloskey's elaboration of her position on epistemology in *Knowledge and Persuasion* is far more satisfactory than in, say, *If You're So Smart*. I therefore do not pursue at length here an argument about the status of McCloskey's truth claims.

8 The notion that, in the absence of direct and unmediated contact with phenomena, we do not interpret texts but instead produce their meaning reinstates as a criterion of knowledge Descartes's fanciful idea that, in order for them to be valid, ideas must "derive from" phenomena. The sense that we construct rather than construe retains a Cartesian correspondence theory of truth as the satisfactory condition of belief. The well-known work of C.S. Peirce and Ferdinand de Saussure – who contend that ideas emerge and make sense as signs, only in differential relation to other ideas – should have dispelled this notion. For

a discussion of the relation between writing and reading texts, in the context of theories of legal interpretation, see Michaels (1985: 678).

9 If Fish makes similar claims in *Is There a Text in This Class?*, he avoids this flawed logic in his more recent work, *Professional Correctness* (1995).

10 Even the best formulated claims for the constructedness of knowledge belie the claim. Resnick and Wolff (1988) think that self-consciousness that their non-essential Marxism is a construction, even a contrivance (60), rather than a claim to absolute truth, elevates their model. In "Division and Difference," these two authors and Amariglio deny that nonessentialist Marxism is the "correct way" to consider economic phenomena (Amariglio *et al.* 1990: 121). They distinguish between illusory positivist economic models and "normative" ones (119). Nevertheless, they clearly believe that their model (or normative construction) best accounts for economic phenomena, precisely because it correlates with the non-unified self and the ineluctability of "uncertainty" that positivist economics has tried to repress but which continually surfaces in positivist discourse. This is an empirical claim, one that evidently precludes others. In general, if you can be a partisan of one account against others, it does not have for you the status of a construction, but of a compelling account.

11 Fish has made this argument about the work of the critical legal scholar Roberto Unger. Unger "conceiv[es] of selves . . . as entities with the capacity of being without content." Such selves, however, would "be selves with no orientation or angle of habitual vision that inclined them in this direction rather than that. They would be selves without a core of assumptions in relation to which . . . things (physical, mental, moral)" take shape. "If [the self] stands free of all confining hierarchies and roles, it is nothing" (Fish 1989: 427–28).

12 Davidson (1980: 51) suggests that descriptions by agents of the causes of their acts "are apt to be trivial and unrevealing," because such descriptions are in fact redescriptions of the action, an account of the same thing under another description. See Davidson's discussion of this point in essays like "Actions, Reasons, Causes, Events," "Agency," and "Freedom to Act," published in *Essays on Actions and Events* (1980).

13 At one point McCloskey suggests that at the least the rhetorical approach is one technique among many for understanding economic texts, and "the more techniques the better" (McCloskey 1994: 307). The circularity of the exhortation to rhetoric, however, means that it isn't a technique at all.

14 Richards in effect abandons his systematic method in the closing portion of *Practical Criticism* (1929). He decides that intelligence is unavoidably "word-dependent" and therefore unable to overcome the preconceptions, habits, and "stock responses" to which we submit and which are imparted through words (322, 295). Given the "inevitable ambiguity" of language, and since our preconceptions and submission to authority "betray" our every word-dependent attempt to surmount our preconceptions, our attempts at understanding consistently result in "bewilderment," a feeling of "chaos" that prompts only reinvigorated resort to prefabricated response (320, 322). At this point, Richards replaces his systematic ideal with what we might call a heroic model of interpretation, in which an "unsupported self" (296), a self having perilously dispensed with its preconceptions, "triumph[s] against odds" (315) and understands language and experience. The criterion for interpretive success now becomes "the

quality of the reading" rather than its "correctness" (327). Richards's only real interpretive counsel now is a Cartesian self-consciousness. Once the self is purified of its beliefs – with belief defined as distorting preconception and a reliance on external authorities – we should develop "a little pertinacity and a certain habit of examining our intellectual . . . instruments" (314). High quality interpretations require an unsupported self self-consciously transcending its context.

15 As Fish (1988: 27) has written, a "point of view . . . is not something you can hold at arm's length [try on] with a view toward rejecting it or confirming it." On the question of whether we can choose our beliefs – and on why we cannot choose them – see Michaels (1983).

16 We might note that McCloskey's recommendation is again wholly modernist in that it too matches the program of Richards, who wants to encourage "qualities of sensitiveness and imagination" (Richards 1929: 213).

17 Klamer himself makes this very point in "Towards the Native's Point of View" (1990a: 23): "We humans act because we experience a *tension*. We have a vague feeling of dissatisfaction (the stomach does not feel as we like it or we feel restless) and we walk to the refrigerator. We read or hear something that does not fit in with what we already know and we begin to think." In this characterization, what motivates action is not the form of stimulation (rhetoric or hunger), but the content of our experience. Rhetoric is not in itself the trigger of change, belief is.

Klamer adds a footnote that both explains what motivates revision and indicates why he seeks a formal mode of inquiry that will guarantee revision. "How are we able to perceive a tension? If something does not fit what I already know, how do I know?" (32 n5). Klamer's last sentence should read differently: If something does not fit what I already know, that's tension. The tension that Klamer so nicely discusses arises precisely when an experience clashes with the organization of experience that feels comfortable to us. Klamer worries, however, that lack of fit means that we by definition exclude or repress unsettling phenomena. Yes, our psyches may manage to disregard some experience that would be unsettling, but it is only because phenomena or experience can register as unsettling that we might (be motivated to) revise our beliefs or conduct. Klamer notes the contingency of revision – the fact that it might not occur and that it depends on the configuration of our beliefs – and seeks greater warrant for revision. He advocates rhetorical analysis as a formal method in order to guarantee disruption of beliefs, the arousal of tension.

18 See Amariglio (1990: 41): "[U]ncertainty unleashes a postmodern reaction to knowledge and rationality." Jacques Derrida makes very different, less formalist claims for the efficacy of deconstruction. In order for it to "intervene" in traditional structures and practices of Western philosophical discourse, he argues, deconstruction requires a "labor" on the part of the practitioner (Derrida 1977: 195). Deconstruction does not deconstruct on its own, and its consequences, if any, result only from an audience's reception of a writer's actions.

References

Amariglio, Jack (1990). "Economics as a Postmodern Discourse." In *Economics as Discourse: An Analysis of the Language of Economists*. Ed. W.J. Samuels. Boston, MA: Kluwer, 15–46.

——, Stephen Resnick, and Richard Wolff (1990). "Division and Difference in the 'Discipline' of Economics." *Critical Inquiry* 17 (Autumn): 108–37.

Backhouse, Roger, Tony Dudley-Evans, and Willie Henderson, eds. (1993). *Economics and Language*. London & New York: Routledge.

Bicchieri, Cristina (1988). "Should a Scientist Abstain from Metaphor?" In *The Consequences of Economic Rhetoric*. Ed. A. Klamer, D.N. McCloskey, and R.M. Solow. Cambridge: Cambridge University Press, 100–14.

Davidson, Donald (1980). *Essays on Actions and Events*. New York: Oxford University Press.

Derrida, Jacques (1977). "Signature Event Context." *Glyph: Johns Hopkins Textual Studies* 1: 172–97.

Descartes, René (1980). *Meditations on First Philosophy*. In *Discourse on Method and Meditations on First Philosophy*. Trans. Donald A. Cress. Indianapolis: Hackett.

Fish, Stanley (1980). *Is There a Text in This Class? The Authority of Interpretive Communities*. Cambridge, MA: Harvard University Press.

—— (1985). "Consequences." In *Against Theory: Literary Studies and the New Pragmatism*. Ed. W.J.T. Mitchell. Chicago: University of Chicago Press, 106–31.

—— (1988). "Comments from Outside Economics." In *The Consequences of Economic Rhetoric*. Ed. A. Klamer, D.N. McCloskey, and R.M. Solow.

—— (1989). *Doing What Comes Naturally: Change, Rhetoric, and the Practice of Theory in Literary and Legal Studies*. Durham, NC: Duke University Press.

—— (1995). *Professional Correctness: Literary Studies and Political Change*. New York & Oxford: Oxford University Press.

Geertz, Clifford (1973). *The Interpretation of Cultures*. New York: Basic Books.

Gerrard, Bill (1993). Review of *If You're So Smart*. *Economic Journal* (July): 1086–87.

Heilbroner, Robert (1988). "Rhetoric and Ideology." In *The Consequences of Economic Rhetoric*. Ed. A. Klamer, D.N. McCloskey, and R.M. Solow. Cambridge: Cambridge University Press, 38–43.

—— (1990). "Economics as Ideology." In *Economics as Discourse: An Analysis of the Language of Economists*. Ed. W.J. Samuels Boston, MA: Kluwer, 101–16.

James, William ([1890] 1950). *The Principles of Psychology*. 2 vols. New York: Dover.

—— (1975). *Pragmatism and the Meaning of Truth*. Cambridge, MA: Harvard University Press.

Jay, Martin (1982). "Should Intellectual History Take a Linguistic Turn? Reflections on the Habermas–Gadamer Debate." In *Modern European Intellectual History: Reappraisals and New Perspectives*. Ed. Dominick LaCapra and Steven L. Kaplan. Ithaca: Cornell University Press, 86–110.

Keynes, John Maynard ([1936] 1964). *General Theory of Employment, Interest, and Money*. New York: Harcourt.

Klamer, Arjo (1990a). "Towards the Native's Point of View: the Difficulty of Changing the Conversation." In *Economics and Hermeneutics*. Ed. D. Lavoie. London & New York: Routledge, 19–33.

—— (1990b). "The Textbook Presentation of Economic Discourse." In *Economics as Discourse: An Analysis of the Language of Economists*. Ed. W.J. Samuels. Boston, MA: Kluwer, 129–54.

Klamer, Arjo, and Thomas C. Leonard (1994). "So What's an Economic Metaphor?" In *Natural Images in Economic Thought: "Markets Read in Tooth and Claw"*. Ed. P. Mirowski. New York: Cambridge University Press, 20–51.

Klamer, Arjo, Donald N. McCloskey, and Robert M. Solow, eds. (1988). *The Consequences of Economic Rhetoric*. Cambridge: Cambridge University Press.

LaCapra, Dominick (1983). *Rethinking Intellectual History: Texts, Contexts, Language*. Ithaca: Cornell University Press.

Lavoie, Don, ed. (1990). *Economics and Hermeneutics*. London & New York: Routledge.

Lewis, Margaret (1992). Review of *If You're So Smart. Journal of Economic Issues* 26: 1310–12.

McCloskey, Donald N. (1985). *The Rhetoric of Economics*. Madison: University of Wisconsin Press.

—— (1989). "Why I Am No Longer a Positivist." *Review of Social Economy* 47 (Fall): 225–38.

—— (1990). *If You're So Smart: The Narrative of Economic Expertise*. Chicago: University of Chicago Press.

—— (1991). "Conditional Economic History: a Reply to Komlos and Landes." *Economic History Review* 128–32.

—— (1994). *Knowledge and Persuasion in Economics*. Cambridge & New York: Cambridge University Press.

Maki, Uskali (1993). "Two Philosophies of the Rhetoric of Economics." In *Economics and Language*. Ed. R. Backhouse, T. Dudley-Evans, and W. Henderson. London & New York: Routledge, 23–50.

Michaels, Walter Benn (1983). "Is There a Politics of Interpretation?" In *The Politics of Interpretation*. Ed. W. J. T. Mitchell. Chicago: University of Chicago Press, 335–45.

—— (1985). "Response to Perry and Simon." *Southern California Law Review* 58 (January): 673–81.

Mirowski, Philip (1994a). "Doing What Comes Naturally: Four Metanarratives on What Metaphors Are For." In *Natural Images in Economic Thought: "Markets Read in Tooth and Claw"*. Ed. P. Mirowski. New York: Cambridge University Press, 3–19.

—— , ed. (1994b) *Natural Images in Economic Thought: "Markets Read in Tooth and Claw."* NewYork: Cambridge University Press.

Peirce, Charles S. (1958). *Charles S. Peirce: Selected Writings*. Ed. Philip P. Wiener. New York: Dover.

Rector, Ralph A. (1990). "The Economics of Rationality and the Rationality of Economics." In *Economics and Hermeneutics*. Ed. D. Lavoie. London & New York: Routledge, 195–235.

Resnick, Stephen, and Richard Wolff, (1988). "Marxian Theory and the Rhetorics of Economics." In *The Consequences of Economic Rhetoric*. Ed. A. Klamer, D.N. McCloskey, and R.M. Solow. Cambridge: Cambridge University Press, 47–63.

Richards, I.A. (1929). *Practical Criticism*. New York: Harcourt.

Rorty, Richard. (1984). "The Historiography of Philosophy: Four Genres." In *Philosophy in History: Essays in the Historiography of Philosophy*. Ed. Richard Rorty, J.B. Schneewind, and Quentin Skinner. New York: Cambridge University Press, 49–75.

—— (1989). *Contingency, Irony, and Solidarity*. Cambridge, MA: Harvard University Press.

—— (1991). *Objectivity, Relativism, and Truth: Philosophical Papers*, Vol. 1. New York: Cambridge University Press.

Rossetti, Jane (1990). "Deconstructing Robert Lucas." In *Economcs as Discourse: An Analysis of the Language of Economists*. Ed. W.J. Samuels. Boston, MA: Kluwer, 225–43.

Samuels, Warren J., ed. (1990). *Economics as Discourse: An Analysis of the Language of Economists*. Boston, MA: Kluwer.

Saussure, Ferdinand de (1969). *Course in General Linguistics*. London: McGraw-Hill.

Solow, Robert M. (1988) "Comments from Inside Economics." In *The Consequences of Economic Rhetoric*. Ed. A. Klamer, D.N. McCloskey, and R.M. Solow. Cambridge: Cambridge University Press, 31–37.

Toews, John E. (1987) "Intellectual History after the Linguistic Turn: The Autonomy of Meaning and the Irreducibility of Experience." *American Historical Review* 92 (Oct.): 879–907.

Veblen, Thorstein (1919). "Why Economics Is Not an Evolutionary Science." In *The Place of Science in Modern Civilization*. New York: Huebsch, 65–89.

Waller, William, and Linda Robertson, (1990). "Why Johnny (PhD, Economics) Can't Read: A Rhetorical Analysis of Thorstein Veblen and a Response to Donald McCloskey's *Rhetoric of Economics*." *Journal of Economic Issues* 24 (December): 1027–44.

Weintraub, E. Roy (1990). "Comment on 'Economics as Ideology' by Robert Heilbroner." In *Economics as Discourse: An Analysis of the Language of Economists*. Ed. W.J. Samuels. Boston, MA: Kluwer, 117–28.

White, Hayden (1978). *Tropics of Discourse: Essays in Cultural Criticism*. Baltimore: Johns Hopkins University Press.

Wisman, Jon D. (1990). "The Scope and Goals of Economic Science." In *Economics and Hermeneutics*. Ed. D. Lavoie. London & New York: Routledge, 113–33.

8

THE ENDS OF ECONOMICS

John Dupré and Regenia Gagnier[1]

The title of this paper is intended to be multiply ambiguous. It raises, first, the question of why we care about the conclusions of economics, why we bother to do economics at all. Second, and given that we do do economics, it is possible that whatever ends economists themselves intend to promote by doing economics might differ from more general goals identified in answering the first question. And third, we may inquire whether economic theories may contain, overtly or covertly, particular economic goals – normative presuppositions about the way economics ought to be practiced. In this paper, we shall offer some admittedly sketchy answers to these interrelated questions. Since we shall suggest that many of the ends of economics are ends that we have little good reason to pursue, we conclude with the question of whether we should advocate, in yet one further sense, an end of economics.

The first question, why economics matters to us at all, seems relatively easy to answer.[2] Economics concerns the provision of our needs and the satisfaction of our desires. It is hard to imagine what could more obviously command our interest. A slightly more sophisticated answer (see, for example, Robbins 1935) is that economics is the study of scarcity. Since we would have no reason to study the provision of needs or the satisfaction of our desires if the objects of these wants were always at hand, this answer is hardly different from the first. This crude characterization of the point of economics needs two obvious qualifications. First, our interest in economics will not be attracted merely by the compelling nature of its subject matter, but requires also that it tell us something useful about that subject matter. We would be grateful for some assistance in addressing our needs and wants. And second, and more important, any particular version of economics will be valuable only if we think it offers a plausible account of what people generally need or want. There is no use in telling us how to provide ourselves with things unless they are indeed what we need or want. Our concern in this paper will be limited to the second of these issues.[3]

This brings us to the second question, the ends of economists.[4] One might naturally answer (especially in the light of some common economic assumptions) that economists want money, fame, power, etc., and that their practice of economics is aimed at the optimal satisfaction of whichever of these goals individual economists wish to pursue. It is, after all, an assumption of much economic theory that economists, as humans, inevitably pursue such self-interested goals. But let us put this skeptical or even cynical answer to one side and assume that there are at least institutionally established norms that determine what kinds of achievements tend to be met with personal rewards, and that these achievements indeed further our pursuit of some economic goals. One would expect the nature of these goals to be a subject of considerable debate among economists. Remarkably, this is not the case. The even more remarkable explanation of this absence is that most economists believe that the core of economics can be developed with no assumptions at all about what an economy should aim to provide.

Here we must enter an important proviso. Throughout this paper we are criticizing the dominant, neoclassical model of economics. A number of models have existed at various times alongside the neoclassical model: Marshallian, and some subsequent, welfare economics; Marxist and Institutionalist economics; development and labor economics; and most recently, feminist economics. Many of our criticisms have been anticipated by one or more of these schools. But there is no doubt that neoclassicalism predominates among professional economists. Many economics departments, at least in the US, see no need to stray beyond the borders of this program.

The possibility of an economics without any particular goals is implicit in the widely assumed distinction between positive and normative economics. The basic presupposition of this distinction is that whereas positive economics tells us of the causal connections between economic phenomena of different kinds, it is up to us to choose what ends we use this knowledge to promote. This distinction has been attacked from both sides. One side (a thesis with which we are highly sympathetic) denies the possibility of value-free causal knowledge in an area so deeply connected with the complexities and conflicts of social life. On the other side, it is now widely held that the goal of economics is somehow implicit in economics itself – that positive economics describes a machinery that needs only to be left alone, unhampered by interfering governments and pernicious monopolists, to produce the economic outcome for which we should strive. This, then, brings us to a third, perhaps covert, sense in which we suggested that economics might have ends.

The political aspect of the second of the views just described finds recent expression in "The End of History?," an essay by Francis Fukuyama (1989) to which, with commentary, an entire issue of Irving Kristol's organ *The National Interest* was recently devoted.[5] Fukuyama offers the "Hegelian" argument that "with the triumph of Western economic and political liberalism" we are witnessing the "end of history as such . . . the end point of mankind's evolution and the universalization of Western liberal democracy as the final form of human government" (3–4). Citing the "spectacular abundance of advanced liberal economies and the infinitely diverse consumer culture made possible by them" (8), Fukuyama announces that political liberalism is following economic liberalism "with seeming inevitability" (10) and that class and race antagonisms are merely "historical legacies of pre-modern conditions" already on the way out. Somewhat ironically, and in contrast to most who see in the triumph of market economics the culmination of human history, Fukuyama conceives of history as reaching merely a factual rather than a desirable end. He concludes on a nostalgic note:

> The end of history will be a very sad time. The struggle for recognition, the willingness to risk one's life for a purely abstract goal, the worldwide ideological struggle that called forth daring, courage, imagination, and idealism, will be replaced by economic calculation, the endless solving of technical problems, environmental concerns, and the satisfaction of sophisticated consumer demands.
>
> (Fukuyama 1989: 18)

Fukuyama's vision of the terminus of human development in the triumph of economic and political liberalism lacks neither historical antecedents nor contemporary defenders. Neither, however, has it been the universally dominant theme in the development of economic thought. In the rest of this paper we shall distinguish two major threads in the early history of economics. One, associated with the great classical figures of political economy such as Smith, Mill, and Marx, considers the division of labor and the development of free markets as a historical phenomenon with certain vital, but nonetheless limited, capacities to contribute to human well-being. Another tradition has tried to interpret these historical developments in a much bolder way, seeing in them not only the means to, but the actual and ideal end of, human development. A key moment in this tradition occurs when political economy gives way to mere economics in the work of late nineteenth-century theorists. We believe that reflection on these contrasting historical threads may illuminate contemporary debates about the intrinsic or instrumental value of economic institutions, especially markets. We shall attempt to draw some conclusions about these debates in the final section of the paper.

Market Utopias

In this section we shall look at some of the historical antecedents for the view that free-market capitalism is the final goal of human history. Unconstrained enthusiasm for the benefits of free markets derives not so much from the early political economists as from the early technophiles who post-dated them. The early systems analyst Charles Babbage, for example, conceived of the universe as one large system of potentially free markets instantiating the "freedom every man has to use his capital, his labour, and his talents in the way most conducive to his interests" (Babbage [1832] 1963: 370). Babbage displays his conception of the relationship between politics and economics when he explains Britain's place in this universal system: to provide the rest of the world with machinery and commodities. Babbage's confidence that British industry will not be threatened by its competitors is predicated on his faith in the British system of government. He writes that "[t]hese great advantages cannot exist under less free governments. These circumstances . . . give such decided superiority to our people, that no injurious rivalry, either in the construction of machinery or the manufacture of commodities, can reasonably be anticipated" (364). In Babbage's view of progress, English people will use time saved by machines to gratify other wants; and each new machine will add new luxuries that will then become socially necessary to their happiness (335).

Babbage's vision raises questions about the fate of workers supplanted by the technological advance he imagines. In particular, he asks whether machines should be made so perfect as to supplant workers suddenly, or rather should be improved slowly to force them out of employment gradually. He concludes that workers should be forced out immediately, so that they will have no choice but to retrain (336). Thus for Babbage humans will be forced to progress at the rate of technological development. Babbage does not anticipate Marx's view that one's labor might shape one's identity in fundamental ways. Rather, he foreshadows postmodern theory by viewing identity as no less fluid and exchangeable than other commodities.

If Babbage was optimistic about human versatility, Andrew Ure thought that the human component of the market system should be subordinated to its role in that system by any means necessary. He propounds "the great doctrine . . . that when capital enlists science in her service the refractory hand of labour will always be taught docility" (Ure [1835] 1967: 368), and he treats workers' failure to conform to the needs of production as infractions of natural law. On workers stopping when they need to, he writes, "Of the amount of the injury resulting from the violation of the rules of automatic labour, [the worker] can hardly ever be a proper judge; just as mankind at large can never fully estimate the evils consequent upon an infraction of God's moral law."

In striking contrast to the picture of factory work handed down to us by Dickens or by autobiographical accounts of workers who were children in the textile industry, Ure describes how the factory system *improves* women and children:

> The children seemed to be always cheerful and alert, taking pleasure in the light play of their muscles, – enjoying the mobility natural to their age. The scene of industry, so far from exciting sad emotions in my mind, was always exhilarating. It was delightful to observe the nimbleness with which they pieced the broken ends. . . . As to

> exhaustion by the [ten-hour] day's work, they evinced no trace of it on emerging from the mill in the evening; for they immediately began to skip about any neighbouring playground, and to commence their little amusements with the same alacrity as boys issuing from a school.
>
> (Ibid.: 310)

Ure also depicts the women who run the power-looms as being beautified by their work:

> Their light labour and erect posture in tending the looms, and the habit which many of them have of exercising their arms and shoulders as if with dumb-bells . . . opens their chests, and gives them generally a graceful carriage . . . and . . . not a little of the Grecian style of beauty.
>
> (Ibid.: 350)

The unqualified enthusiasm for the growing economic system we find in Babbage and Ure did not find its way into the mainstream of economics until around 1870, when it entered as a corollary of the marginalist revolution, which initiated the rise of *neo*classical economics. Unlike Babbage and Ure, however, the proponents of marginal analysis largely ignored the internal workings of the mechanisms of production to focus almost exclusively on consumption. The concern for the well-being of workers common to both the technophiles and the earlier political economists ceased to be considered relevant to economics. Henceforward labor, regardless of whether the workers who performed it were cheerful and alert, or tended toward the Grecian ideal of beauty, concerned economics solely as a factor of production and as a marketable commodity.[6]

A number of crucial developments occurred at this well-studied point in the evolution of economics. One trend that reached fruition was the supposition that an adequate economic theory should be fully mathematized. Paradoxically, this trend did not coincide with a move to measure utilities quantitatively.[7] On the contrary, a major implication of marginalism was that appropriate economic variables (e.g., cost and revenue, utilities derivable from different products, or work vs. leisure) could be equated at the margin without concern for the total or average values of those quantities. Thus a great perceived virtue of the movement was that it enabled the mathematization of economics without the actual measurement of most economic variables. A consequence of this situation with particular relevance to the present discussion is that it no longer seemed necessary for economists to compare the utilities of different persons. Subsequent developments have taken economic theory even further from the concrete realities underlying individual utilities. First, the replacement of cardinal by ordinal theories of utility implied that different levels of utility could only be ranked, not measured. And finally, the theory of revealed preference provided a behaviorist reduction of the individual's ordinal utility function, again moving economic theory away from the real internal pleasures and pains in which the theory of utility had originated.

Fundamental to the application of marginal analysis is the assumption that the marginal utility of any good declines with the quantity of it acquired. It might naturally be inferred from this assumption that the marginal utility of income, reflecting the total of all goods consumed, must also decline. This would in turn suggest that utility could be increased by transferring income from the wealthy to the poor. Strangely enough, this conclusion has not been widely embraced by economists either in the late nineteenth or in the late twentieth century. One might cynically suggest that at this point we should consider the personal ends of economists who are, after all, almost invariably wealthy. But other strategies are available, and can be found even in the writings of late nineteenth-century economists.

One obvious possibility is to claim that the wealthy generally have a greater capacity for deriving utility. The wealthy, in this view, must differ from the poor in regard to basic psychological capacities. (Perhaps, it is often suggested, that is why they are rich.) This strategy, which obviously requires that one believe in interpersonal comparisons of utility, was pioneered by F.Y. Edgeworth in his *Mathematical Psychics* (1881). Edgeworth argued that in calculating the amount of utility economically possible in a given society we must weigh "the comfort of a limited number" against "numbers with limited comfort" (7). He opted for the comfort of a limited number on the principle that the capacity for pleasure *evolves*. Thus men have more capacity for pleasure than women, Europeans have more than non-Europeans, and so on. Thus the greatest happiness, mathematically speaking, requires the allocation of resources not to the masses with their relatively low capacities, but to the most highly evolved. As Edgeworth puts it, "In the general advance, the most advanced should advance most" (68). "In fact," he writes in a bizarrely mixed Darwinian metaphor, "the happiness of some of the lower classes may be sacrificed to that of the higher classes. . . . Contemplating the combined movements we seem to see the vast composite flexible organism . . . by degrees advancing up the line of evolution; the parts about the front advancing most, the members of the other extremity more slowly moving on and largely dying off" (71).

The mainstream of economics, however, was able to achieve the same consequences without such obviously self-serving assumptions. The declining utility of wealth and the threatened demise of scarcity can be staved off provided only that the satisfaction of every lower order want creates a want or wants of higher order. This is the approach taken by economists such as Carl Menger and Stanley Jevons, thereby ensuring that scarcity would be the inevitable condition of humankind, and that choosing between scarce commodities could remain the species' primary occupation.[8] Since at every level of wealth there will still be wants to satisfy and market choices to make, psychological subjectivism can still remain wholly agnostic as to whether the loaf of bread for a starving man will produce more satisfaction than a second yacht for one more fortunate. Thus for Menger (1950), civilization is identified with the proliferation of higher order goods and insatiable wants. There is no memory of Adam Smith's use of the distinction between "civilization" and "barbarism" (discussed below) to criticize the human consequences of excessive industrialization. Modern economic man would henceforth be known by the insatiability of his desires; to be on the road to civilization, the indolent races of savages need only be inspired by envy to desire his desires and imitate his wants. Thus Jevons (1888: 182) could ask "whether the creating of wants be not the likeliest way to produce industry in a people? If Irish peasants were accustomed to eat beef and wear shoes, would they not be more industrious?".

It is easy to see here the historical roots of twentieth-century economic man, for whom insatiability and the endless pursuit of commodities have become human nature. Thus the "seeming inevitability" of Fukuyama's "spectacular abundance of advanced liberal economies and the infinitely diverse consumer culture made possible by them" (Fukuyama 1989: 8). Economic man's social milieu, capitalist consumer society, became no longer one historical stage, as it was for Mill or Marx (see below), but, as for Fukuyama, its culmination. Modern economic man reveals his Reason, his level of civilization, and his personal tastes or preferences, by performing the fundamental human task of choosing rationally from the universe of goods on display. The terms are those of our contemporary economic debate – rational choice, revealed preference – as are the methods: methodological individualism, subjectivism, and behaviorism.

Markets as means

Before about 1870, it is possible to trace another tradition in political economy. Although Adam Smith is most widely known for his metaphor of the Invisible Hand, and therefore as the originator of the idea that unregulated markets can automatically provide socially optimal outcomes, this is far from the full picture of Smith's views. Indeed, even more widely cited in the massive scholarly literature on Smith than the passage from Book IV of *The Wealth of Nations* where he introduces the Invisible Hand is the passage from Book V where he compares the brutalizing and divisive effects of civilization with the simple but pleasant equality of "barbarous" societies. It should be noted that for Smith "civilization" is a technical term designating a society characterized by technological superiority based on the division of labor. Its counterpart, "barbarism," meant, by contrast, little or no industrial technology, but often complex capabilities at the individual level. As Smith notes, the "civilized" man "whose whole life is spent in performing a few simple operations . . . has no occasion to exert his understanding, or exercise his invention. . . . He . . . generally becomes as stupid and ignorant as it is possible for a human creature to become." This destruction of their "intellectual, social, and martial virtues" is the necessary lot of "the labouring poor, that is, the great body of the people" in all civilized countries unless, in some way, it can be ameliorated by the educational efforts of the government (Smith [1776] 1965: 734–36). This is clearly a much less sanguine picture of the industrial machine than the ones presented by Babbage and Ure.

Smith, of course, believed that the "moral sentiments" of empathy and sympathy were as innate to humankind as the economic virtues of self-interest and the desire for wealth. Indeed "sympathy" can be seen in the early political economists as underlying the possibility – increasingly rejected in the aftermath of the marginal revolution – of interpersonal comparisons of utility. The particular danger Smith perceived in the development of market society was that the great material gains such a society made possible might be paid for by a decline in the ability of humankind, or at least workers, to exercise those faculties of reason, imagination, and sympathy on which ethical behavior depended. Thus what Menger and Jevons identified as essential human nature is precisely the human type that Smith feared market society would produce.[9]

As we noted, Smith hoped that these dangers might be averted by sufficient public investment in education. J.S. Mill, on the other hand, argued that education under capitalism would propagate hedonistic and self-interested citizens and eventually drive out "moral sentiments" like sympathy and altruism. In the final two books of his *Principles of Political Economy* (1848), Mill unequivocally condemns the goal of continual economic growth, arguing that economic man's competitive struggle for accumulation and even self-interest itself is merely part of one stage – the industrial stage – toward progress, and by no means the end. He concludes his argument with the well-known statement that "It is only in the backward countries of the world that increased production is still an important object: in those most advanced, what is needed is a better distribution" (Mill [1848] n.d.: 496–97). Here and elsewhere, the United States is Mill's chief illustration of failure to progress beyond accumulation. He expresses his distaste for its national materialism with a characteristic disapproval of reproductive growth (Mill was an obsessive defender of family planning): "They have the six points of Chartism, and they have no poverty: and all these advantages seem to have done for them is that the life of the whole of one sex is devoted to dollar-hunting, and of the other to breeding dollar-hunters" (496). Mill concludes that he does not share traditional political economy's fear of the stationary state that will follow the full globalization of market competition. And, like Smith, he questions whether industrial technology will benefit much of humankind. It is the only passage in Mill that Marx ever praised:

> Hitherto it is questionable if all the mechanical inventions yet made have lightened the day's toil of any human being. They have enabled a greater population to live the same life of drudgery and imprisonment, and an increased number of manufacturers and others to make fortunes. They have increased the comforts of the middle classes. But they have not yet begun to effect those great changes in human destiny, which it is in their nature and their futurity to accomplish.
>
> (Ibid.: 498)

Mill was concerned less with gross production than (in keeping with the earlier tradition of political economy) with the relations of production, especially gender and class. Thus while Mill clearly saw technological progress and market society as potential, though not yet actual, instruments of progress, they were certainly not ends in themselves as they were for first the technophiles and later the neoclassical economists.

Finally, Karl Marx insisted on the fundamental importance of human labor to human nature. For Marx, the way in which human labor transforms the material world for human ends is what constitutes human nature; the loss of control of their own labor experienced by workers under capitalism is thus a profoundly dehumanizing alienation. Marx contrasts capitalism with communism (the political system that will result from the collapse of capitalism) in a way remarkably redolent of Smith's contrast between barbarism and civilization, though Marx reverses the historical sequence:

> For as soon as the division of labor comes into being, each man has a particular, exclusive sphere of activity. . . . [H]e is a hunter, a fisherman, a shepherd, or a critical critic . . . ; while in communist society . . . society regulates the general production and makes it possible for me to do one thing today and another tomorrow, to hunt in the morning, fish in the afternoon, rear cattle in the evening, criticise after dinner, just as I have a mind, without ever becoming hunter, fisherman, shepherd, or critic.
>
> (Marx [1867] 1967: 160)

However one views Smith's lost Eden and Marx's anticipated Utopia, the contrast between the classical political economists' vision of human flourishing and the neoclassicalists' increasing abstraction of all specific content from their conception of human nature could not be sharper.

Political economy, past, present, and future

Several important points emerge from the preceding historical remarks. The first is that the revolution that began in political economy in the late nineteenth century, in addition to its technical aspects (marginalism and ordinalism) and its methodological aspects (the insistence on formal mathematical methods), contained a vital normative component. Symbolized by the terminological move from "political economy" to "economics," this normative component amounted essentially to the internalization of the goals of economics. Instead of being seen as a means of producing the material sufficiency fundamental to a good society, economics came to see itself as embodying the social aims of efficiency and ever-increasing material abundance. Employing, whether consciously or not, this standard for legitimating claims about what is socially important, economics has been instrumental in constructing an account of human nature. Thus evolves economic man, the rational maximizer of utility derived from consumption of material goods, for whom the society at which economics aims is indeed the ideal. Moreover, this account has been so successful that economic man, sometimes dressed as an exponent of rational choice, now threatens to colonize law, ethics, sex, familial relations, and heaven knows what else.[10]

At least as far as professional economics is concerned, it is evident that these normative assumptions have been as widely adopted as have the technical and methodological innovations. Despite Mill's skepticism, few question whether economic growth is of itself valuable to a society. Yet surely the declining living standards of most Americans during the so-called economic boom of the 1980s (see Mishel and Frankel 1991) is enough to show that economic growth does not by itself constitute social progress. Though few economists would defend gross accumulation against the need to redistribute wealth as crassly as Edgeworth did, appeals to a naïve subjectivist psychology continue to ground skepticism about interpersonal comparisons – and to yield the same inequitable consequences.

We noted earlier in this paper how remarkable it is that economics could be conceived as a subject amenable to investigation without a prior determination of the social goals to which it was intended to contribute. Our discussion of the marginalist revolution aims to throw some light on the historical process by which this conception developed. One explanation we have suggested is that certain views of the social good, together with correlative assumptions about human nature, have become deeply embedded in the fabric of economic theory. Although most of these ideas about society and human nature seem quite implausible when explicitly stated, their embedding in a prestigious "scientific" theory has made them both influential and invisible.

A more self-conscious neglect of the normative foundations of political economy can be found in the standard distinction between positive and normative economics. It is not just (though this is significant) that normative economics continues to be seen as an intellectual backwater, as lacking the power, rigor, and theoretical depth of positive economics. It is rather that the very distinction implies – contrary to a natural intuition that economics is a normative discipline – that there is a value-free aspect of economics.

The picture of value-free economics implied by the separation of positive and normative economics can usefully be drawn in a different way. The economic system may be conceived of as a huge machine. What it provides for us in the way of material outputs depends on our ensuring that it is correctly put together (i.e., with maximally unconstrained markets) and then on our feeding the appropriate inputs (labor, capital, raw materials) into it. Normative questions arise only after we have got as much as we can out of the economic machine and must then decide what to do with it all. Such a picture prompts several deep objections. First, certain social goals relevant to this hypothetical machine have nothing to do with the quantity of its output. For example (and apart from somewhat technical, though obviously important, issues concerning externalities), we think here of the failure to view labor as anything more than a marketable commodity or a factor of production. Central to Marx's critique of political economy was the insight that people's labor is fundamentally important to them.[11] Smith also makes this very clear in his fascinating discussion of the many factors besides wages that relate to the desirability of various kinds of work ([1776] 1965: Bk I, ch. x). Even Ure evidently thought it important to claim, against apparently all evidence, that to be a cog in the great economic machine was a highly desirable position.

But it is not just that economics inadequately conceives of the range of values to which the economic machine is answerable. In many respects the whole machine analogy is deeply misleading. The analogy supposes, for example, that the nature of the parts is antecedently determined, and that these therefore determine what kind of machine it is possible to construct. But one of the main reasons to consider the history of economic theory is to note that the conception of economic man, who, as consumer and producer, provides the basic parts of the economic machine, is a quite recent and contingent conception. Moreover, as both Marx and Mill were at pains to note, the construction of people who resemble the economic model results from the capitalist economic mode of production. As an obvious example, in contemporary Western society, the advertising industry spends billions of dollars "educating" people about new wants they can learn to satisfy. To the limited extent that people do indeed conform to the model of human nature assumed by the normative presuppositions of economic theory, this may be largely because the economic system has made them that way.

More generally, one of us has argued at length that science is hampered by adhering to the remnants of an increasingly untenable mechanistic world view (see Dupré 1993a). Economics is a science in which mechanistic metaphysical assumptions are both prevalent and strikingly implausible. In addition to supposing that the parts and qualities into which social or biological machines should be analyzed are given by nature, mechanism assumes a deterministic, or at least complete, causal structure. The obvious inapplicability of this assumption to economic models has been central to methodological discussions in economics at least since Mill. Giving up these assumptions allows us to see that what kind of economic system we aim to develop is wholly contingent, and that this economic system affects what kinds of people we become. More tentatively, we would like to suggest that the extreme technophilia in the prehistory of economics is far from coincidental.[12]

Let us conclude by returning specifically to the questions of the ends of economics raised at the beginning of this essay. Certainly our conclusions contradict views such as Fukuyama's that freeze history in the state envisaged by current economic theory. But although we reject current attempts to extract social goals directly from the content of contemporary "positive" economics, we do not believe that there can be a study of economics that does not explicitly acknowledge at least a partial conception of the social good. What is needed, therefore, is something that could be recovered from the tradition of political economy out of which neoclassical economics grew in the late nineteenth century: an economics in which discussions of the social good and its relation to different modes of economic organization is an integral part.[13] Thus, in a sense, we do call for an end of economics. But we also hope for a more humane science of political economy.

Notes

1 This paper has benefited from comments on an earlier draft by Daniel Hausman and Debra Satz.

2 We do not address directly the possibility that the point of economics might be solely the disinterested pursuit of knowledge. This view would lead to the conclusion that economics has not been very successful (see, e.g., Rosenberg 1992; Dupré 1993b).

3 The first question is addressed in Dupré (1993b).

4 This topic has perhaps been most systematically explored in the field of economic rhetoric. See Klamer (1984); Klamer *et al.* (1988); McCloskey (1985). See especially Craufurd D. Goodwin's distinctions between the economist as philosopher, as priest, and as hired gun (Goodwin 1988: 209ff).

5 A more extended defense of such a position is found in Friedman (1962). With more space, we would have much more to say about the cynicism of Friedman's views on democracy and progress. Fukuyama further developed his views in *The End of History and the Last Man* (1992).

6 As mentioned in our caveat above, among the dissenters from parts of the dominant neoclassical model are certain labor economists. There is a tradition in labor economics, especially among neo-institutionalists, in which the conditions and welfare of workers are taken much more seriously. This tradition, however, lies on the margins of the dominant paradigm, and indeed is difficult to reconcile with that paradigm.

7 Ironically, since he is so renowned for his contributions to the formal theory of neoclassical economics, Marshall (1961 [1890]) strongly resisted this move to formalization.

8 For a more detailed study of the shift in value from the political economists to the

neoclassicals as seen in their differing conceptions of economic man and of scarcity, and of the historical arguments of this paper generally, see Gagnier (1993).

9 A more recent, but related, discussion of the importance of the ways that markets of various kinds, but especially labor markets, contribute to the production of particular kinds of people can be found in Samuel Bowles (1991).

10 Prominent examples are Posner (1992) on sex; Philipson and Posner (1993) on the epidemiology of AIDS; and Gauthier (1986) on ethics. The poverty of current economic methodology for addressing social issues is clearly illustrated in Nobel Laureate Gary Becker's celebrated *Treatise on the Family* (1981). From simplistic assumptions obscured by a thicket of algebra and sparsely ornamented with empirical claims emerge occasionally remarkable policy conclusions. To take one example, Becker concludes that progressive taxation may increase inequality. The progressive tax in Becker's model, an asymptotic approach to a flat rate, would not impress an advocate of income redistribution. Nevertheless, Becker tosses into the algebra soup of his current model the argument that such a tax might increase the coefficient of variation of income. Many years of training are required to extract any sense from this kind of activity, yet its very unintelligibility is surely part of its rhetorical effectiveness – perhaps the whole of it. This work (and that of Philipson and Posner) is criticized in detail by Dupré (1995).

11 Our views on work are further explored in Gagnier and Dupré (1995, 1996).

12 The ways in which neoclassical economics developed in self-conscious imitation of physical science, specifically physical theories of energy, in the nineteenth century are documented in detail by Mirowski (1989). A notable economist who insisted on the radical difference between economics and natural science, and even on the essential normativity of the former, was John Maynard Keynes.

13 Neva Goodwin (1991) argues that something like this is implicit in the largely neglected parts of Marshall's work on welfare economics.

References

Babbage, Charles ([1832] 1963). *On the Economy of Machinery and Manufacture*. New York: Augustus Kelly.

Becker, Gary (1981). *A Treatise on the Family*. Cambridge, MA: Harvard University Press.

Bowles, Samuel (1991). "What Markets Can – and Cannot – Do." *Challenge* 34.4: 11–16.

Dupré, John (1993a). *The Disorder of Things: Metaphysical Foundations of the Disunity of Science*. Cambridge, MA: Harvard University Press.

—— (1993b). "Could There be a Science of Economics?" *Midwest Studies in Philosophy* 18: 363–78.

—— (1995). "Against Scientific Imperialism." In *Proceedings of the Philosophy of Science Association 1994*. Ed. D. Hull, M. Forbes and R.M. Burian. 2: 374–81.

Edgeworth, Francis Y. (1881). *Mathematical Psychics*. London: C. Kegan Paul.

Ferber, Marianne A. and Julie A. Nelson, eds. (1993). *Beyond Economic Man: Feminist Theory and Economics*. Chicago: University of Chicago Press.

Friedman, Milton (1962). *Capitalism and Freedom*. Chicago: University of Chicago Press.

Fukuyama, Francis (1989). "The End of History?" *National Interest* 16 (Summer: 1–18).
—— (1992). *The End of History and the Last Man*. New York: Avon.
Gagnier, Regenia (1993). "On the Insatiability of Human Wants: Economic and Aesthetic Man." *Victorian Studies* 36.2: 125–53.
—— and John Dupré (1995). "On Work and Idleness." *Feminist Economics* 1: 96–109.
—— and —— (1996). "A Brief History of Work." *Journal of Economic Issues* 30: 553–59.
Gauthier, David (1986). *Morals by Agreement*. Oxford: Oxford University Press.
Goodwin, Craufurd D. (1988). "The Heterogeneity of the Economists' Discourse: Philosopher, Priest, and Hired Gun." In *The Consequences of Economic Rhetoric*. Ed. A. Klamer, D.N. McCloskey, and R.M. Solow. Cambridge: Cambridge University Press, 207–20.
Goodwin, Neva R. (1991). *Social Economics: An Alternative Theory. Vol. 1: Building Anew on Marshall's Principles*. New York: St. Martin's Press.
Hausman, Daniel M., ed. (1984). *The Philosophy of Economics*. Cambridge: Cambridge University Press.
Jevons, William Stanley ([1871] 1888). *The Theory of Political Economy*. London: Macmillan.
Keynes, John Maynard ([1938] 1984). "Letters to R.F. Harrod." In *The Philosophy of Economics*. Ed. D.M. Hausman. Cambridge: Cambridge University Press, 300–2.
Klamer, Arjo (1984). *Conversations with Economists: New Classical Economists and Opponents Speak Out on the Current Controversy in Macroeconomics*. New Jersey: Rowman & Allanheld.
——. Donald N. McCloskey, and Robert M. Solow, eds (1988). *The Consequences of Economic Rhetoric*. Cambridge: Cambridge University Press.
Marshall, Alfred ([1890] 1961). *Principles of Economics*. New York: Macmillan.
Marx, Karl ([1867] 1967). *Capital*. Vol. 1. New York: International Publishers.
McCloskey, Donald M. (1985). *The Rhetoric of Economics*. Madison: University of Wisconsin Press.
—— (1990). *If You're So Smart: The Narrative of Economic Expertise*. Chicago: University of Chicago Press.
Menger, Carl ([1871] 1950). *The Principles of Economics*. Glencoe, IL.: Free Press.
Mill, John Stuart (1984). "On the Definition and Method of Political Economy." In *The Philosophy of Economics*. Ed. D.M. Hausman. Cambridge: Cambridge University Press, 52–98.
—— ([1848] n.d.). *The Principles of Political Economy*. London: Routledge.
—— (1987). *On Socialism*. New York: Prometheus.
Mirowski, Philip (1989). *More Heat Than Light*. Cambridge: Cambridge University Press.
Mishel, Lawrence, and David M. Frankel (1991). *The State of Working America: 1990–91 Edition*. Armonk, NY: Sharpe.
Philipson, Tomas, and Richard Posner (1993). *Private Choices and Public Health*. Cambridge, MA: Harvard University Press.
Posner, Richard (1992). *Sex and Reason*. Cambridge, MA: Harvard University Press.
Robbins, Lionel (1935). *An Essay on the Nature and Significance of Economic Science*. 2nd edn. London: Macmillan.

Rosenberg, Alexander (1992). *Economics – Mathematical Politics or Science of Diminishing Returns*. Chicago: University of Chicago Press.
Smith, Adam ([1759] 1907). *The Theory of Moral Sentiments*. London: George Bell.
—— ([1776] 1965). *An Inquiry into the Nature and Causes of the Wealth of Nations*. New York: Modern Library.
Ure, Andrew ([1835] 1967). *The Philosophy of Manufactures*. London: Frank Cass.

Part III

ECONOMICS OF THE IRRATIONAL

9

A PORTRAIT OF *HOMO ECONOMICUS* AS A YOUNG MAN

Susan F. Feiner

> Few textbooks contain a direct portrait of rational economic man. He is introduced furtively and piece by piece. . . . He lurks in the assumptions, leading an enlightened existence between input and output, stimulus and response. He is neither tall nor short, fat nor thin, married nor single. There is no telling whether he loves his dog, beats his wife or prefers pushpin to poetry. We do not know what he wants. But we do know that, whatever it is, he will maximize ruthlessly to get it.
>
> (Hollis and Nell 1975: 53–54)

Introduction

Certainly for a hundred years, and on some readings since the days of Adam Smith, the *dramatis personae* of mainstream economics have been self-interested and egoistic actors for whom the dual spurs of competition and pleasure-seeking have motivated all behavior. *Homo economicus* (*a.k.a.* Rational Economic Man), reared in the Cartesian nursery, nourished by a diet long on atomism and short on empathy, has generally been treated as a rather transparent agent. Some have criticized this one-sided perspective on human behavior by pointing to the likely demise of any society (or community or family) in which self-interest is the only (or even the dominant) affective state (Frank 1988). Interestingly, criticism of Rational Economic Man for being a superficial "stick of a person" has been leveled by practitioners both inside and outside the mainstream. But both of these characterizations miss a great deal.

The omnipresence of *Homo economicus* in the worldviews of professional economists, as well as in the ersatz economics of far too much contemporary politics, tells us quite clearly that this character has feelings, depths, and sensitivities with which a great many people identify. For if *Homo economicus* were as superficial or flat as has been claimed, we would be hard-pressed to explain the passion with which he and his worldview are defended. Thus, those of us concerned to understand the bases on which identifications with *Homo economicus* occur must delve beyond the manifest content of the rationality of economic man to discover the latent, repressed contents of his unconscious.

Today even the defenders of economic correctness would probably be willing to admit that: (a) the orthodox definition of economics as "the study of the allocation of scarce resources to the infinity of human wants" is both partial and culturally determined; and (b) the traits of economic actors map (too perfectly to be coincidental) onto traditional notions of masculinity.[1] An early discussion of the connection among economics, methodology, and the politics of identity showed how positivist claims about objectivity had the effect of marginalizing economic questions of concern to women and people of color (see Feiner and Roberts 1990). That this exclusionary move should continue to be at the center of critical scrutiny is not surprising:

> In economics the triumph of Positivism was the triumph of Utility. Man, illumined by the Enlightenment and anatomized by the utilitarians, was an individual bundle of desires. He was simply a complex animal, no less part of nature than anything else and no less subject to discoverable empirical laws. His behavior was to be explained as a series of attempts to get what he wanted. Whether his wants were metaphysical, religious, ethical or merely selfish was not the point. For, scientifically speaking, it could simply be said that he was seeking the satisfaction of his desires. Judgments of value were irrelevant, except insofar as it could be asked scientifically whether the means chosen would secure the end, given the impact of the behavior of each man on the aspirations of others. The rationally calculated, long-run optimum of each contributes to the long-run optimum of all. The calculation is the maximizing of utility.
>
> (Hollis and Nell 1975: 48)

In short, the narratives of *Homo economicus* are fraught with multiple meanings. In addition to whatever insight into the nitty gritty of economic relationships that can be gleaned from the plenitude of maximizing models in which *Homo economicus*[2] is principal actor, these stories also carry forward the humanist project in which Man (the conscious, knowing, unified, and rational subject) is the master of his fate. When students, the public, or policy makers step into the world of mainstream economics they do so as subjects endowed with these properties – consequently, they recognize themselves. Acquisition of the skills needed to become a producer/consumer of mainstream economic knowledge thus involves the development of an empathic resonance between the reader and his or her economic text. And, it seems to me, understanding how such texts limit the range of available subject positions plays some role in resisting the powerful forces of socialization.

A first attempt at understanding this process motivated an earlier essay of mine on "the perfect market" (a metaphor central to Max U's world) in which I demonstrated a connection between markets and fantasies about mothers (Feiner 1995). Although the parallel has not been noticed until recently, both perfect markets and perfect mothers meet all of our desires immediately, with no frustration and no anxiety. That this is developmentally a very immature view of things is expressed in the now famous definition given by Lionel Robbins in 1935: economics is "the science which studies human behavior as a relationship between ends and scarce means which have alternative uses" (Robbins 1952: 16). Translated into the language of economics textbooks, this means that economics is "the study of the allocation of scarce resources to the infinity of human wants." Note how the external world is perceived as subject to scarcity while the wants and demands of the self are perceived as limitless; this view of the relationship between self and other reproduces an infant's view of things.

This paper will further explore the possibility that economic relationships, experienced (and represented) as relationships of people to markets, express fears and anxieties similar to those experienced in our earliest contacts with the outside world. Indeed, the vicissitudes of markets, in their effects on the lives of people who depend on them for their livelihoods (and this includes almost everyone), are not unlike the vicissitudes of our mothers. Insofar as markets vacillate between generosity, availability, and affirmation on the one hand, and withholding, scarcity, and punishment on the other, who among us is not at some deep level reminded of our profound dependency upon forces we cannot control? The prospect that markets may fail us tends to awaken our earliest horrors and fears of total abandonment. This essay hopes to show how identification with the character(s) populating economic stories (or fantasies) helps to contain the socially experienced anxieties arising from our collective dependence on markets.

Desidero ergo sum

> There is also a psychological element in the survival of equilibrium theory. There is an irresistible attraction about the concept of equilibrium – the silent hum of the perfectly running machine; the apparent stillness of the exact balance of counteracting pressures; the automatic smooth recovery from a chance disturbance. Is there perhaps something Freudian about it? Does it connect with a longing to return to the womb? We have to look for a psychological explanation to account

> for the powerful influence of an idea that is intellectually unsatisfactory.
>
> (Robinson 1962: 77–78)

Exploring the ignored and denied dimensions of *Homo economicus* reveals an inner life replete with trials, agonies, and intense longings. Plumbing the psychic depths of Rational Economic Man will provide insight into the seductive power of the discipline's meta-narrative: that behavior rooted in narcissistic self-interest, competition, and cold, scientific rationality will inevitably lead us to a promised land of optimal output, growth, and efficiency.

We can show that orthodox economic narratives perform a soothing, maternal function by revealing their fundamental alignment with romantic fictional forms. As we will see, those elements of the neoclassical story which give clues to the romantic orientation of the text are simultaneously fraught with information about the emotional (affective, psychological) orientation of the protagonist – *Homo economicus*. Some standard features of romances include: (a) the protagonist sets off on an impossible quest or mission, the completion of which will save the kingdom/family/community (sword and grail variations on this theme are well known, so is the sexed nature of the imagery); (b) the protagonist is disciplined and/or constrained by outside (exogenous) forces – e.g., parents, civil society, or the state; or (c) the protagonist is divided between good and bad, and these two strong but opposed sides of the self battle for control (Brantlinger 1976: 19–45). As we will see, each of these conditions figures prominently in Max U's world.[3]

Although this theme is developed at length elsewhere, two points are essential to the rest of this paper. First, it is usual to associate mothers or mothering with warmth, caring, and connectedness. Yet markets are quite the opposite: they are cold and impersonal. In markets the cash nexus is the only possible connection. This reversal (or reaction formation) is a defense mechanism that undoes anxieties about dependency relations since it shows us that we don't need connection or empathy to survive and flourish. The economic world seen through the eyes of Rational Economic Man is frequently represented as its opposite, so that whatever problem *you* care to identify – poverty, discrimination, famine, deforestation, or urban decay – *HE* sees only the inevitable result of market forces. Economic theory does permit regret and lament, but not remedial action, since any attempt to improve conditions will only make things worse. The result is paralysis: the world is not perfect and any use of human, visible hands to mold socio-economic outcomes to desired specifications is seen as misguided if not downright perverse.

The second point requires an examination of some technical aspects of economic stories. A key feature of perfect-mother fantasies is that they

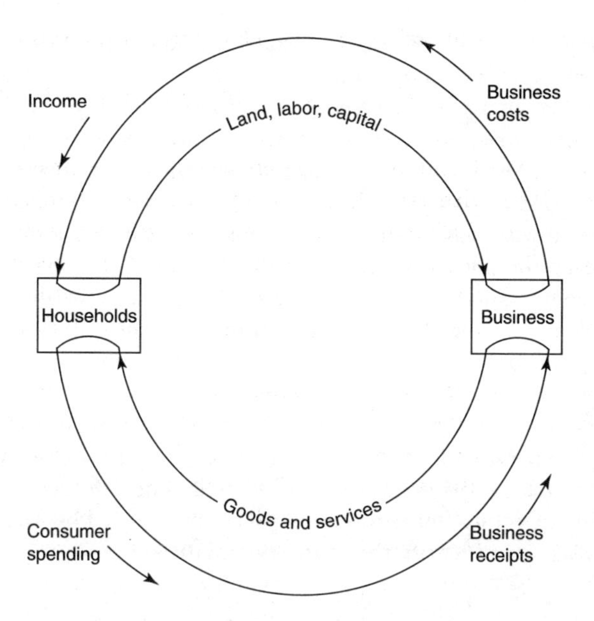

Figure 9.1 The circular flow. The circular flow diagram shows the income received and the payments made by the two sectors of the economy, firms and households

"mirror" infants' needs and desires exactly (see Chodorow 1989). This vision of pervasive, omnipresent empathic mirroring occurs over and over in neoclassical economics. The circular-flow model, one of the first taught in the introductory class, affords a fine example of this.

As Figure 9.1 shows, what households want, firms have; what firms have, households want. That no mismatches take place, that no mismatches *can* take place is ensured by the two-fold nature of the flow. Side one: households "own" factor services (land, labor, and capital) which are needed by firms; in exchange for their factor services, households receive income. Side two: firms own the goods and services which have been produced; households purchase these with the income received for their factor services. Notice how this enforces "the apparent stillness of the exact balance of counteracting pressures."

As the frictionless working of market adjustments creates a discursive space in which difference is eclipsed, the perfect symmetry of household and firm behavior amplifies the "silent hum of the perfectly tuned machine." *HE* will maximize utility, subject to constraints. Firms will maximize profits, subject to constraints. Utility and profits are just the stuff of economic life, and in consequence firms become analytically indistinguishable from individuals.

The famous battle of the Cambridges (Massachusetts and England) reveals another instance of mirroring. The subject of this debate was the logical (mathematical) coherence of Max U's representation of production.[4] To make a long story short, there is only one (very restrictive) condition under which models of the economy will *in general* tend toward situations of equilibrium in all markets simultaneously. In such a state there is no involuntary unemployment (!); consumers get exactly what they want; firms purchase all the inputs needed to produce what consumers want; interest rates are at the precise level to accomplish all of this; firms earn zero economic profit; and incomes are at the correct level to ensure that all that is produced can be purchased. To guarantee this sanguine state of affairs the theory must contain the assumption that there is only one commodity: the outputs produced by firms must be of the same stuff that firms use as inputs. When what goes in is exactly what comes out, difference is obliterated.

The tendencies to represent things or relationships as their opposite, combined with pervasive, omnipresent mirroring, secure a fantasy image of a world at rest, at equilibrium, at peace with itself. The defensive nature of this narrative provides clues to the intense anxiety experienced by Max U. Further scrutiny allows us to identify the sources of this anxiety.

The inner object world of Max U

> – Tell us, Dedalus, do you kiss your mother before you go to bed? Stephen answered: – I do. Wells turned to the other fellows and said: – O, I say, here's a fellow says he kisses his mother every night before he goes to bed. The other fellows stopped their game and turned round, laughing. Stephen blushed under their eyes and said: – I do not. Wells said: – O, I say, here's a fellow says he doesn't kiss his mother before he goes to bed. They all laughed again. Stephen tried to laugh with them. He felt his whole body hot and confused in a moment. What was the right answer to the question?
>
> (Joyce [1916] 1968: 14)

We return now to the way Max U perceives himself and his world.[5] For *HE* all of existence, every possible thought, action, or planned action bears some relationship to these three questions: (a) How much and what shall I consume? (b) How much time shall I devote to paid employment? and (c) How much of current income shall I set aside as savings? The questions are interdependent: if Max doesn't want a lot of stuff to consume he faces considerably less pressure to work to earn the income needed to purchase the goods he desires. If Max works anyway, he can – by virtue of his abstention from current consumption – save, thereby assuring himself high levels of consumption in the future (when he may choose not to work). Or if Max owns factors of production in addition to his labor power, he may choose to rent or lend them, thereby securing non-wage income. Thus, *the* problem for Max is:

given his level of desire, what choices must he make to ensure the highest possible level of satisfaction (or utility) now and in the future?

The analytics of the object relations school of psychoanalysis can be deployed to make sense of this orientation to the world. Virtually all authors within this school take as a starting point the view that the utter dependency of infants on their parents (usually the mother) creates an internal field of relatedness which unfolds and grows through complex processes of interaction between the baby and its significant others. One result of this process is that "people react to and interact with not only an *actual* other but also an *internal* other, a psychic representation of a person (or several people) which in itself has the power to influence both the individual's affective states and his overt behavior" (Greenberg and Mitchell 1993: 10; emphasis added). It is not difficult to find traces of these psychic representations in *HE*'s affective states and behavior.[6]

The view that human development is fundamentally relational has at its core the idea that from the very beginning infants imagine that their mother's insides are filled with magical substances and objects. The move from fantasies about mother's insides to fantasies about the great big superstore in the sky requires little imagination: what was imagined by infants to be inside mother is imagined by Max to be inside markets. Infants seek these objects through relatedness with their mothers; Max seeks these objects in the market. In the baby/caretaker interplay, babies come to introject these objects, which represent the infant's relations to and perceptions of mother. These perceptions have both good and bad aspects, resulting in babies envisioning themselves as similarly split:

> The child cannot do without parents, yet living in a world in which parents, the constituents of one's entire interpersonal world, are unavailable or arbitrary is unbearably painful. Therefore . . . the first in a series of internalizations, repressions, and splits takes place, based on the necessity for preserving the illusion of the goodness of the parents as real figures in the outside world. The child separates and internalizes the bad aspects of parents – it is not they who are bad, it is he. The badness is inside him; if he were different, their love would be forthcoming. . . . He takes upon himself the "burden of badness." The "badness," the undesirable qualities of the parents – that is, the depression, the disorganization, the sadism – are now in him. These "bad" features become bad objects, with which the ego identifies. The child has purchased outer security at the price of sacrificing internal security plus illusory hope. When the child experienced the "badness" as outside, in the real parents, he felt painfully unable to make any impact at all. If the "badness" is inside him, he preserves the hope of omnipotent control over it.
>
> (Greenberg and Mitchell 1993: 170–71)

Our examination of the choices at the center of Max U's life will discover a similar splitting, as well as other indications of developmental problems. Theorists in the object relations school argue that when the movement from infantile dependence to mature dependence is blocked, one crucial manifestation of such blockage is a clinging to infantile objects and the relations to caretakers which they represent:

> No one can ever completely give up these objects since we all carry within ourselves the traces of our earliest experiences. Thus in the ongoing, never-ending transition from infantile dependence to adult relatedness the central conflict is between the developmental urge toward mature dependence and richer relations, and the regressive reluctance to abandon infantile dependence and ties to undifferentiated objects (both internal and external), for fear of losing contact of any sort.
>
> (Ibid.: 162)

The didactic tales of *Homo economicus* are replete with examples of this "regressive reluctance." His world reflects "ancient internal attachments and allegiances to early significant others. The re-creation of the sorrow, suffering, and defeat are forms of renewal of and devotion to these ties" (ibid.: 174). This latter may seem puzzling: how can the perpetual "maximization of utility" re-create sorrow, suffering, and defeat? As we will see, the very choices which Max is driven to make represent the infantile splitting of the world into good and bad objects; the endless pursuit of an unattainable goal; and the inescapable discipline of the adult world. In a horrifying way the choices of Rational Economic Men become Sophie's Choice: impossible, yet they must be made; and once made the choosers are perpetually haunted by that which they have given up; seeking absolution, they are compelled to repeat these renunciations through all time.

As was sketched above, three questions (how much and what to consume? how much to work? and how much to save?) constitute the constellation of choices open to our friend Max. These choices are envisioned by *HE* to be simultaneous. On the one hand, *HE* chooses how to spend his (limited) income to purchase the goods and services which will maximize his utility (given his exogenously determined tastes and preferences, and his exogenously given endowments). These choices underlie the demand curves of economics textbooks. On the other hand, *HE* must make some supply-side choices. Here, how much time is devoted to working (and thus not to leisuring) and how much of current income is devoted to saving (and thus not to spending) will determine how much income is available (in the current period) to spend on goods and services. I will take up Max's view of each of these choices, beginning with the "demand side" choice of consumption and ending with the "supply side" choices of working and saving.

Max's notion of consumption has some peculiarities which are worth exploring. First, we note that consumption contains all the other choices (to work or play; to save or spend) since Max only works or saves to get more income, which will in turn allow him to consume more. But putting that aside for the moment, what does consumption entail for Max? Consumption is the final, ultimate destiny of every entity in the external object world. All goods and services end their independent existence as they are ingested, becoming a part of Max U. The boundary between outside and inside disappears. By consuming that which is not *Homo economicus*, Max U recreates the world as a part of himself. But following from the principle of non-satiation, no matter what is consumed, or how much of it can be taken in, there is always a tomorrow in which more is better.

This perspective on consumption represents the replaying of relationships with enticing, exciting objects that constantly promise satisfaction and fulfilment but never deliver. Max's name for the representation of his desire tells us a great deal: that which is wanted, the various combinations of goods and services which will satisfy Max, are known as "indifference" curves. Think about the ambivalence of this message: "I want, yet I am indifferent."

As Figure 9.2 shows, desire radiates through an infinite universe in which Max recognizes only two types of relationships. Since some combinations of goods yield the same psychic satisfaction, these goods stand in a relation of indifference to all other combinations of goods (along each of the curves depicted above). But because Max experiences pleasure in response to changes in quantity, there are combinations of goods which are preferred to others (moving out to the north-east in the figure). Max can assume only one of these positions *vis-à-vis* each unique combination of goods potentially available in the cosmos. So Max is torn. On the one hand he christens the combinations of what he wants "indifference"; yet at the same time he insists that more is preferable to less. Consequently, no amount of stuff, none of the goods found in the market (its maternal "supplies"), can ever be enough. The void within can never be filled and so Max U is compulsively driven to repeat his attempt to ingest the world.

We note too that in this drive to incorporate the whole of the world into himself the only barrier to the success of Max's project is his income constraint. Max wants seventeen Bentleys; houses in The Hamptons, San Francisco, and Paris; vintage champagne; and of course toothpaste, socks, and plenty of clean underwear. Even if he were Donald Trump he couldn't get all of what he wanted because each item sells for a price and his income isn't infinite.

A short algebraic exposition is necessary. If we take the price of each good desired (P) and multiply this by the number of units of the good desired (Q), then the product (PQ) must be the amount spent on that good. There will be a product (PQ) for each good desired: $P_aQ_a + P_bQ_b + P_cQ_c + \ldots + P_nQ_n$. The sum of all the PQs can't exceed total income (Y). The simple two-good case can be stated as: $P_aQ_a + P_bQ_b = Y$.

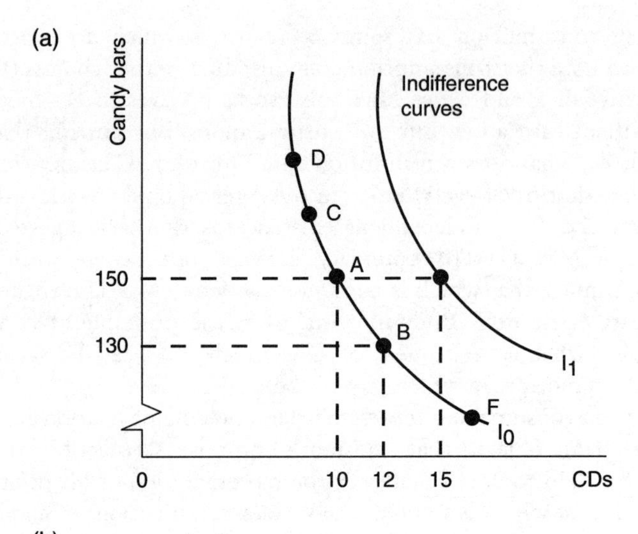

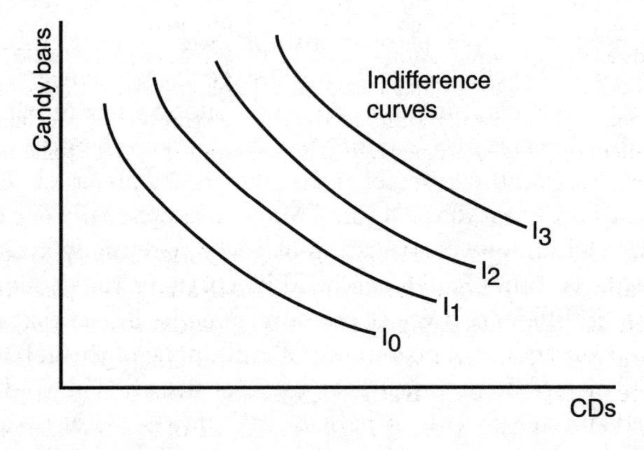

Figure 9.2 Mapping desire

(a) Two indifference curves. Each indifference curve traces a combination of goods among which an individual is indifferent. These two reflect Max U's taste for CDs and for candy bars. He is just as well off (has an identical amount of utility at points on the indifference curve; A, B, C, D, or F)

(b) Multiple indifference curves. By definition, an indifference curve describing Max U's tastes can be drawn through any point in the diagram. Four of the infinite number of possibilities are shown here. Because more is better, Max U will prefer indifference curves that are higher (and out to the north-east), like I_3, to those that are lower, like I_0.

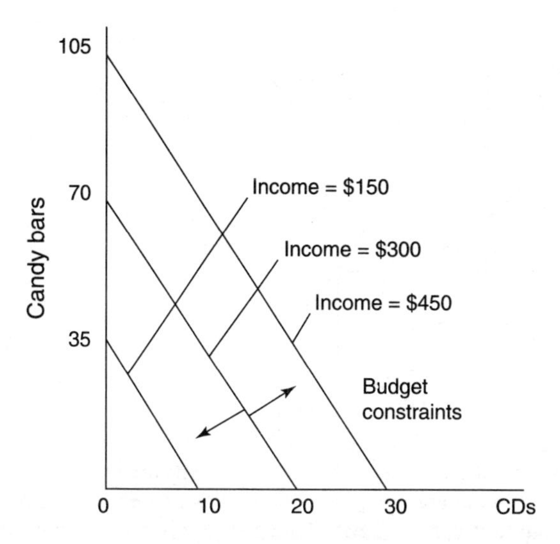

Figure 9.3 The budget constraint for Max U when he consumes only two goods. Max U's budget constraint separates those combinations of goods he can purchase from those which are not affordable, given the prices of the goods and his income. Along the budget line Max spends all his income on these two goods. Points above the budget constraint cannot be reached by Max, while points below the constraint do not exhaust Max U's income (so they are not optimal, although they are available)

In Figure 9.3 the expression ($PaQa + PbQb = Y$) is linear, and solving for the intercepts allows us to draw the budget line. If Max spends all his income on good *a*, then he can't buy any good *b*. In algebraic terms: if $PaQa = Y$, $Qb = 0$. So the largest amount of Qa that Max can purchase (given these prices and his income – each is data from the outside world) can be written as: maximum $Qa = Y/Pa$. Likewise, if Max spends all of his income on good *b*, then he can't buy any good *a*. In algebraic terms: if $PbQb = Y$, $Qa = 0$. So the largest amount of Qb that Max can purchase (given these prices and his income – each is data from the outside world) can be written as: maximum $Qb = Y/Pb$. The two points (maximum $Qa = Y/Pa$ and maximum $Qb = Y/Pb$) are the intercepts of a straight line which is determined by forces larger than and external to Max. Thus Max, like many a romantic hero is disciplined (constrained) by society.

As shown in Figure 9.4, if Max can't always get what he wants, it is because he is thwarted by parental power. This stylized fact leads Max U to believe that *every* aspect of life can be represented as a problem of constrained maximization: marriage, fertility, going to college, drug use, where to live, whether to have a pet, what to do for dinner next Tuesday, whether to act altruistically, how to arrange a financial portfolio, enclosing the common

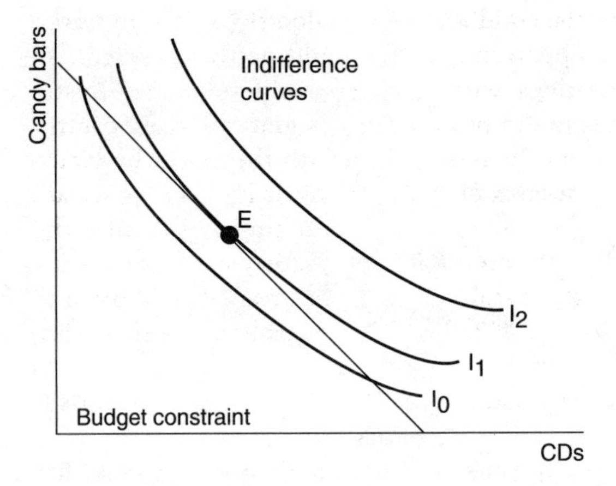

Figure 9.4 Constrained maximization. Max U, like all other consumers, will purchase the combination of candy bars and CDs which maximizes his total utility. Graphically, he will move along the budget constraint until he reaches the highest possible indifference curve (point E in the graph). At point E, the budget constraint and indifference curve I_1 are tangent

fields, going on strike, the objectives of a "central plan," murder, rape, and nuclear war.[7] *Naturally*, choices about working and saving fit this mold as well.

We are now in a position to interrogate Max's view on the question of how much time to devote to work and leisure respectively. What strikes us instantly is the "good"/"bad" splitting that characterizes this perception. There is on the one hand the world of leisure, fun, and play – a child's world, filled with the immediate gratifications of activities that are pleasurable in themselves. In stark contrast is the world of work, which is for Max U an unpleasantness to which he is compelled (unless he has the good fortune to have enough unearned income to be able to avoid laboring). Because working is one of only two ways to get an income, Max must renounce the immediate pleasures of childhood and enter an adult world in which pleasures are not derived from the activities themselves, but are instead dependent upon satisfaction achieved in other realms (sublimation). He does not work because work has intrinsic value or merit or pleasure to him (indeed if it did he would get paid less [!] according to the theory of compensating wage differentials); instead he works to get the income needed to act on his desires in the market for final goods and services. Work, and thus wage or salary income, is one way to ensure access to the symbolic mother: without income those magical substances inside mother are beyond reach:

> If the other is available for gratifying, pleasurable exchange, the child will enter into pleasurable activities. If the parent offers only painful,

> unfulfilling contacts, the child *does not* abandon the parent to search for more pleasurable opportunities. The child needs the parent, so he integrates his relations with him on a suffering, masochistic basis. The child attempts to protect what is gratifying and control what is not gratifying in the relationship with the parent by establishing compensatory internal object relations. It is in the "obstinate attachment" of the libidinal ego to the exciting object that the child preserves his hopes for fuller, more satisfying contact with the parent. The emptier the real exchange, the greater his devotion to the promising yet depriving features of his parents which he has internalized and seeks within.
>
> (Greenberg and Mitchell 1993: 173; emphasis added)

Max has many brothers, cousins, and uncles. In most respects they are just like him. In fact, the only way to tell them apart is by their tastes and preferences, including their attitudes toward time and money. Some of Max's relatives behave like ants, others behave like grasshoppers. Ants are always aware that winter is just around the corner and that all energy must be devoted to storing, gathering, and holding supplies for the coming cold, dark months (which will be spent underground). But the grasshoppers don't get it. They live in the here-and-now, content to enjoy long summer evenings playing the fiddle, dancing, and singing. The future orientation of ants is in marked contrast to the present orientation of grasshoppers, and as a result ants have a special role in the world. Their virtuous renunciation of current enjoyments (including bodily pleasures) makes us all better off since their abstemious withholding is the driving force behind accumulation and growth.

What part of the body does this vision valorize and privilege? Since the founding of psychoanalysis, saving money and hoarding have been symbolically associated with anality. The meaning of anality varies across psychoanalytic schools, but one element remains constant: the idea that infants store-up (or hoard) their feces because expelling them is pleasurable. Once again Max U sees the world as "good" and "bad." Saving, which requires withholding, deprivation, and frustration, represents the adult world of disciplining parents into which one must move if one is to have access to (m)other. Spending, like playing, is the immediate world of children in which gratification and satisfaction are at hand now.

Some comments on the ambivalence embedded in this view of work/play, save/spend are in order. Saving and working are "bad" (since they represent the withholding and exciting aspects of parents), yet they are necessary if you want to get "goods." Playing, in contrast, is "good" (since it represents gratification), yet it is "bad" since the more one plays, the less likely one is to get "goods." The simultaneity of these meanings expresses ambivalence, and guilt is not far behind: playing and not working, spending and not saving, are activities for which children are frequently punished. If Max U were to play and spend he would be similarly punished. His intense longing for the gratification inherent in these childlike activities produces anxiety: "Where there is anxiety, there will almost certainly be found a mechanism of defense against that anxiety" (Bordo 1991: 75). The principal mechanism of defense for Max U is the centrality of consumption: his ability to take in the whole of the external world obliterates differences like outside/inside, good/bad, and pleasure/pain so that Max can deny difference and merge with his fantasy mother.

Conclusion

regression run.[8] Beyond supply and demand, past the bend in general equilibrium to the spot where we can hear the complaint "It's time to get beyond *Homo economicus*, that stick figure of a man, to someone real, like Bovary" (McCloskey 1985: 66). But this portrait of Rational Economic Man, like the bourgeois drama in which he is principal actor (and his clones the supporting cast), hides more than it reveals. *Homo economicus*, the Hobbesian mushroom man *par excellence*, seems to epitomize the competitive, self-interested, isolated individual – shrewd, calculating, and devoid of sentiment, the personification of capital.

But wait: Who was that masked man? Will the really rational agent please stand up? Can we unmask him? Dare we strip away the fantasies which make us unwitting partners in his dance of denial, dread, and damnation? Each of us has been to the market – The Temple of The Goods – lair of *Homo economicus*. Peering in, whom do you see? The Man in the Gray Flannel Suit? Robinson Crusoe? Ebenezer Scrooge? Or Stephen, as

> he had begun to grope in the darkness of his own state. From the evil seed of lust all other deadly sins had sprung forth: pride in himself and contempt of others, covetousness in using money for the purchase of unlawful pleasure, envy of those whose vices he could not reach to and calumnious murmuring against the pious, gluttonous enjoyment of food, the dull glowering anger amid which he brooded upon his longing, the swamp of spiritual and bodily sloth in which his whole being had sunk.
>
> (Joyce [1916] 1968: 162)

Clues strewn liberally through the didactic tales of *Homo economicus* (textbook economics as autobiography) reveal an intensely romantic young man like Stephen for whom consumption, working, and saving express aspects of an infant's world. The textual creation of a boundary-less state is a metaphor for the symbiosis of the mother–child unit, while the representations of working and saving as "bad" and playing as "good" symbolize the child's reaction to authority and power. Simultaneously the exaltation of consumption and saving privileges oral and anal pleasures. This romance evokes memories of an early state in which choices were very limited and autonomy was totally contingent. Inside, in love, incest, indifferent, now watch the[9]

Notes

1 Feminist economists have shown how standard methodologies and typical stories of the discipline are constructed by and through the male gaze. See, for example, England (1993); Grapard (1995); Nelson (1993); Pujol (1995); and Strassman (1993).

2 At this point I've used *Homo economicus* or Rational Economic Man as proper nouns nine times. Both terms are accurate, but each is difficult to type or to say. (Try saying *Homo economicus* three times fast.) Two revealing abbreviations spring immediately to mind: HE and REM (those physical manifestations of the dream state). But a better name is available. Anyone who has taught or studied economics has written the phrase Maximize Utility a million times. In preparing a textbook on the subject, Deirdre (Donald) McCloskey and Arjo Klamer coined the real name of our protagonist: Max U.

3 My psychoanalytic interpretation of economics has frequently been misunderstood as an analysis of individual economists. This is not what I am up to. I am not suggesting that the personal psychological perspectives of economists play determining roles in shaping the unconscious life of the fictive agents whose lives they script. I believe that causation runs in a rather different direction. Despite the fact that economists articulate economic theories, these theories take their shape as much from general social affective orientations as they do from the inner life of economists.

4 This debate was very technical and its details are not especially relevant here. An accessible presentation can be found in Feiner and Roberts (1990). In neoclassical economics production occurs within firms, yet each firm is the proverbial black box: inputs go in, and outputs come out, but almost no attention is paid to what actually goes on to make this happen. True, economists do specify the techniques of production – the engineering relationships that obtain between inputs and outputs – but the actual activities of production receive virtually no attention. Economists refer to something called "entrepreneurship," but the analysis of this is generally left to business professors.

5 An aspect of Max that frequently gives pause to students is his implausibility: an agent with perfect information, able to rank all choices in a single bound as he effortlessly calculates the costs and benefits of every action (including those in the future)? NOT. While this characterization may indeed be at odds with how people "really" act, I don't want to take issue with it here. Instead I will focus on the inner life implied by Max U's representation of, and relation to, the three choices that describe, fill, and limit his life.

6 One of the more profound consequences of this perspective for mainstream economics is that it undercuts the notion of individuality outside the web of human connectedness. In object relations theory it is impossible to have personality ouside the relational field, and in this sense the very analytic category

of atomistic individuals becomes an impossibility. Even the separative selves who dominate neoclassical economics exist in relation to one another. Their relatedness is, however, mediated by things. But it is nevertheless a relationship.

7 Now you know why economists and students of economics have written "Max U" ten jillion times.

8 James Joyce's *Finnegans Wake* (1939) opens with an incomplete sentence that begins "riverrun, past Eve and Adam's" (3).

9 It ends with the beginning of the same sentence: "A way a lone a last a loved a long the" (628). The point is to suggest the endless cycles of human history, figured throughout the text as a dream.

References

Bergmann, Barbara (1995). "Becker's Theory of the Family: Preposterous Conclusions." *Feminist Economics* 1: 141–50.

Bordo, Susan (1991). *The Flight to Objectivity: Essays on Cartesianism and Culture*. Albany: State University of New York Press.

Brantlinger, Patrick (1976). "Romances, Novels, and Psychoanalysis." In *The Practice of Psychoanalytic Criticism*. Ed. Leonard Tennenhouse. Detroit: Wayne State University Press. 19–45.

Chodorow, Nancy (1989). *Feminism and Psychoanalytic Theory*. New Haven, CN: Yale University Press.

England, Paula (1993). "The Separative Self: Androcentric Bias in Neoclassical Assumptions." In *Beyond Economic Man: Feminist Theory and Economics*. Ed. M.A. Ferber and J.A. Nelson. Chicago: University of Chicago Press, 37–53.

Feiner, Susan F. (1995). "Reading Neoclassical Economics: Toward an Erotic Economy of Sharing." In *Out of the Margin: Feminist Perspectives in Economics*. Ed. Edith Kuiper and Jolande Sap. New York: Routledge, 151–66.

—— , and Bruce Roberts (1990). "Hidden by the Invisible Hand: Neoclassical Economic Theory and the Textbook Treatment of Women and Minorities." *Gender and Society* 4.2: 159–81.

Ferber, Marianne A. and Julie A. Nelson, eds. (1993). *Beyond Economic Man: Feminist Theory and Economics*. Chicago: University of Chicago Press.

Flax, Jane (1983). "The Patriarchal Unconscious." In *Discovering Reality*. Ed. Sandra Harding and Merrill Hintika. New York: Reidel, 245–81.

Frank, Robert (1988). *Passions within Reason: The Strategic Role of the Emotions*. New York: W.W. Norton.

Grapard, Ulla (1995). "Robinson Crusoe: the Quintessential Economic Man?" *Feminist Economics* 1: 33–52.

Greenberg, Jay, and Stephen Mitchell (1993). *Object Relations in Psychoanalytic Theory*. Cambridge, MA: Harvard University Press.

Hollis, Martin, and Edward Nell (1975). *Rational Economic Man*. Cambridge: Cambridge University Press.

Joyce, James (1939). *Finnegans Wake*. New York: Viking.

—— ([1916] 1968). *A Portrait of the Artist as a Young Man: Text, Criticism and Notes*. Ed. Chester G. Anderson. New York: Viking.

McCloskey, Donald (1985). *The Rhetoric of Economics*. Madison: University of Wisconsin Press.

Nelson, Julie A. (1993). "The Study of Choice or the Study of Provisioning? Gender and the Definition of Economics." In *Beyond Economic Man: Feminist Theory and Economics*. Ed. M.A. Ferber and J.A. Nelson. Chicago: University of Chicago Press, 23–36.

Pujol, Michelle (1995). "Into the Margin!" In *Out of the Margin: Feminist Perspectives in Economics*. Ed. Edith Kuiper and Jolande Sap. New York: Routledge, 17–34.

Robbins, Lionel (1952). *An Essay on the Nature and Significance of Economic Science*. 2nd edn. London: Macmillan.

Robinson, Joan (1962). *Economic Heresies: Some Old Fashioned Questions in Economic Theory*. New York: Basic Books.

Strassman, Diana (1993). "Not a Free Market: the Rhetoric of Disciplinary Authority in Economics." In *Beyond Economic Man: Feminist Theory and Economics*. Ed. M.A. Ferber and J.A. Nelson. Chicago: University of Chicago Press, 54–68.

10

BANISHING PANIC

Harriet Martineau and the popularization of political economy

Elaine Freedgood

In the first three decades of the nineteenth century, a number of liberal British intellectuals attempted to popularize the "laws" of classical political economy in the hope, as the Victorian statistician William Farr put it, that "knowledge [would] banish panic" – that a better understanding of economic laws would quiet the growing unease of the middle and upper classes and the growing unrest of the laboring classes over an increasingly deregulated and industrialized market economy.[1] Harriet Martineau's *Illustrations of Political Economy* (1832–3) was among the most successful of such works. Published in nine pocket-sized volumes, the *Illustrations* consist of stories about the happy endings that await those who place their faith in a market left to its own "natural" workings. A narrative method that invests heavily in plot and economizes severely on character and detail allows the stories to pick their way through the minefield of Britain's new economy, speedily and systematically revealing the signs of growing stability and prosperity that lie just beneath its very troubled surface.

Like the economists she popularizes, Martineau represents economic laws as counterparts of the inevitable and immutable natural laws of the physical sciences and (largely implicitly) of God as their metaphysical author. The fact of immutable laws meant that there was no need for human intervention, even in the face of what might appear to be the disastrous effects of the market. God and science joined, in the theory of classical political economy as in Martineau's popularization thereof, to assuage cultural anxiety about the effects of a fully industrialized capitalism: economic and social relations are not humanly made, nor are humans responsible for, or even capable of, improving these relations.

T.R. Malthus's use of numbers, for example, made the conclusions in his 1797 *Essay on Population* seem like an absolutely inescapable outcome of biology.[2] And from the realm of the natural, it was only a short leap to the realm of the providential. Stefan Collini describes the way in which, in the work of Malthus:

> [e]conomic laws seem to be equated with God's laws in an effort to deliver the *quietus* to any prospect of beneficial change in social and political circumstances; human devices of any kind seem puny and helpless in the face of Nature. It is not so much a case of economic laws, but of biological necessity determining social and political arrangements.
>
> (Collini *et al.* 1983: 70)

Yet in the first three decades of the nineteenth century, a universe arranged by nature or by God was not particularly apparent. Social unrest, manifested in machine breaking, rick burning, and rioting; the power and danger of technological innovations from railroads to power looms; the unpredictability and severity of market cycles; and a tradition of dependence on the resources, labor, and markets of increasingly rebellious colonies, contributed to a sense of contingency and uncertainty in all classes, even at moments of considerable prosperity. All that was solid continually threatened to melt into air. The "laws" of classical political economy rationalized the frequently cruel effects of industrial capitalism, and their promise of regularity offered relief from the anxiety that the new contingencies and uncertainties in this form of capitalism produced.

In its promise of meaning and predictability classical political economy functioned like a cosmology: it attributed to its world a not entirely knowable, yet nevertheless reliable, structure and dynamics. And yet cosmological thinking has been relegated by a number of contemporary theorists to the realm of primitive, or pre-modern, thinking. In the work of Marshall Berman, Anthony Giddens, and Niklas Luhmann, to name but three, modernity is characterized by an acceptance of risk, an acceptance of the world as an irremediably uncertain place.

Classical political economy, especially as it is represented in Martineau's tranquilizing tales, suggests that the presence of risk produced panic rather than acceptance in the culture of Victorian modernity; the ongoing need to eliminate risk is registered in narratives – fictional and theoretical – that attempted to make the enduring and unendurable presence of uncertainty bearable by analyzing, explaining, predicting and in this way expunging it. Risk-reducing laws – not only of economics, but of history, politics, biology and public health – began in the early nineteenth century to circulate and take hold of imaginations groping for order in a world turned upside down by the unprecedented pace of change set in motion by industrialization. The cosmological consolations provided by these "laws" are most apparent in their popularized forms, in which promises of stability and order are proffered with unambivalent confidence.

Martineau, in the obituary she wrote for herself, contended that she could "popularize" but "neither discover or invent"(quoted in David 1987: 27). This essay will attempt to identify the ways in which her popularization of political economy did in fact change the theory it purported to explain. The changes Martineau made in classical theory – her discovery and invention of an inordinate amount of good news in the "dismal science" – were precisely what enabled the *Illustrations of Political Economy* to offer powerful consolation to Britons caught up in the immense change that marked the first thirty years of the nineteenth century. Martineau's tales suggest an important division of textual labor between popular, fleeting accounts of political economy and the more enduring works on the subject. The latter – the works of Smith, Ricardo, and Malthus as well as of novelists like Dickens, Eliot, and Gaskell – did not explain industrial capitalism as a utopia-in-progress: indeed, Ricardo's account of the conflicts inherent in class relations and Malthus's depressing view of the deadly outcome of healthy human sexuality suggest that the market is a tragic but inescapable mechanism. The "industrial" novels of the period also depict the market as an evil for which individual relationships and the comforts of the private sphere promise a palliative if not a cure.[3] Martineau repackages tragedy as error: her tales provide immediate consolation for their middle-class readers because they suggest that the pains of capitalism are due to misunderstanding and wrong action; obedience to the laws of the market will eventually lead to prosperity for all classes.

The *Illustrations* could not, however, provide enduring consolation because they offered utopian resolutions to real problems: the work declined in popularity during the 1840s, and fell into a long obscurity from which it has only recently, and tentatively, begun to recover. Although, as the title *Illustrations* suggests, the tales aspire to realism, they are actually more like myths in that they offer a "stable unifying philosophy by which to interpret a given subject matter" (Preminger 1986: 156) – here, the subject matter of Britain's new market. For Martineau to resolve her plots in terms of the conventions of realist fiction would require her to provide humanly made and idiosyncratic solutions to the problems of a "free" market. Instead, her plots are resolved by laws, and these laws operate according to the reliable and providential mechanisms of the market. She has no use for the individualistic, idiosyncratic plotting typical of realism; rather, her fictions strive to be what is finally an impossible and inefficacious generic hybrid: realist myth.

The swiftness with which Martineau's plots resolve the problems they depict may also have contributed to their inability to assuage panic in the long term. Janice A. Radway (1991), in her study of late twentieth-century romance reading, reports that the texts regarded by the readers she interviewed as "failed romances" made the mistake of delivering pleasure and relief before they had evoked "equally powerful feelings of anger and fear" (157). There seems to be, in reading that is done for relaxation and for relief from life's tribulations, a need for anxiety to be heightened before it is relieved: perhaps because of this temporary heightening, the relief is more intense and more lasting. Although my theory of the Victorian psychology of reading must necessarily be a highly speculative one, I wonder if Martineau's readers did not question whether or not they had truly earned, in the attenuated emotional labor required to read her tales, the happy endings she so readily provides.

Her law-governed plots, I will argue later in more detail, work like short-acting drugs: they take effect quickly for readers in need of easily understandable solutions to overwhelming and complex problems, but they wear off just as quickly, requiring additional doses of short-term relief but also of texts that provide more complicated and therefore longer-acting solutions to the problems at hand. The intense but short-lived popularity of the *Illustrations* attests to their ability to provide helpful explanations and short-term relief of anxiety to a wide variety of readers. By 1834 the monthly sales of the series had reached 10,000, several times that of many of Dickens's novels, which at 2,000 or 3,000 per month were considered highly successful:

> [Readers] as diverse as Victoria and Coleridge waited anxiously for each new number. Sir Robert Peel sent a private letter of congratulations and Richard Cobben publicly endorsed the work. Members of Parliament and cabinet ministers showered the author with bluebooks and suggestions for new tales to pave the way for legislation.
>
> (Blaug 1973: 130)

Martineau was clearly regarded as an author who could not only banish panic, but could also shape public opinion with her narrative method.

Because of their headlong rush to soothe an anxious reading public, Martineau's tales reveal, in clearer outline than their more enduring fictional and theoretical counterparts, the political unconscious of their moment: the utopian over-reaching of the stories insistently directs us "to the informing power of forces or contradictions which the text seeks in vain wholly to control or master" (Jameson 1981: 49). The repeated swerve, in tale after tale, from illustration to myth is a measure of the anxiety that attended the precarious triumph of the Victorian middle class and the first "free" market. Readers afflicted by this anxiety apparently could not bear the ambiguity, ambivalence, and inevitable remainder of conflict that inhere in realist fiction: they needed certain and complete relief, even if such relief could not last.

It is noteworthy that Martineau, who became so successful at addressing cultural anxiety, described her childhood as plagued by phobias: "panic struck at the head of the stairs, and I was sure I could not get down; and I could never cross the yard to the garden without flying and panting, and fearing to look behind, because a wild beast was after me" (Martineau [1877] 1984: 1. 10). This disabling anxiety is relieved by the discovery of "laws" – first the Necessitarian doctrines of Unitarianism (Webb 1960: 80) and then the laws of political economy:

> I finally laid hold of the conception of general laws. . . . My labouring brain and beating heart grew quiet, and something more like peace

> than I had ever known settled down upon my anxious mind. . . . From the time when I became convinced of the certainty of the action of laws, of the true importance of good influences and good habits, of the firmness, in short, of the ground I was treading, and of the security of the results which I should take the right means to attain, a new vigour pervaded my whole life, a new light spread through my mind, and I began to experience a steady growth in self-command, courage, and consequent integrity and disinterestedness.
>
> (Martineau [1877] 1984: 1. 109–10)

Martineau's world becomes secure, and the ground under her feet is guaranteed in its firmness by the existence of laws that dictate "results." Predictability and solidity replace her vertiginous sense of the contingency and fragility of the world around (and under) her. Her tales of political economy impart this sense of a predictable and solid economic and social structure, and her confident optimism was no doubt a significant ingredient in their remarkable success.

In addition to her own experience of anxiety, and a consequent empirical understanding of how anxiety might be relieved, Martineau also had her own experience of the vicissitudes of the market. In 1826 she and her family were bankrupted by a bad investment. This bankruptcy propelled her from part-time, amateur writing into a full-time literary career. The bright side of bankruptcy was that it provided her with "scope for action": "I began to feel the blessing of a wholly new freedom. I, who had been obliged to write before breakfast, or in some private way, had henceforth liberty to do my own work in my own way; for we had lost our gentility" (ibid.: 1. 141). The iron laws of political economy rescued Martineau from the iron laws of middle-class domestic economy and a woman's place within it: instead of having to hide and minimize her work, she now could, indeed had to, engage in it openly and productively. For Martineau, the invisible hand of the market was mercifully impartial; it brought disaster down upon her and her family, but it also enabled her, as a middle-class woman, to regain financial security and attain literary celebrity by writing a series of tales that explain and defend the system by which she had paradoxically been both victimized and liberated. We can thus understand Martineau's unbridled enthusiasm for *laissez faire* and also her considerable credibility as an apologist for it: she could preach the doctrine of submission to its laws from her own difficult, but rewarding, experience.

The *Illustrations* are a series of tales designed to educate a wide audience about every facet of political economy, from capital accumulation to colonialism, from taxation to free trade. Martineau's work is radical, in the middle-class Victorian sense of the word: she tries to return to fundamentals, even if this return proves to be disturbing. She is protective of social order, in other words, but not necessarily of *the* social order. Her radicalism and her feminism are expressed in the tales with a logical force that suggests at once the depth of her commitment to certain kinds of reform and an equally strong commitment to the very political-economic status quo that prevents such change.[4]

In the first tale of the *Illustrations*, "Life in the Wilds," set in southern Africa, a group of marauding Bushmen prey on a British settlement, steal all the "capital" of the British, and turn the settlers from a "state of advanced civilization to a primitive condition of society" (Martineau 1832: 1. 5). Martineau, in an explanation unusual for any Victorian, portrays the Bushmen's revenge as the result of European colonization, in effect partially placing the responsibility on the apparent victims:

> The Bushmen were the original possessors of much of the country about the Cape, which the British and the Dutch have since taken for their own. The natives were hunted down like so many wild beasts. This usage naturally made them fierce and active in their revenge. The hardships they have undergone have affected their bodily make also; and their short stature and clumsy form are not, as some suppose, a sufficient proof that they are of an inferior race to the men they make war upon. If we may judge by the experiments which have been tried upon the natives of various countries, it seems probable that if Europeans were driven from their homes into the mountains, and exposed to the hardships of a savage life, they would become stunted in their forms, barbarous in their habits, and cruel in their revenge.
>
> (Ibid.: 1. 4)

Martineau rejects the biological tenets of Victorian racial theory, and puts forward an environmentalist explanation for the condition of the Bushmen. By bringing the Bushmen into a three-dimensional foreground, rather than leaving them in the background as part of the menacing African scenery, Martineau complicates considerably the apparently simple implications of her tale. In order to demonstrate "primitive accumulation," Martineau has "primitives" reduce the English settlers to primitivity, but she also makes the behavior of the primitives an understandable response to the brutalities of colonization.

One effect of this complication is that the virtue of the English characters in her story is impugned from the beginning. Although Martineau effaces the agency of the colonizers by using the passive voice ("the natives were hunted down like wild beasts"), it is nonetheless clear that the hunters of the Bushmen were people like the settlers. There are thus two conflicting parables here. The first parable teaches that aggression is dangerous: the legitimate anger of the colonized emerges in an act of revenge that, in turn, reduces the colonizers to the condition of the primitive colonized. This parable is partially disavowed by a second one in which it is shown that the English can never be reduced to a truly primitive condition because they have the experience of economic development and thus whatever else is taken from them, "the intelligence belonging to a state of advancement remains" (ibid.: 1. 22). The English settlers recover from primitive economic conditions rapidly because of this irremovable intellectual capital. But it is precisely the imperial impulse, a crucial ingredient in the "intellectual capital" of the British, that has brought them to Africa in the first place. So although the virtue of the settlers may be undermined, their security and self-sufficiency are not. The aggressions of colonized peoples may be understandable, but the good news is that such people will never be able to vanquish their colonizers. The triumphalism of imperial thinking is subdued but not extinguished in this complicated, troubling, but finally supportive construction of the colonizing enterprise.

In Martineau's argument about the environmentally caused inferiority of the Bushmen, the Bushmen have been victimized, but the fact is that they are now inferior to the British, who therefore have a right to keep the land their forebears took. Nonetheless, the environmentalist argument has been made, and it can be easily transferred to others – to women, for example, who have been made into weak non-participants in public affairs, but who are not a biologically inferior gender any more than the Bushmen are a biologically inferior race. Martineau, Deirdre David (1987: 32) has argued, "engineers her feminism so that it serves the ideological aims of that same social class for whom she performs her legitimating role." The ideology that justifies imperialism and colonialism is left intact by this tale; essentialist ideas about race, and other "biological" categories like gender, are opened to question.

The settlers' loss of all capital provides a situation in which the evolution of an economy can be narrated at a fast-forward pace. The settlers are, in general, models of British industriousness, and immediately set about hunting, gathering, and making tools. But one character, Arnall, a former shopkeeper, is distressed at being reduced to a "labourer," because he has a "very limited notion of the meaning of the word" (ibid.: 1. 35). It seems as if Arnall may be a threat to the community because of his selfish unwillingness to work. True to the tenets of Adam Smith, however, Arnall's pursuit of his own self-interest turns out to benefit the community at large: Arnall conceives of a plan for catching buffalo and antelopes by digging a pit that may be used as a snare. "This magnificent plan entered Arnall's head one day when he was thinking how he might distinguish himself in a genteel way, and show himself a benefactor to the settlement without sacrificing his dignity" (56). Thus even the vanity of a man like Arnall benefits the larger community, even though it initially appears to be anti-social.

As soon as tools are fashioned, a spontaneous division of labor occurs. Three boys manufacturing bows and arrows divide the work such that each boy does whatever he can do best. The division of labor leads to the invention of machinery because "men, women and children are never so apt at devising ways of easing their toils as when they are confined to this sort of labour, and have to give their attention to it" (ibid: 1. 77). Martineau represents manufacturing, the division of labor, and the invention of machinery as processes that are as "natural" and spontaneous as child's play. The boys naturally divide their labor, and spontaneously think of devices. These effects of capital are represented as flowing from the worker, and as resulting in a decrease of "toil"; specialized labor and the use of machinery as a source of increased profit for the manufacturer, and alienation and unemployment for the worker, are conveniently elided.

Martineau uses her de-civilized settlers to show that what the English regard as necessities are in fact luxuries that result from an ever-increasing and universally beneficial division of labor. Mr. Stone, the voice of political economy in the tale, longs for one of his wife's Dorsetshire pies, but he is well aware that

> there must be an extensive division of labour before even that single dish can be prepared. To say nothing of what has already been done in our fields in fencing, ploughing, sowing, and trenching, there is much work remaining in reaping, threshing, and grinding, before you can have the flour. Then the meat for your pie is still grazing, and must be brought home and slaughtered and cut up. Then the salt must be got from the lake yonder; and the pepper, – what will you do for pepper?
>
> (Ibid.: 1. 80–81)

The upshot of this conversation is that even the breakfast of an "English washerwoman has cost the labour of many hundred hands," and is the result of a vast international division of labor and colonization. The tea, for example, comes from the East Indies and the sugar from the West Indies. The intended effect of this tale on its laboring-class readers is absurdly clear – without realizing it, they are all basking in the luxuries of a highly evolved economic system:

> Our countrymen little think how much the poorest of them owes to this grand principle of the division of labour. . . . They little think how . . . many kings and princes of countries less favoured than theirs would be glad to exchange their heaps of silver and gold for the accommodations of an English day labourer.
>
> (Ibid.: 1. 82)

Such pronouncements indicate the extent to which Martineau was entirely unfamiliar with the actual accommodations of an English day-laborer. This unfamiliarity may also explain the lack of popularity of Martineau's work among the laboring classes, who, particularly in the 1830s, rejected the teachings of classical political economy in general, and hers in particular.[5] Martineau's work was much more widely read by the middle classes, who were undoubtedly relieved to learn of this luxurious standard of living among a class of people who gave every appearance of being in a state of desperate want.

The second tale of Volume 1, "The Hill and the Valley," is set in a "wild district of South Wales" where the landscape is suddenly and violently transformed by the building of an ironworks. The first character we meet, old Armstrong, is appalled by the ugliness of the works; he values his solitude and the beauty of the previously unspoiled nature around him. Initially, Martineau represents his position as unassailable and unobjectionable. Slowly but surely, however, this seemingly unarguable position is shown to be mistaken. First, Martineau brings in the more moderate and reasonable views of the other inhabitants of the hill and the valley, who "thought it would be an advantage to have so many people settled there as could be provided with employment" (ibid.: 1. 18). But it is Mr. Wallace, the manager and part-owner of the works, who, through a favorite device of Martineau's, the friendly conversation, corrects Armstrong's backward-looking ideas. Mr. Wallace calmly and cordially demonstrates the points at which Mr. Armstrong's objections are either incorrect or grievously selfish. Armstrong, for example, believes that factory workers are like slaves; Mr. Wallace points out that, unlike master and slave, capitalist and worker are bound together by a "mutual interest" in productivity. Armstrong keeps his savings in his mattress, refusing to invest them; Wallace shows that the investment of capital is an important act of social generosity, almost of charity. Mr. Wallace himself experiences "great pleasure" in going around the ironworks to see how "the employment of his capital afforded subsistence to nearly 300 people, and to remember that the productions of their labour would promote the comfort and convenience of many hundreds or thousands more in the distant places to which the iron of this district was carried" (21). The industrial capitalist is represented as a benevolent *pater familias* who provides for his "children," who include both laborers and consumers. There is no intimation that Mr. Wallace is himself making a considerable profit. Profit, which appears only as collective wealth, is symbolically socialized in Martineau's account of *laissez faire*, making it closer to Owenite socialism than to Ricardian capitalism. The individuals who usually populate accounts of classical economics are transmogrified in Martineau's fiction into a collective body, each member of which benefits all other members by full participation in the capitalist enterprise.

Martineau attempts to make this socialized, moralized version of *laissez faire* believable through her choice of narrator. Mr. Wallace is the grandson of a laborer, who "by his skill and industry . . . managed to earn rather more than was sufficient to feed and clothe his family of four children," and was thus able to save and invest his money, and rise "out of labour" (ibid.: 1. 19). This is a cornerstone of Martineau's economic optimism: laborers who think like capitalists can save enough money to become capitalists. This is a truly grotesque idea, and one to which both the reform novels and the social investigations of the 1840s respond, with unsparing descriptions of laboring-class poverty.[6] Martineau, like many of her fellow Britons, failed or refused to know the actual conditions of what Disraeli aptly named the "other nation" of the poor.

Part of the persuasive force of Martineau's tales derives from her apparent willingness to give anti-industrialist and anti-capitalist views a full hearing. She stints nothing, for example, in her representation of Armstrong's compelling complaints about "the ugliness of smoke, and rows of houses, and ridges of cinders" (ibid.: 1. 37). He appeals to Mrs. Wallace, as a "lady of taste," to second his aesthetic objections. Mrs. Wallace, however, is much more a woman of principle than a lady of taste:

> It was true that a grove was a finer object at this distance than a cinder-ridge, and that a mountain-stream was more picturesque than a column of smoke; but there was beauty of a different kind which belonged to such establishments, and to which she was sure Mr. Armstrong would not be blind if he would only come down and survey the works. There was in the first place the beauty of machinery. She thought it could not but gratify the taste to see how men bring the powers of nature under their own control by their own contrivances; how the wind and the fire are made to act in the furnaces so that the metal runs out in a pure stream below; how, by the application of steam, such a substance as iron is passed between rollers, and compressed and shaped by them as easily as if it were potter's clay and then cut into lengths like twigs.
>
> (Ibid.: 1. 37)

Martineau uses gender here to great advantage. She has a female character explain to a male one that the beauty of the ironworks lies in its manly power. The implication is that Armstrong not only has anachronistic ideas, but that his nature-worship verges, perhaps, on the effeminate. Mrs. Wallace elaborates a new industrial aesthetic, which celebrates the beauty of "contrivances" that can subject nature to human needs. The fact that a woman can discern the beauty of the ironworks vouches for it in a way that a male endorsement could not, given the middle-class Victorian division of labor, a division in which, generally, men produced and women decorated. Mrs. Wallace's industrial aesthetic threatens to blur and even cancel the separation of public and private space in which the typical division of labor took place, a separation that dictated an ugly and dangerous public sphere for which compensation could be found in the beauty and security of the private sphere. Mrs. Wallace's ability to define the beauty of the ironworks suggests that the public sphere, if interpreted correctly (by women), may possess many of the virtues of the private one.

In Mrs. Wallace's description of the physical processes of iron production, technological domination "gratif[ies] taste." Adorno and Horkheimer (1991: 57) have described the anxious origin of this pleasure: "All power in class society is tied to a nagging consciousness of its own impotence against physical nature and its social descendants – the many. Only consciously contrived adaptation to nature brings nature under the control of the physically weaker." The "nagging consciousness of impotence" must be repressed with tales of triumph. The ability of this repression to succeed depends on the ability of authors like Martineau to generate excitement about and appreciation of such things as ironworks. Moreover, although this excitement and appreciation are produced by the sight of human (male) domination over the physically stronger forces of nature and labor, the example of such machinery could easily function as a paradigm for the possibility of the physically weaker controlling the stronger in other combinations: man over iron can be imaginatively transmuted into woman over iron, or woman over man *and* iron. Such representations of the industrial conquest of the natural world suggest that the power of middle-class men over nature – and "the many" – is potentially available to middle-class women. It is not surprising that classical political economy, which unequivocally supported the advance of technology, would have a strong appeal not only to Martineau, but to many women who were held psychically and economically hostage within the Victorian family structure by those whose power is shown here not to be essential at all, but rather only a mechanical addition that women could deploy just as effectively.

Back in the valley that has become happier because of the employment provided by the iron works, the price of iron suddenly drops by half and new machinery is introduced to cut costs. Many workers are thus unemployed and machine-blaming and -breaking ensues. Martineau does not evade the common objection that machinery, no matter how profitable, is wrong not only because it causes unemployment, but because it is simply too dangerous. She steers the plot directly into this controversy:

> It soon happened, most unfortunately, that a boy, who had in charge the management of some part of the new machinery, was careless, and put himself in the way of receiving a blow on the head, which killed him on the spot.
>
> (Martineau 1832: 1. 92)

The syntactic strategy of this sentence places the responsibility for the death of the boy squarely on the dead boy himself: he "put[s] himself in the way of receiving a blow on the head." Moreover, he was "in charge" of the machine and "careless." In a curious conjunction of states of mind, the boy is described both as not paying attention and as putting himself – which connotes deliberation rather than carelessness – in the way of receiving this fatal blow to the head. The reader can allay his or her own fear of machinery by choosing the most comforting conception of the boy: as either fatally absent-minded or fatally stupid. The machine is rendered passive and benign in this account, able to hurt only those who put themselves in the way to be hurt or who fail to take the minimum amount of care necessary not to be hurt.

In general, Martineau argues, machinery benefits everyone because it saves labor and capital and thus leads to the production of more capital that will lead to the employment of more labor. Mr. Wallace tells his workers that "we could not have employed any of you for the last six months, but for the saving caused by the new machinery; and . . . now it is gone, we can employ none of you any longer" (ibid.: 1. 131). Workers who break machinery thus have their causes and effects confused: falling prices, not machinery, produce unemployment. Martineau promises that machinery will eventually lead – and the timetable here is a considerable sticking point for both fictional and actual workers of the period – to more employment by increasing the amount of capital available for investment.

This is a significant deviation from classical theory: Ricardo, in the third edition of his *Principles of Political Economy and Taxation* (1821), had conceded that workers had been correct to view machinery as their enemy: "the opinion entertained by the labouring class, that the employment of machinery is frequently detrimental to their interests, is not founded on prejudice and error, but is conformable to the correct principles of political economy" (Ricardo [1821] 1990: 392). He maintained, however, that mechanization must be implemented to the fullest extent possible if British manufacturers were to remain competitive in the international market. He thus admitted class conflict to be an incurable feature of industrial capitalism. This tragic vision is necessarily suppressed in Martineau's utopian fiction of a strict harmony of class interests.[7] To retain this hopeful fiction, she must return to Smith as the most optimistic, or least tragic, theorist of *laissez faire*. She thus uses classical theory selectively, discovering its truths according to a formula expressed by the protagonist of her novel *Deerbrook* (1839): "What can religion be for, or reason or philosophy, whichever name you call your faith by, but to show us the bright side of everything?" It is this anti-realist credo that ultimately undermines the representational power of the *Illustrations*, and weakens the work's ability to assuage cultural anxiety: the bright side can usually take care of itself; it is the neglected dark side that demands explanation, and Martineau could not illuminate that darkness except by reference to economic laws that were guaranteed to be working, however invisibly, toward a happy equilibrium.

Lest they escape her readers, Martineau makes explicit at the end of each story the principles it was intended to illustrate. At the end of "The Hill and the Valley" we thus read:

> Since Capital is derived from Labour, whatever economizes labour assists the growth of Capital.
>
> Machinery economizes Labour, and therefore assists the growth of Capital.
>
> Machinery, by assisting the growth of Capital, therefore increases the demand for Labour.
>
> The interests of the two classes of producers, Labour and Capital, are therefore the same; the prosperity of both depending on the accumulation of Capital.
>
> (Martineau 1832: 1. 139)

Martineau's presentation of universally beneficent economic laws ignores the sophistication of existing radical analyses of political economy. By the 1830s such analyses had condemned *laissez faire* economic practices as chronically harmful to the laboring class.[8] The audience whom Martineau could satisfy, for a time at least, were those elements of the middle and upper classes who were anxious about the security of their own class standing and, perhaps at some level, guilty about the effects of an unregulated, expanding industrial capitalism. For these readers, the blatant pursuit of self-interest could be justified as a socially salutary course of action, since on Martineau's account, both the accumulation and the investment of capital were socially as well as individually beneficial.

Martineau thus appropriates and transforms the Smithian doctrine of self-interest. In her reworking, self-interest is simply equal to social interest. In Smith's version, the "Invisible Hand" of the market leads individuals "to promote the wealth of their nation." Although Smith abhors "self-conscious social interest" as an "affectation" (Smith [1776] 1976: 47), he does not, in marked contrast to the nineteenth-century economists, dispense with the need for "moral sentiments" in the economic and political sphere. In his vision, sympathy and empathy constrain commercial activity in socially useful ways; in the vision of nineteenth-century *laissez faire*, the checks and balances of the market are purely economic, divorced from both psychological and ethical considerations.[9] Martineau cannily reconnects economic and moral realms by suggesting, among other things, that investing for one's own profit is also a charitable act in that it raises the level of employment and of wages. She thus finds a way to dissociate aggressive, self-interested commercial behavior from guilt and anxiety.

In the late 1830s, the growing immiseration and discontentment of the laboring classes seriously challenged the idea that the pursuit of individual gain would or could increase public well-being. To prop up this idea required a thorough renovation of the ethic of social compassion. To this end, Martineau takes on one of the thorniest issues confronting *laissez faire*: the poor laws. "Cousin Marshall" is a tale that asks "What is charity?" and answers by debunking the apparently kind but actually cruel ideas behind the eighteenth-century poor laws.

At the opening of the tale a poor woman and her children, the Bridgemans, have been burnt out of their home. Mrs. Bridgeman's sister, Mrs. Bell, has been corrupted by too much government assistance and has consequently lost her sense of self-reliance as well as a sense of responsibility for her own family. She will scarcely aid her homeless sister, and, when her sister dies, will not take in her nieces and nephews. Mrs. Bell not only has no mercy on her nieces and nephews; she claims that her own dead son is still alive (although she does admit he is "beyond hope") in order to collect charity from the parish and food from the neighbors. Cousin Marshall, although a more distant relative, is not on relief, and consequently has a greater sense of social responsibility and family feeling. He takes in two of the four Bridgeman children, but the other two must go to a workhouse.

At the time of the *Illustrations*, the only poor relief Martineau favored was free education, "the enlightenment of the mind" (Martineau 1832: 3. 132). She took the only position truly consistent with a Malthusian-influenced *laissez faire* doctrine: that the government's responsibility to the poor was to decrease their numbers. Martineau, with her cost-effective use of character, tells us only enough about the Burkes to make them convincing opponents of government relief for the poor: they are a compassionate, charitably active, non-industrial brother and sister who argue against all relief except free education. Mr. Burke is a surgeon who cares for the poor, and his sister is a regular visitor at the local workhouse, and thus a comforter of the unlucky Bridgeman siblings. It is the people who are most in touch with the poor, and who care most about them, Martineau's characterizations suggest, who oppose the poor laws. The Burkes know at first hand that the present system of charity is morally ruinous in that it destroys "family values," and economically ruinous in that it will eventually impoverish everybody by "sinking," rather than investing, capital.

Martineau abandoned this strict *laissez faire* position on poor laws a year later, and was commissioned by Lord Brougham of the Society for the Diffusion of Useful Knowledge to write a series of tales popularizing the New Poor Law of 1834, *Poor Laws and Paupers Illustrated* (1833–4). She came to favor the provisions of the New Poor Law, which, although more stringent than the old Poor Law, still provided considerable relief. And although it gained the support of many *laissez faire* advocates, the New Poor Law, which replaced "outdoor" relief with the indoor relief of the workhouse and the administrative apparatus this entailed, occasioned "the most important extension of government power and of the administrative apparatus of the state in more than half a century" (Himmelfarb 1984: 166).

Laissez faire in theory and government intervention in practice together gained prominence as complementary and necessary parts of the Victorian "free" market. But the theory of *laissez faire* liberalism had constantly to disavow the fact that the economic sphere, "as a sphere of continued and rapid change, has as its necessary condition the power of the modern state" (Giddens 1984: 198). Indeed, two historians of state formation assert that state intervention in this period actually "enabled, accomplished, stabilized, [and] regulated into dominance that market on which *laissez faire* theory depends" (Corrigan and Sayer 1985: 118). This need for a powerful state repeatedly threatened to reveal that the market was not in fact self-regulating and that the evolution toward equilibrium that classical political economy (at its most optimistic) promised needed to be directed by the state. Martineau, like many liberals of the period, exhibited, particularly in her changing view of the poor laws, an increasing awareness of the risks that inhere in an unregulated, increasingly industrialized market, including the ability of sudden changes to create a domino effect of unemployment, poverty, indigence, unrest, and, quite conceivably, revolution. For industrial capitalism to survive, these risks had to be contained by government agencies created to collect information about the poor and minister to them in a consistent and "scientific" manner. The stage was set for the reform movements of the 1840s.

The severity of a deteriorating social reality crowded in upon all classes in the late 1830s and early 1840s. The excessive optimism of writers like Martineau finally prevented works like the *Illustrations* from banishing the panic of the middle and upper classes and quelling the anger of the laboring classes over the instability and cruelty of the economy. The cosmological consolations of popular political economy were limited in their duration by their attempt to totalize too tidily a particularly recalcitrant social reality. The rapid-fire plots of Martineau's fiction, which dispatch problems with an initially reassuring alacrity, begin to suggest, because of this need to move with such speed and thoroughness, the severity of the problems at hand. Panic might be banished by such tales, but the banished panic will return, and a new text, with a new set of consolations, will be needed to assuage it. The power and brevity of many popular texts can be explained by a pharmacological metaphor: their consolations, like the effects of strong but short-acting drugs, take effect quickly, but also wear off quickly. Panic thus returns, to be treated by new, "short-acting" texts – as popular and ephemeral works on political economy were replaced to a great extent in the 1840s by the best-selling and also largely ephemeral literature of reform.[10] Modern cosmologies, as they are circulated in modern myths like those of Martineau, must be highly disposable and readily replaceable, keeping pace with the multiplying and multifocal anxieties of modernity, Victorian and otherwise.

Cultural anxiety also requires the longer-lasting resolutions found in more enduring canonical works, both literary and economic. Dickens and Gaskell, for example, were acutely critical of the consequences of Britain's new economy, but their fictions allow for more complication and conflict than do Martineau's, and therefore, I would suggest, for more enduring relief of cultural anxiety (and, by extension, for the endurance of the very economy they criticize). They represent England as fraught with difficult and even dangerous social, political, and economic problems, problems that are not readily solvable. Their readers must experience and endure problems over time, including class conflict and violence, family dissolution, poverty, and homelessness. Anxieties are thereby raised before they are relieved – a procedure that Radway (1991), we recall, found critical to the success of romance novels in providing their readers with emotional satisfaction. The conflicts that the novels of Dickens, Gaskell, and other writers of realist fiction depict, and the contradictions that they do not thoroughly resolve – poverty persists, the location of value remains uncertain, possessing wealth continues to threaten character, the values of home are entirely incompatible with those of the market – require readers to perform significant emotional and intellectual labor in the process of reading, and that labor perhaps buys them a modicum of tranquility about certain aspects of the reality they have engaged, at the safe distance fiction provides.

We can readily find a parallel process in economic theory, specifically in the third edition of Ricardo's *Principles of Political Economy*, when he admits that the use of machinery is not after all in the interest of the laboring class and thus may inspire anxiety in his readers about the just workings of a *laissez faire* economy. In the ensuing arguments about Britain's need to remain competitive in world markets, Ricardo asserts that machinery must be retained and class conflict tolerated. This text of "high" theory can tolerate, and expect its readers to tolerate, discomfort long enough to achieve a resolution that retains some conflict rather than resolving all of it with flimsy optimism and artifice. Ricardo's very partial resolution of the machinery question is sufficiently grounded in social and psychological actualities to remain convincing in the long term. Such difficult resolutions can treat the residue of panic that resists the too-sweet blandishments of popular, ephemeral texts like Martineau's. But it is in the blandishments of texts like Martineau's *Illustrations of Political Economy* that the acute conflicts of the Victorian political unconscious are most available to interpretation, unresolved and unobscured by the long-acting and long-lasting conceptual structures of the nineteenth-century canons of political economy and fiction.

Notes

1 Quoted in Cullen (1975: 36). See also Jane Marcet, *Conversations on Political Economy* (1816), and G.R. Porter, *Progress of the Nation* (1836). Karl Polanyi (1957: 83) has argued that it was not until the Poor Law Reform of 1834,

which established a competitive labor market by abolishing the "right to live" allowances of the Speenhamland system, that the British economy became a "self-regulating" market economy.

2 "The [apparent] numerical precision," Gertrude Himmelfarb (1984: 127) writes, "gave an authority, a mathematical exactitude, and certitude to the theory which enhanced its appeal and was almost mesmerizing in its effect."

3 See Gallagher (1985).

4 See Hobart (1994) for a discussion of the "menacing implications of a feminist politics that uncritically values liberty, equality, and *fraternity*" (249).

5 According to Webb (1955: 100), "the working-class press gave no quarter to the popular conceptions of political economy, and they did not carry on their attack in ignorance." For working-class critiques of classical political economy, see also Stafford (1987). Nonetheless, it is of course difficult to characterize such a large and various thing as "working-class opinion." My intention here is to suggest the fact of considerable and thoughtful working-class resistance to *laissez faire*. Webb (1960: 124) describes the circulation of the *Illustrations* as "almost entirely middle class."

6 Elizabeth Gaskell's *Mary Barton* (1848) seems a particularly acute response to Martineau's representations. It is noteworthy that in the preface Gaskell disavows her own participation in such a debate, asserting "I know nothing of Political Economy or the theories of trade" (1972: lxxx). See also Edwin Chadwick's Report on the *Sanitary Condition of the Labouring Population of Great Britain* ([1842] 1965), a work that refutes Martineau's account of the beneficence of the "free" market economy with unintended but nonetheless compelling vigor.

7 Catherine Gallagher (1985: 61) has argued that Martineau had a partially tragic vision of *laissez faire*: she bound her laboring characters in "chains of necessity, depicted their suffering and advised acceptance." I am arguing that the scheme of the tales is to convince laboring-class readers that if they accept economic laws, and work in harmony with them, their chains will fall away – their chains, in other words, are their ignorance of economics and their consequent mistaken sense of class conflict.

8 See Stafford (1987).

9 Simon Dentith (1983: 185) argues that the nineteenth-century version of classical political economy succeeded in "establishing an area of discourse independent of moral considerations."

10 Chadwick's 1842 *Sanitary Report*, for example, sold between 10,000 and 20,000 copies, and Florence Nightingale's works on nursing and hospitals went through numerous editions.

References

Adorno, Theodor, and Max Horkheimer (1991). *Dialectic of Enlightenment*. Trans. John Cumming. New York: Continuum.

Berman, Marshall (1982). *All That Is Solid Melts into Air: The Experience of Modernity*. New York: Simon & Schuster.

Blaug, Mark (1973). *Ricardian Economics: A Historical Study*. Westport, CT: Greenwood.
—— (1978). *Economic Theory in Retrospect*. 3rd edn. Cambridge: Cambridge University Press.
Chadwick, Edwin ([1842] 1965). *Sanitary Condition of the Labouring Population of Great Britain*. Edinburgh: Edinburgh University Press.
Collini, Stefan, Donald Winch, and John Burrow (1983). *That Noble Science of Politics: A Study in Nineteenth Century Intellectual Politics*. Cambridge: Cambridge University Press.
Corrigan, Philip Richard D., and Derek Sayer (1985). *The Great Arch: English State Formation as Cultural Revolution*. New York: Basil Blackwell.
Cullen, Michael J. (1975). *The Statistical Movement in Early Victorian Britain: The Foundations of Empirical Social Research*. New York: Barnes & Noble.
David, Deirdre (1987). *Intellectual Women and Victorian Patriarchy: Harriet Martineau, Elizabeth Barrett Browning, George Eliot*. Ithaca: Cornell University Press.
Dentith, Simon (1983). "Political Economy, Fiction and the Language of Practical Ideology in Nineteenth-Century England." *Social History* 8: 183–99.
Gallagher, Catherine (1985). *The Industrial Reformation of English Fiction 1832–1867*. Chicago: University of Chicago Press.
Gaskell, Elizabeth (1972). *Mary Barton*. New York: Putnam.
Giddens, Anthony (1984). *The Constitution of Society: Outline of the Theory of Structuration*. Berkeley: University of California Press.
—— (1990). *The Consequences of Modernity*. Stanford, CA: Stanford University Press.
—— (1991). *Modernity and Self-Identity: Self and Society in the Late Modern Age*. Stanford, CA: Stanford University Press.
Himmelfarb, Gertrude (1984). *The Idea of Poverty*. New York: Knopf.
Hobart, Ann (1994). "Harriet Martineau's Political Economy of Everyday Life." *Victorian Studies* 37: 223–52.
Jameson, Fredric (1981). *The Political Unconscious: Narrative as a Socially Symbolic Act*. Ithaca, NY: Cornell University Press.
Luhmann, Niklas (1979). *Trust and Power*. New York: John Wiley.
—— (1993). *Risk: A Sociological Theory*. Trans. Rhodes Barrett. New York: de Gruyter.
Martineau, Harriet (1832). *Illustrations of Political Economy*. 9 vols. London: Charles Fox.
—— ([1877] 1984). *Autobiography*. 2 vols. London: Virago.
Polanyi, Karl (1957). *The Great Transformation: The Political and Economic Origins of Our Time*. Boston, MA: Beacon.
Preminger, Alex, ed. (1986). *The Princeton Handbook of Poetic Terms*. Princeton, NJ: Princeton University Press.
Radway, Janice A. (1991). *Reading the Romance: Women, Patriarchy and Popular Literature*. Chapel Hill: University of North Carolina Press.
Ricardo, David ([1821] 1990). *On the Principles of Political Economy and Taxation*. 3rd edn. Ed. Piero Sraffa. Cambridge: Cambridge University Press.
Smith, Adam ([1776] 1976). *An Inquiry into the Nature and Causes of the Wealth of Nations*. Ed. Edwin Cannan. Chicago: University of Chicago Press.

Stafford, William K. (1987). *Socialism, Radicalism and Nostalgia: Social Criticism in Britain, 1775–1830*. Cambridge: Cambridge University Press.
Webb, R.K. (1995). *The British Working Class Reader 1790–1848: Literacy and Social Tension*. London: George Allen & Unwin.
—— (1960). *Harriet Martineau: A Radical Victorian*. New York: Columbia University Press.

11

"LIBIDINAL ECONOMICS"

Lyotard and accounting for the unaccountable

Brian P. Cooper and Margueritte S. Murphy

Jean-François Lyotard's *Libidinal Economy* first appeared in France in 1974, in part as a response to Deleuze and Guattari's *Anti-Oedipus: Capitalism and Schizophrenia*, published two years earlier. Like *Anti-Oedipus*, *Libidinal Economy* is an attempt to wed economic analysis and psychoanalysis, wildly revising and, in Lyotard's case, reviling Marx and Freud along the way. Unlike *Anti-Oedipus*, *Libidinal Economy* has had little impact in any field, other than to alienate Lyotard's Marxist friends, if we are to believe the author himself, who in 1988 reflected: "The readers of this book – thank god there were very few – generally accepted the product as a rhetorical exercise and gave no consideration to the upheaval it required of my soul. . . . Its rare readers disliked the book, which passed for a piece of shamelessness, immodesty, and provocation" (Lyotard 1988: 13–14).

It is indeed an execrable book, embarrassing in its graphic descriptions of the "so-called" body, contradictory in its refusal of critique while indulging in scathing critiques, and generally unruly in terms of organization of thought and connections among thought sequences. (Using Lyotard's own terms, one might say that its dominant formal principle is flux propelled by and culminating in "intensities" or exclamatory affirmations.) All this is doubtless due in part to Lyotard's own desire to deploy a style – or a "writing" – driven by libidinal energies: in effect to put into practice the anti-theory theory that he expounds. Despite these flaws, which make the book at times nearly unreadable, there are genuine insights and a general direction of thought that well warrants the attention of anyone seeking to define an anti-essentialist economics, and to describe economic "events," like panics, that seem to evade economic analysis.

To clarify Lyotard's project, we will begin by briefly comparing a few of his basic terms and premises with those of Deleuze and Guattari in *Anti-Oedipus*. As their title implies, Deleuze and Guattari critique the Oedipal model for introducing lack into desire and thereby belying the productive powers of the unconscious:

> The fact is, from the moment that we are placed within the framework of Oedipus – from the moment that we are measured in terms of Oedipus – the cards are stacked against us, and the only real relationship, that of production, has been done away with. The great discovery of psychoanalysis was that of the production of desire, of the productions of the unconscious. But once Oedipus entered the picture, this discovery was soon buried beneath a new brand of idealism: a classical theater was substituted for the unconscious as a factory; representation was substituted for the units of production of the unconscious; and an unconscious that was capable of nothing but expressing itself – in myth, tragedy, dreams – was substituted for the productive unconscious.
>
> (Deleuze and Guattari 1983: 24)

Their figure for the working of the unconscious that produces "flows of desire" is "desiring-machines," and economic or "social production" "is purely and simply desiring-production itself under determinate conditions." That is, the libido invests the forces of economic production directly, without any sort of mediation or transformation.

Lyotard takes his cue from *Anti-Oedipus*, claiming that "the libido never fails to invest regions, and it doesn't invest under the rubric of lack and appropriation. It invests without condition" (Lyotard 1993: 4). Hence for Lyotard the power, ubiquity, and dissimulated nature of libidinal investments. Like Deleuze and Guattari, he denounces the "theater of representation," and then goes on to challenge the representational space of Western metaphysics going back to Plato and St. Augustine, putting in question the conceptual itself, as well as the representational space of capitalism, all of which masks the libidinal pulsions, or drives, informing human production. His figure for this universal libidinal drive is the "great ephemeral skin," a Moebius band with neither inside nor outside, hence no volume to suggest a theatrical space. This band itself, of course, is to be considered a fiction; otherwise, it would enter the realm of representation.

Among Lyotard's more contemporary targets is semiotics. Essentially he accuses semiotics of the "dematerialization" of things, with the sign as a substitution that, for Saussure, does not lead to signification but to a metonymic system whereby signification is always deferred – hence to the infinite "postponement of the signifier." Lyotard would replace the signifier/signified relationship with the figure of the "tensor," which includes the sign and all the intensities invested in the sign without the "lack," that is, the emptying out of signification occasioned by the deferral inherent in semiotics. But ironically, in the eyes of the libidinal economist, "dematerialization" is also productive – a channeling of libidinal energies; it is

> in the same space and time, the cartography of a *material* voyage, of new regions of sonorous, but also chromatic, sculptural, political,

> erotic, linguistic space, being, as a result of the *mise en signes*, conquered and crossed by the trails of influxes, offering the libido new opportunities for intensification, the fabrication of signs through "dematerialization" providing material for the extension of tensors.
> (Ibid.: 44)

Thus, semiotics dissimulates its libidinal investments; it abstracts pieces from the pulsional band, yet this dissection is also "an opportunity for a refinement and an intensification of the passages of affects" (ibid.).

The libidinal economist finds a similar operation in the workings of capital: both the dissimulation of libidinal energies in the systems described by political economy and the channeling of energies through such description and any policies, like mercantilism, thereby enacted. Lyotard maintains that he neither seeks to interpret, analyze, or critique capital, for to critique "is to maintain oneself in the field of the criticized thing and in the dogmatic, indeed paranoiac, relation of knowledge" (95) and to erect the metaphysical "theater" that Lyotard would abandon (3). Rather, he wishes to describe capital's operations by redescribing political economy and its theory of exchange. This theory, as summarized by Lyotard, sees exchange as "an exchange in the sense of two contracting parties each intending to swap two objects of equivalent (marginal) utility" (92). Lyotard's alternative view has two crucial foci: the affirmation of singular events as against system and, a related theme, the affirmative violence wrought by the unaccountable (and excessive) in libidinal investment. For Lyotard, political economy, in its efforts to "explain" the operations of capital, crushes singularity in order to render an organic unity, all elements of which will be comparable: value is defined, in political economy as in a semiotic system, relationally. For Lyotard, every exchange involves a libidinal excess over and above exchange and entails an incommensurability – not an equivalence – not captured by the accounting methods of political economy.

Championing singularities against totalizing systems of account, as Lyotard does, may in fact preclude anything but description. Yet a glance at the history of economic thought shows us that the unsettling effects of desire were once a major preoccupation of its practitioners, particularly in the nineteenth century. The problematic role of sexual desire demarcated the limits of the Malthusian population debate; it was a commonplace that the wants and desires of civilized man stoked the fires of capitalist production and consumption, indeed defined such a man as civilized. And the probability that speculative desires, so necessary for economic growth, would grow to unhealthy proportions, thus setting off periodic crises, haunted ninteenth-century analysts. The language of desire has receded from economic discourse, supplanted by the reign of "well-ordered preferences." Notable exceptions to this rule occur in the reaction to moments of evident disorder such as the wreckage wrought by financial crashes or the aftermath of speculative bubbles. But even at such moments desire reappears as a rational, orderly, and ultimately explicable operation.

In contrast to the economists, Lyotard seeks not to explain but to describe the singularities called "panics." For Lyotard, money has two forms – account and credit – with three functions: homeostasis, dynamic equilibrium, and disequilibrium. In this paper, we will focus mostly on homeostasis and disequilibrium.[1] Political economy is predicated upon nullification, upon crushing the singularity of libidinal investments as part of the process of creating the equivalences necessary for exchange. This form of nullification is the accounting system for payment money, what Lyotard calls the great concentrator, the device requisite for homeostatic regulation in capital. The great concentrator seeks to stabilize, *immobilize* the social body and achieve a state of totality "which would have its unity in itself and where the 'truth' of political economy would finally prevail, in this case a reproduction conforming to nature" (215). Lyotard cites Piero Sraffa's organic standard commodity as the "truth" of political economy as accounting system. To the list of "truths" we can add Debreu's mathematical formalism of the Invisible Hand, a formalism which proves the existence of the core of Walrasian general equilibrium.

As Lyotard indicates, in political economic accounting systems the regulative and deregulative functions are both manifest. A recent example of this regulative function is the US Federal Reserve's abandonment of policy by rule in favor of discretionary measures as the principal means to keep the economy on a steady, non-inflationary growth path.[2] For Lyotard, even such an arbitrary attempt to stabilize belies the "madness" of the great concentrator and the "madness" of political economy (214–15). There are, moreover, occasional manifestations of "crises" or blatant eruptions of libidinal, mercantilist "zeal," constitutive of speculative movements of capital, which are normally hidden by the reproductive function of capital. Indeed, for Lyotard, mercantilism may always be a part of the workings of capital in that the two uses of credit – reproductive and "looting" – are "dissimulated together" and it is only during crises, which are like "hysterical attacks," that these two uses of credit become discernible (223). Mercantilism (jealousy) operates as an anti-system or anti-matter predicated on exhausting and killing through plunder, pillage, or conquest of the body it feeds upon. Mercantilism, then, is a zero-sum game. Recent speculative attacks (coordinated by whom or by what? computer programs?) on European currencies such as the franc and lira are instances of the zero-sum character of the movements of speculative capital. The losers in these cases, aside from those caught holding the wrong type of money, are national governments. The identity of the state and its putative policy independence are called into question as speculative capital introduces disequilibrium into the system through its mercantilist edge.

As examples of movements of capital that manifest speculative jealousy or "zeal" Lyotard discusses the financial crises of 1921 and 1929 and the oil crisis of 1973. Here we will look briefly at economists' attempts to "explain" what happened during a similar, more recent financial crisis. The report of the Brady Commission, appointed by President Reagan to investigate the stock market crash of October 1987, assigned blame for the crash to technical matters. Philip Mirowski (1994) summarizes the rejection of the Brady Commission report by economists and policy makers in the following manner: by fixing blame on technical matters, the report failed in its juridical role, which is to "determine which calamitous transgressions were Natural and which were Social, to reduce the complexity of the transgression to an anthropomorphically comprehensible phenomenon, the better to mete out blame and punishment accordingly." Consequently, the report failed to reassure market participants that order could be restored. The specific responses of the economics discipline, Mirowski (1994: 475–76) notes, were manifold and unsuccessful:

> Alas, rejection of the Brady Commission narrative did not mean that the neoclassicals had a better narrative with which to replace it. . . . Every possible permutation of the Natural and the Social in the neoclassical toolbox was floated at one time or another. One proposal was that the share market remained rational and efficient, even on October 19 and 20: In other words, the 500-point drop just meant people had revised their estimation of the fundamentals over the weekend; or in cruder terms, market crashes are Natural. Another option resonant with the roaring 1980s was that the crash was somehow the government's fault, even if the precise mechanism was obscure; this was the ever-popular scenario of the Social frustrating the Natural. Another variant of the Unnatural (or Preternatural?) thwarting the Natural was Robert Shiller's widely quoted claim that a vast wave of mob psychology, a weekend crisis of confidence, had swept over the investing populace. . . . Finally, in a desperate resort to epicycles, some liberal economists attempted to temper the Natural with the Social by maintaining that if the market were left to the professionals, it would be as efficient as the neoclassical model maintained, but the presence of "noise traders" – that is humble, simple individual investors – kept inducing Unnatural disturbances in the rational prices.

As attempts to domesticate crises, or as explanations which would serve to re-establish order, each of these neoclassical stories was unsuccessful. They failed because, Mirowski observes, save for the first story ("there was no panic"), they remain inconsistent with notions of general equilibrium or homeostatic regulation.

Yet each story Mirowski recounts has a venerable history in analyses of financial crises. The last, invoking the presence and survival of "noise traders," resembles Walter Bagehot's anxiety over the presence of evolutionary atavisms – including ignorant traders stuck in the "cake of custom" – which would lead to financial panics (de Long *et al.* 1990, 1991).[3] Bagehot usefully illustrates the differences between economists' narratives and Lyotard's descriptions of commercial crises: the former emphasize the efficient functioning of well-ordered desire, its functioning disrupted only occasionally by the stampede provoked by herd mentality; the latter stress desire's ubiquity and violence, attributes signaled by traders' "mere love of activity." Bagehot sought to chart a new set of bodily analogies for bankers and economists to describe the working of the Victorian money market, displacing the problematic image of the circulatory system with an analogy to the nervous system, and describing commercial panics as a "species of neuralgia" rather than as consequences of "overflowing blood." Timothy Alborn (1994: 191) describes Bagehot's evolutionary narrative of the progress of civilization, outlined in *Physics and Politics* (1872), as one that begins with prehistoric savages

> whose active biological impulses spur them onward to forming small groups. From these groups nations are formed among individuals who excel at imitating leaders, creating the "cake of custom" that is vital to national character. Finally the "age of discussion" develops tolerance among individuals in those nations (like England) lucky enough to make it to the final stage of civilization.

Bagehot sought to warn bankers of the presence of both types of atavisms within the money market: the "cake of custom" or imitative activity associated with herd mentality, and the impulse to action or what Bagehot termed the "disposition to excessive action" (Bagehot [1872] 1889: 567).[4] While present-day economists tend to conjure the first as a "cause" of panics, Bagehot considered that commercial panics were caused "in some degree . . . by the urge to get rich; but in a considerable degree, too, by the mere love of activity" where the usual signs of mercantilism – hoarding and demanding gold from banks – prevailed. Bagehot feared a return of English capitalism to the unhappy organic unity of the savage, mercantilist state if the bad speculators had it too much their way.

A popular present-day variant of the efforts by academic economists to render panics as "business as usual" consists of describing panics as the outcome of a game between market participants. We can play the game too. Let's describe the information sets and strategies of two sets of participants in the game of capital: the Federal Reserve, on the one hand, and economists and market analysts on the other. Both players' tasks include world-describing and world-making, structuring agency so as to prevent and contain panics, and providing *ex post facto* assurances of the order underlying crises. The equilibrium game of capital generates the following questions: what signs does the Fed read as a basis for action? And how do economists and market analysts read the Fed? We state these two questions because descriptions of the workings of financial capital, whether popular or academic, take the recursive approach standard in strategic analyses. That is, market players analyze the Fed, knowing that the Fed in turn analyzes market participants' analyses of the Fed, and so on. The Fed is a diligent collector of both physical and psychical data on the "health" of the economy. If we are to believe his statements on the untrustworthiness of the former, Alan Greenspan relies more on intuition, by responding to bankers' and businessmen's anecdotes and narratives, than on quantitative evidence in his attempt to anticipate both inflation and inflationary expectations while, simultaneously, hoping not to set off a spiral of self-fulfilling expectations.

So economists read the Fed and the Fed reads market psychology – the condition of its "nerves," its bouts of amnesia and the like – even though, to paraphrase Greenspan's lament, we economists are not trained in psychology. Two recent descriptions of speculative disequilibrium serve, in fact, to illustrate the tendency of social scientific discourse to repress considerations of unruly individual and market psychology. Each focuses on the strategic aspects of market participants' actions, substituting rational decision-making for analogies of body functions. Notably, the rhetoric of these analyses relies on a shift from the language of psychoanalysis to the seemingly neutral, scientific language of economics and decision science, implying order rather than disorder. The first paper replaces a model of rational expectations which generates "schizophrenia" in its traders with "monopolistic competition" (Kyle 1989); the second replaces a "mania–distress–panic" paradigm of market crises with the paradigm of "action–attribution–regulation" (Abolafia and Kilduf 1988). In avoiding psychological speculation, these papers typify the way in which analysts redescribe panics as no more than the normal problem of coordinating traders' rational desires and rational actions.

For Lyotard, however, recasting panics as outcomes of strategic decision-making is simply accounting work that allows the analysts' work to proceed.[5] He departs from the economists by foregrounding the ever present potential for money's functions to erupt into panics – the unaccountable. By highlighting the role of mercantilist *jealousy* in producing crises, Lyotard sounds more like the nineteenth-century speculator who, commenting on attempts to corner various Wall Street markets, observed that "hardly a week goes by without a recurrence of these singular phenomena."[6] Lyotard (1993: 228–29) writes that panics occur when looting creates an increasing inequality of wealth, which in turn

> [creates] between one piece and the other of the libidinal patchwork a more and more hateful jealousy with regard to intensities. . . . Take the crisis of 1929, one sees the mercantilist machine there on a large scale. Should the powerful impulsions of looting be at work from one end to the other, should in capital the excess of

> what is without a counterpart come to light, there is the event, there its affirmativity.[7]

Lyotard quotes J. Néré on the reason for the extent of speculation on credit, the operations of "the mercantilist machine," in the crisis of 1929: "There is a lack of basic information to answer this." To which Lyotard responds:

> There is in fact no response to the question of a displacement of libidinal inscription. That intensity, that force is then instantiated in the securities trade and considered as exchangeable things, rather than the production of consumable commodities, is no more explicable than the fact that the libido lodged in the genital zone moves toward the anus or the ear. Call it regression if it makes you any happier. The eroticization (in this banal sense) of the Stock Market is not to be explained, but taken note of.
>
> (Ibid.: 236)

As an example, Lyotard takes note of the trade, credit, and inflationary movements of the crisis of 1921, an "event" anticipating the crisis of 1929.

When commenting on these movements in the crisis of 1921, Lyotard uses the standard technical language of a market analyst. Yet when he borrows an example cited by Keynes, in which a Moscow grocer hurries to exchange currency for cheese, as a more stable store of value, his language shifts. In this episode:

> [one] enters another, vertiginous time, made of *as many times as there are exchanges*. . . . Every encounter of the cheesemonger with roubles must be imagined as an unbearable event which he flees. . . . And from one flight to another, there is no continuity. From one heap of notes to the other, there is no identity, not even simple quantitative difference.
>
> (Ibid.: 231)[8]

Crises reveal the fiction of the social body. They reveal as well the duplicity of economic signs in the use of currency, including the duplicity of time: the logical time of the system is iterative, atemporal, continuous, hence logically reversible; while the time of the event is singular, that is, discontinuous.

As instances of the reversal of the logic of exchange, these "vertiginous" events – which send money, goods and individuals scurrying hither and thither – represent "immoderation" and "economic amnesia." This economic amnesia ("*a-metry* [*amétrie*], anomie" [233]) may be incomplete, having as it does "a direct similarity with the passage of influxes on the pieces of libidinal patchwork. . . . [I]t manifests all the characteristics of the pulsional 'disorder' affecting the body of reproduction: the running Muscovite cheesemonger is an effect of partial pulsional motion" (233).

But partial amnesia is evident in the logic and operations of capital even during its normal functioning. As the *New York Times* has observed, "The financial markets, with their notorious absence of a long-term memory, began to worry about inflation again, despite any objective basis for the concern and a big inflation-fighting increase in short-term interest rates by the Federal Reserve on Tuesday" (22 August 1994: D3). If the space-time of reproduction always and everywhere faces the jeopardy posed by singularities, so too does its logic, the reproduction of space-time.

Thus, Lyotard's libidinal economics may not exactly account for financial crises and panics, but it does situate them as part of the unaccountable in market activity, eruptions that make clear the libidinal investments in the use of credit. And if we look for a moment at the question of economic agency, we see other ways in which *Libidinal Economy* serves as a provocative corrective to conventional views of economic behavior. The assault on *Homo economicus*, or Arjo Klamer's updated version, "Max U," has been heavy in recent years, especially by feminist economists like Nancy Folbre and Heidi Hartmann, Ulla Grapard, Julie Nelson, Diana Strassmann and many others, and we laud this critical examination of the all-too-masculine assumptions about the economic subject. As Amariglio and Graham (1993) note, the sexism built into neoclassical theory also pits masculine reason against the passions emanating from the desires of the body, too often conceived of as feminine.[9] From a neoclassical point of view, this story has a "happy" ending: reason tames desire, or bodily needs and desires are mediated by the rational decision-making process that characterizes economic activity in progressive societies.[10]

But this ongoing narrative of individually based homeostasis receives occasional jolts during periods of inexplicable, ongoing slumps in consumer demand, or eruptions of speculative crises. Clearly, Lyotard's post-Freudian economics turns the conventional picture of the economic actor on its head: desire, all along, we realize, has driven not only market activity without mediation, but also the rationalization that has accompanied such activity, which produces economic theory. Yet we are already misconstruing Lyotard by positing an individual economic actor, for, as a good Postmodernist, Lyotard long ago relinquished belief in the unified subject. Indeed, he critiques Marcel Mauss's concept of the gift, itself a critique of political economy, by noting that Mauss's symbolic exchange "presupposes a subject, a limit of his proper body and property, and the generous transgression of this property" (Lyotard 1993: 122). Lyotard's depiction of the libidinal skin as a Moebius band strategically posits libidinal forces without an individual body, particularly without a head – a condition of acephalia, as Lyotard calls it. Hence, desire is everywhere and has no bodily center. (Lyotard also critiques Freud for his focus on genital origins in the aetiology of neuroses

– 186.) Body parts and proper names – or, to quote Lyotard, "Sarah, Birgit, Paul, the liver, the left eye, the cold, hard neck" – are all "singular effects" juxtaposed on the pulsional band (18). Like his great precursors Marx, Nietzsche, and Freud, Lyotard makes the body basic to his philosophy; yet, as he says in response to Marx, there never was an organic body.[11]

Lyotard's metaphysics of desire, however, does not itself escape a naturalizing and totalizing impulse. We see this in his assertion that political economy dates from the time of the Lydians, inventors of the system of gold coinage and hence of the system of money exchange, who also initiated the practice of selling their daughters into prostitution, an activity that took the daughters out of the function of reproduction, committing them to sterility and to "the circular game of the exchange market as goods and proprietors of goods" (168). Lyotard comments: "You understand that what is in question here, is, at the infinite limit, the introduction of all the parts of the 'entire' labyrinth of the pulsional body into the circle of exchanges"; thus "each parcel of the great labyrinthine band may be turned to cash in the *Milieu* (*Mitte*). *And it is precisely this which is at issue today in universal capitalism*" (169). If the buying and selling of the Lydian daughters' body parts anticipates capitalism, as Lyotard proposes, then the libidinal band becomes too literal in this early model and puts its status as pure figure in question. Thus Lyotard is guilty of the naturalization he would avoid, as the nostalgia for the organic body – for which Lyotard castigates Marx – is implied by the figure of the Lydian daughters before prostitution.[12]

While all libidinal investments are affirmative and a source of *jouissance* in the framework of *Libidinal Economy*, the introduction of the prostitution of Lydian daughters as the forerunner of capitalism also surely implies some ethical issues that *Libidinal Economy* would elide. Similar ethical reservations lie beneath Lyotard's "description" of the looting and plundering inherent in the speculative use of capital. Lyotard himself saw this problem quite clearly later, remarking in *Peregrinations*:

> Unfortunately, following nothing but the intensities of affects does not allow us to separate the wheat from the chaff. Because everything has value according to its energetic force, the law might not exist and the monk might be really a devil. . . . The monk I tried to become should have reminded himself that the polymorphic paganism of exploring and exploiting the whole range of intensive forms could easily be swept away into lawful permissiveness, including violence and terror.
>
> (Lyotard 1988: 15)

Thus, not only does Lyotard's metaphysics of desire fail to embrace and celebrate *jouissance* unequivocally in all its forms, as he claims it does, but, in retrospect, an older, repentant Lyotard recognizes the real dangers of giving desire free rein, of making desire a law unto itself.

Without embracing the Dionysian impulse, as does Lyotard, we do want to note once more the inadequacy of conventional economic discourse to explain or represent the underlying "psychology" of currency speculation, panics and crises, and even the normal functioning of financial markets. While *Libidinal Economy* is, in part, a diatribe against the space of representation, it also makes evident the limitations of representation in economics, illuminating the discipline's equivocal relationship with the problematics of desire. Foucault remarks on the subversive potential of psychoanalysis, with its notion of the unconscious, in relation to the other social sciences:

> Whereas all the human sciences advance towards the unconscious only with their back to it, waiting for it to unveil itself as fast as consciousness is analysed, as it were backwards, psychoanalysis, on the other hand, points directly towards it, with a deliberate purpose – not towards that which must be rendered gradually more explicit by the progressive illumination of the implicit, but towards what is there and yet is hidden, towards what exists with the mute solidity of a thing, of a text closed in upon itself, or of a blank space in a visible text, and uses that quality to defend itself.
>
> (Foucault 1973: 374)

Libidinal Economy uses the premises of psychoanalytic thought to point to "a blank space" in the "visible text" of economic discourse. The book may fail utterly to rewrite this economic text productively or even coherently, but the blank space remains.

Notes

1 For Lyotard, credit money enables dynamic equilibrium or growth. As the basis for the system's expansion, credit, which is an advance of time, "has no specifiable meaning: it could have one only if one admits the existence of a cosmic clock, the hours of which would be commensurable with the time of the system" (Lyotard 1993: 225). Lyotard notes that secondary or tertiary production are barely rooted in cosmic time at all. "Here the credit of time is only a process of expansive regulation, an arbitrary act by which a power to include new energies in the system is delivered. The capacity to deliver such powers constitutes the power of all powers" (ibid.). The time of credit is basically atemporal, logically reversible, proceeding as it does by analogy:

> The history of growing capital is only analogous to itself: the new commodities introduced at the time of the cycle $n + 1$ are to the money advanced as those of the cycle n are to the money then in circulation. Credit in its (re)productive usage rests on this analogy: the future it opens up is no different from the past. The one and the other are

identical in principle, this is why they are reversible, and this is how the creditor can buy his future.

(Ibid.: 226)

2 The Fed gave up targeting the monetary measure M2 to focus instead on interest rates and market psychology. M2 is defined as currency plus demand deposits (equal to M1) plus time and savings deposits at commercial banks other than large certificates of deposit. M2 became increasingly unreliable as a sign and means of controlling the economy's liquidity as international capital mobility increased and new forms of money and financial intermediaries proliferated in the 1980s. An additional factor in the abandonment of M2 was that policy was predicated upon the behavioral assumption of stable money velocity, an assumption violated with grievous results in the 1982–3 slowdown in the American economy. Of course monetary stability is not the only policy instrument and target for the Fed. The Federal Reserve Act of 1978 charges the Fed with pursuing "maximum employment, stable prices and moderate long-term interest rates." The Fed interprets these policy goals as a set of numerical targets: a 2.5 per cent annual growth rate, consistent with the natural rate of economic expansion; zero inflation; and the natural rate of unemployment, a residual, determined by the other policy variables.
3 Our analysis of Bagehot here also borrows from Alborn (1994), cited below.
4 The phrase "herd mentality," like Keynes's "animal spirits," nicely captures Bagehot's sense of atavism as a mix of the mental and the physical.
5 Lyotard stresses that in game theory what is important is not the analyst but "the criteria for the calculation of losses and gains, damages and interests," calculations that produce the negotiating subject and allow exchange to take place (Lyotard 1993: 174–77).
6 Quoted in Gordon (1991: 16). We might see in Lyotard's remarks conflating "credit money" and "speculative use of credit money," and his consideration that speculation is normal and integral to the normal functioning of markets, nothing more or less than the "modern view" of the economists. Of course "normal" speculation for Lyotard is not a sign of markets functioning in a well-coordinated, predictable fashion according to the efficient markets hypothesis but of a libidinal energy in all markets that is unpredictable because of the singularity of the "event" – that is, of each investment.
7 For the sake of clarity, we have slightly amended the translation here and in one other instance to conform more closely to the original French.
8 Lyotard quotes from Keynes's 1923 *Treatise on Money* and writes that Keynes's description is that of a "true libidinalist."
9 As Amariglio and Ruccio (1994) point out, the body rarely makes an appearance in the present-day discourse of economics.
10 This is not to say that taming desires was not a preoccupation of classical political economy as well. For an example of such preoccupation, see Freedgood.
11 Terry Eagleton (1990: 197) remarks that Marx, Nietzsche, and Freud are revolutionary in their reconstruction of "everything – ethics, history, politics, rationality – from a bodily foundation."
12 In this "history" of libidinal economy, the Lydians serve as a foil to the homosexually oriented Greeks, who "prostitute their penises" in order to

reproduce the citizenry; the Lydians "take an immense step forward over the Hellenes" by extending market participation – or sterile and marketable rather than procreative sexuality – to women (Lyotard 1993: 168).

References

Abolafia, Mitchel Y., and Martin Kilduf (1988). "Enacting Market Crisis: the Social Construction of a Speculative Bubble." *Administrative Science Quarterly* 33.2: 177–93.

Alborn, Timothy L. (1994). "Economic Man, Economic Machine: Images of Circulation in the Victorian Money Market." In *Natural Images in Economic Thought: "Markets Read in Tooth and Claw."* Ed. Philip Mirowski. Cambridge: Cambridge University Press, 173–96.

Amariglio, Jack, and Julie Graham (1993). "Gendering and Fragmenting the Economic Subject." Paper delivered at the "Out of the Margin" conference, Amsterdam, 2–4 June.

Amariglio, Jack, and David Ruccio (1994). "Modern Economics: The Case of the Disappearing Body?" Paper delivered at the Conference on New Economic Criticism, Cleveland, OH, October.

Bagehot, Walter ([1872) 1889). *Physics and Politics*. Ed. Forrest Morgan. Hartford: Travelers Insurance Company. Vol. 4 of *The Works of Walter Bagehot*. 5 vols.

Debreu, Gerard (1959). *Theory of Value: An Axiomatic Analysis of Economic Equilibrium*. New York: John Wiley.

Deleuze, Gilles, and Felix Guattari (1983). *Anti-Oedipus: Capitalism and Schizophrenia*. Trans. Robert Hurley, Mark Seem, and Helen R. Lane. Minneapolis: University of Minnesota Press. First French edn 1972.

de Long, Brad *et al.* (1990). "Noise Trader Risk in Financial Markets." *Journal of Political Economy* 98: 703–35.

—— (1991). "The Survival of Noise Traders in Financial Markets." *Journal of Business* 64: 1–19.

Eagleton, Terry (1990). *The Ideology of the Aesthetic*. Oxford: Basil Blackwell.

Foucault, Michel (1973). *The Order of Things: An Archaeology of the Human Sciences*. New York: Vintage.

Freedgood, Elaine (1999). "Banishing Panic: Harriet Martineau and the Popularization of Political Economy." In this volume.

Gordon, John Steele (1991). "The Corners of Wall and Broad." *American Heritage* 42: 16–18.

Kyle, Albert S. (1989). "Informed Speculation with Imperfect Competition." *Review of Economic Studies* 56.3: 317–55.

Lyotard, Jean-François (1988). *Peregrinations: Law, Form, Event*. New York: Columbia University Press.

—— (1993). *Libidinal Economy*. Trans. Iain Hamilton Grant. Bloomington: Indiana University Press. First French edn 1974.

Mirowski, Philip (1994). "The Realms of the Natural." In *Natural Images in Economic Thought: "Markets Read in Tooth and Claw."* Ed. Philip Mirowski. Cambridge: Cambridge University Press, 451–83.

New York Times (1994). "Tracking the Markets." 22 August: D3.

Sraffa, Piero (1960). *Production of Commodities by Means of Commodities*. Cambridge: Cambridge University Press.

Part IV

ECONOMIC ETHICS

Debts and bondage

12

MONTAIGNE'S *ESSAIS*

Metaphors of capital and exchange

Nancy P. Epstein

Christopher Smith enters a discussion of Montaigne and money with the claim that "the *Essais* display little awareness of economic problems, whether in their immediate or their theoretical aspects" (Smith 1981: 147). This is not quite true. While economics does not make up the principal theme of any single chapter, Montaigne demonstrates his concern with the problematics of money and exchange through a studied concern to avoid them. In the first chapter of her book, *Les Essais de Montaigne: miroir et procès de leur temps* (1984), Géralde Nakam outlines the nucleus of Montaigne's ideas about economics. It is evident from her presentation, as from Montaigne's own testimony, that a complex psychology of exchange informed his relationship with the mercantilist economy as well as his social and intellectual relationships. These relationships in turn laid the groundwork for Montaigne's own textual psychology, making it one of the earliest instances of a bourgeois individualist subjectivity – in spite of his antagonism to bourgeois culture.

In "Of Three Sorts of Intercourse" Montaigne refers to relations with women, with male friends, and with books as "commerces" – thus metaphorically as systems of exchange. It is true, Nakam notes, that the metaphorical use of economic vocabulary was already commonplace in the sixteenth century (Nekam 1984: 61). But this is no reason to ignore its use in the *Essais*. On the contrary, a study by Philippe Desan reveals the importance of the economic model for the Renaissance text precisely because of its universality:

> It appears that ways of apprehending social relationships, as well as all forms of human activity – including the arts and literature – have straddled the economic mode of organization ever since the end of the sixteenth century. The literary text from then on was approached and organized as a commercial object and thought of itself strictly as merchandise. It is thus normal that not only the content of a literary work but also its structure would be tightly linked to the economic sphere.
>
> (Desan 1988: 84)[1]

Desan argues that the restructuring of economies at the taking-off point of mercantilism was reflected in a restructuring of discourse itself on an economic model (ibid.). This restructuring, still resisted in the sixteenth century, was complete by the seventeenth. Montaigne, though aloof and disdainful of market processes as they functioned in the exchange of goods and services, embraced and exploited the rich potential of their logic and vocabulary in discourse and intellectual exchange. This is reflected in the content of his *Essais* as well as their structure, which, as Desan shows, is modelled on the account book, or "*registre.*"

In a more recent study, *Les Commerces de Montaigne* (1992), Desan attempts to outline and explain all of Montaigne's attitudes towards mercantilism and towards social intercourse in the light of the confusion, widespread in sixteenth-century France, between the role and status of the noble and the merchant classes. For political and economic reasons, entering the nobility and taking advantage of its privileges had become increasingly easy for wealthy bourgeois to do. At the same time, maintaining noble rank, for many rural gentry of ancient lineage, was increasingly difficult.

The reason for this, and the key (for Desan) to Montaigne's attitudes about money, was the ancient but still cherished code barring the nobility from participating in commercial activity. Only by reaping the revenues of their rich agricultural holdings or by military conquest could the so-called *noblesse d'épée*, or nobility of the sword, maintain their wealth and their rank. If their land holdings were too poor or too small or not well-managed, their choice was between poverty or plying a trade and losing their titles. The resulting increased social mobility, both upwards and downwards, led to a general confusion in sixteenth-century France between "true" (ancient, earned by military or other service to the throne) and "false" (or recently acquired) nobility.

Desan succeeds easily in demonstrating Michel de Montaigne's concern with this issue and his pride in the fact that his ancestors had acquired their estate more than one hundred years before his time. Three generations, or one hundred years, constituted by convention the minimum amount of time for which a family had to "live nobly" to be considered true nobility (Desan 1992: 38). Given that concern, Desan places Montaigne squarely in the camp of those gentry for whom nobility was signified above all by a lifestyle conforming to the values of virtue and honor; Montaigne would not let himself or his name be sullied by association with the increasingly favored bourgeois values of personal gain and shrewdness (86).

These principles shaped the essayist's relationship both to matters of commerce and to the spheres of social and textual exchange. According to Desan, Montaigne resisted all association with commercial activity and avoided bourgeois values in his actions but could not refrain from employing their vocabulary in his discourse (83). This situation locates Montaigne in a unique position on the cusp between the values of pre-capitalist and capitalist society. Marcel Mauss was among the first anthropologists to dispute the notion that pre-capitalist societies simply had no economies. He recognized that all societies had economic markets governed by rules of exchange. However, those rules shifted importantly with the advent of capitalism. As Deleuze and Guattari point out:

> exchange is known, well known in the primitive socius – but as that which must be exorcised, encasted, severely restricted, so that no corresponding value can develop as exchange value that would introduce the nightmare of a commodity economy. The primitive market operates through bargaining rather than by fixing an equivalent that would lead to a decoding of flows and a collapse of the mode of inscription on the socius.
>
> (Deleuze and Guattari 1983: 185)

Montaigne would thus have been in the position of making a last stand for the defense of the socius against the commodification of culture; he resisted the trend towards exchange value over use value.

Montaigne provided his own analysis of his unique relationship with money in "That the Savor of Goods and Ills depends in large part on the Idea that we have of them." He recognized three separate stages of his development, the first of which was his "insouciant," or "carefree," phase roughly corresponding to the years of adolescence and young adulthood, prior to the death of his father. During this time he spent liberally money that came to him by chance; he owned nothing. He borrowed freely, but felt indebtedness to be "an annoying burden" (Montaigne 1925: 1. 81). The concept of debt represents to Montaigne a diminishing of the freedom of independent action. It is a bond of obligation, and therefore infringes on the autonomy of the self. Montaigne's preoccupation with debt is not in itself surprising. Owing money was a brand new phenomenon with the generalization of money economies, and by the sixteenth century, according to Nakam (1984: 28), there existed what amounted to a crisis of debt resulting in record numbers of personal as well as state bankruptcies.

With Montaigne, who was himself never in real danger of insolvency (ibid.: 38–43), debt is the fundamental relationship in all but extraordinary social bonds, and is in his own analysis a psychological phenomenon. Paying back was experienced by Montaigne as a source of pleasure, in part a consequence of the pleasure it gave to the lender: "I feel a pleasure that flatters me in doing a good action and pleasing another" (Montaigne 1925:1. 81–82). Conversely, much of the heaviness he experienced from outstanding debts must have been due to the real or imagined displeasure of the other; debts bind self to other by bonds of mutual displeasure. Montaigne experienced financial obligation as a social phenomenon, just as he conceived of social interactions of all types in the vocabulary of commercial exchange.

Montaigne's second phase was a period of relative financial (and emotional) avarice. He recognizes, at least in retrospect, that his fears are irrational, calling them "futile and fallacious imaginings" (1. 83). They center around the fear of loss. On all his travels and at home Montaigne keeps near him a "*boyte*," or coffer, wherein he stores his savings. This he guards jealously, suspecting treachery from without (highwaymen) and from within (servants). He hates to withdraw from it. Though the real situation of the time justified some concern, Montaigne's continual mental preoccupation with the loss of this object was irrational and he recognized the fact.

Nakam has cleverly linked this object of loss with another lost object, Montaigne's friend La Boétie, who had died a few years before the death of Montaigne's father and the first writing of the *Essais*. "In the old titles," she observes, "the name La Boétie was spelled Boyt or Boyte (and later Boytie, La Boytie, La Boitie). Montaigne wrote La Boitie. By sealing shut his '*boyte*' [box or coffer], Montaigne acquits himself of a debt, and seals off at the same time, preserves, that which is *dearest* to him" (Nakam 1984: 47). The link with La Boétie is two-fold: both a link of preservation and a link of debt. The bonds of obligation linking human beings in social commerce do not dissolve automatically with the death of one or the other party.

This again is characteristic of economies that do not know the fixed exchange value of a money economy, those economies in which exchange is still a mechanism for social cohesion. Marcel Mauss (1950: 167) observes that "one of the first groups of beings with whom mankind had to contract and who by definition were there to contract with mankind were the gods and the spirits of the dead. In effect, they were the true owners of the things and the goods of this world." He had already perceived that the gift in these tribal economies was never truly a gift but always entailed the imperative either to give back or to pass on, to keep the goods and the spirits of their creators in circulation or else face death, expulsion from the group, or a serious loss of stature. He recognized that this imperative was truer than ever when it came to debts owed to the dead: "it is with them [the dead] that it was the most necessary to exchange and the most dangerous not to exchange" (ibid.). Montaigne's special concern with debts to the dead is thus not out of character with his affected nobleman's disdain of money economies and commercial activity.

It is no accident that during this second, "stingy" phase Montaigne learns to appreciate the difference between use value and exchange value: "when you are accustomed to a certain pile [of money]," he observes, "it is no longer at your service" (Montaigne 1925: 1. 84). He consistently prefers use value, as in "Of Coaches," where he compares the use made of gold by the Aztecs and by their Spanish conquerors. The former, for whom "the use of coin was entirely unknown" (4. 94), valued gold for its aesthetic properties and made of it works of art, beautiful and practical, like a throne, to be passed on from generation to generation. This is in stark contrast to the conquistadors, representatives of a mercantile economy, who melted down these objects of beauty to mint them into coins that could be "circulated" and "dispersed" (ibid.).

In the third phase of his development, Montaigne cured himself of his miserliness by a healthy dose of expenditure. During a seventeen-month voyage through Italy he spent, according to Nakam's (1984: 43) estimates, the equivalent of one year's income. From this point on he was able to find a balance between the evil of luxury and the evil of miserliness. "I live from day to day," he says, "to buy pleasure" (Montaigne 1925: 1. 85). In other words, he settles on that which has use value.

Too much pleasure, however, is not a good thing if to obtain it one must mortgage something of the self. To go into debt, to be obliged to another (and, equally, the reverse – to give more than is received, to have others obliged to the self) is to relinquish a share of one's independence, which Montaigne chose to avoid whenever possible: "I hold in mortal hatred the being beholden to another or having another beholden to me. I eagerly make use of every means in my power to do without the kindness of another before making use of it on any occasion or need, whether trivial or important" (4. 166). Desan reads Montaigne's avoidance of relationships involving either gain to or loss of the self once again in light of the struggle between bourgeois and noble values. To *profit* from a relationship (necessarily at the expense of the other, in sixteenth-century logic) is to think like a merchant, whereas to sacrifice self for another is noble; to refuse either gain or loss in relationships is thus to walk a tightrope, balancing the opposing values of two social classes in conflict (Desan 1992: 91). Desan relates Montaigne's stinginess with the capital of the self to his (anti-mercantilist) preference for use value: "One must guard oneself against those exchanges [*commerces*] which are solely for the purpose of extracting personal profit. Montaigne engages in an economizing frugality of the self so as to avoid (ex/s)pending himself in useless fashion" (ibid.: 94).

This desire for preservation of the capital of self situates Montaigne at the origins of an economy of relationships that Hélène Cixous (1981) wishes to see brought to an end. Her critique is of the masculine economy, as described by Freud, functioning in capitalist society. Although Montaigne resisted the encroachment of capitalist values in his day, his texts embraced capitalism's metaphors and thereby structured his personal economy as a bourgeois one, making him an appropriate target for Freudian and post-Freudian analysis. Cixous associates the economy of debt with male psychology, which for her is almost always negative. While it may not be particularly fruitful to polarize psychologies into the "masculine" and the "feminine," the model of social relations here outlined very accurately describes Montaigne's attitudes as he portrays them himself:

> Giving: there you have a basic problem, which is that masculinity is always associated – in the unconscious, which is after all what makes

> the whole economy function – with debt. Freud, in deciphering the latent antagonisms between parents and children, shows very well the extent to which the family is founded . . . on a fearful debt. The child *owes* his parents his life and his problem is exactly to *repay* them: nothing is more dangerous than obligation. Obligation is submission to the enormous weight of the other's generosity, is being threatened by a blessing . . . and a blessing is always evil when it comes from someone else. For the moment you receive something you are effectively "open" to the other, and if you are a man you have only one wish, and that is hastily to return the gift . . . to be nobody's child, to owe no one a thing.
>
> (Cixous 1981: 48)

"To owe no one a thing" is a recurrent wish in the *Essais*. The debt metaphor straddles the parallel realms of the economic and the social. But it does not do so unconsciously, as Cixous's remarks may suggest. Montaigne is entirely conscious both of his antagonism to monetary indebtedness and of the way in which his attitude towards debt extends to all sorts of exchanges he deems unequal. His attitude towards debt defines his attitude towards social relationships, as outlined in "Of Friendship."

In this chapter of his *Essais* Montaigne compares the structures of various sorts of social intercourse – between lovers, husbands and wives, brothers, in ordinary friendship, etc. – with the one ideal relationship: the perfect friendship. All other relationships are tainted for him by their association with the world of commerce. Sometimes they literally involve commercial exchange, as in the marriage contract. At other times the association is only metaphorical. Montaigne confounds the two, understanding all relationships in terms of preservation or exchange regardless of whether they involve money. "Of Friendship" is peppered with economic vocabulary.

The ideal friendship, as Montaigne imagines it (although he claims to be describing only what he has actually experienced in his relationship with La Boétie), has nothing to do with commerce at all. To Montaigne profit is fundamentally destructive. In "One Man's Profit is another's Loss" he writes that "no profit is made save at a loss to someone else, and by such a reckoning we should have to condemn every sort of gain" (Montaigne 1925: 1. 142). Note the use of the conditional: it would be necessary to condemn gain if it were not a natural law, for according to atomist philosophy nothing can be created but from the matter released when something else is destroyed. Yet what Montaigne allows as a natural law in the marketplace he excludes from his fantastic vision of the ideal human exchange. There can be no place for profit in true friendship: "all those companionships which pleasure or profit, or public or private needs, beget and nourish, are in so far less beautiful and noble, and in so far less true friendships, as they introduce another cause and end and fruit into friendship than friendship itself" (1. 246).

True friendship of the ideal kind thus cannot exist between fathers and sons. This relationship is based on inequality and, ultimately, as Cixous observes above, on the debt of life that sons owe to fathers. The "natural obligations" sons owe their fathers, Montaigne writes, diminish the relative proportion of devotion that they may give out of "[their] own choice and free will"; and free will for Montaigne constitutes the only possible basis for true friendship (1. 248).

A fear of debt and of consequent inequality is a psychological effect of specific socioeconomic structures. Montaigne writes almost obsessively, especially in "Of Vanity," of his free will, liberty, and independence. He wishes to rely on no one but himself. This sentiment may stem from the helplessness he felt at being reliant upon the good will of his neighbors, both Protestant and Catholic, for protection of his estate from the ravages of pillaging armies during the wars of religion (4. 149). "I improve [*cultive*] myself," he writes, comparing himself to a crop – a commodity, the commodity of the self – "that I may find thus the means to content myself should all else abandon me" (4. 165). In this he displays the landowner's desire for economic self-sufficiency – his suspicion of any economic system that could lead to greater interdependence. Montaigne refers to the example of Eleus Hippias, who learned all the trades himself (cooking, barbering, shoemaking, etc.) so as not to have to depend on commodities made and sold by others. Insofar as the family (among sixteenth-century nobility) constituted an economic structure that entangled its members in webs of interdependence, Montaigne felt it to be more of a burden than a support.

Montaigne blames patrilineal inheritance – with its splitting (*partages*) of properties and flow of goods (*meslange de biens*) – which leads to one sibling prospering at the expense of impoverishing the other, for alienating brothers who might otherwise be friends. The same goes for husbands and wives, for in Montaigne's social class at this time marriages were made for other ends than love. They were a social and economic alliance between two families, each negotiating for its own profit, and thus were not amenable to the disinterestedness that Montaigne requires of true friendship: "in friendship there are no dealings or transactions save with itself," he writes (1. 249). When used to designate forms of social interaction, the terms "dealings" and "transactions" are wholly negative for Montaigne; he believes in the possibility of communication unmediated by unequal exchanges. Thus it is that he disdainfully dismisses marriage as "a bargain [i.e., a transaction] . . . which is ordinarily entered into for other objects" (ibid.).

This is not to say that marriage and family have no place in life. Rather, they play a role exterior to the economy of the self, which must be preserved against their intrusion. In "Of Solitude" Montaigne comments that he doesn't envy those who, to be always in the public eye, surrender their privacy; he must have his study to retreat to from the responsibilities of the household and the bonds of mutual obligation and interdependence that tie him to its other occupants. "All of us who can must have wives, children, property, and, above all, health," he writes, "but not be so attached to them that our happiness depends on them; we must reserve for ourselves a private room, all our own" (1. 319). The reason he gives for the necessity of preserving the capital of self is remarkable. He readily admits in this passage, written during his stingy period following the deaths of his father, best friend, and first child, that one must work hard to learn to enjoy one's self so as to be able to go on with life, should wife and children and property be lost in this world where nothing is certain or permanent.

That follows exactly the pattern outlined by Cixous. Man, she says, who fears debt and inequality, and who takes back immediately that part of himself that was offered (as bait, after the model of Don Juan) – man mourns precisely in order to recover what was lost: "When you've lost something and the loss is a dangerous one, you refuse to admit that something of your self might be lost in the lost object. So you 'mourn,' you make haste to recover the investment made in the lost object" (Cixous 1981: 54). Montaigne, fearing or anticipating death, makes haste to recover the investment before the loved object is even lost: "Love this or that," he writes, but "espouse nothing but ourselves; that is to say: all else may belong to us, but not so combined and united with us that it can not be detached without flaying us, and tearing off with it a part of our flesh" (Montaigne 1925: 1. 320–21).

There is, then, a certain greediness at the root of Montaigne's thought, particularly during what he himself recognized as his avaricious stage. Not only are human relationships understood in economic terms, but economic discourse itself – talk about money – often can and should be read as metaphoric for something psychological.

At the basis of Montaigne's psychology during the period when he began to write the *Essais* lie the sentiments of debt, of loss, and of the need for preservation, inspired by the series of losses he had endured during the previous decade. The loss that receives the most explicit attention is that of his closest friend, La Boétie. In "Of Friendship" Montaigne discusses the nature and circumstances of this friendship, elevating it in memory and imagination to the level of myth. He contrasts it sharply not only with the contractual and economic bonds of marriage and blood relations, but also with ordinary friendships – "acquaintances and familiar relations formed by some chance or convenience [*commodité*]" (1. 251). Again, economic bonds are undesirable in human interaction. They distance rather than link "souls" because any amount of obligation tying people together diminishes the degree to which their association is entered into by free will. "*Volonté*" is for Montaigne the sole basis for true friendship.

The way in which Montaigne describes his feelings upon being drawn into friendship with La Boétie is fascinating. "*Volonté*" is a key word, and yet it is an involuntary "volonté," as he relates the sensation of being pulled "irresistibly" into this bond:

> it was I don't know what quintessence of all this blending which, having completely possessed itself of my will, led it to plunge into and lose itself in his; and having completely possessed itself of his will, led it to plunge into and lose itself in mine, by force of a like eagerness and impulse. I say "lose" with truth, for it left us nothing that was our own, or that was either his or mine.
>
> (1. 252)

Perfect understanding does not escape a vocabulary of exchange, but instead pushes exchange to its outer limits: all items exchanged are now jointly owned. In a complete merging of property, bargaining is no longer necessary, or even possible. There can be no question of obligation: the other has become as much self as the self, so obligation to the other does not involve any transfer of goods. There is no exchange of currency for goods, for goods are now possessed jointly by all; all that remains is to make use of them, *jouissance*, pure use-value.

Thus, the metaphors of giving and receiving, of debt and obligation, of commerce, can only describe the ideal interaction negatively, by way of contrast. True friends "can not lend or give anything to each other" (1. 254). But if they could give to one another, Montaigne continues, it would be the giver who would be obliged to the receiver to repay the gift of receiving (ibid.). He envisions, perhaps, a sort of giving that does not entail *giving up* anything, either goods or freedom – a "giving that doesn't take away, but *gives*," to use Cixous's (1981: 51) terms. In her dichotomy this idyll of a relationship that is not tied to the economy of debt and recuperation is a characteristic of the feminine – which she hopes one day will be universal. But does Montaigne's ideal relationship really escape the system of giving and taking back? If so, only by a sort of cop-out: in giving to the perfect friend, one gives up nothing, but instead immediately, in fact, simultaneously, takes back a gift for the self, because the other is the self. The perfect friend is "[he] who is not another – he is myself" (Montaigne 1925: 1. 256). The relationship can continue, unmediated by any "commerce" external to the economy of the self, two subjects existing as one, until one friend dies.

Then, it is time to recuperate, however, and in a hurry, because such a death represents a loss of the self, and this is the most dangerous loss of all. Montaigne admits that since La Boétie's death any pleasure simply increases the pain of his loss, since the lost part can no longer share the pleasure: "We halved every thing; it seems to me that I steal from him his share" (1. 258). So Montaigne feels indebted to the dead, on the one hand, and must pay them back; on the other hand, he must preserve what has been lost and reincorporate it into the living self. He speaks on several occasions of the debt he feels he owes to his father, and in "Of Vanity" he acknowledges what to him, apparently, is a very important consideration: that he has "paid" his friends the friendship and gratitude he owes them as faithfully as ever, or more so, since their deaths.

How has he paid back the dead? How can he fulfill his obligation to the dead while at the same time taking back his investment in them? The key is preservation. Montaigne admits to an obsession with preserving relics of the dead. Particularly when it comes to his ancestors, he says: "I preserve so far as I can from the inroads of time [their writing, their blood, their Bibles]." In his preface "To the Reader," written after the last of the essays, Montaigne expresses the hope that his writings will be similarly guarded by his friends and family after his death and that "by this means, they may cherish more completely and more vividly the knowledge they have had of me" (1. 3). In this sense, books "conserve" the capital of the self, the capital of the author. Like the gold of the Aztecs, they are raw material that has been made into art and preserved as treasures to be handed down from generation to generation. They are a commodity with use value as well as exchange value. As Desan (1988: 84) notes, by the sixteenth century all texts understood themselves as "merchandise." The *Essais* are no exception.

Montaigne himself compares books to money, or wealth: "I enjoy them, as misers their treasures," he writes (3. 284). He is aware of the commodity value of his own books as well. In "Of Repenting" he writes of how it amused his neighbors to see him in print, and of how his "worth" increased as his reputation spread beyond his neighborhood (3. 260). But books are implicated in commerce in more ways than one. They have a value on the market and bring profit to publishers. They also have value for and bring profit to readers. Women, Montaigne advises, will derive "various benefits [*diverses commoditez*]" from reading history: it will be comforting, educational, profitable. For himself he prefers books "that move me with pleasure, or that comfort me and advise me how to order my life and my death" (1. 326). The latter function of consoling and counselling is also a function of friends. Commerce with books, then, is like commerce among friends. However, for Montaigne books are better than friends. The commerce of books is the third of the "Three Sorts of Intercourse" he treats in a chapter by this title, the third chapter of Book 3 of *Essais*. (The first two are the commerce of ordinary social intercourse with men, and the commerce of women.) It is also the least threatening of the three: "intercourse with books, which is the third sort, is much more sure and more ours" (3. 283). This is because it requires the least expenditure of the capital of self. Borrowings from books need not be paid back, or can be paid back at nearly no cost.

There is one particular book that is a better friend to Montaigne than all the others because it requires absolutely no expenditure of the capital of self. This is of course his own book, his "*registre*," or account book, in which he records credits and debits of thought. Even words are currency. They mediate the exchange of "our desires and our thoughts" (2. 81). "False speech," a lie, is like "false money"; it causes transactions to fail, communication to break down, commerce to be disrupted: " if [the word . . . the interpreter of our souls] deceives us, it severs all our intercourse [*commerce*]" (2. 81). The commerce of thought in books can be carried out without the need for mediation by the "servile and annoying custom" of the rites of social intercourse with the living. The *Essais* themselves represent commerce with, and a preservation of, the thoughts of the dead. "All the dealing that I have with the public in this matter," Montaigne writes, "is that I borrow the tools of their writing. . . . As compensation, I shall perhaps prevent a pound of butter in the market-place from spoiling" (2. 78). The "public" is the public of dead correspondents, of other authors. Montaigne's commerce with them (as usual in his "interpersonal" relationships) is one of borrowing and repayment. What he borrows is their thoughts and words; what he returns is their preservation. He compares his text to an envelope or protective casing that preserves the quoted texts within it from melting into oblivion. He keeps the goods in circulation.

In preserving the ancients from oblivion, Montaigne also honors and preserves the memory of those to whom he is most indebted: his father and La Boétie. The capital of their thought is preserved in the text, not directly, but by the medium of their influence on its author – through the currency of books. Montaigne owes more to his father than just the already imposing debt of life. He owes both to his father and to La Boétie something that is equivalent to the debt of life for a writer; he owes them the debt of his life *as* a writer. For more than anyone else, they were responsible for encouraging Montaigne's literary pursuits. His father directed his unique and slightly uncouth education. Montaigne knew Latin, he tells us, before he learned French, and he read the ancient authors before the moderns. Ancient Rome was more familiar and perhaps more real to him than the geography of his own neighborhood, and its inhabitants were his childhood companions (3. 201). He maintained the relationship as an adult: it is their "commerce" that heads the entries of his "account books." His father was also responsible for prompting his first literary effort (a translation of Raymond Sébond) and for providing a household always full of visiting intellectuals.

From his commerce with La Boétie Montaigne gained an example of a contemporary who was already an accomplished writer and philosopher, he gained a partner for stimulating intellectual exchange, and he gained literally half his books. In "Of Friendship" Montaigne tells us La Boétie willed him his entire library "when death was at hand" (1. 246). So part of the debt owed to this friend, to "[him] who is not other," is a debt of books. Indeed, Montaigne is indebted to a particular book, La Boétie's *La Servitude volontaire*, for bringing them together in the first place (ibid.). His *Essais* began as notes in the margins of these and other books. They began, in other words, as commerce with the dead – the dead authors read and loved, and formerly discussed, by a dead friend. By preserving and protecting the words of the ancient writers he quotes, Montaigne also preserves the memory of their former readers, and he preserves his own investment in their thought. All this began during his self-proclaimed period of avarice. The hoarding of money was accompanied, and later replaced, by the hoarding of thoughts and words. Nakam (1984: 48) describes this tendency as Montaigne's "eagerness to preserve everything, an eagerness which only writing, in the end, was able to satisfy".

The *Essais* preserve the memory of a friend, they represent commerce with "friends," and, in a sense, they also played the role of friend to Montaigne. Nearly all of the characteristics he enumerates of ideal friendship apply equally well to commerce with books, particularly his own books. Perfect communication of wills (*volontez* [*sic*]), the absence of "words implying separation and difference – benefit, obligation . . . and their like," the complete merging of property, etc. (Montaigne 1925: 1. 254) – all apply to the author's relationship to his *Essais*, that "book of the same substance as its author" (2. 78). In fact, what the *Essais* ultimately share with the perfect friend is their avowed identity with Montaigne's self. The perfect friend *c'est moi* because there can be no losses and no losers in a transaction with the self. The only possible "loser" in an autobiographical transaction is, as Desan (1992: 270) has noted, the reified author of earlier passages, corrected or overridden by messages from the more mature author of the later passages. Through his corrections and additions to his own texts, Montaigne was able to accumulate capital for his living self at the expense of earlier selves. These two relationships, with La Boétie and, after his death, with the text of the *Essais*, were the only two that allowed Montaigne to conserve his self. The "*boyte*," symbolic of the preservation of capital, represents La Boétie during Montaigne's years of mourning. In some sense the *Essais* themselves replaced the "*boyte*" as the coffer preserving the great "fortune" of a friendship so rare that it is unlikely to "occur more than once every three centuries."

In summary, Montaigne understood the logic of the money system well enough to conceive of other relationships in terms of currency and exchange. He was preoccupied with the psychology of debt, was keenly aware of his own need to "conserve" the capital of self, and judged all sorts of relationships in terms of whether they threatened or secured this commodity. The self and the self's investments in high-yield relationships had to be preserved and protected at all costs. Montaigne was aware both of his earlier urge to protect capital in his "*boyte*" and of his later desire to preserve memories of himself for his family and friends after his death.

The stoic in search of the contemplative life, more inclined to commerce with the dead than with the living, Montaigne retreated to the solitude of his study. He cut himself off from the commercial activity of the town and from ties with townspeople, going so far as to resign his seat on Bordeaux's parliament because even the legal profession was a trade and thus not worthy of a true nobleman. He even distanced himself from friends and family whose intercourse struck him as tainted with overtones of monetary obligation. By thus severing every social and economic tie to the capitalist marketplace, he hoped to demonstrate the legitimacy of his claim to nobility.

The ironic outcome of this effort was the emergence in a literary text of one of the earliest examples of bourgeois subjectivity. As Marcel Mauss (1950: 258) shows, it was the emergence of money economies (with fixed equivalencies) that would sever the act of exchange from the social obligations that such exchange had carried in precapitalist societies. The resulting notion of individual interest became the cornerstone of capitalist economies. Montaigne, the anti-capitalist, anti-bourgeois intellectual, produced a text that preserved his individual interest, his ego, from dispersal on the winds of trade.

Note

1 English translations from the French of Philippe Desan, Géralde Nakam, and Marcel Mauss are my own.

References

Cixous, Hélène (1981). "Castration or Decapitation?" Trans. Annette Kuhn. *Signs: Journal of Women in Culture and Society* 7: 41–55.

Deleuze, Gilles, and Félix Guattari (1983). *Anti-Oedipus: Capitalism and Schizophrenia.* Trans. Robert Hurley, Mark Seem, and Helen R. Lane. Minneapolis: University of Minnesota Press.

Desan, Philippe (1988). "Quand le discours social passe par le discours économique: les *Essais* de Montaigne." *Sociocriticism* 7: 59–86.

—— (1992). *Les Commerces de Montaigne: le discours économique des* Essais. Paris: Librairie A.-G. Nizet.

Mauss, Marcel (1950). "Essai sur le don." In *Sociologie et Anthropologie.* Paris: Presses universitaires de France.

Montaigne, Michel de (1925). *The Essays of Montaigne.* Trans. George B. Ives. Ed. Grace Norton. 4 vols. Cambridge, MA: Harvard University Press.

Nakam, Géralde (1984). *Les Essais de Montaigne: miroir et procès de leur temps.* Paris: Librarie A.-G. Nizet.

Smith, Christopher (1981). "Montaigne and Money." In *Montaigne and His Age.* Ed. Keith Cameron. Exeter: University of Exeter Press, 147–57.

13

SADE'S ETHICAL ECONOMIES

David Martyn

Recent criticism has underscored the difficulty of coming to terms with the ethical consequences of literary interpretation. On the one hand, criticism seems unable to avoid ethical judgments. Tobin Siebers (1988: 1), recalling the etymological senses of the word *criticism* – "to cut" or "to distinguish" – argues that literary analysis is obliged to make critical choices that reveal a certain character or ethos: "literary criticism is inextricably linked to ethics." On the other hand, to embrace a deliberately "ethical criticism" would seem to compromise the disinterestedness that, beginning with Kant, is often held up as a prerequisite for aesthetic judgment. An interest in certain moral values threatens to restrict the freedom that is required for unprejudiced rhetorical or formal analysis. Stephen Heath (1990: 129), for example, writes of "a feeling that moral terms are an irrelevant weakening of analytic rigor." Criticism, it would seem, can neither avoid ethics nor reconcile itself to the idea that it must promote a specific moral agenda.[1]

A possible way out of this double bind might be to center the discussion of ethics and literature on economic structures: circular exchange, sharing, stealing, giving. Focusing on economic structures would seem, on the one hand, to preserve all the advantages of remaining comfortably within the confines of formal analysis, for an "economy" is a law governing a system of value and exchange that is by nature formal or formalizable. At the same time, however, the phenomenon of exchange is necessarily tied up with issues of generosity and magnanimity, issues that seem, in other words, to be inherently ethical in nature. As Marcel Mauss's ([1925] 1954: 76) essay on the gift demonstrates, analyses of systems of exchange, of give and take, seem of themselves to lead to "ethical conclusions."

If articulating ethics with economics seems a good way to face the ethical dilemma of criticism, then two authors who might lend themselves particularly well to such an attempt are Sade and Adam Smith. The philosopher most closely associated with the law of supply and demand, Smith also wrote *The Theory of Moral Sentiments* (1759) in which many of the same structures that he later used to describe the mechanisms of the market function as the principles of a system of moral judgment (Raphael and Macfie 1976: 20–25).

Sade, that most radical of eighteenth-century moralists, also has a particular interest in economic structures that has long been an emphasis of critical interpretation (Barthes 1971; Hénaff 1978). The interest of a confrontation between Smith's *Theory of Moral Sentiments* and Sade's *Justine, ou Les Malheurs de la vertu* derives in part from the fact that the analysis of ethical interaction in economic terms seems to lead, in the two books, to diametrically opposed conclusions.

For Smith, ethics are essentially economic in nature. While David Marshall (1986: 167–92) rightly insists on the theatrical aspects of Smith's moral philosophy, the privileged paradigm of ethical interaction in Smith is the marketplace. When distinguishing other human feelings from those sentiments he considers to be specifically moral, Smith often insists on the economic structure of moral sentiments as their defining characteristic. Love, for example, does not figure in Smith's system as a moral sentiment, whereas gratitude does precisely to the extent that it is inscribed in a strictly balanced system of give and take. Whereas love, Smith writes, is pleased with the good fortune of the person loved "without regarding who was the author of his prosperity," the feeling of gratitude demands that one be personally instrumental in promoting the happiness of one's benefactor (Smith [1790] 1976: 68). Gratitude, it would seem, is like a debt that has been incurred and that must be acquitted. Analogously, Smith uses the same argument to distinguish the feeling of hate, which he does not qualify as moral, from the specifically moral feeling of resentment: whereas hatred is satisfied by the mere knowledge that one's enemy has suffered some misfortune, the moral feeling of resentment demands that one be oneself the cause of one's enemy's distress (69). Gratitude and resentment are both forms of recompense: they strive for a proportionally balanced compensation in a circular pattern of give and take.

Like Smith, Sade is also keenly aware of how moral sentiments enter into closed economies of exchange. But while Smith speaks approvingly of the economic structure of moral sentiments, Sade sees the economy hidden behind moral behavior as discrediting the very notion of virtue. More in the tradition of La Rochefoucauld – an author Smith takes issue with in the 1759 edition of his *Theory* ([1759] 1971: 470–89) – than in that of Smith's Anglo-Saxon influences, Sade compares ethics to economics in order to show how seemingly virtuous behavior derives in fact from a calculating self-interestedness:

> And in my view the value of the virtuous sentiment further deteriorates when I remember not only that it is not a primary natural impulse, but that, by definition, it is a low, base impulse, that it stinks of commerce: *I give unto you in order that I may obtain from you in exchange* [*je te donne pour que tu me rendes*].
>
> (Sade, *J.L.* 143–44; *Oc* 8. 181–82)[2]

Because the benefactor receives a return on his or her good deed from the person benefited, he or she can no longer lay claim to a selfless act of generosity. Whether the return occurs as a material recompense – one good turn deserves another – or merely as an expression of gratitude, the "good deed" in Sade is caught in an exchange economy that reveals behind its outward appearance of magnanimity the pettiness of a contract or a deal. "*Je te donne pour que tu me rendes*": the gift of the benefactor, for Sade, is like the potlatch that Mauss ([1925] 1954: 31–45) describes in his analysis of the gift among indigenous tribes of northwest America, in which the gift anticipates the obligation of gratitude it incurs. Far from being a generous act of goodwill, the gift as potlatch is an act of aggression and humiliation, a means of impoverishing and enslaving the one benefited.

Sade's *Justine* appears in this light as an extended attack on precisely the kind of economic ethics of gratitude that Smith espouses. Like Smith, the character Justine invokes the law of exchange as the principle that should govern moral interaction: "[D]eign to remember," she implores Roland, "that I saved your life, that, moved by gratitude for an instant, you seemed to offer me happiness and that it is by precipitating me into an eternal abyss of evils you acquit my services" (*J* 668; *Oc* 3. 237). But for Justine's libertine persecutor, the economic structure of beneficence is not one of exchange between self and other, but between self and self:

> What, pray tell, do you mean by this feeling of gratitude with which you fancy you have captivated me? . . . Be more reasonable, wretched creature; what were you doing when you came to my rescue? Between the two possibilities, of continuing on your way and of coming up to me, did you not choose the latter as an impulse dictated by your heart? You therefore gave yourself up to a pleasure? How in the devil's name can you maintain I am obliged to recompense you for the joys you give yourself?
>
> (Ibid.)

Justine's "gift" in aiding Roland is a pleasure she gives to herself. One is reminded of similar passages in La Rochefoucauld that expose the vanity of beneficence and generosity: "What we call generosity is most often nothing but the vanity of giving, which we value more than what we give" ([1665] 1967: 67, no. 263; translation mine, as elsewhere when quoting French-language sources).

Roland adopts this critique and pushes it still farther. Beneficence is not just a form of selfishness; it is a potlatch that is designed to humiliate the person being benefited:

> [I]s not he who receives always humiliated? And is this humiliation not sufficient payment for the benefactor who, by this alone, finds

> himself superior to the other? Is it not pride's delight to be raised above one's fellow? Is any other necessary to the person who obliges? And if the obligation, by causing humiliation to him who receives, becomes a burden to him, by what right is he to be forced to continue to shoulder it? Why must I consent to let myself be humiliated every time my eyes fall upon him who has obliged me? Instead of being a vice, ingratitude is therefore a virtue in proud spirits. . . .
>
> (*J* 669; *Oc* 3. 238)

Far from being generous, beneficence is a form of usury: sufficiently recompensed by the giver's own vanity, by the gift the benefactor "gives to himself," the "good deed" selfishly demands the services of the other's gratitude as well. Even worse, by anticipating the obligation of gratitude, beneficence humiliates the person benefited. This hidden economy of the good deed is expressed in the play on the word that Roland uses to describe the act of beneficence: "to oblige" (*obliger*) means both to bind or to constrain and, as when one speaks of an "obliging young fellow," to please, to gratify, or to help. The notion of *obligeance* equates helping with constraint, gratification with enslavement, beneficence with obligation; it proclaims every favor to be the creation of a debt. Justine, Roland claims, manipulates this ambiguity of *obligeance* to her own advantage. Readers of Sade justly emphasize how male sexual desire functions as an instrument of subjugation; but it is not quite true, as Nancy Miller (1980: 58) writes, that Justine "remains the passive object of a masculine will to domination by the powers of the phallus," for Justine has her own means of obligating others. Her acts of chastity also function, albeit unsuccessfully, as a mechanism of domination.

Hence the ethical economy of *Justine* would seem, at this point, to be the precise inversion of Smith's ethics of gratitude and resentment. Such an inversion is possible because Smith's moral theory is a symmetrical system of values that can be either positive or negative. "To reward," Smith writes, "is to recompense, to remunerate, to return good for good received. To punish, too, is to recompense, to remunerate, though in a different manner; it is to return evil for evil that has been done" ([1790] 1976: 68). The symmetry of the equation makes it easy to invert: Sade's novel also tells of a system of recompense, but of one in which evil is returned for good that has been done. As Philippe Roger (1976: 176–77) observes, in the exchange economy that Justine confronts "every act of assistance merits reward, even if, for the retribution, several currencies are valid."

But while the values are inverted, the law of a balanced, closed economy of exchange still holds. Justine's good deeds are *never* repaid in kind; they always earn her exactly the opposite of what she expects. Indeed, Justine's negative "recompense" is figured explicitly by the text in economic terms: "[I]t is by precipitating me into an eternal abyss of evils you *acquit* my services" (*J* 668; *Oc* 3. 237; emphasis added). Justine's persecutions are an acquittance; the law of recompense, far from being annulled, has only been inverted. The more charitably Justine "obliges" others, the more viciously she is punished. Punishment follows upon virtue with the necessity of a rational law. Despite the reversal, then, Justine's moral interactions are still governed by an economic law of exchange.

As a result of this lawful regularity, Justine is able to remain conscious of the ethical economy of recompense despite the fact that she never receives the reward she expects. Indeed, the consciousness of the consistent injustice with which her behavior is recompensed often allows her to derive an immaterial compensation for her persecution. "[T]he recompense," she consoles herself, "is in your heart, whose innocent pleasures are worth more than all the remorse that torments your enemies" (*Oc* 7. 240). Justine is always able to find a recompense for her own virtue. Although her immediate recompense is a negative one, the initial injury is ultimately eclipsed by the pleasure she derives from the consciousness of having acted virtuously. In terms of a material recompense, Justine's suffering, as Angela Carter (1980: 52) observes, has no exchange value (52); but insofar as the immaterial pleasure of the heart "is worth more," her suffering is not merely compensated but earns a return with interest. Far from being unjust, the ethical economy that recompenses good deeds with evil ones allows for a semiotic displacement of recompense that produces a surplus value in the ultimate compensation of virtue. The more Justine perceives her interactions with others as a pattern in which evil is returned for good received, the more her persecution will function inevitably as a material sign that measures and records the extent of her martyrdom, giving her the "pleasure" of the "recompense" in her "heart" that she values above all else.

Hence, as long as virtue is defined by an economy of recompense, it does not really matter what form the recompense takes. Whether reward or punishment, a recompense that is proportionally related to the extent of Justine's beneficence can function as a *sign* that determines and records the measure of her virtue. This sign can then be used to re-establish a system of positive rewards: "[I]f Providence renders difficult my career in life," Justine tells herself, "'tis in order to compensate me in a better world" (*J* 481; *Oc* 3. 47). Like positive recompense, negative recompense keeps tally; it assigns a quantifiable value to virtue in a formalized algebra that assures the possibility of just reward. Whether it is deferred to a transcendent realm or merely transposed into the immaterial pleasure of a clean conscience, compensation is bound to ensue as soon as actions are inscribed in a closed economy of exchange.

It is this inevitability of recompense that motivates Sade's relentless critique of the ethics of beneficence. Inasmuch as any kind of recompense, whether positive or negative, is capable of transforming beneficence into a vain or self-interested action, it would follow that beneficence can never be a virtue. For Sade, there can be no ethics of the gift. If the ideal of virtue is a moral gesture without return, or an interaction that escapes the confines of a closed economy, then, Sade's novel seems to say, there can be no virtue in beneficence.

This does not mean, however, that there is no possibility at all in Sade of a moral gesture without return. Beneficence is not the only tenor of moral interaction, and although beneficence is always caught in a system of exchange and return, the same does not necessarily hold true for other moral actions. In Sade, the possibility arises that what cannot be attained in beneficence can be attained in its opposite: in injury and in maleficence.

It would at first seem, of course, that inverting the values of maleficence and beneficence would not alter the underlying structure of moral exchange itself. Leo Bersani and Ulysse Dutoit (1985: 39) have argued that sadism mirrors theories of benevolent sympathy to the extent that both sadism and sympathy depend on an introjective identification with the other: like sympathy, the libertine's cruelty is a means of internalizing the other's agitation in order to procure a masochistic pleasure. Both cruelty and kindness seem to follow a circular trajectory – what Bersani and Dutoit (1979: 25) call "the fantasmatic circuit by which the subject appropriates the other's 'violent commotion'" – in which the passion is returned to the self by means of an identification that is always experienced as pleasurable.

However, one can observe in both Sade and Smith a curious asymmetry in the relationship between beneficence and maleficence. One would expect that, for Smith, injury provokes vengeance in the same sort of closed economy in which kindness calls for gratitude. But what Smith says of gratitude, that it is a duty that approaches "nearest to what is called a perfect and complete obligation" – one is obliged to feel grateful – he does not say of resentment: one is not obliged to feel resentful. Resentment is one of the "unsocial passions"; while it may be perfectly justified, it does not earn the sympathy of an impartial spectator as readily as does the passion of gratitude (Smith [1790] 1976: 34–38). As a result, Smith argues, resentment, if it is to be consistent with propriety, must be held to a minimum, whereas strong expressions of gratitude are considered perfectly decorous (40). The injury incurred must be very great before the lack of resentment will be considered a sign of stupidity or insensibility, whereas even the slightest want of gratitude will be considered a defect (27). Gratitude, in short, seems a sentiment "of which the rules are the most precise" (174), whereas resentment is much more loosely tied to its cause.

One finds the same asymmetry between the economies of beneficence and maleficence in the text of an author – the *Maximes* of La Rochefoucauld – who is much closer to Sade than is Adam Smith. In a maxim on the potlatch of beneficence that seems, at first sight, to set up a perfectly balanced chiasmus between beneficence and injury, one notices, upon closer scrutiny, an underlying lopsidedness: "Men tend not just to forget acts of kindness and of injury; they hate those who have obliged them, and cease to hate those who have abused them. The task of rewarding good and of avenging evil seems to them a form of servitude to which they do not willingly submit" (La Rochefoucauld [1665] 1967: 10, no. 14). Here, in a twist of thought common in Sade and typical of La Rochefoucauld as well, the economy of beneficence and gratitude is reversed: far from being grateful, one hates those who have done one a favor. On the other axis of the chiasmus, however, no such reversal takes place: we do not love those who have injured us, we merely cease to hate them. The link between beneficence and resentment is not mirrored by a corresponding link between maleficence and gratitude. Whereas the person who has been benefited is constrained to react, reversing his gratitude into its opposite, the injured person is free to abstain from reaction altogether. As a result, the evil deed ends up being less of an imposition than the good deed: the good deed requires an onerous form of recompense, whereas the evil deed is allowed to be forgotten.

As Blanchot (1963: 47) has observed, the maxims collected in Sade's works make those of La Rochefoucauld seem feeble by comparison. In *Justine*, the asymmetry La Rochefoucauld observes in the economies of injury and beneficence is promoted to the rank of a moral principle in the theories propounded by Roland, who takes what he wants and gives nothing to anybody, and who does not involve himself in the closed systems of give and take that characterize all of Justine's beneficent dealings with others. Responding to Justine's plea for mercy, Roland replies:

> And what right have you . . . to expect me to sweeten your circumstances? Because of the fantasies I am pleased to put into execution with you? But am I to throw myself at your feet and implore you to accord favors for the granting of which you can implore some recompense? *I ask nothing from you, I take. . . .* [O]*wing only to myself what I take hold of*, and never exacting from [a woman] anything but submission, I cannot be constrained, in the light of all this, to acknowledge any gratitude toward her. I ask them who would like to compel me to be thankful whether a thief who snatches a man's purse in the woods because he, the thief, is the stronger of the two, owes this man any gratitude for the wrong he has just done him. . . .
>
> (*J* 679; *Oc* 3. 248–49; emphasis added)

The economic paradigm of Roland's ethics is not the gift, as it was in the case of Justine, but the theft. Whereas the beneficence of the gift establishes a contract of give and take, the theft subverts the closure of such a system: the theft is all take and no give. Roland's apology for theft is framed in just these terms: he does not embrace thievery out of some natural maliciousness, but explicitly because it does away with all forms of recompense. A donee receives, but owes also gratitude; a thief receives and owes nothing. A gift is an exchange, a theft is not. While Mauss ([1925] 1954: 34–35) and Bataille (1970–88: 7. 70) can argue that the institution of exchange originates not in barter but in the gift, it would be more difficult for an anthropologist to trace the institution of exchange back to the practice of thievery.

Sade's valuation of theft above gift is often seen as a central element of his thought. For Josué Harari, Sade's antipathy for the gift is what lies at the base of his approbation of incest. Incest circumvents the necessity of entering into a form of social interaction in which women are "given" or exchanged, and inasmuch as the incest taboo, according to Lévi-Strauss, is what accomplishes the passage from nature to culture, Sade's sanction of incest functions to undermine the reciprocal system of exchange that is the very foundation of culture (Harari 1987: 172–81). Frances Ferguson (1991: 5), analyzing what could be called another form of "gift" in Sade, the intergenerational bequest, also argues that Sade's antipathy for this kind of "giving" is part of his anticulturalism: Sade attacks the institution of inheritance in part because it assures the continuation and propagation of a culture that is not so much a "gift" as it is a form of indebtedness. Similarly, critics who read Sade's antipathy for forms of giving as an expression of his "antipathy to contracts" (Deleuze 1967: 67) also attribute it to a sociocritical intent. Sade's insistence on theft, Hénaff (1978: 243–51) argues, debunks the myth of the social contract: what pretends to be a universally reciprocal pact for the benefit of all is revealed to be a historically specific mechanism designed to favor a privileged few. But if Sade's antipathy for the gift is part of a general rejection of culture and societal interaction, a mechanism "that permits the constitution of an individual subject outside the circle of exchange" (Harari 1987: 181), then it is hard to explain the proliferation in his works of microsocieties that are based largely on the dictate to enter into circuits of give and take, to engage in an exchange of objects – pain, pleasure, excrement, urine, semen – that is arguably a form of social interaction. The Sadian libertine is not free to withdraw from the society of others: as Klossowski (1967: 129–36) points out, the libertine cannot renounce the other without giving up his own identity as torturer.

Hence, instead of reading Sade's approbation of theft as a form of social critique, one should perhaps read it in the context of a specifically ethical critique of traditional, Christian notions of benevolence. Like the gift, the theft is a form of social interaction; but unlike the gift, the theft is a morally encoded transfer that proceeds in a single direction. It obeys a different moral economy. In the terms of Georges Bataille's economic theory, the "gift" of beneficence, insofar as it prizes production and conservation, could be said to conform to the notions of an "*économie classique*," whereas theft and injury, as forms of unrecuperable loss and destruction, are responsive to the exigencies of what Bataille calls the "*économie générale*." This difference is an ethical one, as Bataille himself emphasizes: the shift from a classical to a general economy occurs as an "inversion of morals" (Bataille 1970–88: 7. 33). "Theft," as Carter

(1980: 83) has observed, "is a moral imperative", for unlike the gift, the theft is a moral gesture without return, without reciprocity. Roland emblemizes this ethic; by profession a counterfeiter, he is a figure for the subversion of reciprocal exchange.[3] At the root of Roland's persecution of Justine one finds not some instinctive cruelty or "sadism" at the level of a natural or perverted human drive, but rather a critical ethics of maleficence. Beneficence and generosity, in Sade's world, appear as petty and calculating, injury and theft as magnanimous and liberal. This is why theft can serve as a paradigm of the moral act.[4]

The economy of gratitude and resentment is not, however, the only dimension in which Sade's novel portrays ethical relations in economic terms. Besides Justine's exchanges of pity, assistance, and beneficence, she also enters into another kind of exchange with others by telling her story. The plot of *Justine* is structured as a series of these acts of narrating: like Diderot's Suzanne, that other great narrator-victim of the French eighteenth century, Justine always tells her tale to everyone she meets. Like her offers of beneficence, Justine's repeated acts of narration also enter into systems of exchange and of recompense; and as in her experiences with the economy of gratitude and resentment, the "recompense" she receives for her narrative offerings is most often the converse of what she expects.

The question arises, therefore, whether the economy of narrative portrayed in the novel follows the same patterns that are established in the novel's treatment of gratitude and resentment. Is telling a story like giving a gift in that it incurs a debt of gratitude? And if narrating is a gift, is it also a form of potlatch in which what poses as a gift is in fact an aggressive demand for recompense? Does the gift of narrative earn gratitude, or does it, like Justine's "good deeds," provoke resentment? Or is narrative not like a gift at all, but rather more like a theft? Is narrating a form of taking rather than giving? To the extent that *Justine* is as much a novel about narration as it is about moral interaction, these are questions which cannot be put aside.[5] We have then not just to ask what ethical economy is *portrayed* in the novel, but more specifically: what kind of ethical economy does the narrative of *Justine* itself *perform*? That Justine should be a narrator at all is something of an anomaly in the world of Sade's novels. Both Barthes (1971: 36) and Hénaff (1978: 29) argue that the dominant characteristic of the Sadian libertine is his speech, his access to discourse, whereas the victim is typically silent. But Justine does not fit this pattern. Justine is a victim – indeed, she is Sade's victim *par excellence* – but as Sade's most famous first-person narrator, she also does more talking than almost anyone else in the Sadian universe. Interestingly, the last of the three versions of the novel, *La Nouvelle Justine*, is written in the third person: it strips Justine of her function as narrator, so that she is made to fit the paradigm of the silent victim. Despite Sade's revision, however, in the earlier version of the novel, Justine is both victim and narrator, and as such, any reading of that text has to confront this anomaly.

At the outset of the novel, Justine's narration functions as her only mode of social exchange. Destitute and unskilled, too delicate to labor, too virtuous to prostitute herself, the only "value" she has to offer in an exchange with others is her story. From the perspective of the libertines she deals with, however, her story has no exchange value. They want her body, not her story, as Justine's first libertine acquaintance explains to her: "When persons of our sort give, it is never except to receive; well, how may a little girl like yourself show gratitude for what one does for her if it is not by the most complete surrender of all that is desired of her body?" (*J* 470; *Oc* 3. 36). In the structure of exchange that has been established at this point in the novel, the body and not the narrative functions as currency.

The economic framework changes, however, when Justine's narrative grows to include the scenes of debauchery to which she has been subjected. Newly endowed with a power to arouse the passions of the libertine, her story begins to assume an exchange value that rivals that of her body and involves her in the very economy of pleasure her morals condemn. While she intends her narrative as a criticism of licentiousness, it inevitably becomes licentious itself. Susan Stewart, by comparing the Meese report on pornography to Sade's *120 Days of Sodom*, has argued that the discourse on pornography is always itself pornographic (1991: 235). Justine's discourse, certainly, functions as pornography: Dom Severino masturbates while hearing Justine's confession and asks her to repeat the obscene details of her past that excite him most (*J* 562–63; *Oc* 3. 130). That Justine complies shows to what extent her story fulfils the tasks her body refuses. The same libertines who are infuriated by her bodily resistance to their desires are delighted with her story: "there's nothing as pleasing as the tale of this girl's exploits!" (*J* 727; *Oc* 3. 297). Indeed, the stringency with which Justine reserves her body from commerce contradicts the indiscriminateness with which she proffers her tale. Even when it is clear that her narrative is going to arouse the same violent passions in her listeners that she tells of in her story, Justine, true to her character, never strays from her habit of describing scenes of lubricity in every detail. When a newly encountered persecutor strips her of her clothes and brutally examines the various organs of her body he clearly intends to molest, she still complies readily when he asks to hear her story: "It was during this scrutiny that he solicited numerous details concerning what had been done to me at the monastery of Saint Mary-in-the-Wood, and *without noticing that my recitations doubled his warmth*, I was candid enough to give them all with naïveté" (*J* 632; *Oc* 3. 200; emphasis added). A prude as regards her body, Justine is excessively promiscuous as regards her narrative.

That Justine's story is an object of exchange does not mean, however, that she masters the laws of the exchange economy her narrative involves her in. As promiscuous as she may be with her story, strictly speaking Justine is not a prostitute of narrative, as Jane Gallop (1981: 60–61) has suggested; for unlike the *historiennes* in the *120 Days of Sodom*, she derives no benefit from her services as a narrator. Indeed, the exchange she makes is most often just the converse: instead of being rewarded for so obligingly arousing her listeners, she is simply persecuted once again. The tormentor to whom Justine narrates her story in the passage just quoted responds to her tale by opening her veins and draining her blood until she faints. It would at first seem, therefore, that Justine's exchange of narrative is recompensed not by gratitude but by resentment: her story earns her only misery.

Indeed, it becomes increasingly evident that Justine's narrating is the ultimate cause of all her misfortune. "Yet further horrors!" she cries before one of the countless scenes of her torture, and the response she gets expresses with a directness and concision typical of Sade's prose the motive of her tormentor: "'That's it: 'tis ordained,' Saint-Florent broke in; 'you know, my dear: the weak yield to the strong's desires, or fall victims to their wickedness: that's all: *that's your whole story, Thérèse, therefore obey {c'est votre histoire, Thérèse, obéissez donc}*'" (*J* 726; *Oc* 3. 296; emphasis added). Justine must suffer, Saint-Florent tells her, *because it is her story*, because it is the story she herself keeps telling. Justine's torturers do in fact base their actions on what Justine herself has told them about her past. Invariably, it is only after they have heard her tale that the libertines persecute Justine; and at times they justify their behavior by referring – in academic manner – to the arguments of Justine's previous torturers, to arguments, in other words, they themselves learned from hearing Justine's tale (*J* 513; *Oc* 3. 80–81). Justine's torturers are all the products of what she recounts, and they treat her in accordance with the role she makes for herself. "Justine's life," Nancy Miller (1976: 222) observes, "is defined and measured solely by what she tells." Justine, in short, is not a character at all but merely an effect of narrative.

It soon becomes evident, however, that this effect is not a predictable one. Although Justine's narrative determines how she is treated by others, this treatment is not always the same. Most often her story leads to her torture; but at other times it elicits sympathy and assistance from her listeners, as when she pleads her innocence to M. S[ervant] (*J* 692; *Oc* 3. 262; see *Oc* 2. 361), or, most notably, at the end of the novel, when she finishes telling her tale to Juliette and Corville. The same story that incites the libertines to torture the teller draws help and understanding from Servant, Juliette, and Corville. Hence, there is no general rule governing the exchanges in which Justine's tale involves her.

But while Justine's narrative earns her varying returns, it always earns her one kind of return or another. And although the reactions to her story may be at times rewarding and at other times vindictive, they seem always to bear a direct proportion to the excessive goriness of her tale. Justine's listeners either persecute her shamelessly or they help her with heart and soul; but in no event do they react mildly. What varies, therefore, is the positive or negative value of the reaction, not the general economic pattern. Like the economy that emerged in the analysis of beneficence and gratitude, Justine's commerce with narration shows again that a reversal in the value of the recompense received does not entail a qualitative break with the economic structure of circular exchange.

Must one conclude that narrative exchange, like the exchange of gifts, is *always* caught in a circular economic pattern? Up to this point, I have considered Justine's narrative as a story that she tells orally in the presence of a listener. This is, however, not the only way in which Justine's narrative functions. Besides being a story to be told, Justine's narrative is also a written text designed to be read. It is not immediately evident that the economics of Justine's oral exchanges will also govern the context of her narrative when considered as a written text. From the reader's point of view, can one say that the text is a gift? Does it do us good to read this book? Or is the text rather more like a theft? Does it rob its readers of their virtue?

It is not at first clear how one could go about answering this question. How is one to isolate Justine's oral narrative from its function as a text to be read? In the novel, Justine's narrative is given in direct speech, enclosed in quotation marks; and throughout the novel, one is reminded by the occasional interventions of her listeners, Juliette and Corville, that Justine is telling her tale orally. Everything one reads about Justine is in the form of oral address. How then can one separate what is to be read from what is to be heard?

One possibility would be to consider Justine's story in its function as a legend. The word "legend," from medieval Latin *legenda*, the neuter plural gerundive of *legere*, "to read," means, literally, "things to be read." Indeed, as Nancy Miller (1976: 224) has observed, the legendary aspect is very much in evidence in the story of Justine. Like the biographies of the saints in the Roman Catholic canon of legends, Justine's is essentially the story of an unflagging loyalty to moral and religious faith in the face of adversity. And as in the stories of martyrs, there is a strong suggestion in Justine's story that she is killed because of her refusal to compromise her sense of virtue. Hence, it may be that by analyzing the legendary character of Justine's narrative, one could isolate its function as a "thing to be read," as a legend, from its form as oral narrative.

It is especially at the end of the novel that Justine's tale takes on the character of a legend. Readings of the end of the novel often center on the violent death of Justine herself (Foucault [1972] 1976: 553–54; Van Den Abbeele 1987: 13–16); one can also choose to focus on the miraculous effects of what survives her death, on her narrative and on her body. The body of the dead Justine, horribly disfigured by the thunderbolt that Providence seems to have cast on to her to ensure that her torments never end, moves Juliette to embrace the principles of virtue that she had ridiculed in her early youth: "[L]eave her here before my eyes, Monsieur, I have got to contemplate her in order to be confirmed in the resolves I have just taken. . . . [T]hat charming girl's incredible calamities, her terrifying reversals and uninterrupted disasters are a warning issued me by the Eternal, Who would that I heed the voice of mine guilt and cast myself into His arms" (*J* 742; *Oc* 3. 311–12). André Jolles (1930: 36) argues that the mental disposition at work in the legend is best expressed in the medieval Latin usage of the word *imitatio*, which he sees as combining the legend's three basic elements: the image or portrait (*imago*); the attempt to emulate (*aemulus*); and the process of transformation or change (due to a popular confusion of *imitari* with *immutare*). In Juliette's reaction to Justine's death, all three of these elements are present: struck by the image of her martyred sister's body, Juliette vows to change her ways and to emulate her sister's virtue. Clearly, we are dealing here with an instance of legend in Jolles's sense of the term. Accordingly, one can read the scene as exemplifying the difference between oral narrative and legend, between what is told and what is written. Told orally, Justine's story could earn Juliette's sympathy but not change her convictions; but once Justine has been killed, her story has become a legend, and like the legends of saints and martyrs, it has assumed the force to transform and convert its readers. Her disfigured corpse takes on the character of a saint's relic: it has a nearly miraculous power or "virtue" of conversion.

Judging from its effect on Juliette, therefore, the legend of Justine would seem not only to be a gift but to be the most generous gift, a kind of offering or sacrifice. Because Justine dies before receiving the recompense due to her for her virtuous life of suffering, the legend of her life can only suggest that she has suffered for those she left behind. In this way, her legend constitutes what one might call a *sacrificial economy*: the recompense for her virtue is deferred and displaced on to the "reader" who survives her, Juliette. But even this most generous of gifts is not without a return: the sacrifice, as Derrida (1992b: 102) shows, is based on the belief in an infinite, divine retribution after death, a belief that institutes a still more effective system of calculable recompense. Sacrifice, like any gift, does not escape the closure of reciprocal exchange.

Other passages in the text, however, seem to suggest quite a different economic pattern. Justine, for example, predicts that her narrative, far from being a "gift" of virtue, will have a devastating effect on its readers: "What discouragement the story of my life will implant in men's souls if ever it is published! O you who may learn it someday, do not divulge it, I beseech you; you would bring despair to the hearts of all those who cherish what is good, and you would incite crime by exhibiting its triumphs" (*Oc* 7. 92). If ever her story is "published," if ever it becomes a text available to the public, Justine fears that it will corrupt its readers. This passage is taken from *La Nouvelle Justine*, where the effect of Justine's death on Juliette is the converse of what it is in the first version: instead of converting, Juliette feels confirmed in her vicious ways when she sees her virtuous sister punished by the heavens (*JL* 1190–91; *Oc* 9. 580). Hence, the later version of the novel represents the "legend" of Justine not as a force of conversion, but as a force of corruption.

This ambivalence in the perlocutionary force of Justine's tale is already present in the earlier version as well, where Justine is acutely aware of what one reader of the novel has called "the sin of narration itself" (Philip Stewart 1987: 197). "I have, perhaps, offended Heaven with impure recitals," she exclaims at the end of her tale, begging her listeners a "thousand pardons" (*J* 737; *Oc* 3. 307). Justine, as Thomas DiPiero (1992: 360) observes, "accomplishes a transgression merely by her use of language." Indeed, since Justine is the narrator of *Justine, ou Les Malheurs de la vertu*, a book that constitutes one of the most "impure" things ever offered to the reading public, her tale may very well be said to "offend the heavens." As virtuous as Justine may be, there is indeed something very offensive about her story. Much of the forcefulness of Sade's novel derives from the paradox that the record or legend of a perfectly virtuous life may itself constitute a heinous crime, that "the reading even of a morally exemplary book might cause something morally deplorable to occur" (J. Hillis Miller 1990: 21). Virtue, it would seem, is not always compatible with the legend of virtue.

For this reason, the legend of Justine has a unique status in the economy of the novel. Justine's acts of narration are unlike all else that she does: aware that she may have "offended the heavens" should her "impure tales" ever be published, Justine *consciously* runs the risk of committing a crime when she narrates her story. Readers of the earliest of the novel's three versions have stressed Justine's incomprehension of the content (Didier 1976: 96) and the irony (Brandt 1981) of her own narrative; but as Béatrice Didier observes, the Justine of the *Malheurs de la vertu* – the version I am considering here – has entirely overcome this naïveté. Unlike Diderot's Suzanne, who describes orgasms without knowing what she's talking about (Diderot [1796] 1972: 205), Justine is fully aware of the licentiousness of the tale she offers her readers, and she does not let this awareness deter her from her drive to narrate. She narrates in utter disregard for her readers. Gallop (1981: 61) has argued that Justine is motivated to narrate by a "certain perverse, non-utilitarian desire to please (to pander to the other's desire)"; I would suggest, to the contrary, that the motive for her narration is the only sentiment Justine has that is not assimilable to the ethics of beneficence that governs all her other actions. Narrating is the only thing Justine does *not* do out of a concern for others. For the first time, she strays from the principles of virtue that had always governed her behavior and acts without being able to control the lawfulness of her act.

The legend, then, is like a theft to the extent that it violates the ethics of beneficence; but its violation follows a less controlled course. The ethics of the theft, as we saw, is based on the possibility of forgetting: the good deed provokes hatred, but injury and theft, in La Rochefoucauld's maxim, are more likely to go unrecompensed, to pass from memory. Such a forgetting is also the condition of possibility of an absolute "gift" that would not provoke a return (Derrida 1992a: 16). The structure of the legend of Justine is a different one: Justine does not forget what she "gives" in telling her tale, but she does not and cannot know whether this "gift" is a virtue or a sin, a gift or a theft. Although much of Sade's narrative may be motivated, as Joan DeJean (1984: 323) argues, by a desire to control the reader, Justine's narration recklessly abandons its reader to the license of its perlocutionary instability.

It is impossible to decide which of the two possible consequences Justine's "legend" will have, to decide whether it will convert, as in the first two versions of the novel, or, as in the third, corrupt its listeners. It is impossible to decide, in other words, whether the transfer constituted by the legend will have been beneficent or maleficent, a gift or a theft. The "gift" (or the "theft") of the legend is blind, blind not only to the identity of the receiver, but to its own value as well. As a result, the legend of Justine cannot be contained in the same pattern of economic exchange that governs the other ethical themes of the novel. Because it cannot be decided whether the legend will corrupt or convert, whether it will constitute a "gift" or a "theft" of virtue, there is no possibility of a return, of a "recompense" that can determine and record the ethical measure of the act of narrating. There is no suitable or adequate "recompense" for the legend, and this is why, as a paradigm of ethics, the legend can escape the economic constraints that make generosity into a form of selfishness and beneficence into a form of vanity.[6]

For Sade, a theft is always more noble than a gift, but better still than thievery is his vision of a legendary crime that is also the crime of the legend, the crime of those who produce what is to be read:

> [H]e is like those perverse writers whose corruption is so dangerous, so active, that their single aim is, by causing their appalling doctrines to be printed, to immortalize the sum of their crimes after their own lives are at an end. They themselves can do no more wrongs, but their accursed writings will cause others to be committed; and this sweet vision that they carry to the grave consoles them upon the obligation, enjoined by death, to relinquish the doing of evil.
>
> (*J* 611; *Oc* 3. 179)

This passage, often cited in studies of Sade (Blanchot 1963: 35; Pfersmann 1983: 87), seems to identify writing as the only possibility of committing an immortal crime, of surpassing the closed economy of give and take from which life seems unable to escape. In order for there to be ethics, in order for there to be an ethical action free of the constraint of proportionate exchange, there must not only be crime, but specifically the crime of making a text.

Derrida (1992a: 100), describing the contradictory conditions of an absolute "gift" that would exceed the confines of an exchange or potlatch economy, associates the problematic of the gift with the problematic of the trace or of the text. As a condition of the gift, the text as trace also entails a certain "economy of death":

> The death of the donor agency (and here we are calling death the fatality that destines a gift *not to return* to the donor agency) is not a natural accident external to the donor agency; it is only thinkable on the basis of, setting out from [*à partir du*] the gift. This does not mean simply that only death or the dead can give. No, only a "life" can give, but a life in which this economy of death presents itself and lets itself be exceeded.
>
> (Ibid.: 102)

In the passage from Sade quoted above, the libertine who writes is said to be consoling himself for the obligation death puts him under to renounce evil. Like Derrida's "gift," then, the crime of the legend is a function of death, of the anticipation of a death whose "obligation" defines life as an economy exceeded only by writing. Writing is an obligation of death; but it remains unclear, in this passage, which of the two antithetical meanings of "obligation" is intended. Death obliges; but is this obliging a service, a gratification, a "gift," the gift of the legend, for example? Or is it a constraint, an enslavement, a depravation, a taking, or a "theft"? The impossibility of deciding between these two meanings is what assures the necessity of ethics as the crime or as the virtue of writing.

Notes

1 In addition to the literature I discuss in this essay, evidence of a renewed interest in literature and ethics can be found in the recent works of Hillis Miller (1987), Nouvet (1991), Critchley (1992), and Handwerk (1985).

2 Citations of Sade's works give the page number of the English translation (unless none exists, in which case the translation is my own), whereby Juliette is abbreviated as *JL* and Justine as *J*, followed by a reference to the corresponding passage in Sade's *Oeuvres complètes*, which is abbreviated as *Oc* and followed by the volume and page numbers. Where necessary, translations have been modified to bring them closer to the original.

3 Reading Baudelaire, Derrida (1992a: 158) argues that counterfeit money is the condition of, or more precisely, the "chance" for a gift that would resist recuperation by a closed system of recompense. Roland does not "give" anything, but it is true that his thievery and his counterfeiting come closer to the ideal of the gift than all of Justine's generosity.

Derrida's analysis of the gift and other forms of expenditure without return, first presented in his reading of Bataille ([1967] 1979: 369–407), cannot be equated with earlier anthropological analyses of symbolic exchange, as Vincent Pecora (1991: 209) claims. Pecora credits Marcel Mauss with having completed, long before Bataille, "much of the antidialectical work" that Derrida attributes to Bataille. In fact, as Derrida's recent critique of Mauss in *Given Time I* shows, the distance separating his notion of the gift from the anthropologist's conceptions of symbolic exchange couldn't be greater.

4 Insisting on the ethical context of Sade's approbation of theft may also cause us

to reassess the significance of his attitude toward the concept of the law. Sade's antipathy for the law has been emphasized both by Deleuze (1967: 77), who views Sade as rejecting the law in favor of an institutionalized anarchy, and by Blanchot (1986: 92), who perceives him as unwilling to submit the principle of destructive energy to a higher legal instance. For Blanchot it is in the revolutionary moment between legal orders, in the anarchical instant when the previous legitimacy has just been abrogated but before a new legality has been instituted, that man attains his true sovereignty. Geoffrey Bennington (1985: 199), adopting Blanchot's observation and altering it to conform to his deconstructive analysis of the law in Sade, relocates the hiatus between legal orders on to the level of language: "the *entre-temps* is not a temporal gap *between* two régimes of law but, *within* a system of law, the silence in the law between the sense and the non-sense of the words." But one can also see in Sade's antipathy for the law an effort to isolate a specifically ethical mode of exchange from the processes determined by laws of nature or of language. Inasmuch as beneficence always provokes a recompense that is ultimately experienced as pleasurable, it sets off a chain reaction as inevitable as the law of cause and effect. As such, it has no claim to the moral status of a gracious or freely inspired act. Maleficence, on the other hand, is often enough portrayed as an act that obeys no higher law. For another, more explicitly "ethical" reading of Sade that also draws on Blanchot to analyze Sade's revolt against the law, see Keenan's (1991) fine reading of *La Philosophie dans le boudoir*.

5 Much of the discussion of "ethics and literature" has centered on narrative: "ethics," writes Hillis Miller (1990: 16), "has a peculiar relation to that form of language we call narrative." For a very different approach to the question of ethics and narrative, see Booth (1988).

6 Hence, the Sadian ethic operative in the legend of Justine differs from the ethics of desire that Lacan (1966: 782), by identifying repressed desire with the moral law, develops in his reading of Kant with Sade. Readings of Sade that draw on a Lacanian ethics of desire are likely to find a figure of ethical strength not in Justine or in her act of narrative but in Juliette, "this a-pathetic rake who [like Antigone] 'doesn't give way on her desire'" (Žižek 1989: 117). A similar ethics of desire informs Michael Shapiro's (1993) reading of Sade with Smith. While I would concur with both Shapiro and Lacan in their affirmation of a Sadian or Kantian–Sadian ethic, I try to approach the issue from a different angle by emphasizing what exceeds systems of closed exchange, rather than what exceeds imaginary or social mechanisms for the alienation of desire.

References

Barthes, Roland (1971). *Sade, Fourier, Loyola*. Paris: Seuil.
Bataille, Georges (1970–88). *Oeuvres complètes*. 12 vols. Paris: Gallimard.
Bennington, Geoffrey (1985). *Sententiousness and the Novel: Laying Down the Law in Eighteenth-Century French Fiction*. Cambridge: Cambridge University Press.
Bersani, Leo, and Ulysse Dutoit (1979). "Merde Alors." *October* 13: 23–35.
—— and —— (1985). *The Forms of Violence: Narrative in Assyrian Art and Modern Culture*. New York: Schocken.
Blanchot, Maurice (1963). *Lautréamont et Sade*. Arguments 19. Paris: Minuit.

—— (1963). "L'Insurrection, la folie d'écrire." In *Sade et Restif de la Bretonne*. Bruxelles: Complexe, 67–101.

Booth, Wayne C. (1988). *The Company We Keep: An Ethics of Fiction*. Berkeley: University of California Press.

Brandt, Per Aage (1981). "Ironie et subjectivité." *Revue romane* 16.1–2: 36–48.

Carter, Angela (1980). *The Sadeian Woman and the Ideology of Pornography*. New York: Harper.

Critchley, Simon (1992). *The Ethics of Deconstruction: Derrida and Levinas*. Oxford: Basil Blackwell.

DeJean, Joan (1984). *Literary Fortifications: Rousseau, Laclos, Sade*. Princeton, NJ: Princeton University Press.

Deleuze, Gilles (1967). *Présentation de Sacher-Masoch: le froid et le cruel*. Paris: Minuit.

Derrida, Jacques ([1967] 1979). *L'Écriture et la différence*. Collection Points 100. Paris: Seuil.

—— (1992a). *Given Time. I: Counterfeit Money*. Trans. Peggy Kamuf. Chicago: University of Chicago Press.

—— (1992b). "Donner la mort." In *L'Éthique du don: Jacques Derrida et la pensée du don*. Ed. Jean-Michel Rabaté and Michael Wetzel. Proc. of a *Colloque de Royaumont*. Dec. 1990. Paris: Métailié-Transition, 11–108.

Diderot, Denis. ([1796] 1972). *La Religieuse*. Ed. Robert Mauzi. Collection Folio 57. Paris: Gallimard.

Didier, Béatrice (1976). *Sade*. Paris: Denoël/Gonthier.

DiPiero, Thomas (1992). *Dangerous Truths and Criminal Passions: The Evolution of the French Novel, 1569–1791*. Stanford, CA: Stanford University Press.

Ferguson, Frances (1991). "Sade and the Pornographic Legacy." *Representations* 36: 1–21.

Foucault, Michel ([1972] 1976). *Histoire de la folie à l'âge classique*. Collection Tel 9. Paris: Gallimard.

Gallop, Jane (1981). *Intersections: A Reading of Sade with Bataille, Blanchot, and Klossowski*. Lincoln: University of Nebraska Press.

Handwerk, Gery J. (1985). *Irony and Ethics in Narrative: From Schlegel to Lacan*. New Haven, CT: Yale University Press.

Harari, Josué V. (1987). *Scenarios of the Imaginary: Theorizing the French Enlightenment*. Ithaca, NY: Cornell University Press.

Heath, Stephen (1990). "The Ethics of Sexual Difference." *Discourse* 12.2: 128–53.

Hénaff, Marcel (1978). *Sade: L'Invention du corps libertin*. Paris: PUF.

Jolles, André (1930). *Einfache Formen: Legende / Sage / Mythe / Rätsel / Spruch / Kasus / Memorabile / Märchen / Witz*. Halle: Niemeyer.

Keenan, Thomas (1991). "Freedom, the Law of Another Fable." In *Literature and the Ethical Question*. Ed. C. Nouvet. *Yale French Studies* 79: 231–51.

Klossowski, Pierre (1967). *Sade mon prochain, précédé de Le Philosophe scélérat*. Paris: Seuil.

Lacan, Jacques (1966). *Écrits*. Paris: Seuil.

La Rochefoucauld, François de ([1665] 1967). *Maximes, suivies des Réflexions diverses*. . . . Ed. Jacques Truchet. Paris: Garnier.

Marshall, David (1986). *The Figure of Theater: Shaftesbury, Defoe, Adam Smith, and George Eliot*. New York: Columbia University Press.

Mauss, Marcel ([1925] 1954). *The Gift: Forms and Functions of Exchange in Archaic Societies*. Trans. Ian Cunnison. London: Cohen & West.

Miller, J. Hillis (1987). *The Ethics of Reading: Kant, de Man, Eliot, Trollope, James, and Benjamin*. New York: Columbia University Press.
—— (1990). *Versions of Pygmalion*. Cambridge, MA: Harvard University Press.
Miller, Nancy K. (1976). "*Justine*; or, The Vicious Circle." *Studies in Eighteenth-Century Culture* 5: 215–28.
—— (1980). *The Heroine's Text: Readings in the French and English Novel, 1722–1782*. New York: Columbia University Press.
Nouvet, Claire, ed. (1991). *Literature and the Ethical Question. Yale French Studies* 79.
Pecora, Vincent P. (1991). "Ethics, Politics, and the Middle Voice." In *Literature and the Ethical Question*. Ed. C. Nouvet. *Yale French Studies* 79: 203–30.
Pfersmann, Andreas (1983). "L'Ironie romantique chez Sade." In *Sade: Écrire la crise*. Ed. Michel Camus and Philippe Roger. Proc. of a *Colloque de Cerisy*, 19–29 June 1981. Paris: Belfond, 85–98.
Raphael, D.D., and A.L. Macfie (1976). Introduction to *The Theory of Moral Sentiments*, by Adam Smith. Oxford: Clarendon Press, 1–52.
Roger, Philippe (1976). *Sade: La philosophie dans le pressoir*. Paris: Grasset.
Sade, Marquis de (1988). *Juliette*. Trans. Austryn Wainhouse. New York: Evergreen-Grove. Translation first published 1968.
—— (1990). *Justine, Philosophy in the Bedroom, and Other Writings*. Comp. and trans. Richard Seaver and Austryn Wainhouse. New York: Evergreen-Grove. Translation first published 1965.
—— (1986–). *Oeuvres complètes*. Ed. Annie Le Brun and Jean-Jacques Pauvert. 12 vols to date. Paris: Pauvert.
Shapiro, Michael J. (1993). "Eighteenth Century Intimations of Modernity: Adam Smith and the Marquis de Sade." *Political Theory* 21: 273–93.
Siebers, Tobin (1988). *The Ethics of Criticism*. Ithaca, NY: Cornell University Press.
Smith, Adam ([1759] 1971). *The Theory of Moral Sentiments*. New York: Garland.
—— ([1790] 1976). *The Theory of Moral Sentiments*. Ed. D.D. Raphael and A.L. Macfie. Oxford: Oxford University Press.
Stewart, Philip (1987). "Meaning and Its Opposite: Order in Justine's Disordered World." *Saggi e ricerche di letteratura francese* 26: 169–98.
Stewart, Susan (1991). *Crimes of Writing: Problems in the Containment of Representation*. New York: Oxford University Press.
Van den Abbeele, Georges (1987). "Sade, Foucault, and the Scene of Enlightenment Lucidity." *Stanford French Review* 11.1: 7–16.
Žižek, Slavoj (1989). *The Sublime Object of Ideology*. London: Verso.

14

FUGITIVE PROPERTIES

Samira Kawash

In the modern liberal tradition, the foundation of the economy and the purpose of the state begin from a single irreducible principle: the principle of property. The "natural right" of property is intimately connected to a particular notion of "person" as political and social subject. In the work of such political philosophers as Locke and Hegel "property-in-person" is the first modality of the subject. Property right is a natural right because it is an extension into the world of the propertied essence of the subject. The modern idea of property and the modern idea of the subject are indissociable.

That some persons might be defined as property seems violently contradictory to the principles of modern liberal society. Yet race slavery is coeval with the rise of these very principles. Rather than viewing race slavery as an aberrant barbarism which anachronistically lingered into the modern era, we need to interrogate the operation of the principles of "property" and "person" that made slavery a viable economic form for hundreds of years. In particular, the system of slavery reveals that "property" and "person" are neither natural nor neutral. The dramatic stories of escape recounted in nineteenth-century American slave narratives reveal the limits of the liberal ideology of property and person by creating a third figure outside this order: the fugitive.

Historians have noted the legal complications arising from the attempt to fix the status of the slave, who is at the same time person and property. Slave codes in the various states recognized both these aspects as they simultaneously insured the owner's right to the slave's labor and product, and imposed certain obligations on the owners for the care and welfare of the slave (Stampp 1956: 192–93; Genovese 1974: 28–37). As property, the slave is wholly subject to the will of the owner. But if the owner's right to dispose of his property is to remain uninfringed by the state, at some point the personhood of the slave must come into conflict with the slave's legal status as property or thing.

To recognize the free will of the slave would require a recognition of the rights of the slave – and slavery demands the slave have none. Not only the efficacy, but also the legitimacy of slavery depends on making "person" absolutely incommensurable with "(human) property." The record of the everyday practice of slavery preserved in slave narratives gives eloquent testimony to the centrality of the denial of the personhood of the slave. While the slave as slave might be viewed as a thing, the slave as person posed intolerable contradictions to a system that recognizes the personality only of those who are legally accorded property in their own person. The success and stability of slavery depended on the power to suppress the tension between person and property embodied in the slave.

The fault lines of this tension are revealed with especial poignancy in an episode in Frederick Douglass's life that followed from the publication in 1845 of the *Narrative of the Life of Frederick Douglass, an American Slave*. The "self-evidence" of the autobiographical *Narrative* was also for Douglass self-exposure; the public and published disclosure of his identity put him in danger of recapture by his legal owner. To insure his safety, Douglass departed for England at the same time his *Narrative* appeared. This was not simply a hypothetical danger: his legal owner Hugh Auld had made public his intention to reduce Douglass to slavery as soon as he returned to America, and engaged agents to watch for his return. Auld demanded $750 for Douglass's freedom. So that Douglass might return unmolested to his wife and family in the United States, his friends raised the money and secured his "free papers."

Newspaper editorials throughout New England expressed dismay when news of this transaction became known: "A romantic storm broke loose among the New England abolitionists! Douglass had 'disappointed' them, 'let them down,' 'stumbled,' 'violated one of the fundamental principles of the abolition movement,' by succumbing to that transaction with a slave-holder, recognizing a fellow creature's 'right of property' in him!" (Starling 1988: 42). The thrust of white objection was that Douglass had legitimated the entire slave system by purchasing his own freedom. The righteously indignant seemed little concerned that the other options for Douglass were permanent exile in England or return to slavery. The presumptuousness of these objections is extraordinary; white abolitionists seemed certain that Douglass would not mind living as a symbol for the cause. One such activist opines: "Douglass, while here, may have been in danger, but we think not in much fear. He is a courageous man, and would have been glad of an attempt at recapture, as another arrow in his quiver against the 'abominable institution' from which he had escaped" (ibid).

These objections reveal the impossibility of the fugitive within the space of slavery: the system of property demands that one maintain an unambiguous relation to its law of division, wholly on one side or the other. Douglass's necessary capitulation to Auld's demand for payment is distressing not simply because he has given in to the tyrants, but because it reveals that there can be no "outside" a system of slavery constituted by property rights. One is owned, or one owns. Douglass becomes a "proper" subject by becoming a *propertied* subject – a subject in full possession of himself.

At the same time, the abolitionists' infatuation with Douglass as fugitive reveals the power of the figure of fugitivity to counter the logic of master and slave. The fugitive is neither, but the price of occupying this non-place between master and slave is silence, invisibility, and placelessness. For the abolitionists, the symbolic value of Douglass is as a man who is another's slave. Douglass as fugitive symbolizes the conjoining of two terms which by definition are mutually exclusive. But in fact Douglass cannot be both a man and a slave; the two terms can only be held together under the sign of "fugitive" and the immanent threat of violence it entails.

The escaping slave not only fled cruelty and oppression; she or he also deprived her or his master of a significant asset. Slave property represented a large portion of the total wealth of the slave states. The reported average value of "personal estate" for slave farms in 1860 (primarily slave property) was $19,828 (Ransom 1990: 62). This was of course one of the principal barriers to peacefully ending the institution of slavery: to free the four million slaves held in the South on the eve of the Civil War would have been tantamount, from the slaveholder's perspective, to a loss of some $3 billion in assets (ibid.: 70). Some masters were willing to allow slaves to purchase their freedom, but few slaves were able to earn the several hundred dollars necessary in their spare "free time."[1] In the decades before 1860, the average price of slaves never fell below $200, and sometimes rose as high as $800. The price of a prime field hand could be considerably higher.[2]

Both the significant monetary value of the slave and the division of the law of property were at play in the popular expression among slaves for escape, "stealing oneself." "Stealing" here exhibits a strange transitivity. Leaving in secret, without the master's knowledge or permission, the fugitive "steals away," an action without syntactical object. But as property, this removal is simultaneously theft: the fugitive steals himself or herself, the subject and object of an action which aims at the removal of this very duality. Both the agent and the object of this theft inhabit the same body; and in this, the enslaved risked capture, severe punishment, even death. In the real, corporeal danger of flight, the enslaved risks the body to regain the body, to rejoin person and property into one subject.

In stealing himself or herself, the fugitive has violated the law of property, has become an "outlaw." But because it is the law of property which has granted to some property in their person and relegated others to the status of property simple, the fugitive's attempt to restore person to property is in the paradoxical situation of being a violation of the law (stealing) which requires for its success the sanction of the law (recognition of the fugitive as subject, that is, as one having property in him- or herself). Thus the fugitive cannot simply transform slavery under the law into freedom under the law. It is only by remaining outside the law that the fugitive escapes the status of (human) property; in flight, the fugitive is no longer property for another, but neither does he or she become property in himself or herself. That one might exist as neither propertied subject nor as property belies the foundational status of the "natural right" of property.

A fascinating tale of escape was published in 1849 under the descriptive and explanatory title *The Narrative of Henry Box Brown, Who Escaped from Slavery Enclosed in a Box Three Feet Long, Two Feet Wide, and Two-and-a Half Feet High, Written from a Statement of Facts Made by Himself*. In the second edition of his narrative Brown (1852) recounts how, after his wife and children are sold to a slave trader, he resolves to gain his own liberty. While praying fervently to God for help, Brown receives an inspiration: "suddenly, the idea flashed across my mind of shutting myself *up in a box*, and getting myself conveyed as dry goods to a free state" (Brown 1852: 51). A friend assents to accompany Brown's box to Philadelphia, in order to be sure the box is kept upright and Brown does not suffocate. Another friend in Philadelphia agrees to call for the box on its arrival, and take care of Brown. Brown describes the box he had made for the occasion:

> The box which I had procured was three feet one inch long, two feet six inches high, and two feet wide. On the morning of the 29th day of March, 1839, I went into the box – having previously bored three gimlet holes for air opposite my face and having provided myself with a bladder of water, both for the purpose of quenching my thirst and for wetting my face should I feel getting faint. . . . Being thus equipped for the battle of liberty, my friends nailed down the lid and had me conveyed to the Express Office.
>
> (Ibid.: 53)

Part of the thrill of this story is the image of being buried alive, nailed into a coffin-like box for what Brown describes as an excruciating 27-hour ordeal. Indeed, Brown plays on this imagery, equating the living death of his journey with the living death of slavery for all those enslaved. When his box arrives at its destination, his friends break open the box. "Then," Brown says, "came my resurrection from the grave of slavery" (57).

The simple narrative of death and resurrection is complicated, however, by the intervention of the box. Despite the resonance of box and coffin in this story, the box is in fact nothing like a coffin: its dimensions prohibit the "laying out" of the dead; instead Brown must curl up, knees to chest, to fit into its 3 ft × 2.5 ft × 2 ft space. This fetal position suggests that the box is also like a womb, in which Brown will slowly incubate into a free man. Through its multiple referents, the box successively reconstitutes Brown as corpse, as fetus, as first man.[3] However, the box is neither coffin nor womb. What is inside is not a man, nor even a slave, but something else. Flight itself, as mediated by the box, removes Brown from the economy of mastery and slavery.

Brown plays on the confusion between sensible man and insensible object in his box:

> Perceiving my box, standing on end, [a man] threw it down and then the two sat upon it. . . . I could now listen to the men talking and heard one of them asking the other what he supposed *the box contained*. His companion replied he guessed it was "the mail." I too thought it was a mail, but not such a mail as he supposed it to be.
>
> (Ibid.: 55)

Brown's pun on the male in the mail marks the way in which the introduction of *a male* is simultaneously a disruption of *the mail*. These observers little expect the mail to contain human cargo. Indeed, could there be any such suspicion, Brown's escape would be blocked. Bernhard Siegert has argued that the modern postal system is both a technology of subjectivity and a technology of property. Beginning in the late eighteenth century, letters began to be understood as private correspondences expressing the personal thoughts and feelings, the "truth of the heart," of the sender: "words had an individual origin in thought. . . . Words were metaphors for ideas formed by the soul – every self thus became the subject of its own discourse *a priori*. Words were now the subject's private property: the pre-condition necessary for the existence of private letters" (Siegert forthcoming). The subject is presumed to precede this expression; the letters that circulate are representations of the subject, not the subject itself. Accordingly, the subject is understood to stand outside of and prior to the circulation of the mail. But Brown's circulation in the mail is not as the product or the property of a prior subject. Brown, simultaneously agent and object of the act of mailing himself to freedom, disturbs the relation of prior, autonomous subject and property that is supposedly reflected in the system of the post. Brown can be delivered as subject only as a result of being sent through the mail; Brown's subjectivity depends on becoming the very mail that is supposed merely to represent the truth of a prior subject. Thus, where the subject is presumed to precede and stand apart from the mail, Brown's ultimate emergence as subject radically upends this relation: Brown is not an autonomous subject of the post; rather, he becomes a subject through the post. While Brown's "delivery" as a free man at the end of his journey affirms the postal logic of the subject by revealing an autonomous subject at the mail's terminus, his presence as the mail exposes the extent to which this subject is a product, rather than a precondition, of the subjectivizing technology of the post.

The troubled and troubling status of Brown in the box continues throughout the journey to mark the space of the box as one difficult to locate or characterize in the terms of property, slavery, or subjectivity. Midway in the journey, Brown's box is transferred from a steamboat to a train:

> When the driver arrived at the depot, I heard him call for some person to help take the box off the wagon and some one answered him to the effect that he might throw it off. But, says the driver, "it

> is marked 'this side up with care.' So if I throw it off I might break something." The other answers him that it did not matter if he broke all that was in it; the railway company was able enough to pay for it. No sooner were these words spoken than I began to tumble from the wagon, and, falling on the end where my head was, I could hear my neck give a crack, as if it had been snapped asunder, and I was knocked completely insensible.
>
> (Ibid.: 55)

Brown is clear that something has indeed been broken by the railworkers' careless treatment of the box. The loss caused by such negligence, however, is not exactly the damaged goods that the workers anticipate. The damage to Brown's body results in the loss of consciousness, a literalized "break" with the past. Can the rail company hope to pay for what has here been lost? One might speculate that if the rail company had been responsible for damage to a slave, the slave's owner would be entitled to compensation for property damaged or lost. But what is in the box? He is no longer a slave, the property of another; yet neither a man who might sue the company in his own right for injuries sustained on their liability. The content of the box at this moment is a blank, a consciousness "completely insensible."

If Brown has in the course of his journey become completely insensible, then we might say that there is no one, in the sense of a conscious being, in the box. While he is no longer a slave, as a fugitive in the box he cannot be a subject. There is barely room for his body in the box; the box is the smallest space in which his body may persist as body, while at the same time being excluded from the regularized spaces of society. When his box arrives in Philadelphia, the friends who receive it are uncertain whether they will find their cargo alive or dead. Brown recalls, "I heard a man say, 'let us rap upon the box and see if he is alive,' and immediately a rap ensued and a voice said, tremblingly, 'Is all right within?' To which I replied, 'all right'" (ibid.: 56). The phrasing of the question of Brown's status is peculiar, in so far as it is not addressed to Brown, the only one who might be able to answer. If Brown were suddenly to burst through the door, rather than arriving ensconced in a box, one might imagine the question to be, rather, "are you all right?" But the interposition of the box unhinges the relation of identity between Brown, his well-being, and the contents of the box. Brown is split between the one who answers, in effect, "yes, all is right within," and the one who is "all right."

Perhaps it might be more accurate to say that Brown is "fractured" or "shattered" by the box. By "shattering," I mean to suggest that the intervention of the box does not produce or reveal the "split subject" conventionally described as the dialectical splitting internal to a self-conscious subjectivity, that is, the split in "I am" between the one speaking and the one being spoken. The shattering of Brown in the box is not the enactment of a splitting of subjectivity which is (in a Hegelian or Lacanian sense) constitutive of subjectivity itself. Rather, this apparent splitting is of a particular sort, symptomatic of the status of the fugitive, or the space of the box as outside the order of master and slave: there is "no one" to whom to address a question, no subject, insofar as subjectivity is assigned and ordered by the categories of master and slave, to hear or to respond. Hence, the impossibility of addressing the question of well-being to its object.

The suspension of subject and object, of sensate man or insensate matter, is resolved in Brown's response, "all right." Not only is he "all right" having survived his ordeal, but all is made right in his simultaneous return to the social order: his friends break open the box on hearing his voice, and he "rose a free man." Emerging from the box, Brown is not only "resurrecting from the grave of slavery," he is equally returning to the realm of subjectivity. What he is in the box is unclear and ambiguous; what he is when he emerges from the box is unequivocal: a free man. The box is a space outside, extruded by and excluded from the space of the social. It is only from the perspective of the box that one recognizes the limits of subjectivity marked out by the relation of slavery. The box is a bounded space which, by being excluded from it, marks the constructedness and boundedness of the space of the social and the subject, which would otherwise appear simply as neutral, natural, and static. When Brown rises from the box he is a "free man"; but the appearance of Brown in the box remains puzzling. In the box, he is not a subject, nor is he free, and yet he is somehow escaped from slavery. Brown's fugitivity is not the same thing as freedom, and yet it bears some relation to freedom. There where there is no subject, can there be freedom? and what sort of freedom would it be? The possibility of freedom, and the relation of freedom to fugitivity, is a central concern in the last slave narrative I want to consider, that of Harriet Jacobs.

Harriet Jacobs's *Incidents in the Life of a Slave Girl, Written by Herself* (1861) now holds pride of place as perhaps the most widely read piece of nineteenth-century American literature written by a woman. Since speculations that it was in fact a sentimental novel written by white abolitionist Lydia Marie Childs were finally put to rest in 1981 by Jean Yellin's publication of Jacobs's newly discovered correspondence, readers have viewed the narrative as exemplifying a specifically textual strategy of resistance and subversion that creates a powerful voice for the black woman from within the discursive constraints that have rendered her invisible. But Jacobs is far more equivocal about her "empowerment" than her contemporary readers seem to acknowledge. Carla Kaplan (1993: 103) has suggested that to insist on Jacobs's textual triumph over her oppressors is to miss the point of the story: "Jacobs is at great pains to dramatize Brent's *inability* to 'subvert' her status, 'assault' her master's domination, wage 'effective' combat, or 'reverse' the power structures which bind her. This is the lived meaning of slavery for Linda Brent. It is this narrative's strongest indictment." Although

Incidents conforms overall to the teleological structure of slave narrative which documents the transformational development from slave to free, Jacobs's circumspection over the possibilities of power or freedom as defined within the terms of the self-possessed individual opens a space within the narrative for a more critical examination of what freedom might mean.

Jacobs's narrative, like Douglass's, ends with freedom. Yet the relation of each to that freedom is markedly different. For Douglass the transformation is absolute and unequivocal: "I was now my own master. . . . It was to me the starting point of a new existence" (Douglass [1845]1987: 150). Jacobs too is free, but her nominal freedom is in fact severely constrained by her continued servitude: "The dream of my life is not yet realized. I do not sit with my children in a home of my own. . . . God so orders circumstances as to keep me with my friend Mrs. Bruce. Love, duty, gratitude also bind me to her side" (Jacobs [1861] 1987: 513). Legal freedom notwithstanding, the promises of possession and self-possession continue to prove elusive for Jacobs. Within the context of a liberal polity founded on principles of property right, it is only as a propertied subject that Jacobs has any hope of rights, protections, or the future that she dreams of ("a hearthstone of my own, however humble": 513). But as a woman and a former slave, such self-possession is deeply compromised. Jacobs's story ends with a freedom marred by the price at which it has been attained, the "bill of sale" that redistributes property and person such that Jacobs's freedom is in fact legally attained as a result of her friend Mrs. Bruce's purchase of her. Mrs. Bruce's insistence that she has paid for Jacobs not to own her, but to free her, offers only a little comfort. Jacobs's dismay at her bought freedom raises the question Douglass necessarily suppresses: Where would a freedom not liable to the threat of purchase lie, and what would it look like? Douglass attempts to neutralize the ambivalence of the freedom available to him as self-possessed subject by availing himself of the power of Enlightenment rhetoric. In contrast, Jacobs insists on the gap between the rhetoric of freedom and its material reality; able to suspend faith in the liberatory promise of the self-possessed subject, Jacobs goes much farther in exploring the limits, boundaries, and exclusions of the order based on property and contract. The persistence of the problem of property as the determinant of personhood in the last pages of Jacobs's narrative suggests that another freedom must escape this insidious economy.

Such an escape is indeed figured in Jacobs's narrative in what she describes as a "loophole of retreat," which is not a flight to the freedom of the north (the freedom of the self-possessed "free man"), but a withdrawal into a space that is simultaneously inside and outside of the economy of slavery. Others have remarked on the multiple valencies of the "loophole" in this narrative as a means of escape: from slavery, from the power and exploitation of Flint and Sands. These readers discover Jacobs's freedom in confinement, concealment, and the power to see and act without being detected.[4] But the nature of this loophole, and its peculiar relation to the economy of slavery and subjectivity, make such a univocal reading difficult to sustain, not simply because Jacobs's experience in the garret is also restricted, constrained, or vulnerable, but because what counts as subjective agency is determined in a way that absolutely excludes the space marked out by the garret, such that the "freedom" of the garret is purchased at the price of the loss of the self. In relation to the constitution of the subject, the space of the garret is not similar to but separate from the space of slavery. The force of slavery depends on its totalizing colonization of every space and every body: either thing or subject, either slave or free. My emphasis on the loophole, rather than on Jacobs's figurations of either slavery or freedom, is intended to emphasize this "colonization" as the production, rather than merely the parcelling out, of space. The separation of places of work and habitation assigned to slave and free populations, the regulations governing modes of movement in public places and thoroughfares, the continual surveillance of the enslaved and the refusal of any space of privacy or retreat were all mechanisms to enforce through spatial practices the fundamental opposition between the wilful person of the master and the will-less property that is the slave. In contrast, the space of the garret is invisible, unsurveilled, unregulated. It is excluded by the space of slavery, and this very exclusion marks the limits of slavery's totalizing premise of opposition between person and property.

Jacobs's retreat to the garret emerges in the narrative as a solution to the inherent contradiction between her disposition as property by Mr. Flint, and the ties of love and responsibility that she maintains with her extended family despite the master's efforts to prevent it. Jacobs's continued sexual victimization and vulnerability make her desperate to escape from her lascivious master, but her solution is not the autonomous flight of Douglass or Brown. Rather, she disappears from Flint by going into hiding. This disappearance seems her best chance; his ongoing and obsessive search for his escaped "Linda," his insistence that he will get her back no matter what the cost, and his refusal even to accept payment for her freedom, make it clear that there is no safe place beyond his reach to which to escape. Even if she could find her way north, she would constantly be hounded by his pursuit; and the likelihood of success of such an attempt is further diminished by the fact that he effectively blocks every exit by which she might flee to a place of freedom. Thus, in lieu of flight, Jacobs's family finds a way to secrete her in its innermost heart. Jacobs lives for seven years in the attic of a small shed in her grandmother's yard. The space is hardly fit for habitation:

> Some boards were laid across the joists at the top [of the shed], and between these boards and the roof was a very small garret, never occupied by any thing but rats and mice. It was a pent roof, covered with nothing but shingles, according to the southern custom for such buildings. The garret was only nine feet long and seven wide. The

> highest part was three feet high, and sloped down abruptly to the loose board floor. There was no admission for either light or air.
>
> (Jacobs [1861] 1987: 437)

Jacobs calls this space, in a chapter heading, her "loophole of retreat."[5] The figurative use of the term "loophole," meaning "an outlet or means of escape," is never far off. In her garret Jacobs has effected an escape without going anywhere, as if the surface of slavery looped back on itself and created a little pocket where Jacobs can be *in*, but not a part of, the goings on of her community. It is, in fact, precisely because she is not anywhere within slavery, but in a pocket outside or alongside slavery, that her safety is guaranteed. Even when she sees Dr. Flint on the street outside, just a few feet away, she feels safe from his reach: "Had the least suspicion rested on my grandmother's house, it would have been burned to the ground. But it was the last place they thought of. Yet there was no place, where slavery existed, that could have afforded me so good a place of concealment" (440). The ambiguity of the syntax of this last sentence is suggestive. On the one hand, it might read: here where slavery existed, there was no other place that could have afforded so good a place of concealment. But the sentence might equally be read: there was no place at all in those places where slavery existed that could have afforded so good a place of concealment; and therefore by implication, this place of concealment is not where slavery exists. The loophole of retreat has shifted into an "elsewhere" where slavery does not exist.

Is this loophole, as Burnham (1993) and others would have it, a "site of resistance"? I must confess that it is difficult for me to see it in such a positive light. The "elsewhere" of the loophole is not an actual place where Jacobs might safely live beyond the reach of slavery. It is at great physical and mental cost that she remains in the garret. Jacobs's descriptions of her experience are punctuated by the progressive atrophy and deterioration of her body. The lack of air, the lack of space, and the ravages of the seasons make her constantly conscious of her body and its continual discomfort. During her second winter in the garret, she comes close to dying: "I had a very painful sensation of coldness in my head; even my face and tongue stiffened, and I lost the power of speech. . . . [My brother] thought I was dying, for I had been in an unconscious state sixteen hours" (444). The deprivation of air, space, and finally consciousness itself is the price of removing herself from the economy of master and slave. The "elsewhere" of the loophole of retreat is an elsewhere nobody, no *body*, can inhabit for long. If the loophole is an escape, it is not a triumph. Jacobs as fugitive cannot be reduced to property, but neither can she be availed of the securities of person. Jacobs as fugitive is, from the totalizing perspective of slavery, "no thing" and "no one."

Jacobs's safety in the loophole is predicated on her exclusion from the social; the condition of her security is simultaneously the absolute deprivation of freedom. The unsustainability of this paradoxical circumstance marks the limits of a reading that would interpret her efforts to deflect Flint's attention as a reversal in the power relations between Flint and herself. If we view the loophole as merely reversing the relation between slave and master, we miss the implications of the loophole as a (non-)place outside slavery and master. This outside is not freedom; in the no place of the loophole, there is no subject, and therefore there can be no freedom. But to say that there is "no one" in the space of fugitivity is not to say that nothing can happen. Jacobs is able to remain secure in this liminal space by effecting ruses that deflect Flint's attention. This activity does not reverse the power between master and slave; rather, it works to secure and maintain the garret as a space apart from mastery and slavery.

The circumstance of Jacobs's body in the loophole reinforces the significance of property in the determination of the subject. In her "loophole," Jacobs is neither slave nor free, neither embodying the property of another nor possessing property in herself. She does not become free simply by withdrawing from slavery; rather, she must be reinserted into the economy of property, first as purchased (by Mrs. Burns) then subsequently as potential purchaser (of a hearth of her own). Freedom is as much a problem as it is a solution at the conclusion of her narrative; that the promise of freedom in property might fail Jacobs leaves open the question of whether this is the only possible freedom. As Carla Kaplan (1993: 116) notes, it is this failure that makes of the narrative an implicit call for political intervention: "Although Brent does eventually get out of her miserable attic hideaway, Jacobs does not escape the impasse this narrative so brilliantly renders. And that is the narrative's point. Her inability to do so makes further – or future – action on our behalf necessary." The future action which slave narrative seemed to call for in its own day was the end to slavery, an action wrenchingly achieved. Yet that cannot be the end, just as Jacobs insists that her freedom from slavery cannot be the end of her own story. The future of freedom is not only Jacobs's nineteenth-century future, it is our future as well. Jacobs's ambivalence in the last pages of her narrative suggests that freedom's future is as yet unknown, calling for further, and future, action.

Fugitivity, as embodied in the figures of Brown in the box or Jacobs in the garret, painfully exposes both the limits of the discursive order of property and person, and the agonizing effects of any attempt to evade or surpass these orders. The self-possessed individual is an ideological fiction, true – but a fiction of sufficient power to enforce its "naturalness" through the more-than-systematic violence that exposes the bodies of Brown and Jacobs to their corporeal limits. Reading the corporeal topography of the space of fugitivity, one becomes increasingly sceptical of the blithe, celebratory invocations of the subversive powers of boundary crossing, nomadism, or excess – all figures that *might* be mobilized to describe the space of fugitivity. The fugitive body exposes, in fact embodies, the violence necessary to preserve order, hierarchy, boundedness, propriety, and property. Thus, the fugitive body cannot simply be read as a force "from the outside" – and if it is a potential or actual source of destabilization or subversion, these possibilities must be carefully thought in and through the displaced and exposed body of the fugitive.

Notes

1 Even slaves able to earn or acquire enough money were often bitterly disappointed when masters took their money and refused to honor the agreement. As Stampp (1956: 197) notes, a slave "could not be a party to a contract. No promise of freedom, oral or written, was binding upon his master." Since legally both the slave's labor and the slave's money belonged to the master, the courts would not recognize as binding any arrangement exchanging the one for the other.

2 See Ransom (1990) for an extended analysis of the relation of the demand for slaves to the price of slaves in the open market.

3 The name of the company that shipped Brown's box was "Adam's Express."

4 See especially Burnham, (1993); Smith (1990).

5 For an extended analysis of the history of the term "loophole," and speculation on Jacobs's possible sources for the reference, see Burnham (1993).

References

Brown, Henry (1849). *The Narrative of Henry Box Brown, Who Escaped from Slavery Enclosed in a Box Three Feet Long, Two Feet Wide, and Two-and-a-Half Feet High, Written from a Statement of Facts Made by Himself. With Remarks upon the Remedy for Slavery. By Charles Stearns.* Boston: Brown and Stearns.

—— (1852). *Narrative of the Life of Henry Box Brown, Written by Himself.* 2nd edn. Boston: Samuel Webb.

Burnham, Michelle (1993). "Loopholes of Resistance: Harriet Jacobs' Slave Narrative and the Critique of Agency in Foucault." *Arizona Quarterly* 49.2: 53–73.

Douglass, Frederick ([1845] 1986). *Narrative of the Life of Frederick Douglass, An American Slave, Written by Himself.* Ed. Houston Baker Jr. New York: Penguin.

Genovese, Eugene (1974). *Roll, Jordan, Roll: The World the Slaves Made.* New York: Pantheon.

Jacobs, Harriet ([1861] 1987). *Incidents in the Life of a Slave Girl, Written by Herself, Linda Brent.* Reprinted in *The Classic Slave Narratives.* Ed. Henry Louis Gates Jr. New York: New American Library.

Kaplan, Carla (1993). "Narrative Contracts and Emancipatory Readers: *Incidents in the Life of a Slave Girl.*" *Yale Journal of Criticism* 6.1: 93–119.

Ransom, Roger L. (1990). *Conflict and Compromise: The Political Economy of Slavery, Emancipation, and the American Civil War.* New York: Cambridge University Press.

Siegert, Bernhard (forthcoming). *Relais: Literature as an Epoch of the Postal Service.* Trans. Kevin Repp. Stanford, CA: Stanford University Press.

Smith, Valerie (1990). "'Loopholes of Retreat': Architecture and Ideology in Harriet Jacobs's *Incidents in the Life of a Slave Girl.*" In *Reading Black, Reading Feminist: A Critical Anthology.* Ed. Henry Louis Gates Jr. New York: Penguin, 212–26.

Stampp, Kenneth (1956). *The Peculiar Institution: Slavery in the Ante-Bellum South*. New York: Knopf.

Starling, Marion Wilson (1988). *The Slave Narrative: Its Place in American History*. 2nd edn. Washington, DC: Howard University Press.

Part V

ECONOMIES OF AUTHORSHIP

15

"A TASTE FOR MORE"

Trollope's addictive realism

Christina Crosby

Reading Anthony Trollope, especially his *Autobiography*, involves an exercise in enumeration. Following his own practice in that book, one can list his forty-seven novels, most of them in three volumes, and his sixteen other books; one may note that his sales sometimes topped 100,000; or count the words (425,000) of *The Way We Live Now*, "probably the longest of his works" (Sutherland 1982: vii). In *An Autobiography* one discovers the exact sum he received for each book published, and is given the grand total, down to the penny, that he earned from those books – £68,939.17.5; and there, too, one reads an account of his mode of production, written he says, "for the benefit of those who may read these pages, and when young may intend to follow the same career" (Trollope [1883]: 1947: 303): to rise every morning in whatever circumstance at 5:30 and to work for three hours; more precisely, after reading over what had been written the day before, "to write with my watch before me, and to require from myself 250 words every quarter of an hour," thus "produc[ing] over ten pages of an ordinary novel volume a day" (227–28). This general scheme is further specified:

> According to the circumstances of the time, – whether my other business might be then heavy or light, or whether the book which I was writing was or was not wanted with speed, – I have allotted myself so many pages a week. The average number has been about 40. It has been placed as low as 20, and has risen to 112. And as a page is an ambiguous term, my page has been made to contain 250 words; and as words, if not watched, will have a tendency to straggle, I have had every word counted as I went.
>
> (Ibid.: 101)

Among those who read Trollope's words these days are academic critics, writers themselves, who cannot fail to be struck by the sheer quantity of his work: 250 words every fifteen minutes! As remarkable, perhaps, is the pleasure Trollope took in writing under such circumstances, for this is writing under compulsion, one might even say addictive writing. "I was moved . . . by a determination to excel, if not in quality, at any rate in quantity," Trollope declares (103). He delights in quantity, which is, of course, illimitable. Thus Trollope is compelled morning after morning to rise before dawn and write with his watch before him; he can never be satisfied, however pleased he may be with his day's work, for the morrow must see him again at his desk.

An Autobiography recounts how Trollope did in fact excel, not only in producing an extraordinary number of books, but in selling his books to his publishers for substantial sums. He gained also a substantial audience. As the powerful critic E.S. Dallas observes in *The Times* for 23 May 1859: "He writes faster than we can read, and the more the pensive public reads the more does it desire to read" (quoted in Smalley 1969: 103). The more Trollope writes, the more he wants to write; the more readers read, the more they desire to read. Readers, it seems, are addicted to reading Trollope, as he is addicted to writing. They can't get enough.

Trollope's writing, then, especially his writing about writing in his *Autobiography*, opens a series of questions about desire and repetition, pleasure and compulsion, and the quality of quantity. For if Trollope is in some sense addicted to writing, he is by no means tormented by his compulsion but rather delights in writing under what he calls "hot pressure." If addiction entails the infinite deferral of satisfaction while inducing intensities of desire and pleasure, Trollope makes that very deferral enjoyable – for himself and for his readers. The particular quality of the Trollopian text is precisely an effect of sheer quantity.

The pleasurable quality of quantity, of deferral, of desire and repetition distinguishes Trollope's work as specifically modern, as part of a world in which quantity counts as never before. While in this essay I can only approach, not account for, the larger dimensions of quantification, I wish to gesture towards developments contemporaneous with Trollope's success: the extraordinarily fast and comprehensive growth of financial credit in the latter half of the nineteenth century, and the hot pressure of an economy dependent on continual expansion. The years of Trollope's unparalleled production are the years when Britain moved with surprising rapidity from an economy based on money to one based on credit; from trade based on the direct exchange of gold sovereigns for goods to a complex system of notes, bills of exchange, bank deposits, checks, and stocks; from unlimited liability, which restricted access to investment, to limited liability, which opened the stock market to anyone with a few pounds to risk. Credit enables one to get (money or commodities) now and pay (more) later; it is a structure of deferral in which individuals, firms, and corporations find themselves increasingly involved, getting more and owing more, renewing bills, deferring payment, over and over, credit pyramiding as the economy expands. Credit is addictive: enterprise expands, and more and more is needed; once you have it, you can't do without it. As Walter Bagehot (1873: 15, 17) declares in his 1873 book on the money market: "English trade is become essentially a trade on borrowed capital, and . . . it is only by this refinement of our banking system that we are able to do the sort of trade we do, or to get through the quantity of it."

Trollope, who (as we will see) imagines writing to be like any other trade, elaborates in literature the logic of "never enough" that keeps him writing and keeps readers reading. He is one of the first and most successful to do so, and still has a hold on readers; his most recent biographer concludes her study by declaring that "[n]ever before, even in his lifetime, have Trollope's books been so well published, so readily available, or so much in demand" (Glendinning 1993: 530). I would speculate further that Trollopian writing, the elements of which I will sketch, has helped to create the demand for narrative which is such a distinctive part of modernity. From Trollope's *oeuvre* one can move to the endlessly repetitive and endlessly enjoyable narratives of TV – the sports games which are always the same and always different, the mini-series which are always familiar yet always new, and so on. While the endless deferrals and "derealizations" of modernity have both an economic and a literary specificity, reading Trollope may help to suggest that writing cannot be abstracted from the economic, any more than the economic can be abstracted from writing.

Because quantity presses so inexorably on readers of Trollope, and because quantity is so celebrated by the author in his *Autobiography*, one is brought inevitably to the matter that he himself poses at the close of that book: the relation between quantity and quality. In a characteristic rhetorical turn he writes: "it will not, I am sure, be thought that, in making my boast as to quantity, I have endeavoured to lay claim to any literary excellence. That, in the writing of books, quantity without quality is a vice and a misfortune, has been too manifestly settled to leave a doubt on such a matter. But I do lay claim to whatever merit should be accorded to me for persevering diligence in my profession" (Trollope [1883] 1947: 303). That turn, the most common trope of the *Autobiography*, is a litotes. For in reading Trollope one does indeed think that the boast as to quantity, made so repeatedly and insistently, is a claim for quality, and "persevering diligence" appears to be inseparable from literary excellence. This is a fine example of the trope of diminution: by depreciating his writing through understatement, Trollope rhetorically enhances its value, giving energy and weight to the idea that quantity and quality, far from being contraries, are in fact the same.[1] Quantity *is* quality, and, moreover, he imagines that literary excellence is precisely the result of his mode of producing literature – a page every quarter hour, three hours a day.

This valorization of his writing is even more striking coming as it does directly below the list of all his books, their dates of publication, and the "total sums received" for them. Indeed, the rhetoric works to establish an equivalence between the sum total of £70,000 (in today's money, about $3,500,000) and literary value, often thought to be unquantifiable.[2] Trollope assiduously affirms the possibility of such an equivalence. As Fontanier (1969: 134–35) has observed, the legibility of litotes depends on the "tone and circumstances of the discourse" in general, since the trope itself appears in a perfectly ordinary grammatical form. Trollope's discourse is what may be called "maximizing," replete with declarative sentences, simple generalizations about the way the world works, and maxim-like statements. Thus, in his *Autobiography* he advances what he calls his "theory" (88) that "the love of money is so distinctive a characteristic of humanity that . . . sermons [preached against it] are mere platitudes called for by customary but unintelligent piety. All material progress has come from man's desire to do the best he can for himself and those about him, and civilization and Christianity itself have been made possible by such progress. Though we do not all of us argue this matter out within our breasts," he continues, "we do all feel it; and we know that the more a man earns the more useful he is to his fellow men" (89). Implicit is the conclusion that the writer of the best books will have the best income, and Trollope, who intends to honor the claims of the real – as opposed to unintelligent or hypocritical convention – is willing to tell this truth.

His "boast as to quantity," then, figured most boldly in the columns of "total sums received," *is* a boast as to quality, a boast that takes the form of depreciation only to enhance the value of Trollope's texts. Indeed, as Walter Kendrick (1980) has closely argued in *The Novel Machine*, an astute and indefatigable reading of Trollope's autobiography and novels, *An Autobiography* develops a perfectly coherent – and perfectly contradictory – theory of literary excellence that establishes Trollope's own productions as the standard by which any writing should be judged. All of Trollope's writing is artfully devoted to making itself disappear as writing, the better to make reality appear as reality. In the words of Trollope, "I am realistic" (189).

To be more precise, in Chapter 12, "On Novels and the Art of Writing Them," Trollope writes, "Among English novels of the present day, and among English novelists, a great division is made. There are sensational novels and anti-sensational, sensational novelists and anti-sensational, sensational readers and anti-sensational. The novelists who are considered to be anti-sensational are generally called realistic. I am realistic" (189). Here again Trollope's rhetoric of diminuation works to reverse the apparent hierarchy in which sensation sets the standard and realistic representation is secondary and derived, for as the argument develops, sensational novels, novelists, and readers are all sublated into the realistic in that realistic novels are devoted above all to character, and character is everything: "It all lies in that. No novel is anything . . . unless the reader can sympathize with the characters whose names he finds upon the pages. . . . Truth let there be, – truth of description, truth of character, human truth as to men and women. If there be such truth, I do not know that a novel can be too sensational" (191).

The "realistic," then, renders the sensational moot. And the unassailable position of the realistic writer is a position Trollope claims with his "boast as to quantity." Trollope was by no means the only abundant Victorian writer. Thackeray, Eliot, and Dickens – to mention only three canonical authors – rival him in length, but none approaches him in absolute quantity. There he stands alone. As he observes, "my literary performances . . . are more in amount than the works of any other living English author. If any English authors not living have written more . . . I do not know who they are" (301). More in amount, his writings are also more realistic, if we take realistic representation to be that form of writing that most assiduously effaces itself as writing: writing that disavows its specificity as writing, art that denies art. Said by his contemporaries to have a remarkable "facility in reproducing conventional life in all its finest details," said to "picture the society of the day with a fidelity with which society has never been pictured before in the history of the world," said by Henry James to instance a "great apprehension of the real," Trollope's writing effaces itself in order to imagine an equivalence between writing and the world.[3]

Kendrick (1980) shows in detail the irresolvable contradictions of Trollope's theory of literature and literary practice, for there is, of course, no way to do away with writing through writing, and no way to overcome the constitutive contradiction of the logic of equivalence: a logic that cannot do without difference, since without difference there is no necessity for equivalence; a logic that equally must make difference disappear in the process of producing an equivalent form. This contradiction keeps in perpetual motion what Kendrick so aptly calls the novel-machine, Trollope's nonstop production of books: "The ingenious economy of the novel-machine is set in motion by the imposition of the real on the written. Unwritten reality must be writable, even though [as Trollope insists] reality is known by its difference from writing and writing is by nature inadequate to reality. There is no synthesis of these antitheses; they are in perpetual disequilibrium, and Trollope's rhetoric aims only at making them work, not sublimating them" (Kendrick 1980: 84).

The distinctively realistic quality of Trollope's texts, then, is an effect of the novel-machine that produces an immense quantity of writing, all of which rhetorically effaces itself in favor of what is posed as its antithesis, reality. Quantity is of the essence, Trollope declares, for the author who pauses to reflect on his text or dally over the composition is paying attention to the wrong thing: the writing, and not the reality it is to convey. "I believe that the work which has been done quickest has been done the best," Trollope declares of his own novels, and his quickly written realistic writing becomes in the *Autobiography* the standard for all good writing: "When my work has been quicker done, – and it has sometimes been done very quickly – the rapidity has been achieved by hot pressure, not in the conception but in the telling of the story" (147). What is true of novel-writing is equally true of writing official Post Office reports. This tireless author was a civil servant for much of his working life, doing a full day of Post Office business after his early hours writing novels. "I took extreme delight in writing [reports]," Trollope declares, "not allowing myself to re-copy them, never having them re-copied by others, but sending them up with their original blots and erasures, – if blots and erasures there were. It is hardly manly, I think, that a man . . . should not be able to exact from himself the necessity of writing words in the form in which they should be read" (237).

What, one might ask, can be the "extreme delight" in writing memoranda and reports? And where the pleasure in exacting necessity? Reading the *Autobiography*, one comes to see that the delight, oddly enough, has to do with submitting to the demands of time; to master writing one must submit to the real, and reality is conceived to be fully quantifiable. "Hot pressure," writing to meet a deadline, produces writing that is done too rapidly to be tricked out in distracting ornament, too concentrated on the task at hand to lose itself in poetic elaboration, too absorbed by the necessity of conveying what must be said to worry about how to say it. Moreover, the very demands of "hot pressure" indispensable to realist writing also induce intensities of pleasure – "extreme delight" – in the writer. The novel-machine is also a pleasure-machine.

Its pleasures, however, are a bit rigorous, requiring that the writer submit to certain negations and limitations – he is at his table every morning at 5:30 a.m., and "allow[s] [himself] no mercy" (227); he must not eat too much, or drink too much, or smoke too much, for "then his condition may be unfavourable for work" (102); he exacts from himself words in their proper form, "not allowing [himself] to recopy them"; he finds lapses in the schedule of his writing to be "a blister to [his eye]" – all of which positively affirm the priority of something other than writing: a quantifiable, measurable real. The realistic writer takes pleasure in being in thrall to this real, as Trollope's delighted accounts of his methodical discipline suggest, for such thralldom is the way to achieve literary excellence.

It would not be too strong to say that the writer gives himself over to an implacable reality of pure quantity, and that he depends for his pleasure on repeatedly acknowledging its demands. Here we begin to see the elements of addiction characteristic of Trollope's writing practice; like the addict he surrenders to the demands of what gives him pleasure, and like the addict he finds both intensities of delight and the impossibility of satisfaction, for those demands are always renewed. One might say he is "alienated," in the sense that he no longer commands or "owns" himself but is mastered by the real. Trollope, however, unlike the hopeless addict, turns this subjection to his account and makes a virtue of necessity since realistic writing, the only writing that induces extreme delight, the very best writing, issues from submitting to the demands of the real. We will return to the question of addiction, but first let us pause to consider a bit further the advantages that accrue to the happily "alienated" realistic writer.

First, he is able to enjoy the virtue of punctuality. "I have not once," Trollope boasts, "through all my literary career, felt myself even in danger of being late with my task" (102). Punctuality and realistic writing go together; indeed, realistic writing is an effect of punctuality, as may be seen from the negative example of Victor Hugo, neither reliable nor realistic. Trollope recounts how he was asked by an editor to give way to "one of Victor Hugo's modern novels," scheduled to appear earlier in a certain periodical, but because of Hugo's failure to deliver on time, now conflicting with the novel Trollope had supplied not only on time, but ahead of time:

> My disgust at this proposition was, I think, chiefly due to Victor Hugo's latter novels, which I regard as pretentious and untrue to nature. To this perhaps was added some feeling of indignation that I should be asked to give way to a Frenchman. The Frenchman had broken his engagement. He had failed to have his work finished by the stipulated time. From week to week and from month to month he had put off the fulfillment of his duty. And because of these laches on his part, – on the part of this sententious French Radical, – I was to be thrown over!
>
> (Ibid.: 272)

Foreign and weak, given to exaggerated moralizing, indolent and unrealistic, Hugo and his failings only emphasize Trollope's successes. Realistic writing, which is to say the only writing Trollope declares to be free of falsification, artifice, and pretense, is writing done with a watch before one and a schedule to be kept. Only under these conditions does reality impose itself with sufficient force to restrain the writer from poetic flights and self-righteous moralizing.

The same logic governs Trollope's famous (or infamous) assertion that an author is no different from a shoemaker or any other workman. When reviewing his career in his *Autobiography* he declares: "I had long since convinced myself that in such work as mine the great secret consisted in acknowledging myself to be bound to rules of labour similar to those which an artisan or a mechanic is forced to obey" (268). In his characteristic mode of (self-valorizing) self-deprecation he writes: "A shoemaker when he has finished one pair of shoes does not sit down and contemplate his work in idle satisfaction. . . . The shoemaker who so indulged himself would be without wages half his time. It is the same with a professional writer of books. . . . I had now quite accustomed myself to begin a second pair as soon as the first was out of my hands" (265). Both writer and shoemaker must work to be paid, and wages are, of course, calculated on the basis of time spent; a quarter of an hour cobbling or a quarter of an hour writing is the same fifteen minutes. This sameness is so important to Trollope because it can save the writer from the dangerous seductions of writing; it can protect him from indulging in poetic phrase-making at the expense of the reality he wishes to picture. Trollope abstracts writing by making it rhetorically equivalent to shoemaking, and in so doing imagines he makes writing more concretely real. The writer, no less than any other workman, is bound to rules of labor that "alienate" him from writing as writing, and bind him to what he imagines to be the real: a set period of time, a certain quantity produced.

The realistic writer delights in this alienation that denies writing its specificity so as to grant it value as the equivalent of the real. On this point, Henry James is a most astute reader of Trollope, his acuity enhanced by his very distaste for Trollopian realism and his championing of a different sort of novel – what one might call "idealist" rather than realist writing.[4] James caustically observes of one of Trollope's mid-1860s novels that it is "a *stupid* book; and in a much deeper sense than of being simply dull. . . . A dull book is a failure. Mr. Trollope's story is stupid and a success. It is essentially, organically, consistently stupid; stupid in direct proportion to its strength. It is without a single idea" (quoted in Smalley 1969: 257–58). Exactly, for the realist writer must make himself and his ideas disappear along with writing as writing; what remains should have a form directly equivalent to a calculable reality. This is what James calls stupidity: writing that is no different from what it represents. "That [the novel] should deal exclusively with dull, flat, commonplace people was to be expected," James allows, "and this need not be a fault; but it deals with such people as one of themselves, and this is . . . a 'damning' fault" (ibid.: 258). Trollope, however, is dedicated to such a disappearance of difference; he aspires to be one with his characters, and with his readers. This is the oneness of a reality unmediated by writing. James says Trollope's writing is "without a single idea," but will not grant Trollope the idea that informs all of his writing. The idea is the realist ideal, namely, that writing take the form of appearance of the real. Trollope is thus deeply interested in writing that deals with people as "one of themselves," writing that is as organically "stupid" as the real itself.

The success of realist writing rests, then, on what Philippe Hamon (1992: 173) has called the "marked redundancy and foreseeability of its content," the notable size of many realistic novels devolving in part from the necessity of "concretizing" character, for example, by describing the "physical sphere of activity" (place of business, church, House of Commons, dining room or drawing room) and detailing the appropriate activities (transacting business, conducting a service, making a speech, giving a dinner, entertaining guests), with the inert objects and familiar functions of these places and activities. As the *National Review* observed of Trollope early in his career, his novels show "an appreciation of minutiae which enable him always to assign to his characters of every class their fitting costume, language, and mode of mind" (quoted in Smalley 1969: 83). These are not the portentous details of sensational writing, but the redundant details of the realistic text. Similarly, the "predilection for all the *ritualised* activities of daily life" that are repeated from day to day in a sequence already known marks realist writing; from one Trollope novel to the next we sit through family breakfasts, dinner parties, and official banquets, attend political functions (Trollope is particularly fond of the House of Commons with its invariable rules of order), travel by train (adhering to a timetable), go fox-hunting (following the rules of the sport), and so on. Foreseeable and redundant, bound to sequential repetition, realistic writing is also characterized by what Hamon calls "detonalization" and "demodalization"; that is, the narrator asserts and describes, and does not italicize, qualify, hesitate, or give way to euphoria (175). Trollope is eminently declarative. If, for instance, a character is to fall in love, for Trollope it suffices to declare the fact. The novel will proceed on that basis with no further ado, with its quotidian rituals and rule-bound events advancing or retarding the love interest. Moreover, his writing is replete with clichés, not only the clichéd language that marks the speeches of the characters, but the clichés of the narrator, all of which admit the limitations of language in order to advance the claims of the real.[5] He is formulaic.

He is thus a most credible author, as the *Saturday Review* is ready to declare in 1862: "Trollope . . . gives almost always a shilling's worth of story for our money. He does not make us pay the discount of philosophical reflections, or reflections of his own mental state" (quoted in Smalley 1969: 144).[6] To be "trustworthy," as even James grants he is, Trollope must eschew the opportunity to enrich himself at the expense of his readers or of the real; to be credible he must not get more than he gives, but rather deal in direct and immediate equivalents: writing = reality. His writing must be, to revert to James's formulation, as stupid as the real itself.

Yet as I have suggested, this devotion to the real is an ideal, however poor in philosophical reflections or psychological cogitations the text seems to be. To recall the words of E.S. Dallas, "the more the pensive public reads the more does it desire to read" (quoted in ibid.: 103). As his irony suggests, there is no time to be pensive, no time to be lost in thought any more for the reader than the writer. Both need more, more writing, to ensure that reality is recognizably real. Empty of "ideas," the novels are full to repletion of the forms of "conventional life." A Trollope novel gives immediate and absorbing pleasure, but when one is finished reading, the pleasure, which is in the immediacy of the reading and not in reflection, fades. To renew it, one must read another, and another.

When Trollope writes of himself as a reader in the *Autobiography*, he turns again to litotes, devaluing ideas and valorizing "something dim and inaccurate," a desire that defies satisfaction. And he ascribes this desire to "most readers" – which in the logic of understatement may be understood to mean all readers:

> For what remains to me of life I trust for my happiness still chiefly to my work . . . secondly, to the love of those who love me; and then

> to my books. That I can read and be happy while I am reading is a great blessing. Could I remember, as some men do, what I read, I should have been able to call myself an educated man. But that power I have never possessed. Something is always left, – something dim and inaccurate, – but still something sufficient to preserve the taste for more. I am inclined to think that it is so with most readers.
>
> (Trollope [1883] 1947: 305)

Both writing and reading are motivated by a lack, the dim and inaccurate something that leaves one unsatisfied and wanting more. This lack comes to be more valued than education or ideas, which turn out to be the end of reading and writing. Just as the realist writer, driven by illimitable quantity, has come to be the best writer in the course of the *Autobiography*, the perpetually dissatisfied reader whose happiness in reading must always be renewed and who anticipates the next book rather than meditating on books past, becomes the best reader.

The realist writer delights in "hot pressure," and his pleasure depends on submitting to the demands of quantity: as soon as one piece of writing is done he begins another; the more he writes, the more he desires to write. And the same is true of readers. Trollope's writing and his writing about writing, not to mention the readers who keep coming back for more, suggest a modern complex of writing/reading/addiction, the pleasures of which are structured by the particular logic of quantity.

Addiction is partly a matter of quantity: one time, even two or three is not enough; one drink, or two, one or two cigarettes, one or two books, is not enough. There has to be more, and the desire for more, but more is never enough. Writing of the modern phenomenon of drug addiction, Derrida (1993) observes that it necessarily involves "the crossing of a quantitative threshold."[7] Surely one can say that Trollope crossed a quantitative threshold not only in his *oeuvre*, but even more importantly in his compulsion to calculate, list, and sum up. Yet more than individual compulsion is necessary for addiction. What Derrida calls "the techno-economical transformations of the market-place, transportation, international communications, etc." must also be in place, quantitative matters as well, to be sure, but on a national and international scale. In *The Long Revolution* Raymond Williams (1961) shows in precise detail the transformations of politics, industry, and culture that distinguish modernity in Britain. In the nineteenth century publishing is fully revolutionized: it is capitalized with stock offerings; advertising drives an expansion of the market, bringing in both funds and readers; production is industrialized; circulating libraries and bookstalls in railway stations make books available as never before.[8] The desire of the "pensive public" for more and more Trollope is an effect in part of these transformations, as is indeed that public itself.

Yet the industrialization and capitalization of publishing, however important, do not in themselves account for the delights writing held for Trollope, nor for the fact that the more the public reads of his writing, the more it desires to read. One needs also to bear in mind the workings of addiction. An addict is one who is enslaved, as is suggested by the etymology of the word: "Latin *addictus*, 'given over,' one awarded to another as a slave . . . *ad-* + *dicere*, to say, pronounce, adjudge" (*American Heritage Dictionary* 1978: 15). "Given over," an addict belongs to someone or something other than oneself, which is to say one is bound to another. One is dictated to.

What could be more delightful to a writer? The words just come. Trollope writes with his watch before him, and finds that "250 words have been forthcoming [every quarter hour] as regularly as my watch went" (Trollope [1883] 1947: 228). Happy man! It would seem that he is inspired, and indeed as Derrida observes, addiction and inspiration are part of literary modernity: not only the introduction of coffee and tobacco – and thus the literary culture of coffee houses so significant in the eighteenth century – but the ingestion of these addictive substances, and many others (alcohol, opium, and heroin come to mind), by writers who desire to be "alienated" from the ordinary, taken out of themselves; to be beside themselves with creativity and spoken to by the gods; to be bound over so as to be emancipated from the constraints of the mundane. Trollope admits to the coffee – his servant brought it to him every morning when he called him from his bed – but punctual and trustworthy workman that he is, he is disdainful of any talk of inspiration:

> There are those . . . who think that the man who works with his imagination should allow himself to wait till – inspiration moves him. When I have heard such doctrine preached, I have hardly been able to repress my scorn. To me it would not be more absurd if the shoemaker were to wait for inspiration, or the tallow-chandler for the divine moment of melting. If the man whose business it is to write has eaten too many good things, or has drunk too much, or smoked too many cigars . . . then his condition may be unfavourable for work; but so will be the condition of the shoemaker who has been similarly imprudent.
>
> (Ibid.: 102)

"*Mens sana in corpore sano*," a healthy mind in a healthy body. Such is Trollope's motto, hardly the words of a writer dependent on wine or tobacco, or anything else, including inspiration. The words that are so regularly forthcoming when Trollope works are the product not of an alienating stimulation, but of his own labor.

Yet Trollope is no less caught up by the structure of addiction. The man who trusts for his happiness chiefly to his work "bind[s] [himself] by certain self-imposed laws," the binding being no less compelling because self-imposed. For Trollope, writing induces "extreme delight," yet this intensity of pleasure is only to be experienced when writing under pressure. Moreover, if Trollope is dictated to by the demands of the real, "the real" has also already been said to be measurable and quantifiable: so many hours of work, so many pages, so many books, so much money. Quantity dictates reality, and reality dictates to the writer. A doubling, originary alienation thus structures writing for Trollope. "I finished on Thursday the novel I was writing," he told his son in 1880, "and on Friday I began another. Nothing really frightens me but the idea of forced idleness. As long as I can write books, even though they be not published, I think that I can be happy" (Glendinning 1993: 488). Trollope is addicted to quantity, afraid only when he thinks that he might be forced to give up adding to his list of books. He has always a taste for more.

The desire for more keeps Trollope writing and equally keeps his readers reading, and its compulsive quality ensures that nothing will change; the compulsion is to repeat.[9] You know what you are getting when you buy a Trollope novel, and that's what you want, but one, it seems, is not enough. The very qualities of the text that make it familiar, even boring, incite a desire for more maximized familiarity. Trollope's novels enthrall with the charm of the obvious, but obviousness itself must be continually renewed.

Trollope is addicted to his work and readers are addicted to his *oeuvre*; both author and readers are caught up in the endlessness of the obvious. More than other modes of literature, perhaps, Trollopian realism impresses on one the necessity of credibility, and suggests how expansive is the production of belief in the real. This credit must be continually extended. Trollope, without seeming to exact from his readers any discount, nonetheless produces writing that keeps one coming back to be renewed. Enthralled by, in thrall to, the obvious, we have always the taste for more.

Notes

1 Litotes is defined by Fontanier (1969: 133): "Litotes, also called understatement, . . . in place of positively affirming a thing, denies completely the contrary thing, or diminishes it more or less, with the intent of giving more energy and weight to the positive affirmation that it disguises."

2 This figure is based on an estimate of pounds to contemporary dollars found in Pool (1993: 21): £1 = $50. This is the middle of three estimates, the low being $20, the high $200, all surrounded by caveats about the difficulty, even impossibility, of making such comparisons between value in the Victorian economy and value today.

3 Quoted in Smalley 1969: 410, 508, 530.

4 For a brilliant, wide-ranging, and subtle reading of the competing logics of idealism and realism in nineteenth-century French literature and culture, see Schor 1993.

5 Kendrick (1980: 67–71) offers an excellent analysis, which I follow here, of Trollope's use of clichés.

6 In nineteenth-century usage "discount" had "reference to the buying and selling of bills of exchange by moneylenders and bill brokers. On the one hand, it referred to the practice of buying a bill at a discount, i.e., a moneylender or bill broker purchased a bill from a creditor before it was due to be paid, giving the creditor less money than he would have received when it was finally due, this difference being the 'discount.' Alternatively, the practice referred to a debtor trying to raise money by writing out a bill directly to the moneylender – only for more than the amount which the moneylender actually gave him" (as glossed in Pool 1993: 298).

7 An "ample supply" must be available, which entails a certain scale of production and distribution; as for consumption, "the technical possibility for an individual to reproduce the act, even when alone" must also be in place (Derrida 1993: 5).

8 Of particular interest are the chapters "The Growth of the Reading Public" and "The Growth of the Popular Press" in *The Long Revolution* (Williams 1961).

9 One might cite Theodore de Banville writing on the demanding pleasures of cigarettes: "the cigarette, which is the most imperious, the most engaging, the most loving, the most refined of mistresses, tolerates nothing which is not her, and compromises with nothing: it [*elle*] inspires a passion that is absolute, exclusive, ferocious like gambling or reading" (as quoted and translated by Klein 1993: 56).

References

American Heritage Dictionary (1978). Boston, MA: Houghton Mifflin.

Bagehot, Walter (1873). *Lombard Street: A Description of the Money Market*. New York: Scribner, Armstrong.

Derrida, Jacques, with *Autrement* (1993). "The Rhetoric of Drugs: an Interview." Trans. Michael Israel. *differences* 5.1: 1–25.

Fontanier, Pierre (1969). *Les Figures du discours*. Paris: Flammarion.

Glendinning, Victoria (1993). *Anthony Trollope*. New York: Knopf.

Hamon, Philippe (1992). "Philippe Hamon on the Major Features of Realist Discourse." Trans. Lilian R. Furst and Sean Hand. In *Realism*. Ed. Lilian R. Furst. London: Longman.

Kendrick, Walter (1980). *The Novel Machine: The Theory and Fiction of Anthony Trollope*. Baltimore, MD: Johns Hopkins University Press.

Klein, Richard. *Cigarettes Are Sublime* (1993). Durham, NC: Duke University Press.

Pool, Daniel (1993). *What Jane Austen Ate and Charles Dickens Knew*. New York: Simon & Schuster.

Schor, Naomi (1993). *George Sand and Idealism*. New York: Columbia University Press.

Smalley, Donald, ed. (1969) *Trollope: The Critical Heritage*. London: Routledge & Kegan Paul.

Sutherland, John (1982). Introduction to *The Way We Live Now*, by Anthony Trollope. New York: Oxford University Press, vii–xxxiv.

Trollope, Anthony ([1883] 1947). *An Autobiography*. Berkeley: University of California Press.

Williams, Raymond (1961). *The Long Revolution: An Analysis of the Democratic, Industrial, and Cultural Changes Transforming Our Society*. New York: Columbia University Press.

16

COMMODIFYING TENNYSON

The historical transformation of "brand loyalty"

Gerhard Joseph

The great brand
Made lightnings in the splendour of the moon,
And flashing round and round, and whirled in an arch,
Shot like a streamer of the northern morn,
Seen where the moving isles of winter shock
By night, with noises of the Northern Sea.
So flashed and fell the brand Excalibur:
But ere he dipt the surface, rose an arm
Clothed in white samite, mystic, wonderful,
And caught him by the hilt and brandished him
Three times, and drew him under in the mere.
Tennyson, "The Passing of Arthur," ll. 304–14[1]

From the beginning to the end of his career, from the lost sword of the juvenilian story "Mungo the American" to the Excalibur of the *Idylls of the King* and the sword in his play *Harold*, Alfred Tennyson explored with marked pertinacity the provenance and meaning of a male sword, the weapon that in Excalibur's case he often gives the gender marking of "he" and "him."[2] It is also true – and A.E. Baker's *Tennyson Concordance* confirms such divided usage – that while Tennyson sometimes refers to Arthur's blade as a "sword," he more habitually calls the weapon that inspired the loyalty of Arthur's knights a "brand."[3] In the argument that follows, I should like to bring together that medievalized use of "brand" with the fact that an edition of Tennyson's works was one of the first books (and the only work of poetry) Frederick Macmillan brought out in 1890 to institute the publishing firm's "net book" policy. Through that influential practice, Macmillan would provide certain books to booksellers and lending libraries on trade terms only if they would agree to sell them to the public at a fixed net price rather than at a highly variable discount, as had hitherto been trade procedure. By instituting such control of retail prices in order to curb the practice of underselling, the Macmillan

Company confirmed, if it did not actually initiate, the modern circulation of the book as a "branded good" by an author with a valued name – Tennyson as a branded commodity of the Macmillan firm just as, say, a razor blade, with its advertising logo of crossed swords, is the branded product of Wilkinson.

Tennyson's interest in the *Idylls* and in "The Passing of Arthur" most specifically is in the gradual process by which cultural authority (i.e., the works of *auctors*, in every sense) gets transmitted from civilization to civilization – from, say, feudal to imperial Britain and beyond.[4] In the historical transformation I posit that makes the pun on "brand loyalty" possible, I will provide an economic context for how the old order changeth, yielding place to new – for how a Victorian sense of an author as consumable brand good evolves out of an earlier notion of *auctorité* implicit in a medievalized reading of "brand" as a non-commodifiable object/sign, one that is incommensurable and inalienable. For in King Arthur's pre-capitalist version of brand loyalty, his insistence that the brand Excalibur not be subject to alienable ownership but merely to cultural "use" and reuse, he prepares for one of the most powerful enabling fictions of our time, Marx's narrative of the West's move from use- to exchange-value, and foreshadows the emergence of a late nineteenth-century imperialist economy, with its ever widening circulation of commodities.[5]

My approach is thus a quasi-materialist one: *quasi*-materialist because I move with conscious eclecticism between material and linguistic categories, between discussions of changes in the modes of production (the economic relationship of authors, publishers, booksellers, and readers) and in signifying practices (the etymological history of "brand"). "Etymologies," Jonathan Culler (1988) has said, "give us respectable puns, endowing pun-like effects with the authority of science and even of truth." In thus responding to what Culler has labelled "the call of the phoneme" (ibid.: 3), I am not suggesting that Tennyson himself was consciously playing on the changes in the meaning of "brand," that he explicitly conceived of himself or that Macmillan's blatantly thought of him as branded by the firm. Rather, I assume that changes in the means of production effect, however indirectly, conceptual changes before manifesting themselves within the speech of individuals, so that a pun on "brand loyalty" may become available only well after the material fact (the emergence of the "branded good" in the trade associations of the 1890s: Levy 1942: 65–76) that generated it. There is thus toward century's end a political unconscious at work, a material shift with ideological and lexical consequences. And Tennyson, the *Idylls of the King*, and Macmillan's net-price edition of *The Poetical Works of Alfred Lord Tennyson* all, willy nilly, participate in that shift and those consequences in the following way.

There are, I would suggest, three reasons why Tennyson habitually prefers "brand" to "sword" in the *Idylls*: first, as the OED tells us, "brand" is a "poetical," deliberately "archaic" term for a sword, and is thus semantically apt for a poem that tries to archaize its materials at every turn. Second, as the OED also shows, the term "brand," with its etymology in the act of burning (from the Old High German *brant*), is suggestive of a flashing in fire or of light, and Excalibur's primary characteristic is such an effect, as when for instance the "brand Excalibur . . . flash[ed] round and round" and "flashed and fell" in the quotation that constitutes my epigraph – it is indeed a "blade so bright / That men are blinded by it" ("The Coming of Arthur," ll. 299–300). Such an instrument may be used to inscribe one's own sign, to put one's own brand upon another. For though the OED gives 1807 as the date of the first use of "brand" as a trademark denoting proprietorship of goods capable of being "plugged" in the modern commercial sense, a king's "dubbing" (from the Old High German for "to plug") of his knights is no doubt a ceremonial displacement of a more primitive branding of the skin denoting allegiance to a liegelord – or even to the Lord.[6] And so third and most importantly, while the word "sword" refers to a material object, the term "brand" is more suggestive of the way that such an object is also a sign, precisely a blade that may have a message of ownership inscribed or branded upon it and that is itself an instrument of further inscription by its wielder.[7]

Thus the essential feature of the sword in Tennyson's juvenilian "Mungo the American" is that it has the letters "F.T." etched into its hilt;[8] likewise the later Excalibur presents itself initially to Arthur as a linguistic effect as much as a material object, as a "privileged signifier," to adopt a post-Saussurian category. For while the words "Take me" are graven on one side "in the oldest tongue of all the world," on the reverse side the words "Cast me away" are "written in the speech ye [Arthur] speak yourself" ("The Coming of Arthur," ll. 300–4). Thus branded itself, the sword is in turn the chosen instrument by which Arthur attempts to brand his knights and queen, to impose his mark upon them and her so that he can will his will and work his work: when the king selects and binds his knights "to his own self," Bellicent, his sister, beholds "from eye to eye thro' all their Order flash / A momentary likeness of the King" (ibid.: ll. 261–70). Such attempts at appropriation are, to be sure, only of temporary avail since brandings (unless we are talking about cattle or casks of wine) fail to take into account the quirky individuality of the brandee, the resistance to branding of the person branded.

For it is Arthur's story alone, ancient legend alone unsupported by an exchangeable material relic in an heir's "treasure-house" (l. 269), that must work its work as unalienated "use," a key and echoing concept in the *Idylls* as a whole. That is, of course, the point of Arthur's exchanges with Bedevere, the last of his knights, who in "The Passing of Arthur" thinks otherwise. Bedevere initially withholds Excalibur from the Lady of the Lake's mere into which Arthur orders him to return it for a fairly vague, sensuous reason: he is dazzled into hesitation by the "diamond sparks, / Myriads of topaz-lights, and jacinth-work of subtlest jewellery" (ll. 225–26). It is during his second denial that Bedevere elaborates a more blatantly acquisitive motivation:

> The King is sick, and knows not what he does.
> What record, or what relic of my lord
> Should be to aftertime, but empty breath
> And rumours of a doubt? But were this kept,
> Stored in some treasure-house of mighty kings,
> Some one might show it at a joust of arms,
> Saying, "King Arthur's sword, Excalibur,
> Wrought by the lonely maiden of the Lake.
> Nine years she wrought it, sitting in the deeps
> Upon the hidden bases of the hills."
> So might some old man speak in the aftertime
> To all the people, winning reverence.
> But now much honour and much fame were lost.
> (ll. 265–77)

We are here yet a long way from what Marx meant by commodity exchange, or for that matter from a money economy that facilitates such exchange. Bedevere has no intention of selling Excalibur, merely of hoarding it for his own purposes: "so might some old man speak in aftertime / To all the people, winning reverence," he says. But reverence for whom? For Arthur or for the "old man" who might well, we suspect, be Bedevere himself? The "honour" and "fame" of line 277 are at any rate for Bedevere specifically tied to an alienable object that can move between persons, whereas for Arthur honour and fame exist exclusive of relics and the world of exchangeable objects, exist as ideal and self-authorized story. It would of course be anachronistic to accuse Bedevere of thinking of the sword as a fetishized and alienated commodity in the economic sense Marx elaborates during the opening section of *Capital* (I, ch. 1, s. 4); however, if only because of a persistently male gendering of the sword as "he," we might have less trouble seeing it as a fetish, as a displacement of the phallus, in the Freudian sense. But if in the "ways the sword gets handled we may find the poet imagining ways of wielding the Arthurian corpus," as Tucker (1991: 326) suggests, the contrast of attitude between Arthur and Bedevere regarding the Lady of the Lake's material good may at least bring Bedevere to the edge of, or at any rate predict, a Victorian sense of authorial property at a time when Britain is becoming "wealthier – wealthier – hour by hour" (Tennyson, "To the Queen," l. 23). Such a reading perhaps merely restates what has often been said of the *Idylls*, that its medievalism is of necessity a markedly Victorian construction. My present take on such a critical truism would be to assert that, in the implied etymological opposition within our own horizon of expectations for a medieval and a Victorian "brand," the *Idylls* uncovers the medieval sources of the material practices of Victorian authorial property rights – or, better, to suggest that such "medievalism" is a conceptual back-formation of those Victorian practices.

There is by this time a vast literature concerning the progress of the notion of intellectual property, one that involves an interplay of philosophic and aesthetic issues on the one hand and of legal, economic, and social questions on the other.[9] There seems to be general agreement these days that the key century for the emergence of the modern European author as "an individual who is solely responsible – and therefore exclusively deserving of credit – for the production of a unique work" (Woodmansee 1984: 426) is the eighteenth. However various the history of that evolution on the Continent, for England specifically the esthetic watershed moment is the celebration of individual authorial genius in Edward Young's 1759 *Conjectures on Original Composition*, while its legal counterpart in establishing the rights of individual authorship is the copyright statute of Queen Anne in 1710.[10] To be sure, the statute affirming the rights of ownership to intellectual property such as book copy was passed on the petition of and in the interest of booksellers, not authors. But once copyright affirmed the legal principle of rights to book copying as alienable property, it was but a short step to the legal right of authors to "their own work," as that historically specific concept would have it. If stationers and booksellers could have a legal right to a copy and a book, why couldn't authors as well?

Although by the Victorian period the concept of authorial property rights had been firmly established, nevertheless Victorian copyright was rarely held exclusively by one party, but was always open to negotiation among booksellers, publishers, lending libraries, *and* authors – and even technical developments in printing could be co-opted by either (or both) author and publisher in their ongoing struggle for control of the literary text (Dooley 1992: *passim*). Such is, after all, the major ethical and social point to Marx's linkage of commodification and alienation (see Marx and Engels 1965): a piece of work becomes a commodity *because* it is subject to market exchange and is therefore alienable. Thus the primary reason Excalibur eludes commodity status within the *Idylls* is that it is not alienable from an Arthur who does not – and never claims to – "own" it: as the Lady of the Lake's twin messages suggest, Excalibur exists only for the social "use" of the person upon whom it is bestowed within any given social order and must be "cast away" so that it may be passed on to the next appropriate bearer once such use within a given civilization is exhausted. And the word to be emphasized in that last sentence is "appropriate." For as Ruskin says in the "*Ad Valorem*" section of *Unto this Last*, "usefulness" in an article depends much more on the virtue of the person using it than on any quality attributable to the article: if usefulness is thus "value in the hands of the valiant. . . . Wealth . . . is 'THE POSSESSION OF THE VALUABLE BY THE VALIANT'" (Ruskin 1905: 88). If that is so, an Excalibur crafted by the Lady of the Lake for a supremely valiant Arthur may be said to constitute the purest fictional example of what Ruskin, if not Marx, meant by use. Furthermore, to the extent that Excalibur *is* intended to move on at some future date within a new cultural order, it may be said to circulate within something closer to a system of gift rather than of market exchange: as Lewis Hyde suggests in the opening pages of *The Gift*, his account of the difference between gift and commodity economies, "the gift" (notwithstanding Bedevere's intention) "must always move" rather than being put "in a warehouse or museum (or, more to the point for capitalism, [laid] aside to be used for production)" (Hyde 1983: 3–4). It must "shine in [personal] use," rather than be hoarded, as Tennyson's dull, rusting Ulysses says when he in turn describes himself as a sword yearning once more to burnish among his fellow mariners rather than stagnate among a "hoard[ing]" race in Ithaca.[11] It must be "passed along" – and usually to a third party, not to the same person who gave it initially (ibid.: 3–4).[12] That is certainly one of the meanings I would assign to the word "passing" in "The Passing of Arthur" – over against the static "death" implied by the earlier title "Morte d'Arthur."[13]

But once the gift moves toward market exchange in a fully commodified sense, the question of who owns what share of a property – say, an intellectual property within the intellectual marketplace – gets highlighted. The progress of copyright law with respect to books in the eighteenth and nineteenth centuries is a history of negotiation among author, publisher, and bookseller for rights within a property (whether that right was construed as a right to a "copy" or a right to an originary "book"). As Norman Feltes (1986) has argued, a climactic change in that history in consolidating the economic power of the publisher *vis à vis* all the other claimants in the right of the book occurred in 1890. It was in this year that Tennyson's final publisher (from 1884–92), Frederick Macmillan, instituted the circulation of the net book, offered through a pricing policy whereby – to elaborate upon my earlier definition – certain Macmillan books under copyright were no longer offered to lending libraries and booksellers at trade terms unless those libraries and booksellers agreed to sell them at a low set price, rather than at a discounted price, to the reading public.[14] (Most Macmillan books were, to be sure, still "subject books," i.e, books subject to discount.)

Feltes's interest is primarily in how the dominant petty-commodity structure of book (especially novel) production in the nineteenth century gave way to a new publishing strategy suited to the larger structures of a newly emergent consumer capitalism, with its shift of emphasis from production to consumption – and how this happened via the net book pricing strategy. Macmillan's policy, Feltes suggests, constituted a reaction not merely to the death of the three-decker novel but also to a wider "conjunctural crisis" (Gareth Stedman Jones's [1976: 52] concept) in the production of books, of which the decline in the profitability of lending libraries, the appearance of new publishers, and the death of the three-decker were all constituents. Frederick Macmillan's response to that crisis, one that was quickly reinforced by other publishing houses and that eventuated in the industry-wide Net Book Agreement of 1899, "the Magna Carta of the book trade" according to Macmillan (1924: 30), had the effect of strengthening the publisher's control over the production of books by curtailing the power of such retailing middlemen as booksellers and lending libraries. By 1924 Macmillan could boast that "it is now the exception for any copyright book to be published 'subject to discount'" (ibid.).

My own addition to the argument would be to emphasize that Feltes's thesis concerning the production of novels applies as well to the production of books of poetry such as the Tennyson volume Macmillan listed in the Christmas number of the *Publishers' Circular* of 1890 as one of the firm's initial twenty net books in various formats and at various prices. The choice of Tennyson as one of the first such authors has to do with his proven reliability as a commodity that would affirm the Macmillan brand under the new economic circumstances of agreement about price levels among publishers. Hermann Levy (1942) discusses the way in which such a development in the 1890s and before was a reflex of the larger development of cartels and trusts in a British capitalism more and more driven by imperialist designs and the thirst for continual expansion: manufacturers, given the general agreement about price levels, were now constantly faced with the need to devise new ways of attracting retail customers, and a primary means was to extend the principle of the patent which creates "branded goods," to be sold at advertised (or in the publishers' terms "net") prices. The practice of the branded good permitted manufacturers not only to punish price cutters but more directly to capture retail customers by creating what economic historians call "consumer insistence" for a particular book – say, a Macmillan book. It is this consumer insistence that was intended to create the quasi-monopoly value of the brand (Levy 1942: 5, 7, 65–76; Feltes 1986: 83–4).

For such a system to work, the books chosen, especially at the beginning of the process, had to be exceptionally attractive ones, "because if the first net book[s] did not sell, [their] failure would certainly be attributed to [their] *netness* and not to [their] quality" (Macmillan 1924: 14). For publishers the name of the author now "becomes a kind of brand name, a recognizable sign that the cultural commodity will be of a certain kind and quality" (Rose 1993: 1). Thus while the very first book Frederick Macmillan chose to launch the firm's new policy was *The Principles of Economics* by the distinguished economist and Professor of Political Economy at Cambridge, Alfred Marshall (announced on 7 August 1890), the choice of Tennyson for the Christmas trade of 1890 was not far behind.

The emergence of the brand should be discussed within the context of the evolution of a commodity culture within Victorian England, a narrative that Thomas Richards (1990) has followed from the Great Exhibition (1851) to the Queen's Jubilee, across Africa, back into the medicine cabinets of Victorian homes, and finally into the thoughts and habits of consumers (see Richards 1990: *passim*). The advertising ditties Richards discusses – meant to sell, for instance, Beacham's pills – suggest that, Matthew Arnold to the contrary, it is not so much serious poetry but rather the work of literature as commodity whose future is immense; it is the commodity which tends to occupy the site at the center of Victorian life once held by religion (Riede 1991: 248). For even serious poetry – with the work of Tennyson as an instance – partook of such commodification by being turned, as part of what Baudrillard (1988) has called a consumption "system" of reified objects, into a Macmillan brand – or such, at any rate, was arguably the publisher's intention.[15] Less prestigious nineteenth-century publishers than Macmillan, such as those who specialized in the mass production of cheap fiction for a working-class audience, had, to be sure, branded a stable of writers with their own names before century's end, as was the case with Edward Lloyd's Penny Bloods of the 1840s or John Dick's Penny Standard Plays of the 1860s (James 1963; Neuberg 1977). In the 1820s and 1830s John Murray and Richard Bentley had worked up the idea of "libraries" in which each volume attained some of its value (and some of its call to be purchased) by being branded and marketed as part of a set. What distinguishes the emerging branded book of the 1890s from earlier nineteenth-century "commodity books" (Feltes's phrase) associated with specific publishers is that it tests an assumed quality, a "reputation-value" of an established, highly prestigious writer as a way of interpellating the "unknown" reader prepared to buy a commodity text, rather than courting the already "known" reader. Instead of appealing to the known but limited market for a petty-commodity text, the branded book of monopoly capitalism tries to extend the market's scope, since within a mature capitalist ethos the market must always be expanding: imperial Britain will ideally become, to repeat the hope of the *Idylls*'s dedicatory "To the Queen," "wealthier – wealthier – hour by hour."

There were of course more expensive Macmillan editions of Tennyson intended for "known" readers and libraries that could afford them – the New Library Edition, at first in nine and eventually in twelve volumes, and especially a Parchment Edition (called the Handmade Paper Edition in Macmillan's accounts) available for the carriage trade and completed in ten volumes in 1893. But Macmillan's one-volume Pocket Edition of Tennyson's works in 1890 at 7*s*. 6*d*. was specifically geared to sell to a wider but not wholly "known" audience, and the fact that 3,000 of a run of 7,000 were sold in 1890, the year of the first printing, suggests the commercial acumen of Macmillan's new policy.

In moving from Arthur's conception of a "brand" to be passed on as a cultural gift to the "brand loyalty" of the modern consumer confirmed for modern publishing by the Macmillan *Tennyson* of 1890, we have, I would argue, a history in small, or at any rate an etymological parable for our times, of the construction of the literary commodity against its medieval back-formation. Tennyson was, of course, very shrewd in his dealings with publishers: his grandfather was notoriously wrong in the anecdote according to which, upon being presented with an early poem, he gave his grandson, the fledgling poet, ten shillings with the words, "There, that is the first money you have ever earned by your poetry, and, take my word for it, it will be the last" (quoted in Ricks 1972: 13). And with authors as successful as Tennyson surely was in the later stages of his life, this wealthiest of Victorian poets is indeed "become a name" not like his Ulysses ("Ulysses", l. 11), but rather a name upon which Macmillan can in turn inscribe itself. In the wake of such a development, we tend to experience even our most serious authors as products of the various entrepreneurial and professional activities that have combined to represent them rather than as figures prior to, figures somehow independent of, such branded representations.

Of course, to undercut the totalizing potential of my argument, the point must also be made that this attempt at branding is only a partial success, that the *book* of serious literature (as distinct from the *copy*) also in some measure evades the intended branding of the publisher. While contemporary readers no doubt saw the branded hack writers of the Penny Dreadfuls as "belonging" to Edward Lloyd's stable, the contemporaries of Tennyson surely thought of him only in passing as a Macmillan author, as readers of, say, Hemingway and Fitzgerald think of such later figures only in passing as Scribner authors. There is, that is, a certain degree of mystification in Feltes's notion of the "commodity book" because of his collapse of the distinction between the commodification of the "book" and that of the "copy." Tennyson sold Macmillan only the right to copy, not the right to the book, which exists as the copy's supplement (in the Derridian sense). The book of serious poetry, as distinct from the copies that a Macmillan may sell, thus finally evades the publisher's goal (in a thoroughgoing Marxist reading) of complete control, of global commodification – and to that extent the publisher's attempt at a branding of the serious writer for the sake of market command will always be something of a failure.[16] Indeed, if the publisher can only buy "copyright" and not the "book," it might even be argued that the commodification of the book, or at any rate of serious literature, can never happen *at all*. For once the idea of copyright gets established as an exchangeable commodity, does "the book" not become something of a romantic mystification, a back-formation or what Baudrillard (see note 6) might call the "alibi" of the copy – as Arthurian/medieval "use" is in large measure a back-formation or alibi of Victorian "exchange"?

Still, whatever the mystifying uses of "use," the ethos of the marketplace, if not as totally hegemonic as a Marxist critic like Feltes asserts it to be, is pervasive enough within our twentieth-century literary/academic community.[17] "Every man imputes himself" – and presumably the Spirit of his Age – in his interpretations, Tennyson said to his friend James Knowles (Knowles 1893: 165). So, to close on a self-imputational note for our own age, one might see the proliferation of academic books, articles, and conferences with well-paid stars as productions within a specialized industry, as exchanges within the highly professionalized and therefore commodified "small world" David Lodge has satirized. The small world indeed of Tennyson studies within which some of us labor may not in these theory-driven, post-humanist, Death-of-the-Author days, be the blue-chip operation it once was. As Lindsay Waters, a senior editor at Harvard University Press, was cited as saying in a *New York Times Magazine* article on the 1990 meeting of the Modern Language Association, while a monograph on Tennyson may move 500 copies these days, Terry Eagleton's *Introduction to Literary Theory* had at the time of the MLA meeting already sold 120,000 copies and counting (Matthews 1991: 59). But even a scaled-back Tennyson operation sustains us laborers within it well enough. It is in this sense that our scholarly examinations and celebrations of individual authors cannot help but be seared with trade, cannot but be driven in part by brand considerations within a literary marketplace. But built into the production/consumption dialectic that marks our professional enterprise is also a self-awareness that may partially redeem us. For we at least *know* that the commodifying impulse, to the extent that we are not immune from it as academic producers and consumers, is the displacement of an earlier notion of loyalty to a different kind of brand that Tennyson celebrates in the *Idylls of the King* – even as he himself lived through the passing of such an ideal, what Derrida would call a Metaphysics of Use or Baudrillard denigrate as an ideological alibi, in becoming one of the very first authors to constitute a branded good five years after the completion of that plangent work. And we understand, plangently enough ourselves, that in the historical inevitability of such institutional commodification, *Bedevere, c'est nous*.

Notes

1 All citations from the poetry are from Ricks's edition (1987).

2 See Joseph (1992: 191–212). Shires (1992: 408) asserts that the sword gets most significantly gendered as male in "The Passing of Arthur," l. 194, precisely at the moment when it is surrendered once more to the female great deep: "Concurrent with the removal of the male hero into the realm of the feminine and maternal, the poem asserts a definition of manliness as the letting go of material objects of masculine authority."

3 According to Tucker (1988: 326), a revision in line 27 of the earliest manuscript of "Morte d'Arthur" (Tennyson Notebook 17 at Trinity College, Cambridge) first records the preference for "brand" over "sword."

4 See Tucker (1991) for the way in which Tennyson "did some of the most interesting ideological work of the nineteenth-century epic by abdicating his own initiative in favor of the authority of legend" (703), grounding his epic in "the sovereign power of innuendo" and social gossip (717). For a reading of the imperialist emphasis within the *Idylls*, see McGuire (1992).

5 The classical instance of the distinction between use- and exchange-value appears in volume I, ch. 1, s. 1 of *Capital*. For the concrete, sensuous, differentiated, inalienable, and incommensurable nature of use-value as over against the abstract, universal, and uniform nature of exchange-value, see Marx (1970: 36). A section

of this "curtain-raiser" to *Capital* develops the distinction in the way most relevant to the present argument:

> Although use-values serve social needs and therefore exist within the social framework, they do not express the social relations of production. For instance, let us take as a use-value a commodity such as a diamond. We cannot tell by looking at it that the diamond is a commodity. Where it serves as an aesthetic or mechanical use-value, on the neck of a courtesan or in the hand of a glass cutter, it is a diamond and not a commodity. To be a use-value is evidently a necessary prerequisite of the commodity, but it is immaterial to the use-value whether it is a commodity. Use-value as such, since it is independent of the determinate economic form, lies outside the sphere of investigation of political economy. It belongs to this sphere only when it is itself a determinate economic form. Use-value is the immediate physical entity in which a definite economic relationship – *exchange value* – is expressed. (Ibid.: 28).

My notion of the use/exchange binary as an "enabling fiction" is indebted to Jean Baudrillard's (1988) thoroughgoing deconstruction of "use" as an ideological *alibi* for a post-lapsarian "exchange." As part of Baudrillard's larger critique of the "imaginary of the sign" (i.e., a mystification of the signifier/signified distinction within political economy), use-value does not constitute a historical *elsewhere* with respect to the system of exchange value; rather, "the fetishism of use value redoubles and deepens the fetishism of exchange value" (71). With respect to the argument that follows, Baudrillard might say that the fetishism of Arthurian (and Tennysonian) "use" redoubles and deepens the fetishism of post-Bedeverean "exchange." In thus allowing at the outset for a deconstruction of my entire argument, I would nevertheless assert that even if we move beyond the mystification of signifier/signified and use/exchange, we cannot for long live within Baudrillard's collapse of all difference, within his global, systemic hyperreal. We must, that is, inevitably construct new binary distinctions by which, if ever so magically, to think.

6 According to Allmendinger (1992: ch. 1), while cattlemen in the American West used brands as signs of economic possession, the cowboys who actually imprinted brands on cattlemen's stock appropriated them in their poetry as symbols of Christian salvation, with God branding the cowboys as members of his favorite herd, the saved.

7 See Tucker (1988: 326): "Tennyson's preferred term for Excalibur is not 'sword' but 'brand' . . . because a 'brand' is a sign, the meaning of which depends in part on the attitude of its user."

8 For a biographical reading of the story that relates this "F.T." to Alfred Tennyson's friendly competition with Frederick Tennyson, one of the three brothers who contributed poems to *Poems by Two Brothers*, see Joseph (1989).

9 I owe my sense of the complexity of that interplay to the papers of a conference on "Intellectual Property and the Construction of Authorship," sponsored by the Society for Critical Exchange on 21 April 1991, at Case Western Reserve University. The proceedings have been published in Woodmansee and Jaszi (1994).

10 On the history of the Anglo-American copyright, see Barnes (1964, 1974), and Patterson (1968: esp. 143–50).

11 "Ulysses," ll. 22–23: "How dull it is to pause, to make an end, / To rust unburnish'd, not to shine in use!"; ll.4–5: "a savage race / That hoard, and sleep, and feed, and know not me."

12 Such an argument assumes that the Arthur who is to "come again" is not merely a return of the Arthur who has died but rather an equivalent of that "old" leader within the "new" cultural order.

13 "Mungo the American" presents a malign mirror reversal of such a benign usage. The story of how Mungo, a Panamanian native – in a subtitle – "found a sword, & after-wards how it came to possession of the right owner, after the space of two years" is a tale about an alienated sword, the sword of a "stranger" who is variously and therefore never definitively identified. Mungo's two-year possession of the sword of a "stranger," the Spanish invader Francisco Tolivarez (the "F.T." alluded to in note 8), has behind it Tolivarez's earlier seizing and "switching" of swords with a member of his regiment, Alonzo Roderigo, yet another "stranger." As I have argued elsewhere (Joseph 1989: 147–56), such parallel appropriative "switches" of the tale suggest an overall air of doubling and displacement within a moral wilderness (and the switches are both thematic and linguistic, both of the sword and of the person to whom the floating signifier "stranger" is applied). For a full discussion of "Mungo" in the context of Tennyson's later "sword" poems, see ibid.

14 Tennyson's most personal relationship within the publishing firm was with Alexander Macmillan, its co-founder, who had brought Tennyson over from Kegan Paul in 1884. But by 1890 Alexander had passed on the active running of the firm to his son George and his nephews, Frederick and Maurice, the sons of his brother Daniel. See Hagen (1979: 158–85).

15 For a relevant discussion of how the development of "brand loyalty" is a correlative of the shifting emphasis from production to consumption within late capitalism, see "The System of Objects" in Baudrillard (1988: 10–28). See also Gagnier (1986) and Freedman (1990) for the ways in which market conditions and artistic production work with and against each other in the last twenty years of the nineteenth century.

16 Linda Austin's essay in this volume describes the way a "hack" writer like James Thomson evaded a simplistic "commodification" when writing for *Cope's Tobacco Plant*, and achieved a measure of freedom within the most extreme of Victorian commercial restrictions.

17 For a less insistently Marxist treatment of nineteenth-century publication practices, see Sutherland (1976). The difference between the materialist approaches of Feltes and Sutherland is, however, only a matter of degree. "There is," Sutherland maintains, "no Victorian novel (and I would include even literary eccentricities like *Wuthering Heights*) which was not materially influenced by the publishing system, for good or ill" (ibid.: 6).

References

Allmendinger, Blake (1992). *The Cowboy: Representations of Labor in an American Work Culture*. New York: Oxford University Press.

Austin, Linda (1999). "Smoking, the Hack, and the General Equivalent." In this volume.

Baker, Arthur ([1914] 1966). *A Concordance to the Poetical and Dramatic Works of Alfred Lord Tennyson*. New York: Barnes & Noble.

Barnes, James J. (1964). *Free Trade in Books*. Oxford: Clarendon Press.

—— (1974). *Authors, Publishers and Politicians: The Quest for an Anglo-American Copyright Agreement 1815–54*. London: Routledge & Kegan Paul.

Baudrillard, Jean (1988). *Selected Writings*. Ed. Mark Poster. Stanford, CA: Stanford University Press.

Culler, Jonathan (1988). "The Call of the Phoneme." In *On Puns: The Foundation of Letters*. Ed. Jonathan Culler. London: Basil Blackwell.

Dooley, Allan C. (1992). *Author and Printer in Victorian England*. Charlottesville, VA: University Press of Virginia.

Feltes, N.N. (1986). *Modes of Production of Victorian Novels*. Chicago: University of Chicago Press.

Freedman, Jonathan (1990). *Professions of Taste: Henry James, British Aestheticism, and Commodity Culture*. Stanford, CA: Stanford University Press.

Gagnier, Regenia (1986). *Idylls of the Marketplace: Oscar Wilde and the Victorian Public*. Stanford, CA: Stanford University Press.

Gray, J.M. (1969). *Man and Myth in Victorian England: Tennyson's "The Coming of Arthur."* Tennyson Monograph. Lincoln, Lincs.: Tennyson Research Centre.

Hagen, June Steffensen (1979). *Tennyson and His Publishers*. London: Macmillan.

Hyde, Lewis (1983). *The Gift: Imagination and the Erotic Life of Property*. New York: Random House.

James, Louis (1963). *Fiction for the Working Man*. London: Oxford University Press.

Jones, Gareth Stedman (1976). *Outcast London*. Harmondsworth, Middlesex: Penguin.

Joseph, Gerhard (1989). "Tales of Two Brothers: Tennyson's 'Mungo the American' and *Balin and Balan*." *Victorian Poetry* 27: 147–56.

—— (1992). *Tennyson and the Text: The Weaver's Shuttle*. Cambridge: Cambridge University Press.

Knowles, James (1893). "Aspects of Tennyson. II: A Personal Reminiscence." *Nineteenth Century* 33: 164–88.

Levy, Hermann (1942). "Branded Goods." In *Retail Trade Associations: A New Form of Monopolist Organization in Britain*. London: Kegan Paul, Trench, Trubner, 65–76.

Macmillan, Frederick (1924). *The Net Book Agreement 1899 and the Book War 1906–1908*. Glasgow: Robert Maclehose.

Marx, Karl (1954) *Capital*. 3 vols. Trans. Samuel Moore and Edward Aveling. Ed. Frederick Engels. London: Lawrence & Wishart.

—— (1970) *A Contribution to the Critique of Political Economy*. Trans. S.W. Ryanskaya. London: Lawrence & Wishart.

——, and Friedrich Engels (1965). *The German Ideology*. Trans. S.W. Ryanaskaya. London: Lawrence & Wishart.

Matthews, Anne (1991). "Deciphering Victorian Underwear and Other Seminars." *New York Times Magazine*. 10 Feb.: 42–43, 57–59, 69.

McGuire, Ian (1992). "Epistemology and Empire in *Idylls of the King*." *Victorian Poetry* 30: 387–400.

Neuberg, Victor (1977). *Popular Literature: A History and Guide*. London: Woburn Press.

Patterson, Lyman Ray (1968). *Copyright in Historical Perspective*. Nashville: Vanderbilt University Press.

Richards, Thomas (1990). *The Commodity Culture of Victorian England, 1851–1914*. Stanford, CA: Stanford University Press.

Ricks, Christopher (1972). *Tennyson*. New York: Collier.

Riede, David (1991). "Guide to the Year's Work in Victorian Poetry: 1990." *Victorian Poetry* 29: 247–54.

Rose, Mark (1993). *Authors and Owners: The Invention of Copyright*. Cambridge, MA: Harvard University Press.

Ruskin, John (1905). *"Unto This Last," "Munerva Pulveris," "Time and Tide," with Other Writings on Political Economy*. Vol. 17 of *The Works of John Ruskin*. Ed. E.T. Cook and Alexander Wedderburn. London: George Allen.

Shires, Linda (1992). "Patriarchy, Dead Men, and Tennyson's *Idylls of the King*." *Victorian Poetry* 30: 401–17.

Sutherland, J.A. (1976). *Victorian Novelists and Publishers*. Chicago: University of Chicago Press.

Tennyson, Alfred (1890). *The Poetical Works of Alfred Lord Tennyson*. Pocket Edition. London: Macmillan.

—— (1987). *The Poems of Tennyson*. Ed. Christopher Ricks. 3 vols. Berkeley: University of California Press.

Tucker, Herbert F. (1988). *Tennyson and the Doom of Romanticism*. Cambridge, MA: Harvard University Press.

—— (1991). "The Epic Plight of Troth in *Idylls of the King*." *ELH* 58: 701–20.

Woodmansee, Martha (1984). "The Genius and the Copyright: Economic and Legal Conditions of the Emergence of the 'Author.'" *Eighteenth-Century Studies* 17: 425–48.

——, and Peter Jaszi, eds. (1994). *The Construction of Authorship: Textual Appropriation in Law and Literature*. Durham, NC: Duke University Press.

17

SMOKING, THE HACK, AND THE GENERAL EQUIVALENT

Linda Austin

To speak of an economy of art, as we now often do, we have had first to exhume its economic base; by this I mean not simply that we have uncovered the material production and exchange of literature, but that we have detected a symbolics of this production and exchange. This symbolics emerges as an aesthetic already inscribed in an economic mode of symbolizing. One odd but telling instance of this – what Jean-Joseph Goux (1990: 125) has called the "ritual dimension" of the economic act – centers on the career of James Thomson, who died in 1882, and involves the still powerful romantic conception of the laborer in the late nineteenth century.

James Thomson, poet and essayist, author of *The City of Dreadful Night*, self-taught in German, French, and Italian, had read widely in continental philosophy and literature. He was an atheist whose favorite English poet was Shelley. After leaving the army, he came to London in 1862 and subsisted by writing for radical and free-thought periodicals. In them he published "cockney" poems about the working classes from their perspective, book reviews, essays satirical of middle-class beliefs and conventions, and translations of his favorite continental poet, Heine. He typifies the general idea of the hack writer: most of his work was short; it appeared in the narrow columns of weeklies; he was paid by the piece; and most important, his range of subject-matter was wide. He would do any kind of work required. In fact, from about 1875 (or as early as 1871) to 1881, he published short, pseudonymous essays in *Cope's Tobacco Plant*, a monthly tradesheet based in Liverpool and sold by subscription at tobacconists' shops for 2*s*. a year. As a regular contributor, Thomson was allowed to write about anything he wanted, with one condition: he had to mention smoking in every piece. How he fulfilled his contract illustrates the compatibility of idealist aesthetics and capitalistic production and exchange in the late nineteenth century for the group of servile writers to which Thomson belonged.

Thomson's main outlet in the 1860s was the *National Reformer: Secular Advocate and Freethought Journal* edited by, the masthead shows, "Iconoclast"

– the pen-name of Charles Bradlaugh. The *Reformer* published Thomson's work under the pseudonym "B.V.". A sampling includes "Sunday at Hampstead," a long poem narrated by a clerk, translations of Heine's poetry, and a number of short essays advancing secularist positions. Like many of his colleagues, Thomson used the word "secularist" as a synonym for "rationalist," and he frequently subjected Christian doctrine to his rationalism, an empirical and often overgeneralized common sense. His New Year's Day piece of 1865 on the Athanasian Creed debunks the Trinity through analogies with mathematics and chemistry ("[T]he chemist does not tell us that oxygen, nitrogen, and carbonic acid are three gases and yet one gas" [1845: 4]). Eventually Thomson quarrelled with Bradlaugh and moved to a rival journal, the *Secularist*. For its inaugural issue of 1 January 1876, Thomson contributed the first installment of a long poem, "By the Sea," and another, "Universal Interaction," and for the next few months worked as the journal's in-house poet, publishing many translations from Heine's work. His essays for the journal chart his own reading in literature and philosophy. Many of them are discursive reviews of biographies or of other essays on Heine, Renan, Schopenhauer, in the style of the *Times Literary Supplement* review-essay. When writing for the *National Reformer* Thomson adopted its prevailing sarcasm, particularly toward literal readings of the Bible and other "irrational" religious practices. Soon he caught the tone of the *Secularist* as well.

The views expressed in the *Secularist* were more pragmatic and populist than the *Reformer*'s. In their "Policy of Contents" in the first issue, co-editors G.J. Holyoake and G.W. Foote announce that their paper will consider only ideas "which can be determined by human reason," by which they mean "the secular purport and value" of their adversaries' positions. The *Secularist* vowed not to debate the existence of God or the literal truth of the Bible, frequent subjects in the *National Reformer*, and to focus instead on the "*uses* of theism, the guidance to be had from revelation" (*Secularist* 1 Jan. 1876: 4). Avoiding any theoretical discussion proved unfortunate; soon petty animosities seeped into articles on unrelated subjects, and the journal became a running record of Secularist Party squabbles. Holyoake resigned from the paper within two months and sided with Thomson's old employer, Bradlaugh. In an open letter to Bradlaugh in June, Foote accused him of "malicious slander against my dearest friend. . . . His name will live when yours is forgotten; his memory be treasured when yours has fled. I would rather touch his hand dead than yours living" (*Secularist* 17 June 1876: 394). Most likely this friend was Thomson. As the articles signed "B.V." reveal, by spring 1876, when the *Secularist* was just four months old, Thomson had become a prominent member of Foote's faction. He had entered a rancorous public exchange through his review of Annie Besant's *Secular Song and Hymnbook*, which Bradlaugh had published under the imprint of the National Secularist Society. According to "B.V.," who was wielding the journal's pragmatic standard, the hymn-book contained no musical accompaniment for the lyrics Besant had collected and was too expensive for its potential buyers, who would have to purchase separate sheet music. "B.V." blamed Bradlaugh for giving the tacit approval of the National Secularist Society to Besant's awkward and embarrassing lyrics, some of which advocated revolution ("To arms! Republicans!": 18 Apr. 1876: 271).[1] A few months later, while reviewing *The Life, Work, and Opinions of Heinrich Heine* by William Stigand, Thomson managed to suggest that Bradlaugh had been blackmailing Holyoake, who seemed mysteriously under his old rival's power (*Secularist* 16 Sep. 1876: 188).

I have mentioned Thomson's part in the secularists' "squibs," their frequent word for attacks in print, to convey the kind of passion with which Thomson wrote for these two journals and to introduce a problem with our understanding of mercenary or hack work, as opposed to art. Of course the separation of the two has been misleading, as Derrida points out in his essay, "Economimesis" (1981); the relationship between the mechanical structure of art and its so-called "free" production is symbiotic. Neither is ever a discrete process. But this false distinction, which pervades idealist esthetics, is especially compelling to fringe writers like Thomson who are forever assessing their position against the idea of art as liberal, free, and non-mercenary. The writer who could publish an essay like "The Athanasian Creed," who could ridicule metaphysics and philosophy in poetry, and could indulge animosities in print for pay, enjoyed a kind of privileged freedom of art as defined in the idealist tradition, and simultaneously, freedom of labor as praised by nineteenth-century idealists like John Ruskin. The romantic theory of labor advanced by contemporary Utopian economists like Ruskin and J.A. Hobson was patterned in part after unitary and idealist notions of the self that permeated lyric poetry (particularly Wordsworth's) earlier in the century. Freedom of expression, which allows the writer to convey him or her "self" in work, assumes at the very least an emotional tie between the writer and his or her production. Of the *National Reformer* Thomson once said, "[I]ts supreme merit consists in the fact that I can say in it what I like how I like; and I know not another periodical in Britain which would grant me the same liberty or license" (quoted in Salt 1889: 54).

He also once remarked, though, that working for the *National Reformer* was "anything but a recommendation" (quoted in Walker 1950: 47n). His journal entries record rejections of his poetry by *Cornhill*, *St. Paul's*, and *Macmillan's*, among others (Schaefer 1965: 7). Ambitious, Thomson felt estranged from outlets he found for his work; they lacked the prestige of the respectable literary journals to which he aspired, even though both his poems and his essays would have offended their readerships. The difference between art and mercenary work was, therefore, reversed in Thomson's mind: hack-work allowed freedom of expression and the liberal play of imagination that depends on this freedom; art constrained both subject and expression. But essentially he defined both hack-work and art primarily as relations of production; they differed merely in social status. After he died, the poet Philip Bourke Marston observed, in a memorial published in the *Athenaeum*, that Thomson "belonged to no special community or brotherhood in art" (quoted in Salt 1889: 55). Marston too conceived of the writer in terms of his outlets, it seems; consequently, in speaking of Thomson he could define him only as someone outside the art world.

The notion of a hack as opposed to an artist arises from the social position of the writer and his or her connection to various institutions; these provide readerships, both during and after the writer's life; and these readers in turn define the nature or esthetic of the work. If both "hack" and "artist" describe similar economic relations of production and exchange, and if necessity and the market compel and restrict all labor, the difference between the artist and the servile writer becomes arbitrary – a matter of current consciousness. What was hack-work to Dr. Johnson is not to us. We regularly deflate the idealist rhetoric about art; the economics of hack-work likewise seem obvious. Yet its underlying esthetic is less so. For at the heart of the hack's relation to production and exchange is a capitalistic and idealist symbolics.

Thomson's official association with *Cope's Tobacco Plant* began in 1875, though he may have contributed articles as early as 1871. His job was to provide material for readers while they were smoking and to remind those who perhaps did not have cigar in hand to smoke. This early form of public relations temporarily removed Thomson from the fractious circles of the secularists, but it brought him closest to the drudgery and estrangement of hack-work. He now assumed various pseudonyms: Mixtures, Sigvat, X. Under these he wrote pieces entitled "Ben Jonson," "Rabelais Compared with Swift," "Edmund Burke," "George Meredith," and "Rubaiyat of Omar Khayyam." They are much shorter and more formulaic than his essays for the free-thought journals. Many of them begin, "so-and-so was born . . ." and continue just as blandly, reading like lifeless imitations of essays in *Blackwood's*. A few "squibs" at secularists appear, but in general the sarcasm that permeated the *National Reformer*'s coverage of politics and religion is gone.

Cope's was neutral in all newsworthy controversy, and at the same time sought the tobacco angle of all issues. The effect of this commercial perspective is sometimes outlandish, as when *Cope's* declares allegiances with Huxley and Swedenborg because they smoke cigars. Occasionally the positions it does take seem to be against its commercial interest. For instance, it deplores, citing Ruskin, the pollution of Roman buildings by the Pope's tobacco-works. Yet there is a method in such perverseness. *Cope's* policy is to promote only the consumption of cigars; accordingly, it sunders itself from production. In its pages the leisurely smoking of tobacco has nothing to do with the conditions of labor or the industrial site, or even the production of forms of knowledge, as I shall suggest later. Smoking is linked with cultivated consumption, not consumption's dirty origins. Smokers can relax and read about Ben Jonson or Huxley in the mediated advertising of its pages and in this state have to absorb nothing but the desire to smoke. Similarly, Thomson's contributions to *Cope's* conceal labor. Their brevity and emptiness suggest minimal effort; they are suitable material for the distracting haze of the smokeroom. In abstract terms, Thomson's work for *Cope's* hypothesizes a condition of leisure for the non-intellectual, relaxed production of words and insinuates the hack himself into the socioeconomic place of smoking club-men. The respectable literary tradition (in packaged or digested form) he offers his readers mystifies the exchange between production and consumption.

Perhaps the one condition of his employment reminded Thomson of his real position as a paid writer for a tradesheet. Maybe after awhile the effort of putting smoking in every piece frustrated and bored him, or maybe he wanted to exploit the literal terms of his employer's stipulation. In testing the limits of his freedom, Thomson defied the intention, if not the letter, of his contract. He wrote some articles about smoking, such as "Gautier as a Hashish-eater," "Shakespeare and Tobacco," and "Tobacco at the Opera." Occasionally, as in "How the Weed Has Been Persecuted," he used smoking to profess his loathing, as a secularist, of religious temperance movements. For most of 1878, Thomson was preoccupied with "Tobacco Smuggling in the Last Generation," a summary of a blue-book report on tobacco duties. The project, which *Cope's* editor John Fraser closely supervised, required much research. In fact, the constraints of subject are nearly always evident in *Cope's*. An article on Carlyle contains this scenario: "As he smoked in his quiet study, and thought over the affairs of Europe, he came to the conclusion that there should be nobody at the head of men unless he was the leader of men" (*Cope's* Apr. 1871: 152). A short biography of William I of Prussia ends with the sentence: "Not in smoke, assuredly, ended the daring and determined schemes of the Smoking King" (*Cope's* Apr. 1872: 301). In an unenthusiastic appeal on behalf of Holyoake, who in 1875 was sick and broke, Thomson pictures him "under a cloud" after "so long smoking ignorance and humbug" (*Cope's* Apr. 1875: 735). In these passages, "smoking" no longer represents *Cope's* product. It implies obfuscation and emptiness in the notices about Holyoake. In the other contexts it means, if anything, destruction. Thomson was hired to link refinement and culture to a physical act, smoking. Presumably he would have to represent the act, but Thomson flouted the condition of his employment and abstracted "smoking" into various signs of negation. The word "smoke," or "smoker," usually had no concrete representational role in Thomson's pieces (nor in the work of any of the contributors).[2]

As far as anyone knows, *Cope's* did not object to Thomson's interpretation of the agreement. In fact it boasted of its association with Thomson after his death, when it collected his articles in one of its "Smoke-room Booklets." In his introduction, Walter Lewin (1889: 12) writes as an apologist for both Thomson and *Cope's*:

> It was much more than an advertising sheet, as its many readers were well aware. It was a literary journal written by men of known ability. It served its primary purpose of advertising Messrs. Cope's tobacco by maintaining a high standard of literary excellence, by which means it found entrance and attracted respectful attention where a mere "trade advertising sheet" would certainly have been disregarded.

Lewin goes on to pay Thomson the romantic compliment of sincerity: "Though he never obtrudes himself on his readers, his personality is stamped on all his work: everywhere and always, whatever be the subject, his writing is a true expression of himself" (15). By endowing his writing with a personal and cohesive identity and stressing a complete tie between personality and work, Lewin anticipates the charge that *Cope's* is a tradesheet and its writers hacks, estranged by their labor. *Cope's*, then, is a site of free expression by men of known ability for respectable readers. "It found entrance," Lewin says, without stating where, presumably into the brotherhood of art. It does not exemplify the anathema of Marx, Ruskin, and William Morris – all the famous nineteenth-century detractors of industrial capitalism.

Thomson describes his own relation to *Cope's* with the romantic model of labor in mind, one which remained for him unattainable. While working on "Tobacco Smuggling in the Last Generation," he privately observed a gulf between the "exterior writing" and the "inner self [which] disclaims all responsibility for it." Yet of his general relationship with *Cope's* he declared: "Payment is fair and regular: I have not to violate my conscience by writing what I don't believe, for I *do* believe in tobacco. . . . On the whole one earns a little money in this way not more wearisomely and rather more honourably than in any other just now open to me" (Leonard 1993: 226; quoted in Salt 1889: 130). This justification, with its discrete content, does not contradict Lewin's account; it merely subjects the unattainable romantic model to the hack's perspective. When the mechanical and mercenary structure of the writing defines the writer's relation to production, the rift between production or "exterior writing" and the "inner self" disappears. If one must, in the view of the romantic economists, "believe in" one's work, Thomson "believes in" tobacco, for he buys and smokes it. Lewin does misrepresent Thomson, however, by exaggerating his personal stamp on the articles in the tradesheet; the writing Thomson did for *Cope's* is as distinctive as the character of encyclopedia entries. It suggests, contrary to Lewin's assertion, that Thomson tried to efface evidence of himself, even though the articles were appearing under pseudonyms.

Thomson, moreover, would not have articulated freedom of expression as an extension of himself, for theoretically at least he did not understand personality in the sense that Lewin uses it, as "persistent identity." In an essay of 1865 for the *National Reformer*, he professes the Hegelian concept of life as continuous motion and concludes that organic development itself precludes our fixed sense of personality. The notion of our own and others' selfhood seemed to him a perverse illusion. In his refusal to accept a unitary self, Thomson expresses conventional British skepticism; he obviously had read David Hume's argument against "personal identity" in *A Treatise of Human Nature* and had written on the philosopher for *Cope's*. A person, to Hume, is "nothing but a bundle or collection of different perceptions," which themselves are ephemeral (Hume [1739–40] 1978: 251). Under his influence, Thomson described personality as an idealistic construction of memory, which he also debunked. As a function, it did not exist; it was only the name given to a composite of irreconcilable moods: "It is only in rare moments of meditation that we can discern how black and profound are these abysses yawning between the successive hours of our life" ("Sympathy," 242). If the idea of a unified personality is rejected, the writer cannot be completely and inextricably identified with his or her labor. The Platonic relation, "believing in," then becomes fluid. In his essays for the freethought journals, Thomson so often uses the word "belief" as a signal of false consciousness that his declaration of belief in tobacco seems disingenuous. And it is, in the context of his Humean skepticism. But in economics this faith has a valid role – as a social or public relation.

In public relations, the object of belief is no longer ideal, or part of one's personality; it is an entity of exchange, an object of current (and roving) desire. In other words, Thomson's beliefs cannot be understood within metaphysics; they are operational. Thus Hegel's organicism was an appealing theory for the hack writer: it erased the "concrete signifying body" and all its laboriousness (Goux 1990: 105). Thus the fragmented subject he describes in his essay on personality supports the simulations of leisure in the writing for *Cope's*. His description of his relation with *Cope's* hints at both disaffection and curtailed ambition: "On the whole one earns a little money in this way not more wearisomely and rather more honorably than in any other just now open to me." Lewin is much more extravagant in his description because he privileges art as an ideal form of expression that transcends production, and because his idea of labor stresses intellectual effort. The dominant romantic, anti-capitalistic political economies did not countenance such indifference toward intellectual or unimaginative work without reducing it to manual labor and decrying its conditions of estrangement. (The nineteenth-century attack on John Stuart Mill for proposing the "economic man" who lives to gratify his desires exemplifies this intolerance.[3]) To imply, as Ruskin and Carlyle had, that work is unethical when not a true expression of the self is extreme by late nineteenth-century standards of capitalism. To claim that such work is alienating ignores the power of economic symbols. If hack-work is a sign of a writer's castration – enslavement to an estranged product, an estranging process, and an alien market – in *Cope's* Thomson reversed his own subjection by abstracting the phallic signs of production and consumption. As a result, he simulated the leisure of smoking and became a smoker himself.

Such a transposition involves a deliberate symbolic seizure. It begins as an act of *ressentiment* and results in an abstract exchange between Thomson and his readers, and between the word "smoke" and its nebulous signified. This is possible in a society that acknowledges a general or universal equivalent of value. In Marx's description, the universal equivalent is "the form assumed in common by the values of all commodities; it therefore becomes . . . exchangeable with all and every of them" (Marx 1967: I. 72). In the history of exchange, this equivalent (which now is paper money) is the culmination of a progressive abstraction that began with the material or relative form, in which the value of one commodity was expressed in some other commodity. By making "x commodity A" equal "y commodity B" in the relative form of value, we "equate the labour embodied in the former to that in the latter," Marx explains. The "expression of equivalence between different sorts of commodities . . . alone brings into relief the specific character of value-creating labour" (ibid.: I. 57). Because the kind of labor involved in the manufacture of A and B may differ (Marx's example is tailoring and weaving), relative value embodies human labor in the abstract. As equations of value became less particular and more unified, value found expression in a single socially recognized form – corn, for example – and eventually in one that sloughed off all matter.

It is this progressive abstraction of economic value that Goux (1990) applies to the cryptophoric symbol. The "'profound' nature" of the symbol parallels that of the general or universal equivalent: it replaces and stands for many absent things, often hidden because they are, for various reasons, unpresentable in a modern society that has "divorced economic practices from their diffuse symbolic valences . . . establishing [the economic] as an independent agency" (Goux 1990: 124, 122). In idealist philosophy as in capitalism, the unpresentable is the material source. In this light, just as "smoking" erases its "institutional genesis" – buying and consuming tobacco – Thomson can, in wielding the general equivalent "smoking," abrogate the "concrete signifying body" (ibid.: 124, 95, 105). When "smoking" reaches its culmination and becomes capable of representing anything – when it stands as the general equivalent of value – idealist philosophy serves the hack's construction of the fragmented self in capitalism. At this limit of symbolization, Thomson conveniently obscures his social relation to the institution, just as smoking loses its history of production in the pages of *Cope's*.

As a professed materialist, Thomson often writes of metaphysics as a deliberate neglect or erasure of the material. An essay of 1876 in the *Secularist* by "B.V.," "On the Worth of Metaphysical Systems," treats idealism as a supplement to all rational demonstration. All system-builders, particularly philosophers, know "that even the most obvious and commonplace so-called facts are undermined by deepest metaphysical doubts. Admitting the relative truth, they must seek the absolute basis; acknowledging the limited fact, they hunger for the universal law" (13 May 1876: 306–8). In this essay, among others, Thomson restates the Feuerbachian inversion, what Goux (1990: 94) elsewhere calls "the idealist optical illusion." Anyone who has read *The City of Dreadful Night* knows how committed Thomson was to a negative idealism, however. Its hold on him is especially noticeable when he uses smoking to mean "nothing." Thomson's materialism, his ambition, and his sense of his own position are completely circumscribed by the metaphysics he ridiculed, and the abstracting tendency of language serves him as well as it does *Cope's*. When characterizing his actual position, Thomson cannot use Lewin's romantic rhetoric; he will not fuse his work with a concept of "himself." Yet this ideal of labor forces him into a distanced, negating statement of his position ("On the whole *one* earns a little money in this way *not* more wearisomely" (emphasis added). The idealist perspective he effects through the general equivalent suppresses Thomson's own labor and all association with actual smoking.

Arguably, when smoking loses all meaning in the tradesheet, it does not inflate into the general equivalent but collapses into an economic symbol and becomes, rather than a negative abstraction, operational currency. So in the text read for traditional, symbolic meaning, "smoking" signifies nothing or everything, but in public relations it is a pleonasm marking a consumer's desire. "Smoking" has flattened, lost all depth as a word. In this light, Thomson's work for *Cope's* anticipates a modern development. Goux (1990: 131) observes: "As the predominant social relation becomes founded on economic surplus value, this relation suffers from a depreciation of meaning." Subjects "come to have only an operational relation to substitution and exchange."

The tension between the idealist inflation of language and its operational role surfaces in *Cope's*. The hierarchical world of literature, its great writers and great ideas, awed the editors of the tradesheet and their hirelings; they felt the rift between a hieratic culture of art and their own enterprise, and they strove to overcome the distinction in columns of newsprint on the "greats" and, more subtly but fundamentally, through an effacing language of general equivalence. Their own relations to production are fraught with the tendency toward abstraction and hierarchy in idealism. But in Thomson's perfunctory writing, this hierarchy dissolves; without an interior or a metaphysics, the abstraction of the general equivalent deflates into a kind of function.

In showing how Thomson, along with *Cope's*, concealed his real links with production and advertising, I do not want to reinforce the impression that he was really an unhappy hack and a closet idealist. For both he and *Cope's* were not only aware of the gap between their roles and what he facetiously called "High Art," but enjoyed exploiting their positions.[4] For a time *Cope's* included with its cigars a "Shakespere Card," picturing the Bard in a swirl of the words "Cope's Smokes for All Ages." Captioned illustrations of the seven ages of man surround him, and each contains a smoker: the schoolboy lights up on the sly, the feeble old man gropes for his pipe. Shakespeare himself holds his pipe upside-down, so that it looks like a pen, and points with it to a scroll headed "The Real Cryptogram." "I come to Cope," it begins; three more lines, connected only by their relation to tobacco, follow. The "real" cryptogram, composed in part of passages from *King Lear*, has lost an identifiable, organic relation to the play.[5] The human element, involving depth of character and its potential transcendence into a symbolic realm, is gone. But this does not mean that the lines express a dehumanized language, in the pejorative and idealist sense of the word. The passages now express a human, economic relation between the "old" cryptophoric regime and the consumption of tobacco. In the final joke on the established hierarchy of literature, the great writer rests his elbows on three books: the top one is a volume of *Cope's Tobacco Plant*; the others are the *Novum Organon* and *Bacon Saved*, both by *Cope's*.

Twenty-four by nineteen inches, the Shakespere Card was too big to be a bookmark. It came to purchasers with their tobacco as a token of the ritual with which *Cope's* invested consumption. To help elevate smoking into a rite of cultivated leisure, the factory tradesheet hired Thomson, the man known for ridiculing religion and metaphysics; he used the metaphysical tendency of representative language to mystify his own social relation to *Cope's* and his audience. Thomson continued to admire the priestly class that the esthetic tradition of a profoundly symbolic language engenders; and he aspired to its ranks through such language in his poetry, but in *Cope's* he was consciously engaged in an economic mode of symbolizing. He wrote for the tradesheet at a time when British political economy had begun to recognize the individual experiences of laborers. Intellectual effort, which even Mill had counted, could vary in a task like writing, depending on the worker's ability and the circumstances. It was possible for composition to be menial rather than cerebral, for a writer to be vacant, not vatic. Thomson's association with *Cope's* was comfortable, according to his various biographers, because he did not mourn the loss of interiority in production. It had meant for Thomson and other hacks conscious subjection within the traditions of philosophical idealism, romantic expression, and political economy. But subjecting idealism and its pantheon of artists to economic symbolizing allowed Thomson and *Cope's* detachment, which could be leisurely and amusing. This was not alienation, but the operational equivalent of transcendence.

Notes

1 See the account of the feud in Leonard (1993: 212–15).

2 Because all pieces in *Cope's* are pseudonymous, I cannot be completely certain that every quotation I have used is by Thomson. But obviously I use Thomson to exemplify the circumstances of many hacks.

3 Artists often were excluded from the general idea of the "economic man" in nineteenth-century political economy, although by including mental exertion as

labor in his *Principles of Political Economy* (1848), Mill, theoretically at least, supported a discussion of the artist as exploited laborer. In the general view, however, the difference between manual labor and artistic production was distinct and accepted, and best seen in imaginative literature like Dickens's *Hard Times* (1854). Toward the end of the century George Gissing would challenge this division in *New Grub Street* (1891).

4 Thomson wrote a long essay, "Per Contra: the Poet, High Art, Genius" (*National Reformer* 19 Nov. 1865), in which he argued, against the idea of artistic vocation, that all artists work chiefly for money and the things it buys.

5 These are Edgar's lines (*King Lear* V.iii.124). The full passage is worth quoting because it enhances the joke: "Yet am I noble as the adversary [Edmund] I come to cope." Sources for the other phrases which Thomson strings together are: "The best comforter": *The Tempest* V.i.58; "To bring forth weeds:" *Antony and Cleopatra* I.ii.113; "That give delight and hurt not": *The Tempest* III.ii.147; "Whose smoke, like incense, doth perfume the sky": *Titus Andronicus* I.i.145.

References

Derrida, Jacques (1981). "Economimesis." *Diacritics* 11: 3–25.

Goux, Jean-Joseph (1990). *Symbolic Economies: After Marx and Freud.* Trans. Jennifer Curtiss Gage. Ithaca, NY: Cornell University Press.

Holyoake, G.J., and G.W. Foote (1876). "Policy of Contents." *Secularist* 1 Jan.: 4.

Hume, David ([1739–40] 1978). *A Treatise of Human Nature.* Ed. L.A. Selby-Bigge. 2nd edn. Oxford: Clarendon Press.

Leonard, Tom (1993). *Places of the Mind: The Life and Work of James Thomson ("B.V.").* London: Jonathan Cape.

Lewin, Walter (1889). Introduction to *Selections from Original Contributions to* Cope's Tobacco Plant. Liverpool: Cope's Tobacco Plant, 9–15.

Marx, Karl (1967). *Capital.* Trans. Samuel Moore and Edward Aveling. 3 vols. New York: International.

Salt, Henry Stephens (1889). *The Life of James Thomson ("B.V."): A Critical Study.* London: A.H. Bonner.

Schaefer, William David (1965). *James Thomson (B.V.): Beyond "The City."* Berkeley: University of California Press.

Thomson, James (1865). "The Athanasian Creed." *National Reformer* 1 January: 4.

—— (1871). "Famous Smokers." *Cope's Tobacco Plant* April: 152.

—— (1872)."Zopf und Schwert." *Cope's Tobacco Plant* April: 301.

—— (1876a). Letter to Charles Bradlaugh. *Secularist* 17 June: 394.

—— (1876b). "On the Worth of Metaphysical Systems." *Secularist* 13 May: 306–8.

—— (1876c). Review of *The Life, Work, and Opinions of Heinrich Heine*, by William Stigand. *Secularist* 16 September: 188.

—— (1889). *Selections from Original Contributions by James Thompson to* Cope's Tobacco Plant. Liverpool: Office of Cope's Tobacco Plant.

—— (1881). "Sympathy." In *Essays and Phantasies.* London: Reeves & Turner, 228–49.

Walker, Imogene B. (1950). *James Thomson (B.V.): A Critical Study.* Ithaca, NY: Cornell University Press.

Part VI

MODERNISM AND MARKETS

18

WHO PAID FOR MODERNISM?

Paul Delany

Why in Chrisst's name we arent all millionaires I dont know.
(Ezra Pound to James Joyce, 22 November 1918)

If we want to know who paid for Victorian fiction, the answer is simple: its readers.[1] Victorian novels were produced almost entirely under direct signals from the market. Publishers paid for a novel in one lump on acceptance of the manuscript, according to their judgment of its success: £3,000, for example, for Trollope's *The Way We Live Now* (1873) or £10,000 for Disraeli's *Endymion* (1880).[2] The novelist provided the middle-class reading public with an agreeable work, which until the death of the three-decker in 1895 was close to being a standard commodity; and the price was a measure of how well the task of literary production had been achieved (Griest 1970).

It was Ezra Pound's aim to establish a modernist literary economy in isolation from the literary marketplace. But someone still had to pay for modernism; my aim here is to show where the money came from, what modernism's supporters expected for their money, and how the practice of modernist writers in England was shaped by the sources of their support. The direct source of money for much of early modernism was a regime of patronage; but I will be arguing that the market was not easily or permanently shunned, even if modernism's relation to it was one of complex intermediacy.

In the last two decades of the nineteenth century, two developments prepared the way for the modernist mode of literary production: a major restructuring of the literary marketplace, and the establishment of an alternative to market forces in what I will call a "rentier culture." The market was changed by a general increase in prosperity, and by the near-universal literacy achieved in Britain by 1900. Mass literacy did not produce sweetness and light, but rather literary production for mass taste. By 1893 the Harmsworth family – which proved most adept at catering to this new market – controlled publications with a circulation of one and a half million copies a week. In 1896 they launched the *Daily Mail* with the slogan "A penny newspaper for a halfpenny" (Bourne 1990: 22, 27). Journalism became the dominant form; even "serious" writers came to depend on it for a substantial part of their income, and *all* writers had to recognize that they were now more a class defined by its relation to the market than a profession defined by its place in a prestige order.[3]

By the 1890s, a huge expansion of the reading public had swept aside the dominant literary formation of the previous fifty years: the three-decker novel that had been directed at an upper middle-class readership and distributed through subscription libraries. Other changes in the literary marketplace included: the recognition of British copyright by the US in 1891; the rise of literary agents in the 1890s; the shift from outright sale of literary property to payment by royalty; the fragmentation of novelistic form after the end of the three-decker; and the relaxation of censorship in consequence of the decline of the circulating libraries. These shifts worked together synergistically to create a new literary system, one that conditioned the creative impulses of all literary people and produced complex secondary effects. It is against the background of this new system that we can best understand Pound's project: not just to "make it new" at the level of the individual work, but also to construct a fully articulated *counter*-system for modernist literary production.

Rentier culture preceded modernism as an alternative to the production of literature for the market. Since at least the seventeenth century, many major British writers – notably Milton, Pope, Keats, Shelley, Byron, Tennyson, Browning – had supported themselves on parental allowances or inherited money. Freedom from mundane economic necessity can be associated with a preference for poetry over prose, and with other kinds of unconventionality such as living abroad and political utopianism.[4] The concept of "rentier culture" connotes a more integrated social position, along with a scaling up from such miniature social formations as the friendship networks of the romantic poets.

It was the massive accumulation of wealth over successive generations in nineteenth-century England that created, in Eric Hobsbawm's terms:

> a class of *rentiers*, who lived on the profit and savings of the previous two or three generations' accumulations. By 1871 Britain contained 170,000 "persons of rank and property" without visible occupation – almost all of them women.
>
> (Hobsbawm 1968: 96–97)

The census of 1911 recorded 52,432 men and 295,712 women as having "Private Means" and "Without Specified Occupations." Since inheritance favored the male heir, these figures must greatly underestimate the number of male rentiers, who presumably would define themselves by some occupation even if most of their income came from the return on their capital. It seems reasonable to assume that British rentier society included at least half a million adults in 1911; and also, importantly, that women were well represented in this group and may even have predominated. E.M. Forster, for example, takes it for granted that the Schlegel sisters in *Howards End* are as common and recognizable a social type as an insurance clerk or a businessman.

As the main consumers of high culture, the rentiers shaped modernism in ways to be discussed in detail below. As producers – I speak here of rentier writers of fiction – they are distinctive for their self-reflexiveness: for finding their characteristic subject matter in their own style of life and moral preoccupations. To put it another way, the rentier class was now large enough to suggest a novelistic rather than lyrical literary representation. We may take Henry James and E.M. Forster as the great senior and junior representatives of rentier culture in fiction; Galsworthy was another significant figure, and Thomas Mann would be their exemplary German cousin.[5] George Gissing both scrutinized it (*The Whirlpool*, 1897) and longed to share its comforts (*The Private Papers of Henry Ryecroft*, 1903). The case of Virginia Woolf is too complex to examine here: she was in differing degrees a rentier, a literary journalist, a best-selling novelist, a literary entrepreneur, and a modernist in the more astringent and experimental elements of her fiction.

Rentier culture distinguished itself from market-sensitive art by elaborating an ethic of *refinement*. It is no coincidence that Henry James wrote his classic defense of the art novel, "The Art of Fiction," in response to Walter Besant, who, as a "good steady man of letters," argued that "he who works for pay must respect the prejudices of his customers" (quoted in Griest 1970: 139). The art novel assumed a certain leisured sensitivity both in its readers and in the characters it represented. Rentier artists were more likely to have roots in the mercantile or financial sectors of the economy; their inherited incomes absolved them from active struggle in the marketplace, but neither were they responsible for a landed estate or a local community. Their separation from the market was expressed in the common Victorian term for them, "the independent classes."

The modernists were also hostile to such marketable talents as Walter Besant or Arnold Bennett, and based their esthetic on resistance to literary commodification. Yet support for this resistance was largely derived – through the mediation of patronage – from the rentier culture; so that the modernists were dependent on the independence of those with greater means than themselves. They were both subordinate to rentier culture and concerned to distinguish themselves from it. If rentier culture offered an escape from the vulgarities of the literary marketplace (including the vulgarity of popular success), and an affinity with the oppositional stance of late Victorian esthetes and decadents, why did it not satisfy the literary aspirations of figures like Yeats, Joyce, Eliot and, above all, Pound? In part, certainly, because they were all outsiders by nationality. They mistrusted the embeddedness of rentier culture in the most privileged stratum of English society, with all the exclusiveness and complacency that were by-products of this status. A culture so intimately linked to the established order could scarcely function as a true avant-garde of the continental type. Further, for an artist to have a private income was largely a question of luck, so it would be difficult to base an ideologically coherent movement on such a randomly distributed resource. Some people who had private incomes would not be modernists, and some people who were modernists would not have private incomes. Early modernism, in defining itself as a movement of cultural insurgency, felt the need to sharpen its differences with the rentiers on one side and commercial writers on the other. Yet this oppositional stance coexisted with a craving, often only thinly disguised, for absorption and acceptance.[6] Culturally, Pound and Eliot both envisioned the re-establishment of a conservative order; Eliot had his own modest private income from his father's estate (with the expectation of more), and both Eliot and Pound married into the British rentier class in the expectation of social and perhaps material enrichment.[7]

Modernism and patronage

Where rentier writing shows a tropism towards refinement, sensitivity and exclusiveness, modernists show a more aggressive and deliberate attempt to make their works "unmarketable." "Modernism," Terry Eagleton (1988: 392) argues, "is among other things a strategy whereby the work of art resists commodification, holds out by the skin of its teeth against those social forces which would degrade it to an exchangeable object." The road away from the market could lead only to some form of patronage – whether self-patronage, from the writer's private income in rentier culture, or patronage from outside supporters of the modernist agenda. Modernism was indeed a "patronage culture"; yet its embrace of patronage entailed two nagging difficulties. One was that literature – unlike the plastic arts – still faced the imperatives of reproduction and circulation, even if this was done outside of mass-market channels. Literary works whose production was supported by patronage were offered for general sale once they were complete, and patrons supported not only individual writers but their distinctive means of distribution: the little magazine and the avant-garde press. It would prove hard to maintain the distinction between a modernist prestige culture whose sole currency was the critical approval of mandarins like Pound or Eliot and a market mechanism that translated approval into cash sales (and, eventually, sales that were very large).[8] Exclusiveness does not conflict with commodification; it may even be the highest form of it. Patronage allowed the young modernist writers to survive while they labored at forms too esoteric for the commercial literary culture. Yet the projects they undertook, in subsidized obscurity, were grandiose in scale and in breadth of cultural reference; their implicit aim was to progress from their avant-garde coteries into the public sphere of the great capitals.

The other problem with modernist patronage was its gender. Those who were active in the Social Darwinist milieu of pre-1914 capitalism – virtually all male – found their primary satisfaction in the struggle itself, rather than in any of the leisure arts. Like Forster's Wilcoxes, they were likely to look down on the cultural sphere as effete and feminized – or, at best, a sphere where their wives or artistic children might pass their time blamelessly.[9] John Quinn was probably the only one of the main patrons of modernism who contributed money that he had made himself. The others either inherited their money or, like Lady Rothermere, spent on culture part of their husband's profits from business. It is not surprising, then, that most of modernism's patrons were women – though this did not inhibit male modernists from biting the hand of the gender that fed them. Andreas Huyssen (1986: 189) has attributed the suspicion towards women of modernist male writers to "the increasingly marginal position of literature and the arts in a society in which masculinity is identified with action, enterprise and progress – with the realms of business, industry, science, and law." The male writer may embrace this marginality, cultivating his "imaginary femininity" through identification with estheticism, homosexuality, or female eroticism and hysteria. From Flaubert to Eliot, Joyce, and D.H. Lawrence, male authors responded to the popularity of "women's" literature by colonizing its emotional territory for the profit of patriarchal high art.[10] Yet at the same time, they resisted feminine cultural hegemony, or even women's desire to speak for themselves: the author of Molly Bloom's soliloquy preferred the actual women in his life to wear long dresses and be silent. When Eliot warned against "the Feminine in literature" he meant women writers and their demands, but also the feminine in American culture that stood for the refinement or repression of male energies (Eliot 1988: 204). Pound explicitly voiced his desire to exclude women from the modernist movement: seeking John Quinn's support for a proposed new review in 1915, he wrote: "You will see that I have included hardly any feminine names. I think active America is getting fed up on gynocracy and that it's time for a male review" (Pound 1991: 41).

Leslie Fiedler has spoken of a nineteenth-century American literary culture that was "simultaneously commercialized and feminized" – to the consternation of "serious" male authors (quoted in Gilbert and Gubar 1988: 143). The purchasing power of the female reader generated the successful female popular author, a constant target for modernist misogyny (ibid.: 146–47). Women's power as consumers and sponsors of art made them, in the eyes of Pound and Eliot, threats to their phallic autonomy. The modernists routinely produced work of *ressentiment* against the milieu that sustained them: generic satires like Eliot's "Portrait of a Lady" or Pound's "Portrait d'une Femme," or personal ones like the treatment of Ottoline Morrell in *Women in Love* and in Huxley's *Point Counter Point*. Another characteristic response was for the male modernist to divide his loyalties between a sexual muse and a chaste patron, by which means he could evade the threat to his masculine image of both sleeping with a woman and taking money from her. Yeats's concurrent dealings with Olivia Shakespear and Lady Gregory, or Joyce's with Nora and Harriet Shaw Weaver, followed this pattern. When the two categories were confused, trouble was sure to follow, as in D.H. Lawrence's triangles with Frieda and Lady Ottoline Morrell, or Mabel Dodge Luhan. Lawrence was unusual in accepting patronage only if he was desperate and paying it back as soon as he could; but accepting it from a woman was especially repugnant to him.

Female patronage allowed Yeats, Pound, Hemingway, and Joyce to wait out the market's early indifference to experimentalism, and to do so in a milieu much more agreeable than the stereotypical garret of the avant-garde artist. Olivia Shakespear, for example, was at the center of a nexus of social support for modernism (Harwood 1989). With her husband's £1,000 a year and some money of her own she gave sexual and social comfort to Yeats. Lady Gregory, his platonic patron, lent him money as needed and lodged him during summers at Coole. Thanks to her, Yeats recorded, he was able "through the greater part of my working life to write without thought of anything but the beauty or the utility of what I wrote. Until I was nearly fifty, my writing never brought me more than two hundred a year, and most often less, and I am not by nature economical" (Yeats 1955: 409). Pound's writing brought much less than £200 a year, and he steadfastly refused to take regular employment. Margaret Cravens apparently gave him £200 a year until her suicide in 1912; two years later, Olivia Shakespear finally agreed that Pound should marry her daughter Dorothy, whose income was also about £200 (Harwood 1989: 144, 179). Humphrey Carpenter (1988: 235) observes that Pound's "access to Dorothy's income inevitably affected the nature of his literary work in the years following the marriage. It freed him not only from the necessity of earning his living but even of considering his audience." This was a freedom that Pound enjoyed for the remainder of his career, as Dorothy, through successive gifts and inheritances, became steadily richer.[11] The long roll-call of women who supported modernism financially or morally makes it evident that, even as male modernists decried the influence of female culture, they were profoundly indebted to it, sometimes even for their very survival as artists.[12]

Patronage and form

Orientation to the market assumes acceptance of an already existing commodity form; patronage enables the writer to produce something relatively unconstrained either formally or temporally. The ideal-typical example is the composition of *Ulysses* and *Finnegans Wake* by a method of gradual accretion, whereby each successive draft of an episode is longer and more complex, and the *Wake* as a whole is an accretion on its predecessor. A similar esthetic appears in the composition of the *Cantos*. Joyce's project of relentless "densification" of an original narrative core could not have been carried through without Harriet Weaver's support. To use up seven years for *Ulysses* and sixteen for *Finnegans Wake* was not a commercial rate of literary production; repeatedly Joyce told his patron that he needed more time, and wanted her to send more money. Without his subsidy Joyce would have had to write more numerous but simpler books, as commercial novelists have always had to do.

Joyce's decisions about form were, of course, over-determined; and financial circumstances can scarcely explain every local particularity of his works. But Harriet Weaver's decision to endow Joyce with a substantial block of capital – effectively without conditions – gave him the security to push his fictional method to its full extension (Lidderdale 1970). In both Joyce and Pound we observe an imaginative ambition to pile up riches; to combine comprehensiveness and fineness of detail to achieve works that aggregate in themselves every formal and thematic resource of their literary era. Distinguishing his aims from those of the Balzac–Zola–Arnold Bennett line of realism, Pound observed that "Not everything is interesting or rather not everything is interesting enough to be written into novels, which are at all but the best a dilution of life."[13] Such novels, written for the market, were unproblematic representations of everyday life that were immediately recirculated as literary commodities. Modernist masterworks, in contrast, issued from a tertiary mode of production in which pre-existing representations were accumulated and re-combined in order to create new values – a process that, both in the financial and literary systems, took place at a remove from the markets that provide for primary needs of consumers.

Modernist production is no longer the representation of a coherent social reality, but a piecing of shards into a structure whose value depends on the labor of reconstruction devoted to it by its author. The ineluctable secondariness of this imaginative work leaves the author with the task of restoring a shattered inheritance, to make it yield something on which to live. The shattering itself is blamed on the industrial and commercial power of the nineteenth century, when "all that is solid melts into air," and European organic society is deprived of its integrity. The modernists, coming at the end of the nineteenth-century regime of capitalist accumulation – and benefiting from it, of course – feared that their time might be one of cultural exhaustion. This sense of dissolution was made literal in Eliot's selling off, during the early 1920s, his shares in the Hydraulic Press-Brick Company, which his family controlled. The company's letterhead proclaimed it "The Largest Manufacturers of Face Brick in the World" but its power and glory meant nothing to Eliot, since he wished only to diversify his holdings and ensure a reliable supplementary income. Just as the rentier withdraws from direct participation in business to cultivate a more refined style of life, so does the modernist take up a secondary or indirect relation to literary production. Yet both rentier and modernist author (and all the more one who occupies both positions) are haunted by their loss of "primary" productivity or usefulness – something that could have been achieved by actual participation in business in the one case, or by success in an unproblematized literary genre in the other.

Modernism and the market

Modern literary theory has proposed the subordination of the writer's subjectivity to impersonal "authorship systems" of genres, ideologies, discourse-formations, and the like. Yet these structuralist models have taken little note of the literary marketplace, whose tendency also is to reduce the author to a "price taker" faced with an established mass taste that he or she cannot easily influence. One of the most imposing manifestations of literary impersonality is that the market has its own preferences in subjectivity, and that any pristine authorial sense of self must be alienated – in both a psychic and an economic sense – in order to be "realized." The only escape from those market preferences, for the modernist author, seems to be through irony, fragmentation, and pastiche. Jameson (1981: 107) suggests that traditional generic writing can only persist in popular rather than high culture:

> [T]he generic contract and institution itself . . . falls casualty to the gradual penetration of a market system and a money economy. With the elimination of an institutionalized social status for the cultural producer and the opening of the work of art itself to commodification, the older generic specifications are transformed into a brand-new system against which any authentic artistic expression must necessarily struggle. The older generic categories do not, for all that, die out, but persist in the half-life of the subliterary genres of mass culture, transformed into the drugstore and airport paperback lines of gothics, mysteries, romances, bestsellers, and popular biographies. . . .

Jameson's argument has been widely influential; but it goes too far in reducing modernist literary practice to a simple reaction against the alienation of subjectivity into commodity. There is an evident difference between the writing practice of a Trollope who writes two thousand words every day before breakfast, and that of a Joyce who takes a day to decide on the order of words in one sentence. Patronage did insulate the modernist writer from the immediate demands of a market that wanted a steady stream of predictable works. Yet modernist works, even if they arrived at the market more intermittently and by a more circuitous route, ended up as commodities too. Just as being a rentier can be said to mystify the relation between an income and its origin, so does literary patronage mystify the relation between the production of a work and its ultimate destination.

In trumpeting that "Nothing written for pay is worth printing. ONLY what has been written AGAINST the market," Pound sought to establish a modernist myth of economic innocence (quoted in Carpenter 1988: 236). The myth has since flourished – in such instances as Van Gogh's inability to sell his paintings, Joyce's difficulty in getting his early works published, or *Under the Volcano* selling three copies in North America in the year of its publication. It proposes an irreducible hostility between the vision of modernist art and the philistine world of popular taste. The paranoid and hermetic features of modernism can then be justified by Nietzsche's maxim that "The strong always have to be defended against the weak." Yet a salient feature of literary modernism is the speed with which it established itself in the literary marketplace that it professed to despise, and the hegemony that it achieved after World War II – and, in spite of the canon wars, still enjoys.[14]

Lawrence Rainey (1989) has examined the "scaling-up" of modernist distribution from avant-garde journals of tiny circulation like *The Egoist* or *The Little Review*, to *The Dial*, and finally to the mass-market *Vanity Fair*. Scofield Thayer and James Sibley Watson Jr contributed $220,000 between 1920 and 1922 to support *The Dial* – money that bought them a key role in the popularizing of modernism in North America:

> When Pound suggested in May and August [1922] that [*The Waste Land*] be published by *Vanity Fair*, his proposal looked forward to modernism's future, to the ease and speed with which a market economy could purchase, assimilate, commodify, and revindicate the works of a literature whose ideological premises were bitterly inimical towards its ethos and cultural operations. These distinct moments were mediated by what, in the early 1920s, was modernism's present: the world epitomised by *The Dial*, a form of production supported by massive and unprecedented patronage which facilitated modernism's transition from a literature of an exiguous elite to a position of prestigious dominance.
>
> (Rainey 1989: 34)

Rainey goes on to argue that these three American journals – *The Little Review*, *The Dial*, *Vanity Fair* – "are best viewed not as antagonists who represented alien or incompatible ideologies, but as protagonists who shared a common terrain, whose fields of activity overlapped and diverged within a shared spectrum of marketing and consumption" (ibid.: 37). The twentieth-century avant-garde is no longer an enclave of artistic integrity, holding itself aloof from the swamp of commercialism; rather, Rainey argues, it "played no special role, possessed no ideological privilege; instead it was constituted by a specific array of marketing and publicity structures that were integrated in varying degrees with the larger economic apparatus of its time. Its typical endeavor was to develop an idiom, a shareable language that could be marketed and yet allow a certain space for individuation" (38).

Rainey's essay is a cogent riposte to the modernist myth of *l'art pour l'art*; but his revisionism – like much New Historicist writing on commodification – is too monolithic. That *The Waste Land* and Pears Soap both benefited from marketing campaigns tells us something about modern culture – but not everything, and the distinctions need to be observed as well as the convergences. The rentier culture out of which modernism emerged was a particular class formation, hostile to "trade," marketing and mass consumption; it mimicked aristocratic values, and followed European (as opposed to American) conventions of "old money" behavior. To assert its separateness and superiority, this class favored modes of consumption that were intangible (in the sense of refinement of manners) or that highlighted exclusive, artisanal or patinated goods (McCracken 1988: 30–43). Much of the rentier style can, of course, be demystified. Commodification affects all classes in the early twentieth century, and a rentier way of life is often underwritten by such occluded articles of manufacture as Tarrant's Black Lead (in Gissing's *In the Year of Jubilee*), the Eliot family's bricks, or the unmentionable object produced by Mrs. Newsome's New England factory in *The Ambassadors*. Nonetheless, the economic milieu that incubated modernism did manage to distance itself from the brute material realities of the literary marketplace where writers like Gissing, Wells, or Arnold Bennett had to make their way.

Pound insistently attacked Bennett because he believed himself to be a fundamentally different kind of writer, and with reason. The complexity and allusiveness of Pound's and Eliot's poetry, their condescension towards everyday life and everyday people – let alone their decision to write poetry rather than fiction – *did* exclude them from the Bennett market. The commercial success of some modernist works in the 1920s could scarcely have been predicted, nor does it make sense to view this success as the pay-off for a deliberate campaign by modernist writers to commodify their productions. The "integration" (Rainey's term) of modernism into contemporary market capitalism occurred in various ways, and as the result of various forces. The market became interested in modernism rather than the other way round: *Women in Love*, *Under the Volcano* and even *Ulysses* ended up as movies after their authors' deaths because they were famous enough to become "properties," regardless of their authors' original artistic intentions. Other modernists saw that they could dilute their style into commercial viability, as in Hemingway's classic trajectory of experimentalism, commercial success, and artistic decline. Rather than expose the marketing of *The Waste Land* as mere commodification, we need to explore in detail the segmentation of the literary marketplace, the nature of the "product cycle" for literary works, and the interaction within the market site of formally differentiated "monetary" and "prestige" systems.

Circulation, refinement, and patronage

An *objet d'art* does not move through the same channels as a mass consumer product; but this differentiation only confirms the market's capacity to value and circulate everything, from a bar of soap to a reputation. The market has always been a sensitive register of the refinement and scarcity of a good: in transgressing the normal expectations of genre, modernist works achieve a particularity – a kind of ontological scarcity – that is a crucial element in their value. In their material embodiment, too, modernist first editions typically sell for at least a hundred times more than the price at which they were first offered. When the work is unique, such as a sculpture or a painting, increases in market value have often taken on a legendary quality of excess. In consequence, those searching for good "investments" try to buy earlier and earlier in an artist's career. The market history of recent decades has conclusively refuted the modernist work's original claim to be an "anti-commodity." It is rather a super-commodity: something whose canonical status rests on a collective evaluation, and whose worth is almost completely dissociated from the original investment in its production.

Modernism's status in the market is achieved as an estimate of *refinement*. Whether published or offered for sale as an object, the exchange value of the avant-garde work of art is measured by its distance from the crude utility of staple and tangible goods; indeed, the highest values in the market have always accrued to things farthest removed from practical use. When we consider the employment of capital, similarly, we observe the gradient from the extraction of raw materials at the periphery, to their working-up in manufacturing centres, and on to tertiary functions of finance and distribution in the metropolis. The task of the economic critic is to try all the links of the chain: to note, for example, how in the 1930s the composition of both *Finnegans Wake* and *The Cantos* was being supported by investments in the Canadian Northern Ontario Railway, a part of the colonial extractive infrastructure traditionally popular with metropolitan rentiers. Canadian Northern 4 percent bonds figured prominently in the investment portfolios of both James Joyce and Dorothy Pound. Neither Joyce nor Ezra Pound would have had the slightest interest in the culture of Northern Ontario, of course – but to reap a yield from a position of distance and disinterest was precisely the point of the London capital market. Frank Lentricchia (1994: 65), expressing a typical kind of New Historicist antipathy to capitalism, has argued that the modern economic order works "to so establish and saturate the conditions of creativity as to eliminate all social spaces that might be hospitable to the personality of idiosyncratic imagination." But the social space of modernism is closer to a final stage of capitalism than it is a genuine site of opposition to it.

Although modernist writing could not exist outside of capitalism, it would be crude to assume that all capitalist commodities comprise a passive, undifferentiated mass. The modern literary marketplace – like market society as a whole – includes many active subcultures of readers and producers. There is a market for detective stories, for pornography, for self-help books, for screenplays, for avant-garde poetry, and so on down the list. All respond in particular ways to market forces, though some works break out of their categories and "cross over" into a wider and more lucrative market segment (as most modernist masterworks eventually succeeded in doing). But just as literary value can be defined as everything in a work that *exceeds* the formal requirements of its genre, so does "high" literature exceed the market conditions under which it is produced. It is not merely that these conditions fail to explain all the specificities of literary works, and the formal differences between them; it is also that, *pace* the new historicism, the status of these works as tradable goods does not render trivial the ability of many of them – *The Way We Live Now*, say, or *The Wings of the Dove*, or *The Waste Land* – to articulate the most searching critiques of market society.

Where modernism should be situated, therefore, is in certain enclaves comprehended by market society, yet with a *relative* autonomy within it. In these enclaves works were "traded" by critics and other "cultural brokers" who determined distribution and reception. Audiences could "invest" in authors according to how their works were "priced" in the stock exchange of modernist reputations. Bourdieu (1984: 1) has spoken of "cultural capital" as a realm opposed in principle to economism: "There is an economy of cultural goods, but it has a specific logic." Yet relative autonomy, in my terms, means that the specificity of the cultural sphere is bounded by its economic constraints. The avant-garde resembles other prestige system proto-markets (marriage, sports, literary criticism) that look implicitly to a settlement day when status tokens from the one market are cashed for banknotes from the other. At the level of material subsistence, the modernist cultural enterprise was supported by real money that necessarily came from the market economy, whether directly or indirectly – from inheritances, patronage, allowances from parents, jobs in Lloyds Bank or the Trieste Berlitz School, and so on.

Modernist patrons and clients alike understood the linkages between the modernist and the commercial literary systems. Scofield Thayer and James Watson, like Lady Rothermere, Lady Ottoline Morrell, Harold Loeb, Nathalie Barney, and many others, used their money – not all of them had a great deal of it – to gain entry into literary circles and bask in the reflected glory of the writers they assisted. But they used their money because they could not have gained entry on their talent, and everyone understood the difference between what patronage could and could not buy. The fact that the people involved in these transactions – writers and patrons – each had something the other lacked, and that the transactions involved money (though more than just money changed hands), does not mean that modernist production was determined through and through by the marketplace in the sense that, say, the novels of Gene Stratton Porter were.[15] A patroness provided "venture capital" for the development of works that were not yet viable in the commercial market; she did not give a reward (as she would have during the renaissance), but made an investment, both in the artist's future development and in the transformation of public taste. Her own profit, if it accrued, would be in literary prestige rather than money, as she gained a position of honor in the living pantheon of modernism.

Pound's relations with John Quinn enable us to correlate cultural practice with a patron's status within capitalism. Among the major patrons of modernism, Quinn, a corporate lawyer in New York, was perhaps the only active man of affairs. His patronage was more opportunistic, more directive, and closer to the market than that of women like Harriet Weaver; but it is ironic that his "masculine" shrewdness produced only modest and cautious support for Pound's editorial schemes. Quinn reserved his serious money for tangible objects: works of art by such artists as Matisse, Brancusi, Picasso, Rousseau.[16] His literary interests found a focus in actual books and manuscripts: he brokered the sale of a manuscript of *Ulysses* to the Rosenbach Foundation in the US, paid $10,000 for Conrad manuscripts between 1911 and 1919, and accepted as a gift from Eliot the manuscript of *The Waste Land*.[17]

Quinn took for granted the implicitly commercial relation between patron and producer in the visual arts. However much the patron might consider himself a friend and benefactor to the artist, at the end of the day a material object changed hands at a price set by negotiation, and the price arrived at was an index of the balance of interest in the relationship. Pound's solution to this awkwardness was that Quinn should only buy from artists whose work was still cheap:

> My whole drive is that if a patron buys from an artist who needs money (needs money to buy tools, time and food) the patron then makes himself equal to the artist, he is building art into the world. He creates.
>
> If he buys even of living artists who are already famous or already making £12,000 per year, he ceases to create. He sinks back to the rank of a consumer.
>
> (Pound 1991: 23)

The trouble with this advice was that the patron expected the artist to *become* famous before long. If he did not, it was a mistake to buy his work; if he did, the patron was simply a shrewd investor who bought in advance of a rise. Pound himself played the same card in urging Quinn to buy drawings by Wyndham Lewis: "As to Lewis, I think his prices will soar like Matisse's when once they start" (ibid.: 26). No line that Pound might draw between poor and rich artists could obscure the desire of any artist to sell high, and of any patron to buy low – as Carter Ratcliff has argued (1991: 147):

> Western art gains its entrepreneurial flavor from the Western self. We define ourselves in competition for economic profits that, thoroughly examined, reveal other aspects – social, cultural, esthetic. Likewise, the most transcendentally esthetic behavior or image reveals motives in some sense economic. The esthetic is an aspect of the economic, as the economic is an aspect of the esthetic.

No one knew this better than Quinn; and Pound knew it too in his own way, hard as he fought to change the actual workings of the economic/esthetic system that he encountered when he moved to London in 1908.

The development of the modernist market niche under the regime of patronage was a relatively brief episode in literary history, enabled by conditions that could never again be reproduced. By 1933 Pound himself was already casting a backward eye at the moment of modernism – though he was not inclined to give any credit to Western capitalism for what had been achieved:

> It is no answer to say that "my" programme in art and letters has gradually been forced through, has, to some extent, grabbed its place in the sun. For one thing, I don't care about "minority culture." I have never cared a damn about snobbisms of writing *ultimately* for the few. Perhaps that is an exaggeration. Perhaps I was a worse young man than I think I was.
>
> Serious art is unpopular at its birth. But it ultimately forms the mass culture.
>
> (Pound 1973: 231)

"Ultimately" is an important term here. New Historicist arguments tend to assume that because the destination of modernism is commodification – in the form, say, of a modernist classic that sells half a million copies a year, or Van Gogh's "Irises" selling for $59 million at Sotheby's – the commodification was implicit in the very moment of conception. But modernist patronage was not just a screen behind which commercialism pulled all the strings of reputation and financial reward; it was rather a specific regime that deserves to be examined, in all its complexity and contradiction, within the historical conjuncture that made it possible.

Notes

1 Most of the major Victorian novelists depended on the literary marketplace for most of their income; a few (especially women) were supported by their families or had private incomes, but success for a novel was closely linked to its popularity in the market.

2 These payments are roughly equivalent to £150,000 and £500,000 in 1996 values.

3 Qualitative changes in status were associated with quantitative shifts: the census category of "Authors, Editors, Journalists" grew from 6,111 in 1881 to 8,272 in 1891, 11,060 in 1901, and 13,786 in 1911 (*Census* 1904). However, this increase of more than double in thirty years is understated, as the figure for 1881 includes "Shorthand Clerks," who in subsequent censuses were moved to another category.

4 Once established, of course, several of these poets earned large incomes from the commercial sale of their works.

5 Strictly speaking, Henry James was a rentier only as a young man. His grandfather was an Irish immigrant who made a fortune of $3 million in upstate New York; James's father inherited an income of about $10,000 a year which made him, as he put it, "leisured for life" (Edel 1987: 4). From early in his career Henry James was determined to earn enough to support himself from the sale of his writings, and succeeded in doing so (Anesko 1986 gives details of his earnings). However, James was shaped by the rentier mentality of creative freedom and disinterestedness, and he found his richest subject matter in the rentier milieu.

6 Wyndham Lewis's obsessive attacks on Bloomsbury defined the pole of opposition; integration with rentier culture was most evident in Yeats's, Pound's and Eliot's marriages.

7 Eliot's financial affairs are too complex to detail here; in brief, he made a substantial income at Lloyds Bank (£650 a year by 1924), which was supplemented with about £250 a year from his inheritance and gifts from his mother and brother.

8 The translation of key modernist works from the cultural margin into canonical best-sellers was linked to the arrival of mass higher education after 1945, and is beyond my present scope.

9 Capitalists who encouraged such family links with the arts were likely to be in tertiary sectors like finance or international trade rather than in manufacturing.

10 See *Madame Bovary*, the "Nausikaa" chapter of *Ulysses*, sections II and III of *The Waste Land*.

11 Dorothy's uncle Herbert Leaf gave her £1,000 in 1928, and her mother gave her £5,000 in 1931. All this money seems to have been put into Italian bonds which became worthless during the war, with the result that Pound had to rely on the $2,000 a year he was given for his propaganda broadcasts. After the war, Dorothy's inheritances from her mother and her uncle Henry Tucker, which had been blocked in London, were released; they amounted to about £40,000 (Harwood 1989: 179–81, 192).

12 Gilbert and Gubar (1988: 147) list the principal female sponsors of modernism (147).

13 Pound (1992: 7). In saying that "Flaubert, Trollope, and towards the last Henry James got through to money" (1973: 155), Pound was presumably identifying a novelistic tradition that was more worthy of being taken seriously.

14 The evolution of the Hogarth Press from the avant-garde to the commercial mainstream – paralleling Virginia Woolf's success as a best-selling author from the mid-1920s on – is a further confirmation of modernism's responsiveness, in the medium term, to market incentives. However, the Woolfs could not give Eliot incentive enough. They were both cultural patrons and publishers of Eliot's early work (the Hogarth Press published his *Poems* in 1919 and *The Waste Land* in

1922); as he became more renowned, he disappointed the Woolfs by moving his books to Faber's (Ackroyd 1984: 153–54).

15 Horace Liveright wrote to Pound in February 1923: "Just think, Eliot may make about $500 on the book rights of this poem. And Gene Stratton Porter makes $40,000 to $60,000 a year out of her books" (quoted in Rainey 1989: 33).

16 In the event, Quinn's collection was auctioned off after his death at a time of market weakness, and realized less than he had paid for it (Reid 1968: 660–61).

17 On Quinn's Conrad purchases, see Meyers (1991: 260, 352). The manuscripts were sold in 1923 for $111,000.

References

Ackroyd, Peter (1984). *T.S. Eliot: A Life*. New York: Simon & Schuster.

Anesko, Michael (1986). *"Friction With the Market:" Henry James and the Profession of Authorship*. New York: Oxford University Press.

Bourdieu, Pierre (1984). *Distinction: A Social Critique of the Judgement of Taste*. Trans. Richard Nice. London: Routledge & Kegan Paul.

Bourne, Richard (1990). *Lords of Fleet Street: The Harmsworth Dynasty*. London: Unwin Hyman.

Carpenter, Humphrey (1988). *A Serious Character: The Life of Ezra Pound*. London: Faber & Faber.

Census of England and Wales: General Report (1904). London: HMSO.

Eagleton, Terry (1988). "Capitalism, Modernism and Postmodernism." In *Modern Criticism and Theory: A Reader*. Ed. David Lodge. London: Longman, 385–98.

Edel, Leon (1987). *Henry James: A Life*. London: Collins.

Eliot, T.S. (1988). *The Letters of T.S. Eliot*. Ed. Valerie Eliot. Vol. 1. London: Faber & Faber.

Gilbert, Sandra M., and Susan Gubar (1988). *No Man's Land: The Place of the Woman Writer in the Twentieth Century*. Vol. 1. New Haven, CT: Yale University Press.

Griest, Guinevere L. (1970). *Mudie's Circulating Library and the Victorian Novel*. Newton Abbott, Devon: David & Charles.

Harwood, John (1989). *Olivia Shakespear and W.B. Yeats: After Long Silence*. London: Macmillan.

Hobsbawm, E.J. (1968). *Industry and Empire: An Economic History of Britain since 1750*. London: Weidenfeld & Nicolson.

Huyssen, Andreas (1986). "Mass Culture as Woman: Modernism's Other." In *Studies in Entertainment: Critical Approaches to Mass Culture*. Ed. Tania Modleski. Bloomington: Indiana University Press, 188–207.

Jameson, Fredric (1981). *The Political Unconscious: Narrative as a Socially Symbolic Act*. London: Methuen.

Lentricchia, Frank (1994). *Modernist Quartet*. Cambridge: Cambridge University Press.

Lidderdale, Jane, and Mary Nicholson (1970). *Dear Miss Weaver: Harriet Shaw Weaver 1876–1961*. New York: Viking.

McCracken, Grant (1988). *Culture and Consumption: New Approaches to the Symbolic Character of Consumer Goods and Activities*. Bloomington: Indiana University Press.

Meyers, Jeffrey (1991). *Joseph Conrad: A Biography*. New York: Scribner's.

Pound, Ezra (1967). *Pound/Joyce: The Letters of Ezra Pound to James Joyce*. Ed. Forrest Read. London: Faber & Faber.
—— (1973). *Selected Prose 1909–1965*. Ed. William Cookson. New York: New Directions.
—— (1991). *The Selected Letters of Ezra Pound to John Quinn 1915–1924*. Ed. Timothy Materer. Durham, NC: Duke University Press.
—— (1992). *A Walking Tour of Southern France*. Ed. Richard Sieburth. New York: New Directions.
Rainey, Lawrence (1989). "The Price of Modernism: Reconsidering the Publication of *The Waste Land*." *Critical Quarterly* 31.4: 21–47.
Ratcliff, Carter (1991). "The Marriage of Art and Money." In *Re-visions: New Perspectives of Art Criticism*. Ed. Howard Smagula. Englewood Cliffs, NJ: Prentice-Hall, 138–52.
Reid, B.L. (1968). *The Man from New York: John Quinn and His Friends*. New York: Oxford University Press.
Yeats, William Butler (1955). *Autobiographies*. London: Macmillan.

19

RHETORIC, SCIENCE, AND ECONOMIC PROPHECY

John Maynard Keynes's correspondence with Franklin D. Roosevelt

Davis W. Houck

> The worldly philosophers change the world with their stories and metaphors. There's work for the econo-literary critic in showing how the rhetoric matters to policy and in distinguishing the good stories of policy from the bad.
>
> (McCloskey 1990: 50)

> Most, probably, of our decisions to do something positive, the full consequences of which will be drawn out over many days to come, can only be taken as a result of animal spirits – of a spontaneous urge to action rather than inaction, and not as the outcome of a weighted average of qualitative benefits multiplied by quantitative probabilities. . . . Thus if the animal spirits are dimmed and the spontaneous optimism falters, leaving us to depend on nothing but a mathematical expectation, enterprise will fade and die; – though fears of loss may have a basis no more reasonable than hopes of profit had before. It is safe to say that enterprise which depends on hopes stretching into the future benefits the community as a whole.
>
> (John Maynard Keynes, *A General Theory of Employment, Interest and Money*)

> Economic laws are not made by nature. They are made by human beings.
>
> (Roosevelt [1932] 1937: 1. 657)

Rarely, it seems, is the term "revolution" or "revolutionary" employed judiciously. Perhaps owing to the need to expedite, and thereby instantiate, that which is at the germinal stages of development, Americans are often eager to usher in "new" eras of thought. We need only look to the "Reagan

Revolution" and its rhetorical acolytes to witness an inchoate revolution, one whose celebrations were muted by unprecedented federal deficits. Occasionally, though, ideas and their progenitors are deserving of the revolutionary label; one such figure is the English economist John Maynard Keynes – a thinker whose vernacular has become so ingrained in the discourse of United States government fiscal policy that it functions as a dead metaphor. In fact, simply to invoke the phrase "government fiscal policy" is to cite the Keynesian idiom. "True" revolutionaries, as Kenneth Burke might argue, are those who literally change the terms of debate.

Economic historians would probably date the Keynesian revolution to passage of the Employment Act of 1946, an act premised on the Keynesian notion of demand-side fiscal management. Not until passage of this historic Act did the executive branch have a legislatively mandated council of economic advisers whose task it was to "fine tune" the economy by means of active measures. As John Kenneth Galbraith (1987: 254–55) notes, passage of the Employment Act of 1946 "was a step of marked importance in the history of economics. It established economists and economic counsel firmly in the center of modern American public administration." The act would be Keynes's monument in the United States.

Yet to gaze worshipfully at Keynes's monument is to ignore the events that preceded it and the way these events coalesced into the Keynesian revolution. In a word, we would miss the rhetorical dynamics inherent in the paradigm shift. In this essay I examine only one event: two letters that Keynes sent to President Franklin Roosevelt in December 1933 and June 1934. The importance of the letters, I argue, lies in the way they illustrate Keynes's unique perspective on economic recovery – a perspective that integrates science and rhetoric. In analyzing the texts I hope to demonstrate the extent to which rhetoric functions as the very ground of economic policy and economic recovery. While this latter point may seem trivial to participants in the "new conversation" between rhetoric and economics, to date precious little attention has been paid to the "potency" of economic discourse outside of academic circles (McCloskey 1985: 72). If rhetoric is as foundational to economics as many conversants claim, might we not move beyond the "intra-tribalism" and critical reflexivity (or narcissism) of academic economists' discursive practices (Klamer 1987: 165; Amariglio 1988: 583)? Self-awareness is a critical first step, of course, but there remains the task of exploring rhetoric's power to construct and deconstruct in the sociopolitical realm (McCloskey 1990: 150; Samuels 1991: 511–24).

Crisis – epistemological, social, political

As the Great Depression reached its apogee, the time was right for economic revolution. Roosevelt's political pragmatism and flexibility steered him clear of any rigid ideological commitments. Perhaps of equal importance were three key situational variables that provide much of the context for the letters: the Great Depression, economists' reactions to it, and Roosevelt's "New Deal."

Economic historians often draw our attention to the event that ostensibly "caused" the Great Depression: the stock market crash of 1929. We should not forget, though, that this event was simply the beginning; by the end of 1933, 1930 looked very favorable by comparison. The national income in 1930, for example, totaled $90.4 billion; by 1933 the figure was under $40 billion (O'Sullivan and Keuchel 1989: 167). A total of 4.3 million people (8.9 percent of the labor force) were unemployed in 1930; by 1933 the figure had risen to 12.8 million – 25.2 percent of the labor force (Norton 1991: 59).

Statistics, though, speak only to measurable data; perhaps more telling is the extent to which capitalism as a viable alternative was being seriously questioned (Adelstein 1991: 160–61; Skidelsky 1979: 29–39). The skepticism pertaining to capitalism was fueled, in part, by the fact that the Depression undermined most of the foundational assumptions of the dominant mode of economic thought, "classical economics" – a school of thought whose orthodoxies constituted "a totem, a manifestation of religious faith" (Galbraith 1987: 219). With its emphasis on scientific methods and mathematical models purporting to establish "covering laws" of market behavior, the classical school of economics was open to the heterodoxies of new prophets.

Aside from its scientistic assumptions, classical economic theory excluded depressions: the market would always experience cyclical fluctuations, but never the deep, prolonged contractions typified by the decade of the 1930s. Classical economists also assumed that the economy was a self-correcting mechanism: contractions would be followed by expansions, and hence government interference with the market's "invisible hand" was seen as heretical. If manipulations were necessary, they would be carried out by the Federal Reserve banks – which by lowering discount rates would foster investment opportunities that in turn would engender more jobs and higher wages. But the economy defied the classical tenets: businesses did not invest despite low interest rates; demand did not increase despite low prices; and, most importantly, the market did not automatically adjust upward. As the Great Depression entered its fourth year, Herbert Hoover was easily ousted by New York's governor, who, at the Democratic National Convention, promised the country a "New Deal."

It would prove serendipitous for Keynes that Roosevelt succeeded Hoover, for, despite his Harvard pedigree, Roosevelt had little knowledge of theoretical economic matters (Norton 1991: 48). As a result of his naïveté, not to mention his idiosyncratic management style, Roosevelt formed what was to become known as the "Brain Trust" to advise him on such matters. Though Keynes was not an official member of this elite academic group, his friend Felix Frankfurter was extremely close to Roosevelt. Equally important was Roosevelt's lack of an ideologically consistent economic policy; his was a series of policies, not a policy. "FDR made up his economic policy as he went along," claims Norton (ibid.), "and at no time had a systematic and consistent policy. He departed from his predecessors chiefly in that he made a greater effort to utilize the resources of economic analysis and advice available to him." Given Roosevelt's pragmatism, Keynes's admission comes into sharper relief: "You remain for me the ruler whose general outlook and attitude to the tasks of government are the most sympathetic in the world" (Keynes 1982: 21. 195). Keynes thought he had found the man capable of carrying out his revolution.

Thanks in large part to Frankfurter's insistence, Keynes drafted his first letter to Roosevelt in December of 1933. Frankfurter hand-delivered the letter to Roosevelt prior to its 31 December publication in the *New York Times*. That Frankfurter may have influenced the style of the letter is illustrated by its highly didactic, if not simplistic, form; Roosevelt was no fiscal expert, as this letter makes clear. Not surprisingly, much of what Keynes advocates in his letter foreshadows the "incendiary" ideas he would later espouse in his seminal work *A General Theory*, whose publication date was less than three years away.

Letter to the President

Though rhetorical critics, particularly textual critics, are loath to "reduce" a text to its propositional level, we must first get a sense of the Keynesian prescription. Such a perusal of the text will facilitate a better understanding of its textual dynamics and nuances. Keynes frames his letter to the President in terms of economic concern: the advice Roosevelt was receiving seemed "confused," if not "crack-brained and queer" (Keynes 1982: 21. 290). Within this context of chaos Keynes presents his view of the problems and their solution. First, the administration was attempting to do too much: reform was getting in the way of recovery. Such reform measures as the National Industrial Recovery Act (NIRA) were "impeding" recovery, having "been put across too hastily" (ibid.: 291). Recovery, in Keynes's view, was premised on increasing the "national output" by increasing incomes "through the expenditure of borrowed or printed money" (291, 292). "Public authority," not individual consumers or the business world, would foster recovery.

Having briefly mentioned the means to recovery, Keynes moves on to detail "two technical fallacies" adversely affecting the administration's economic policy (292). The first fallacy involved the administration's efforts to increase output by "deliberately" and "artificially" increasing prices through the imposition of price floors. The creation of higher prices was a "serious misapprehension of the roles prices could play in economic recovery" (ibid.). A second set of fallacies involved the "crude economic doctrine" known as the quantity theory of money, whose proponents argued that increased output and incomes could be obtained by increasing the quantity of money. Such an assumption was akin to "trying to get fat by buying a larger belt" (294). Keynes argues further that the same set of assumptions was responsible for the "gyrations of the dollar," since the administration wrongly held that a "mathematical relation" existed "between the price of gold and the price of other things" (ibid.). Keynes concludes his nine-page letter by offering three immediate courses of action: (a) avoid "wide or meaningless fluctuations in the dollar"; (b) create a large quantity of government-sponsored loan expenditures; and (c) reduce the rate of interest on long-term government bonds (296).

For all we know, Roosevelt may have indeed "reduced" Keynes's letter to its propositional content; yet to leave the letter at such a level is to miss the rhetorical subtlety of a "lucid and resourceful master of English prose" (Galbraith 1987: 232). A close reading of the text reveals a highly nuanced integration of scientific principles with rhetorical practices – an integration upon which "economic recovery" is constructed and premised. More specifically, Keynes discursively constructs an economic recovery by combining scientific terminology with an economic logic premised on the strategic use of presidential rhetorical practices. In Keynes's account, economic recovery is contingent on both scientific principles and rhetorical practices – a combination which may have appealed greatly to the recently elected President.

Despite economists' claims about Keynes's heresies, he was well ensconced within the then-prevailing model of economic thought – physics (Heilbroner 1986: 249). Less well known is biographer Charles H. Hession's claim that Keynes's scientism was buttressed by a rhetorical understanding of economic behavior. In his biography, Hession insightfully notes that Keynes conceptualized economic equilibrium as a shifting or dynamic one, wherein "changing views about the future are capable of influencing the present situation" (Hession 1984: 271). Such a rhetorical/prophetic view of the economy and economic change, abetted by the vernacular of science, is fundamental to understanding Keynes's correspondence with Roosevelt.

Keynes's belief in the redemptive powers of science is exemplified in his very first sentence: "You have made yourself the trustee for those in every country who seek to mend the evils of our condition by reasoned experiment within the framework of the existing social system" (Keynes 1982: 21. 289). The "evils" of which Keynes speaks, of course, are those of the Great Depression; but the method of "reasoned experiment" can "mend" such evils. Redemption can be achieved, moreover, within the current "system." Note that recovery is initially presented as an object, one whose constitutive parts are both knowable and amenable to laboratory-like manipulations. While this opening sentence foregrounds the rationalism of science, it also "de-radicalizes" Keynes by clothing his revolution in the garb of conservatism.

Keynes also attends in his opening remarks to classical economists' ill-reasoned assumptions. Assuming the voice of many Englishmen, they believe that "the best hope lies in your ridding yourself of your present advisers to return to the old ways" (290). Such a "wait to see" attitude is anathema to Keynes's "own view" (ibid.).

In the body of the letter, Keynes distinguishes between recovery and reform, and argues which should be privileged. While recovery is to be preferred, the reason offered underscores Keynes's understanding of the rhetorical nature of economic success: "It will be through raising high the prestige of your Administration by success in short-range recovery that you will have the driving force to accomplish long-range reform" (ibid.). Economic success, in Keynes's account, functions as the equivalent of persuasive argument for long-range reforms. The merger of rhetoric and science is unmistakable: a rhetoric informed by past successes is the "driving force" that engenders change.

But despite even "wise reforms," such measures might "impede and complicate recovery" (ibid.). Why? In answering the question, Keynes again emphasizes the link between rhetoric and recovery: reform "will upset the confidence of the business world and weaken its existing motives to action before you have had time to put other motives in their place" (ibid.). As Keynes makes clear, especially in the second letter, business confidence is fundamental to recovery; more importantly, such confidence is fostered by rhetorical means, a strategic placement of motives to action. If the business world is not persuaded to take action owing to low confidence, recovery will remain at a purely theoretical level.

The present state of low confidence, claims Keynes, owes much to the reformist goals of the NIRA – goals, not coincidentally, hostile to traditional business practices of allowing market forces to determine price and quantity supplied. Thus, Keynes concludes that the NIRA is not only not part "of the technique of recovery," but actually "impedes" it (291). That Keynes conceptualizes recovery as a "technique" adds further weight to his aim of "reasoned experiment." Recovery is not a whimsical enterprise, but a systematic series of rational moves. Additionally, such moves can be located within the nexus of mathematical models. Keynes notes that an "increase of output [the object of recovery] cannot occur unless by the operation of one or other of three factors": increased consumer spending; higher wages paid by the business world; or government sponsored expenditures (ibid.). Since each of the three factors' "values" to recovery can be approximated in advance, Keynes concludes that only the "third factor" will yield "the initial major impulse" (ibid.). Thus, not only has Keynes effectively quantified the recovery into "factors," but he also claims to know the value that each factor represents.

As Keynes moves to talk about the "two technical fallacies" affecting the administration's reasoning, he again borrows from the scientific lexicon to juxtapose his solution with the administration's. In this instance, though, Keynes invokes "nature" to legitimate his recovery plan: "rising prices caused by deliberately increasing prime costs or by restricting output have a vastly inferior value to rising prices which are the natural results of an increase in the nation's purchasing power" (292). The administration is guilty of artificially increasing prices, while the Keynesian prescription would simply allow nature to run its course. So not only does Keynes construct a technique of recovery premised on scientific principles and mathematical factors, but once in place, the recovery would follow a natural (predictable) course. Thus Keynes can logically contextualize the "autumn set-back" as the "predictable consequence of the failure of your Administration to organize any material increase in the new loan expenditure during your first six months in office" (293).

The second technical fallacy adversely affecting the administration's economic policy is the quantity theory of money, which Keynes likens to "trying to get fat by buying a larger belt" (294). Again the fallacy is reducible to mathematical terms: "It is a most misleading thing to stress the quantity of money, which is only a limiting factor, rather than the volume of expenditure, which is the operative factor" (ibid.). Owing to the logic of the quantity theory of money, the administration was again attempting to subvert the laws of nature, this time by increasing and decreasing the dollar "at an entirely arbitrary pace" (ibid.). Under Keynes's prescriptions, valuation of the dollar "should follow the success of your domestic price raising policy as its natural consequence" (ibid.).

The three solutions that Keynes recommends are premised on rhetorical and/or scientific grounds. The first solution Keynes suggests, that of controlling the dollar's exchange rate, is highly rhetorical: the mere act of presidential speech will engender recovery:

> You can announce that you will control the dollar exchange by buying and selling gold and foreign currencies at a definite figure . . . with a right to shift the parities at any time, but with a declared intention only so to do either to correct a serious want of balance in America's international receipts and payments or to meet a shift in your domestic price level relative to price levels abroad.
>
> (Ibid.: 296)

"Announcing" and "declaring" will be sufficient to restore monetary tranquillity both at home and abroad (295, 296).

Keynes's second course of action, premised on the scientific grounds of physics, calls for "a large volume of loan expenditure under government auspices. . . . The object is to start the ball rolling. The United States is ready to roll towards prosperity, if a good hard shove can be given in the next six months" (296). Once underway, the recovery would simply follow the natural forces along a downward sloping path; the recovery would presumably gain added force and momentum with each passing day.

The final solution Keynes offers is "the reduction of the long-term rate of interest," a solution that merges science and rhetoric (297). Specifically, lower interest rates can be attained by the Federal Reserve System's "deliberate engineering" of open-market policy (ibid.). The long-term rate of interest on government bonds can easily be reduced to 2.5 percent simply by "engineering" the change. Once such a manipulation is actualized, positive results would necessarily ensue since the business community would translate lower rates of interest into increased confidence, which, in turn, would stimulate investment and production.

Keynes's concluding paragraph is synechdochic of the letter as a whole:

> With these adaptations or enlargements of your existing policies, I should expect a successful outcome with great confidence. How much that would mean, not only to the material prosperity of the United States and the whole world, but in comfort to men's minds through a restoration of their faith in the wisdom and power of government!
>
> (Ibid.)

Keynes's optimism about the future is directly informed by his faith in science; after all, prediction is perhaps the ultimate end of scientific reasoning. But ever the rhetorician, he also understands the non-material, psychic benefits that recovery would engender – a mentality both the cause and consequence of material prosperity. Thus, despite his predilection for the scientific, Keynes clearly fathomed the all-important human variable in the larger economic equations.

What effect, if any, did Keynes's letter have on Roosevelt? Unfortunately, according to Arthur M. Schlesinger, Jr. (1960: 405), we have no record of his reaction to the letter. That Keynes's letter did, however, have an impact, at least on some government officials, is suggested by journalist Walter Lippmann's 17 April 1934 letter to Keynes. In the brief correspondence, Lippmann informs Keynes, "I don't know whether you realize how great an effect that letter had, but I am told that it was chiefly responsible for the policy which the Treasury is now quietly but effectively pursuing" (Keynes 1982: 21. 305). Keynes's rhetorical mission to the President was not complete though. Lippmann adds:

> Our greatest difficulty now lies in the President's emotional and moral commitments to the N.R.A. and to the various other measures which he regards as the framework of a better economic order. As they are being administered, they are a very serious check to our recovery. . . . Nobody could make so great an impression upon the

> President as you could if you undertook to show him the meaning of that part of his policy
>
> (Ibid.)

Keynes would take Lippmann up on his advice, but not before visiting the United States to receive an honorary degree from Columbia University and to survey the economic landscape. Perhaps more importantly, Frankfurter scheduled a meeting between Keynes and Roosevelt on 28 May 1934. Each participant has left fairly detailed accounts of the meeting. Though Roosevelt wrote to Frankfurter, "I had a grand talk with K[eynes] and liked him immensely," he confided to Frances Perkins that "He [Keynes] left a whole rigamarole of figures. He must be a mathematician rather than a political economist" (Schlesinger 1960: 406). Keynes was much less ambiguous in his remarks on Roosevelt. To Perkins he noted that he had "supposed the President was more literate, economically speaking" (ibid.). And, less tactfully to Alvin Johnson: "I don't think your President Roosevelt knows anything about economics" (ibid.). Despite the mutual skepticism, Keynes agreed to Lippmann's request, writing a shorter letter to Roosevelt published in the *New York Times* on 11 June 1934.

Agenda for the President

Economically speaking, the second letter is very similar to the first: Keynes emphasizes the need for government-sponsored loan expenditures, lower rates of interest on government bonds, and new agencies to supervise and coordinate the federal government's fiscal activities. The rhetorical means to such ends are also similar: scientific principles in conjunction with effective presidential rhetoric would facilitate economic recovery. But Keynes adds a new weapon to his rhetorical arsenal: a prophetic voice empowered by the recent past. Importantly, however, this addition is not divorced from Keynes's "rhetorico-scientific" view of economic recovery; rather, this view which, as the first letter indicates, privileges prediction, had itself been vindicated during the intervening five months. Thus Keynes could rightfully speak with an air of certainty about the immediate economic future.

Keynes's second letter lacks the formal artistry and eloquence of his first. His purpose in writing the letter – "to consider the prospects rather than the past" – is disavowed in the very next paragraph as he discusses in some detail the administration's support of the NIRA and the Agricultural Adjustment Administration (AAA). Additionally, perhaps in lieu of his apparent disenchantment with Roosevelt, the letter lacks an addressee and ends abruptly without a conclusion.[1] Such ostensible faults, however, should not predispose the critic to overlook the intricate rhetorical dynamics at work – and how such dynamics construe economics, economic recovery, and Keynes's relation to them.

Keynes is much more explicit in the second letter as to why the business world will not, of its own volition, lead the nation towards "normal enterprise." The answer Keynes provides implicates rhetoric's role in times of economic crisis: "the important but intangible state of mind, which we call business confidence, is signally lacking" (Keynes 1982: 21. 324). Significantly, material conditions are not as important as are "perplexity and discomfort" in stifling economic recovery. Rhetoric is fundamental to alleviating such psychic wounds: "If the President could convince business men that they know the worst, so to speak, that might hasten matters" (ibid.). Keynes's message to Roosevelt is clear: persuasive, optimistic rhetoric can function as a self-fulfilling prophecy.[2] Aside from presidential rhetoric, "the mere passage of time" and the "experience of improving conditions," Keynes adds, function as potentially suasory vehicles. Thus, for Keynes, changing perceptions are the *sine qua non* of changing material reality.

In addition to changing the manner in which the business world perceived the economy, Keynes's more overtly "material" solution for economic recovery – government expenditures – is advanced in the scientific vernacular: "the measure of recovery to be achieved will mainly depend on the degree of the direct stimulus to production deliberately applied by the Administration. . . . [T]his must chiefly mean the pace and volume of the Government's emergency expenditure" (325). It is no trivial linguistic matter that Keynes refers to the economy as "measurable" by "degrees" of "stimulus." Such a representation of the economy resembles a Skinnerian economic behaviorism wherein economic outcomes are known far in advance. The scientist must simply determine "pace and volume" – variables which Keynes claims to know.

Knowledge of what the economic future holds functions as Keynes's theme for the remainder of the letter. Whereas Keynes's first letter is pedagogic in tone, his second is much more prophetic; didacticism has been replaced by divination. Yet Keynes's economic prophecies are based on the past five months of economic activity. The administration, chronicles Keynes, having seemingly followed his advice in the form of higher government expenditures, produced an "excellent" effect on business (ibid.). "But then came what seems to me to have been an unfortunate decision. The expenditure of the Civil Works Administration was checked before the expenditure of the Public Works Administration was ready to take its place" (ibid.). Not maintaining the level of public expenditure has resulted in ground being lost. If Roosevelt would simply follow Keynes's provisos, "I should be quite confident that a strong business revival would set in by the autumn" (325–26). Keynes's economic theology is quite clear: higher spending in the present will lead to economic salvation in the near future. As such, Keynes assumes a distinctly late twentieth-century voice – that of economic prophet.[3]

Prophets, of course, are judged by the accuracy of their prognostications; true prophets have history on their side. That Keynes is such a prophet is underscored by his final paragraph. He notes:

> Some five months ago I wrote that the relapse in the latter half of 1933 was the predictable consequence of the failure of the Administration to organize new loan expenditure on an adequate scale and that the position six months later would entirely depend on whether the foundation had been laid for larger expenditures in the ensuing week. . . . As I predicted the fruits of this have been enjoyed, and I estimate that there has been an improvement of something like 15 percent in output, incomes and employment. . . . But latterly, the expenditures have been declining and, once more as a predictable result, a recession of 3 percent and perhaps 5 percent is impending.
> (Ibid.: 328–29)

Keynes skillfuly positions himself as a true prophet, having vindicated his December plan of action. How, though, does Keynes position his audience? Roosevelt and his administration are positioned clearly as faithless sinners for having ignored the "true" prophet in favor of the false prophet of classicism (balanced budgets) and, as a result, forcing the rest of the country to suffer. Keynes emerges from the letter unscathed, having vindicated himself and, perhaps more importantly, his novel view of market behavior.

As with the first letter, Keynes's second letter received the eye and the ear of the administration. As Schlesinger (1960: 407) details, newspapers across the country attributed the increase in government spending directly to Keynes's letter. Schlesinger, however, in perhaps a moment of historiographical *angst*, downplays Keynes's influence: "it cannot be said either that spending would not have taken place without his intervention or that it did take place for his reasons. In 1934 and 1935 the New Deal was spending in spite of itself" (ibid.). Schlesinger does concede that "Keynes strengthened the President's inclination to do what he was going to do anyway" (ibid.). Keynes's influence on the administration would multiply exponentially with his soon-to-be published *magnum opus*, *The General Theory of Employment, Interest, and Money*, after which there was "a widespread conversion to Keynesianism" (Hession 1984: 299). Yet, with his two letters to Roosevelt, Keynes served notice to the administration and to the United States that revolution was right around the corner – a corner the administration would turn during both the "Roosevelt recession" of 1938 and the entry of the United States into World War II.

Though "influence" is implicated in any act labeled "rhetorical," I have been more concerned with Keynes's *efforts* at influence – how he attempted to constitute economic recovery and advance such a creation to the President. Unlike many of his contemporary colleagues, Keynes recognized that "good rhetoric" can function as the very ground for improved economic activity; as such, Keynes can rightly be heard in nearly all presidential economic discourse in the twentieth century, where optimism, vision, confidence, hope, and positive economic indicators are the standard *topoi*. Perhaps most importantly, Keynes recognized that consumers were not bits of data whose behavior could be assumed away under the auspices of a rationality quotient. Good science had to be accompanied by good rhetoric in Keynes's economic cosmology. Science could take care of the numbers and the forecasts, but rhetoric addressed to consumer uncertainty and expectations set the equations in motion.

Rhetoric holds important implications for economic policy; more importantly, as Keynes clearly recognized, rhetoric can function *as* the policy. Rhetoric, particularly presidential rhetoric addressed to a mass (or macro-economic) audience, can enliven the "animal spirits" and thereby provide a vital impetus to economic activity and economic recovery. Herein Keynes speaks loudly and perhaps with some reproach to the "rhetoric of economics movement" – a movement whose collective voice often speaks to a rigidly circumscribed set of rhetorical issues. In addition to epistemic justifications, argumentative efficacy and exegesis of academic economic texts, an emphasis on rhetoric and rhetorical criticism can shed significant light on economic activities in a world far removed from University Drive or College Avenue – a world in which "the behavior of the economy is determined by human beings" (Arndt 1984: 112).

Notes

1 Keynes's detachment from Roosevelt is emphasized further by what is not stated: Keynes never addresses the President by name, nor does he even begin the letter with a formal salutation; instead, Keynes impersonally entitles it an "Agenda for the President."

2 McCloskey (1991: 298) would appear to have Keynes in mind in writing: "We can in fact (and in word) create prosperity by declaring it to be just around the corner. One is tempted to conclude that economies and economics are 'mere' matters of words, that announcing a five-year plan or a new economic policy is the same thing as achieving it." Similarly, Galbraith (1961: 21) states: "[b]y affirming solemnly that prosperity will continue, it is believed, one can help insure that prosperity will in fact continue. Especially among businessmen the faith in the efficiency of such incantation is very great."

3 For an intriguing look at the relationship between economics and theology, see Nelson (1991).

References

Adelstein, Richard P. (1991). "'The Nation as an Economic Unit': Keynes, Roosevelt, and the Managerial Ideal." *Journal of American History* 78: 160–87.

Amariglio, Jack L. (1988). "The Body, Economic Discourse, and Power: An Economist's Introduction to Foucault." *History of Political Economy* 20: 583–613.

Arndt, Helmut (1984). *Economic Theory vs Economic Reality*. Trans. William A. Kirby. East Lansing, MI: Michigan State University Press.

Galbraith, John Kenneth (1961). *The Great Crash*. Boston, MA: Houghton Mifflin.

—— (1987). *Economics in Perspective: A Critical History*. Boston, MA: Houghton Mifflin.
Heilbroner, Robert L. (1986). *The Worldly Philosophers*. 6th edn. New York: Simon & Schuster.
Hession, Charles H. (1984). *John Maynard Keynes*. New York: Macmillan.
Keynes, John Maynard ([1936] 1953). *A General Theory of Employment, Interest, and Money*. San Diego, CA: Harcourt, Brace, Jovanovich.
—— (1982). *The Collected Writings of John Maynard Keynes*. Ed. Donald Moggridge. 30 vols. Cambridge: Cambridge University Press.
Klamer, Arjo (1987). "As If Economists and Their Subjects Were Rational." In *The Rhetoric of the Human Sciences*. Ed. John S. Nelson, Allan Megill, and Donald N. McCloskey. Madison: University of Wisconsin Press, 163–83.
McCloskey, Donald N. (1985). *The Rhetoric of Economics*. Madison: University of Wisconsin Press.
—— (1990). *If You're So Smart: The Narrative of Economic Expertise*. Chicago: University of Chicago Press.
—— (1991). "Voodoo Economics." *Poetics Today* 12: 287–300.
Nelson, Robert H. (1991). *Reaching for Heaven on Earth: The Theological Meaning of Economics*. Savage, MD: Rowan & Littlefield.
Norton, Hugh S. (1991). *The Quest for Economic Stability: Roosevelt to Bush*. 2nd edn. Columbia: University of South Carolina Press.
O'Sullivan, John and Edward F. Keuchel (1989). *American Economic History: From Abundance to Constraint*. 2nd edn. New York: Harkus Weiner.
Roosevelt, Franklin D. ([1932] 1937). "The Governor Accepts the Nomination for the Presidency, Chicago, Ill. July 2, 1932." In *The Public Papers and Addresses of Franklin D. Roosevelt*. Vol. 1 Ed. Samuel I. Rosenman. New York: Random House, 647–59.
Samuels, Warren J. (1991). "'Truth' and 'Discourse' in the Social Construction of Reality: An Essay on the Relation of Knowledge to Socioeconomic Policy." *Journal of Post-Keynesian Economics* 13: 511–24.
Schlesinger, Arthur M. Jr. (1960). *The Politics of Upheaval*. Boston, MA: Houghton Mifflin.
Skidelsky, Robert (1979). "Keynes and the Reconstruction of Liberalism." *Encounter* 52: 29–39.

20

A MAN IS HIS BONDS

The Great Gatsby and deficit spending

Michael Tratner

In the 1920s, there was a remarkable shift in the way the average consumer allocated money: savings shrank and debt blossomed. Before World War I, the average American had 6.4 percent of income in savings; by 1925, this was down to 3.8 percent (Olney 1991: 48). As one historian of consumer finance puts it: "Such a sharp decline in the personal savings rate is astounding, and particularly since the 1920s were rather prosperous years and we usually expect savings rates to climb, not fall, during periods of prosperity" (ibid.: 49).

The cause of this change in savings was a roughly equal change in the amount people invested in objects bought on time, particularly automobiles, but also "major durables" such as refrigerators: during the same period, such investment doubled from 3.7 percent to 7.2 percent of average income. These numbers may seem fairly insignificant, but they provide statistical evidence of a remarkable change of attitude: within a few years, going into debt stopped being dangerous and became completely normal. To see that this change in economic morality has consequences for literature, just think how consumer debts are portrayed in nineteenth-century novels, where those who borrow are always courting disaster. Some characters do succeed in living while continually in debt, but they are usually comical or satiric figures. In *The Great Gatsby*, however, both the narrator and the main character trade in money – they sell bonds – and that fact seems a minor part of their portrayal. Fitzgerald created brokers in quite a few of his works, drawing on his own financial history.[1] Selling bonds, which in effect is the business of encouraging others to become money-lenders, is a normal occupation in Fitzgerald's world. Bond selling may seem a minor version of money-lending to focus upon, but bonds held a prominent place in the American psyche in the 1920s, because the government itself had been so visibly involved in selling bonds during the war. The book even connects Gatsby's illicit bonds and the federal government in the phone call to Gatsby's house at the end, which says that government agents had arrested "Parker" after tracking the phony bonds all the way from New York. Nick gets that message, in effect reassuring him that the bonds he sells for Probity Trust are protected by the government. Nick, of course, is not the embodiment of probity, and one suspects that his bonds are not as pure as Liberty Bonds. In 1925, private loans and lenders were still suspect, but they were rapidly becoming a normal part of life. *Gatsby* participates in this disorienting transformation.[2]

Consumer credit exploded in the 1920s due to two developments: the mass production of automobiles, and government legislation that legalized lending practices which had been condemned for centuries. As one business historian put it, until the 1920s "there were no good loan sharks. They were all bad until converted by the law" into eminently respectable businessmen (Walter S. Hilborn, quoted in Michelman 1970: 152). Normalizing debt brought about a rapid transformation of economic morality, a process that caused considerable anxiety. Legislators feared that once people realized that they could own without first saving, they would lose all moral fiber. As one critic of legalized borrowing put it:

> The crime of installment selling is that it is causing manufacturers, advertisers, merchants and consumers to go more madly after material things to the neglect of the things of the spirit. One becomes addicted to installment buying as he [*sic*] would become addicted to liquor or gambling or any other vice. . . . The installment business is making our citizens dishonest and unreliable. Those traits of thrift, industry and reliability which created America are fast becoming obsolete. . . . People fail to realize that a thin veil separates carelessness from crime. I believe that the sales of automobiles on "easy terms" is in part responsible for the present serious state of the nation's morals.
>
> (Roger Babson, quoted in Michelman 1970: 211)

The distinction and similarity between carelessness and crime is central to the novel, and is connected repeatedly to automobiles: Daisy and Tom Buchanan and Jordan Baker are all described as "careless," and all three are involved in similar kinds of auto accidents. Jordan also says that Nick is careless, and his name – Carraway – certainly supports her charge, though he does not have an auto accident. The book makes us focus intently on the morality of all these people, and we are left with a distinctly ambivalent feeling about them. Nick's summary judgment about Tom and Daisy is that they are careless, and this judgment seems one with Nick's decision not to reveal that Daisy is the one who drove the car that killed Myrtle Wilson – as if she were not quite criminally guilty. In contrast to these careless people is Meyer Wolfsheim, who is clearly criminal. Wolfsheim does not merely cheat in a golf game; he fixes the whole World Series. He does not merely hit people by accident with a car; he has them killed and wears human teeth as cufflinks. By making his gangster Jewish, Fitzgerald raises the old stereotype of the Shylock, as if money-lending underlies all Wolfsheim's crimes. Gatsby, trying to change partners from the world of Wolfsheim to the world of Daisy, is seeking to cross the line from crime to carelessness, the line separating loan sharks from finance companies.

To coin a phrase, we could say that Gatsby is trying to move from illegitimate to legitimate bonds. The pun operates quite directly in the novel: Daisy is both the ideal marital partner and a representation of a certain kind of wealth. She is always in white, and her most important feature, for Gatsby, is her voice, which is described as a "promise" and as "full of money" (Fitzgerald [1925] 1992: 120). When the two kiss, his "visions" are wedded to her "perishable breath" and the "incarnation was complete" (112). What incarnates and makes real his fantasies is that breath "full of money," which is different from what he gains from his relation to Wolfsheim: Daisy promises clean, white, legitimate money.

To achieve the promise of legitimate money, Gatsby enters the world of illegitimacy, borrowing both money and his identity. His acts of borrowing are surrounded with danger, and the plot ends with his dying because he is mistakenly held responsible for the auto accident that killed Myrtle. When the person who actually caused that accident, Daisy, escapes punishment herself because she is one of the careless rich, it might seem that the book is warning people about the dangers of involvement with the rich, warning readers to be careful and not to imitate Gatsby. However, the onus falls more on the rich for having excluded Gatsby than on Gatsby: the book seems far more to be trying to imagine a way to allow Gatsby to incarnate his visions, to love Daisy, without having to enter the world of illegality and without being endangered by the powerful acts of the rich. In other words, Fitzgerald is seeking some way to reduce the carefulness required of the poor, to allow some of the carelessness of the rich to become the norm in the nation – but without the violence and corruption that seem entwined with that carelessness.

Fitzgerald is participating, albeit anxiously, in the economic transformation going on in the 1920s, when a new kind of carelessness – borrowing and spending – was being encouraged as a better route to wealth than saving. To quote another literary source published the same year as *Gatsby*, Theodore Dreiser's novel *The Financier*: "It was not his idea that he could get rich by saving . . . , from the first, he had the notion that liberal spending was better" (Dreiser [1925] 1961: 19). Spending even became a moral good; to quote an economist, Simon Patten, from the same years: "The non-saver is now a higher type than the saver. . . . I tell my students to spend all they have and borrow more and spend that. It is foolish for persons to scrimp and save" (quoted in Rodgers 1978: 120). Patten may be a bit excessive, but his advice to spend rather than save was typical of a wide range of writers on economics in the early twentieth century. In 1909, John Hobson declared that "the highly extolled virtues of thrift, parsimony and savings were the chief culprits for prevailing industrial maladies" (Hobson [1909] 1974: ix). John Maynard Keynes brought such arguments into economic orthodoxy, writing in his *General Theory* that "the growth of wealth, so far from being dependent on the abstinence of the rich, as is commonly supposed, is more likely to be impeded by it" (Keynes 1936: 373). People need to release their desires by spending if they and the nation are going to achieve the promise of money.

Gatsby attempts to live out such an economic theory: to win that voice "full of money" – Daisy's – he simply spends, lavishly. The most emotional moment between the two lovers reveals precisely that spending is the key to Daisy's heart. Daisy is moved to tears only once, in Gatsby's bedroom, when he throws dozens of his shirts all over his bed: "Suddenly, with a strained sound, Daisy bent her head into the shirts and began to cry stormily. 'They're such beautiful shirts,' she sobbed, her voice muffled in the thick folds. 'It makes me sad because I've never seen such – such beautiful shirts before'" (Fitzgerald [1925] 1992: 98).

Given that she is crying on the bed of a former lover, we might interpret her words as having little to do with the shirts at all, but it certainly seems that what breaks through her emotional reserve is precisely his having spent so much money for beautiful shirts. It isn't even his taste that is being celebrated, because he has just said, before he started throwing out his shirts, "I've got a man in England who buys me clothes. He sends over a selection of things at the beginning of each season, spring and fall" (97). These shirts represent the sheer expenditure of vast amounts of money to be attractive – an expenditure far greater than will ever be visible on Gatsby's actual body. His house and his huge closet of shirts exist entirely to attract Daisy: he achieves a seduction by sheer quantity of spending. What one expects to see in the bedroom is Gatsby's great desire for Daisy – perhaps represented by some extravagantly expensive gift – but that is Tom Buchanan's method of seducing Daisy, not Gatsby's. Gatsby seduces Daisy not by spending on her, but simply by spending on everything and everyone. Gatsby's parties represent the general willingness to spend money that is stimulated and created by the "promise of money." People will spend if they believe that they can attract the kind of money that had seemed reserved for the rich. If Daisy embodies the promise of money, Gatsby embodies immense desire. Indeed, Gatsby's monetary history enacts the cycle that easy money promised – desire that had been inhibited is released by the easy, almost illicit money of credit (in his case, literally illicit bonds); that desire released is "effective demand" or spending which then stimulates the whole economic system to produce licit money – symbolically, Daisy. Spending illicit money is a method of gaining access to the world of licit money, as spending on credit is a way of gaining an unmortgaged return.

Those economists who advocated spending concluded that the problem could never be solved by simply getting the rich to spend more. There needed to be more people spending money – the desires of the masses had to be released as well. Gatsby represents this goal as well: for one thing, he grew up locked out from the world of money, and opens the way for all sorts of people to enter the world of spending through his immense parties. Nick compares these parties to "amusement parks" (45), places for everyone to indulge in wild fantasies for a few dollars. Gatsby's parties seem to be purely a waste of money, but it is just such "waste" that is deemed necessary by economists such as Keynes to keep the boom of the 1920s going. During the Depression, Keynes wrote that if the government were to spend money on anything at all, even "digging holes in the ground," it would restore the boom of the twenties; of course, he also recommended more "magnificent" projects (Keynes 1936: 221). Gatsby's mansion and his parties and his shirts are magnificent unnecessary projects, and their effect is exactly what Keynes wants – they stimulate everyone involved, increasing demand. Though Gatsby gives immense quantities of commodities away, the result of his parties is to make people want more. His parties, like credit, lend people easy means of indulging in the pleasures of the rich. Perhaps a better analogy for Gatsby's house than the amusement park would be the department store, which, like the amusement park, emerged around the turn of the century to provide magnificent, palatial environments open to people of all classes. Daisy's ecstasy at seeing so many beautiful shirts provided by professional buyers is of course the central emotion department stores aim to produce.

Department stores and amusement parks contributed to a new image of the economic system. Instead of seeing production and scarcity as the crucial elements defining wealth, the economic theories that advocated spending postulated a general abundance, a vast reservoir of valuable commodities that need only be distributed or put into circulation. The image of the basic economic problem facing America then became in effect a department store full of beautiful shirts with no customers – underconsumption – rather than a group of people fighting over too few shirts or over the methods of making shirts.

Underconsumption theorists argued that there was a blockage in the free flow of the abundant reservoir of goods, and the culprit causing this blockage was precisely the economic morality of saving and restraint. If people let go, rather than hold back, relax rather than strain, they would get more. In the most common metaphor for this theory, one that has become absolutely central to the business pages of every newspaper, the economic system is compared to an automobile, a powerful engine that one does not "construct" via labor but that one keeps running via various throttles and brakes. The acts that release wealth are thus not the hard acts of labor, but the small acts of regulating a powerful engine. People are not the squirrels in cages keeping the economic wheels moving; rather they are sitting on plush seats and merely have to push certain levers and buttons to go much faster than they ever could in their squirrel cages. Wealth emerges from nowhere – it's just there in the system.

The image of an abundance available for the taking, if only people would relax and take it rather than holding back, pervades not only economic thinking but also religious and medical thought in the early twentieth century. In his study of the transformation of the work ethic into a "spending ethic" in America from 1850 to 1920, Daniel Rodgers (1978) notes the commonness of images of abundance around the turn of the century, and sees these images as closely tied to new forms of morality: "The metaphor of abundance as insinuated into religion and psychology in the counsel to unclamp the will, to open the gates to life – giving a rush of instincts and energies – . . . essentially shifted the grounds of ethics" (122). Rodgers quotes religious writers such as Ralph Waldo Trine, who wrote that "Opulence is the law of the universe . . . an abundant supply for every need if nothing is put in the way of its coming" (110). In these theories, a huge reservoir of grace waits to pour down over those who know how to release the bounty of heaven; one does not need to work hard and refrain from indulgence to gain everything valuable. The end of the work ethic brings with it, according to Rodgers, a shift away from "self-discipline, self-denial, obedience, and chastity" (121).

Rodgers's notion of a shift away from chastity draws attention to the changes in sexual attitudes that parallel the changes in economic and religious attitudes. In twentieth-century sexology, sexual activity became, like spending, something with the potential to build up rather than drain the individual (Birken 1988: 37). Wilhelm Reich's (1978) theories are peculiarly close to certain passages in *Gatsby*, though I am not trying to show any direct influence between Reich and Fitzgerald. Reich's and Fitzgerald's texts converge because they both developed out of an early twentieth-century constellation of views about the sources of value and energy in humans and in societies that marked a change away from the economics and sexuality of scarcity toward an economics and a sexuality of letting go, of "spending" – or, we might say, of applying the throttle to the social and individual engines.

Reich developed a consumerist theory of sexuality in which pleasure becomes quite literally the "productive process in the biological system" (Reich 1961: 260). Pleasure releases energy that is nearly divine: Reich calls it "cosmic" or "orgone" energy, and credits it with maintaining mental and physical health. He explains that "the living organism contains orgone energy in every one of its cells, and keeps charging itself orgonotically from the atmosphere by the process of breathing" (264). The orgone energy becomes usable only through sexual pleasure, through orgasm; the key issue in each person's life is thus "the manner in which an individual handles his bio-electric energy; how much of it he dams up and much of it he discharges orgastically" (ibid.).

One phrase in *The Great Gatsby* that seems quite close to Reichian language is the description of Jay Gatsby as pursuing an "orgastic future" (Fitzgerald

[1925] 1992: 189). Edmund Wilson changed this phrase to "orgiastic future" in an edition published after Fitzgerald's death, thereby altering the focus from orgasm to orgy.[3] Wilson's alteration seems a mistake, as Gatsby's orgies, his parties, function only as a means to bring Daisy to him. The orgies are only preludes to the single perfect relationship. Gatsby believes that if only he and Daisy can break through the dams set up by social codes, the two will join together in a magnificent explosion, releasing all the instinctual energy inside them in a single moment, a magnificent orgasm. The novel anticipates the result of this complete release in the description of what would happen when he kissed Daisy "and forever wed his unutterable visions to her perishable breath": "the incarnation" would be "complete" (117). Gatsby envisions an "orgastic" moment when the barriers separating the human and the divine break down: when his and Daisy's bodies meet, the sexual contact ought to release "cosmic" forces (to use a Reichian term), incarnating the American Dream.

Another Reichian image in the novel occurs very early, and rather strangely ties together the ideas of drawing health from the air, learning the mysteries of credit, and writing literature:

> There was so much to read, for one thing, and so much fine health to be pulled down out of the young breath-giving air. I bought a dozen volumes on banking and credit and investment securities, and they stood on my shelf in red and gold like new money from the mind, promising to unfold the shining secrets that only Midas and Morgan and Maecenas knew. And I had the high intention of reading many other books besides. I was rather literary in college – one year I wrote a series of very solemn and obvious editorials for the Yale News – and now I was going to bring back all such things into my life.
>
> (Ibid.: 8)

In Reich's theory, the way to draw health from the air was to tear down inner dams that kept parts of the individual repressed. In this passage, books on credit promise to perform a similar function, to release hidden parts – new money – of the mind that will allow one to acquire wealth as if one were pulling it from the air. The promise of unfolding shining secrets may not seem sexual, but the rest of the novel reveals that it is the sexual secrets of the rich that Nick will discover far more than any economic ones. Furthermore, soon after this passage, Gatsby appears, looking at the "silver pepper" of the stars, "to determine what share was his of our local heavens" (25). Gatsby seems to know how to bring down the heavenly abundance: through pursuit of an "orgastic future" that is both economic and sexual. His peculiar behavior fits very well with theories promoting the release of dammed up economic and sexual energy by writers such as Wilhelm Reich and the underconsumptionists.

But Gatsby finally is not a Reichian or an underconsumptionist: both the orgastic future and the economics he pursues are not at all "new" but quite nineteenth-century. Yes, he spends to attract money, and he seems willing to violate some rules of sexual restraint, but even as he seeks to seduce a married woman what he wants is somehow to recover the old nineteenth-century ideal of marrying her, and, even more, of having her somehow recover her virginity, so that he becomes the only person she has ever loved. Reich argues that full release of orgastic potential means that people would not be restricted to "one partner" (Reich 1961: 132). But Gatsby will not accept such a conclusion: he holds to the nineteenth-century morality of complete ownership, failing to understand the new sexuality and the new economics that his actions anticipate: he wants to take Daisy from "old money," from Tom Buchanan, but in order to have her in exactly the way Tom has her. Gatsby's spending is an image of a new economics, but his personal morality is not: note, for example, that though he provides endless liquor for his guests, he does not drink. He is a highly disciplined, restrained individual who dreams of an "orgastic future" when he can fully possess Daisy, taking her away from Tom. Gatsby does not want to be a borrower or a lender: he wants to be an owner, or, perhaps, a revolutionary. He wants to take all the value away from the "old" families and then fully possess it himself.

Gatsby's nineteenth-century morality also appears in the discipline he imposed upon himself as a youth, his Benjamin Franklin method of getting ahead by planning out every minute of his life. The book ends up suggesting quite strongly that such discipline is no longer useful. In his belief in a kind of bodily discipline, Gatsby is quite like Tom Buchanan. But bodily discipline no longer produces health; it is no longer possible to be a self-made man, even physically: Tom's "sturdy physical egotism no longer nourished his peremptory heart" (Fitzgerald [1925] 1992: 25). Tom ends up seeking through sexuality the nourishment his egotism fails to provide: he has an affair with Myrtle Wilson because she has the one thing he lacks: "an immediate perceptible vitality" (30). The book is about searching for this "vitality" in a sexual relationship, searching for some reservoir of energy to tap, precisely in order to become a physical self, to have a body: Gatsby searches for Daisy to provide the "body" to "incarnate" his visions. But Gatsby mistakes what Daisy will provide, thinking that if he has her he will become self-possessed. In this novel, as in the economics of deficits, self-sufficiency is no longer possible and no longer a model of strength. It becomes rather a form of weakness; a person, a business, a government becomes stronger or richer when it knows how to borrow. As Van Wyck Brooks put it in the 1920s, "economic self-assertion [is] to a large extent a vicious anachronism" (quoted in Rodgers 1978: 121). People do not build up their own bank accounts or their own bodies: both need "vitality" from others.

One rather amusing example may help illustrate what is at stake here. Nick says that "almost any exhibition of complete self-sufficiency draws a stunned tribute from me" (13). Such a display is very rare, and in fact entirely an illusion. He makes that comment to describe Jordan Baker sitting so precisely balanced that she seems as if "buoyed upon an anchored balloon" (12). All that is left of self-sufficiency is this image of balancing in the air. The self-made person is no more than a self-inflated balloon.

The novel marks a move away from the ideal of self-possession to a world of partial possessions, of joint ownership. Daisy and Gatsby could be united, and the dream realized, if only he did not require her to be entirely "his." She is willing to live in a world in which she has loved two men, but Gatsby is not. The novel ultimately moves away from Gatsby toward another system, a world of small pleasures for everyone, without the "complete" orgasm that would blow up the system and take money (or pleasure) away from those who now have it. This alternative is suggested by Nick Carraway's relationships: Nick doesn't need to marry Daisy to have a relationship with her because he is her second cousin once removed; he has casual sex with Daisy's friends and lends his house for Daisy's tryst with Gatsby. He only borrows Gatsby's wild pleasures, and so doesn't have to pay fully for them; the novel shows us as well how to borrow the pleasures of the rich. Investing in Nick's company rather than Gatsby's, we get a lower interest rate: Nick is a much less "interesting" character than Gatsby, but his words and his bonds are much easier to acquire. If we stick with Nick, we have safe access to the world of wealth: we do not have to repress our "drives" to wealth and pleasure because Nick knows how to use the throttles and brakes to keep our engines humming without going out of control. If Gatsby is like a car out of control, economically and sexually, Nick is, in contrast, "slow-thinking and full of interior rules that act as brakes on [his] desires" (63–64). This may sound like Victorian morality, but his brakes do not repress his desires or his drives; they only slow them down.

Nick speaks of the brakes on his desires during a scene in which he begins a relationship with Jordan Baker. His way of entering this affair is a perfect example of his controlled use of his drives – his controlled driving, we might say. The issue of uncontrolled actions pervades their conversation. They have been discussing carelessness; in particular, Jordan proposes that a careless person is in danger only if she meets another careless person. Nick's line about his interior brakes implies that he is not careless, and so Jordan feels free to be careless around him. In other words, Nick's "brakes" serve to allow other people who interact with him to be careless – just as a bond salesman depends on his reputation for utter probity to induce others to be "careless" enough to borrow money through him. Later, when Nick leaves Jordan, she says she made a mistake, that he is careless and did hurt her. But his behavior throughout their relationship has been neither completely lacking in care nor completely careful – he has not allowed himself fully to care for her, nor to indulge himself without any cares at all. He has been care-less, having a lesser degree of care: his affairs are regulated indulgences, investments without very much interest, paying off in small pleasures. Nick is a person who understands how to stimulate effective demand without releasing the explosions of wildly excessive demand: sexually he can indulge desires without the explosions of feeling that lead to marriage or to dangerous liaisons; economically, he can indulge the desire to spend (or help others indulge by lending them money) without stimulating the explosive desire to have everything, the excessive demand that leads either to inflation or to revolution.

The novel contains some suggestions of revolutionary thinking; at least one critic has claimed that Fitzgerald is in fact presenting Marxist theory (Posnock 1984: 201–14). I would not go so far, but the dream of the full transfer of wealth from the rich to the poor, from the insider to the outsider, from Anglo-Saxon American old money (Tom Buchanan) to ethnic *arriviste* (James Gatz), is a revolutionary goal hovering around the edge of this novel. The danger of revolution was felt to be quite real in America in 1925, only eight years after the Russian Revolution and six years after the "Red Scare" of 1919, when hundreds of immigrants were deported for supposedly advocating communist revolutions.[4] The fear of immigrants taking over the country was very strong in the 1920s, and blurred together concerns about Tammany Hall Bosses, gangsters, Jews and revolutionaries. A series of laws were passed in the 1920s that cut off the stream of immigrants, particularly reducing Jewish immigration. Gatsby, who changes his name and gains power through illicit Jewish connections, would easily raise in the minds of 1920s readers these concerns. How can a poor boy with a foreign-sounding name join in the American dream? Must he turn to crime? To revolution?

There is even a rather intriguing connection between fears of socialism and automobiles: in 1906 President Woodrow Wilson said, "Nothing has spread socialistic feeling in this country more than the automobile . . . , a picture of the arrogance of wealth" (quoted in Michelman 1970: 204). One of the ways in which the US avoided socialist revolution was through the cheap car, available to everyone through easy credit, so that the automobile no longer became a marker of wealth. The novel thus raises the issue of the relation of automobiles, ostentation, and working-class anger: the gas-station worker named Wilson (Fitzgerald is probably not referring to the President, but it is an odd coincidence) seeks over and over again to buy Tom Buchanan's car to fix it up, resell it and make money. But instead of letting the workers profit from his wealth, Tom uses them. Tom's affair with Myrtle Wilson is the cause of the anger that animates Mr Wilson, the anger of the workers at being used and cast into the valley of ashes. And Tom's wife Daisy kills Myrtle, thereby turning Wilson's brooding anger into violent action, which Tom then misdirects at Gatsby. There is a whole conspiracy, acted out in a strangely accidental way by Tom and Daisy, to divert the working-class Wilsons' anger at being used by the rich Buchanans onto the ostentatious Gatsby. The novel thus enacts the response to working-class discontent that was being carried out in the 1920s by the whole country. The novel criticizes the mainstream rich Buchanans for their heartlessness, but it kills Gatsby, the upstart who wants to take money (i.e., Daisy) away from the Buchanans. In the 1920s in America, there was a critique of the rich for their heartlessness, but this did not lead to socialism. Instead, it led to welfare, a limited, controlled, regulated transfer of wealth that had little to do with altering the behavior of the rich. At the same time, the evils of the system had to be blamed on someone, so there was an intense focus of government action and newspaper articles on immigrant revolutionaries and immigrant gangsters during the decade: foreigners could be blamed for working-class anger and for unfair distributions of wealth. The government could be against revolution and against immoral wealth; at the same time class divisions could be diffused into ethnic ones, with the promise of Americanization replacing the hope of upward mobility. After the anger of the working-class Wilsons is deflected from the mainstream upper-class Buchanans onto the corrupt *arriviste* with ties to gangsters, Nick goes home to lend money in a regulated way and to write this novel, in effect replacing Gatsby's amusement park parties with this amusement, this novel, read by millions, giving everyone access to dreams of wealth for a few dollars.

The disaster that ends this novel seems prophetic of the Depression, which could suggest that the novel is criticizing the wildness of the 1920s and advocating a return to nineteenth-century restraint. When Nick returns to the Midwest, there is a feeling of returning to stability and restraint, even to Victorian morality; he says he ends up wanting the world to stand at "moral attention forever" (6). Such an ending would seem to point toward Hoover's method of solving the Depression: tightening up the money supply and constricting borrowing. But such an interpretation ignores how hard the ending works to resurrect Gatsby. The book does not end with Nick returning to hard work; instead, he is going to build his fortune out of literature, as he imagined when he visualized taking health from the air. He is going to publicize the life of Gatsby, to seek a way to extract what is valuable from Gatsby and separate that value from its criminality and explosiveness and violence. The method is a literature of controlled indulgence in fantasy, combined with the controlled borrowing and controlled credit of Probity Trust. The book ends with a Keynesian solution to the danger of crashes: stimulation of spending through low interest rates and government deficits. Everyone is allowed a little bit more money than he or she has earned or saved; everybody's life becomes a little bit more "interesting," a little bit more like Gatsby's.

This novel does in a sense reveal the secrets of how to draw health and wealth from the air, the secrets Nick sought in moving East. The book ends with a whole rash of revelations, most of which have little to do with credit – except one final message about bonds that Nick acquires accidentally by picking up a phone in Gatsby's house after Gatsby has died. Nick hears that "Young Parker's in trouble. . . . They picked him up when he handed the bonds over the counter. They got a circular from New York giving 'em the numbers just five minutes before. What d'you know about that, hey? You never can tell in these hick towns" (174). This conversation provides the only solid evidence of Gatsby's criminal endeavors, and it is striking that it should be about bonds, Nick's specialty, and about the relationship of New York to the other "hick towns" around the country, just before Nick decides to leave New York. The phone call seems a message to Nick about the dangers of illicit bonds and about the ubiquitousness of government regulators. It suggests that Nick's involvement in bonds will be safe, will allow him to gain wealth "from the air" (from interest) without falling into the explosive world of Gatsby and Wolfsheim.

Government regulators succeeded in doing what Gatsby failed to do: allowing certain individuals to use money raised from what had been criminal endeavors (loan sharking) as a means of becoming intimate associates of the most respectable and well-off people: the success of government regulations made those selling credit as fresh as a Daisy instead of as smelly as a Wolf. Soon after this novel was published, the government became an active partner of legal money-lenders, borrowing on a huge scale, adopting wholeheartedly the virtues of deficit spending as throttle and brake to keep the economy moving, to keep just the right "velocity of money," to keep the world of the rich "interesting" but not too "interesting." By the 1930s, borrowing and lending had become the norm of all business and government financing, and full ownership or full payment out of earnings or taxes had become rarities. Everyone knows now that mortgaged or leveraged property is more stimulating to the economy and to the "owner" than property fully paid off. Objects of desire become, then, most stimulating when borrowed, not when fully possessed, so the world becomes a place of abundant partial satisfactions, carelessly acquired and carelessly tossed aside. Such is life in the age of deficits.

Notes

1 Richard Lehan (1990: 70–77) examines in some detail Fitzgerald's interest in brokers.

2 While little has been written about the role of credit in *Gatsby*, Richard Gooden (1986) has characterized Fitzgerald as participating in the transition from early to late capitalism.

3 Matthew Bruccoli notes this change in his notes to the edition of *Gatsby* I have been citing (Fitzgerald [1925]1992: 192).

4 John Higham (1955: 224–28) documents the deportation of immigrants in reaction to the Red Scare of 1919.

References

Birken, Lawrence (1988). *Consuming Desire: Sexual Science and the Emergence of a Culture of Abundance, 1871–1914*. Ithaca, NY: Cornell University Press.

Dreiser, Theodore ([1925] 1961). *The Financier*. New York: Dell.

Fitzgerald, F. Scott ([1925] 1992). *The Great Gatsby*. Ed. Matthew J. Bruccoli. New York: Macmillan.

Gooden, Richard (1986). "Money Makes Manners Make Man Make Woman: *Tender Is the Night*, a Familiar Romance?" *Literature and History* 12.1 (Spring): 16–37.

Higham, John (1955). *Strangers in the Land: Patterns of American Nativism 1860–1925*. New Brunswick, NJ: Rutgers University Press.

Hobson, John ([1909] 1974). *The Crisis of Liberalism*. Hassocks, Sussex: Harvester.

Keynes, John Maynard (1936). *The General Theory of Unemployment, Interest and Money*. London: Macmillan.

Lehan, Richard (1990). The Great Gatsby: *The Limits of Wonder*. Boston, MA: Twayne.

Michelman, Irving S. (1970) *Consumer Finance: A Case History in American Business*. New York: Augustus Kelly.

Olney, Martha (1991). *Buy Now Pay Later: Advertising, Credit and Consumer Durables During the 1920s*. Chapel Hill: University of North Carolina Press.

Posnock, Ross (1984). "'A New World, Material Without Being Real': Fitzgerald's Critique of Capitalism in *The Great Gatsby*." In *Critical Essays on F. Scott Fitzgerald's* The Great Gatsby. Ed. Scott Donaldson. Boston, MA: G.K. Hall.

Reich, Wilhelm (1961). *The Function of the Orgasm*. New York: Bantam.

Rodgers, Daniel T. (1978). *The Work Ethic in Industrial America, 1850–1920*. Chicago: University of Chicago Press.

Part VII

CRITICAL EXCHANGES

21

LITERARY/CULTURAL "ECONOMIES," ECONOMIC DISCOURSE, AND THE QUESTION OF MARXISM

Jack Amariglio and David F. Ruccio

Symbolic Economy? Libidinal Economy? General Economy? Political Economy of the Sign? Textual Economy? The Economy of Desire? These and other current formulations appear to be extremely popular and productive in the broad fields of literary theory and cultural studies. It is legitimate to ask, however, about the relation of these formulations to the concepts and constructs of economic theory proper, or at least to what can be regarded as "official" economic discourse.

Immediately, though, we note that these formulations have only a tenuous relationship to the discourses that comprise the "mainstream" of the economics profession, most importantly the varieties of neoclassical and Keynesian thought that have been dominant in the field for the past century. And while such terms as libidinal economy, symbolic economy, and the like mostly have had their origin in dialogue and debate with Marxian theory and/or what is called institutionalism (here we are referring largely to the writings of Thorstein Veblen, Karl Polanyi, and those who have built up a "substantivist" economic anthropology in opposition to what they call "formalist" economics), here again the present relationship between these discursive forms and those of heterodox, radical economic theory is less than certain.

Let us put our point bluntly. Designators such as "libidinal economy" and the others are almost entirely alien (perhaps unfortunately) to those trained within the academic discipline of economics. That is, these terms have not, and we believe would not, be treated as deserving of serious attention by most professional economists. Two short anecdotes may convey the depth of the problem here. First, a British friend and colleague recently tried to get her cohorts in her economics program (some of them, at least, renegades in relation to economic orthodoxy) to read and discuss Lyotard's *Libidinal*

Economy. As she reported to us, they couldn't get past the title (about which, she said, Lyotard ought to be given some reward for just that response), and were, of course, outraged that anyone would have the audacity to pass off such usage as a serious attempt to "talk" economics (which, incidentally, Lyotard occasionally and insightfully does in that wild and often infuriating book).

Second, we, like all the other authors in this collection, attended the conference in Cleveland organized by Mark Osteen and Martha Woodmansee (along with Deirdre McCloskey) for the Society for Critical Exchange in 1994. Despite the fact that the overwhelming majority of professional economists invited were people already nicely disposed to think, write, and talk about the relationship between economic concepts, discourses, and forms of writing and literary/cultural tropes, and despite the fact that this proclivity makes most of us oddballs within our own field, we were frequently confronted by our economics colleagues, sometimes in good cheer, but other times not, with their own discomfort regarding the lack of knowledge and understanding about "economics" displayed (or so they thought) by the literary and cultural theorists in attendance. We heard several times from our economist friends and colleagues – that is, when they chose to complain, which, to be fair, wasn't all that often – that there appeared to be among the non-economists little familiarity with the vast amount of economic theory of the past century and certainly deep ignorance of what professional economists have been writing about in the wake of the neoclassical, marginalist revolution of the late nineteenth century. In its place, the complaints continued, there was an embarrassment of riches in the frequent "misuses" of the terms and understanding of "economics" (not to mention "the economy," that shadowy figure that rears its ugly but enormous head in the last instance in the form of references to "late capitalism," "consumer society," and other such terms). Our disciplinary colleagues complained that they had expected to encounter literary and cultural theory in which the leading figures of economics and the main schools of thought might at least be engaged. Instead, they continued, they were greeted with "economists" such as Lyotard, Foucault, Derrida, Baudrillard, Bataille, Goux, and others, many of whom have little if any knowledge (or so it was alleged) of economics proper. A recent paper by Regenia Gagnier and John Dupré (1995) begins with a report on two "provocative comments" made at the conference by McCloskey: "First, she said that the trouble with most literary critics who claim to do economic criticism is that their understanding of economics too often ends with Marx. It is as if she observed, "an economist proposed to intervene in literary or cultural debate but her knowledge of that debate ended with Matthew Arnold." This paraphrase captures a sentiment that could have come from the mouths of most economists present at the conference, and even from those whose sympathy with Marxism (and not neoclassicalism) is evident and sincere.[1]

We should convey, of course, our own experience in the economics profession, lest some of our readers might think we see ourselves as outsiders in this *mise-en-scène*. In fact, since we have written for at least fifteen years on such thinkers as Foucault, Lyotard, Derrida, Althusser (especially Althusser), and still others, our own work has been treated in much the same way by many of our colleagues.[2] Recently, for example, one of us was told that he deserved to teach in a liberal arts college (but not in a top rank graduate economics program) because he really doesn't do economics. An example of this lack, the speaker went on to say, was the fact that we gave this individual a paper which discusses the economics of uncertainty and its connection to postmodern thought and, sinfully, referred several times to Lyotard, who, as the speaker asserted (gleefully, we might add), is utterly incomprehensible and, in any event, absolutely irrelevant to what economists do. And the other of us was just as recently informed that when he comes up for promotion, he had best not have any literary critic write on his behalf since, of course, this would only indicate the degree to which his work was also "not economics."

Now, of course, there is a long-standing tradition in the economics profession, and indeed in many professions, especially those with the Big Science envy, in which the definition and explication of the "core" of the discipline is a primary means to define out of existence any and all discourses currently not in favor. Indeed, despite claims that most economists (like scientists) occupy themselves just "doing" economics, our experience is that much time and effort is spent in defining what is in and what is out of the discipline. As Foucault explained lucidly in his discussion of discursive formations and their constitution, acts of exclusion are practiced (in the form of the "positivities" or the statements that are actually produced within these formations) as a normal part of such discourses (hence, this is one way in which the power/knowledge nexus is produced and experienced). In economics, the defining away of heterodox traditions as not economics is so well entrenched that it comes almost as second nature to economists to label most differences not immediately recognizable as within the "core" as being outside of their discipline (see Amariglio *et al.* 1990). Of course, the disposition of such pronouncements has a chilling effect on challenges to orthodoxy, and it is no accident that alternative points of view (such as Marxism, for instance) are regarded as coming from and belonging to another discursive planet, certainly not the terra firma of economics.

In another paper (Amariglio and Ruccio 1994) we have called attention to one way in which such acts of exclusion have been formalized within academic economics. Ironically, the formal definition of the problem and the consequent setting out of the proper boundaries for legitimate economics have come from one of the most iconoclastic of economists (and the one, paradoxically, most responsible for touching off the current shock of interest in the relationship between economics, literary forms, and culture), Deirdre

McCloskey. In McCloskey's textbook (written, we acknowledge, before her conversion to the "rhetoric of economics") entitled *The Applied Theory of Price* (1985), McCloskey begins with a discussion of the economics practiced by the majority of trained professionals and with the difference of this body of thought from what she terms "ersatz economics." The latter term, as McCloskey uses it, is meant to refer to the economics of the non-economist, the "man in the street" (this is, in fact, McCloskey's inglorious phrase). It is meant, as well, to differentiate what many academics not "in" economics regard as common-sense economic ideas and policies from those that the majority of economists, using their scientific toolbox, are able to muster and, mostly (she asserts), agree upon.

To bring us back to our point of departure: there is little question that for many economists formulations such as "libidinal economy" would fall into McCloskey's category of ersatz economics. And here we include the estimation of most heterodox economists of our acquaintance, since many of our radical colleagues, we have sadly learned, are eager to be Big Scientists too and are only too ready to act as disciplinary police, a veritable comprador class within the profession. But such an appraisal, we think, is unjustified, not only because it comes from those who have shown little willingness to entertain the possibility that the formal, axiomatic hypertechnics of contemporary mainstream economics is, like all other formations, a discourse with epistemological and methodological norms that can be and have been severely challenged. It is unjustified as well because it buys into the exclusive privilege of those certified as experts in constructing a discourse that can produce economic thinking and present coherent ways of constituting economic ideas and policies.

Now, we do not think of ourselves as romantics who see every alternative to the mainstream and every pronouncement of "common folk" (even other academics) as containing the real truth that is being concealed by ideologues who are simply protecting their domain of power. For us, the mad person's discourse or statements emanating from the so-called "man on the street" have no epistemological privilege in revealing a blunt truth that the experts are too blind or too partial to see. Rather, we are interested in the ways "ersatz economics" and those formations produced mostly in sites distant from academic economics' headquarters are, in fact, discourses whose rules of formation and regularities in the production of economic knowledge can be discussed.

Without elaborating this point further here (time and space prevent us from saying much more), let us, then, assert the following: that while symbolic economy, libidinal economy, and some of the other formulations have little direct connection to academic economics (the economics of the official discipline), they are indeed productive of economic knowledge and, as such, provide yet additional ideas and theoretical formulations that are largely alternatives, self-consciously or not, to the neoclassical orthodoxy that rules the academic economic roost. But having said this, we also believe that there are ideas and insights to be found in these terms and movements that both bear upon and borrow from neoclassical theory and, even more, from Marxian and other heterodox traditions. Insofar as this is true for us, we turn then to consider (briefly) some of the main strengths and weaknesses in our view of these formulations. That is, we argue that there are incommensurabilities and homologies alike.

In making our evaluation, we turn our eyes primarily on the questions of the specificity of the contribution to economic thought, on the relation of this contribution to the larger field, and most importantly for us, on the ways in which these contributions intervene in the debates and differences that already exist within the confines of the existing profession. Let us say that one issue in which we are keenly interested is the extent to which these formulations are understood as an "anti-economics." On this last score, we are mostly concerned with *which* economic discourses "within" the discipline such terms as libidinal economy oppose, partially reformulate, or extend.

Additionally, since our own familiarity with the economics of literature and with the use of "economy" in cultural studies began with our readings in the 1970s of the "modes of production" tradition within Althusserian Marxism – as employed by such scholars as Pierre Macherey, Terry Eagleton, Michel Pêcheux, and others to discuss the discursive construction of texts as well as their overdetermined literary and political effects – we are interested in looking at how the more recent formulations relate to this earlier movement. And, finally, since in the end our interest is in how such formulations can inform Marxian theory, and certainly Marxian economics, we wish to view the possible productivity of these forms through the lens of non-determinist Marxism, a development within our field in which we have played a small part from its inception in the 1970s (Amariglio *et al.* 1996). We will try to touch, if ever so briefly, on these issues in the remainder of our paper.

Despite the fact that, as we are aware, such terms as libidinal economy, symbolic economy, general economy, and so forth are often posed in opposition to one another (let alone to other "economic" discourses), we will treat them here as having certain similarities that bear notice. If our blurring of the distinctions flattens out the discussion, it is nonetheless useful for us to see how these formations, coming from somewhat similar sources during a bounded time period, are in some sense epistemic in nature. That is, just as Foucault (in *The Order of Things*, 1973) found the common rules of discursive formation that permitted the putatively alternative economic frameworks of Marx and Classical Political Economy to emerge more or less at the same time, so we hope to contribute to a similar genealogical study of symbolic economy and the like.

Of course, the first problem we run up against is the issue of the metaphoricity of the terms "symbolic economy" and the others. Quite a few other writers have worried about the use of "economy" in mixed company.

The problem is compounded by the question of what it means to say, as it has been related to us, that the term "economy" is simply or merely a metaphor in current literary/cultural writings. That is, economy, so it is claimed, is used not in its "restricted" sense (of designating an object – "the economy" – or a set of relations – production, circulation, and consumption of "material" goods), but instead is a borrowing of the term to highlight the play of signifiers, the production and circulation of meaning, and so forth.[3]

We can make little sense out of this distinction since, for us, one dimension of an economic discourse is, in fact, its "internal" overdetermined production of the objects of its analysis. Likewise, the difference between metaphor and its other is so vexed a question (and one that again often leads back to the assertion of a "real" – in this case, an economy – outside of language which is represented faithfully by some discourses in which metaphor plays a minor part, but not in others, in which metaphor dominates) that we do not believe in the possibility of resolving the problem of what form of language appropriately constitutes the object of economic theory. We can add to this the argument, which we have found in numerous texts, that the term "economy" has a long history (most roads lead back to Aristotle, we have found), and that its various uses to describe textual play, as well as market behavior and perhaps much else, is nothing particularly new.

In any event, what we do notice about the variety of terms that are currently in vogue is that they are different from most "official" economic discourses since they bring within their orbit new objects of economic analysis and new ways of seeing economic activity that have, for at least a century or two now, been relegated to the realm of the non-economic. It is a contribution, no doubt, that the problem of representation, for example, has been seen to be at the core not only of artistic/literary practices (in their limited senses, at least), but also of debates over value, price, and money in the history of economic thought. That exchanges are constituted as semiotic systems, and that money can be reduced to a universal equivalent *qua* transcendental signifier, are ideas that, while not new, do give economists ways to contemplate the role meaning production has in the constitution of exchange value. And, of course, for those economists who are dissatisfied with the standard neoclassical dictum that the determinants of taste (culture, for example) have no importance for economic theory, such investigations into the deep ways in which symbols and meanings are produced, represented, and/or performed in economic transactions are potentially of great importance.

Of course, the differences between such terms as libidinal economy and symbolic economy are crucial here since those claiming that economic activity (and particularly commodity exchange) is a sign system like any other must believe in the possibility of determining meaning through representation, no matter how unstable and dissimulated it seems. In contrast, Lyotard, Bataille, and Derrida – to take three other distinct thinkers – suggest the impossibility of transcendental signifiers or at least the destruction of meaning and representation through "libidinal" or "general" economies and their offspring. Whether meaning or its impossibility is at stake, however, the new literary/cultural "economies" do bring the issue of representation squarely back into economic discourse, and they do so by problematizing the distinction between culture and economy that remains central to much mainstream economic thought.

A note of caution here, though. As Koritz and Koritz point out in their contribution to this volume, the move of extension (some might regard it as a form of disciplinary imperialism) has been matched during the past thirty years by the work of some neoclassical economists who have tried to show that in the realm of culture – the "outside" of the economy – outcomes and actions can be, and are, in fact, guided by rational economic choice. Thus everything from choice of religion, belief in heaven, and gift giving, to suicide, substance abuse, marriage and reproduction decisions, has been subjected to the maxims of rational economic behavior, particularly maximization of expected utility. All of these phenomena are discussed as further examples of the productivity of economic analysis to order the entire universe where preference, choice, and bargaining are in play (this universe turns out to be quite large and growing, as the rapid expansion of game theoretic models partly suggests).

To be clear, as Koritz and Koritz nicely argue, the move to break down the distinctions between the sphere of economy and the sphere of culture through such ideas as "symbolic economy" have their corollary in the work of Gary Becker, and many others, which shows that economic theory – in its neoclassical form – is capable of "making sense" out of seemingly "irrational," or "non-economic" cultural and institutional elements. In the hands of the economic imperialists, the principles of rational choice are shown to operate (or at least should operate) in the "efficient" allocation of such scarce "cultural" resources as marriage partners, entrance to heaven, and the like. Since, in the last instance, professional economists are little interested in the sources or origins of choices, let alone their social constitution, the "cultural" analysis that results is mostly concerned with the predictive value of the analysis and the policy (or personal) prescriptions that result. Culture, in this world, is a result of individual choices and negotiated by rational, self-interested agents.

In the jockeying for position of these different ways of relating economics and culture, one thing oddly stands out. In our estimation, the interesting similarity between the neoclassical approach and those demarcated by general economy and the like lies in the production of a general theory in which a single principle (libido, symbolic interaction, excess, phallus, meaning, choice, etc.) establishes a transcendent reign or field of play for all other elements that surround it. Indeed – and this is certainly true of the different ways in which "general economy" has been used – there is a movement to subsume to some principle (in Bataille's case, for example, to the principle of expenditure of energy or excess) other social aspects or even other more "restricted" economies. That is, some of these theories universalize and reduce the spheres in the play of forces by attaching them to some essential principle or other. While we are sure that we will meet with some objection, we think we can establish the various essentialisms and reductionisms at work in Lyotard's libidinal investments, in the concept of the gift that is so crucial to many of these current "economies" from Mauss and Bataille to Sahlins and Baudrillard, in Goux's notion of the general equivalent (which often boils down to the symbolic order of the phallus), and in various other formulations. A few brief examples will have to suffice here. We will use Lyotard's *Libidinal Economy* as our guide to show, in cursory fashion, the essentialisms at work in the concepts of the gift and of symbolic exchange as well as to show the reductions in Lyotard's own presentation of the libidinality of all economies.

Lyotard's *Libidinal Economy* is noteworthy in presenting relentless attacks on reductions, especially those in radical and Marxian political economy, and also reproducing, at a different level, forms of reduction that undo the "ambivalence" that accrues from libidinality. His criticism of Marx, for instance, is brilliant in its attack on the infinitude of desire that marks the incompleteness of Marx's text and in analyzing Marx's longing for a lack of closure because of his obsessive fascination with the body of capital. Likewise, Lyotard is prescient in his repudiation of the organic unity of capital and capitalism, and anticipates much of the anti-essentialist Marxism that we refer to later in the paper (three examples of which would be Resnick and Wolff 1993, Cullenberg 1994, and Gibson-Graham 1996). Think for a moment of the iconoclastic, resolute anti-essentialism (or postmodernism) that characterizes Lyotard's picture of "the supple viscosity of capitalism as fragments of the body, as connected-disconnected singularities, as amnesia, decentered and anarchic, as harlequinade, as metamorphoses without inscription, as the undoing of totalities and totalizations, as ephemeral groupings of unforeseen affirmations" (Lyotard 1993: 103). Or again, the chase of Marx in *Capital* both to seek closure and to live libidinally in its absence: "the work [*Capital*] cannot form a body, just as capital cannot form a body" (ibid.: 102).

Lyotard soon turns his attention to the critique of political economy in the hands of Baudrillard and others. And here, once again, Lyotard insists on indeterminacy. He chides Baudrillard, after crediting him with a most brilliant "critique" of Marx's productionism (in *The Mirror of Production*, 1975, and *A Critique of the Political Economy of the Sign*, 1981), for basing his attack on an alternative theory of origin and essence, that of symbolic exchange. This move by Baudrillard – which he largely shares with Deleuze and Guattari, Bataille and others, most notably including economic anthropologist Marshall Sahlins – depends crucially on a theory of "primitive society" in which the economy (construed by political economy as a mode of production) does not exist, or is dominated in its construction and effects by the realms of symbolic actions, power and culture.[4] The theory of non-productivist, primitive society has many dimensions, but some of the most relevant here refer to primitives as living in a state of libidinal excess in which desire is both transparent and formative of the entire regime of social relations. Key here as well is the theory of the gift, as gift exchange (and the forms of reciprocity that characterize it) is said to be at one and the same time the basis for an alternative "economy" and an anti-economics. Lyotard comments acidly: "How is it that [Baudrillard] does not see that the whole problematic of the gift, of symbolic exchange, such as he receives it from Mauss, with or without the additions and diversions of Bataille, Callois, Lacan, belongs in its entirety to Western racism and imperialism – that it is still ethnology's good savage, slightly libidinalized, which he inherits with the concept" (106). And, moving on to the main point, Lyotard reacts with justified skepticism that such libidinality is lost in capitalism, that it is somehow outside of it, and stretches back into an imaginary past, a lost world of desire and excess, "an externalized region where desire would be sheltered from every treacherous transcription into production, labour and the law of value" (107). Baudrillard's political economy in which symbolic exchange and desire are discovered as either the underlying or the alternative, inaugural social event reinscribes the determinism (and theoreticism) – the recourse to a first and determining principle and to the procedures of theoretical evaluation – of political economy.

Of course, the problems of the cultural determinism and the romanticism of the theory of the gift and primitive society, at least in the hands of French post-structuralists, are rather well known.[5] Theories that use gift exchanges in primitive society as the historical basis for establishing a non-economic "economy" (or at least a political economy not written from the perspective of capital and markets) have always reduced reciprocity, symbolic exchange, and the like to inaugural moments of sociality that are historically and logically prior to "production" and market exchange. [6] All such efforts to establish the gift as *the* initial social act are led by the notion that meaning itself is what is at stake in gift-giving in primitive societies, and that all social relations and their efficacy as forms constituted in/of social control depend for their inception upon the prestations and struggles for power and prestige of the gift. The discourse of the gift at one and the same moment attempts to subsume all later economic forms and to create an imagined space for an alternative to all-pervasive capitalism, which then stands out as the deformation of sociality itself. As David Cheal remarks in *The Gift Economy* about what he calls "elementarist" approaches to the gift, most commentators "overlook the fact, described by Simmel, that the same form of behavior may have many different meanings according to the local context, and it may therefore appear in a wide range of interaction episodes with different social effects" (Cheal 1988: 3). Thus, the search for universal first principles in the fact of the gift may collide not only with professional ethnographic evidence, but even with the logical point that the same event may be differently constituted in different discourses.

While Lyotard thus establishes himself as a champion of such anti-reductionisms and particularities, his retort that "every political economy is libidinal" is likewise problematic, since it is unclear whether he means this as a statement of universal empirical fact (either about all societies or about all discourses) or as a provisional position about the discursive category. Surely Lyotard can attribute libidinality to any and all social formations, but the basis for this is not presented as a discursive choice (or, as Resnick and Wolff would say, an "entry point"). Rather, Lyotard tries to win the reader over by asserting that "there is as much libidinal intensity in capitalist exchange as in the alleged 'symbolic' exchange" and that while "there is no primitive society," it is also true that "capitalism is . . . a primitive society, or: the primitive society is also a capitalism" (109). This last point is put to good use when he claims that "there is no external reference, even if immanent, from which the separation of what belongs to capital (or political economy) and what belongs to subversion (or libidinal economy) can always be made, and cleanly; where desire would be clearly legible, where its *proper economy* would not be scrambled" (108). But we are left as well with the assertion, no less universalizing, of the omnipresence of libido and its extensions, its "intensities and ambivalences" always already present and constructive/destructive in society, so much so that, once again, as Lyotard proceeds, he subordinates political economy and much else to its reading if not its effects.

In looking both at Lyotard's criticisms and his own lapses into universalism, the similarity with the neoclassicalism of Becker and his colleagues is striking: all these theorists try in some way or other to establish the prior regime of a key principle (even if it is simply representation) in determining the general and specific forms in which economy appears. This is true, as we have shown, even when the object is to find a sphere that defies economic logic, such as all those valiant attempts from Deleuze and Guattari to Baudrillard and Bataille and the cultural/economic anthropology organized around Mauss's notion of the gift that seek to escape the constraints of commodity space. These various attempts locate in use value, in primitive exchange, in reciprocity, in desire and pleasure, in excess and violent destruction of meaning and things and so on, the power either to oppose or to elude the workings of the capitalist market and the notions of utility, scarcity, and reproduction that are thought to be the staples of "economic theory" proper.

The positing of an other space outside of capitalism interestingly occupies the central place in the cultural/literary economies. Or at least, the various economies that are proposed reduce capitalism if they can by a formal subsumption of capitalism's purportedly all-encompassing logic to a higher or different logic, that of semiotics, pure expenditure, libidinality, etc. The othering of capitalism and the formal economic logic that is said to characterize it (in this view, we should add, neoclassicalism is seen as nothing more than the expression or representation of a logic imposed by "the economy") – the positing of an alterity, an outside – is important to the workings of the cultural/literary economies, even when the all-pervasiveness of the rule of capital is acknowledged.

On this last point, several recent papers (Mirowski forthcoming, Barberet 1994, Koritz and Koritz in this volume) argue that such figures as Derrida, Lyotard, and Bourdieu in fact see the impossibility of escaping from markets and capital. For example, both Mirowski and Barberet call attention to Derrida's view of the impossibility of the gift and its ultimate reinscription within a field of exchange (of equivalents? this is left in doubt) either because reciprocation of the gift is required or because of the ultimate destruction of the reciprocal social relations that the gift purportedly makes possible. Mirowski shows that the whole edifice of gift theory (and not just Derrida's version) has a fatal fault since the very explanation of the relational aspect of gift giving has left it vulnerable to such claims as Derrida's and certain neoclassical economists' that the gift cannot be the means to initiate an alternative economy that escapes the logic of exchange.[7] As an aside, the impossibility of the gift for Derrida can be read as of a piece with his other recent appreciation of Marxism (Derrida 1994), in which the grand deconstructor has recourse to an omnipresent global capitalism that consumes everything in its wake, as a non-discursive, hegemonic figure haunting the scene still left unresolved by the supposed demise of Marxism and socialism.[8] In other words, the figure of an unrequited capitalism still invigorates even the most acute critics of presence, and in this way, ironically, those who render the new "economies" as eventually surrendering to the rule of capital join forces with those more persistent Marxists who recognize the hegemony of capitalism even in the postmodern culture that has given rise to all these theories of dispersion, play, desire, and diaspora.

Thus, the literary/cultural economies that have recently found favor are caught in the tension between the desire to uncover the realm in which markets, capital, and self-interested rationality have not penetrated and the fear that such a space is no longer discursively possible.[9] This may explain another interesting feature of the literary/cultural economies: the use of figures of exchange, circulation, distribution, and consumption as the primary means by which the "economy" of texts, etc. is rendered. This quite deliberate shift from production and labor to exchange and consumption can be read, of course, differently – not simply as a retreat from production and a concession to the victory of the market. As we say above, the paradox of much of the "New Economic Criticism" is that such terms as exchange and circulation are turned against themselves to show that the limited uses of these figures in conventional economic discourse cannot capture either the broad range of meanings and effects that they give rise to or the fundamental rules governing their emergence as discursive and non-discursive events. Yet, there is also no doubt that while theorists of libidinal economy and the like may have some indistinct notion of mainstream economic theory as their imagined nemesis, this opposition is more distant than the one in which Marxism – or at least certain versions of it – is the prime target.

On this score, both the debt owed to Marxism and the sustained argument with it are clearly evident, as many other commentators have pointed out. There is no mistaking the fact that, at least for the French post-structuralists, Marxism was the economic theory with which they were most familiar and against which they developed their views on economy and political economy. The references to Marxian or Marx-inspired terminology are abundant: use-value vs. exchange-value, mode of production, realization crises, commodity fetishism, alienation, and so forth join more recent references to late capitalism, global capitalism, consumer society and the like. The criticisms of Marxism, or at least some of its variants, are also apparent. Marxian political economy stands accused of privileging value over exchange value and exchange value over use value (and thereby relegating the question of desire, pleasure, and even need to a secondary, or tertiary derivative status); it is faulted for being, consequently, "productionist" (emphasizing labor and production over leisure, consumption, and just plain destruction); it is criticized for making class the *sine qua non* of economic analysis in preference to the multiplicity of other economic and social constitutive elements (including language and libido); it is eschewed because it places too much emphasis on the processes of reproduction and conservation rather than excess and expenditure; and much, much else. It is thus interesting to note that the movement away from the Marxian literary theory of the 1970s and 1980s championed by Macherey, Eagleton, and Jameson has had the effect of resituating an "economic" approach on the basis of entry points and essences that have been much more the domain of neoclassical and other mainstream approaches within official economic discourse.

That is, the history of economic thought demonstrates that for nearly 150 years there has existed a sharply delineated debate between a Marxism dedicated to explicating the crucial role of production and labor in the appearance and deployment of commodities, money, and capital and a neoclassical alternative in which exchange is generally privileged as the site at which value, price, and profit are determined. The opposition of "objective" to "subjective" theories of value is precisely located within this debate, with Marxian economists, in the past, routinely arguing that value is substantial because rooted in labor, and the neoclassicals responding that value is established in the interaction between individuals, each of whom orders preferences according to personal tastes that determine his/her value calculations. Thus, in the neoclassical view, value is determined "in the market" as a result of these supposedly "subjective" calculations; in contrast, Marxist orthodoxy has insisted on a labor theory of value in which value is determined in the process of production and only "realized" in the realm of exchange. Hence, some Marxist and other Left social and cultural theorists have worried aloud that the rise of the new "economies" in preference to the older forms of Marxian economic theory will unwittingly (or openly) end up supporting the neoclassical "subjectivist" view, thus enshrining preference, utility, and individual choice (now dressed up in the new-fangled clothes of libido, desire, pleasure, consumption, leisure, and so forth) as the fundamental principles upon which any economic discourse needs to be established.

Though we too have some trepidation about this possibility, since we have worked for quite a while to unmoor economic discourse from these essential underpinnings, we welcome the new ways of reformulating economic theory, and particularly Marxian economic theory, to take account of these developments. Let us therefore conclude with some thoughts on the contribution that these literary/cultural economies have made and can make to Marxian economic thought.

First, we state the perhaps obvious point that Marxian economics can benefit and has benefited from the rethinking of culture and language at the heart of economic activity and economic discourse. Marx's own work on commodity fetishism was a beginning of such a project – one dedicated to "reading" and performing forms of subjectivity and identity constituted by the play of signs and the play of economic forces within which commodities circulate. Additionally, Marxian economic theory can gain and, in some traditions, has gained considerably from the attacks on humanism, historicism, and representation that have been part and parcel of the deconstructive turn in cultural/literary theory and the new "economics" to which it has given rise. The notion of rupture, of epistemological break, of overdetermination, of the play of forces and signs, of the critique of strictly "economic" reasoning, and much else, has emerged not only in the writings of the French post-structuralists, but often in relation to the new economic concepts that they have championed. And these have enlivened Marxian thought generally and Marxian economic thought in particular. The effects of these concepts on the schools of Marxism that have followed in the footsteps of the Frankfurt school, Lukàcs, and especially Althusser (here we are referring to non-determinist Marxism) have been considerable.

There is also no question that much of the work has been a necessary and productive corrective to the forms of reduction and essentialism practiced by orthodox Marxists. As Baudrillard, Deleuze and Guattari, and others have shown, Marxism has suffered badly both theoretically and in the politics to which it supposedly gives rise in subordinating consumption and circulation to production, in its anthropology of labor, in its neglect of a theory of desire (and the connection of desire to both labor and consumption), and so forth. The reintroduction of the desiring body as a supplement to the laboring body in Marxian theory is also long overdue. Also long overdue is the problematizing of production and reproduction in the light of the concept of "excess" (which is certainly distinct from the Marxian notion of "surplus," since this latter concept is understood as the outcome of productive activity and the basis of productive expenditure). One task for Marxian economic theory may be to consider unproductive expenditure (in Bataille's sense) as more than just a particular disposition of "the surplus" whose effects are mostly unimportant or, worse, to be decried because they include both destruction and social reproduction in the same moment. Another may be to produce theories of consumption and distribution that rival the elaborate treatment of production within the Marxian corpus.

An additional contribution has been and may continue to be the elucidation of the postmodern moments of Marxian economic thought by highlighting the indeterminacies and uncertainties that are unleashed with such terms as "general economy," "libidinal economy," and the like. Lyotard and Derrida, for example, are particularly important to theorizing the deferral and evaporation of fixed and stable meanings as they are thought to occur in the economic realm (which includes the economies of texts). The fragmenting of economic subjects, institutions, and actions – the tendency toward dispersal, recomposition, and endless deferral – calls attention to the conjunctural, fragile nature of most economic events and behaviors. So, while some have bemoaned the "anti-theory" that such fragmentation, indeterminacy, and particularization may set off, Marxian thought, especially that informed by the problematic of the overdetermined conjuncture, stands to gain by enriching its original insight of the ever-active historical constitution of all persons and things.

The particularization of economic events is, by the way, clearly intended by Lyotard in his *Libidinal Economy*. As Brian Cooper and Margueritte Murphy so clearly set forth in their essay in this volume, Lyotard's emphasis in that text on the particular occurrence of economic crises as a materialization of libidinal investments surely is meant as an antidote to general theories of crisis in which the crisis is both articulated and resolved as a crisis in representation. Likewise, Lyotard's theory of exchange is one in which "singularity" is affirmed in contrast to Marxian (and other) political economy. This contrast is captured by Cooper and Murphy in their report that, "for Lyotard, political economy, in its efforts to 'explain' the operations of capital, crushes singularity in order to render an organic unity, all elements of which will be comparable." They go on to state that "for Lyotard, every exchange involves a libidinal excess over and above exchange and entails an incommensurability – not an equivalence – not captured by the accounting methods of political economy." Thus, as Cooper and Murphy note, Lyotard's "execrable book" "warrants the attention of anyone seeking to define an antiessentialist economics."

Without the apparatus of the libido and the resort to such excesses, though, it is possible to see a similar anti-essentialist move in the non-determinist school of Marxian economic thought to which we belong. Indeed, in many ways, members of this school have gone far to deconstruct the given economic concepts and categories from an older, more orthodox Marxism in the light of the new "economies." Readers can get a taste of this work by perusing some of the texts cited below.[10] For lack of space, we present just two examples.

Bruce Norton's work overturns the old Marxian notion of capital accumulation as the determinant of capitalist dynamics. In its place, Norton shows the varying circumstances in which capitalism may or may not promote accumulation, when accumulation may or may not end a cyclical downturn, when profit maximization may and when it may not contribute to accumulation, and so on. Norton's work, conducted as a sustained critique of the essentialism of the monopoly capital and Steindl schools within Marxian economics, challenges entirely the longstanding view that capitalism and its historical development cannot be understood without grounding its "dynamic" in the forms and processes of capital accumulation. Norton, therefore, shares much with those cultural theorists who view the narrow focus on accumulation, dynamics, and progress to be so much teleological and economistic baggage of the long determinist tradition in Marxism. Norton goes so far as to challenge the prevailing assumption that the capitalist firm is primarily motivated by the drive to accumulate. In contrast, Norton has indicated that disaccumulation may characterize the "motivation" of the capitalist firm, as such firms may in fact transform themselves and enhance their profitability by becoming (at least partly) banks, retailers – not exploiters of wage labor – and so forth. While disaccumulation is not equivalent to pure expenditure (since profit is still at stake), it is not too far from Norton's thinking to entertain the possibility of a rationality of the capitalist firm for which "unproductive expenditure" is a major outcome, if not the driving force.

Perhaps equally attuned to the more general movements of anti-essentialism that have occurred outside of both economics and Marxism, J.K. Gibson-Graham has incorporated into her feminist Marxist critique some of the insights of literary/cultural economies. But, also in contrast to many of these formulations, Gibson-Graham argues that the fact that capitalism is seen as dominating or determining most if not all economic and social events in the world today can be attributed mostly to the way capitalism is itself constructed as a concept. In a manner akin to Lyotard's depiction of the viscosity of capitalism and the impossibility of capital as an (in)organic body, Gibson-Graham shows that much Left/Marxian discourse is chiefly responsible for capitalism's being understood as a large, singular, integrated, expansive, and unified economic system in comparison to which all other economic events (particularly forms of non-capitalism) are small, partial, insufficient, and incomplete. Gibson-Graham radically transforms the existing model of capitalism – seeing it as a fragmented and partial set of economic processes and institutions, lacking any necessary unifying drive or logic – and creates a theoretical space for the proliferation of non-capitalist class and economic processes in contemporary societies.

We acknowledge that cultural/literary economies are constituted in ways that present obstacles for non-determinist (or postmodern) Marxian economic thought because of the essentialisms often present in which desire, power, culture, textuality, and so forth are found to provide an ultimate unifying force (if only as a unified "principle of dispersion"); because the critique of productionism and the revivification of exchange has almost entirely displaced class and labor; because general economy and the like are marred at times by naïve anthropology (this is especially true of the frequent recourse to a pre-modern/modern distinction in establishing the veracity of such ideas as the gift) informed by theoretical humanism, and so forth. We leave for another paper a more complete discussion of these obstacles. Yet we are also convinced that the productive interplay of these notions of economy and Marxian economic thought is at a beginning. Unlike our neoclassical brethren, that is, we regard the different discourses of economy discussed here to be ones that can and do inform existing traditions within the economics proffered by its professional practitioners, and it is in that spirit that we hope to participate in the continued "critical exchange" that the editors of this book have done so much to make possible.

Notes

1 To be evenhanded, we should also report that not a few literary and cultural scholars were chagrined at the barely rudimentary level of understanding that the economists had of literary figures, debates, and traditions in literary and cultural theory, and much else that has characterized diverse developments in these fields for a similar length of time. It is news to economists, for example, that such seemingly elementary terms as metaphor, narrative, genre, and so forth have been the objects of roaring debates and disagreements over decades (centuries?) such that little agreement is often evinced amongst literary and cultural theorists about the meaning and use of these terms (not to mention that they emerge in alternative critical approaches in highly differentiated forms). For economists who think that talking about "rhetoric" or "stories" or "symbolism" or any comprehensive term in literary and cultural theory is simply a matter of paying attention to how texts are written, how persuasion works, or how meaning is made, the critique of representation, to take just one example, is a mindboggling affair.

2 Yet, of course, we are not alone. Among others, Judith Mehta (1993, 1994) has found productive use for Derrida, Lyotard, the theory of the gift, and much else in her illuminating work on game theory. Mehta's work is all the more notable because it brings to bear deconstructive techniques and concerns for the indeterminacy and the plurality of meaning in an area in economic thought – game theoretic models – which is considered on the cutting edge of economic "science."

3 One useful discussion of the concept of economy as it relates to the notion of "general economy" that appears in the writings of Bataille, Derrida, and others is Plotnitsky's *Reconfigurations: Critical Theory and General Economy* (1993).

Plotnitsky's thorough treatment of this concept in his book only gestures, however, at its relation to usages within the field of "political economy." While Plotnitsky distinguishes between the use of general economy as an "exchange-management cluster" (which he finds in the history of political economy) and as a reference, metaphorically, to thermodynamics and the expenditure of energy, his aim throughout most of his book is primarily to explicate the latter use and not the former.

4 For a related criticism of Sahlins's cultural determinism as a substitute for Marxian political economy, see the brief comments in Amariglio *et al.* (1988) and Amariglio (1984).

5 Marc Augé, the Marxist anthropologist, calls attention in his *The Anthropological Circle* (1982) to the "phantasy" that haunted the French anthropologists and philosophers most responsible for reinscribing this romanticism. In acerbic and cautionary tones, Augé states that "with the help of fashion (and under pressure from a demand that actually epitomizes the unease of an epoch or a society) a greater and greater number of increasingly picturesque savages are paraded before us. These savages live better than we; they know better than we do the secrets of both life and death and the mysterious texture of the real, and how to see and turn away from the sterile schemata of analytic thought" (4).

6 In Amariglio's (1984) doctoral dissertation, the epistemological problem of an economic anthropology alternative to Marxian political economy is presented via an extended critique of Sahlins, Baudrillard, and of much Marxian anthropology and Marxist discussions of "primitive communism." In some important ways, this criticism parallels the views that Lyotard puts forward in his discussion.

7 Gudeman (forthcoming), though, attempts to answer Mirowski in a forceful defense of reciprocity and its continued possibility for serving as the inaugural concept in an alternative "political economy." In *The Social Meaning of Money*, Viviana Zelizer (1994) raises the important question of the problem of a simple dichotomy between gift and market exchange. This dichotomy is clearly at play both with Derrida and with Mirowski, since the impossibility or possibility of the gift is dependent upon whether or not it collapses into market exchange (not to speak as well of the issue of the "impossibility" of market exchange). While continuing to preserve the distinction, Zelizer remarks that at least for market transfers, "there are multiple types of modern transfers rather than a single market exchange of commodities. Gifts constitute a range of transfers distinct from payments and entitlements and corresponding to a different range of social relations" (78). The plurality of forms of gifts and commodities, of course, begs the question of when the "borderline" has been crossed, but it also suggests the constitution of most if not all transactions of these types as always hybrid and overdetermined.

8 In their penetrating discussion of *Specters of Marx* (see Gibson-Graham 1996), Julie Graham and Kathie Gibson have focused on Derrida's adoption of an all-too-familiar Marxism, in which there is no escape from the ever-spreading tentacles of capitalism.

9 Mark Osteen has pointed out to us that, of course, there is no escaping from "self-interest" in much of the literature on the gift and prestation. Rather, an economic interest is replaced by a political interest in acquiring power or social control in the potlatch and other such forms of unbalanced reciprocity. Now, the question

of whether this substitution eludes "self" interest is open to debate. But in the absence of a reconceptualization of the self through which it might be shown that when the stakes are economic, then "selfdom" – its constitution as an interest – is produced, in contrast to the production of something else when the stakes are non-economic, the substitution does not eliminate the possibility that self-interest is operating in either case.

10 See especially Resnick and Wolff (1993); Gibson-Graham (1996); Ruccio (1988); Amariglio and Ruccio (1994 and forthcoming); Norton (1988, 1995); Wolff *et al.* (1982); Garnett (1995).

References

Amariglio, Jack (1984). *Economic History and the Theory of Primitive Socio-economic Development*. Dissertation. University of Massachusetts.

——, and David Ruccio (1994). "Postmodernism, Marxism, and the Critique of Modern Economic Thought." *Rethinking Marxism* 7, 1: 7–35.

—— and —— (forthcoming). "The Transgressive Knowledge of 'Ersatz' Economics." In *What Do Economists Know? New Economics of Knowledge/New Knowledge of Economics*. Ed. Rob Garnett. New York: Routledge.

Amariglio, Jack, Antonio Callari, Stephen Resnick, David Ruccio, and Richard Wolff (1996). "Nondeterminist Marxism: The Birth of a Postmodern Tradition in Economics." In *Beyond Neoclassical Economics: Heterodox Approaches to Economic Theory*. Ed. F. Foldvary. Aldershot, Hants.: Edward Elgar.

——, Stephen Resnick, and Richard Wolff (1988). "Class, Power, and Culture." In *Marxism and the Interpretation of Culture*. Ed. Cary Nelson and Lawrence Grossberg. Urbana: University of Illinois Press.

——, —— and —— (1990). "Division and Difference in the 'Discipline' of Economics." *Critical Inquiry* 17: 108–37.

Augé, Marc (1982). *The Anthropological Circle*. Cambridge: Cambridge University Press.

Barberet, John (1994). "'And of course Marx . . .': Derrida's *Given Time I*." Paper presented at the conference on New Economic Criticism at Case Western University, Cleveland, October.

Bataille, Georges (1985). "The Notion of Expenditure." In *Visions of Excess: Selected Writings, 1927–1939*. Ed. Allan Stoekl. Trans. Allan Stoekl, with Carl R. Lovitt and Donald M. Leslie Jr. Minneapolis: University of Minnesota Press.

—— (1986). *Erotism: Death and Sensuality*. San Francisco: City Lights.

—— (1988). *The Accursed Share*. Vol. 1. New York: Zone.

Baudrillard, Jean (1975). *The Mirror of Production*. St. Louis: Telos.

—— (1981). *For a Critique of the Political Economy of the Sign*. St Louis: Telos.

Cheal, David (1988). *The Gift Economy*. London: Routledge.

Cooper, Brian, and Margueritte Murphy (1999). "'Libidinal Economics': Lyotard and Accounting for the Unaccountable." In this volume.

Cullenberg, Stephen (1994). *The Falling Rate of Profit*. London: Pluto.

——, David Ruccio, and Jack Amariglio, eds (forthcoming). *Postmodernism, Knowledge, and Economics*. New York: Routledge.

Derrida, Jacques (1978). "From Restricted to General Economy: A Hegelianism without Reserve." In *Writing and Difference*. Trans. Alan Bass. Chicago: University of Chicago Press, 251–77.

—— (1992). *Given Time: I. Counterfeit Money*. Trans. Peggy Kamuf. Chicago: University of Chicago Press.

—— (1994). *Specters of Marx: The State of the Debt, the Work of Mourning, and the New International*. New York: Routledge.

Foucault, Michel (1973). *The Order of Things*. New York: Vintage.

Gagnier, Regenia, and John Dupré (1995). "Economists, Marxists, Critics: Whose Economics?" Paper presented at session entitled "(Un)settling Accounts: New Languages of Economic Criticism" at the Modern Language Association Meeting, Chicago, December.

Garnett, Robert F. (1995). "Marx's Value Theory: Modern or Postmodern?" *Rethinking Marxism* 8, 4: 40–60.

Gibson-Graham, J.K. (1996). *The End of Capitalism (As We Knew It)*. Oxford: Blackwell.

Goux, Jean-Joseph (1990). *Symbolic Economies: After Marx and Freud*. Trans. Jennifer Curtiss Gage. Ithaca, NY: Cornell University Press.

Gudeman, Stephen (forthcoming). "Greek Gifts." In *Postmodernism, Knowledge and Economics*. Ed. S. Cullenberg, D. Ruccio, and J. Amariglio.

Koritz, Amy, and Douglas Koritz. "Symbolic Economics: Adventures in the Metaphorical Marketplace." In this volume.

Lyotard, Jean-François (1993). *Libidinal Economy*. Reprinted Bloomington: Indiana University Press.

McCloskey, Donald N. (1985). *The Applied Theory of Price*. 2nd edn. New York: Macmillan.

Mehta, Judith (1993). "Meaning in the Context of Bargaining Games – Narratives in Opposition." In *Economics and Language*. Ed. Willie Henderson, Tony Dudley-Evans, and Roger Backhouse. New York: Routledge, 85–102.

—— (1994). "Cooperation Between and Within Firms: Reflections on the Giving of Gifts." Discussion Paper no. 9402. Economics Research Centre: University of East Anglia.

—— (forthcoming). "A Disorderly Household: Voicing the Noise." In *Postmodernism, Knowledge and Economics*. Ed. S. Cullenberg, D. Ruccio, and J. Amariglio. New York: Routledge.

Mirowski, Philip (forthcoming). "Refusing the Gift." In *Postmodernism, Knowledge and Economics*. Ed. S. Cullenberg, D. Ruccio, and J. Amariglio. New York: Routledge.

Norton, Bruce (1988). "Epochs and Essences: A Review of Marxist Long-wave and Stagnation Theories." *Cambridge Journal of Economics* 12: 203–24.

—— (1995). "Late Capitalism and Postmodernism: Jameson/Mandel." In *Marxism in the Postmodern Age*. Ed. Antonio Callari, Stephen Cullenberg, and Carole Biewener. New York: Guilford, 59–70.

Plotnitsky, Arkady (1993). *Reconfigurations: Critical Theory and General Economy*. Gainesville: University Press of Florida.

Resnick, Stephen, and Richard Wolff (1993). *Knowledge and Class: A Marxian Critique of Political Economy*. Chicago: University of Chicago Press.

Richman, Michèle (1982). *Reading Georges Bataille: Beyond the Gift*. Baltimore, MD: Johns Hopkins University Press.

Ruccio, David (1988). "The Merchant of Venice, or Marxism in the Mathematical Mode." *Rethinking Marxism* 1, 4: 36–68.
Sahlins, Marshall (1972). *Stone Age Economics*. Chicago: Aldine-Atherton.
Wolff, Richard, Bruce Roberts, and Antonio Callari (1982). "Marx's (not Ricardo's) Transformation Problem: A Radical Reconceptualization." *History of Political Economy* 14: 564–82.
Zelizer, Viviana A. (1994). *The Social Meaning of Money*. New York: Basic Books.

22

REPLY TO AMARIGLIO AND RUCCIO'S "LITERARY/CULTURAL 'ECONOMIES', ECONOMIC DISCOURSE, AND THE QUESTION OF MARXISM"

Regenia Gagnier and John Dupré

We are a philosopher and a literary critic who for the past few years have been involved in discussions with both centrist ("neoclassical") economists and those on the margins of their discipline, including feminist economists and institutionalists, as well as radical economists, both determinist and non-determinist. We have also been writing articles aimed at clarifying (*pace* McCloskey) the modern history of economics to non-economists. We have discussed some of that history in relation to mechanism in our contribution above; here we will briefly summarize the history in order to respond to two questions posed by Jack Amariglio and David Ruccio. They ask about "the specificity of the contribution [of 'literary/cultural economies'] to economic thought." From our familiarity with their work outside this volume, we know that the new symbolic and libidinal economies have indeed informed their non-determinist, postmodern economic theory. For example, they have tried to include in economics re-evaluations of the experiences and distributions of pleasure and pain, work and desire, hierarchies of taste, emotions and reason, passions and interests, sex, race, and class. They have reconsidered the desiring body of neoclassical economics and contrasted it with the laboring body of political economy. They have commended neoclassicalism for positing that there is no "truly human" body and for displacing the body as origin of value – as it was in the classic labor theory of value. They distinguish this dispersed map of the body – in which the consuming body or its functions is distinct from the producing body or its functions, and none is subsumed into a higher unity – from the organic unity of the body they see in Adam Smith or David Hume. They have also deconstructed essentialisms in both Marxism and neoclassicalism, including the essentializing of markets, planning, the subject, and knowledge, while insisting on the historical contingency of all categories.

In this paper, they further raise two questions concerning the contribution of literary/cultural economies to economic thought. First, they wonder whether economism – the "imperialist" colonization of all disciplines, even of all human phenomena ("the choice of religion, belief in heaven, gift giving, suicide, substance abuse, marriage and reproduction decisions, and much else"), by economic analysis – and the new symbolic economies are not equally reductionist, since each claims to hold the key to all mythologies, either in rational choice theory (neoclassicalism), libidinal investments (Jean-François Lyotard), the gift (Georges Bataille), the general equivalent (Jean-Joseph Goux), or representation itself (Jean Baudrillard). Second, they speculate whether these new economies do not often share the specific reductionism of neoclassical economics itself.

As stated, we shall approach these questions through the relevant history, for non-economists should know what they are subscribing to when they adopt economic models. The history of modern economics is best encapsulated in the transition from political economy to neoclassicalism.[1] The single most important insight of classical political economy was that the division of labor was the source of differences between people. People may or may not identify with a social or economic class: in Britain in the nineteenth century they often did, in the US today they typically do not. But most people's subjective and objective identities are centrally related to whether they make nails, automobiles, books, contracts, breakfast, hotel beds, or music. The fact that the division of labor also reflects major social divisions of race, gender, and ethnicity, and internationally reflects relations of domination and subordination between nations, is also crucial in establishing individual identities. That the political economists themselves ignored the unpaid labor of women in their assignation of value is of paramount significance in the history of economics (see Pujol 1992), but it does not diminish the magnitude of their original insight into social relations.

Second, the political economists were concerned about the negative consequences of the division of labor. Adam Smith proposed government mechanisms to ameliorate British workers' deterioration in what he called the social, intellectual, and martial virtues. J.S. Mill feared that competitive individualism would drive out sympathy and altruism. And Karl Marx and Friedrich Engels – who criticized political economy while adopting some of its fundamental categories – put alienation and atomism, respectively, at the center of working and bourgeois life. Despite their penchant for discovering economic laws and for depicting a self-interested maximizer of material advantage called Economic Man, the political economists also believed that economic systems made kinds of people and that the division of labor, as John Ruskin said, also divided people from one another.

Third, the political economists did not believe that markets were the end of history. Markets were viewed as one stage of growth, but economic growth was no more an end in itself than beauty was to their contemporaries in esthetics (the so-called "political economists of art"). Smith thought that free trade, if it ever happened (which he thought unlikely), would lead to world peace (the "doux-commerce" thesis). Mill thought that once production reached a certain level, society's primary concern should be with more equal distribution and indeed thought that the appropriate level of production had already been reached in 1871. Political economy entailed a theory of social relations in a world in which scarcity was perceived to be a relationship between productive forces and nature, and in which markets were appropriate to but one stage of the development of those productive forces.

For many exponents of neoclassical economics, markets *were* the end of history, and objective, or intersubjective, social relations were replaced by subjective introspection on utilities – or, technically, in Pareto's term, "ophelimities" (desires rather than needs). These could be ranked but not measured and could not be compared across persons or groups (for example, classes). Human beings were no longer perceived primarily as producers but as consumers; human freedom was defined less as the freedom to be or create than as the freedom to choose between objects of consumption. And scarcity was less a relation to nature than a psychological condition of insatiability in the endless pursuit of material goods. Most of this transition in the history of economics occurred between 1870 and the 1930s.

This new notion of humankind as consumers introspecting on their choices and preferences in the pursuit of material goods was the distinguishing feature of modernity – the end of history – that was then used to differentiate and objectify others. Notions of civilization, barbarism, "non-competing groups," and other hierarchical descriptions of people ceased to refer to contingent divisions of labor or advanced technologies and came to be seen (often with support by eugenics or anthropology) as innate differences. Societies as well as individuals were known by the quality of their desires – their "tastes" – as revealed in their choices or preferences. Unlike values, which can be discussed and rationally debated, in modern economics there is no disputing about tastes.

Although it was not until the 1930s that the social bases of political economy were finally obliterated from the science of economics, this evisceration was grounded in the social conditions of the late nineteenth century. These included the expansion of technology and production that led to a "culture of abundance" (in Birken's [1988] terms); the professionalizing of economics as an academic discipline heavily influenced by psychology and the calculation of pleasure and pain (see Small 1991; Birken 1988; Maloney 1985)[2]; the mathematizing of economics as a "scientific" response to the unequal distribution of wealth at a time when the rise of labor unions and the Labor Party challenged the social status quo; the corollary increase of abstraction that shifted focus from actual workers and their environments to statistical variation in the labor market (see Mitch 1994)[3]; and a merger of economic and anthropological theory at the height of British imperialism, which imported into economics racist and cultural ideologies from which political economy, with its insistence on the division of labor and advances in technology, had been relatively – but only relatively – distant (see Stocking 1987, 1995; Kuklick 1991).

One of us has described elsewhere how this shift in economics was simultaneous with a shift in esthetics (Gagnier 1993, 1995). Substantive theories of esthetics, both the ethical (Kant or Mill) and the political economic (Ruskin or Morris), made way, again in the period after 1870, for esthetic formalism. Esthetics began to focus less on objective, or intersubjective, social relations (the classic "plots" of the nineteenth-century novel), and more on individual psychology. Esthetic theories based on creative production were replaced by those positing the autonomy of the critic or consumer of the work (the Oxford critic Walter Pater exemplifies this shift).

We can now take up the question posed by Amariglio and Ruccio: whether the new symbolic or libidinal economies that they welcome into a more pluralist economics will not "end up supporting the neoclassical 'subjectivist' view, thus enshrining preference, utility, and individual choice (but now dressed up in the new-fangled clothes of libido, desire, pleasure, consumption, leisure, and so forth) as the fundamental principles upon which any economic discourse needs to be established" – not just at the expense of Marxian economic theory, but at the expense of need itself in favor of the pleasures of what Fukuyama (discussed in our essay in this volume) has called "the spectacular abundance of advanced liberal economies and the infinitely diverse consumer culture made possible by them." Ruccio and Amariglio have "some trepidations" about this possibility. We have some, too.

We can illustrate our concerns by referring to a recent highly positive reading of neoclassicalism, Lawrence Birken's *Consuming Desire: Sexual Science and the Emergence of a Culture of Abundance 1871–1914* (1988). Birken argues that in slowly abandoning the bourgeois system in which only property-ownership, production, and labor bestowed individuality and citizenship, in favor of a (theoretical) system of sovereign, desiring, perfectly competitive "ids," neoclassical theory extended the ideology of democracy further than it had been extended before. Just as an ethic of work and need was abandoned in favor of an ethic of pleasure and desire, late Victorian sexology saw an increased ambivalence about gender centered in reproduction and envisioned instead an objectless, all-desiring genderlessness, a polymorphously perverse sexuality. Although he frequently nods to the Foucauldian thesis that the discourses of sexology have been as repressive as liberating, Birken calls this society of individuals freely pursuing their individual desires "democratic" and "consumerist" interchangeably.

Although such an argument has its appeal after two decades of post-modern theory, we have reservations about it. First, we must note that the *desire* to consume or to express one's individuality through consumption is not the same thing as the *power* to consume. In *The Joyless Economy*, the economist Tibor Scitovsky points out that there are two kinds of power in consumer society: individual wealth to consume what one desires ("the eccentric millionaire") and the power of the mass to fulfill its desires through pressure for mass-production (Scitovsky 1976: 7–9). Thus while Birken acknowledges that the consumer ideology he equates with democratization was an effective desire ("effective demand") for only a small elite, Scitovsky shows, and we would agree, that mere desire cannot be called democratic unless accompanied by power. Although the mass of people may be said to have power, this power is not the power to exercise individual choice and therefore not the power to make individual desire effective. Such reservations make one uncomfortable with Birken's characterization of women's consumer "choices" as feminist praxis (Birken 1988: 145), and with his suggestion that "the sexualization of women and children may have constituted a symbolic representation of their . . . claim to citizenship." Birken even sees this sexualization as a form of positive "subjectification" (149).

Birken's celebration of individualism, desire, choice, consumption, markets, and other fetishes of professional economics begins to show how such appropriations of neoclassicalism (for all its virtues in correcting an overemphasis on production) tend toward reductionism (and, as we shall argue below, idealism). What is good about a pluralist or postmodern economics is that, rather than essentializing a single category as the key to all economies, it considers people as both producers and consumers, workers and wanters; as both biological and cultural, both emotional and rational, at once social and self-interested; as creatures horribly vulnerable to pain but also desiring pleasure; as creatures with bodies – and minds – both desirous and laboring, who take pleasure in competition but also long for security, and who find value in both use and exchange, both planning and markets. And these dichotomies should be understood not as mutually exclusive alternatives, but as defining the poles of a continuum, or even as interacting.

We do not intend to question the achievements of economics in developing, for example, a theory of distribution through a price mechanism (which we take to be the core of neoclassicalism). Our point in the remainder of this reply is to indicate the limitations of this theory when applied outside its narrow arena. The supposition that the power of rational choice among ranked preferences is the essential property of human nature seems to us disastrous. First, as we have discussed at length elsewhere (Gagnier and Dupré 1995, 1996), the understanding of labor as a commodity gives only the most partial insight into the importance of work to human life. The neoclassical shift from viewing humans as producers to viewing humans as consumers has tended to reduce work to no more than a disutility to be traded for an optimal basket of commodities. But as both Mill and Marx argued, and as remains obvious to those with the good fortune to do work that is not mere drudgery, satisfying labor can be an essential ingredient of highly rewarding human lives. Moreover, as the political economists' attention to the division of labor made clear, the nature of one's work is fundamental in defining one's role and status in society and, subjectively, one's sense of identity.

Second, unfashionable though this may have become, we will still defend the importance of the traditional Marxist emphasis on needs. Contemporary neoclassical economists often maintain that distinguishing needs from other desires is intolerably paternalistic, and that individual choosers should be left to decide which of their wants are more or less important. This presumption reveals the extent to which neoclassical economics is an idealist theory: the choosing mind, essential to this conception of human nature, is only accidentally related to a biological body whose flourishing depends to an important degree on objectively determinate conditions. In reality, of course, only after these objective conditions for biological flourishing are met is there any possibility for the exercise of meaningful choice among options.

Third, and perhaps most important, humans are not anti-social, individualistic monads. It is ironic that contemporary individualism has derived much of its ideological support from biology, particularly human sociobiology. For if there is one uncontroversial fact about human behavioral biology, it is that humans are social animals. Neoclassical economics might provide a sufficient account of our species if we were, say, rational sharks, but it does not offer an adequate description of the highly gregarious, interdependent social primates that we in fact are. Moreover, concern for the well-being of others is not, as contemporary economic theorists sometimes suggest, an eccentric taste, but a central feature of most humans. Although we do not deny that a society sufficiently committed to acquisitive individualism might eventually go far in eliminating altruism, we also do not welcome this possibility. As Susan Feiner argues in her essay in the present volume, and as many other radical economists have also begun to show, *Homo economicus* is not a rational human, but a seriously defective one.

These remarks are not, we repeat, intended to deny either the value of economic theory in its proper place or the potential importance of the satisfaction of desires to human life. The point is rather to insist that an adequate economics or, better, political economy, must place the mechanism for the distribution of goods within a much wider context that considers many other conditions for human flourishing. The satisfaction of desires must be seen as subordinate to the provision of needs; the latter might be better served, at this stage in history, by a planned system than by market mechanisms. And contrary to the standard practice of contemporary economics, evaluation of the importance of maximal satisfaction of desire cannot adequately proceed without some account of the etiology of desires. Here the contributions of cultural studies and critical theory to a deep account of tastes have an obvious and central role to play.

Notes

1 A bibliography of the classic texts in the history of economics that we refer to can be found in our essay in this volume.

2 Some would trace the neoclassical calculus back to Bentham. This seems to us mistaken. Bentham was interested in utility for the greatest number, not the individual's marginal utility, and this required that he make interpersonal comparisons, which he did not hesitate to do.

3 The theory that mathematization is a response to class warfare comes out of a discussion between the authors and the economist Samuel Bowles.

References

Birken, Lawrence (1988). *Consuming Desire: Sexual Science and the Emergence of a Culture of Abundance, 1871–1914*. Ithaca, NY: Cornell University Press.

Gagnier, Regenia (1993). "On the Insatiability of Human Wants: Economic and Aesthetic Man." *Victorian Studies* 36.2: 125–54.

—— (1995). "Is Market Society the *Fin* of History?" In *Cultural Politics at the Fin de Siècle*. Ed. Sally Ledger and Scott McCracken. Cambridge: Cambridge University Press, 290–310.

——, and John Dupré (1995). "On Work and Idleness." *Feminist Economics* 1: 96–109.

—— , and —— (1996). "A Brief History of Work." *Journal of Economic Issues* 30: 553–59.

Kuklick, Henrika (1991). *The Savage Within: The Social History of British Anthropology, 1885–1945*. Cambridge: Cambridge University Press.

Maloney, John (1985). *Marshall, Orthodoxy and the Professionalisation of Economics*. Cambridge: Cambridge University Press.

Mitch, David (1994). "Victorian Views of the Nature of Work and its Influence on the Nature of the Worker." Paper presented at the conference "Victorian Work," University of California at Santa Cruz, 4–7 August.

Pujol, Michele (1992). *Feminism and Antifeminism in Early Economic Thought*. New York: Gower.

Scitovsky, Tibor (1976). *The Joyless Economy: An Inquiry into Human Satisfaction and Consumer Dissatisfaction*. New York: Oxford University Press.

Small, Ian (1991). *Conditions for Criticism*. Oxford: Oxford University Press.

Stocking, George W. Jr (1987). *Victorian Anthropology*. New York: Free Press.

—— (1995). *After Tylor: British Social Anthropology 1888–1951*. Madison: University of Wisconsin Press.

23

SYMBOLIC ECONOMICS

Adventures in the metaphorical marketplace

Amy Koritz and Douglas Koritz

In *Keywords* Raymond Williams (1985: 90) outlines three currently common uses of the word "culture." The first and last of these uses situates culture in the production or appreciation of the intellectual, spiritual, and esthetic. The second use refers to "a particular way of life," and potentially includes both material and symbolic production. Williams – and the field of cultural studies he helped invent – has been particularly interested in *relating* rather than contrasting the symbolic and the material. Does the current tendency to refer to realms of symbolic practice and signification in terms of symbolic *economies* achieve such a relation, or simply conflate the two via metaphorical sleight-of-hand? The deployment of economic language to describe the circulation of cultural practices, tastes, and styles, which is supposed to refer the cultural to the economic in order to assert the impossibility of extricating the one from the other, has become a powerful and privileged way of understanding culture. Does culture, when understood as a symbolic economy, become economic, *tout court?*

Economics, as Deirdre (Donald) McCloskey (1990) has argued, is a form of storytelling. Economic stories, however, are frequently taken as true and can have direct consequences in the material lives of individuals. Further, all narrative genres carry with them ideological implications and place limits on what it is possible to do, think, or be within their boundaries. The heroine of a conventional romance novel, for example, always ends up part of a couple, and never does that couple consist of two women. Narrative, according to Jerome Bruner (1991: 4–5), is the most important tool we have for making sense of our experience; as such it not only represents reality, but also helps *constitute* it. Metaphor, in turn, is fundamental to narrative to the extent that the conceptual building blocks of narrative are deeply metaphorical in nature. Metaphors such as "argument is war," or "time is money" shape the ways we think and act. As Lakoff and Johnson (1980) have noted, such metaphors are culturally and historically specific, and they not only enable certain ways of thinking and acting, but make alternatives (e.g., conceiving of an argument as a dance) difficult to see or comprehend.

The term "culture" once referred to essentially economic activities, as in agriculture, and attained its modern meaning via its metaphorical use in the description of the arts (Williams 1985: 87). Using economic metaphors to describe and explain culture perhaps merely returns the term to its etymological roots, except that under advanced capitalism the economics of culture is far from bucolic. Our concern is that a complex and subtle array of human endeavors and experiences may be in danger of being subsumed into economic modes of explanation.

In fact, major economic paradigms are well advanced in subsuming the cultural. In the neoclassical theories of new family economics, the cultural domain and its symbols are given material existence by positing all, or at least many, cultural processes as exchange. A cultural trait, symbol, etc. is deemed to have, at least in principle, a quantifiable value via its equation with the traits and symbols for which it is traded. At times these bundles of culture are further equated with objects more traditionally viewed as economic, e.g., commodities or money, as in divorce proceedings. Indeed, in the work of Gary Becker, a Nobel Laureate in Economics and the father of the new family economics, this becomes explicit. For Becker, all social processes become exchanges of owned properties culminating in a reflexive property – the individual – that has property in itself.

Given this totalizing impulse within economic theory, the prevalence and persuasiveness of the metaphorical treatment of culture as an economy by cultural theorists should be approached with some caution. If culture is nothing but the marketplace – even though this marketplace is now conceptualized in terms of symbolic economies – only questions and positions consonant with the economic field and its paradigms can be asked or assumed. Thus here we address the problems that the appropriation of economic language for cultural analysis entails from two directions: neoclassical economics, represented particularly by the work of Gary Becker, and the influential cultural theory of Pierre Bourdieu. The neoclassical school of thought dominates economics both in the professional and in the popular imagination and discourse, and Becker's work is centrally located in that school. Pierre Bourdieu, in contrast, offers a general theory of social practice that attempts to employ economic language while rejecting economic reductionism, but which, we argue, finally offers little resistance to the hegemony of economic explanations of cultural practices. What is sacrificed in both Bourdieu's and Becker's accounts of culture is the possibility of what Lyotard has called the differend, a concept that acknowledges the limitation of the economic to a specific kind of narrative, and its ultimate untranslatability into other genres of discourse.

Bourdieu has developed a subtle and complex picture of a world in which practice is a function of a specific relationship among what he calls "habitus," "capital," and "field." As explained in *Distinction* (1984), this relationship can be written [(habitus) (capital)] + field = practice (101). The nature and function of a habitus is perhaps best described as a set of dispositions or ways of perceiving and appreciating phenomena, along with behaviors consonant with those perceptions and appreciations. Any individual will share with a class of others conditions of existence that in turn "produce homogeneous systems of dispositions capable of generating similar practices" (ibid.), including similar esthetic tastes and lifestyles. Thus the habitus shared by most readers of this paper generates a response of visceral disgust to the eating of grubs and insects by human beings. The semi- or unconscious, non-calculating nature of the habitus is important, since it is the basis for Bourdieu's rejection of economistic interpretations of his work. A field, in contrast, is a structured space that functions according to laws specific to it. In the case of works of art, for example, what accounts for the relative status of specific works and their producers is not, according to Bourdieu, the power of influential individuals or institutions (e.g., galleries, journals, publishers), but "the field of production understood as the system of objective relations between these agents and institutions and as the site of struggles for the monopoly of the power to consecrate, in which the values of works of art and belief in those values are continuously generated" (Bourdieu 1993: 78). Capital, finally, is what agents wage this struggle with and fight to maintain the value of. Besides economic capital, Bourdieu identifies two important kinds of capital in the struggle to gain and maintain distinction: cultural capital and symbolic capital. Symbolic capital refers to prestige and celebrity, while cultural capital has more to do with knowledge, taste, and expertise. There may or may not, in his view, be a positive correlation between the possession of economic capital and any other kind. In fact, sometimes one *loses* cultural capital in consequence of gaining economic capital. In abstraction from a specific field, capital is an empty category. That is, the particular nature and location of capital cannot be determined outside the conditions governing each field – what counts as capital in the academic field differs from what counts as capital in the economic or political fields.

The economic field, the educational field, the cultural field, and so on are all relatively autonomous, but they all work in the same way – that is, they are *structurally homologous*. In each case struggles over the power to define what counts as symbolic or cultural capital are waged between agents and institutions in order to secure the status quo or destabilize it. Analyzing the relations between fields as homologies rather than identities is supposed to guard against the threat of economic reductionism posed by Bourdieu's choice of vocabulary. At the same time, he is explicit in his desire to develop a theory capable of analyzing "all practices, including those purporting to be disinterested or gratuitous, and hence non-economic, as economic practices directed toward the maximizing of material or symbolic profit" (Bourdieu 1977: 183). As Randal Johnson (1983: 8) puts it, every field entails specific interests and investments which "can be analyzed in terms of an economic logic without in any way reducing them to economics."

The possibility of maintaining this distinction between the logic and language one employs, on one hand, and the field from which they emerge, on the other, is, we believe, questionable. Bourdieu wants to deploy the rhetorical and explanatory power of economic metaphor while denying that a fundamental identity between "homologous" structures is implied by that rhetoric. If this economic rhetoric is meant as metaphor, then terms normally understood as economic must be redefined to distance their cultural and symbolic meanings from their economic meaning. Thus economic language such as "exchange," "market," and "capital" must be modified into "cultural exchange," "cultural market," and "cultural capital," and suitably redefined. The difficulties in this project can be illustrated by the questions that arise from the fact that the normal usage of these terms is squarely within economics: Does cultural exchange take place in a generalized abstract market in which symbolic attributes are generally available to those willing and able to pay? Are these symbolic commodities scarce? Is the market perfectly competitive? Is cultural capital quantifiable? Gary Becker, and mainstream economists in general, would answer these questions with an emphatic "yes," based on economic meanings and logic.

In Becker we have the apogee of an axiomatic, totalizing exchange paradigm. Not only are "economic" processes such as production and distribution conceptualized in terms of exchange, but all social interactions are as well. Production, strictly speaking, would be for Becker a wholly individual activity. The "production" that takes place in a factory, for example, would be a special case of individual production together with exchange among individuals directed by a "production function" or recipe embodying necessary technical relations among the several inputs. The purpose of individual production, whether it is of a loaf of bread or a symbolic good – Becker (1974: 1067), interestingly enough, suggests "distinction" – is to maximize utility. The only legitimate way for one individual to gain utility from the endowments and production of others is through mutually advantageous exchange. Likewise, all social interaction is exchange *by definition*; therefore, individuals always act *as if* they were exchanging. Whether people are conscious of making these exchanges is from Becker's perspective irrelevant. Each individual uses his or her endowment of various types of capital, all quantifiable in monetary terms, for direct exchange or to produce other economic, cultural, or symbolic commodities that contribute directly to utility or may themselves be exchanged. Family members, for example, "act 'as if' they 'loved' all other family members, even when they are really selfish" (ibid.: 1063). "Love," in Becker's theory, exists when an individual's utility function includes someone else's well-being as an argument.

Further, power asymmetries among exchangers are systematically ignored within a Beckerian discourse. Narrowly conceived, the neoclassical framework does not and cannot admit unequal exchange of any sort. If persistent power asymmetries are widely observed, they are attributed to the incursion of extra-economic elements, that is, to market imperfections such as government regulation or monopoly power that interfere with the free market. In *The*

Economics of Discrimination (1971), for example, Becker argues that competition within the marketplace will cause racial and gender discrimination to evaporate of their own accord. Those who persist in discriminating, he reasons, will face higher than normal costs and thus receive lower than normal returns, weakening their economic viability. In the long run (apparently the very long run), non-discriminating behavior will prevail. In short, the economy is a self-correcting mechanism that if left to itself will enable individuals to achieve the greatest possible utility for themselves subject only to the constraints imposed by their endowments of human and material capital and commodities.[1]

While the modifications to Becker's neoclassicalism needed to make an economic metaphorics plausible in the cultural sphere include addressing systematic power asymmetries and other market imperfections, the difficulties we see in adopting a neoclassical economic rhetoric and substance – whether done consciously or not – in the service of cultural criticism precede the question of power asymmetries. They are deeply embedded in the requirements of the economic field in general, and specifically in the assumption of a maximizing, self-interested, rationally calculating subject that is fundamental to mainstream and even much heterodox economic theory.[2] These difficulties further derive from an epistemological stance in which social interaction, conceived of as exchange alone, is understood by deduction from maximizing first principles. In this respect Bourdieu and Becker seem to share more than Bourdieu at least is willing to acknowledge, since both assume human subjects to be motivated in the first instance by a desire to maximize – though in Becker the object of maximization is utility, while in Bourdieu it is distinction. These neoclassical assumptions cannot be easily erased, even when their inadequacy to human behavior and institutions is recognized, because they persist in the logic (or more profoundly, in the narrative and metaphorical coherence) of economic discourse.

One of the results of this axiomatic strategy is to devalue most people's views of their own way of life, or at best to legitimize only one vocabulary for articulating those views (which may amount to the same thing). A privileged authority is granted to those who study and accept neoclassical assumptions. In this context, there is no accessible vocabulary for motivations other than self-interest. Cooperation or community become very difficult and complex concepts. This would not much matter if no one outside a small cabal of economists felt obliged to define community in terms of neoclassical assumptions. Increasingly, however, states like New York require a semester of mostly neoclassical economics in high school. Such a requirement only reinforces the legitimacy of acting out of self-interest, adding yet another impediment to the very necessary and very difficult task of building inner-city communities. Studies of undergraduates indicate that, if anything, a major in economics only exacerbates the inability to conceive of acting on any other motivation (see Frank *et al.* 1993).

Another consequence of their adopting economic language is that cultural critics like Bourdieu lose control over the meaning of their words. Terms like "market," "profit," and "capital" are defined first and foremost in the discipline of economics. Furthermore, the orthodoxy of the neoclassical system is closely policed within the discipline. Even the distinguished macroeconomist Alan Blinder was sharply criticized when he suggested, at a meeting of the American Economics Association, that in order to understand the price-setting process we should ask those who make pricing decisions. The objection, of course, was methodological. Reports of individuals about what they do cannot produce knowledge in neoclassical economics. Knowledge, in this approach, is extended either by bringing more powerful logical (i.e., "mathematical") techniques to bear, or by using empirical evidence to decide between competing propositions, each of which is *logically derived* from first principles, previously proven axioms, or other "empirically sustained" derivative propositions. Only the language of utility maximizing exchange can make for meaningful and "scientific" statements about the economy (or culture) – even when the statements come from the discipline's own elite. Such theories, of which Becker's work is an exemplar, cannot admit the possibility that culture (or some aspects of culture) might somehow be subject to a logic different from that of economics.

The intuitive feeling of the inadequacy of, say, Becker's definition of love to what many of us experience when we are in love gives rise to a situation described by the French philosopher Jean-François Lyotard as a "differend." He defines a differend as "a case of conflict between (at least) two parties that cannot be equitably resolved for lack of a rule of judgment applicable to both arguments" (Lyotard 1988: xi). If, for example, what we feel when we are in love cannot be expressed within the rules of the genre of discourse within which the rightness of our description of love is to be judged (in this case Becker's theory of social interaction), then, according to Lyotard, a wrong has been done to us: "A wrong results from the fact that the rules of the genre of discourse by which one judges are not those of the judged genre or genres of discourse" (ibid.). To take another example, in current legal and economic discourse a worker is presupposed to speak of his or her work as if it were a commodity, owned by the worker, which is exchanged on the market. Failure to use this language is to remove oneself from the field of reference – there is no other way to become a plaintiff in a labor dispute. Does this mean there is no other way in which a worker might be a victim? In Lyotard's words, "By what well-formed phrase and by means of what establishment procedure can the worker affirm before the labor arbitrator that what one yields to one's boss is *not* a commodity?" (10). While Lyotard tends to overstate his case, since much labor law is designed to address exactly this problem, the necessity for legal redress itself suggests the power the economic genre has exerted in defining the nature of work.[3]

The larger point to be drawn from Lyotard's theory of the differend is that the partiality of any specific genre of discourse – such as the economic genre – implies that (a) not all human experience can be encompassed by any one genre, and (b) that any discourse will silence, by making them unrepresentable, aspects of experience not encompassed by its particular genre. Work, as Lyotard notes, "does not belong to exchange, to the economic genre. It is a concatenation of genres of discourse" (174). To make it unrepresentable except as exchange is to make the human experience of work unrepresentable in terms, for example, of contemplation, transformation, or discovery.

In other ways as well, the view of exchange and the theoretical strategies of the dominant economic paradigm make adopting its language problematic for cultural theorists. In the first place, it is easy to use the language of economics without much awareness of how doing so situates one's argument in relation to the neoclassical paradigm. What looks progressive from the perspective of cultural studies may be rather reactionary economics. Second, even a thinker as well informed as Bourdieu cannot control the power of neoclassical assumptions about human nature that his use of economic language calls forth. Thus Bourdieu is constantly forced to distance his work from interpretations based on what are effectively neoclassical assumptions.

Bourdieu's is not a subversive use of economic language. Indeed, by using economic language, his cultural theory gains some of the privileged status accorded *res economica* in Western culture without taking responsibility for its use by placing it in the context of economic discourse. To be sure, this would not be an easy undertaking. Economists' definitions are given priority by academics and lay people alike. In such a tightly controlled discipline as economics, in which heterodoxy among the cognoscenti is not gracefully tolerated, why would the words of an interloper from sociology, cultural studies, or worse, literary studies be given credence sufficient to break the "deaf isolation" that, as Klamer and McCloskey (1988) have lamented, characterizes the discipline? At the very least, such circumstances suggest that cultural critics should resist privileging an economic rhetoric that permits their work to be easily digested by the neoclassical project. At the same time, the meaning and use of economic language is too important to leave solely to economists. It is therefore important that cultural critics engage economists on their own ground. Bourdieu's use of the term "capital," when compared to an economist's use of the same term, illustrates the difficulty of this task.

Any economic discourse must grapple with processes whereby capital is rendered as a homogeneous quantity. Few would doubt that the phrase "more capital" makes sense, at least in a capitalist system. Yet that which is capital is itself qualitatively diverse. Thus for Becker an individual's capital consists in his or her endowment of natural and acquired abilities and knowledge (human capital), material property that lasts more than one time period, and "social environment" – all quantified via money and prices. From this stock of capital derives a flow of "social income" which is "the sum of a person's own income (his [*sic*] earnings, etc.) and the (flow of) the monetary value to him [sic] of the relevant characteristics of others" (Becker 1974: 1063). Bourdieu might object that he has no need to quantify heterogeneous capital into a single aggregate, since his usage is metaphorical. But an economist of any school of thought does not have this luxury. While economists disagree vehemently over the definition of capital (see Harcourt 1972), all agree that it must be quantifiable in order to be meaningful. The rules of the economic field require unifying the diverse class of things called "capital" into a homogeneous, not merely homologous, quantifiable aggregate.

Bourdieu himself argues that his economic language should not be understood as located in the economic field. Thus "capital" for him means any storable form of power capable of use in a given context. In fact at times Bourdieu uses the term interchangeably with "power" (Bourdieu 1990a: 111–12; 1986: 243). What constitutes capital, as well as the rules for its use, is field-specific. Why, then, invoke and therefore privilege the economic field by giving its language priority when one's meaning might be just as well served by a less specialized term such as "store of power"? If "capital" as an instrument in the pursuit of distinction is no more than a powerful and suggestive metaphor to describe that which might just as easily be described in terms of a different metaphorics – say that of health and disease – then we have to ask what drives the choice, and we might add, the persuasiveness, of Bourdieu's economic vocabulary.

Bourdieu's use of economic rhetoric, whether meant metaphorically or not, offers little resistance to totalizing economic theories such as Becker's – despite Bourdieu's attempts to distance himself from such theories. He argues against economistic and reductionist readings of his theory on two grounds. First, he rejects the neoclassical assumption of a fully rational subject primarily motivated by economic self-interest (Bourdieu 1990a: 108ff). But, as Elizabeth Wilson (1988: 54) has pointed out, Bourdieu's theory seems to assume a competitive subject in search of distinction (or "capital" in its various forms) as the pre-eminent quality of human subjects (and their institutions) rather than as the product of a particular context. Substituting "distinction maximization" for Becker's "utility maximization" makes clear the homology between the two theories. Second, Bourdieu (1990a: 111) insists that the *homology* between the economic and other fields not be reduced to an *identity*:

> The charge of economism which is often brought against me consists of treating the homology between the economic field . . . and the fields of cultural production . . . as an identity, pure and simple. . . . The reduction of all fields to the economic field . . . goes hand in hand with the reduction of all interests to the interest characteristic of the economic field. And this twin reduction brings the accusation

> of reductionist economism or of economistic reductionism to a theory whose major purpose is undoubtedly to avoid economistic reduction.

Admittedly, a homology is not to be equated with an identity; but Bourdieu nonetheless effectively privileges the terms in which the homology is couched. His consistent use of economic language, together with the fact that economic motivation is already powerfully privileged in Western culture, makes it difficult to maintain the distinction between homology and identity. The usefulness of a concept such as the differend is precisely in the refusal of a privileged discourse that grounds the similarities among fields and practices, for once such a discourse exists its dominance becomes practically unassailable, despite the best intentions of its author.[4]

Bourdieu has in fact given the economic field some degree of conceptual priority, as when, in "The Forms of Capital," he acknowledges that economic capital is, "in the last analysis," at the root of other forms (Bourdieu 1986: 252). Or in the following statement from *The Logic of Practice* (1990b: 122):

> The theory of strictly economic practices is a particular case of a general theory of the economy of practices. Even when they give every appearance of disinterestedness because they escape the logic of "economic" interest (in the narrow sense) and are oriented toward non-material stakes that are not easily quantified, as in "pre-capitalist" societies or in the cultural sphere of capitalist societies, practices never cease to comply with an economic logic.

Further, the two assumptions arguably most fundamental to his vision of human agents and society – the pursuit of maximum distinction and exchange interactions in competitive markets – both become evident through the economic metaphorics of this theory and demonstrate the proximity between Bourdieu's theory and the central assumptions of neoclassical economics.

This seems to us to have real and dangerous political implications. At one time not too long ago, the insertion of economics into discussions of literature and the arts was a sign of a Left, oppositional, critical practice that called into question the separation of high culture from the marketplace. It is this impulse that seems to drive Barbara Herrnstein Smith's deployment of the economic in *Contingencies of Value* (1988). On the one hand, as Fredric Jameson (1991: 193) has noted, it is no longer necessarily the case that the economic carries this political weight in literary studies. On the other, the dualistic opposition between market and culture that Smith attacks is by now, we would argue, a straw man among those who think seriously about culture. If economic rhetoric is no longer functioning in cultural theory to identify the writer's political commitments, and, further, if neoclassical economic theory is all too willing to, in effect, take such rhetoric at its word, then the political implications of its use have changed.

The economic genre is a particularly powerful one in our culture, and therefore just what is assumed or disallowed by it carries a great deal of weight. It may in fact not be all that difficult to persuade people that everything they do is best described in terms of utility maximizing exchanges between themselves and others. But to the extent that we persuade them of the dominance of the economic in their lives and actions, we risk erasing the possibility of thinking – and finally acting – in any other terms. As Lyotard (1988: 178) has pointed out, not all questions can be asked within the conceptual context allowed by the economic genre, including some of the most important – such as, for example, "*What ought we to be?*"

Notes

1 Despite the tendency within neoclassical economics to ignore power asymmetries, they can be integrated into a Beckerian framework while leaving both its core assumptions and key conclusions untouched. Neoclassical economists can maintain the assumption of individual utility maximization that underpins their theory by blaming power asymmetries on the optimizing decisions of victims themselves. Examples include childbearing, vocational and consumption choices, and directly or indirectly granting others (e.g., movie stars, sports heroes) disproportionate power. Perhaps the most common and pernicious explanation for persistent asymmetries consonant with the neoclassical framework is that they arise from inherent genetic differences among individuals. In general, however, the neoclassical model downplays the importance of inequities in the exchange relation by arguing that as factors such as asymmetric information and incomplete markets become significant, they create incentives that lead to their amelioration.

2 Even economists deeply critical of some neoclassical claims retain this stance. Some feminist economists, for example, have adopted a bargaining-power framework in the analysis of the family that amounts to a Beckerian theory with power asymmetries, collective action and endogenous preferences (see McCrate 1988, 1990). Even coherent economic theories consistent with the core assumptions of neoclassical theory are ruled out of the neoclassical court because they eschew the tendency toward equilibrium and contradict the normative claim that "free" markets are the best form of social organization.

3 See Dupré and Gagnier's first essay in this volume for a critique of the economic reduction of labor to commodity or "factor of production" in the context of a larger argument against the viability of a non-normative economics. We should note here that our use of Lyotard's theory is intentionally selective. The logical extension of the concept of the differend arguably leads to extreme fragmentation and quietism, positions with which we do not sympathize. On the other hand, to take seriously the possibility of an untranslatable abyss between discourses provides a welcome corrective to totalizing intellectual tendencies.

4 John Guillory, a sympathetic and subtle reader of Bourdieu, expresses discomfort at the way the "specificity of the esthetic experience . . . seems to disappear altogether into the 'esthetic disposition,' the mode of consumption" (Guillory

1993: 332). Just at such a point we would wish to invoke a differend. Hubert Dryfus and Paul Rabinow (1993) critique Bourdieu's attempt to create a unified science of social meaning on several grounds that point toward a similar discomfort.

References

Becker, Gary S. (1971). *The Economics of Discrimination.* 2nd edn. Chicago: University of Chicago Press.

—— (1974). "A Theory of Social Interactions." *Journal of Political Economy* 82.6: 1063–93.

—— (1991). *A Treatise on the Family*. Enl. edn. Cambridge, MA: Harvard University Press.

Bourdieu, Pierre (1977). *Outline of a Theory of Practice.* Trans. Richard Nice. Cambridge: Cambridge University Press.

—— (1984). *Distinction: A Social Critique of the Judgement of Taste.* Trans. Richard Nice. Cambridge, MA: Harvard University Press.

—— (1986). "The Forms of Capital." In *Handbook of Theory and Research for the Sociology of Education*. Ed. John G. Richardson. New York: Greenwood, 241–58.

—— (1990a). "A Reply to Some Objections." In *In Other Words: Essays Towards a Reflexive Sociology*. Trans. Matthew Adamson. Cambridge: Polity, 106–19.

—— (1990b). *The Logic of Practice.* Trans. Richard Nice. Cambridge: Polity.

—— (1993). *The Field of Cultural Production.* Ed. Randal Johnson. New York: Columbia University Press.

Bruner, Jerome (1991). "The Narrative Construction of Reality." *Critical Inquiry* 18.1: 1–21.

Dryfus, Hubert, and Paul Rabinow (1993). "Can There be a Science of Existential Structure and Social Meaning?" In *Bourdieu: Critical Perspectives*. Ed. Craig Calhoun, Edward LiPuma, and Moishe Postone. Chicago: University of Chicago Press, 35–44.

Frank, Robert H., Thomas Gilovich, and Dennis T. Regan (1993). "Does Studying Economics Inhibit Cooperation?" *Journal of Economic Perspectives* 7.2: 159–71.

Guillory, John (1993). *Cultural Capital: The Problem of Literary Canon Formation.* Chicago: University of Chicago Press.

Harcourt, Geoffrey (1972). *Cambridge Controversies in the Theory of Capital.* New York: Cambridge University Press.

Jameson, Fredric (1991). *Postmodernism, or, The Cultural Logic of Late Capitalism.* Durham, NC: Duke University Press.

Johnson, Randal (1983). "Editor's Introduction: Pierre Bourdieu on Art, Literature and Culture." In Pierre Bourdieu, *The Field of Cultural Production.* Ed. Randal Johnson. New York: Columbia University Press.

Klamer, Arjo, and Donald N. McCloskey (1988). "Economics in the Human Conversation." In *The Consequences of Economic Rhetoric.* Ed. Arjo Klamer, Donald N. McCloskey, and Robert M. Solow. New York: Cambridge University Press, 3–20.

Lakoff, George, and Mark Johnson (1980). *Metaphors We Live By.* Chicago: University of Chicago Press.

Lyotard, Jean-François. (1988) *The Differend: Phrases in Dispute*. Trans. George Van Den Abbeele. Minneapolis: University of Minnesota Press.

McCloskey, Donald N. (1990). "Storytelling in Economics." In *Narrative in Culture: The Uses of Storytelling in the Sciences, Philosophy, and Literature*. Ed. Christopher Nash. London: Routledge, 5–22.

McCrate, Elaine (1988). "Gender Difference: the Role of Endogenous Preferences and Collective Action." *American Economic Review* 78: 235–39.

—— (1990). "Labor Market Segmentation and Relative Black/White Teenage Birth Rates." *Review of Black Political Economy* 18: 37–53.

Smith, Barbara Herrnstein (1988). *Contingencies of Value: Alternative Perspectives for Critical Theory*. Cambridge, MA: Harvard University Press.

Williams, Raymond (1985). *Keywords: A Vocabulary of Culture and Society*. Rev. edn. New York: Oxford University Press.

Wilson, Elizabeth (1988). "Picasso and Paté de Foie Gras: Pierre Bourdieu's Sociology of Culture". *Diacritics* 18.2: 47–60.

INDEX

Note: page numbers in italics refer to illustrations